Contents

CHAPTER 1   IN THE BEGINNING

It has been largely accepted for many years that the team we now all know as Rotherham United was founded in 1884, but that does not seem to be the precise date to which the roots can be retraced. When any club, no matter what the sport, has been in existence under a previous name, it is always difficult to define exactly when it was formed and there are many arguments for the justification of defining varying years.

The most commonly quoted date is 1884, but that is not the case, for both Rotherham Town and Thornhill United were in existence before then, and the Author's research has not thrown up any real validation for that year's claims. After Thornhill had changed its name to Rotherham County, it became stronger than its 'Town' counterpart, so consequently it has generally been accepted that the club was the forerunner of the present 'United'. But it is only fair that equal recognition should be given to Rotherham Town, for they were the first team from the town to play in the Football League, so descendants from that club could claim with some justification that they were the originators.

So, should it be 1870, when a Rotherham team first came into being, 1877 when Thornhill played its first game, or 1925 when United finally became one club following the amalgamation of the two others? It is definitely not 1884 - despite the fact that the present club celebrated its centenary in 1984! The Author's opinion is that 1925 should be recognised as the birth of *Rotherham United*, but 1870 should be accepted as the date when football was really established in the town.

The seeds had actually been sown in 1867/68, when the first president was the Rev. J.J. Christie M.A., the Grammar School headmaster. The hon.secretary was Henry Hart and the committee consisted of Messrs. John Fawcett, John Mason, T.W.Badger, G.D.Owen, R.R.Sharp, J.W.Bellamy, G.W.Kemp and W.G.Haggard.

The rules of the club appear strange and amusing now. A few samples:-
" *That the season shall commence in November and end in April and that practice days be Wednesday and Saturday.*
" *That gentlemen wishing to join shall be proposed and seconded by members of the committee at one meeting and balloted for at the next, one black ball in three to exclude.*
" *That the subscription shall be two shillings and sixpence, due on the first day of December each year.*
" *That the captain of the club has sole management of the matches and the selection of the teams, subject to the approval of the committee".*

The laws of the game also had an amusing look about them:-
" *After a goal is won the losing side shall kick off and goals shall be changed but if, in playing a match, half the specified time shall expire without a goal having been obtained, the sides shall change goals, the kick off being from the middle, in the same direction as at the commencement of the game.*
" *A goal shall be won when the ball crosses between the goalposts, under the tape, not being thrown, knocked or carried.*
" *When the ball is in touch a player of the opposite side to that which kicked it out shall kick it in from here it went out, and no player shall be allowed within six yards of the ball until kicked.*
" *Any player between an opponent's goal and goalkeeper (unless he has followed the play there) is offside and out of play. The goalkeeper is that player on the defending side who for the time being, is nearest to his own goal".*
(The latter was known as "goalie-wag" even until recent years)

But it would appear that the first game did not take place until December 1870 when the following advertisement was placed in the *Rotherham and Masborough Advertiser*:-

However, it was not until 1872 that a team appeared with the name 'Rotherham', when Wanderers took to the pitch at Jarvis' Field which belonged to the tenant of the Red Lion Hotel and it subsequently became known as the Clifton Lane Cricket Ground.

There were some other teams playing at the time but Wanderers were into decline and in 1878 the strangely named Lunar Rovers came into being with the title coming as a result of most of their games having to be played by moonlight. This was because the team had been formed by shopkeepers and others and as they had no afternoons off, they were compelled to play their games after work.

Rovers started their playing days in the Clifton Grove area of Middle Lane, later moving to the Doncaster Road end of Middle Lane, eventually moving to Clifton Lane to share the ground with the cricketers.

In 1882, Rovers felt a name change would be appropriate and they became known initially as 'Rotherham Club', with Captain Stoddart (event-ually to become Colonel Sir Charles Stoddart) taking over as President while Walter Musson became the captain.

With several other teams setting up - such as Clifton Wanderers, Holmes Rising Star, Kiln-hurst and Mexborough - Rotherham Club were eager to show that they were the town's leading team and they entered all the important cup competitions by 1884 and were drawn at home against Nottingham Forest in the English Cup competition. But the offer of money to switch the game to their opponents ground proved to be more enticing with them receiving the princely sum of £17.10s to concede home advantage plus a dinner at the Maypole.

Forest won the game 5-0. The following season Rotherham were drawn at home again with the famous Notts County and home advantage was sold again - for £30 - before the team were on the wrong end of a 15-0 thrashing.

Keeping track of Thornhill, they played their first game on 4th October 1877 off Greasbrough Road, and it was in 1882 that they settled down at the Red House Ground around half a mile from their roots. But they could offer little in the way of facilities for spectators at the ground which was situated near the junction of Henley Grove Road and Park Street and for the dressing rooms, the Red House Inn was used at the intersection of these roads. Both the ground and the public house have long since disappeared owing to industrial development and new roads with the old centre spot more or less in the roundabout where Henley Rise meets the ring road dual carriageway.

Meanwhile, the Rotherham club were exiled from Clifton Lane with the cricket club looking to increase the £5 rental and the footballers moved just down the road to Cocker's Field near Sherwood Crescent off Wellgate. But this venue was far from satisfactory for there was a very pronounced slope and it was felt that it was not conducive to playing good football and the stay lasted just a few months before another move took them to the West End Ground near Ickles. Here the pitch was much more suitable, but unfortunately accessibility was not so and they quickly settled their differences with the cricket club and moved back into Clifton Lane.

A stand capable of accommodating 500 specta-tors was erected and following the acquisition of the name "Town", they gradually started to achieve better things both on and off the pitch with finances gradually getting better.

In the 1887/88 season, Town defeated the powerful Ecclesfield 5-2 and went on to reach the final of the Wharncliffe Charity Cup, in which they were beaten but not disgraced by Sheffield Wednesday, although the occasion was marred by some unsavoury incidents. Contro-versy arose as to whether the pitch was fit for play after it had been cleared of snow and

Rotherham responded to suggestions that the game should be played as an exhibition by insisting that it was, *"the final or nothing".* Their demands were met but not until they had been kept hanging around for an hour in the cold while the Wednesday players were waiting in the warmth and comfort of the dressing room.

An interesting story is told of that particular time of a visit of the Rotherham Club to play a game in Doncaster but only six of the chosen players turned up at the station. Not to be deterred by this skeleton of a side, captain Walter Musson would not abandon the trip and he said he would find some substitutes and immediately recruited three.

One was a gentleman called Fitzpatrick, another was Mr Tovey, who was later to become Town Clerk of Doncaster, and a third was a prisoner who was on his way to serve time at Wakefield but how it came that his services were enlisted is unknown. He was a footballer of some note and his custodian must have been a football enthusiast for he allowed the handcuffs to be removed to don the football garb. All ended satisfactorily, for Rotherham, short-handed as they were, won the game and the prisoner-come-footballer continued his journey to the then Her Majesty's vegetarian Hotel in Wakefield. The club was generally credited as being the first to import players from over the border when Mr George Hague and honorary secretary Mr Arthur Wordsworth visited Dumfries in their search for players. Unfortunately Mr Hague made himself conspicuous by wearing a Tam-O-Shanter which was intended to impress the Scotsmen but this only made it easier for them to identify the English poachers. They were threatened with being thrown into the main street fountain and were compelled to take refuge in their hotel.

Leaving by the back door, they arrived at the station only to be greeted by a crowd of angry men several hundred strong, who were intent of doing them bodily injury. Again compelled to take refuge, they availed themselves of the station master's kindness and remained in his office until all was clear. They were two tired men when they departed from Dumfries, having left Rotherham on Friday night after a hard day's work, by the midnight train, arriving in Dumfries at 7am. Leaving Scotland in safety late on Saturday night, they arrived in Rotherham on Sunday morning having for their trouble the satisfaction of knowing they had secured a full back named Halliday and a centre-half named McKie, both players of exceptional merit.

Momentum gradually picked up and in 1888/89, the highlight of the season was a visit from Preston North End when a crowd of around 4,000 saw Town beaten 3-1 with the goal from Johnny McCormick. Later that season Rotherham lifted their first major success when they beat Staveley at Bramall Lane to win the Sheffield and Hallamshire Challenge Cup and they were welcomed back to the town amid scenes of wild excitement as they paraded on a wagonette.

The following season saw the inception of the Rotherham Charity Cup and the formation of the Midland League, following the success of the introduction of League football in England. Town were founder-members of the Midland League, and they played their first league game at Clifton Lane against Sheffield Club on 14th September, when the home supporters were rewarded with a 3-1 victory.

At this time another local team came into existence with the emergence of Rotherham Swifts who had been founded by Fred Micklethwaite, late goalkeeper and secretary of the Town club and their rise matched their name.

There was little love lost between the two clubs as can be highlighted by an English Cup third qualifying game played at Swifts' Holmes ground with it being abandoned ten minutes before the end of extra time with neither side having scored. The replay took place at Clifton Lane and Town were leading 2-1 six minutes from the end of extra time when bad light again stopped play. The Swifts refused to concede defeat and so the final minutes were played out at the same venue a few days later when Town added another goal. At the initial match at the cricket ground, the Town goalkeeper, Wharton, finished in hospital after being kicked by a spectator, the Swifts team were pelted with mud and Rab Howell, one of Swifts star players, was struck on the head with an umbrella! Who says crowd violence has only come into being in the 90's?

Swifts quickly folded when four of the players, Howell, Mick Whitham, A.Watson and Frank Salkeld left to form the nucleus of Sheffield United to go on and achieve renown in the football world.

After beating Swifts, Town were beaten by Sheffield United but they gained revenge by beating them in the final of the Sheffield and Hallamshire Cup with over 5,000 spectators watching a McCormick goal give Town the win at Clifton Lane after a goalless draw at Bramall Lane.

Finances started to put a severe strain on the club in 1890/91 - and it's just the same over a century later - and matters were not helped by other clubs not turning up for scheduled games. Royal Arsenal sent a wire to say they would not turn up on Christmas Day 1890 and Town were awarded £5 compensation by the English Association despite claiming £17.

Then £12 was wasted on a journey to Staveley, Kidderminster failed to appear at Clifton Lane and Warwick County cried off - both these had a £10 penalty imposed with Rotherham agreeing to take half the amounts on condition that the return games were played at Rotherham, but they never did take place.

In January 1891 the club's deficit was £247 and after an appeal for subscriptions, the debt had been reduced to £64 at the end of the season, but it came as a surprise in August that year that the club were upping the stands and their other property at Clifton Lane to move to Clifton Grove. Gate receipts for the season amounted to £270 from which £152 accounted for players' wages but the danger of the club folding was averted. The last game played at the cricket ground was against Burnley on 18th April in front of around 1,000 spectators who watched a single goal home victory.

At first there was some disquiet from the locals surrounding the new ground for it was situated

off Middle Lane just south of Clifton Grove opposite Gladys Street, in a residential area. But the fears of the residents of having a football ground in their midst were allayed except for the occupants of six houses in Clifton Grove who had their view to the south blocked by the covered stand that had been rapidly moved from the cricket ground.

An open stand, three quarters pitch width long, was erected at the Middle Road end where the entrance to the ground was located. It was a piece of flat land, formerly tenanted by Silas Garner, and even though it was furrowed, it was a big area and nine foot high hoardings were erected to get the ground ready for action by 5th September 1891 for a reserve team game by 'Rotherham United', as the second string were named.

Two days before that, the team earned themselves a place in football's history books when it was reported that they were the first ever to score with a penalty kick. Spot kicks had only come into being that season, and on Thursday 3rd September 1891, Rotherham Town were awarded one in the morning match at Darlington St. Augustine's, with Albert 'Buck' Rodgers stepping up and finding the back of the net.

Several factors had lead to the move from Clifton Lane, not least of which were the difficulties arising over the renewal of the tenancy with the new owners of the Clifton Lane ground - The Racing Company.

The last straw was the announcement by the company that they intended to use it on days when the football club would normally have attractive home games with considerable monetary benefit - namely Statutes Monday and the Saturday previous to it. The proximity of Clifton Lane to the Herringthorpe racecourse made it a convenient parking area.

One of the advantages of not needing to share a ground with the cricketers was that the football club could arrange matches in future during the month of September.

The opening competitive first team match at the new home was played on 26th September 1891 when Grantham Rovers were the visitors in the Midland League game, when an attendance of 3,000 watched a 2-2 draw. The figure dropped to 1,000 two weeks later but this drastic reduction was put down to poor weather. But the club continued to do well in their new surroundings and they went on to win the League championship following a last match 4-1 victory against Wednesday Old Athletic, cheered on by 4,000 fans. During the interval former captain Walter Masson paraded a goat across the ground with the animal bedecked in fancy trappings with the motto *"Play up Rotherham"*.

Thornhill United - Rotherham Charity Cup winners in 1893/94. (Back): Bob Ridge (Trainer), W.Pennington, Tom Sharp, Tom Bates, W.Temperton (Linesman). (Middle): Jack Bray, Tom Brooks, E.Heppenstall. (Bottom) S.Frost, Harry Garnett, A.Green, W.Fowler.

Things were looking up for the club, by now they had become a limited company - with the year's profit yielding £158 - but some controversy was caused in the Rotherham camp by a rule passed at a meeting of the Midland League to the effect that a fourpenny "gate" was to be acknowledged everywhere during the following season.

This, though was a time of ambition for the club:- improvements had been made at Clifton Grove and a cycle track round the ground was proposed, having in mind the safety of those, *"who don't enjoy being run down on the roads"*, while those who enjoyed an alcoholic beverage before or after a game were catered for by the granting of an occasional licence for the sale of intoxicating drink on the ground for the Christmas holiday matches of 1892.

Town made history in September of that year when they had the distinction of being Liverpool's first opponents at Anfield in a friendly game, but they lost 7-1.

The fourpenny gate had its adverse effect on the attendances in 1892/93 and the shareholders were asked for the whole of the uncalled-up part of the subscribed capital. But this did not deter the team on the field and they lifted the championship for the second successive season when they clinched the title with a 3-1 win over Loughborough, with the attendance estimated somewhere between 4,000 and 6,000.

The championship flag was presented after an 8-0 win against Mansfield in the last match of the season, with the Borough Temperance Band in attendance, and they became the first team to win the title in successive seasons. The playing record for the season was:- played 24, won 19, drawn 3, lost 2, goals for 80, against 28, points 41, and when the number of clubs in the Second Division of the Football League was increased from twelve to sixteen in 1893, Rotherham Town was one of the newcomers elected along with Liverpool, Newcastle United and Woolwich Arsenal.

The first game ended in a 1-1 draw at Lincoln City, and Town then visited Small Heath where they were beaten 4-3 in Birmingham, when Alf

Pickering, the club's best forward broke his leg. McCormick sprained his ankle and these injures, together with subsequent ones, were to have a lasting effect.

The first home Football League game took place at Clifton Grove on 9th September 1893 when Grimsby Town were the visitors but the game took place in an atmosphere of apprehension and doubt. There was some unease at the insistence of the railway company in running a special train from Grimsby, with the fear that the possible contagion of the cholera that had reached the port from the continent. An attempt was made by the Bench at the Rotherham Borough Police Court to impede the proceedings by refusing to grant a licence for the day of the match, but the game was played, the railway excursion came, and Town were 4-3 winners. That unfortunately was one of only six victories - only one away from home - and Town finished next to bottom and had to apply for re-election.

Bootle had dropped out prior to the start of the previous season to create a vacancy and with Northwich Victoria not re-applying for membership, this left just Manchester City (who had been renamed from Ardwick) and Town to stand. City sailed through with 20 votes but Rotherham dropped out with 15 votes, beaten by Midland Leaguers Leicester Fosse with 20. Bury (from the Lancashire League) and Burton Wanderers (Midland League) took the other two vacancies with 17 votes each.

However, on 11th June the Management Committee received a letter from hard up Middlesbrough Ironopolis resigning from membership, so having earned more votes than any of the other unsuccessful applicants, Rotherham were invited back into the fold. Town's first act was to complain quite justifiably that ten of their first twelve matches were away from home!

At the annual general meeting, it was disclosed that the total of match receipts for 1894/95 was £482, less than half that of the previous season. Attendances had been effected by the "Coal War" which broke out during the summer of 1883 and dragged on until November, and with many people out of work due to the miners'

dispute, most people in the area had little money to spend on football matches.

The amount spent on players' wages had been halved, affecting the standard of play, as was reflected by the final position in the League table.

The £100 loss for the year was attributed to lock-out in the coal trade and fortunes were slightly better during the 1894/95 season when at least the club finished just above the re-election line. Notable successes included a 6-1 home win against Walsall and a 5-2 triumph against Lincoln, with the last two games both providing victories. But any thoughts of making further progress were shattered when the first three games of the following season all ended in defeat, and after the encouragement of some success in the qualifying rounds of the English Cup, came a staggering blow from the landlord, Mr R.J. Bentley of Brewery fame. He entered a distraint for rent due and the news of the action spread about town. This had a disastrous effect on the gates with rumours spreading that the club was about to fold and all the players were leaving.

In February 1896 attempts were made at the Borough Police Court to get an order against the club but the court had difficulty in serving the summons as the club was having a rapid succession of secretaries. Town were then having trouble in fielding a full eleven players for their games and at the end of January, they sent a letter to Port Vale explaining that unless the necessary train fares were remitted, the team would be unable to travel. It looked serious for Town when this was reported to the League until some friends of the club came to the rescue enabling them to travel, but even then they did so with only ten players.

An appeal for subscriptions was mounted to try and keep the club afloat and prevent them from being the first Football League club to fold up during a season and it just brought in enough funds to succeed. A benefit performance at the Theatre Royal, a benefit match and a "Grand Ball" all helped the club to survive until the end of the season when they finished next to bottom.

The last home game - a 2-2 draw against Lincoln City - took place on 16th March 1896 in front of a crowd of just 300, and it was estimated that 100 of those came from Lincoln!

At the season's end it was announced that only £550 had been taken at the gate for the first team matches and with players' wages alone accounting for £470, £77 was lost on the season. Even the AGM in August was poorly attended and the club didn't even bother to apply for re-election to the Football League. So Rotherham Town just quietly died and it was not long before the Clifton Grove ground was turned into a housing site which it remains to this day.

There was a marked reluctance by many people in undertaking to raise another representative football club in the town and prominent officials formerly connected with the game intimated that they, *"would have now't no more to do wi'it"*.

Town's demise saw some of their players move to other local clubs, with Kimberworth Bible Class taking a couple, but this was the time for Thornhill United to take centre stage as the leading club of the area and while Town had been playing in the Football League, they had been making progress themselves.

Suddenly they could envisage that they were well placed with teams in the Sheffield Alliance and South Yorkshire Leagues but the poor condition of their Red House ground did not help them.

What happened then to the Town players? - Hempsall signed for Thornhill while two newly elected clubs to the Second Division of the Football League - Blackpool and Gainsborough - took on Porteous (T), Wilkinson and Webster. Porteous (D) and Reid went to Darwen and Bryant to Newton Heath, the forerunner of Manchester United.

But we were soon to see the basis being laid down for the formation of another Rotherham team and a meeting was held in March 1898, presided by Town's last chairman, Mr N.Gibbs, with a view to forming a new Rotherham Club and joining the Midland League. The Odd-fellows Hall was filled to overflowing but nothing came of the meeting until later in the same year, when Rotherham Tradesmen's Thursday Football Club came into being. They were allowed to use the Pigeon Cote Ground at Holmes - former home of the Swifts - at a nominal fee of £1 and they wore the chocolate and blue colours used by Town in its early days.

But the following year two minor clubs in the town - Rotherham Casuals and Rotherham Grammar School - combined to become Rotherham Club and they joined Thornhill in the Sheffield Association League while they went on to change their status to a semi-professional one. They played at Clifton Lane, and with growing support it became necessary to raise embankments around the ground, so when the racecourse closed down, the committee decided to buy the grandstand and move it to their ground. But when they pulled it down for removal, the stand was found to be rotten and they just had to make the best job they could of it.

In 1903 Rotherham Club won the Sheffield Association championship with Thornhill as runners-up and both were admitted to the Midland League to begin a period of intense rivalry that was to last 22 years until they finally joined together to form one club.

Ground standards in the League were being raised and Rotherham started getting complaints that their Clifton Lane ground sloped in an unfair way to the advantage of the home team, so, threatened with the possibility of being thrown out, they set to work to level the ground.

In 1904 Clifton Lane was brought by three enterprising gentlemen who floated the concern into a limited company - the Rotherham Athletic Company Limited - holding the lease of the ground for 21 years with 3,200 shares of £1 being allotted. The football club were to pay £80 per year and the cricket club £50 and the precaution was taken of adding a condition to the lease giving the football club permission to play the minimum width approved by the English Football Association.

Rotherham's top two clubs, around the turn of the century
(Top) An un-named Thornhill United team group, and
(Below) Rotherham Town
Back - J.Sharpe, A.Greenwood, W.Newsom, G.Stacey, A.Philips, W.Bank, J.Pilgrim, W.Bramham, T.Sorsby.
Front - O.Smith, H.Waldron, W.Hodgkiss, J.Simpson, H.Sorsby, E.Roddis, M.Woollen.
Bottom - H.Grummitt, J.Sanderson.

freely gave of their labour and loaned timber and other materials, the ground was levelled and then transformed into an up to date enclosure. Two old stands from the Red House ground were made into one which was put up on the Rotherham side of the ground and some fifty loads of ashes were daily tipped in the ground from neighbouring works. It was estimated that when they had finished, the new ground, which was leased from the Midland Railway Company, would be able to accommodate a crowd of 15,000 with comfort. The first game to be staged at Millmoor was on 2nd September 1907 when County beat Leeds City reserves 3-2 in a Midland League fixture.

Trustees were appointed for the football club, and in April 1905 rules were adopted, the first being that the club would, in future, be known as Rotherham Town Football Club. This went against the grain as far as Thornhill were concerned and they argued that since they had been in existence much longer than the present Rotherham Town, they had every right themselves to use the name Rotherham.

And so they became Rotherham County - the name taken from the fact that the town was a county borough. County felt that they were the more senior club and they took a step forward to prove this when they moved to a new ground after things had come to a head in the 1906/07 season when they were prevented from playing cup-ties on their Red House ground as it did not comply with the regulations of the English F.A.

So in 1907 they moved to Millmoor which was described as *"a grass plot of not much practical utility"*, sandwiched between works premises and cottage property, passed on one side by the Midland Railway and on the other by the corporation trams. It had an alarming slope, but thanks to the efforts of officials and friends who

The 1907/08 season saw County make a bright start but it was Town who grabbed the limelight when they became the first Rotherham side ever to qualify for the competition proper of the English F.A. Cup. They had to progress through six ties in the preliminary and qualifying rounds before going out with honour, beaten 1-0 by West Ham at their Boleyn Castle ground.

But fame brought it's penalties and several players left Town to join other clubs - skipper Harrop went to Liverpool and Layton and Jones to Aston Villa. This began the decline of Town and in the years preceding the outbreak of the first world war, County came into their own. They won the Midland League championship on four successive seasons, between 1911/12 and 1914/15, before wartime conditions forced the temporary abandonment of normal league football. Meanwhile, the affairs of the Town club were reaching crisis point. At the commencement of the 1913/14 season, the club owed £247 and later, in March 1914, the secretary, Mr John Jones sent out a communication indicating that

Four personalities from the era:

Top: (Left) One-time captain Everard Turner. (Right) 'Bunkie' Merryweather. Below: (Left) Trainer Mick Whitham who returned to Rotherham. (Right) Walter Bramham

unless the sportsmen of Rotherham rallied to their assistance, the directors would have no alternative but to close down.

It was decided to wind up the company and form a syndicate to take over the assets and the lease of the ground, with a committee being set up for the purpose of getting in subscriptions.

According to the F.A., Town did not exist but eventually they were re-admitted to the Midland League and an appeal was made by Councillor George Gummer to raise £1,000 to assist the club over its financial problems.

In defence to the greater claims of the war, Rotherham Town ceased operations, but County carried on during this period and at the request of the Football League played what was designated "War Time Football", no wages being allowed to be paid to any player and a large proportion of the "gate" receipts being devoted to charitable objects.

Professional players were bound by no club and the Millmoor outfit had the services of several famous exponents of the game including Wm. Hibbert (England) and Wilfred Lowe (Scotland) - Two internationals.

The successful County team of 1911/12:
(Back): Billy Hodgkiss (trainer), Sammy Hopkinson, H.Hibbert, A.Brooks,
Charlie Hopkinson, W.Ashmore, A.Bluer, Tom Sharp (secretary).
(Front): Frankie Lee, Herbert Lloyd, Tommy Hakin, J.Thompson, W.Palmer.

As reward for their Midland League achievements, Rotherham County applied for admission to the Second Division of the Football League when it was resumed after the war, in 1919, and extended to include 44 teams.

Their application, which received 28 votes, was championed by the Mayor, Alderman Gummer who spoke so eloquently on the club's behalf that he brought this report from the Athletic News:- *"The defeated were amazed at Rotherham's success. Well, Rotherham have a Mayor who is an advocate of football. Just for the moment he is the best Mayor we know.*

"It was not so much as a spokesman for the club as the Mayor of the town that Alderman Gummer appealed for support. He referred to the drab lives that men had to live in industrial centres and went on to say that there was no attraction that could come up to football".

Town also had the temerity to apply for admission but they were turned down with most of those present at the League meeting being under the impression that there had been no Rotherham Town in existence since the Clifton Grove set up became defunct in 1896.

But they did manage to get back into the Midland League, although this caused some consternation, owing to a ruling of the league that no two clubs belonging to one town should play at home on the same day. A clash of fixtures was inevitable as County's reserves were to play in the Midland League as well.

A consequence of County being admitted to the Second Division was the decision to run the club as a limited liability company in order to provide security against financial loss and to support carrying out of the necessary ground improvements.

A meeting in June 1919 carried unanimously the resolution that, *"the club be converted into a company limited by shares with a capital of £5,000",* and a prospectus was published and a subscription list opened in September 1919.

With the prospect of 25,000 - 30,000 crowds, County shelved their original costly schemes regarding increased accommodation to spend money on securing players for their Second Division campaign.

Goalkeeper J.Branston came from Grimsby, centre-forward "Teddy" Glennon from Sheffield Wednesday and in October 1919, the enterprise of the directors was rewarded when they brought off the double signing of right full-back Harry Millership and Masborough born Herbert Lounds, both players coming from the ostracised Leeds City club. Millership, who cost £1,000, was capped by Wales a few months later, in February 1920 - the first Rotherham player to be selected for international honours.

Rotherham County's first match in the second division was against Nottingham Forest, when 10,000 emotional spectators at Millmoor saw the home team win 2-0, but this early form was not maintained, County ending the season in 17th position (out of 22) with 34 points from 42 games.

Nethertheless the club performed quite well, in often difficult circumstances, as was highlighted by the problems encountered in fulfilling a Monday game at Fulham. The trip started on Sunday afternoon, with a rest for the night being made at Bedford, and the journey continued to London the following morning.

After the game, Monday night was spent in London, and the whole of Tuesday was taken up covering the 170 mile journey back to Rotherham. It was 6.30 p.m. on Tuesday evening when the players arrived back in the town after ten hours of travelling including stoppages for refreshments, with £100 eaten up in the travelling costs.

How we should be grateful for motorways today!

During the summer of 1920, Rotherham County erected a new stand to accommodate 1,500 people at a cost of £4,000 after the chairman, Mr R.H.Nelson, had devised a scheme for raising money by offering for sale £5 souvenir tickets. Although the stand had not been completed, it was in use at the beginning of the 1920/21 season while at the other end of town Rotherham Town were one of 24 northern and midland clubs who met at the King's Head Hotel in Sheffield on 15th May and unanimously passed a resolution in favour of the formation of a Third Division of the Football League.

However, the Third Division that came into being comprised of only clubs from the First Division of the Southern League and the AGM of the League shelved the formation of a Northern section until the following year. The directors and supporters of Rotherham Town had set their hearts on justifying their claims for admission to the proposed new section and, following County's lead, it was suggested that a new limited company should be formed in order to provide a solid foundation for the club. It was thought that without the expenditure of a good deal of money, a good team could not be put together, and there would have to be a considerable outlay in carrying out the contemplated alterations to the ground.

Improvements were needed to the playing pitch and a new stand with seating accommodation housing dressing rooms and offices was planned. Concrete terracing which would provide room for 20,000 spectators was envisaged and looking to the future, the directors had made arrangements with the Rotherham Athletic Company to enter into a tenancy of the ground lasting until 1947.

The cat was put among the pigeons when the admission charge for Town's Midland League games was increased to a shilling and this led to a reaction from the supporters that it was too much, but the officials of the club were satisfied with the receipts of the opening game of the 1920/21 season, despite the attendance being smaller.

The ambitious Midland League clubs were put in an awkward position when the powers-that-be ruled that resignations had to be sent in by 1st March 1921 - before the date of the Football League meeting which was to decide the formation of the Northern section. Confident of success, Town duly resigned, but their hopes were shattered when their 13 votes were not enough to gain them admittance to the Football League and this led to bitterness at the AGM of the Midland League. However, Town did succeed in obtaining re-election to the Midland League and they stubbornly decided to carry on, using what money they could scrape together for the signing of new players.

The year 1920 had ended on an unhappy note for County with the resignations of Mr Nelson and Mr Roper, and during the season there were many injuries and illnesses among the players.

During the 1921 summer, the levelling of Millmoor was undertaken although not everyone was in favour of the money - £1,000 - being spent in this way, but it had become necessary following complaints from other teams, also in fulfilment of a promise made to the Football League when County were elected to the Second Division. "Hillside Crescent" disappeared and new brick buildings were put up along with additional terracing which it was estimated, would increase the capacity by around 8,000 to 30,000.

All the hard work during the summer was rewarded when the team had a more successful 1921/22 season, for they finished in 16th position, three places higher than the previous campaign. They did, however, boast the best defensive home record in the division with a meagre seven goals conceded, and in the whole of the four sections only Darlington were able to match this number. Ironically the home playing record was identical to the previous season, with eight victories, nine draws and four defeats, while two more away wins were recorded.

Amalgamation of the town's two football teams was first hinted at in the early months of 1922 when representatives of the Football Association and the Football League were present at meetings of shareholders of the two clubs when the fatuity of Rotherham trying to support two separate clubs was pointed out. It was felt that the weaker one would have to go and there were also reports that the Midland Railway Company required the Millmoor ground for new sidings, but these were denied.

Town were certainly in need of some help for their income was falling short of expenditure and the officials found themselves in a similar position to that of their Clifton Grove predecessors. Attendances at matches were so discouraging that players were asked to submit to a reduction in wages and they were given the freedom to join other clubs, significantly, two players moved to County.

After struggling to complete their league programme, Town tendered their resignation from the Midland League while County had experienced their own share of financial hardship and were not in a position to bail Town out.

Hopes of an amalgamation into one club to be known simply as Rotherham were dashed with bitterness when Mr G.W. Parkin, a director of the Town club, expressed himself as being sick and tired of professional football. So Town had to go it alone again. They were allowed to withdraw their resignation from the Midland League, although it meant that they had to find an entirely new team and arrangements were made for them to share the Clifton Lane ground with another revived club - Rotherham Amateurs.

The season proved to be even more difficult for Town, for receipts were disappointing and rumours were prevalent that there was a likelihood of the club becoming defunct at the end of the season. Town finished second from bottom with only 22 points from 24 matches, but expenditure had been kept down to a minimum and on the strength of this, the officers of the club with almost foolhardy bravado, decided to carry on.

For Rotherham County, the 1922/23 season ended in almost complete disaster. In April 1923, The Football League appointed a commission of inquiry which came to the conclusion that the Rotherham County Football Club had made illegal payments to an amateur - G.W. Cook - when signing him from Bishop Auckland. The League wielded the big stick by fining County £50, cancelling the registration of the player and suspending four of the club's officials for a period of twelve months. The club was also fined £25 for violating League rules in respect of the registration of a player who was on Leeds United's retained list - J.Lambert - but the ultimate calamity came at the end of the season when Rotherham County's many flirtations with relegation met with the inevitable result.

The club had made their first appearance in the FA Cup proper, but they made their exit in the first round, going down to a single goal defeat against Chelsea at Stamford Bridge. The team had spent the previous week in special training in Brighton, and for the Rotherham spectators the chance to visit the capital city was something not to be forgotten.

Arriving at King's Cross station some three hours before kick off, they endulged in some sightseeing and attracted great attention from the locals with their Yorkshire accents. After the match they called in at a well known restaurant hoping to obtain a substantial meal. But to their disappointment they dropped in on a 'tea dansant', and all they could get in the foodline was a cup of tea, sandwiches and a few cakes. One of the members of the party called for the waiter, and having asked for the menu all the infomration he could elicit from this worthy 'foreigner' was, *"twice four"*. Not knowing what the waiter meant, the Rotherhamite replied, *"right-ho"*, and a few minutes later was presented with a bill for 24 shillings!

County won their last match of the season against Blackpool only to find that their efforts had been in vain and they went down, with

Wolverhampton Wanderers, into the Northern Section of the Third Division. That meant that County no longer had voting powers on League matters as they were now regarded only as associate members.

Using what money was raised from a Bank Holiday sports carnival, Town entered into the 1923/24 season with ambitions that again came to nought; they finished as wooden-spoonists in the Midland League to rule out any further thoughts of applying for League status. Fortunately for Town, there were several resignations from the Midland League so they did not have to apply for re-election but that League became a mere shadow of its former self.

County, meanwhile were pulling themselves together, ending the 1923/24 season in fourth place - thanks mainly to a 9 match unbeaten run in January and February - and the public in general and the business people in Rotherham in particular were urged to take up the 1,679 shares that had remained un-allocated, with the need for financial backing following a season's loss of £1,400.

The end is near for Rotherham Town 1923/24 season players and officials.

Back row (left to right):—C. Smalley, W. Gill, W. Jowett, W. Brammer, H. Douglas (hon. sec.), A. Hobson, T. Townsend, E. Haggar. Third row:—L. Binks, E. Whitchurch, C. O. Bretnall, L. Johnson, F. G. Wainwright, L. M. Bedford, C. Hazeltine, W. Hawley. Second row:—J. Burnley, F. Bevan, S. Williams, A. Taylor, S. Abbott, F. A. Laycock, F. Rose, G. Sharman (team manager). Front row:—A. Perry, G. W. Wilde, C. Mayor, R. Duckenfield, E. Pennington, F. Moorhouse, Hodgkiss (trainer).

Former player Herbert Lounds won a court case against the club in January 1924 when he applied for compensation following a knee injury he received whilst playing against Hull City on 21st October 1922. His average weekly wage was £8 at the time, and he was paid £6 per week until 5th May 1923, before an agreement was reached that Lounds would receive £1-15 weekly and costs, after the club admitted liability.

The promotion hopes of Rotherham Town and County for the season 1924/25 were not to be realised for at the end of the season County were no fewer than eleven points adrift at the bottom of the table with just 21 points from 42 matches, while Town fared little better. The latter finished in twelfth position out of 15 Midland League clubs with 22 points from 28 matches and it proved to be their last season with the long awaited amalgamation finally taking place.

An appeal by Town to the local business houses in December 1924 failed to bring sufficient response and the County directors, bearing in mind their own none too rosy outlook, approached members of the Clifton Lane organisation. This time there were more positive results, with the new formation agreed by both parties in early March 1925. A meeting of the Town club passed resolutions in favour of the appointment of a liquidator for the purpose of winding up the company. For every three shares in the Town club two were to be granted in the United organisation, the capital of which was to be increased to £8,000 in order to cover the issue. An early April County programme issued the following statement, designed to clarify the situation for everyone.

"These are momentous days for Rotherham football and especially for those who are entrusted with its control. They are days of change and from the process of transition, there is to emerge a Rotherham United club - an organistaion with a new name, a strong and virile body and with a determination to realise high ambitions.

"A new start is to be made and given the support of the public, success will be met with. It is this support that is earnestly asked for and needed. Old and new friends of Rotherham football, whether they have in the past favoured Millmoor or Clifton Lane, or both grounds, are asked to rally round the new standard which is to be raised.

"Between now and the end of the present season - not many weeks remain for its close - an effort to rally the forces that can fight for the retention of League football in Rotherham is to be made. Financial help is necessary before the work of re-organistion can be pushed on with and the public is to be appealed to for this monetary assistance. If everybody will contribute a little, the task will be accomplished and we shall commence next season with brighter prospects than ever before".

Mr W.G.Parkin was appointed to the Board of Directors of the new club and one of his last acts as chairman of the Town club had been to entertain the players of the club and their wives to dinner in celebration of their winning the Sheffield Challenge Cup and to mark the passing out of existence of the Rotherham Town Football Club. Taking no chances, the County directors obtained a lease on the Clifton Lane ground thus precluding any possibility of the Athletic Company granting a lease to people who might inaugurate another Rotherham Town Football Club. The ground was retained as a "nursery" and for use by the third team in the Sheffield Association League.

Two events marked the end of this chapter in the history of football in Rotherham; at an extraordinary general meeting of the shareholders of the County club, held at Millmoor on 27th May 1925, a resolution was passed changing the name of the company to "The Rotherham United Football Club", and at the annual meeting of the Football League a few days later, Rotherham United were unanimously re-elected - or was it elected? - to the Northern Section of the Third Division of the Football League.

The meeting which took place in London proved to be a mere formality with Rotherham United gaining 42 votes, Tranmere Rovers 32, Mansfield Town 13 and Blyth Spartans 3 with the first two clubs being elected. Rotherham were represented by Mr E.J. Jenkins and Mr J.Thorpe (directors) and Mr J. Briggs (secretary).

The first change that took place was the announcement that the new United team would wear different colours with the former black and white colours of County being replaced by black and gold jerseys with a black lined V, black cuffs and white knickers.

A new signing was also made quickly with T.W. Brelsford, a well known half-back, joining Rotherham from Barrow. He had spent eight seasons with The Wednesday and he declined to re-sign for Barrow owing to the inconvenience of travelling the long distance to and from his home in Sheffield. Rotherham had to pay Barrow a fee for his transfer but it was thought that he would prove a great acquisition with his extensive experience.

The annual general meeting of the club was held towards the end of June when the chairman Mr W.Wordsworth looked forward to the club entering a new era, and he said the club would continue to bring in new players in an attempt to get the club back into the Second Division.

In fact J.Lee, who had previously played with Hull City and Chelsea, had been signed that day and negotiations were going on with another, but the club was in debt to the amount of £5,493-2s-4d and to try and offset this, a Shilling Fund had been set up. But that met with a poor response from the Rotherham public who had become disillusioned with football in the town after the previous season's poor displays on the pitch.

Season ticket prices were announced - £2-2s-0d for a seat in the front of the stand - and the new season was anticipated with great enthusiasm with several practice matches scheduled to take place.

But after last season's poor showing there was also an air of caution about, and despite the poor results which had led to the re-election situation most of the players had been retained, with five

newcomers brought in to try and strengthen the club. The practice game emphasised that United had far more reserves to call on.

And so the long awaited new season got under way with Rotherham United playing its first game at Bradford on 29th August 1925, with three newcomers, Brelsford, Glew and Hodgetts, in the line-up. But what a comedown it was for them - beaten 6-1 - and what's more, clearly outplayed with only centre-forward Hammerton and goalkeeper Mehaffy matching their opponents. It was Hammerton who had the distinction of scoring United's first ever goal but the supporters were not disheartened, even if they had been unprepared for such a scoreline, and they turned up in great numbers for the opening game at Millmoor, against Tranmere Rovers two days later.

There were in fact between 7,000 and 8,000 spectators for the first home game and they witnessed a much improved performance which led to a 2-0 victory and everything in the garden looked rosy. The optimism spilled over into the next game when Grimsby Town were the visitors with the 2-1 victory being the second game in a four match unbeaten run which was regarded as a good achievement, with injuries already starting to have a serious effect, particularly the one which sidelined centre-forward Jack Hammerton.

It had been an encouraging start but local tradesmen had still not dipped into their pockets as deeply as was hoped for, when they were asked to give increased financial support to the newly amalgamated club. But the directors bravely pursued a progressive policy and the search for the players who could bring success to the club was stepped up considerably, although it was very refreshing to see the emergence of Jackie Bestall who was usually the best player on view.

Things started to go wrong though when a 5-1 defeat at Halifax was quickly followed by another, by the same scoreline, at Durham and that led to the resignation of secretary-manager Mr J.Briggs and the directors who selected the side for the next game against Hartlepools United made several changes. A five figure attendance at Millmoor witnessed a draw against local rivals Doncaster Rovers, after beating Hartlepools, before the club at last succeeded in the transfer market with the signing of Ernest H.Goldthorpe from Manchester United at the end of October, and it was expected that he would provide the goals.

However, he played in just two games which both ended in defeat before his leg gave way and he agreed to cancel his agreement with the club in order not to be a burden on the club's finances. One of those games was against Nelson which ended with the referee reporting the club for bad behaviour, but an inquiry into the allegations of misconduct by the spectators only led to the posting of notices around the ground warning against a repetition.

Fortunes then took a big swing for the better with five successive victories - two of them coming in the F.A. Cup to give the team their best ever record in the competition. A fine display disposed of Halifax in the first round and that success gave United a mouth watering tie against Doncaster Rovers in the second round, in a game which aroused more excitement than on any previous occasion.

Between 5,000 and 6,000 Rotherham supporters made the journey to Doncaster and those who stayed at home were reported to be uneasy until they had heard the result which was a 2-0 away win. The many United followers enabled Doncaster to establish a new attendance record for the ground with the 13,764 people present paying a total of £817 15s 3d. The cup victories heartened the club's followers, re-kindled the fire of enthusiasm but more importantly it took them to the stages of the competition never reached before, as they could now complete with the aristocrats of the game.

The draw for the third round pitted Rotherham against First Division Bury at Millmoor and it would be the first competition proper game ever to be played in Rotherham. It was anticipated that the record receipts figure of just over £1,000 would be broken. That had been established on 1st November 1920 when 21,000 spectators saw Rotherham beat The Wednesday

in a Second Division League game. The build up to the big cup game could not have been worse as Rotherham suffered five successive defeats - one of them a 6-1 hammering at Chesterfield.

The poor run of defeats did not dampen the enthusiasm of the locals, though, and the demand for tickets for the reserved sections of the stand was so great that they were all sold over a week before the game.

United put up one of their most gallant ever performances in the F.A. Cup before they went down 3-2 to Bury, who at the time were one of the most talked about teams in the land, but the home team took enormous praise for their performance. There had been no more interesting a match played at Millmoor up to that time, with the game full of thrills and good football.

There was a disappointing feature to come out of the epic and that was the attendance with expectations of a record crowd not being realised, and the final figure being 16,442 who paid receipts of £965. Various reasons were given for the official figures falling short of the estimates with one being that many people were kept away in the belief that the ground would be too crowded and another that the game would be too one-sided in Bury's favour.

So it was a case of back to the bread and butter of the League, but matters were not helped regarding the attendances particularly for a home game against Halifax when it was reported that over 8,000 Rotherham people travelled to Sheffield to see the Blades lose 2-1 to Sunderland in the fourth round of the F.A. Cup. Inconsistent form followed United until the end of the season, but in late February there was a surprise off the pitch when it was announced that the whole of the playing staff had been placed on the transfer list with the coffers in great need of replenishing.

Expenditure in the amalgamation scheme with Rotherham Town had been very heavy. It was the time of the year when clubs were on the look-out for new players and with stories of the financial plight gathering pace, it was rumoured that the club might even break up. But that was not the case as was indicated by the fact that offers of £1,800 and £700 for two players were rejected as being too small, but the club reached the end of their first ever season as Rotherham United in 14th place with 41 points from their 42 games.

When the accounts were revealed in the middle of June a loss on the season of £1,956-1s-8d was announced, but this deficit was not as bad as many people had predicted thanks to strict economies which included a reduction in the wages and salaries list of £600 compared to the previous season. In his report at the subsequent annual meeting, chairman Mr W. Wordsworth said he thought the amalgamation with Town had been a disaster financially having had to pay off Town's debts, but he was convinced there was a much better future ahead.

In an attempt to attract more spectators to Millmoor all season ticket prices were reduced as the club looked forward to the new campaign with great anticipation. Most of the previous season's players were still at the club but some newcomers had been introduced, the main one being the signing of Harold Pantling from Sheffield United.

He was an international half-back, while the "giant" Bernard Chambers elected to join Rotherham in preference to any of the numerous other clubs who were after him, and the two new recruits both played in the opening game, at home to Crewe Alexandra. That game produced a home win and it was followed two days later with another victory at Millmoor, this time against Wrexham to put Rotherham where they had never been before - at the top of the northern section of Division Three.

Star performer in those two early wins was the youthful Albert Oakton from nearby Dinnington, but the whole team performed well, particularly considering that injuries had reduced them to only eight players at one stage in the game against Crewe. And the attendances were much better than had been expected with the coal trade dispute still leaving many people unemployed, although the club were unable to reduce admis-

sion prices as they wanted to do as these were governed by the Football League.

In addition to topping the table for the first time, another record was established for it was also the first time that a Rotherham team had started a season in the Football League with two successive wins. The financial difficulties the spectators were enduring was emphasised by a lot of them trying to gain admission through the boys' gate - half price - and trouble threatened causing the club to take such steps to put a stop to the practice.

The good start, though, wasn't maintained and defeats against Nelson and Chesterfield led to the directors making several changes for the visit to Ashington with new signing Pantling left out and a local amateur, Roland Bentley, came in to replace centre-forward Fergusson. It was some reward with a 4-4 draw but the main worry for the directors was the large number of football followers who were electing to travel to watch football in Sheffield rather than turn up at Millmoor, to leave the financial purses rather strained.

Letters continued to pour into the Rotherham Advertiser from dissatisfied fans, but all efforts to recruit new players were halted by the exorbitant fees clubs were demanding for players and great importance was placed on another good cup run in view of the unenviable financial position.

The club had started with a big debit bank balance and that had increased during the season, but the cup game ended in a disappointing defeat at Lincoln who won 2-0.

Jackie Bestall was sold to Grimsby Town a couple of days before the cup-tie to produce much needed income which would help to pay the wages, and it was reported that his transfer represented a good piece of business with the fee said to be just short of four figures. Despite all the monetary troubles United were in a midtable position going into the Christmas holiday games, but they only took one point from three games as they went into a spell of ten games without a win.

Sheffield United were knocked out of the F.A. Cup at the first time of asking by Arsenal in the third round and it was hoped that their exit would lead to more Rotherham people watching matches at Millmoor in preference to Bramall Lane.

One way of trying to arouse greater interest was tried prior to the game at Millmoor against Bradford on 28th January, with the introduction of community singing accompanied by the Rotherham Borough Band whilst the well-known local musician Charles Elsom led the affair. Rumours were spreading rapidly that several Rotherham players were being lined up to leave the club to ease the ever increasing financial burden and it came as a huge disappointment when the proposed move of Ramsden to Nottingham Forest did not materialise. A 5-0 home win against Ashington lifted the gloom a little but that was one of only three wins from the turn of the year until the end of the season.

A measure of the indifference that the local support was generating for United was emphasised by the fact that on the day they were playing away at Southport, Rotherham Boys attracted a crowd of over 8,000 when they beat Scarborough at Millmoor in the semi-final of the Yorkshire Wylie Schools competition - a figure more than double the usual to watch Rotherham.

In compliance with the Football League regulations the retained list had to be announced before the 17th April and Rotherham underlined the fact that their team was not good enough by offering new contracts to only seven players - at a salary of £208 per year. Another seven followed suit the following week and it was something of a relief when the season ended with United in 19th position out of 22 clubs but at least they did not have to go cap in hand and apply for re-election.

What's more there was some very welcome additions to the coffers with Ramsden, who hit 11 goals that season, being transferred to Manchester United. Also an important signing was made behind the scenes with Billy Heald taking over as secretary/manager some four years after he joined the club as assistant secretary, and he

was to play a big part in the running of the club for many years.

The 1927/28 season got off to a bad start with a 2-0 defeat at Stockport County and with ten minutes of their next game against Tranmere Rovers to go, they were trailing by one goal to nil and most of the 5,000 crowd had given up hope of any reward. But two late goals gave Rotherham their first win of the season and they quickly followed it by beating Barrow a few days later to raise hopes of better times to come.

The dark clouds on the industrial horizon had been lifted and the carping critics on the terraces were implored to give their team better backing with the expectancy that better results would follow from it. There was an immediate reward with a victory against Rochdale who had won all four of their League games up to that point, while off the field a new office was built and what's more it did not cost the club a penny as the material and work were generously given.

The organisation of the club was hit by the deaths of two directors within a short time of each other - Mr Joe Steeples and Mr W.H.Ball - who had both worked hard for the club forming part of the Board of management.

A handful of indifferent results were followed with resounding wins against Hartlepools United and Doncaster Rovers - the latter in the Sheffield and Hallamshire County Cup - and suddenly a new spirit was manifesting itself in the town, but it didn't last long with the next League victory not arriving until Chesterfield were beaten on 27th December, some seven games after the previous success.

As if the finances weren't under enough strain, a hurricane caused severe damage to the ground with about £100 worth of damage being done to the hoardings which were demolished on several sides of the ground. The repair work obviously could not be delayed but just where would the money come from? An appeal was made to the supporters and collecting boxes were put in place at the ground but the response amounted to £2!

The gloom on the financial front was lifted, though, with a remarkable debut from a new player, Thomas Hall who made the kind of entrance to a Rotherham career which it is doubtful if it has been matched since. He had been spotted playing for Darnall WMC and had scored 27 goals, netting at least three times in every game before hitting four goals in his first game in Rotherham's colours. Hall played his first match as an amateur against Wigan Borough, but he made such a tremendous impact that he signed professional forms immediately after the game.

The F.A. Cup again offered itself as a way of bringing much needed income into the club and the first round draw pitted Rotherham against Spennymoor United who declined the offer to switch the tie to Millmoor, leaving a long trip to Durham. A draw brought them back to Millmoor where a crowd of 5,043 paid receipts of £268 14s 9d to watch Rotherham go through to the next round with another away tie, this time at Bradford City. Around 1,400 Rotherham supporters made up part of the 9,503 crowd and with their rattles, trumpets and lusty lungs, they cheered their team to victory.

A home tie against Exeter City was the reward with hopes high that the previous record crowd of 20,000 would be broken with only one other tie due to take place in South Yorkshire, with The Wednesday's game against Bournemouth looking the least attractive.

By some strange means, Rotherham United were referred to as "The Saddlers" down Exeter way, and this was something of an insult to the colliers, the steel workers and the brass workers of the area. But the big day was to be a disappointment all round with United squandering a two goal lead to be held to a 3-3 draw and they lost the replay four days later. What's more, by being beaten, Rotherham lost the chance of a huge game in the next round, for the next round draw gave the winners a mouth watering clash against the famous Blackburn Rovers.

The game at Millmoor eventually attracted 15,425 spectators with £824-5s-0d receipts and the replay drew a crowd of 11,085 (£777).

The club received praise from Mr A.Green of the Brook Green Tavern, Exeter who wrote:-
"I have been requested to write on behalf of my party from Exeter to thank Rotherham United's club supporters for the enthusiastic welcome they gave them. They all say they have never met a more sporting and unbiased crowd in all their travels. Their only complaint was that after travelling all night and standing in the rain all afternoon watching the match, they had to leave Rotherham wet through with the thoughts of another ten hours' travelling and could not get a drink because the licensed houses did not open before their train left. They think that the Rotherham magistrates should show a little more consideration to their visitors on such occasions. Good luck to Rotherham United".

Performances on the field continued to be moderate but the club was dealt a severe blow at the end of February 1928 with the sudden death of 71-year-old William Wordsworth who had been chairman and had devoted such an enormous amount of his time into establishing Rotherham United in the Football League.

Tributes for him poured in for he had been regarded as the navigator who had to steer his ship through the troublesome seas and it was felt that the worries of the task had hastened his end. Six of the club's players acted as bearers at his funeral.

Under the gloom still hanging over his death, Rotherham players surpassed themselves the following Saturday with a fine performance which gave them a win at Hartlepools and the weight of the blow the players might have expected would handicap them, had the opposite effect.

It was a relief in many ways when the end of the season arrived following the heaviest defeat of the campaign - 6-0 at Ashington - in the penultimate game, and it saw a benefit game staged for full-back Jackson's reward for his loyal service to the club.

A friendly game was staged against Grimsby Town - his reward was an attendance of 523 who paid just over £24 and with £3 to be deducted for entertainment tax, the cost of printing, services of police, Town's travelling expenses and a few other items, there was precious little left for Jackson. Some benefit!

Team building plans for the 1928/29 season went ahead during the summer and United made what they considered to be an import-ant signing when they secured the services of 20-year-old Richard Gallyer who came to Millmoor after playing for two seasons in Liverpool's Central League side. After playing in the Midland Combination, the reserves made a welcome return to the Midland League and this was looked upon as financially rewarding, as there would be less expense in travelling than there had been in the other league. The club could also anticipate better gates with local clubs Barnsley, Chesterfield and Doncaster Rovers all coming into the Midland League where, of course, Rotherham County had enjoyed such success.

The Millmoor Lane stand under construction early in the 1928/29 season.

It looked as if Rotherham had lined up a new signing at the end of June when the transfer papers were despatched to the home of the Scottish player concerned, but when these were not immediately returned it later transpired that he had changed his mind after agreeing terms with Rotherham, in favour of a Football League club in the south.

The financial statement presented at the annual general meeting revealed a loss on the season of just over £30, which was considerably better than the previous deficit of more than £1,000 with the improvement mainly attributed to much increased receipts from Cup-ties.

Presiding over the meeting as chairman for the first time was Mr. John Thorpe who was well known and well respected in the highest circles of English football. As a member of the old Thornhill United club and director of both Rotherham County and United, he had a longer official association with Rotherham football than any other individual.

Several newcomers were in the Rotherham squad that looked forward to the 1928/29 season with great hope, but one of them - J.Hastings, a half back from Spennymoor - wasn't available for the first few weeks as he was banned by the Football Association for being involved in payments for amateurs before his move to Millmoor. But hope was soon turned to despair with an opening day 11-1 defeat at Bradford City, a scoreline which remains as Rotherham's heaviest ever defeat and it was described as astounding, staggering, bewildering, and discouraging, being confused with a cricket score.

To their credit, though, the players quickly put this dreadful opening behind them as they went on to record their best start in the Football League with three wins and two draws from the next five matches to put them in fourth position.

Meanwhile, after an indifferent start to the season the reserves started to string together some good performances and they notched up a fine 2-0 win at Millmoor against Nottingham Forest in front of a crowd of 3,000, and off the pitch plans were laid for the provision of a new covered stand on the enclosure with the supporters helping to meet the costs. These plans were subsequently approved, although it was decided that the structure would be erected on the popular side of the ground instead of the enclosure, at a cost of several hundred pounds. The new stand was 130 ft long, 35 ft wide, and accommodated 1,800 spectators at no additional charge apart from the normal ground admission.

The stand was designed by one of the directors - David B. Jenkinson - and special care was taken to avoid any obstruction to the view of the spectators, there being only two intermediate stanchions. No rivet holes were cut, giving economy in material, especially in tension members and joint connections, which it was claimed were stronger than rivetted joints. The type of structure followed American practice and it was stated to be the first of its type in Great Britain.

Injuries took their toll with the next four games all ending in defeat, and only four more victories were recorded in the sixteen games played before the turn of the year.

1929 started on a better note with a fine 3-1 win at Accrington Stanley, but an overnight journey to Barrow the following week left them on the wrong end of a 4-0 result, before the new Millmoor Lane covered stand was used for the first time for the visit of Hartlepools United on 19th January.

Inconsistency was again to prove to be a stumbling block for United, as they recorded fine wins against Wigan Borough (4-2) and Nelson (4-0), but they fell away to their second double figure thrashing of the season when they were beaten 10-1 at South Shields. Just before the victory against Nelson, United had an expensive and fruitless journey to Crewe when Gresty Road was judged as being unfit for play, but not until the Rotherham players had arrived at the ground. Such was the delay in reaching Manchester owing to frozen railway points, that the train to Crewe had already departed when the Rotherham players arrived in Cottonopolis. As there was no other trains to Crewe for several hours, some other means of transport had to be found with taxi-cabs eventually being used to complete the 20 miles to the ground.

Even then matters did not go smoothly, for one of the vehicles carrying four players got lost, before everyone eventually arrived just before 3pm, only for the referee to decide that the pitch was unfit for play in its frozen condition.

On the day the first team were crushed at South Shields, the reserves were beaten 7-2 at Millmoor by York City and the third team were thrashed 8-0 by Firbeck Colliery in the Sheffield Association League to make it a real disaster Saturday.

Fears were raised that the club would become involved in the battle to keep out of the re-election zone, but there was some encouraging news regarding the future in April 1929, when it was announced that Stanley Davies, the famous Welsh international forward, had been engaged as team manager.

This indeed was an important and bold step, for Davies had been capped 19 times by Wales and had previously played for Rochdale, Preston North End, Everton, West Bromwich Albion, Birmingham and Cardiff City, in addition to much active service during the war, when he won a string of medals - including the Military Medal and the Croix de Guerre. What's more he went on to play during the summer for Rotherham's Yorkshire Council cricket team as a medium pace bowler. His appointment was something of an innovation, for the directors had previously run the club, but Davies was given "carte blanche" in team management.

At least the season ended on a high note with the best win of the coming in the very last game - a 5-0 victory at Millmoor against Rochdale - and it was the only time United hit five goals in one game all season. Perhaps Stanley Davies was having an effect already!

Much work was carried out in the close season with Davies busily recruiting new players and appointing a new first team trainer in Charles Slade, who for the past two seasons had acted as trainer to the Folkestone Rowing Club. He was a well known former footballer who had spent nine seasons with Huddersfield Town and three with Middlesbrough. Time was also spent during the summer in making Millmoor look spic and span, but when the accounts were produced, they yet again showed a loss on the past season - this time over £1,952.

There was another addition to the Millmoor scene at this time with the opening of the Millmoor Hotel, on Thursday, 15th August 1929, and this hostelry has, of course, served Rotherham supporters ever since, firmly establishing itself as the headquarters for the supporters club. Among the newcomers to the club, were Joseph Little, Thomas Harris, G.Munden and Vic Wright,

Action from the Lincoln match in September 1929. The Millers centre-forward Wright is challenged by an Imps defender. Wright scored in this match to earn a 1-1 draw.

predominantly forwards, as Davies looked to remedy the problems in that department.

The 1929/30 campaign got off to a high scoring 5-4 defeat at Tranmere Rovers, but two wins and a draw from the next three games renewed the optimism that had filled the air at Millmoor prior to the start of the season.

A heat wave with extremely high temperatures saw Rotherham beat Halifax Town, when the star performer was centre half Andy Smailes. He was to be associated with the club for many, many years, as trainer and manager, and his name will crop up frequently in the later chapters.

With the financial millstone of the payment of the new stand still hovering, the Auxiliary Committee made themselves responsible for clearing off the debt with their "penny on the ball" scheme proving popular.

Results, though, did not go particularly well and at the end of October 1929, the club was rocked by rumours that it was unable to carry on due to financial difficulties, that all the players had been put up for sale, and the reason given that this situation had been brought about by poor support. There subsequently proved to be no foundation in these rumours, apart from a confidential letter which was circulated to other Football League clubs to the effect that certain players were available.

As far as the poor support was concerned, nothing could have been further from the truth for gate receipts were regularly on the increase with £300 being exceeded on several occasions, and season ticket sales had been the best for some considerable time.

The season continued to have its ups and downs with a 7-1 defeat at Southport followed by an F.A. Cup win against Ashington, when a crowd of 6,537 paid a total of £336 12s 3d - a figure which was very welcome to the Millmoor coffers. The second round saw Rotherham draw 3-3 at Scunthorpe before winning the replay 5-4 and that was a mightily important victory, for it took them through to the third round of the competition for the fifth time, with an attractive home tie against Nottingham Forest to look forward to.

The youngest ever team that Rotherham had fielded warmed up nicely for the Cup-tie against the Forest team - which occupied a mid-table Second Division place - by winning 5-0 against Tranmere Rovers, but a 5-1 defeat at Hartlepools then did nothing for the confidence.

Come F.A. Cup day everything ended in great disappointment, with the visitors notching up a comfortable 5-0 victory. But there was some consolation in that the attendance of 15,862 paid a total of just over £900. The game was played in appalling conditions and there was a feeling that the referee might have abandoned it after the interval with a blinding blizzard prevailing, and the light getting ever poorer. But that could not be blamed for the final outcome, as Rotherham were three down at half time.

There was some consolation the following week when United beat Barrow 7-0, and it was the first time they had hit so many in a Football League game. Four of the goals came from Munden, taking his tally to 17 - a number not approached by any Rotherham player in recent earlier years - while he also became the first Rotherham player in a League game to hit a quartet. Manager Stanley Davies was further honoured when he received a telegram inviting him to play for Wales against Ireland in Belfast, but he was unable to prevent a 7-0 defeat.

No less than 53 goals were conceded in the next 12 games to bring the season towards a miserable end, and the team eventually finished in 20th position after letting in no fewer than 113 goals in their 42 games - a huge letdown after the season had started with such optimism. This was a position just two points and one place above having to apply for re-election.

At one stage manager Davies was the subject of such abuse from the crowd when he was playing for the reserves - necessary since he had only ten other players fit enough to turn out - that he wrote an open letter to the "Advertiser" saying that he would never kick another ball for Rotherham. And it was not long before he severed his connection with the club altogether, when he issued a statement towards the end of March 1930 which said: *"In consequence of my inability to manage the affairs of Rotherham United Football Club, in a manner which in my opinion is necessary, I am reluctant to have to place my resignation in the hands of the directors."*

So ended another era in the club's history as a sorry season came to its close, but one highlight was the goalkeeping feats of Emery who faced ten penalty kicks, but was beaten only once, with another going wide, and saving the other eight.

To wind up the season the team then went on a six match tour of Denmark where they covered themselves in glory with a string of victories.

During the close season, in the summer of 1930, an appeal was launched to raise money for the club, and it was led by no less than the Mayor - Alderman E.Cruikshanks J.P. He consented to act as honorary chairman of the special organising committee which planned to raise £2,000. Steady progress was made towards this goal which was proved necessary again when the accounts revealed a loss on the season of over £864, but that was a considerable improvement on the previous season's £1,952 deficit. On a brighter note, the tour to Denmark realised a profit of £103.

There had not been a great deal of activity on the transfer front before the new season was due to get underway, until two days before the big kick-off, when Reg Freeman was signed from Middlesbrough for what was described as a substantial fee - and what a servant to the club he turned out to be. The season got off to a good start with two wins and a draw from the opening three games, and attendances were very encouraging, but it turned out to be yet another topsy-turvy time as far as results were concerned. Two important new signings were made - goalkeeper James Harris from Manchester City and centre forward William Hick from Notts County - and they had an immediate lifting effect on the team. Hick in particular proved to be a valuable asset, scoring eight goals in his first four games - including two hat-tricks - and he went on to record no less than five trios while tallying 30 goals in 32 League and Cup appearances.

Vic Wright hit four goals in an 8 - 1 win against Accrington Stanley at the beginning of October, but ten days later he was sold to Sheffield Wednesday, the current League champions, for what was said to be a record fee for the Rotherham club, although the exact amount was not specified. Around the same time, Thursday 16th October 1930, the inaugural meeting of the Supporters Club took place at the Millmoor Hotel and a few days later Bramley became the first branch to be formed, being quickly followed by Parkgate, Rawmarsh and East Dene.

The supporters quickly gave themselves the name, *"The Merry Millers"*, so that is how the nickname which was eventually used for the team was actually brought into existence. It was not long before they moved their headquarters to the Travellers Rest on Main Street, but there was a good reason for this as the club chairman Mr Thorpe had just become *"genial boniface"*. The club gradually increased in numbers and had reached over 400, with regular meetings being held to help to raise money which would be passed on to the football club.

An example of the type of concert the supporters held at the Masbrough Co-operative Hall to entertain their members, consisted - Miss A.E.Holland (soprano), Miss M.Jenkinson (violinist), Miss M.Pollard (elocutionist), Mr.F.Davison (baritone), Mr.H.Bramham (bass), Mr.R.Ganicott (baritone), Mr.E.Challener (comedian) and Mrs. J.Cook (accompanist) - that beats a disco any time!

There was to be no repeat of the previous season's F.A. Cup exploits, for Rotherham went out of the competition at the first hurdle suffering a humiliating 2 - 1 defeat at Midland league Newark Town, and the rot set in immediately as 21 goals were conceded in the first five games in December as the old defensive failings returned. After two successive wins at the beginning of 1931, a seven match sequence without a victory rang the alarm bells again as the team languished third from the bottom, with the threat of having to go cap in hand, with an application for re-election looking near once again. However, only one defeat was suffered in the last 11 matches to dispel those worries, and Rotherham finished in a much more respectable 14th position.

The dogs are paraded prior to the first race at Millmoor

And there was a financial boost when it was announced that greyhound racing would take place during the summer months at Millmoor, when the final obstacle was removed with the owners of the ground, the L.M.and S.Railway Company, giving their consent. The first meeting took place on Monday, 11th May 1931. This provided additional revenue which was vital to the club, for it was becoming increasingly difficult for the majority of football clubs to find the money to pay the summer wages, although for the first time since they had been playing Third Division football United actually made a profit. The sum of £781 was indeed a substantial one and it signalled a time for congratulations all round.

Many new players were signed during the summer - not all of them with Football League experience - and the number on the books rose to 24. Everyone in the district held the belief that there had been a re-awakening at Millmoor and that a really serious attempt was about to be made to lift Rotherham to a higher pinnacle than it had previously reached in the Third Division.

Even a practice match between the "Reds" and the "Blues" attracted an attendance of over 4,000, and it was felt that no other club in the Northern Section would be able to attract better support. Yet for all this optimism, the club had plummeted to despair by the end of October with just three wins from the opening 13 League games, and attendances had slumped to just over

3,000, raising questions about the possible collapse of the club. Not enough money was coming in via gate receipts to keep the club on an even keel and there were grave fears that the club was heading in the same direction as the old Town team had done in 1926.

Suddenly some form was found with seven victories from the last ten games which removed the fear of re-election, and the supporters were given the rare treat of a game at Millmoor against opponents from Holland, Almelo who had been the Dutch champions five years previously. Rotherham won 3 - 2.

A measure of the difficulties the club had encountered during the season was highlighted by the fact that no fewer than 29 players were used, and the weak playing strength was demonstrated by the fact that the reserves finished bottom of the Midland League. More surprisingly, perhaps, in view of the perilous financial situation was the fact that a considerable amount of money for season tickets was still outstanding and all those who had not paid were asked to "stump up" as soon as possible.

Within a couple of weeks of the end of the season, the directors issued an appeal for financial assistance to the public of Rotherham for help since there was a real danger of the club losing its Football League status. To compound the problems the Football Association suddenly decided that football grounds should not be used for greyhound racing and this created an immediate problem for Rotherham as they had just granted another 12 months tenancy to the local greyhound company. But the F.A. amended the wording of their resolution stating that no club should be controlled or financed by greyhound racing, and it was felt that the payment of rent should not be classed as financing the club.

The accounts confirmed what everyone had been expecting after such a struggle to balance the books, when a staggering loss of over £2,155 was declared to increase the total deficiency to a massive £14,230, a figure at this time which was a real millstone for any football club to have round its neck. Not surprisingly, it was a very quiet close season as far as bringing in new players was concerned, in fact the crippling wage bill had to be reduced to prevent a repetition of more hard times.

Season tickets were issued to anyone who paid a ten shillings deposit. The opening game produced a 1 - 0 home win against New Brighton but it was another season of struggle with an appalling away record, for it failed to produce a single win on opponents grounds. There were also a couple of hefty defeats as Rotherham lost 8-0 at Crewe and 9-2 at Mansfield, while the best victories were a 5-0 triumph against Crewe in the return game and a 6-1 win against Halifax in the final match.

There was no cup joy either as United went out in the first round, soundly beaten 4-0 at Chester. Therefore it could well have been regarded as something of a success by finishing in 17th position at the end of the 1932/33 season, although the club had the unenviable record of being the only Football League team not to have won an away match.

Wages had been kept at an absolute minimum, but the finances improved with the transfer of centre half George Bratley to Sheffield Wednesday with Rotherham receiving a substantial fee in addition to Victor Wright returning to Millmoor. He had always been popular with United's supporters following his move from Bristol Rovers to Rotherham at the commencement of the 1929/30 season, but after little more than one season, he moved to Wednesday.

The start of the "Merry Millers" - Officials of the Supporters Club in September 1931. (Front): P.Bird, E.Prestidge, F.Shaw, C.Taylor, E.Evers & R.White. (2nd Row): H.Bennett, R.Callear (Asst.Sec.), E.Foster (Vice-Pres.), Ald. E.Cruikshanks JP (Pres.), F.Yates (Chair.), C.Danton (Sec.) & J.Fergusson (Vice-Chair). (3rd Row): S.Callear, Sneath, Bratley, E.Smith, Evers, Fowler, L.Fergusson (Top): R.Bartholomew, C.Bray, J.Hayes, C.Rawlings, J.Waller, J.McNulty, E.Ellison.

The curtain was also drawn down as regards greyhound racing at Millmoor with the last meeting taking place on 29th July 1933, and although the income would be sadly missed, there would be no more complaints, particularly from visiting teams, for the track cut up a portion of the playing area.

The annual Football League meeting considered several new proposals, including the increasing of the number of clubs to be promoted and relegated, the introduction of numbered shirts and a "sixpenny" gate for the unemployed, but all were defeated as they did not receive the necessary two thirds majority.

The strict economy measures the club had instituted paid dividends when a surplus of £575 was revealed with the players' wages having been drastically reduced as there had been a 50 per cent cut in training expenses

and players' requisites, but gate receipts were down again.

The usual campaign of summer recruiting was carried out, although of course this was governed by the available money and one newcomer was winger George Raynor who was signed from Mansfield Town. He was to go on and make a long career in football both as a player and manager.

Another acquisition was W.Burkinshaw who was signed from Falkirk in the face of strong opposition from a string of other clubs, and the question was raised as to how Rotherham had managed to achieve this transfer. He acquired a job at the stove grate works of Yates, Haywood and Co., and it just so happened that the managing director of that firm was a Rotherham follower!

Any hopes of any success were soon thrown out of the window when the first victory was not achieved until the eighth match of the season, and at the end of a long hard campaign, the team finished next to the bottom and had to go cap in hand to apply for re-election. There was some consolation in that the previous season's dreadful away record was improved with five successes on the team's travels, and at least there were not any heavy defeats as had often been the case in the past, but this time round the team had a poor home record. The first win at Millmoor was not achieved until 18th November and only five were managed throughout the whole season.

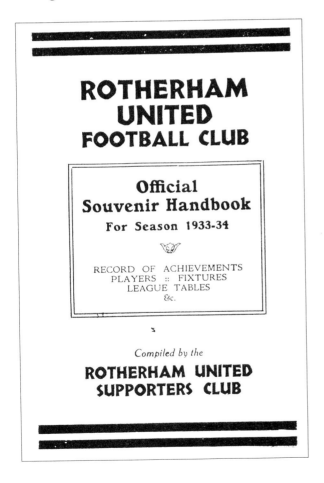

ROTHERHAM UNITED FOOTBALL CLUB

Official Souvenir Handbook

For Season 1933-34

RECORD OF ACHIEVEMENTS
PLAYERS :: FIXTURES
LEAGUE TABLES
&c.

Compiled by the

ROTHERHAM UNITED SUPPORTERS CLUB

The 1933/34 season saw the introduction of the new Northern Section Cup which was brought into being for clubs no longer involved in the F.A. Cup - a forerunner of the Associate members, Leyland Daf, Auto Windscreens Shield, etc. - and Rotherham beat Barnsley in the first round before going out at Chesterfield in the second. The season ended just as badly as it had started with no wins in the last eight games and come the beginning of May, morale was at a very low ebb.

The highlight of the season came in the F.A. Cup for after disposing of South Bank St Peters in the first round, United pulled off a fine win over Coventry in the second, and the draw for the famous third round gave them a real plum draw - Sheffield Wednesday at home. During the week before the cup game, an important move was made with the appointment of Reg Freeman as player/manager in an attempt to bring greater organisation to the team. For some considerable time the directors had been responsible for running the team and in recent weeks they had been very lacking in tactical awareness, which explained the reason why the players invariably left the field much more leg weary than their opponents. Andy Smailes took up the post of trainer.

Freeman's experience as a player started with Harrowby in the West Cheshire League before he moved on to Northern Nomads. He also played for Yorkshire Amateurs against the Corinthians, and in 1919 he went to Oldham Athletic where, after playing one game as an amateur in the reserves, he was included in the first team and remained with the Latics for nearly three seasons. While with Oldham he was an ever-present, and also captained the side, before moving to Middlesbrough with whom he remained for ten seasons before coming to Rotherham in August 1930.

But there was to be no early joy for Freeman who saw his team put up a gallant battle before Wednesday won 3-0, although record receipts were taken from the 20,198 attendance which fell just short of the previous best - 21,000 in 1921 when Sheffield Wednesday were also the opposition in a Second Division game. As had happened in that earlier game, a section of the barriers gave way, but no one was seriously hurt although a few people were treated for minor injuries.

The season drew to its close with something of a sour taste with the penultimate home game seeing United beaten 3-1 by Wrexham in what was described as the poorest performance in a bad season, with team selection being queried.

The last home game, versus Mansfield on the 5th May, produced a crowd of only 1,324, which remains as the lowest League attendance at Millmoor since Football League records have been kept.

Most people were under the impression that Reg Freeman's advice was always followed, yet the chairman, Mr. Edgar Jenkins, publicly stated that the team chosen by the selection committee was not recommended by Freeman. The strange state of affairs was further highlighted by the fact that Mr Jenkins stayed away from the game as a token of objection regarding the selection!

Fears of not gaining re-election to the Football League did not materialise when the only two applicants were Rotherham United and Rochdale who had occupied the bottom two positions. Nelson sent in a provisional application but this was not acceptable to the Football League.

Freeman spent the summer months wisely recruiting new players and his first signing was a goalkeeper - J.Clough - who had been a regular member of Brentford's Second Division team, and others included Leslie Heelbeck from Wolverhampton Wanderers,

Dick Duckworth from Chester, and James Reid, a left winger from Southport.

It looked to be the same old story when the first win of the 1934/35 season did not arrive until the seventh game, but Freeman had a set pattern which he stuck to, and he brought off a fine season for the town to celebrate, with the eventual ninth position being the best United had achieved upto that time.

Once that first victory had been notched up, things looked up considerably with 7,000 being present for the next game, and by April, gates had rocketed to an incredible 20,195 for the match against Doncaster Rovers at Millmoor. Three days after 27,506 (a Third Division Northern Section record) had watched the two teams battle it out at Belle Vue.

With improved displays on the pitch, rumours were often ripe that other clubs were watching Rotherham players, but there was nearly a transfer off the pitch in November 1934. The L.M.and S Railway Company offered the freehold of the Millmoor ground for sale by auction, but it was withdrawn when the bidding had reached £4,800 after starting at £3,000. The ground was let to the club by the railway company at a rent of £100 per year with the current lease starting on 1st May 1932 for three years. It was advertised as being in an excellent position either for continued use as a sports ground or racing track, or for development purposes.

The aforementioned lease obviously expired in 1935, and there was a real worry for the club when an intimation was received by the club from the owners, that the rent was to be trebled and the lease would in future be only from year to year. The complete facts were placed before the Borough Council in the hope that they might help in some way, even possibly by buying the ground, a situation which was not unknown as several clubs had grounds at that time which had been purchased by the local councils.

A piece of land in Eldon Road, originally purchased by the corporation for the purpose of a public playing field was suggested as a site for the United's ground should the worst happen, but it seemed to be a poor alternative. The Eldon Road ground was not as accessible, and its preparation to make it suitable would cost almost as much as the purchase price of Millmoor, but nevertheless the council agreed to the site being leased to the football club.

The question of a suitable ground had, of course, been a troublesome one ever since a Rotherham football team had been in existence, but it was disastrous to think that the problem had arisen again, just as United had put together the best team they had had since going down from the Second Division. Chairman Jenkins started to think positively about moving to Eldon Road, where he could visualise a stadium with a 30,000 capacity in a thickly populated area which was still being developed.

At its next meeting, the council agreed to loan the Eldon Road land to Rotherham United at a rental of £50 for the first three years, £100 for the next seven and an option of a further lease for ten years on terms to be agreed upon. But there was no necessity to implement this agreement, when in late February 1935, the railway company yielded to the pressure of public opinion and amended their terms which were accepted by the football club. These included a longer lease and a substantially reduced rent compared with the original terms. This allowed the club to concentrate on affairs on the field again and there was even talk of gaining promotion, but this was not be, although it turned out to be a very good

season with much of the credit due to manager Reg Freeman. The team did though achieve one notable distinction, and that was not conceding a single penalty kick throughout the whole season.

The annual meeting of the Football League raised a couple of interesting possibilities, but both were rejected as once again they did not obtain the necessary two thirds majority. Everton had proposed that a two referees' system be introduced and Derby County had suggested that four clubs instead of two be promoted to and relegated from the First Division and two each from the Third Divisions promoted to the Second.

The summer of 1935 saw big improvements made to the Millmoor ground with the stand on the enclosure side being re-covered, re-painted and re-sheeted, and a lot of other work was carried out to make the ground spick and span for the new season.

In addition to having a good season on the pitch in the season just ended, the club made a profit of £1,600, the first time they had made such a sum.

No less than eleven new players were among the squad that prepared for the 1935/36 season, with an air of unheard optimism circulating the area that the team could mount a serious challenge for promotion to capitalise on the success of the season just ended. As well as having made the ground look smart and in a good state of repair, workers had almost completed the building of a players' gymnasium which was expected to be of great value, although there was still around £80 of the £150 cost to be raised.

As usual, the team had a bad start with the opening three games all ending in defeat, before a 5-0 home win against Southport got the season swinging, three of the goals coming from William Dickinson. That was the first of three wins on the trot and a sequence of League games which saw just a single defeat in 11 matches, and with the team building up an ever increasing reputation for playing good football. They approached the Christmas games in seventh position, eight points behind leaders Tranmere Rovers, while in the F.A. Cup they had disposed of Cheshire League Champions Wigan Athletic at Springfield Park in front of 15,550 spectators. That win gave United a second round tie against Third Division Southern Section Watford, with the first game ending all square at Millmoor before an attendance of 12,700. Rotherham bowed out of the competition in the replay through the only goal of the game, which was not without incident.

United hit the woodwork on several occasions and claimed they had scored a second half equaliser when Dickinson sent a shot crashing against the Watford bar, with many people being of the opinion that the ball had actually hit the inside of the net. However, the referee thought otherwise and ordered play to proceed.

A 6-0 home win in March against Rochdale, with Roland Bastow hitting four of the goals - the second time in the season he had notched a quartet - was the highlight of the season, while the last two games both ended in defeat. The penultimate fixture was a 4-1 setback at Crewe, but that was nothing compared with the final match when United suffered an 8-2 hammering at Mansfield Town.

The Football League authorities came close to courting with disaster during the season, for they became embroiled in a bitter battle with the companies who ran the football pools which had become very popular. The officials were making attempts to outlaw this practice and they planned to scrap the original fixture lists and the matches for the following Saturday were to be kept secret until the preceding Friday.

Imagine the problems that would have caused with very little time being available to make all the necessary arrangements. The worst scenario was actually put into practise for a couple of weeks, but attendances soon slumped and the Football League were persuaded to see sense and the fixture lists reverted to normal.

The League authorities were in the news again at the June meeting when a two-thirds majority was reached to bring in the promotion and relegation of four clubs between divisions but the joy for the reformers was shortlived when it was discovered that a three-quarters majority was needed.

Once again the accounts made depressing reading with a loss of £897, but an interesting point was the fact that Rotherham paid a total of £936 in gate percentages to visiting clubs while they received only £643 from the clubs they visited.

Chesterfield gained promotion at the end of the last season to leave Rotherham with no real local derby, as Barnsley and Doncaster Rovers had also gone up in recent years, so once again the summer recruiting was done with the aim of joining them in the higher status and to renew local battles. The new players included Ralph Pedwell- a left winger from Barnsley, James Winn - an inside forward from Southport, Reg Kilsby - an outside right from Scunthorpe, Fred Hanson - an outside left from Crystal Palace and Arnold Bramham - a centre forward from Notts County.

For a pleasant change the 1936/37 season got off to a good start with a 3-0 home win against Gateshead in front of a 6,000 crowd, and even though the second match saw a 2-1 defeat at Hull, the team were said to be unlucky as they played, *"some great football"*. But the early season promise was soon shattered with a heavy defeat at Darlington, followed by a dull goalless draw at home to Hull, before five successive League victories restored pride and hope after the team had been subjected to considerable barracking from the so-called supporters.

Two games saw a barrage of goals, for following a 6-0 home win against Halifax Town - with Brown hitting a hat-trick - Rotherham battled out a thrilling 4-4 draw at Millmoor against Hartlepools United in the first round of the F.A. Cup. Brown grabbed another three goals in a game which saw Rotherham leading 4-2 with only 20 minutes to go, but the visitors fought back to earn a replay which they won 2 - 0. There was some consolation in the attendances with 11,552 watching the first game and over 8,000 witnessed the replay.

The dawning of 1937 could not have brought a worse possible time to Millmoor, for the club went through a spell of 13 League and Cup games without a win to leave them floundering at the bottom of the table. But five wins (four of them in successive games) and a draw from the last nine games lifted them to a final 17th position and one of safety.

As a reward for winning those four games on the trot, the players were treated to a day out in the Dukeries before taking tea in Nottingham, and staying on in that city to watch the Nottingham Forest v. Tottenham Hotspur game in the evening. For another treat the players had spent a day the previous week on the Sitwell Park Golf course - goodness knows what the reward would have been if they had kept on winning!

No one managed an ever-present record as 24 players were called upon, although Ernest Smith had the most consistent record, playing in every game after signing for the club in October. Goalscoring was a problem, not for the first or last time, with three players - Smith, Pedwell and Bastow - claiming 55 goals between them, out of a total of 77. Pedwell left to join local rivals Doncaster Rovers, but United were happy with the deal as far as financial terms were concerned, for an incoming recruit was goalkeeper Harold Sleight who the previous season had made 16 Third Division appearances for Carlisle United. As the rebuilding continued another departure saw Leslie Heelbeck, who had been captain for the previous three seasons, join his home town club Scarborough. When the League met once again the "four up four down" proposal was rejected.

Instead of the expected heavy financial loss, outgoing transfers resulted in the club showing a small profit, although it was still in heavy debt to the tune of over £12,400.

Dependence for the 1937/38 season was principally placed in the hands of younger players for the days of a high outlay on new players had to be

There were some new faces, including :- W.Murray, J.Clarke, E.Humphrey, J.Lynch, J.Larkin, W.Brown, H.Sleight.

brought to an end, after previous excursions into the transfer market had not had their desired effect. There had been a time when big transfer fees were paid for players, including £1,000 (twice) and £400 (several times).

In an attempt to attract spectators to the ground, there was no increase in the price of season tickets. In fact, the club went even further by offering what amounted to hire purchase terms through the co-operation of local firms who deducted weekly sums from their employees wages, and when all the season ticket money had been collected they forwarded it to the football club. This scheme had already been successfully adopted at Messrs R. Jenkins and Co. Ltd., and it enabled a number of workmen to take out season tickets when they would otherwise not have been able to do so.

Lo and behold! Rotherham United won their opening two games of the 1937/38 season and that was something they had not achieved since 1930, and though they lost the third game, the next two also ended in victory to set in motion a season which was to become the best ever for Rotherham United up to that time.

Injuries soon took their toll and they led to the early debut of James Mills who made rapid strides after joining the club, to finding his way into the first team. A native of Bramley, he had played the previous season with Dinnington but felt he was not making much progress, so he turned up at Millmoor one morning and smilingly asked for a trial. He was quickly nicknamed "Smiler" and he shaped up so well in his trial that he was put in the reserve team for the match against Shrewsbury Town at Millmoor before being successfully thrust into the first team.

Rivalry was renewed with Doncaster Rovers, and 18,000 fans turned up at Millmoor to

see a 2-2 draw with the difference in the cost of the two teams showing a vast difference. Rovers had spent a massive £18,000 putting their team together, while United's players had not cost the proverbial "brass farthing".

With crowds on the increase and after experiencing some problems from the highly attended Doncaster game, new turnstiles were introduced down Millmoor Lane which would accommodate boys and ladies in one gate, and half time admissions to the ground through another.

A 5-0 defeat against League leaders Lincoln City was a big disappointment as the season was gathering momentum and raising more thoughts about promotion, but this proved to be just a temporary setback as United went the next nine League matches without being beaten again, to move into the New Year full of optimism.

The F.A. Cup saw United beat Burton Town after a replay in the first round, but they went out in the second suffering a surprise 3-1 home defeat against Aldershot. But it was a very Merry Christmas with two wins against Chester to see Rotherham move into 1938 level on points with leaders Tranmere Rovers - both teams had 27 points from their 20 games. Two matches into the New Year and things had got even better, for these games produced three more points, to give them a two points lead at the top of the table. It was the very first time in the history of Rotherham football that the town had been able to boast a team at the top of their section, but the euphoria soon came to an end as a defeat at Oldham in front of well over 17,000 spectators saw Hull City take over at the top.

The end of January arrived with Rotherham having slipped to fourth position, but two successive 1-0 victories - against Doncaster

*The players pictured during a day's golfing at Sitwell Park in February 1938.
(Back): Birkett, Hawkins, Courts, Bramham, Hanson, Haigh, Mills, Smailes (Trainer).
(Front): Reid, Curry, Clarke, Lynch, Smith*

Rovers at Belle Vue (attendance 20,618) and against Rochdale at Millmoor - lifted them to joint top again with Tranmere Rovers. Could they get promotion? That was the question gripping the town, but it was virtually answered in the negative when only one win was recorded from the next seven matches to see those dreams vanish.

During this less than productive spell a vital game was played at leaders Hull City when an 18,000 crowd were thrilled by an amazingly fast game, and though the sun-baked ground and gusty wind were all against good football, the match was far and above the usual Northern Section standard. Rotherham's stamina was remarkable and it looked as if their week's stay in Bridlington had worked wonders for them, but they could only manage a 1-1 draw.

As a gesture of goodwill and to raise money for the Rotherham Hospital Reconstruction Scheme, United played an exhibition match against a team of former Rotherham players at Millmoor with the opposition team comprising: Black (Mansfield Town), Ford (West Ham), Fieldsend (Scarborough),

Coleman (Frickley), Jolly (Scarborough), Heelbeck (Scarborough), Reid, Bestall (Grimsby), Dickinson (Southend), Fenoughty, Murray. Among the players who had to cry off through injuries and other reasons were Victor Wright (Plymouth), George Raynor (Bury),Burbanks (Sunderland), Rhodes (Accrington), Williams (Worksop), Pedwell (Doncaster) and the famous goalkeeper George Swindin of Arsenal. There was an attendance of 4,000 who saw the visitors win 5-0, thanks to the lethal shooting of Billy Dickinson - who hit three goals - and the artistry of Jackie Bestall.

So the season ended with United in sixth position, the best they had ever achieved under that name with Tranmere Rovers snatching the title. Just how could the success be followed and even bettered, for having had a taste of the top, the town was now seeking the ultimate goal of promotion to the Second Division. Manager Reg Freeman was confident that his side could do even better, and while many other Third Division clubs had been spending money during the summer, Rotherham had only brought in a few newcomers and they would rely mainly on their well tried players, all of whom had been retained.

What a start they made to the 1938/39 season! The opening game saw Rochdale thrashed 7-1, with Arnold Bramham hitting four goals. He added another two in the next game, a 4-1 win against Crewe, to leave United sitting the top of the table with a vastly better goal average than those of Oldham and Carlisle, who had also won their first two games. It was three wins out of three, with Bramham hitting the only goal of the game at York, before a crowd of 17,613 saw Rotherham lose their unbeaten record against Barnsley at Oakwell. A 20,000 crowd was present at Millmoor a week later, only for Barnsley to complete a winning double, before the United team came crashing down to earth with a real bump, on the wrong end of a 7-1 scoreline at Gateshead. They were mesmerised by the wizardry of Hughie Gallacher, and the famous Scot, the holder of many international caps, went nap with five goals.

That match was followed by a comfortable 5-1 home win against Hartlepools United, but the team seemed to return then to their more inconsistent form which saw four goals scored on a couple of occasions while conceding the same number in two other games. One of these was in a 4-1 F.A. Cup first round defeat at Hull at the end of November. After two Christmas draws with Doncaster Rovers, 1938 drew to its close with the team in a mid-table position, but with chairman Edgar Jenkins explaining that the club had been fighting financial difficulties for 15 years. He said this problem could only be addressed in three ways - donations, income from gate receipts and transfer fees. The chairman said many people had been calling for Second Division football but the public of the district needed to play their part.

1939 did not get off to a very auspicious start with a heavy defeat at Stockport, and injuries had bitten so hard that the team to play at Hull was very much a weakened one. But the journey to the Anlaby Road ground proved to be a fruitless one as the game was called off due to snow on the pitch, and the team were soon on their way back home. Snow and frost had turned the pitch at Wrexham into a skating rink the following week and there must have been some doubt in the referee's mind as to the wisdom of allowing the game to be played. It might have been to Rotherham's advantage if it had not gone ahead as they lost 2-0 to make it six seasons since they were last successful at that venue.

It was seven League games into the new year before United recorded their first win - a 3-1 victory against Oldham at Millmoor - and results for the remainder of the season were just about on an even keel, which left the club in a mid-table 11th position when the season ended at the end of April.

Manager Reg Freeman came close to leaving the club in February after he received a tempting offer to take over at Stockport County, but the news that he preferred Millmoor to Edgeley Park came as a great relief for Rotherham followers, as he was considered a vital cog in the rebuilding process which was taking place at Millmoor.

One or two changes were made by the Football League at their annual meeting, including the introduction of players' numbering going through with very little opposition, and it was thought that this would please the supporters of all clubs. The four up and four down proposal rceived its usual rejection with the First and Second Division clubs unwilling to take the risk, although it would create greater interest in the lower divisions.

The 1938/39 season turned out to be the last normal one for eight years, and the various competitions which took place during the Second World War have not been included in any official appearances and scoring records, but the results are shown elsewhere in this book.

The usual preparations took place in the summer of 1939 with one particular signing looking to be a very good one, that of the move to Millmoor from Sheffield Wednesday of Mark Hooper. Hooper was a very experienced forward who should have been able to bring the best out of Rotherham's younger players, for he would also undertake coaching duties.

The club made a good profit of £1,811 on the previous season, but this was entirely due to the transfer fees they received amounting to £2,672, for without these of course there would have been another loss.

If the club had not had to pay any entertainment tax they would have been very much in the "black", and it is interesting to note that since they came into League football in 1919/20, a massive £29,372 had been contributed to the National Exchequer via that means.

United opened the 1939/40 season with a 3-1 defeat at Tranmere but followed that by beating York City 2-1 at Millmoor in the second game. The third match was also at Millmoor, and it was played through continuous rain, and ended in a 2-2 draw against Darlington.

But it turned out to be meaningless as the Government then announced that all gatherings and amusement - whether outdoor or indoor - which involved large numbers of people congregating together would be prohibited until further notice.

CHAPTER 4   AFTER THE WAR YEARS

The resumption of full time football in readiness for the 1946/47 season was welcomed with great relief, and no little amount of hope, for Rotherham had done well during the war years when players were frequently borrowed from other clubs.

United did very well indeed in the last war-time season, and crowned it by winning the Third Division North Cup and the Third Division East championship. This heralded the beginning of a ten year spell which would be remembered as Rotherham's most successful era in the Football League.

May 1946

"Smiler" Mills (the United captain), about to receive the Third Division North Cup from Mr. C.W. Cuff, president of the Football League.

Before the season started, though, there was a disappointment with the news that Ronnie Burke had signed for Manchester United, having scored 14 goals in 17 games during the previous season.

The Third Division clubs fixture list for the 1939/40 season was adopted for 1946/47, but before it could get underway there was a dispute to be settled with centre forward Walter Ardron, who had indicated that he wanted to leave the club.

But it was clear that Rotherham wanted him to stay and help achieve their aim of getting into the Second Division. After consulting with both the Football League and the Football Association, it was made clear that

without the club's consent, Ardron could not move to any other club and that was unlikely to be granted.

A record fee was paid to secure the transfer of Albert Wilson from Crystal Palace. He was a Rotherham man who had also played for the local YMCA. "Sheeny", as he was to become known affectionately in Rotherham, went on to serve the club for many years as player, trainer and groundsman - he was a dedicated servant.

The news everyone had been anxiously waiting for duly arrived a couple of weeks before the start of the season when it was revealed that Ardron had finally re-signed for the club, to provide even more optimism about the possibility of gaining promotion. Admission charges were set at 2/6d (12½p) for the enclosure and stand, and what value the spectators were to get for all the games played at Millmoor.

The season opened with successive away wins at Tranmere and York, and to underline the enthusiasm there was about in the town, the attendance at Millmoor on the opening day to watch the reserves beat Hull City 5-0 was no less than 2,500! For the first home game, there were 14,887 present as Rotherham convincingly beat Darlington, and the first point was not dropped until the fourth game. That slight set-back was quickly followed by two more wins, and the expectancy that had already been generated was underlined yet again with the reserves attracting an attendance of 3,247 for their game against Denaby United.

But even those five wins and a draw from the first six games was not enough to put Rotherham on top of the table, for Doncaster Rovers occupied that position, and there was to be a battle royal between the two clubs for the remainder of the season.

An unexpected 4-0 defeat at Lincoln saw Rotherham slip down to fourth spot, but that was to be the last setback until January 4th - which produced an unbeaten run of 13 League and Cup games. The unprecedented success of the team - they just couldn't stop winning at Millmoor - led to the reforming of the Supporters Club at the beginning of November 1946, and this was widely welcomed as they had been out of existence for several years.

Crewe Alexandra and Scunthorpe United were beaten in the first two rounds of the F.A. Cup, and December was to be a testing time with a game against leaders Doncaster Rovers, followed by two against second placed Chester, on successive days at Christmas. The game at Belle Vue ended in a 1-1 draw, the teams shared four goals equally at Chester, but then United beat the Cheshire outfit 3-1 at Millmoor on Boxing Day. Acting on the advice of the Home Office following the Bolton disaster the previous year, the local police force informed United that there was to be a limit of 18,000 for this game, and it was designated an all ticket affair.

These were all sold without any problem with the ones on sale at the ground having been disposed of within 24 hours, while several thousands more were made available at the Odeon cinema, which was completely ringed by queuers, and many more could have been sold.

The year 1946 ended with a resounding 6-0 home win against Tranmere, and 1947 got off to an equally impressive start with a 6-1

New Year's Day 1947 versus York at Millmoor City 'keeper Fergusson punches clear from McLean.

win against York City at Millmoor - just imagine, 12 goals in the space of five days. Two disputed goals led to a surprise 4-3 defeat at Darlington, before the big clash with First Division championship favourites Wolverhampton Wanderers at Molineux in the F.A. Cup third round saw a crowd of around 45,000. Wolves - boasting such players as Stan Cullis, England's top centre half, and Jesse Pye, the Treeton born player - had rocketed to fame with no fewer then five internationals in their side.

As it turned out the home side won 3-0, but Rotherham won high praise from the national press, and Cullis said that Rotherham were better than at least ten teams that Wolves had met already in the First Division - praise indeed.

Returning to the bread and butter of the League a few days later, Rotherham crashed in another six goals, this time against Halifax to give them 24 League goals in the last five games. It was the third successive home game in which United had netted six goals. Representatives from many First and Second Division clubs were flocking to watch Rotherham, but the club were determined to hang on to their players, and even turned down an offer of £6,000 for one of them.

They could afford to do so from a financial point of view, with consistently very high gates, and with £1,000 to come from the F.A. Cup pool. It was anticipated at that time, that the club would be out of debt by the end of the season, for the first time for almost 15 years.

The occasional defeat did not dampen spirits, but the away record was nowhere near as invincible as the home one, and the victory at Crewe on 8th February was the first since early November, although many of the away games had ended in draws. After the Crewe game just one more was played between then and 22nd March. With the country deep in snow for many weeks, and the enforced lay-off, this resulted in a struggle for the clubs to pay their bills with no income being generated.

In a spell of five weeks, Rotherham had a total of just £70, yet because of the snow clearing work, their expenses were considerably higher, while meetings of the Football League and the F.A. hinted at the cancellation of outstanding fixtures. Fortunately, this threat was not carried out and the season was eventually extended into the middle of June, with the resumption after the enforced break finally going ahead in late March.

United carried on where they had left off, i.e. by winning, and they made it five victories on the trot, after beating Carlisle at Millmoor. After a defeat at Southport, they added eight more and a draw in the next nine games. The last of that superb sequence was the 8-0 thrashing at Millmoor of Oldham Athletic, and it remains in the memory, as it was the first game the Author ever saw.

Over 20,000 fans watched Rotherham beat Doncaster in a vital promotion battle at Millmoor, but the win was not enough for United to catch their near neighbours, and they had the top spot sewn up before the end of the season.

That left Rotherham in the runners-up place, and facing a last home game of the season looking to make it 21 wins out of 21 (home) games to equal the record which had been established by Brentford. Albert Wilson gave United the lead, but they were shocked when the visitors hit two goals to take a surprise advantage, although Len Hainsworth pulled Rotherham level a minute before the interval. Not long into the second half Gladstone Guest grabbed the lead again, only for Rochdale to spoil the party by pulling level once more, and they survived a torrid last 20 minutes when the game had all the excitement of a cup-tie. But all Rotherham's efforts came to nothing as they failed to grab a winner.

It was still a remarkable achievement, particularly in view of the fact that all the players had other jobs as well as being part time players. The final home League record read: played 21, won 20, drawn 1, lost 0, goals for 81, goals against 19. The average attendance for the 25 League and Cup games played at Millmoor was 13,160, and on only two occasions did the numbers fall below five figures.

During the summer Albert Wilson put in a transfer request which was kept quiet by the club, but he moved on to Grimsby Town for a fee which was a good deal more than United had paid Crystal Palace only a year earlier, but he would be difficult to replace having scored 22 goals in the past season.

The club was not yet in the situation of having all their players as full-timers, and that hampered pre-season training somewhat as many of them worked down the pit, so training was not as regular as might have been wanted. Once again Walter Ardron kept everyone on tenterhooks by delaying his re-signing until the week before the new season was due to begin, but the question on everyone's lips was - could United go one better than the last season and gain promotion?

Ronnie Thompson took Wilson's place for the 1947/48 opening game at home to Gateshead, but Gladstone Guest was missing from the line-up as he was serving a suspension carried over from a reserve games at the end of the previous season. More than 12,000 supporters watched the match, but Rotherham were held to a goalless draw, before winning 5-1 at Oldham three days later, with all the goals coming from different players. The highlight of United's display was the brilliant form of centre half Horace Williams, and it was felt that if he were playing for a First Division team, then he would be considered for a place in the national team.

The first defeat did not come until the sixth game of the season - at York - but that was soon forgotten as United crushed Carlisle 7-2 at Millmoor, with Ardron hitting four of the goals, but the home game against Southport three days later could not have been in more marked contrast as the team put up an inept performance, to lose 2-0.

No less than 11 games had been played by the end of September, and this put a strain on the players most of whom had other jobs, and in fact after an evening game against Accrington, one of them needed a taxi to take him straight to work on the night shift. Even so, Rotherham were among the front runners, just one point behind leaders Wrexham. After notching up good wins against Bradford City and Barrow, it was a superb result to beat the Welshmen 6-0, and move to the top of the table. That lofty perch was held only until the following Saturday when Rotherham lost at Halifax, but they regained the lead again by winning the next two matches with victories over Rochdale and at New Brighton.

After their successes of the previous year, Rotherham were exempted from the first two rounds of the F.A. Cup, so they played friendlies against Queens Park Rangers - winning the home game but losing the away return meeting - before a poor December saw them play four matches without winning any; three ended in draws. Off the pitch there was some good news with the announcement that an offer had been made to the L.M.S. Railway Company for the purchase of Millmoor, and negotiations continued after the owners turned down the original offer.

The New Year's Day game saw York City sent home empty handed, with Rotherham's two points putting them back at the top of the table, and the attendance was lifted to almost 17,000 by the offer of a ticket for the forthcoming F.A. Cup-tie against Brentford. Hartlepools were also sent home empty handed, and empty pocketed after thieves broke into the visitors dressing room during the game. Rotherham reimbursed the players for the money they had stolen.

Manager Freeman took the opportunity of watching Brentford (of the Second Division)

on a couple of occasions, but there was no special training routine with most of the players having been working during the week. Despite putting on a good show and having most of the possession, Rotherham were beaten 3-0, in front of a capacity 22,000 crowd, although it was alleged that many more got into the ground. United missed the services of Jack Grainger - the Author's all time favourite Rotherham player - on the right wing as the team who had been relegated from the First Division the previous season, made their greater experience pay dividends. And there must have been something about Rotherham which appealed to the Brentford supporters, for one of them wrote to the Mayor asking for a girl friend with a view to marriage. He had three replies forwarded to him by the Town Clerk's Department, but there is no record to say if any ended in wedlock!

Left free to concentrate on the League, Rotherham slipped up when losing 5-3 at Hull (almost 30,000 were there), before launching a magnificent spell of nine wins and a draw from the next ten matches. The last three games of that run were over the Easter holiday period, when all were won in the space of four days, and it was hardly surprising that the six points took Rotherham to the top of the table.

They were level on points with Lincoln City - 51 points from 36 games each - but United had a better goal average, and the teams swopped places again the following week when Rotherham lost by the only goal of the game at Rochdale. There was a good away following, but unfortunately the United supporters behaved rather badly hurling abuse at the management and players after the match, implying that they had lost deliberately as they did not want to go up.

This was an accusation which was to be levelled at the club on many occasions in the next year or so, but it was really without any justifiable reasoning.

Three more victories on the trot, including a six goal win against New Brighton, put Rotherham in the lead yet again and set the scene for a real promotion battle with nearest rivals Lincoln coming to Millmoor for the penultimate match. It was an all ticket game and the queues started to form in the morning, even though they were not on sale until 6pm, with supporters limited to two tickets each. But even under those restrictions hundreds of supporters were disappointed.

A home win would book Second Division football for Rotherham while a draw or an away win would leave the issue in doubt. But it all went wrong for United as City won 2 - 0 to complete a winning double. The visitors scored both their goals inside the first nine minutes, with the first one shrouded in controversy, when two Lincoln players - looking to be offside and the linesman actually flagging - only for the man in charge to allow play to carry on. The last match saw Rotherham win at Accrington Stanley, but Lincoln took the title one point in front of United.

It was a frustrating situation, as the champions had four points fewer than Rotherham had gathered the previous season, when they also finished runners-up. A similar situation was to arise yet again the following season, when Rotherham were second for the third successive season. This time Hull went up, with a points tally better than Lincoln had achieved a year earlier.

Rotherham's 95 goals haul during 1947/48, was 12 more than any other League club, and they gained more points than the winners of the First and Second Divisions - Arsenal and Birmingham City respectively - all teams playing 42 games in those days. The average home League attendance was around 14,000, and the club was expected to make a good profit, but still the ambition of getting into the Second Division had eluded them. There was, however, some consolation, for on Friday, 7th May 1948, the contract for the sale of the Millmoor ground to Rotherham United was signed for a cost of £5,500, for what was considered to be a bargain price. The total land secured was 23,260 square yards, and several plans were immediately put in the pipeline to increase the capacity and improve the accommodation for the spectators.

Rotherham's Mayor (Mr.C.Bosworth) kicks-off in the Amersfoort match

The team went on a four match tour to Holland where they carried on their success by winning three of the games, the defeat being a 2-1 scoreline against a Dutch XI containing nine internationals, while the victories were against Amersfoort, the East Netherlands F.A., and Ajax who were beaten 4-0 - it would be difficult to imagine a similar result today!

Architects spent several weeks surveying Millmoor and prepared long term plans for extensions which would make the ground capable of accommodating 40,000 spectators. The first stage was planned to be at the top of the ground with a proposal that it would go almost up to the main road with a high reinforced concrete wall, and with an extensive Spion Kop which would hold at least 10,000, with access being from passages underneath. The club offices would be transferred to that area, and it was possible that the dressing rooms would be transferred to the Millmoor Lane side, which would then become the main stand side. Ambitious plans indeed but whatever happened to them?

The club successfully applied for admission to the Yorkshire League, where they would play a third team, and a new recruit joined the Rotherham ranks - goalkeeper John Quairney - from Girvan who played in the Scottish Ayrshire League. He was signed by chairman William Watt and his director brother James who were on holiday in Scotland. One or two players had still not re-signed by the middle of July, and their reluctance was hard to understand as United were paying their players more than many Second Division teams, and as much as some from the First Division. There were 31 professionals on the books at the start of the 1948/49 season, but only six of them were full time, with the newcomers including Colin Rawson from Peterborough and Norman Noble from Ransome and Marles - both players who were to play important roles in the future.

Points lost at the start of the previous season proved to be vital in the failed promotion bid, so it was important to improve, and to not leave things to a late good run in. To give the team a boost, a £9,612 profit from the previous season was announced, and what a start the team made to the new one!

Six straight wins, including a 7-0 mauling of Tranmere Rovers at Millmoor put Rotherham well in front in the table, and after dropping a point against Barrow, they promptly won the next two to give them 21 points out of a possible 22, before the first defeat came at Darlington in game number 12. Walter Ardron had celebrated his son's birth 12 months earlier, by scoring four of the side's seven goals against Carlisle, and he repeated the feat on his boy's first birthday, by netting all four goals in Rotherham's 4 - 1 win at Hartlepools.

From their earliest days in the Third Division, Rotherham had never been successful against Darlington, and the first defeat of the season left Rotherham tantalisingly close to creating some new records. Had they won, they would have equalled the best ever start to a Football League season by any club; another away win would have levelled Doncaster Rovers' record of seven successive away wins, and the record of Darlington being the only team Rotherham had then yet to beat, would also have at last been broken with an away victory.

To their credit, Rotherham were not in the least bit put off their stride by this defeat and promptly won their next five matches to give them 31 points out of a possible 34 in 17 matches, but still supporters continued to moan and blame the lack of activity in the transfer market and the old gripe of not wanting to go up. Just how that complaint could justifiably be directed at a team with such an impressive record defies comprehension.

A surprise 6-1 loss at York was turned round in the next game at Carlisle, where the home side took a tenth minute lead but hat-tricks from Wally Ardron and Tom Lowder, on his debut, led to a brilliant 8-1 Rotherham win.

Over 54,000 spectators watched Rotherham lose 3-2 at Hull on Christmas Day, and there were more than 22,000 at Millmoor the following day for a goalless draw, when Rotherham bid farewell to what had been a quite magnificent 1948. That result, again in front of a 22,000 crowd, left Rotherham three points in front of City at the top of the table, but they had played two more games.

The F.A. Cup brought relief from the tension of the promotion battle, and Darlington were the visitors to Millmoor for a third round tie when injury prevented Jack "Nutty" Edwards from playing; it was the first time he had been missing for 77 games. His place was taken by Norman Nobble who scored one of the goals which gave United a home tie in the fourth round against First Division Burnley who had won the Cup in 1947.

The queues and many telephone calls from fans wanting tickets for the Cup game, provided another reminder of how dilatory the directors had been in putting in hand the much needed ground extensions at Millmoor. The police limit was again set at 22,000, with the visitors receiving an allocation of 4,125 and it was obvious that demand would far exceed the supply, with the Supporters Club expressing their dissatisfaction as they were told they would not be allocated any tickets. The 5,000 members of the club stated they were just requesting one ticket each, but when they was rejected they threatened to disband and give the money they had in the bank to charity. At least some concession was granted to the supporters who were making the long trip to Barrow on the day the tickets were to be put on sale, for they were promised a ticket when they purchased their train ticket.

Some of the animosity had arisen because requests from supporters to be able to buy season tickets for other parts of the ground - apart from the stand - at the start of the season had been turned down, but if it had been agreed then all season tickets holders would have been guaranteed a ticket for such games as the Burnley Cup-tie, and the present ill feeling would have been avoided.

Both League games prior to the Cup-tie ended in Rotherham victories - the win at Barrow was the tenth away success of the season - but the big day did not produce an upset, with Burnley winning by the only goal of the game, although it was Rotherham who did most of the attacking as they put up a fine performance.

Burnley 'keeper Strong punches clear from a ruck of players in the Cup-tie.

After bowing out of the Cup, the disappointment was increased when Hull took over at the top, following a poor United display which led to a home defeat by Wrexham, and once again there was unrest on the terraces.

It was felt that promotion would have been achieved a year earlier if there had been a bold move in the transfer market, and it certainly could have been this season with a change of heart. Hardly any other club in the Football League had spent less than Rotherham in the transfer market in the post-war years, but demands to know what was being done, both in securing better players and in building a better Millmoor, fell on deaf ears. The doubt and disappointment of the public was reflected in the lowest home attendance of the season - 12,495 - for the win against Stockport, but even so 1,500 travelled to Halifax for the next match, when their team lost.

Victories came against Bradford City and Darlington, after the Yorkshiremen had done Rotherham a favour by beating Hull, and the possibility of signing Charlie Tomlinson from Sheffield Wednesday came to nothing as the Hillsborough club wanted Danny Williams as part of the deal, and that was out of the question. After a defeat at Rochdale, Rotherham then went on another of their long unbeaten runs, playing ten games without being on the losing side, in the run-in to the end of the season.

At long last it was revealed that the ground extension plans would increase the capacity to 30,000, and work was planned to commence a couple of months later, but on the field the good run came too late to prevent Hull from grabbing the title, despite a good Easter return by United of five from a possible six points. One of the holiday games was at Doncaster, where the 32,000 plus crowd included around 8,000 who had made the journey from Rotherham.

So for the third season on the trot Rotherham had to settle for second place, but the team went off on their travels again with another tour to Holland, where they won two, drew one and lost one of their four matches. United actually tried to sign one of the Amersfoort players, but

goalkeeper Brits declined Reg Freeman's offer. At the conclusion of their Dutch tour, Rotherham then made a spot of history by becoming the first English League club to play a German side since the war when they met Hanover. Rotherham lost 5-1 but that was largely due to the fact that they had just completed a 12 hours road journey.

Ponstijn scores the first goal for Holland, in the 3-2 defeat in Rotterdam.

The end of June saw Walter Ardron move to Nottingham Forest for a five figure fee. His long association with the club had begun when he joined from Denaby in 1937, the following year he went to Derby, but returned to Rotherham in 1941. He was a prolific scorer who netted 233 goals, including four in a match several times, and netting 33 times in the season just finished. In 1946/47, he set up a club record with 40 goals. Ardron gained representative honours when he played for the F.A. XI against the Army, and Rotherham certainly got value for the £750 they paid for him. He would become a full time player at Forest having left the railway service.

Agreement was reached between the directors and the supporters club with the latter being allowed 4,000 places for any all-ticket game, which suggested that almost 1,000 members would be unable to take advantage of the offer. But unfortunately the directors refused to consider the sale of season tickets for all parts of the ground.

Jack Selkirk became a full time player, and there was activity in the incoming transfer market at last with the news that Ken Bower, Darlington's centre forward had moved to Millmoor. Rotherham supporters should remember him, as he scored the two goals which saw Darlington inflict Rotherham's first defeat the previous season.

For the eighth successive year the accounts revealed a profit, this time amounting to £2,050 - and the Ardron transfer fee did not come into those figures - which left the club in a healthier state than any football club in Rotherham had ever been.

The junior side would take part in the newly formed Northern Intermediate League, and the first team's 1949/50 season kicked off with a 2 - 2 home draw against Wrexham. It was the same scoreline at Oldham a couple of days later, before the first win of the season came in the third game with a 4-1 triumph at Accrington Stanley. But the first defeat quickly followed, Oldham winning by the only goal of the game at Millmoor. It was nowhere near as good a start as had been experienced the previous season, and with the defence conceding too many goals, manager Freeman stepped up his search for new players after three home defeats had been sustained by the end of September - as many as were lost at Millmoor in the League in the previous three seasons put together.

Gates were also down, but a new signing was made in the middle of October when left winger Jimmy Rudd joined from Leeds United - now there was a player who had

the most incredible ball control skills. The Author well remembers watching him display some superb ball artistry in training, and he was to play a big part in the following season's success. He went straight into the team which beat Hartlepools United 5-1, Gladstone Guest grabbing a hat-trick.

But a good run could not be put together as had been done so often in the last few seasons, and there was only the occasional good win, such as the 6-0 triumph against Accrington Stanley. The halfway stage of the season was reached with 21 points from 21 matches. The year 1949 came to an end with successive 2-0 wins at Tranmere and Mansfield, but the club was rocked by the transfer requests of five players, including Gladstone Guest, who eventually happily resolved his problems and remained at Millmoor.

So it was into another decade, and although the fifties did not bring immediate success to Rotherham, it was to be an era that will be etched into the record books, as just about the most memorable one in the football club's history. The first game in the New Year was an F.A. Cup third round tie at Bury - Rotherham had been exempted to that stage again - and it turned out to be a nine goal thriller, with Rotherham making an exit from the competition at this first hurdle.

If there was such a thing as honour in defeat, then that is what United deserved for the way they battled against Second Division Bury, whose architect of the victory was none other than Harold Bodle who had left Millmoor as an 18-year-old for £1,500. The home side were two up after 33 minutes, and they added a third just before the interval to make it look as if the game was all over, bar the shouting, at half time. But Jimmy Rudd pulled a goal back ten minutes

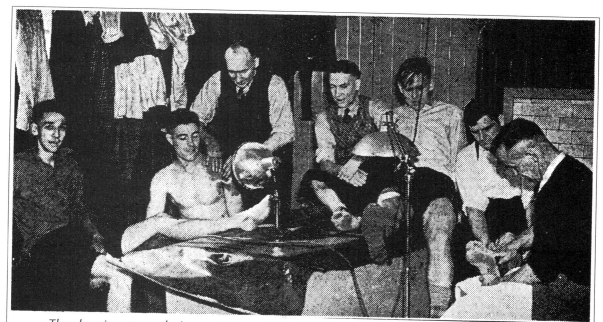

The dressing room during an injury crisis - 1949/50 season. United players - Edwards, Selkirk, Shaw, Bower and Williams - receive treatment from Andy Smailes and Mark Hooper.

into the second half when he lobbed the keeper, and five minutes later Rotherham were awarded a penalty, only for Gladdy Guest to shoot wide with the spot kick.

So instead of making it 3 - 2, two minutes later Rotherham were 4-1 down, following a Bury breakaway, before United began to show amazing courage as they fought back into the game. The Bury defence was literally played to a standstill, with a series of sweeping raids, and it was only a matter of time before Rotherham found the net again with Ken Bower hitting a goal after his earlier shot had hit the post. Jack Grainger started to mesmerise the Bury left back and it was from one of his corners that Norman Noble headed home to put Rotherham just one goal behind, and with nine minutes left they still hammered away.

Three minutes later, hats were flying in the air as Jack Shaw crashed in the equaliser to finish off a whirlwind attack, but with thoughts of being in Monday's Cup draw now in everyone's mind, tragedy struck two minutes from time. Rudd wasted a free kick

when he put the ball behind for a goal kick, only for the Bury keeper to boot it upfield. After blocking one attack, George Warnes, the Rotherham keeper, kicked the ball straight upfield instead of wide down the wings. The ball was played back, and as Horace Williams tackled Massart, it struck the Bury player and he went on to score. But to rub salt into Rotherham's wounds, he admitted after the match that the ball had, in fact, hit him on the hand.

Over 30,000 saw Rotherham lose at Doncaster, and United were unable to get themselves involved in the promotion race even though they managed a few convincing wins on the way to the end of the season which saw them finish in sixth position. It was interesting to see Horace Williams played up front towards the end of the season, for he had played over 300 games as a defender, but he demonstrated his versatility in his new role by by scoring seven times in eight matches.

The Football League decided that they would extend the two Third Divisions for the next season and Scunthorpe United and Shrewsbury Town were brought into the Northern Section, although the introduction of the latter raised some queries for it looked as if a wiser move might have been to switch Nottingham Forest from the Southern Section.

More unrest was to sweep the town with the usual inactivity in the transfer market and with the new season just five weeks away, Rotherham were one of the few clubs in the country who had not signed at least one new player, while in contrast a couple had departed from Millmoor. It was reported that a club had offered £20,000 for Jack Grainger, but this was scoffed at, while there was some concern about the fact that Danny Williams had not re-signed and he was left out of the practice match at Millmoor.

The poorer attendances the previous season showed up in the accounts, for a profit of just £669 was announced, with gate receipts down by as much as £6,104, and there was a feeling that this downward trend would continue unless some new blood was introduced.

Danny failed to settle his differences before the season got underway, with a trip to Oldham, and there was little hope among the spectators of achieving any success in the season about to kick off - how wrong all those doubters were proved to be!

A 5-4 win at Oldham was followed by a goalless home draw against Stockport County, and the goals poured in again when Wrexham were given a 5-0 beating in a game which saw Len White score on his debut. Gladstone Guest was outstanding in the away win at Stockport and there was good news with Danny Williams finally putting pen to paper again, and so remain a Rotherham player. The first defeat of the season came in the sixth match at home to

Tranmere, and after beating Mansfield two more followed in quick succession.

Bogey team Darlington won at Millmoor yet again, but five wins on the trot followed, and in one of them - a 3-1 victory against York City - Gladstone Guest marked his 100th consecutive League game by scoring two of the goals. October also saw the start of some prolific scoring by Jack Shaw who had been switched to centre forward after several cries that lack of goals was letting the team down, and by the end of the month talk of promotion was again very much in the air, with Rotherham playing some brilliant football.

With rivals Tranmere and Gateshead losing on the last Saturday of October, Rotherham could have gone to the top of the table, but they too went down - losing 3 - 2 at home to Crewe - but that was to be the last League defeat until 10th March. The fabulous run of 18 League games unbeaten, which still stands as the club's record, started with a 2 - 1 win at Halifax, the sixth away win of the season. And after beating Hartlepools at home, the seventh followed with a victory at Rochdale. Jack Shaw scored one of the goals - his tenth in the previous six games.

Rotherham were back to playing in the first round of the F.A. Cup this season, and when the draw was made they were given an away tie at Darlington, where they had never won, but confidence was quite naturally sky high in view of their recent form.

They travelled north in a coach with the registration number GET 7 and that is just what the team did as they put on a magnificent display of football to win 7-2, with Jack Shaw hitting five of the goals, an individual record which still stands today. All this came after Darlington had taken a 36th minute lead, and the reward was a mouth watering home tie in the second round against Walter Ardron's Nottingham Forest, who were leaders of the Third Division Southern Section.

Sandwiched in between the cup games was a League match at Shrewsbury, which gave Rotherham their seventh successive away win in League and cup matches, and took them to the top of the table.

But all attentions were turned to the game against Forest, which was a 22,000 sell-out. Tickets changed hands at exorbitant prices, with the club being made to regret the fact that the ground extension plans had not already been brought to bear.

The game attracted great attention with Universal News filming the match for it to be shown at the Odeon cinema later in the week, and it was to be featured on BBC TV's Sports Parade. There was plenty to feature as well, for Rotherham again turned on the style and won 3-1, with Jack Shaw hitting all three goals to take his tally for the season to 24, with 19 of them having come in the last ten matches. Yes, 19 in ten matches!

With everyone hoping for a third round draw against a First Division team, there was a tinge of disappointment when only a Second Division team came out of the hat, but the consolation was that it was near neighbours Doncaster Rovers, so the prospect was of another sell out crowd at Millmoor.

Snow prevented the following week's game against Oldham from going ahead, but at least it gave the players the chance of a rest before they resumed, and they gained a goalless draw at Wrexham and then won 4-0 at Bradford Park Avenue on Christmas Day.

A strange thing happened for the Boxing Day return game at Millmoor against P.A., for Rotherham had to make a team change, with Jock Quairney coming in to replace Danny Bolton in goal, after the team had been unchanged for 17 matches. The winning, though, just went on and on with Bradford, Scunthorpe and Accrington all being beaten, leading to Doncaster's cup visit. United had to do without the services of the injured Gladstone Guest whose absence halted a run of 125 consecutive League and cup games.

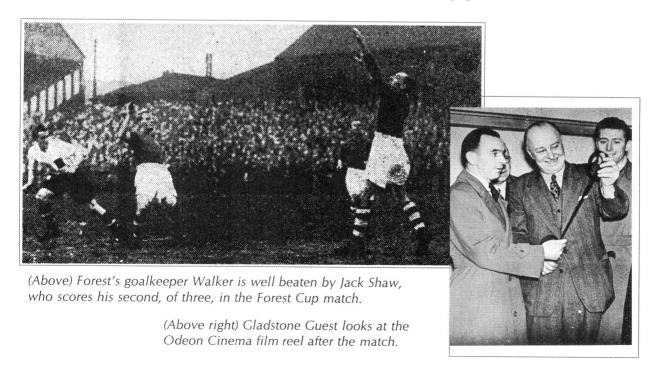

(Above) Forest's goalkeeper Walker is well beaten by Jack Shaw, who scores his second, of three, in the Forest Cup match.

(Above right) Gladstone Guest looks at the Odeon Cinema film reel after the match.

Rovers went in front thanks to a 16th minute penalty converted by Miller, but goals from Jack Shaw and Danny Williams gave United the win that earned them a fourth round tie at Hull City, another Division Two team.

A Jack Grainger goal led to a single goal victory at Southport, and then came successive draws at Mansfield and Darlington where the equaliser came from the penalty spot in the last 15 seconds, thanks to Nobby Noble. He was to become famous for spot kicks - more later! After these two draws, the players went to Bridlington for a few days to prepare for the game at Hull where the team were to be backed by the unbelievable support of 11,000 travelling fans. Jimmy Rudd failed a fitness test so his place on the left wing was taken by young Len White but the team went down to a 2-0 defeat in front of a crowd of 50,040, against a side whose players included Raich Carter, as skipper, and Don Revie.

It was Rotherham's first defeat for 16 League and cup matches and the effects of the cup game obviously took something out of the players for they could only manage a home draw against Southport three days later. It was back to winning ways, though, with a 3-0 home win against Barrow being followed by a 6-2 victory at Millmoor against Accrington, with three more goals coming from Shaw, to end a barren spell of only one goal from seven matches - and all this after Stanley had been two up. That made it ten wins out of the ten matches between the two clubs since the war, before a frolic in the Bootham Crescent mud saw Rotherham come from two goals behind again to earn a point in a 3-3 draw.

Following on from this was a comfortable 5-0 win against New Brighton, but the crowd came in for some "stick" as the attendance surprisingly dropped by over 1,000 from the previous game. Rotherham then went to Valley Parade to meet Bradford City who were three up just after the half hour mark, before United started off on yet another of their now famous "Houdini " acts. After a Noble penalty had reduced the arrears just before half time, they went on to complete a wonderful comeback by hitting the winner in the last minute to give them a 4-3 victory and two valuable points.

The unthinkable then happened - United actually lost a League game to end their 18 League match unbeaten run - with Gateshead winning 2-1 at Millmoor, despite Shaw's 40th goal of the season. But there were still 12 matches left to ensure promotion - and Rotherham only lost one of them - quickly recovering to win two and draw one of the next three games. In those days the Easter holiday programme always included two games against the same team and the fixture list could hardly have thrown up a better pairing than Rotherham and their closest rivals for promotion, Carlisle United.

The Good Friday game ended goalless at Brunton Park, for Rotherham to maintain their five point lead with 54 points from 36 matches, compared to Carlisle's 49 from 36, Lincoln on 47 from 34 and Mansfield 45 from 34.

The Saturday game gave Rotherham a home win against Halifax and they extended their lead to seven points after beating Carlisle 3-0, in a game played in pouring rain, but this did not prevent the two teams from putting on an absolute classic and if the author was asked which was the most memorable Rotherham match ever seen, then this would be the one. Carlisle were the best team that had visited Rotherham for some time - hardly surprising when their manager was Bill Shankly - and they deserved full credit for making the game such a spectacle.

It was a case of "after the Lord Mayor's parade", when United lost at Hartlepools the following week, but there was to be no slip up in the quest for promotion with six wins and a draw from the last seven matches.

Off the field the club had their application for a licence to carry out improvement work at Millmoor restricted to the £1,300 which would strengthen the Millmoor Lane wall, so they decided to make a personal appeal to the Ministry of Supply in Leeds in anticipation of next season's bigger crowds.

Promotion was clinched at Lincoln with another two home games to follow, and scenes of jubilation followed the last match when Oldham were beaten at Millmoor as the Northern Section Shield was presented to Gladstone Guest.

It is well worth taking a closer look at the final record of a magnificent season, which eventually finished with a points tally of 71 points from their 46 games - the equivalent in modern times of 102 points. They scored a phenomenal 103 goals and conceded 41 with an incredible 15 away wins record, and had five players who completed all 46 games.

Three more missed just one game while one played 41 and another 40. United failed to score in only six games, while opponents were prevented from scoring in 22 games.

It certainly was a season to remember for ever. And it didn't end there for a "Festival of Britain" match was played against Irish team Waterford, and Rotherham cruised to a 9-2 win. They then went on a tour to Malta where they opened with a 2-0 victory against a Combined Services team, played on a shale pitch. The second game, against Hibernians (Malta), ended in a 14-3 Rotherham win. The final record was:- played 5, won 4, lost 1, goals for 25, against 7; scorers were Guest, Grainger, White 6 each, D.Williams, Noble and Tomlinson 2 each, H.Williams 1. Immediately upon their return from the sunshine, a celebratory dinner was held when it was announced that there was now a Malta branch of the Supporters Club.

The Northern Section Championship Shield, and a promotion cake presented to the players in the dressing room. From left: Rawson, Rudd, Gibson, Guest, Noble, Shaw, Grainger and manager Freeman. (Inset bottom right, Freeman and Chairman Mr.W.Watt).

The main fear looking towards the tilt at the Second Division was the feeling that Millmoor would not be big enough on many occasions, but full confidence was placed in the ability of the players who had taken United to promotion with no newcomers brought in. There were only 14 full time professionals on the books with skipper Gladstone Guest and keeper Danny Bolton being the only regular first teamers still working, after Danny Williams had given up his job at Silverwood Colliery.

FOR YOUR HELP IN PUTTING ROTHERHAM BACK ON THE MAP!

The attendance was a bit disappointing with just over 17,000 present, for the public had always responded to previous criticism by saying that they would always support a Second Division side, but the crowd was short of the expected full house. The opening goal of that victory came in unusual circumstances when Cardiff defender Baker gathered a Jimmy Rudd shot with both hands for Norman Noble to accept the chance to score from the penalty spot.

Baker's explanation after the game, was that he thought that the referee's whistle had blown! A virtual capacity crowd was at Millmoor to see Doncaster Rovers beaten, before a defeat at Coventry, a draw at Everton and a home win against Southampton set up a visit to Hillsborough.

Pessimism was abundant amongst the Rotherham public when the 1951/52 season got off to a losing start with a home defeat by Nottingham Forest, but they were soon silenced when two days later Rotherham won 4-2 against Cardiff City at Ninian Park with a display of sheer brilliant quality. The victory was against a team which boasted five current Welsh internationals, and the previous season City had lost just one home match and conceded only 20 goals in the process.

Unfortunately that form could not be carried into the next game, a defeat at Brentford, but the double was completed against Cardiff when they made a quick return visit to Millmoor.

The gate at Goodison Park was 44,838, and the Southampton game received the rare treat of being broadcast as BBC's commentary game. It ended in a comprehensive 4-1 win despite the fact that Colin Rawson was taken off injured after only eight minutes, to leave United to battle on with ten men for the remainder of the game. There were no substitutes then, of course.

Before that, though, there was the shock news that Jimmy Rudd's transfer request had

A header from Jack Shaw soars over the Everton bar, in the 3-3 draw at Goodison Park.

been granted. But in some quarters it was not so much of a surprise because there had apparently been some dressing room disharmony, with the feeling that despite his twinkling feet, Rudd did not always play as a team man. Rawson's absence - it ended a run of 54 consecutive League games for him - led to the first change in the defence in 23 League matches.

Five special trains carried 5,000 Rotherham supporters, and a similar number travelled by road, to form part of the 54,846 crowd, the largest any Rotherham team had played in front of.

And they were treated to a real spectacular - a match remembered it as if it were only yesterday.

Shaw again, this time he turns around jubiliantly to herald the Millers first goal at Hillsborough.

For a long time Rotherham had been regarded as the poor relations in South Yorkshire - especially by Sheffield newspapers - but they were full of praise after witnessing a 5-3 away win, with young Peter Wragg opening the scoring for the visitors with his first league goal. Praise was heaped on Rotherham by the national papers and here are some of the quotes:

"I goggled with surprise at them, what a combination." - Daily Mail.

"About the best ever to come out of the Third Division. It's all there, cool, calculated craft with intensive team spirit." -Daily Herald.

"Cold figures are an injustice to Rotherham. Wednesday were played out of the game. Would have given First Division teams a fright." - Daily Mirror.

"Rotherham cruised to victory with a copybook display that made it hard to believe Wednesday were in the First Division last season and Rotherham the third." - Daily Express.

"Wednesday could not have complained if their deficit had been more crushing. Rotherham won because they were a streamlined force." - News of the World.

"In a feast of goal conscious football Rotherham gave their neighbours a rare lesson in the finer arts of soccer team work." - The People.

Praise indeed.

But the victory had it's repercussions the following week when Leeds United were the visitors to Millmoor, for the fans turned out in force and hundreds were locked out when the gates were closed with 21,252 inside the ground. Just for the record, Rotherham cruised to a 4-2 win, to move up into third position in the Second Division table.

It was up into second the following week when Rotherham came from a goal down to beat West Ham United 2-1 at Millmoor, but Rotherham's success was beginning to have a serious effect on local junior football. Two local competitions had to be abandoned, and many other clubs were experiencing difficulty in fielding teams as their players preferred to go and watch United, with even 'Steel, Peech and Tozer' and their 7,000 employees being unable to raise a team on Saturday afternoons.

Big crowds were becoming the norm for Rotherham games and it was no exception when they went to Bramall Lane for a clash with the top two teams in the division, the attendance topping 52,000 in what was the highest at any game in the country that day. In fact such was the Rotherham attraction that the figure was 3,000 higher than the gate which had watched the game between the two Sheffield teams a couple of weeks earlier. But Rotherham lost the chance to go to the top of the table when the Blades won by the only goal of the game, although they might have earned a point if Norman Noble had not hit the post with a penalty kick.

Massive crowds watched Rotherham thrash Barnsley and draw at Hull, before Blackburn Rovers were the next to feel the force of the United attack at Millmoor, as they were sent packing empty handed. Successive wins at Queens Park Rangers and at home to Notts County kept up the confidence. A three goal lead built up after only half an hour was squandered in the game at Hull, while the victory against Rangers at Shepherd's Bush was watched by top administrator (later Sir) Stanley Rous and England team boss Walter Winterbottom, who were both full of praise for Rotherham's performance.

Five points out of a possible six were taken from games against Notts County, Luton

Town and Bury, a trio of games which saw Rotherham sitting proudly on top of the table. They hit that spot after beating Notts County, and the top half of the table looked like this:

	P	W	D	L	F	A	Pts
Rotherham United	17	11	4	2	43	24	24
Sheffield United	17	10	4	3	51	31	23
Brentford	17	9	4	4	23	13	22
Cardiff City	17	9	5	3	29	20	21
Luton Town	17	7	3	7	30	24	21
Doncaster Rovers	18	7	5	6	29	22	20
Nottm Forest	18	6	4	8	33	27	20
Sheffield Wednesday	18	8	6	4	39	35	20
Leicester City	17	6	4	7	35	29	19
Leeds United	17	7	5	5	26	24	19
Birmingham City	18	5	5	8	20	24	18

While the success was seemingly never ending, great criticism was being placed at the club's feet at practically every home game, with accusations that the ground was not fit to house Second Division football, although an extension had been completed and work was due to start on the second phase of the Spion Kop adjoining Millmoor Lane. There was soon the good news that the Kop was to be extended even further, backwards towards the road, which meant the removal of the unsightly wooden hoardings, and what's more the capacity would soon be around 25,000.

Every game had now to be treated as a cuptie, with most teams trying to do their best to stop these "Northern Section upstarts". But nevertheless the pole position was Rotherham's for three games, before they came unstuck with a bang, losing 5-0 at Swansea Town, although the defeat did not cost them the leadership. That happened the following week after a defeat at Forest, and December continued to be a poor month, when after drawing against Brentford, Rotherham lost the two Christmas games to Birmingham City but they recovered to win the last game of the year at Doncaster. That win lifted Rotherham back up to fourth, after they had dropped down to eighth, before they turned their attention to the F.A. Cup with a home third round tie against Bury who were beaten 2-1.

The next home game was against Sheffield Wednesday on 26th January 1952, and the date marked a special place in the history books for it was the first time a game had taken place under the new ground capacity, which the Chief Constable - Mr R.Hall - set at 25,000.

The attendance for the Wednesday game actually finished at 149 above that figure, which broke the previous highest which had stood for 32 years, also in a game against Wednesday. Despite the poor conditions with a thin covering of snow on top of a bone hard pitch, the teams served up a thrilling match as they shared six goals. But the following week, United's worst display for a long, long time saw them lose in the F.A. Cup fourth round at Swansea. For those who believe in superstitions, Rotherham's mascot cat "Snowball" was killed in a road accident just before the cuptie, and Rotherham took 13 players with them to Swansea.

There was some consolation with the news that Jack Grainger had been included in the England 'B' squad for their forthcoming game against Holland, but the rot had set in and successive League defeats at Leeds, West Ham and at home to Coventry burst the bubble well and truly. The defeat against Coventry, one of the division's struggling clubs, started to ring the alarm bells. Although Rotherham were in eighth position, so tight was the whole division that they were only eight points above bottom club Queens Park Rangers, which raised thoughts of being involved in a relegation battle.

This was something that had been unthinkable a couple of months earlier, but to their credit the team quickly banished any such thoughts as they mounted a six match unbeaten run starting with a home win against Sheffield United. Again the new 25,000 capacity was topped, and there was a good attendance two weeks later when Hull City were the visitors. But where did 10,000 spectators disappear to for Rotherham's next home game against Queens Park Rangers when there were just over 9,000 present to see a home win? That victory suddenly raised hopes that Rotherham could get back into the promotion race, for they were only three points behind leaders Sheffield Wednesday, with six games left to play.

Those late hopes were still alive when Notts County were beaten at Meadow Lane, but a disastrous run of five successive defeats well and truly killed them off, as the season which had often promised so much, finished in an ignominious way. Even so, the final ninth position was a very creditable performance in their first season in the Second Division, after being in the doldrums for so long, with the success being reflected in the average home gate which was well in excess of 18,000 .

Rumours that he was about to be transferred to promoted Sheffield Wednesday, were quickly refuted by Jack Grainger himself, while Reg Freeman busied himself enquiring about possible newcomers, but most clubs seemed to be more interested in swop deals than sales.

The Supporters Club had gone from strength to strength during the season, and at their annual dinners they requested permission from the club to raise their membership from 6,000 to 8,000, but the fans had to look forward to increased prices for the new season ahead following raised government taxes. Season ticket holders would have to pay £6 compared to the old £5, while en-

closure day admission charges went from 2s 6d (12½p) to 3s (15p), but the club claimed that they had a greater proportion of cheaper admission charges than any other ground in the First or Second Divisions.

Millmoor amenities again came in for some criticism, with the apparent lack of any work being undertaken to improve them during the Summer, even though it was pointed out that the likes of Accrington Stanley and Crewe Alexandra could provide concrete terracing. Behind the scenes there was some alteration with the back of the stand tidied up, and on a strip of land which was subsequently made available, a wooden building was to be provided for use as offices for the manager and secretary. The re-arrangement enabled the club to enlarge the visitors' dressing room by taking in the old office.

There were few fresh faces when the players reported back for training, but among them were Terry Farmer, a centre forward from Gainsborough Trinity, and left winger Dennis Pell from Methley, while Charlie "Shadow" Tomlinson moved out to Worksop Town.

Now coming near the end of their illustrious careers, the two Williams'. Danny and Horace, were to amass 669 appearances between them.

There was quite a lot of gloom in the town and district concerning the prospects for the future, but Rotherham had always had more than it's fair share of "Dismal Desmonds", and it was down to the old guard to try and get the club off to a good start. But the club was to be rocked by a huge bombshell before the season could get under way, with the news that manager Reg Freeman was leaving to take up the manager's position at Bramall Lane with Sheffield United. After 21 years of devoted service to Rotherham United, during which he lifted them from the depths of despondency and poverty, to the comparative heights of affluence, he deserved the chance to move on. It was no secret that he could have moved several times to a number of fashionable First Division clubs but until now he had always turned them down.

Freeman began as a player in 1931, and took over as manager two years later on the eve of a cup-tie with Sheffield Wednesday. More than any material resources, he had introduced into the Millmoor camp, a spirit and companionship which was second to none. His policy of taking raw material from the South Yorkshire industrial belt was to become an integral feature of life at Millmoor. Freeman's friend and companion through so many of the dark years, Andy Smailes, was given the task of stepping into his shoes with Mark Hooper moved up for the time being to first team trainer.

The opening game of the 1952/53 season saw the inauguration of commentaries to the Doncaster Gate and Moorgate hospitals, and they listened to the accounts of a draw against Birmingham City.

Injuries caused a few changes for the midweek game at Notts County, with Terry Farmer coming in to make his debut, but the team slipped to a narrow 2-1 defeat. Subsequent losses at Luton and at home to Notts County, left United with a single point from their opening four games - hardly the start the new manager was looking for.

Former player Albert Wilson was appointed as second team trainer, and he at least had the consolation of knowing that his charges were at the top of the Midland League with seven points from their first four games.

The first team revival got underway though, with a home win against Leeds United quickly followed by a superb victory at Southampton, where manager Smailes' bold stroke in introducing 20-year-old reserve team left winger Dennis Gee paid rich dividends, for he was one of the successes of the match. Injuries to other players had meant Jack Grainger was having to play at centre forward but this had its compensations, as it allowed Len White to play more often on the right wing.

A three goal lead built up after 34 minutes at Home Park against Plymouth Argyle seemed to have set the seeds for another win, but somehow the home side got back into the game and urged on by the mighty roar of their crowd, they staged a remarkable comeback to win 4-3. Fears about being stuck at the wrong end of the table were quelled when a home draw against Southampton followed this defeat, and that was to be the forerunner of six successive victories.

This sequence included away wins at West Ham United, Lincoln City and Blackburn Rovers, and it was probably more than a coincidence that it happened just as left winger Walter Rickett was signed from Sheffield Wednesday to solve one of Rotherham's problem positions. Norman Noble was sidelined for at least six weeks after undergoing an appendicitis operation and his absence allowed young Malcolm Hussey to make his debut.

Rickett got on the scoresheet at West Ham and Lincoln, and as the momentum gathered pace, promotion talk was suddenly in the air again as Rotherham moved up into fourth position.

Leaving Bullcroft pit after a day shift, Lennie White is congratulated by manager Bedford (right) on the player's selection for the F.A.XI.

There was cause for further celebration when first White and then Grainger were selected to play for the F.A. XI against the RAF and the Army teams, with their selection being well deserved. Grainger headed a goal from White's cross in the 4-1 win against the Army at Leeds.

Grainger was in superb form against Nottingham Forest, but he could not prevent a home defeat, although United were at their brilliant best when they beat Everton at Goodison Park to record their fifth away win of the season - more than any other club in the First or Second Divisions.

The biggest win of the season thus far, a 4-1 beating of Brentford, included a Jack Grainger hat-trick, before Rotherham reached the Christmas programme with a run of inconsistent results. One of these, though, entered the record books, for the

attendance at Millmoor on 13th December 1952 for the 2-0 home defeat against League leaders Sheffield United, was 25,170 and this still remains the highest ever gate at Millmoor. The week before Rotherham had lost 1 - 0 at Huddersfield and that was the first time they had failed to score that season.

United were well beaten at Birmingham, but they came back with a bang on Boxing Day when they walloped Bury 6-1, but lost the return game the following day. The dawning of 1953 could hardly have been celebrated in a better way than winning 4-1 at Bramall Lane against Sheffield United, and Gladstone Guest had cause to rejoice as he cracked home two of the goals including his 100th peace-time Rotherham goal.

The victory could have been even more emphatic but Rotherham missed a penalty, with Grainger's shot being hit with such ferocious power that when it hit the crossbar, the ball rebounded over the top of the stand to finish in Bramall Lane!

The F.A. Cup third round saw Rotherham handed what looked a straight forward home game, against Third Division Colchester United, but they were held to a 2-2 draw, before avoiding an embarrassing elimination by winning the replay. League defeats followed against Leeds and Plymouth before what must surely rank as Rotherham's best ever achievement in their long history, namely an F.A. Cup fourth round win at Newcastle United, who had been the Cup winners for the previous two seasons.

The supporters had made an unsuccessful plea to the North-East club to make the game an all ticket affair to ensure they would get into the ground, but they received no co-operation so decided to set off at 6am to ensure they would have no problems.

Danny Williams (left), 'Keeper Jock Quairney and Dennis Warner combine to stop Vic Keeble, in the memorable F.A.Cup victory over Newcastle United.

Rotherham stayed at Tynemouth from the Wednesday onwards, to prepare for the game against the Geordies who had won 13 successive F.A. Cup-ties, and their preparations were hampered with doubts surrounding the fitness of Jack Grainger. He recovered in time to take his place in the starting line-up, and proceeded to play a vital role in an unforgettable day as Rotherham went on to win, on an extremely windy day.

Straw had been used to protect the pitch from the frost - no undersoil heating in those days - and even though Rotherham had been the better side they went in at half time all square with neither side having found the net. The home side went in front early in the second period, but then Rotherham hit them with three goals, two from Grainger and one from Rickett, to pull off the shock of the season.

There was a Grainger Road in Newcastle, and in it a Grainger Cinema which was showing *"The Quiet Man"*, but the Magpies were unable to keep Rotherham's Grainger quiet, and he had such an effect on them that £30,000 was offered for him immediately after the match.

The Newcastle programme issued some prophetic words for it stated: *"It may be that Rotherham have no history as giant killers but there always has to be a first time"*, and it also quoted: *"There could be no more inspiring opportunity than a game against the cup-holders of two successive seasons."* Perhaps they half expected their own demise after all!

That famous victory took Rotherham into the fifth round for the first time ever, and they were rewarded with a home tie against another First Division team, Aston Villa - that looked easy after Newcastle.

But there was to be no repetition of the giant-killing act, and Villa won 3-1, in what was to be Len White's penultimate game for Rotherham, for he moved to Newcastle a few days later for Rotherham's record fee - well over the £10,000 Nottingham Forest had paid for Walter Ardron.

Ever since the cup-tie, Newcastle had been trying to persuade Rotherham to let Jack Grainger go, and after having their £30,000 bid turned down, they made an amazing open cheque offer. Newcastle continued to watch Grainger, but when they came to terms with the fact that Rotherham would not sell, they moved in for White, who went straight into their first team to play against Liverpool. What's more, he went on to give them many years of loyal service.

The end of the cup run really heralded the end of Rotherham's season, for they only won two of their last 13 League games, but drew seven of them, to produce a final 12th position. Before the season ended there was an important new signing, with centre forward Ronnie Burke joining Rotherham from Huddersfield Town. It may be remembered, that he had guested for United during the war, and the club were greatly disappointed when he decided to join Manchester United instead of Rotherham.

Burke's arrival compensated in some ways for the departure of Colin Rawson, who moved to Sheffield United, and it also made up for the failure to sign McCurley from Colchester. Burke showed what a useful acquisition he would be by scoring six goals in seven matches, as the season drew to its close.

But special mention must be made of the last game of the season - it was the semi-final of the Sheffield and Hallamshire County Cup, and ended in a 7-0 Rotherham win against Sheffield Wednesday.

The first newsworthy announcement to emerge from Millmoor after the season's end, was that plans were afoot to bring in four separate stages of improvement, starting with the concreting of the terracing on the whole of the stand side, and the consequent elimination of the wooden sleepers and the wide pathway dividing the old terracing. It was intended to pull down the old iron railings enclosing the playing pitch and substitute a neat concrete wall.

At the top end of the ground, it was hoped to add a third and smaller concrete bay at the entrance to the stand side of the ground. For this work the Supporters' Club's second allocation of £1,000 would be a part contribution. Fourth item on the agenda was the development at the bottom end of the ground, involving going back almost to the railway line and banking up a space about equal to that at the top end of the ground. With that work completed it was thought Millmoor should house considerably more than 30,000.

Three officials of the club, whose combined service amounted to around 75 years, were recognised for their efforts by the directors who presented them each with a cheque said to be for substantial amounts. They were secretary William Heald - with the club for almost 30 years - manager and former trainer Andy Smailes - 24 years, and Joe Maguire who had been chief scout with around 20 years under his belt.

The playing pitch was increased in size to 115 yards by 75 yards, and the turf received some special treatment, but the ground improvements only went on at a slow pace.

On the playing side Jack Shaw moved to Sheffield Wednesday, but great things were expected of Ronnie Burke, while Ian Wilson - a left winger signed from Chesterfield - was expected to solve what had persistently been a problem position. To make room for him Walter Rickett moved to Halifax Town for a modest fee.

The 1953/54 season opened on a Thursday night at Millmoor, where Rotherham were beaten comfortably by Blackburn Rovers, and that was followed by a defeat at Leeds. But a comprehensive 5-0 home win against West Ham United set the wheels in motion. A Ronnie Burke goal was enough to beat Birmingham, but the erratic form was demonstrated again with setbacks against West Ham and Nottingham Forest.

Jack Selkirk came into the side for the first time to help to spark the team into a win against Fulham, and something like the best form returned as the team reeled off nine games without defeat. In fact eight of those games ended in victory, with the second one against Luton Town having a 6pm kick off to combat other local sporting activities. The decision proved to be a wise one with the biggest attendance since the opening day of the season.

The gates continued to rise as the winning run went on, and manager Andy Smailes demonstrated his determination for success when he put in a bid for Leeds United's Albert Nightingale. The player lived in Rotherham, but the Elland Road outfit kept increasing their price so the deal fell through.

Another Burke goal gave Rotherham a win against Bury on 10th October to lead to more celebrations, not just for the win but because the two points took the team to the top of the table. It was quite a magnificent effort considering that they had been next to the bottom at the end of August, and they stayed top following a win at Oldham. But the team was knocked off its perch the following Saturday when Everton were victors at Millmoor, in front of the highest

crowd of the season - 18,860. That was to be the first of four successive defeats as Rotherham continued to display their inability to stay with the pace-setters again.

As a break from League football, Rotherham had a midweek trip to Grimsby where they had their first experience of playing under floodlights - Tuesday 17th November 1953 - and they shared four goals.

The poor run of form was ended with a draw in a game against Bristol Rovers, which was the visitors first visit to Millmoor, and that point was followed by successive wins at Brentford and at home to Derby County, who were on the wrong end of a 5-2 scoreline. That was at the beginning of December, but the rest of the month was best forgotten as the team picked up just one more point from four games. By then, though, Rotherham's long search for an experienced forward had come to an end with the signing of Third Lanark's inside forward John Henderson, which ended Andy Smailes' length and breadth scouring of the country. Third Lanark was at that time a Scottish League team, who are now no longer in existence.

The year ended with Rotherham in eighth position with 27 points from 26 games - a poorer position than in either of the previous two seasons. There was only a small away following for the opening game of 1954 at Birmingham, but they were rewarded with a United win which helped to whip up some enthusiasm for the trip the following Saturday to Bristol City in the third round of the F.A. Cup.

On form and League positions, the game should have been an away win as City were still in the Third Division, and the game ran true to form with Jack Grainger hitting all three Rotherham goals in their 3-1 win.

Jack Grainger

The goal-scoring winger went on to make 352 appearances for the Millers.

While the F.A.Cup game was going on the juniors were entertaining Manchester United in the F.A. Youth Cup at Millmoor, and there was a crowd of 7,200 present, but they had to settle for a goalless draw. The reward for the first team's success was a visit to West Bromwich Albion in the fourth round and that presented a daunting task with Albion one of the favourites to lift the trophy.

The Hawthorns was capable of holding 65,000 spectators, which gave little anxiety for the Rotherham followers who were intending to follow the team, but before then United had to face Nottingham Forest in the League at Millmoor. That ended in a comfortable 3-0 home win with Jock Henderson having a fine game and another point was gathered the following week at Luton, to put Rotherham in confident mood for the trip to the Midlands. But there was to be no repetition of the famous exploits at Newcastle, as Albion won easily, before Rotherham maintained their good League form with successive wins against Plymouth Argyle and Swansea Town.

The match at Vetch Field saw Rotherham turn on some excellent football but their return journey the following day was not without its mishaps, for there was the sight of directors, officials and players pushing the bus to the brow of a hill after it had run out of petrol. Then the view of Danny Williams running like a harrier out on a morning exercise, while he dashed for an emergency supply of petrol. To cap it all, the bus became stranded in the floods at Beighton before they reached their destination!

Foreign opposition in the shape of F.C.Wien from Austria - Rotherham seemed to be one of the pioneers of European football - paid a visit to Millmoor only to be comfortably beaten 4-0.

Thoughts of promotion were still very much in the air, for with 11 games left Rotherham were in sixth position, only three points behind leaders Leicester City. Two disappointing defeats at Bury and Everton didn't help the prospects, though, but those two games were sandwiched by a really convincing 7-0 home victory against Oldham Athletic, who were the victims of a Ronnie Burke hat-trick, his first for the club. However, the fans had not turned out in very good numbers, for the 11,686 crowd was Rotherham's lowest of the season, and it was also the worst of the day in the Second Division, so it was beginning to look as if the supporters had already abandoned hopes of going up.

That old failing, lack of consistency raised it's ugly head again, before the run in entered April with United still in sixth position. But they were now too far behind leaders Everton to harbour any thought of going up, although they were on course for a best ever final position. The team did not experience another defeat in their final six matches, and they signed off in style with a fine win against local rivals Doncaster Rovers at Millmoor, and on the way they notched up their 700th League post-war goal, a figure which was well ahead of any other team.

The final position of fifth was a really notable achievement and it underlined the fact that Rotherham had become a force to be reckoned with since they gained their place in the Second Division. Yet strangely in those three seasons, the average attendance had gone down, although this was a decline which was not only happening at Millmoor as it was prevalent throughout the whole of the Football League. One reason for it was thought to be the fact that the League constantly rejected the four-up four-down proposal, for it meant that many teams had virtually nothing to play for during the closing weeks of the season, and the game in general needed a fillip. This seems to be a ready made answer for any critic of the latterday end of season play off system.

At the annual general meeting in August, 84-year-old chairman Williams Watt announced that he was relinquishing the post after being in that office for 15 years, although he said he intended to carry on serving as a director, something he had done for the past 35 years. He was subsequently replaced by Mr Reg Cooper who had been a member of the Board for almost 25 years.

The burning question was, could Rotherham improve yet again and attain a higher place in the 1954/55 season that was about to begin? The eventual answer was to be very much in the affirmative, as the club went on to enjoy its best ever season, and they were to come so close to achieving the ultimate aim of a place in the top division.

Little change had taken place during the close season to the playing squad when they opened with a home game against newly promoted Ipswich Town, who were beaten 3- 2, and Leeds United proved to be no match for Rotherham in the second game. A double was quickly completed against Leeds United to give the team an excellent start to the season, but the question was

raised in the "Advertiser" as to why the attendance was only 17,799, pointing out that the figure was quite disconcerting; the ground can't even accommodate that number now!

The victory against Leeds was the first of four wins on the trot, with Ronnie Burke hitting all four goals in the defeat of Bury, which took the team into second place with 12 out of a possible 14 points, to herald a superb start to the campaign. Then came some good news and some bad news for the spectators. The good was an announcement made on Monday 13th September 1954, in the form of an official club statement which read: *"The directors propose to proceed immediately - if and when the necessary licences can be obtained - with the provision of cover for the whole of the Masborough Street end of the ground. The work will entail considerable cost but the directors feel the additional cover to be provided will contribute to the amenities of the spectators."* The bad news came as the statement went on: *"On completion of the work, it is proposed to increase the price of admission to that part of the ground to 2s 6d each."*

Mr Cooper then outlined further plans to build up the railway end and eventually provide the same kind of cover. Here at last was some positive thinking to improve the facilities.

Disappointment quickly followed, though, with a home defeat at the hands of Doncaster Rovers, but a point was gained at Bury five days later. League leaders Luton Town were the next team to visit Millmoor, and they went home empty-handed after being beaten 2-0, to be replaced at the top of the table by none other than - Rotherham United. A win at Hull consolidated the lead, before Rotherham went to Anfield to meet Liverpool, where a 3-1 defeat saw Rotherham knocked off the top of the table by

Blackburn Rovers. But the Millmoor lads bounced straight back to form by thrashing Bristol Rovers, who were just two places behind second placed United.

That comprehensive win catapulted Rotherham back to the top to set up a battle royal with second placed Blackburn, which the Lancashire side won, but there was some consolation for Rotherham in that the national press were giving them some glowing reports with one or two suggestions that Rotherham were playing some of the best football in the country. And this was with a mainly home produced team who played with a great deal of local pride. This was underlined by the fact that Rotherham players were in the eyes of the England selectors, with Jack Grainger earning selection for the Football League XI to play the Army, while full back Peter Johnson was picked as a reserve. The latter's rise to stardom had been meteoric, for it was only two years earlier that he attracted the attention of the United manager while playing for Rawmarsh Welfare, and he had only become a full time professional in March of the previous year.

The representative honours continued to come Rotherham's way when Grainger, Johnson, Jack Selkirk and Ronnie Burke played for Sheffield in an Inter-City match against Glasgow, with Grainger scoring one of his teams' five goals.

Rovers started a trio of games which brought Rotherham no points at all, before a win against Notts County took Rotherham back into fourth position and that was held when United twice came back from being a goal down to beat Derby County. Two draws, a win and a defeat led Rotherham to Christmas, when two wins in three days against Lincoln City brought the year to a happy end. It was the first time in the Second Division that United had won both their

Christmas games, although it took an injury time Gladstone Guest goal to clinch the second victory. The new cover at the Kop end was ready for the Christmas Day game, a week ahead of schedule.

So Rotherham went into 1955 in third place, but the two League games played in January both ended in defeat, and after beating First Division Leicester City at Millmoor in the third round of the F.A. Cup, Rotherham bowed out at the next stage, also at Millmoor, with Luton Town recording a comprehensive 5-1 win. Town were to become one of Rotherham's least favourite teams before the season ended.

February started with a convincing victory at Doncaster, a fine achievement in view of the fact that four players, Danny Bolton, Terry Farmer, Dennis Churms and Tony Reeson had stepped up from the reserves to cover for injuries, and loss of form as far as keeper Jock Quairney was concerned. Then came a crunch game at Luton, where the homesters won 4 - 0, a result which was to have such vital importance at the end of the season. If only Rotherham could have avoided defeat.

Hull City kindly scored both the goals to give Rotherham a 2-0 win in the next game as United maintained third position, which they promptly lost by losing to a disputed goal at Bristol Rovers, claiming that the ball had not crossed the line when it came down off the crossbar. Free-scoring League leaders Blackburn Rovers - they had banged in 98 goals in 32 matches - were the next visitors to Millmoor, but they were given a taste of their own medicine when a Terry Farmer hat-trick led the way to a tremendous 5-1 Rotherham win. That closed the gap between Rotherham and both Luton and Blackburn to four points, but United took just one point from a draw at Fulham from their next two matches.

Had the chances of promotion gone? It looked as if they might have done when Rotherham lost at Notts County, but they returned to that city a few days later to record a 2-0 victory and set off a magnificent string of seven successive wins. Derby County, Forest - again after they were two goals up - West Ham United, Stoke City, Plymouth Argyle, and Swansea Town were swept aside. With two matches left, four points would guarantee Rotherham the championship.

THE LEAGUE TABLE—DIVISION II											
		HOME					AWAY				
	P.	W.	D.	L.	F.	A.	W.	D.	L.	F.	A.	Pts
Luton Town	41	18	2	1	55	18...	4	6	10	30	35...52
STOKE CITY ...	41	12	5	4	38	17...	9	5	6	31	21...52
Rotherham	40	16	1	3	53	21...	8	3	9	35	41...52
Birmingham ...	40	14	4	3	55	22...	7	5	7	29	22...51
Leeds United ...	41	14	4	3	43	19...	8	3	9	24	33...51
Blackburn ...	41	14	3	3	72	30...	8	2	11	41	48...49
Notts. County ...	41	13	3	4	44	26...	7	3	11	28	44...46
West Ham ...	40	12	4	4	46	27...	6	5	9	27	41...45
Bristol Rovers ...	41	15	3	2	50	21...	4	3	14	23	47...44
Middlesbrough ...	41	13	1	7	48	31...	5	4	11	23	49...41
Swansea	41	14	3	3	55	26...	2	6	13	28	55...41
Liverpool	40	11	6	4	53	35...	5	3	12	36	53...41
Bury	41	10	5	6	44	35...	5	5	10	32	36...40
Fulham	41	10	5	5	45	26...	4	6	11	30	50...39
Notts. Forest ...	40	8	3	9	28	28...	8	3	9	27	30...33
Doncaster ...	40	10	5	4	34	26...	4	2	15	23	61...35
Hull City ...	41	7	5	9	30	35...	5	5	10	14	31...34
Lincoln	40	8	6	6	39	34...	4	4	12	28	44...34
PORT VALE ...	40	9	6	5	30	21...	1	5	14	16	50...31
Plymouth ...	41	9	4	7	27	26...	2	3	16	28	56...29
Ipswich	41	10	3	8	37	28...	1	3	16	19	62...28
Derby County ...	41	5	6	9	36	34...	1	3	17	14	48...21

The positions,
as shown in the Port Vale programme.

Thousands went by train (including the Author) and other means of transport, to Burslem for the game against Port Vale, but the home side were to become the party-poopers, for they stole a single goal victory - but that was only part of the story. Whether it was the tension of the occasion no one will ever know, but Rotherham failed to produce their best form in the first half which ended goalless - and that could well be enough if the last games finished like that.

Then a few minutes into the second half, Gladstone Guest and Ian Wilson combined to put Terry Farmer through, only for the striker to be brought down by Cheadle, with the referee having no hesitation in awarding a penalty. This is it, thought all the Rotherham fans, Division One here we come. Norman Noble stepped up, let loose a terrific shot, but King's fist connected with the ball and it flew away to safety. Poor old "Nobby" looked a disconsolate figure and he was - unjustly - after that incident, always remembered as the player whose penalty miss kept Rotherham out of the top bracket. That is hardly fair on a player who gave great service to the club, and he should be remembered for all the good things he did.

Anxiety set in after the miss and Jock Quairney caused a gasp when he dropped the ball in front of Done. Ten minutes later came another devastating blow when Noble headed away only for the ball to be held up in the strong wind, and Stephenson burst through on the left. Jack Selkirk was beaten to the tackle, and when Frank Marshall cut across, all he could do was to concede a corner kick which soared over to Smith who headed home to give Vale the lead.

Even though there was still half an hour to go, United looked beaten from then on, and despite creating some hectic pressure in the last five minutes they could not find an equaliser. It was a very quiet journey home, even more depressing when it was discovered that other results at the top had not gone Rotherham's way. So there was just one home game left, a re-arranged encounter with Liverpool, with United needing to win 16-0 to go above Luton Town; and Birmingham City due to play at Doncaster on Wednesday.

The game turned out to be the season's classic as Liverpool were routed by a team which pulled together as one single unit from the first to the final whistle, to finish in superb style with a 6-1 win.

Ian Wilson netted four of the goals to become the first Rotherham winger ever to hit that number in one match, and so thousands trooped off to Belle Vue two days later, nurturing hopes that Donnie could beat Birmingham.

It was not to be, though, as City won 5-1, to clinch the title leaving themselves and Luton in the two promotion places, with Rotherham in third position; but all three teams had the same number of points - 55. United's goal average was the worst of the three, and to rub salt into the wounds - which have never really healed - in modern day rulings, Rotherham would have finished as champions with their 94 goals tally being the best of the three!

There was scant consolation in winning the County Cup with Sheffield United and Sheffield Wednesday both being beaten, but the team could look back proudly at a wonderful season which is still the best ever in the club's history.

After making such progress following promotion to the Second Division, it would be a very difficult task to improve yet again, but before thoughts were concentrated on the new season, the club had to withstand all the usual accusations that they did not want to go up as they could not afford it. An accusation that had no truth!

Plans to carry out the extension work at the railway end came to a full stop with the club unable to negotiate a suitable price with the railway company for the necessary vacant land. This was rather a strange decision by the landowners as the area of ground was frequently subject to flooding and the lines had been taken up.

Jack Selkirk announced his retirement, and one by one the players who had made Rotherham United the talk of the country since

the war were disappearing, with only Gladdy Guest and Danny Williams of the old school still playing first team football. Danny Bolton was the next to announce his retirement, while it was revealed that Lol Morgan and Ken Keyworth would both become full time professionals. Disappointingly no work was being carried out on the ground apart from the painting of the dressing rooms by Albert Wilson and Mark Hooper.

Before the new season got under way there was a change of heart from Selkirk, and he was persuaded by Andy Smailes to carry on playing with the "Stag's" new employer agreeing to keep his job open for him.

It was basically the same side that had ended the previous season as the one which got the 1955/56 campaign underway, but it was, perhaps, asking a little too much for the team to produce the same kind of results. In fact, they were in marked contrast for only one win was recorded in the first 11 matches to leave the team languishing third from the bottom of the table, and the attendance for the home game against Fulham on 1st October was a mere 12,879 - the lowest of the day in the Second Division.

Efforts were made to bring in new players but it was an old one who Andy Smailes attempted to bring back to Millmoor, although he got no joy with Sheffield Wednesday refusing to do a deal for Jack Shaw. A Terry Farmer goal was enough to bring a long overdue win, with Bristol Rovers being beaten at Millmoor. A few games later the team at last put a run together with no defeats in seven matches, including a victory against Sheffield Wednesday at Hillsborough.

Three successive defeats and a draw brought the year to a miserable close, although there was some consolation in that the home draw against Doncaster Rovers on New Year's

Eve was seen by over 15,000, the highest since Barnsley had been the visitors in early September.

Third Division Scunthorpe United opened 1956 with a visit to Millmoor in the third round of the F.A. Cup, and they pulled off a surprise by holding Rotherham to a draw, before winning the replay 4-2 when Norman Noble was sent off. The early cup exit was a financial blow - for Scunthorpe earned themselves a game against Liverpool in the next round - since the gates at Millmoor were down, with 42,000 fewer supporters than the previous season having watched the first 13 home games.

In an effort to get his team back on the winning trail, manager Smailes made a bold bid to sign Jimmy Hagan from Sheffield United, but the player declined to move after it had looked as if he would sign for Rotherham.

Improved form was shown in the next two away games with a win at Notts County and a draw at Fulham, but there was a snow enforced long break of three weeks before the team got back into action, with three successive defeats against Forest, Wednesday and Leicester.

The win at Meadow Lane deserved special mention for the team contained youngsters Roy Silman, Malcolm Hussey, Brian Jordan and Ken Keyworth, with all four playing a big part in the victory. With dwindling finances, a decision was made not to dabble in the transfer market, so the future of the club seemed to rest in the hands of youngsters such as this quartet. But Silman suffered a nasty injury, although his absence was softened by the return of Guest who had been out of first team action since October.

Relegation fears were ever increasing, but they were dispelled when the Easter pro-

gramme saw United win three out of three to ensure safety, with the teams below them having played several more matches, and it was a good job they took such a good return of points from the holiday games for the remaining seven games all ended in defeat. Five of those disastrous last seven matches were played at Millmoor, and it was significant that the attendance for the final game was just 5,415, the lowest the club had experienced since gaining promotion. United finished fourth from bottom, five points better off than relegated Plymouth.

The season was in such marked contrast to the previous one, and it underlined the debt owed by the club to Gladstone Guest, for his absence for a long part of the campaign brought home what a key role he had played in the past as schemer in chief and skipper.

At the beginning of June, secretary William Heald announced his retirement - he had served with the club for 33 years and had signed on over 1,000 players, his place was taken by assistant secretary Len Holmes. There was little summer news from Millmoor until the players reported back for training, but it did emerge that work had eventually begun at the bottom end of the ground with 10,000 tons of rubble being tipped for banking.

Youth was to be given its chance for the 1956/57 season with no new big signings, although there was much regret among the supporters when Gladdy Guest moved to Gainsborough Trinity, after rejecting the offer of player/coach with the second team at Millmoor.

There could have been no more attractive opposition for the opening game than local rivals Sheffield United, but it wasn't a very good day for Rotherham with the Blades recording a comfortable 4 - 0 win to herald another poor start to the season. In fact it was their worst in Division Two as they were anchored to the bottom in early September.

The first win did not come until the seventh game of the season when Nottingham Forest were beaten, and the next home game saw Rotherham hit Swansea for six before they conceded six at Stoke a week later. The Swansea game saw the debuts of two new players, for the long search for some new blood had proved successful in the end with the signing of inside forwards Roy Stephenson from Burnley and Bobby Brown from Barnsley, for a combined fee of around £8,000.

Danny Williams
Cause for celebration - the holder of the club record
459 League appearances (between 1946 and 1959)

After another home defeat, against Middlesbrough, there seemed to be some light in the dark tunnel with a comprehensive 5-1 win at Notts County, with a hat-trick from Peter Johnson being the third of four games without defeat. The team were slowly climbing the League table, when they suddenly found their shooting boots, crashing home 13 goals in two successive games starting with a memorable 7-2 win at Bramall Lane.

It was memorable not just for the scoreline but for the fact that it was the very first time that Rotherham had played a League game under floodlights (Saturday 15th December

1956), after having experienced them several times in friendly matches.

The next game saw United crash six goals past Bristol City, but after drawing both Christmas games against Barnsley, Blackburn Rovers pulled off a narrow victory in the last game of the year. A single goal victory against Port Vale got 1957 off to a better start but Bristol City quickly brought an end to Rotherham's cup hopes for the season, and victories by West Ham United and Nottingham Forest set the alarm bell ringing again.

There was a bombshell when it was announced that the club were prepared to receive offers for Jack Grainger, Frank Marshall and Ken Keyworth, and if the right offers were received the players would be sold.

The explanation given was that the club were short of cash and because of dwindling gates, could not pay its way. Although several clubs showed an interest in the trio, no definite approaches were received, and it seemed to be a sign of the times and an indication that the days of the inflated transfer market was a thing of the past.

Ray Dixon had been banging in the goals for the Midland League table topping reserves, and he was given his first team chance which he marked by netting one of the goals in a seven goal thriller which gave Rotherham a narrow victory against Fulham. February turned out to be quite a successful month with three wins out of four matches - one of them was at Middlesbrough where a certain Mr Clough was kept off the scoresheet by Nobby Noble. The six points consolidated United in a comparatively safe eighth from the bottom position. By the end of the season they had slipped another two places but still managed to steer well clear of the relegation battle.

There was still no move for the transfer listed players, but one departure saw Jack Selkirk leave Millmoor to become player/manager of King's Lynn - he had given loyal service to the club since 1944.

In an effort to combat the financial problem the Rotherham and District Sportsmen's Association came into being with their aim to raise money, not only for Rotherham United but also for other sporting associations such as Rotherham Town cricket club. But the precarious state of the finances did not prevent close season work from going ahead at the railway end where the old stand which was in a dilapidated condition, was pulled down to make way for new terracing, with plans to make it covered accommodation.

The gloomy situation was, in fact, confirmed when the accounts were issued, for they showed a loss of over £7,000 on the season giving an overall debit of £512 - a disappointing situation considering the success of recent seasons.

Jack Grainger had moved to Lincoln City, so Barry Webster was given his chance on the right wing for the 1957/58 season's opening game against Doncaster Rovers, while new boy Malcolm Stephens, a close season signing from Brighton, was given a place in the first starting line-up.

In marked contrast to the previous season, the new campaign got off to a good start with Doncaster being beaten at Millmoor, followed by a creditable draw at Middlesbrough, which gave renewed heart for what was widely acknowledged as a hard battle ahead. The form was held long enough to record a fine away win at Ipswich, but then Middlesbrough gained revenge by winning 4-1 at Millmoor in the return fixture.

It looked as if the old left wing problem would raise it's head again when Keith Bambridge received his National Service calling up papers, and it seemed likely that he would soon be unavailable for regular selection.

Three points were taken from a possible four in games against Huddersfield and Liverpool, before 4-1 scorelines saw Rotherham lose at Stoke but beat Bristol City, to lead into a sequence of just one point from the next five games. The team had had an enforced break, though, when a 'flu virus went through all the staff and the Football League agreed to postpone a game with ten players sidelined with the illness. Attendances were on the decline and there were less than 9,000 at the Bristol City game, but one theory which was put forward was the fact that many employees in local industries were putting in a lot of overtime work, including Saturday afternoons.

It seemed ironic, therefore, that work at the bottom end of the ground should reach its halfway stage at a time when gates were down. The concreting of the terracing had been completed and the next phase was to put on the cover. The cost would be £10,000 and with the club not being able to meet its costs from gate receipts, the Sportsmen's Association would have to provide considerable help.

At the beginning of November there was some surprise news on the night before the game at Barnsley, with Roy Stephenson moving to Blackburn Rovers at a fee of £6,000, and reserve centre half Peter Madden was brought in to take his place at inside left. The gamble was not a success as the Tykes won the game comfortably, but Andy Smailes' hopes of bringing in Sheffield United's Glyn Jones as Stephenson's replacement brought little joy as the Blades had injury problems of their own and were not prepared to release Jones at that time.

December was a depressing month for Rotherham with just one point from six matches, but at last there was some activity in the transfer market with the acquisition of Ken Twidle from Retford Town for a fee of £1,000. He had to make the big step up from the Yorkshire League to the Football League, but he came with the reputation of being a prolific scorer with 23 goals already that season to add to his 40 from the previous one.

Twidle was joined by Jones, who eventually made the move from Bramall Lane, and Albert Broadbent who moved from Sheffield Wednesday with Peter Johnson going to Hillsborough in part exchange. But they all had little immediate impact as Rotherham went into 1958 as a struggling side, fifth from the bottom of the table. Albert Broadbent - now there was a player who had the kick of a mule from a dead-ball situation.

January proved to be no better a month than December had been, with an F.A. Cup exit at Blackburn followed by just one point from the next available four. The newcomers were not eligible for the cup-tie, so 19-year-old Brian Sawyer had to be

specially flown home from his R.A.F. unit in Germany to play. When key players Danny Williams and Roy Lambert suffered injuries, the transfer of Terry Farmer to York City further depleted the playing strength. Three wins out of four matches lifted the gloom in February, which had started with Rotherham fourth from the bottom, and it was probably no coincidence that defender Norman Noble was pushed up to centre forward.

A blizzard caused the abandonment of the home game against Cardiff City with the game goalless, but it was a blizzard of a different kind which hit Rotherham at Millmoor, as Sheffield United stormed to a 6-1 win. Even worse was to follow in the next game, as United were walloped 8-0 by West Ham, but the two heavy defeats were soon put into the background as 4-1 and 5-2 wins against Barnsley and Swansea respectively saw March bring an avalanche of goals.

The beginning of March unfortunately saw the death of 87-year-old William Watt who had been the club chairman for 15 years and a director for over 35. Together with his brother - the late John - he had kept the club going in the dismal days of the 1930's when United were at a low ebb with a massive £15,000 overdraft.

The massacre by the London team was the heaviest experienced by Rotherham in the Second Division - for the second successive week - and it prompted another player recruitment drive. Nothing materialised, however, with Walter Kelly refusing the move from Doncaster Rovers and Rotherham rejecting Liverpool's £10,000 bid for winger Barrie Webster, even though they could have dome with the income, stating that they wanted £15,000.

The crowded Easter glut of fixtures brought nothing but despondency with the three games all ending in defeat as 13 goals were conceded, and relegation fears loomed up yet again following successes by some of the other struggling teams. Rotherham were fifth from the bottom with only five matches left, but the two wins gained from these were enough to ensure safety albeit by the narrow margin of three points.

It had been a very disappointing season and at the end of the campaign, the greatest source of satisfaction was the fact that United had escaped from relegation. The team had constantly been chopped and changed for various reasons with the same eleven lining up on only four occasions. Defensively the team had their worst ever Second Division season, conceding 101 goals in their 42 league games, while at the other end Webster was top scorer with a modest 12 goals.

Attempts by several clubs to secure the services of wing half Ken Keyworth ended when First Division Leicester City signed him for £10,000 and the former Grammar School lad went on to play in an F.A. Cup final at Wembley, thereby following in Len White's footsteps. The fee came in handy to enable manager Smailes to sign Bobby Foster and Ken Waterhouse from Preston North End with enough left in the kitty to see the club through to the beginning of the

next season. There was another departure when long serving Norman Noble left to join his former skipper Gladstone Guest at Gainsborough Trinity, where he would also join forces with yet another former Rotherham player, Dennis Warner.

Despite the poor showing on the pitch, the club's accounts revealed the healthiest balance for several years with over £10,600 to be carried forward, this was due mainly to £7,000 which was received from the Sportsmen's Association and the fact that entertainment tax had been abolished.

There were 18 full time professionals on the books in addition to around 20 part-timers when the 1958/59 season got underway, but the club might have been better to field them all at the same time when they were thrashed 6-1 at Bristol City on the opening day. The reserves incidentally were now playing in the newly formed North Regional League and they got off to a winning start by beating Hartlepools United 5-1.

If the previous season had been a struggle, the new one was to prove to be even more so as the team managed only ten wins - just one away from home - and they came perilously close to going down as they finished just one point above Grimsby Town. There were sequences of 11 and eight games without a win, and the best run they managed to put together covered five matches at the end of March and in April, a string of games which coincided with the arrival of Alan Kirkman from Manchester City.

The season was not without it's upheavals either, because on 13th October manager Andy Smailes tendered his resignation, to end a link with the club which had been in existence since September 1929 with him serving as player, trainer and manager. Smailes, who was 63 at the time, considered it was in the best interests of the club for a new manager to be appointed after he had severely criticised the players for their performance in a home defeat against Brighton.

Former players Gladstone Guest and Jack Selkirk were among the names bandied about as Smailes' possible replacement, before it emerged that the favourite for the post was George Raynor who had played for Rotherham and was coach to the Swedish national team before taking over as manager at Skegness Town. In the meantime the directors selected the team in consultation with trainers Albert Wilson and Mark Hooper, but their choice gained scant reward, for it suffered a 5-0 defeat at Sheffield Wednesday. Smailes had still not been replaced a month after his departure so the directors decided it was time to advertise the vacancy, with many applications subsequently being received.

By the end of November the team had slumped to the bottom of the division with just 12 points from 18 matches to leave the new boss with a difficult task in front of him. It turned out to be Tom Johnston who was eventually appointed, at the beginning of December, after relinquishing his position of player/manager with Central Alliance League club Heanor Town.

Tom Johnston

Johnston brought new hope to the club, but he had a hard job in front of him and six successive defeats underlined that fact.

An economy "weeding out" took place as the season progressed and at one stage there were 12 players on the transfer list, but the League position did not improve and the team were still stuck at the bottom at the end of February. But they managed to climb the table during that successful April and just scraped enough points together to avoid the drop, although defeats in all the last three matches left the final outcome too close for comfort.

The discovery of the season was probably Ken Waterhouse who had been signed as a forward, when he scored a couple of goals before being dropped, placed on the transfer list, turned into a wing half, taken off the list, and restored to the first team for an unbroken run of 13 matches.

That was the fourth successive season in which United had had to fight a battle against relegation so just what could be done to prevent a fifth campaign on the trot to avoid the drop? There certainly wasn't much money about to rectify the problems, for despite a total of £14,000 being received from the Sportsmen's Association, a loss of over £600 was reported with the wages bill going up by more than £4,700. With that being the case, Tom Johnston pledged the future of the club in his youngsters and with that in mind he set up two youth teams, one would play in the Northern Intermediate League as usual in addition to a team of 15 and 16 year-olds in the Sheffield Intermediate League.

Stalwart Danny Williams was appointed as coach with a special brief to teach and encourage all the young players, and they could have no better person to look up to for he had given great service to the club.

nough money was made available to buy centre forward Bill Myerscough from Aston Villa and he made a scoring debut in the 1959/60 season's opening game, a 3-3 home draw against Charlton Athletic, although Rotherham squandered a three goal lead and that was followed by a sharing of the points at Derby County. Alan Kirkman hit two goals in the win at Bristol City to give him five goals in the first three games as he continued in the same form which had helped the club to stave off relegation at the end of the previous season.

In September it was revealed that the directors were looking into the possibility of installing floodlights at Millmoor, and that would enable all Saturday matches to kick off at 3pm, but the club would be one of the last in the First and Second Divisions to introduce this facility.

After a dismal display in a defeat against Derby County, it was somewhat a surprise when Johnston made no team changes and his faith in the team was rewarded when after slipping to a single goal defeat at Plymouth, Rotherham launched a 15 match unbeaten run which took them by Christmas into second position, with talk of promotion very much in the air.

United were two points behind Aston Villa with a game in hand and one of the secrets of the success had been a settled side. One of the highlights of that unbeaten run was a 3-2 win at Sheffield United, after the home team had been two up at half time, to record Rotherham's fourth away win in six matches.

Brian Sawyer was a constant source of transfer speculation as his promising form attracted the attention of some of the bigger

clubs, but all overtures were rejected as he was considered to be a vital member of the club's future.

If the win against Sheffield United was a notable one, an even more telling victory saw leaders Aston Villa sent home empty handed. A mouth watering game to look forward to was the F.A. Cup third round which had given Rotherham a home tie with mighty Arsenal. It was decided to issue vouchers which would guarantee a ticket for the cup game, but not for the first time the plans did not seem to be very well laid when they were given out at the reserves game, while many supporters were watching the first team at Lincoln!

Twelve months previous to Christmas 1959 the outlook looked bleak, but suddenly it was very different, before everyone was brought down to earth with a double defeat against Middlesbrough at Christmas. The disappointment of that two match setback was soon put into the background however, with a 3-1 home win against bottom of the table Bristol City, but quite naturally all the attention was focused on the Cup-tie against the mighty "Gunners".

Apart from being treated to steaks at a local restaurant, and playing golf on Wednesday, the players followed their normal training routine for a game which revived fond memories of the 1953 win at Newcastle, with all the tickets sold days beforehand. But it seemed that Rotherham were on their way out of the F.A.Cup at the first hurdle for the fifth year in succession when they were trailing 2-0, with only 20 minutes to go, before a tremendous comeback saw them snatch an equaliser and come close to grabbing a late winner.

Arsenal took a 30th minute lead when Julians headed past Roy Ironside, and the visitors increased their lead in the second half when Danny Williams had the misfortune to deflect the ball past his own keeper. Rotherham were given a lifeline when Brian Sawyer took a Keith Kettleborough cross from the right to crash a shot into the net from the edge of the penalty area, and with Arsenal rocked back on their heels, Alan Kirkman's dribble was stopped when Wills used his hands. A penalty kick was awarded and Billy Myerscough accepted the responsibility of the occasion to score - although keeper Standen got his hand to the shot - to give United a well earned replay at Highbury, for they had often looked the better side.

At their own stadium, on a treacherous frozen surface, Arsenal launched a blistering opening assault and could well have been three up in the opening 15 minutes, but they had to wait until two minutes before the interval for Bloomfield to give them the lead. Any thoughts of this leading the way to an easy home win were soon confounded when Barry Webster hit a 60th minute equaliser, to leave the teams deadlocked again despite playing 30 minutes extra time.

Rotherham chairman Reg Cooper won the toss for the choice of venue for the second replay and he quite naturally chose Sheffield Wednesday's Hillsborough ground, but before the third game could take place the Millers were bought down to earth by losing at Scunthorpe.

However, on the Monday night all roads led to Sheffield 6 and the crowd of over 56,000 caused traffic jams of huge proportions. On the pitch though it was virtually one way traffic as Rotherham showed their more illustrious opponents how to play, and a superb exhibition of scintillating soccer gave the minnows a well deserved 2-0 win.

It took Rotherham just seven minutes to go in front with, Kettleborough hitting the vital goal to round off a brilliant move, and Arsenal were powerless to stem the tide of the rampant Rotherham side. Danny Williams was an inspiration in a game which was virtually all over when Sawyer prodded home a second goal after 15 minutes. There was never any hope of Arsenal producing the type of rally that United had come up with in the first game.

Over 138,000 spectators watched the trio of games and produced receipts in excess of £21,000, with the attendance at Highbury - 57,598 - still remaining as the highest a Rotherham team has played in front of.

The reward for the famous victory was a home tie against Brighton and Hove Albion, with this game also requiring three games, before the South Coast club went through when they trounced Rotherham 6-0 in the second replay, which was ironically played at Highbury.

The fact that the original tie ended in a draw caused some exceptional foot slogging for 39-year-old Alex Kasic, a Yugoslavian who worked at Dinnington Colliery, for he had said to his mates that if that was the result, then he would walk to Brighton for the replay, and true to his word he did just that!

The cup marathon over, Rotherham could focus all their attention on maintaining their promotion challenge, and to help them in that quest they used some of the money from their exploits to sign 24-year-old Eddie O'Hara, a left winger, for around £5,000 from Everton. But six League matches without a win severely dented those hopes and the poor run continued, to leave Rotherham in a position of looking easy meat for their Second Division opponents, with accusations of a broken team spirit being responsible for the decline.

A single goal victory against Sunderland on 19th March was only the second in the League since mid-December and only another two were recorded before the season drew to its close with Rotherham finishing in eighth position. That could have been so much better for they had still been in third spot at the beginning of April, but a poor Easter killed off prospects of finishing in a high enough position to earn the club a slice of the talent money which was paid out to the top four teams.

During the summer, Billy Myerscough moved to Coventry City for a fee of around £6,000, and Roy Silman quickly followed by moving to Barnsley for what was described as a "reasonable" fee.

The 1960/61 season opened on a successful note with single goal wins against newly promoted Southampton and Lincoln City, but United could not keep up their winning ways with goalscoring problems denying them a place among the division's front runners. A sequence of six draws from seven matches gave them an average of around a point a game by the end of October, but by then Rotherham had won at Leicester City in the first game of the newly formed Football League Cup.

One of the scorers in that 2-1 victory was George Darwin who made it his third successive scoring game since signing from Derby County, but he was injured in the cup match, to bring an abrupt end to his Rotherham career. The League Cup was, in fact, to become Rotherham's one success in an indifferent season which rarely reached any heights in the League, and the F.A. Cup saw United well beaten at Birmingham after scraping a 1-0 win against Watford in the third round.

Bristol Rovers were beaten at Millmoor in the third round of the League Cup on 23rd

November 1960 - a date which marked another landmark in the club's history, as it was the first senior game to be played under the new floodlights. They had actually been switched on for the first time in a reserve game two days earlier when a crowd of 2,947 watched Rotherham beat Darlington 3-0.

Shortly after, Keith Kettleborough was sold to Sheffield United for £12,000, but he was hardly missed as his former colleagues pulled off a 5-2 win against Luton Town the following day, the first time they had hit five goals in a match since the 1957/58 season. Most of the Kettleborough money was spent in recruiting striker Don Weston from Birmingham City and he soon became the crowd's favourite by hitting the only goal of the Christmas game against Liverpool on his home debut.

Despite the success in the League Cup, there was some cause for alarm regarding the League position, as 1961 got under way with Rotherham ninth from the bottom, but only four points in front of basement club Lincoln City. Three points from games against Ipswich Town and Scunthorpe United - beaten 4-0 - relieved some of the anxiety before a convincing 3-0 win at Millmoor against Portsmouth took Rotherham into the semi-finals of the League Cup.

This was to be a two-legged affair with the draw giving United home advantage in the first game against Third Division Shrewsbury Town, who pulled off a shock to reach that stage by beating Everton. The history-making first ever League Cup semi-final duly took place at Millmoor on 21st March, and two goals from Brian Sawyer and one from Alan Kirkman gave Rotherham a slender 3-2 lead to take into the second leg.

It had been expected that the lead would have been more convincing but it proved to

Chatting over the old times of the 1950/51 (Third Division North) season:
Cliff Wright (Director), Gladstone Guest, Charlie Tomlinson and Danny Williams

be just enough eight days later when United held Town to a 1-1 draw at Gay Meadow, with Don Weston's extra time goal making Rotherham the first team ever to win a place in the final of the competition. Town had levelled the scores at 3-3 on aggregate after just fifteen minutes, and the next 105 saw a stern stamina test before the issue was decided.

Rotherham had the distinction of staging the first leg of the first final, at Millmoor, with Monday 1st May scheduled for the game against either Burnley or Aston Villa. However, this date had to be changed as the two teams still in the competition took their semi-final into a third game, and worse was to follow when the Football League then decided that the final would be held over to the start of the following season. Villa eventually fought their way through.

This decision caused great objections from Millmoor, quite naturally, for the club had to refund the money they had already taken for the sale of final tickets and it was hinted at, that Villa should forfeit their place and the trophy be awarded to Rotherham.

The League programme ended with United hitting 14 goals in their last four games, but only one of them ended in victory so the fifteenth position was again something of a disappointment.

A close season tour to Finland got off to a good start with a 4-0 win against VII Purin Riepas - a First Division team - thanks to a Ken Houghton hat-trick and a goal by Don Weston, and they went on to complete a one hundred per cent winning record from their four matches.

Declining gates, the season's average was around 9,700, forced Rotherham into a re-think about ways of combatting the attraction of having two Sheffield clubs playing in the First Division, and when the fixture list was issued, they plumped for the experiment of staging four Friday night home matches.

A couple of promising youngsters were signed from Scotland, with Bill Cassidy joining from Rangers and Alex Wilson from Clyde, while Eddie O'Hara moved back to his homeland and Falkirk. As usual, though, there wasn't much money available to be thrown around on transfer fees, and without the help of the Sportsmen's Association - who had made donations of £14,000 during the financial year just ended - the club would have made a loss of £4960.

There were, however, no new faces in the team which got the 1961/62 off to a winning start at Stoke, to warm the team up for their long awaited League Cup final first leg game against Aston Villa.

Goals were scored by Barry Webster and Alam Kirkman early in the second half, but United came close to going to Villa Park with just a one goal advantage when Villa were awarded a penalty. But Roy Ironside helped to protect the lead by saving Lynn's spot kick.

A convincing 4-0 home win against Bristol Rovers underlined manager Tom Johnston's pre-season hopes of success, but there then came a heavy defeat at Middlesbrough before a fine 3-1 win at Leeds United took Rotherham to Villa Park for the second leg of the Cup final.

The opening 45 minutes saw fast end to end football with Villa having a slight territorial advantage although there had been little sign of them scoring until the home side hit

Rotherham with two shock goals. The first came after 67 minutes, when O'Neill scored before Burrows quickly added a second. Don Weston failed with three gilt edged chances to put Rotherham back in front on aggregate, and after some heavy Rotherham pressure, the game went into extra time with United again pounding away at the Villa goal. With just ten minutes remaining, Villa snatched the trophy with a shot from Mc-Parland which hit the underside of the bar on it's way into the net to rob Rotherham of the glory.

The League Cup - which the Millers so nearly won in the competition's first season.

But the season was to produce another successful League Cup campaign, which started with a win at Darlington in the first round, before Luton Town were disposed of in the second, thanks to a 2-0 victory at Millmoor after a goalless draw at Kenilworth Road. That game wasn't without it's trials and tribulations for the team only got to the ground ten minutes before the kick off after the coach driver had been misdirected, following a meal break at St Neots.

League form was again showing some inconsistency with three successive wins followed by two defeats on the trot, one of which was a 5-0 drubbing at Walsall, before an unbeaten seven match run took Rotherham to third place in the League by the end of November.

Preston were earlier beaten 3-0 at Millmoor in the third round of the League Cup after a goalless draw at Deepdale. to line up a fourth round meeting against Yorkshire rivals Leeds United.

Winger Brian Taylor had been bought from Birmingham City and manager Johnston wanted to buy two more players, but he was told the coffers had been scraped clean and the only way open to making any more signings was to sell first, with Peter Madden being a possible departure. A familiar story!

The Friday night experiment saw a thrilling 3-3 draw against Huddersfield, and it looked as if the League Cup run had come to an end for Rotherham when they could only draw at home against Leeds, with that game followed by two League defeats.

Don Weston was again the match-winner in the Boxing Day game against Liverpool but 1962 saw an early F.A. Cup exit with United losing 4-3 at Huddersfield Town. The Millers were gallant in defeat though, for Roy Lambert was injured in the first few minutes and it was only a goal two minutes from time that eventually gave Town their victory.

The injury ruled Lambert out for the remainder of the season and his absence was a bitter blow for Rotherham as he had been an ever-present up to then, but the team pulled well together to beat Leeds twice within the space of four days - once in the League and once in the replay of the League Cup. The latter victory led to a fifth round game

against Blackburn Rovers, but one goal was enough to thwart Rotherham's hopes of reaching the semis again.

Another Friday night win - this time against Leyton Orient in early March put Rotherham into fifth position, but then came a depressing run of ten games which saw nine defeats and one draw, to well and truly put paid to hopes of a high position. This dreadful run was only halted by a last match of the season win at Huddersfield, but some consolation had been the emergence of youngsters such as Albert Bennett and Ian Butler, two players on whom the future success of the club could well rest.

Worried chairman Reg Cooper launched an inquiry into what the supporters wanted, after six successive defeats had seen the attendance plummet to just over 4,000, and manager Johnston wielded the big axe leaving out, in turn, experienced players such as Alan Kirkman, Don Weston, Roy Ironside and Lol Morgan. Mr Cooper was deluged with letters from supporters, while Johnston answered the criticism by stating that the public were too impatient and he had a number of young players coming up who would blend into a promotion team.

But the disharmony that had a detrimental effect on the team did not end there, for Don Weston and Lol Morgan were put on the transfer list at their own request, while part-timers Keith Bambridge and Peter Perry were demanding interviews with the management. Weston was quoted as saying he would rather play for a minor team for nothing so that he could at least enjoy his football rather than continue at Millmoor with things as they had been over the previous weeks.

Meanwhile, work started on a proposed three storey block on the front of the ground to incorporate a new entrance and offices, with a new directors' room to be built on the top level - if finances permitted; obviously they didn't.

Barry Webster was sold for £5,000 to Bradford City towards the end of June and former playing hero Danny Williams was asked to take overall charge of the juniors, but he dropped a bombshell by stating that he was severing his long relationship with the club. A native of Thrybergh and an ex-pit boy, he joined Rotherham in 1942 and made a total of 621 first team appearances before taking charge of the reserves, with only illnesses preventing him from topping the 700 mark.

The money which had been received for Webster was soon splashed out on signing striker Hugh McIlmoyle from Leicester City, while Perry moved out, joining York City.

But transfer activity was soon overshadowed by a managerial change, with Tom Johnston being released to allow him to accept a more lucrative offer from Grimsby Town, and hero Danny Williams needed little time to consider the opportunity of accepting the challenge of taking over.

The new manager had already realised the future of the club could well rest in the hands of some young, local, lads and he soon signed on Chris Rabjohn, Harold Wilcockson and Barry Lyons, who were all to play important roles in the next few years.

Relegated from the First Division the previous season, Chelsea opened the new campaign with a 1-0 win at Millmoor, but Rotherham quickly put that defeat behind them by pulling off a thrilling 4-3 win at Elland Road against Leeds United. Alan Kirkman hit a picture goal to snatch the victory six minutes from time after they had led 3-0 at half time, only for the home side to pull level. That was the first of four straight League wins, which included another against Leeds to complete a winning double, and the gate for this match was very encouraging as it easily topped 19,000.

Young Albert Bennett marked his first appearance of the season by hitting two goals in Rotherham's 4-2 win against Sunderland in a game which saw the soaked-to-the-skin spectators give the team rapturous applause.

That euphoria was halted by a 5-1 defeat at Bury, and after going down at Walsall in the following game, United beat Bristol City in the League Cup at Ashton Gate, where 17 year-old Frank Casper made his debut.

The reserves were taking the season by storm and they dropped just one point from the first eight games, in which they scored 31 goals, and that was the main reason for attracting a crowd of 2,713

Kirkman scores the winner in the League match at Elland Road, Leeds.

for the game against Gateshead which saw Rotherham win 3-2.

Danny Williams was determined that none of his players would be sold and he received backing from the board who rejected an offer from Tom Johnston's Grimsby Town, who were prepared to pay three times the fee that Rotherham had done for Alan Kirkman. West Ham United were beaten in the League Cup but Rotherham's progress was stopped abruptly at Ewood Park where Blackburn Rovers won 4 - 1.

There was an unsavoury incident at Millmoor in early November in the game against Portsmouth, when Pompey's left back Wilson punched out a goalbound Keith Bambridge shot, but to the amazement of everyone in the ground, the referee did not award a penalty.

One spectator jumped the wall at the railway end and ran to the centre circle to register his protest to the referee, who for the remaining 20 minutes of the game had to withstand a continuous vocal protest from the crowd. At the end of the game Mr Langdale of Darlington was escorted off the pitch by Danny Williams and two ranks of policemen.

Yet again Rotherham slumped when they were making reasonable progress, with a run of eight League games producing nothing better than three draws, and after beating Luton Town just before Christmas, Rotherham were beaten again on Boxing Day at Stoke.

By then there had been a couple of comings and goings with Don Weston moving to Leeds United and Brian Sawyer switching to Bradford City in an exchange deal which brought John McCole to Millmoor. The other new recruit was Jimmy Blain who arrived from Southport.

Heavy snow meant that the first game of 1963 did not take place until 20th February when Rotherham were beaten 2-0 at Watford in the F.A. Cup third round, and following the long lay-off, it was decided to extend the season by two weeks. To all intents and purposes that defeat left Rotherham with little left to play for in the remainder of the season but the team were rocked by a serious injury to John McCole who fractured a leg in a game at Derby County towards the end of April. In addition to it being an individual blow, it was also hard on Albert Bennett who was learning a lot from having McCole playing alongside him, and the youngster had hit a purple scoring patch.

Hugh McIlmoyle was sold to Carlisle United for £4,000 but his departure came as no real surprise since he had not been able to hold down a place in the first team. He had been placed on the transfer list at his own request stating that he wished to move South - he obviously wasn't very good at geography! Another departure saw Ken Waterhouse's move to Bristol City - would you believe it declining gates had dropped to 8,000 (!) - helped prop up the finances yet again, although the club maintained that none of their up and coming young players would be sold. To keep the club out of financial difficulties, it was reported that average gates of 13,000 were required - a pipedream in recent years.

The team had to settle for 14th position, but there was better news for the reserves who were winners of the North Regional League with seven points to spare, and they scored 89 goals in their 32 matches.

Once again the club had cause to thank the Sportsmen's Association for their season's total donations of £13,000, which led to an eventual profit of over £10,000, and the chairman warned that if low attendances continued it may necessitate the selling of players. That threat was carried out immediately, with the departure of Brian Taylor to Shrewsbury Town for £4,000, but Danny Williams indicated that he would be keeping that money in reserve, stating that he thought the present squad of players were good enough to deal with the job in hand.

The 1963/64 season got off to a poor start with successive defeats at Bury, Leeds United and at home to Manchester City. It was not until the seventh game of the season that the first victory was recorded, when a 1-0 home win against Cardiff City was notched up, before Alan Kirkman was sold to Newcastle United for £12,000 to show a considerable profit for Rotherham. He had been on the transfer list during the summer but settled his differences at the start of the season saying that he had no desire to move.

Another win against Middlesbrough came in the next game and Grimsby Town were beaten at Blundell Park in the second round of the League Cup to give the young team some confidence. John McCole made a welcome return to action following his fracture injury the previous season, with an outing for the reserves at the beginning of October, and he had an unusual partner playing up front alongside Gordon Morritt who was the second string regular 'keeper. He played a game at centre half, and in the next moved to centre forward where he promptly netted two goals.

But McCole's comeback lasted just 55 minutes before he suffered another injury, and his leg had to be put in plaster again, although there was no further fracture. Unfortunately McCole was unable to return to full fitness and after returning to action again with the reserves he subsequently moved to League of Ireland club Shelbourne on a free transfer during the following summer.

That left United with a very young forward line but the Millmoor babes showed a great deal of promise, with Barry Lyons, Albert Bennett, Brian Tiler, Frank Casper and Ian Butler being very much coveted by Danny Williams. At times they lacked experience, but at others they demonstrated their skills, as they did in beating Plymouth, before making further progress in the League Cup by overcoming Coventry City. That win gave Rotherham a home tie in the fourth round against Millwall, who were despatched back to the South on the wrong end of a splendid 5-2 scoreline.

The first away League win of the season was produced with a fine 4-1 victory at Derby County at the beginning of December when the club were pleased to learn that Albert Bennett had decided not to proceed any further with his rumoured transfer request after Danny Williams had outlined to him that he was an important part of the club's future. The League Cup exploits came to an end with a defeat at Stoke and the team followed this by suffering a heavy defeat at Manchester City, but a winning double was recorded against Northampton Town over the two Christmas games.

First Division Burnley provided Rotherham's first opposition in 1964 when the teams met in the third round of the F.A. Cup at Turf Moor, and the visitors did very well indeed to gain a 1-1 draw against a side who fielded six full internationals. The second game took place at a packed Millmoor - Chief Constable Mr Morris considered that too many people were in the ground - and the visitors took a 21st minute lead, but two goals from Barry Lyons looked like leading Rotherham to an upset.

But with just over 20 minutes left to play, full back Colin Clish suffered a fractured leg and Burnley pulled level against the ten men, after 77 minutes, before snatching the winner four minutes from time. The Millmoor attendance was 24,233 to give an aggregate 50,000 figure for the two games.

A few weeks later the injury bogey struck again when 'keeper Roy Ironside had to be carried off after only 15 minutes of the game at Scunthorpe and Brian Tiler took over between the posts for the remainder of the game which ended in a 4-3 defeat. Ironside's absence allowed Gordon Morritt to come into the first team and fortunately he had just played a couple of games in goal for the reserves after hitting 21 goals in his spell as centre forward.

Morritt subsequently asked to be taken off the transfer list, as did Lol Morgan who regained his place in the first team as Clish's replacement, and when the Millers faced Portsmouth in mid-February, they turned out a team which had not cost a single penny in the transfer market with seven of them having progressed through the Rotherham Intermediate League.

Rotherham had always been in a comfortable League position during the season but they were unable to mount a serious promotion challenge despite pulling off some good results. A 5-0 win against Charlton Athletic topped the pile, in a game which saw Albert Bennett score two goals for the fourth successive match. But the season ended with a heavy 6-1 defeat at Southampton, although Rotherham still finished in a creditable seventh position, the best for nine years.

For the coming 1964/65 season it was decided that the Friday night experiment would be thrown into touch, with the feeling that nothing had been gained by the switch of a handful of matches, and when visiting fans were generally prevented from travelling. A credit balance of almost £55,000 was reported after the year's accounts revealed a net profit of almost £12,500, with the money received yet again from the Sportsmen's Association (£9,000) contributing to improving ground amenities, particularly the covering of the terracing in front of the main stand.

It was the same squad of players who got the season off to a start with a point from a goalless draw at Preston, which was the forerunner of a fine opening with five wins coming in the next six matches. This sequence gave the team their best opening for 13 seasons, and a single goal victory against Portsmouth in the middle of September lifted them to the top of the table.

The spirit of the side was epitomised by the fightback that saw the team beat Charlton 3-2 after being 2-1 down with only 15 minutes left, and the good form continued with a home win against Cardiff City, which lifted the Millers to become table-toppers again.

Rochdale had been disposed of in the second round of the League Cup, but Rotherham made their exit from the competition in the next round when they were beaten 2-0 at Swansea after drawing 2-2 at Millmoor. This defeat seemed to have something of a knock-on effect on the team, and they struggled to maintain their challenge among the division's leading pack with the ability of someone like John McCole sadly lacking. He was the type of player who could not only hold the young forward line together and score goals, but also inspire and bring on the young players.

Ken Houghton had hit all three goals in the win against Cardiff, but only one more League win was achieved from the next eight games, which included a 6-1 thrashing at Southampton, to make The Dell one of the club's least favourite grounds, having been beaten by the same scoreline on the previous visit.

United had dropped down to 12th place at the beginning of December, and with injuries to several key players weakening the side, it was obvious that some fresh blood was needed. That was introduced for the game at Coventry City, where former Rotherham player Ken Keyworth made his debut for the home side, following his free transfer from Leicester, and the new £10,000 signing from Wolverhampton Wanderers - John Galley - had the perfect debut. He grabbed a hat-trick in a 5-3 Rotherham win and was on the target as well on his home debut, a 2-2 draw against Preston North End.

Danny Williams was making efforts to bring in other players to strengthen the squad, but he was always met by a request for a player exchange with his youngsters in big demand, and Danny flatly refused to let any of them go.

Rotherham started 1965 with a home win against Crystal Palace but the New Year exploded with the sale of Ian Butler to Hull City for £45,000, a United record, and worse was to follow when a few days later Ken Houghton went to the same club for the same fee. With Albert Bennett fully expected to move to Newcastle within a few days, it looked as if the heart had been ripped out of the team which had so much going for it, and quite naturally the townsfolk were far from happy with the situation.

Manager Danny Williams was hardly thrilled to bits either for he had always pledged to keep his starlets, but Bennett's move did not materialise and Lincoln City were soundly beaten 5-1 in the third round of the F.A. Cup to demonstrate that there was life after B. and H. after all. Some of the money received from the Hull bound pair was spent on signing John Hellawell from Bradford City and a couple of weeks later wing half Robin Hardy moved from Sheffield Wednesday.

First Division Wolverhampton Wanderers had home advantage in the fourth round of the F.A. Cup, but Rotherham were not overawed by their more illustrious opponents as they fought superbly to gain a 2-2 and a replay at Millmoor. Wolves had only equalised in the last minute at Molineux, but they made no mistake in the replay winning 3-0 in front of a crowd of 22,555 who were made to wonder why the Wanderers had not been able to finish the tie at the first time of asking. The day after that cup defeat, Rotherham was in the news again with the sudden resignation of manager Danny Williams and the transfer request by skipper Peter Madden.

Williams indicated that he wanted to devote more time to his family, although he would stay on to the end of the season, and the opportunity had arisen to purchase a bungalow in Bournemouth after he had been contemplating the possibility for some time. But it surely wasn't just coincidence that his resignation came so quickly after the sale of two players, for he had always maintained that he would not sell any of the home grown players.

Any new business commitment reasons for his departure held no weight, when he was appointed manager of Swindon Town, in the middle of June, to show that he was not getting out of football as had been hinted and Williams' replacement was quickly lined up with 37-year-old Jack Mansell set to take over as coach. A former Sheffield Wednesday trainer-coach, he was at the time the coach to the Dutch Division One team Telstar, but the following week it was announced that he could not obtain his release from Holland so the vacancy would be advertised.

So despite spending more and more time at his new south coast base, Danny Williams was still in charge when the season drew to

Keith Pring
jumps for joy as he
puts Rotherham in the
lead in the F.A.Cup at Wolves

its close with Rotherham finishing in 14th position. Eventually it was Mansell who did in fact take over, at the beginning of June, and the chance to become his replacement in Holland was given to Darlington player-manager Lol Morgan who of course was a former Rotherham player himself, but he rejected the invitation.

Close season activity at Millmoor saw behind the scene improvements, including new changing rooms and a gymnasium, with some new seating being installed in the stand. Meanwhile, on the playing side, Roy Ironside and Brian Jackson moved to Barnsley on free transfers.

Peter Madden came off the transfer list again and it was announced that the club would go on a three match pre-season tour to Holland to give the new boss the chance of seeing the players in action.

The expected move of Albert Bennett to Newcastle United finally took place towards the end of July 1965 for a fee of slightly under £30,000, when it had looked at one stage as if he would move for much more.

Watched by his new manager, Joe Harvey, Albert Bennett signs for Newcastle United.

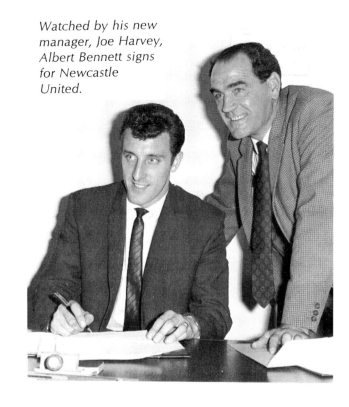

Football kit is switched to cricket whites in July 1965. (Back) Wilcockson, Carver, Galley, Chappell, Madden, Tiler. (Front): Lambert, Morritt, Lewis Purshouse (Vice-Chair.), Wilson.

The tour saw Rotherham lose 2-1 against Mansell's former club Telstar, beat Edo of Haarlem 5-0, and lose 1-0 at Eindhoven. The new manager said he was well satisfied with the performances, with youngster Les Chappell in particular showing a lot of promise.

That form was enough to earn Chappell a place in the team which opened the 1965/66 season, with a 2-1 defeat at Bristol City, and there were no changes at all in the first seven games. There was, however, another change behind the scenes to herald the start of the new season, when Eric Purshouse took over as chairman from the late Reg Cooper. The new man took up the reins after being a director for 23 years. A shrewd business man, Mr Purshouse immediately declared that the club would not go lightly into the buying of players, and he was to keep a prudent hold on the club's purse strings for the remainder of his term of office. Throughout this time he gradually increased the club's financial backing with some astute dealings in the stock market.

One of Mr Purshouse's first tasks in his new position was to announce a credit balance of £38,275 which was, of course, greatly assisted by outgoing transfer deals, despite the wages bill going up by almost £3,000. Entertainment was soon to become the hallmark of Mansell's new team and a 4-1 win at Leyton Orient was quickly followed by a thrilling 4-3 win against Wolves. But that was nothing compared to the 6-4 home win against Cardiff City a few days later when Bobby Williams hit a hat-trick.

The player was on the scoresheet again in an away win at Derby, before Watford were beaten in the second round of the League Cup. A single goal win against Southampton was followed by a humiliating 6-1 thrashing at bottom of the table Bury, with Rotherham a mere shadow of the team who had played so well in the opening matches of the season.

Plans were announced which would enable youth clubs and youth teams to take advantage of the new gymnasium facilities at Millmoor with manager Jack Mansell intending to be on hand to offer advice regarding each club's own particular worries.

Following the drubbing at Bury, Rotherham were well beaten by 4-0 at Middlesbrough, where Les Chappell became the first ever United substitute to be used, when he came on for Keith Pring at the start of the second half. The date was Saturday, 9th October 1965.

Five days at the Lilleshall training centre revitalised United and they cruised to a 5-2 win at nearby Shrewsbury in the third round of the League Cup, but they went out in the next round when West Ham United - Bobby Moore, Martin Peters and Geoff Hurst were in the team - were 2-1 winners at Millmoor.

Goals poured in again when Preston North End were beaten 6-3 at Millmoor, with the visitors becoming the first side to use a substitute at the ground when Lapot replaced Watt, on 30th October, while the first Rotherham substitute to be put into action at home was John Hellawell who replaced Frank Casper after 40 minutes of the 2-0 win against Plymouth Argyle. The date on that occasion was Saturday, 13th November 1965.

Full back Harold Wilkinson attracted the attention of Tottenham Hotspurs' manager Bill Nicholson who spoke to the Rotherham manager and chairman without any transfer figure being mentioned but nothing materialised.

The first home defeat of the season came in dramatic fashion in December when Rotherham were leading 3-0 at half time against Birmingham City, before the visitors staged a remarkable comeback to win 4-3. But United, nevertheless, reached Christmas in seventh place with 24 points from 21 matches - six points behind leaders Huddersfield Town. New Year's Day 1966 saw Rotherham get off to a fine start with a comprehensive 4-1 home win against Middlesbrough, but successive away defeats at Plymouth Argyle and Manchester City left them in need of the win which came next - a 3-0 home victory against Crystal Palace.

The draw for the third round of the F.A. Cup gave United a home tie against Southend United, who at the time were the only team to have only played in the Third Division. But Southend were far from easy opponents, and it needed an own goal to clinch a 3-2 Rotherham win with the rewards for the victory being extremely beneficial, with a plum tie against Manchester United at Old Trafford. Manager Jack Mansell pledged that his team would play the attacking style of football they had produced throughout the whole season, although perhaps the thrill of playing at the big stadium weighed heavily on the players' minds as they only took one point from games against Bristol City and Coventry City.

The National Sporting Centre at Lilleshall was used for special training by Rotherham, and a backing of around 12,000 supporters saw the Millers put up a great performance to hold the big guns of the star-studded Manchester team to a goalless draw with both sides hitting the woodwork.

Talking point number 1: Chappell forces the ball home, only for the 'goal' to be disallowed

A packed Millmoor saw Matt Busby's team pull off a 1-0 win in the replay three days later, but the game was full of controversy with the feeling that the visitors had stolen the game and Rotherham had been robbed of at least the chance of extra time.

Talking point number one came when Rotherham were denied what at first looked to be a perfectly good goal by Les Chappell as he scrambled the ball home after John Galley had crossed from the left.

Talking point number 2: John Galley slips the ball past Harry Gregg, only for Nobby Stiles (right) to clear from under the bar.

Referee Jack Taylor of Wolverhampton had no hesitation in signalling the goal and even 'keeper Harry Gregg kicked the ball down the middle to the centre spot. But the cheers in the Rotherham throats were stifled when, after a lengthy consultation with a linesman, Mr Taylor awarded a free kick to the visitors for what, he later explained, was an offside decision.

Shortly before half time Manchester had another let-off. This time Gregg could only punch out a header from Chappell, and the ball struck Galley on its way into the net, only for Nobby Stiles to pull it back. But it looked as though the ball had crossed the line before Stiles pulled it on to the underside of the crossbar, whereupon it was scrambled to safety by the relieved Manchester defenders.

England winger John Connelly went on to grab the only goal of the game, but Mr Taylor is still reminded of the day the fans thought he "did" them whenever he visits Millmoor. Perhaps it was a pity that a certain Russian linesman who was to grab the headlines several months later in the World Cup, had not been officiating at Millmoor to get his practice in!

After the euphoria of the epic cup-tie had died down, Rotherham were, of course, left to concentrate on their League programme and there was to be no detrimental effect on the team following their fine exploits, for they launched a ten match unbeaten run. It started with a goalless draw at Cardiff for whom David Carver made his home debut after moving to Ninian Park from Millmoor for £12,000 a couple of weeks previously.

With one eye on the future a special ground's committee was established with some futuristic plans in mind, such as double-deck stands around the entire Millmoor perimeter, but of course, nothing

further materialised from these ambitious thoughts. The supporters were given genuine hope, though, when a rights issue of shares was announced by the club with a three-for-four offer for the big holders and one-for-one for those with a holding of less than four. A total of 3,645 shares of the original 8,000 had been held in the company since its formation in 1925, but the directors felt the time was right to offer them to existing holders. They were issued at £1 0s 6d (a premium of 6d), with the income all earmarked for the double decker stands, with seating on top and standing below.

One game in the unbeaten run was a home match against Bury, who were one up at half time, but the Millers came back to win 2-1 with the visitors' goal coming from a certain George Kerr; more of him later.

Despite this good run, Rotherham had just too much leeway to make up and their chances of reaching the top disappeared when they were beaten at home by leaders Manchester City, in an all-ticket game, but United still finished in a creditable seventh position.

Around £500 was spent installing new drains to the Millmoor pitch, while an early departure from the playing staff was 'keeper Gordon Morritt who moved to South African club Durban City for a small fee. He was quickly replace by Alan Hill who made the short move from Barnsley for £12,000, while 18-year-old Les Surman was signed from Charlton Athletic as further goalkeeping cover.

Behind the scenes the finishing touches were put to the gymnasium which had cost around £35,000, improved refreshment and toilet facilities were also introduced, while new turnstiles were added down Millmoor Lane, which was to be concreted.

The team undertook a pre-season tour to the South, with matches at Oxford, Bournemouth and Peterborough on the way back, with mixed results. But the 1966/67 season opened with a convincing 3-1 win at Millmoor against newly promoted Millwall. Four more games were played before the next victory arrived - a 4-2 win against Plymouth - and former Rotherham player Ken Houghton hit the only goal of the game against Hull City at Boothferry Park.

Indifferent League form was forgotten when Frank Casper scored the game's solitary goal, to give the Millers a win against Sheffield Wednesday at Hillsborough in the second round of the League Cup, but they went out in the next round at Northampton.

A superb fightback from a two goal half time deficit against Birmingham City at St Andrews gave Rotherham their first away win of the season, but they were unable to maintain a winning run and December produced just two victories from six matches. Earlier, winger Barry Lyons moved to First Division Nottingham Forest for £40,000, and he had fully earned his chance to play at a higher level after some outstanding displays, but Frank Casper's transfer request was turned down. Shaun Goater - as Rotherham's first Bermudian player - was nearly preceded by 19-year-old goalkeeper Granville Nusum, who saved enough money for his air fare and accommodation, after being recommended to Jack Mansell by coach Alan Harker, but it would appear that nothing came of his trial.

No League victories were recorded in January 1967, with that month being highlighted by two cup-ties against non-league Nuneaton Borough in the third round of the F. A. Cup. They had earned the title of giant-killers after disposing of Swansea Town in the previous round, and 17,000 fans were packed into their Manor Park ground for the first game against the Millers, which ended 1-1. Drama came to the proceedings when Rotherham 'keeper Alan Hill was carried off, to be replaced between the sticks by John Galley. There were almost 23,000 at Millmoor for the replay, which Rotherham struggled to win, but they did so thanks to a goal from full back Harold Wilcockson, to earn Rotherham a home game against Birmingham City.

Up to that time fund raising and the running of the refreshment bars had been the responsibility of the Supporters Club, but that was taken out of their hands in February. The club became responsible for the continuation of this lifeline, without which a loss of £500 per week would have been realised. And so the Rotherham United Development Association came into being, with the introduction of a weekly bingo and Golden Goal competition. Shortly after, the disgruntled Supporters Club announced that they were disbanding as a gesture against how the affair had been handled by the club. But instead, they soon settled their differences, and actually handed over to the club a cheque for £2,500 as a mark of their continued support.

The cup-tie against Birmingham at Millmoor was goalless and City won the replay 2-1, but again there was controversy when Rotherham had what looked to be good goals disallowed, with players other than the scorers being adjudged to be offside.

The last two months of the season fizzled out without a great deal of interest apart from the battle to stave off the threat of relegation, but Rotherham finished too close to the bottom for comfort as they had to settle for 18th position, only six points better off than relegated Northampton Town, who recorded a winning double against the Millers. The season ended with a 3-0 home win against Bury who finished bottom, and the game marked the debut - as substitute - of David Bentley who became the youngest ever player to play for Rotherham in the League with his 17th birthday not due until 30th May.

The directors immediately gave their urgent attention to team strengthening, with chairman Eric Purshouse expressing the opinion that the club had been fortunate to retain its place in the Second Division, and he asked for a display of urgency from the first match of the forthcoming season. The chairman immediately backed that pledge for team strengthening with the acquisition of centre back Bill Thompson from Newcastle United for a fee of £17,000, but no sooner had Jack Mansell completed the deal, than the manager himself left Rotherham to become boss of Boston Beacons in America. His departure from Millmoor was quickly followed by Frank Casper who was sold to Burnley for £27,000, but the board made no immediate moves to replace Mansell, for assistant manager Fred Green initially took over the managerial responsibilities.

A working profit on the year of just under £2,000 raised the club's surplus to £17,272, but none of that money was spent on new players as the 1967/68 season got off to a losing start with a depressing 3-0 home defeat at the hands of Crystal Palace.

A one goal win at Notts County in the first round of the League Cup raised false hopes as the first five League games all ended in defeat. That obviously left Rotherham anchored firmly at the bottom of the table, and the first victory did not arrive until the sixth game when David Chambers gave them a fourth minute lead at Plymouth to leave them clinging on desperately for the rest of the game to secure the win.

A creditable draw was notched up at Norwich in the second round of the League Cup, but after beating Cardiff at home in the League, United lost at home to the Canaries in the replay with John Galley missing a penalty kick which would have brought the teams level. The next ten matches brought a solitary victory and it was obvious that something drastic had to be done to try and halt a rapid slide towards the Third Division. The signing of Billy Hodgson from Derby County failed to stop the rot, while another recruit was Charlie Crickmore, a left winger who cost £20,000 from Gillingham, which took the outlay for players to £60,000 on four newcomers since Jack Mansell left.

Bids of around a total of £80,000 for Chris Rabjohn and Brian Tiler were rejected, with Nottingham Forest and West Bromwich Albion both trailing the pair, but it was on the managerial front that Rotherham sought to make a change, and Chesterfield's Jim McGuigan was offered the post. He didn't accept, but Rotherham immediately made the football world sit up by appointing the famous Tommy Docherty as team boss.

The Scottish international had left Chelsea as manager, under something of a cloud, and it was regarded as something quite sensational when he accepted the job at 'little' Rotherham. With bonuses, Docherty could earn around £5,000, the same as he received at Chelsea when he signed a five year contract with them the previous June, but the new manager and all Rotherham people were incensed by an article which appeared in the London Evening Standard by a certain David Jenkins stating that Rotherham was a place where the pigeons flew backwards to keep the mud out of their eyes.

Certain other southern based newspapers took photographs behind the stand which did Rotherham's image no good whatsoever, but Docherty was quick to defend his 'new' home and Jenkins was invited to Rotherham. Despite being shown the better side of the

New manager Tommy Docherty gets into training with some of his new players (from left): Alan Hill, Laurie Sheffield, (Docherty), Harold Wilcockson, Brian Tiler and Chris Rabjohn.

town, he refused to retract a single word of his article. No wonder southerners have not been held in such good stead in the area!

Within five days of his arrival at Millmoor, Docherty splashed out £27,500 on securing the services of Johnny Quinn from Sheffield Wednesday, and he was to be the first of a host of 'ins and outs'. John Galley departed to Bristol City - where his goals were to save his new team from relegation - and after pulling off a goalless draw at Millwall, the attendance for Docherty's first game shot up to over 15,000. But they were sadly disappointed as Hull City were 3-1 winners, and it was not until his seventh game that the manager saw his charges pull off a victory, by beating Preston North End 1-0 in the last game of the year, rather appropriately against the team with which Docherty had made his initial impact as a player. A

player in the Preston side was none other than the current joint manager Archie Gemmill.

No matter what the value of Mr Docherty's wheelings and dealings turned out to be, there is no doubting he pulled off a master stroke on 2nd January 1968, when he signed David Watson from Notts County with Keith Pring going the other way, and a £2,000 cash adjustment in Rotherham's favour. Watson went on to have an illustrious career for England, and he must surely rank as the best player Rotherham have ever produced.

But Watson made an ignominious debut, as Rotherham were stuffed 6-0 at Queens Park Rangers but that was to be the launch pad of something of a recovery with the next nine matches seeing four wins and five draws. Sandwiched in between was a superb cup run which began with the defeat of Wolves at Millmoor, thanks to Jim Storrie's first Rotherham goal since signing on 29th December from Aberdeen.

Before the next round at Aston Villa could take place, a specially convened meeting was held to give shareholders the chance to meet Mr Docherty, and he stated that he 'was here to stay' as he had signed a five year contract. He was then instrumental in engineering a unique five man transfer deal with Rotherham players Harold Wilcockson, Colin Clish and Chris Rabjohn moving to Doncaster Rovers while Graham Watson and Dennis Leigh came the over way, in addition to the Belle Vue club receiving £10,000.

More than 33,000 spectators were at Villa Park for the cup-tie, and it was Storrie again who grabbed the headlines when he headed the only goal of the game from substitute Steve Downes' cross five minutes from time. That put the Millers into the fifth round for only the second time in their history, with a game against Leicester City at Millmoor attracting a crowd of 23,500, where they saw a 1-1 draw.

The gates at Filbert Street for the replay were closed long before the kick off, with more than 41,000 inside the ground, and there were hundreds of Millers fans among those who could not get in. It was reported that more than 10,000 had travelled from South Yorkshire, and they witnessed their team put up a great display before losing 2-0 after extra time.

By the end of March, United had given themselves a chance of avoiding relegation as they climbed to third from the bottom, but Bristol City had played two games fewer and they made this advantage count as Rotherham were unable to avoid the drop, while City escaped.

So ended 17 successive seasons in the Second Division, and the feeling was that if Docherty had arrived a month earlier, then his team would have retained their status. As soon as the season ended, work was started to extend the main stand which was taken right up to the gymnasium wall, with the addition of 400 seats, while final planning approval was granted for the building of a social club on the forecourt of the ground.

The juniors went on a continental tour, with matches in Holland and Germany, bringing three trophies home with them, but the latter stages of the planned tour - to include Yugoslavia - were called off due to an ever increasing injury list.

Arrangements were made for the club to use Herringthorpe Stadium for their outdoor training, after having used Firth Vickers ground at Tinsley for the previous few seasons. But there was to be a return to the old situation of not much money being available, owing to the fact that the previous season produced a deficit of almost £42,000.

There were, though, a couple of new faces in the squad which flew off to Ireland for a friendly game against Ballymena, with Alan Gilliver having joined from Blackburn Rovers in a straight swop for Les Chappell, and Graham Leggatt - a former Scottish international teammate of Docherty's - moved on a free from Birmingham City.

Before training got under way, the Doc was busy completing the signing of full back John Breckin, the Wingfield schoolboy who had played for Rotherham Boys the previous season - no reminders are needed on what happened to this blonde haired youngster.

Expectancy and hopes were high, but following a 3-3 draw at Orient in the opening League fixture, an early exit was made from the League Cup, with a defeat at Fourth Division Scunthorpe United.

Players continued to come and go, but the club were reasonably placed at the end of September on the back of a seven match unbeaten run, before October produced just one victory. Once again there was speculation that skipper Brian Tiler would be on the move, with two First Division clubs having made enquiries, but it was Docherty himself who sprang a surprise by leaving Millmoor for Queens Park Rangers on Wednesday, 6th November 1969 - a matter of days short of completing a year. He had always made out that he would fulfil the five years of his contract but he maintained that he could not afford to turn down the offer he had received from the First Division club, and so his turbulent reign came to an end.

More than two dozen players had been involved in moves during that time, during which Rotherham had gathered 18 points from their 17 matches - exactly double the total of the previous season from the same number of games - but now in a lower division.

The townsfolk were quite naturally shocked by Docherty's sudden departure and it was first team trainer Jim McAnearney who took over initially. He guided the team through to the second round of the F.A. Cup thanks to a replay win at Millmoor against Hartlepool.

The stand-in manager was not as successful in the second round as United went out against Mansfield at Field Mill after drawing at Millmoor.

Incredibly Docherty's reign at QPR lasted just 28 days before he walked out on them over a dispute about the fee required to sign Brian Tiler, and there was some speculation that he would return to Millmoor, but that was quickly ruled out by chairman Eric Purshouse. He said that the club had been comparatively wealthy when Docherty arrived but now they could not afford him. As it turned out McAnearney was given the job on a permanent basis in mid-December with a pledge that his team would play attacking football.

A lot had already happened in 1968 but it hadn't finished yet, for Docherty was appointed manager of Aston Villa and he helped to ease the financial crisis he had created at Millmoor by signing Tiler for £33,000. It certainly wasn't the end of the transfer moves, with Billy Griffin coming in from Workington and Graham Watson moving back to Doncaster, to be soon followed by the arrival from Charlton - for £5,000 - of winger Jimmy Mullen, but life certainly quietened down at Millmoor.

The season ended in mediocrity with the Millers finishing in 11th position - hardly surprising in view of everything that had gone on.

The first newcomer to arrive in the summer was 20-year-old Neil Warnock who moved from Chesterfield without any fee being involved, and that was not to be unexpected in view of the warning issued by the chairman. Mr Purshouse underlined the problems when he stated that the club was in very desperate straits through a cash shortage, and he emphasised that this situation had been brought about by the fact that the previous manager had been given a free hand to negotiate with the players and the club made to pay the consequences.

There was a thrilling opening to the 1969/70 season with a 4-3 win against Bury at Millmoor, and progress was made to the second round of the League Cup thanks to a 2-0 win at Bradford Park Avenue. There were almost 14,000 spectators at Millmoor to see Doncaster Rovers sneak a single goal victory, and four games had been played without a win when Rotherham travelled to Bolton for the second round of the League Cup.

The game at Burnden Park ended in a goalless draw and a third game was needed to decide the outcome when the teams shared six goals after extra time at Millmoor in the first thrilling replay. Manager Jim McAnearney won the toss for the right to stage the second replay, and it took place at Millmoor just two days later when Trevor Womble scored the night's only goal to give the Millers a home tie against Burnley.

When that game took place, at the end of September, Rotherham had won just two of their opening nine League games, but once again they needed a replay to settle the issue. However, this time they went out in the replay, at Turf Moor.

Another venture had got off the ground with the opening on Thursday 4th September 1969, of the Windmill Club - originally to be named the Millmoor Club - with more than 400 applications for membership having been received.

It was agreed that David Watson's second transfer request would be granted, for two reasons. One, of course, was the financial situation, and the other being that Watson himself quite naturally wanted to play at a higher level.

After the League Cup exit, a national newspaper carried stories of dressing room discontent, but this was vigorously denied by the club who took immediate action to try and halt the slide down the table by signing John Fantham from neighbours Sheffield Wednesday for £6,000. But his debut could not prevent a 3-0 defeat at Bristol Rovers, and six more games were played before another League win was recorded.

Before then the Millers had pulled off a comfortable win at Notts County in the first round of the F.A. Cup with two of the goals coming from Steve Downes who was benefitting a great deal from the experience of Fantham alongside him. Downes, in fact, turned down the chance of a move to Oxford United after a fee of £20,000 had been agreed, and Rotherham found some money to buy David Lill for £4,000 from Hull City as the team slipped perilously close to the wrong end of the table.

An offer of £44,000 from Sheffield Wednesday for David Watson was turned down with the comment that Millmoor was not a 'bargain basement', and the League position improved somewhat after six successive draws were followed by five wins and another draw, with an F.A. Cup win against Workington sandwiched in between.

The attacking policy, with the use of two orthodox wingers in Neil Warnock and Jimmy Mullen, was one of the main reasons for this fine run, before Sheffield Wednesday (under manager Danny Williams) came player searching again. This time their target was Steve Downes, but Rotherham rejected their £30,000 bid, and did the same when the Owls increased the offer to £35,000, but only to accept it when it was upped yet again - this time to £40,000 - so Downes moved to Hillsborough on 23rd December. His departure meant the 'No Further Sales' notices were posted at Millmoor, and the good news emerged that David Watson had taken his name off the transfer list.

Peterborough United were surprise F.A. Cup third round winners at Millmoor in the opening game of 1970, but the good League run continued and 5-0 plus 3-0 wins against Barrow and Plymouth Argyle took the sequence to 18 matches - it still stands as a club record best - together with a similar spell in 1950/51 to date. The run came to a halt with a 2-1 defeat at Bury, when Rotherham had climbed up to sixth position, only five points behind leaders Orient.

As often happens when a defeat comes along so did two more in the next three games to wipe out any optimistic promotion hopes, but there was some honour for the club when 17-year-old Trevor Phillips was selected to play for the England Youth team.

That was to be the forerunner of much attention for young Phillips, with a posse of clubs watching him regularly, including Manchester City's Malcolm Allision and Liverpool's Bill Shankly, but Rotherham stuck to their no sale policy.

There was to be no Easter egg for the Millers as they lost all three holiday games and two more defeats followed immediately. So with a home win on the last day of their topsy-turvy season, a final placing of 14th was Rotherham's fate. That last game, a 3-1 victory against Rochdale, marked David Watson's first for the club at centre forward, where he was to bring more success the following season.

A season of indifference did not go without its high moments, though, for the Millmoor Kop choir were rewarded by winning the competition - beating off Liverpool's challenge - which was organised by the BBC, the Football League Review and the Ford Motor Company. The reward for 30 lucky members was an all expenses trip to Milan for the European Cup Final, and they even got to meet the victorious Feyenoord team in addition to laying their hands on the famous trophy. It is believed that the competition was never held again, so that leaves Rotherham the undefeated champions for the last 25 years!

The first team pool was strengthened by the signing of midfielder John Bettany from Barnsley and he took his place in the team which opened the 1970/71 season with a 4-2 defeat at Shrewsbury Town. Amends were quickly made by recording a League Cup win at Barnsley, and another local side, Doncaster Rovers, were beaten at Millmoor. It was in fact quite a promising start to the season, despite the opening day defeat which turned out to be the only one out of the first eight League games with Watson playing up front. He did so with a great deal of success, none more so than when he netted a hat-trick against Rochdale in a 5-1 Rotherham win.

Both Watson and Trevor Phillips were strongly linked with Sunderland who regularly had representatives at Rotherham matches, and it seemed just a matter of time before Watson, in particular, would leave the club.

Four successive 1-1 draws provided the run-up to a first round F.A. Cup-tie at non-Leaguers Great Harwood, where wet weather prevented the game from taking place until Tuesday afternoon. A shock result looked a possibility when the minnows took an early lead with virtually their first attack, but Rotherham recovered to make no mistake with a 6 - 2 win.

The team was pitted against non-League opposition again in the second round with a visit to Grantham, but it was hardly an ideal build up for Rotherham when they suffered a 5-0 thrashing at Tranmere in their previous game. But United made no mistake in the Cup, winning 4-1, with the opening goal coming from a thunderous shot by David Watson in what turned out to be his last Rotherham game.

David Watson

A couple of days later he was finally on the move - to Sunderland - for the £100,000 fee Rotherham had quite rightly insisted on. It was, of course, Rotherham's first ever six figure deal and it represented a handsome profit for a player who had cost the club virtually nothing. But all Rotherham fans could tell from the first time he played at centre half, that Watson would be something special. Rotherham met Wolves in that match, in the F.A. Cup in January 1968, and Watto had Derek Dougan in his pocket throughout the whole game.

The F.A. Cup draw provided some compensation for Watson's loss, as Rotherham were given a plum home game against Leeds United. A small amount (£8,000) of the Watson money was spent on signing Rod Johnson from Doncaster Rovers (how these two clubs used to feature in transfer deals), and he made his debut in the Boxing Day defeat against Chesterfield, the first loss at home for 12 games.

A frozen, rutted pitch twice caused the postponement of the Leeds United Cup-tie, so Rotherham warmed up for it by drawing 2-2 against Halifax Town, with the Elland Road outfit coming to Millmoor on Monday 9th January. 24,000 spectators crammed into the ground with record receipts of £7,666-8s-0d. being produced. That attendance has not been bettered since, and in the present climate of ground restrictions, never will be.

The home team did themselves proud as they went on to have another crack at the First Division leaders in a goalless draw which might have produced an upset had John Fantham not squandered a glorious second half scoring chance. The game will stick in Rotherham fans' memories for a long, long time, not only because of the way their side battled, but also because they will recall that Jack Charlton appeared (on two occasions) incredibly lucky to have been allowed to stay on the field. First he flattened David Bentley, and then he grabbed substitute Trevor Phillips by the scruff of the neck, but on both occasions he escaped punishment thanks to the lenient attitude of referee Jim Finney.

So two days later it was off to Elland Road, only for thick fog to necessitate the game being called off, yet again, less than an hour before the scheduled kick off. The week's delay suited the Leeds team as they had some injury doubts which had cleared up when the game took place, it seemed to be following the expected pattern when Peter Lorimer gave the home side a 27th minute lead. But the Millers were not deterred and shook the home crowd rigid when goals from Trevor Womble and David Bentley put them in front at the interval.

After the break, with the strong wind behind them, Leeds managed to come back to scrape a 3-2 win, but it was the gallant Rotherham team who grabbed all the glory.

More activity in the transfer market took place a few days later with central defender Ray Mielczarek (later to become known to the home fans as 'Milk Check') moving from Huddersfield Town for £25,000, and midfielder Eddie Ferguson who joined Rotherham from Dumbarton for £6,500. Then just before the transfer deadline Carl Gilbert came in from Bristol Rovers for

LEEDS UNITED
WHITE SHIRTS 3
WHITE SHORTS

1. SPRAKE, Gary
2. REANEY, Paul
3. COOPER, Terry
4. BREMNER, Billy
5. CHARLTON, Jack
6. HUNTER, Norman
7. LORIMER, Peter 2
8. CLARKE, Allan
9. JONES, Mick Belfitt
10. GILES, Johnny 1
11. MADELEY, Paul

Sub. Bates

Referee :
Mr. J. FINNEY
Hereford

Linesmen :
Mr. W. I. COOPER
Preston
(Red Flag)

Mr. A. PORTER
Bolton
(Yellow Flag)

ROTHERHAM UNITED 2
RED SHIRTS
RED SHORTS

1. TUNKS, Roy
2. HOUGHTON, Bill
3. LEIGH, Denis
4. HUDSON, Chris
5. HAGUE, Neil
6. SWIFT, Trevor
7. WOMBLE, Trevor 1
8. LILL, David
9. FANTHAM, John
10. BENTLEY, Dave 1
11. MULLEN, Jim

Sub. Phillips

The programme team line-ups for the Cup replay...
... and the star-studded Leeds team in opposition.

£17,000, and he went on to score four goals in nine appearances before the season finished, with Rotherham in eighth position.

Four players, Pat Wright, Neil Warnock, John Bettany and John Fantham, were given free transfers, with David Lill put on offer. There was good news on the financial front with the announcement of a profit of over £2,000 following the previous year's £9,700 loss.

Speculation mounted that manager Jim McAnearney was leaving to take over at Watford, but nothing came of it and he was at the helm when the 1971/72 season got under way with a League defeat at Blackburn and a home defeat against Sheffield Wednesday in the League Cup.

United got on the winning trail by beating Barnsley, but the next four games all failed to produce a victory before, Bradford City were beaten. That was the third game of a 14 match unbeaten League run, the highlight of which was a 4-0 win against Swansea City, with Carl Gilbert hitting all the goals.

Table-toppers Aston Villa were beaten at Villa Park in front of more than 30,000 fans and to further strengthen the squad Bobby Ham was signed from Preston North End for £10,000. Neil Hague was put on the transfer list after some disciplinary problems with the manager, and it was not long before he was on the move to Plymouth Argyle for a bargain £13,000, just two days after he had scored Rotherham's last minute winner in a 4-3 victory.

But all attention was focused on the F.A. Cup first round game at Frickley Colliery, who quickly refuted suggestions that the tie should be switched to Millmoor. A 9,000 figure was set for the Westfield Lane ground but in fact only 5,824 entered for the game which took place on a bitterly cold day. Rotherham were fortunate to gain a replay in a 2-2 draw with David Bentley grabbing an equaliser in the second minute of injury time. Carl Gilbert hit three of the goals which gave the Millers a comfortable 4-0 win in the replay, and a home tie against York City in the second round was the reward.

The long unbeaten run came to an end with a defeat at Rochdale, before the York game ended all square, with Rotherham winning the replay at Bootham Crescent, although they needed extra time to do so. The rewards for that late win did not seem particularly mouth-watering for it threw up a third round trip to Fourth Division Bury, but it did, of course, present a realistic passage to round four.

The first home game of 1972 attracted an attendance of almost 10,000 for the vital clash with fellow promotion contenders Bournemouth, with the points being shared in a goalless draw. It needed some heroics by goalkeeper Roy Tunks, and a last minute equaliser from Carl Gilbert to gain a replay against Bury at Gigg Lane, but the replay had to be postponed as a result of snow. That gave Rotherham a little breathing space for they had been struggling with a number of injuries which still severely effected the team. When the game took place on the following Monday it was a makeshift Millers which turned out. Trevor Womble played at full back, Trevor Phillips turned out in the number four shirt and Mick Leng

played at left back, his third position in nine games. But the team battled superbly in difficult playing conditions, with Trevor Swift in particular producing a sterling performance, despite suffering from a stomach virus.

That win led to around 5,000 Millers followers making the journey to White Hart Lane for the fourth round game against Tottenham Hotspur, but the game was virtually all over when the home side took a two goals lead after just 17 minutes. That ended the scoring but Rotherham never really threatened to get back in the game and they could well have suffered a heavier defeat, although they did have the consolation of sharing some hefty gate receipts provided by the 36,903 crowd.

Left free to concentrate on trying to improve their current fifth league position, Rotherham won two and drew one of the next three matches, while they recruited winger Norman Whitehead from Rochdale for £10,000.

The next seven matches only produced four points, all from draws, to leave Rotherham too far behind the leading pack to catch them up. Since they were only able to take one point from matches against leaders Aston Villa and fourth placed Notts County, this proved a decisive factor. These two games were both staged at Millmoor and attracted attendances of over 26,000 on aggregate. Good wins against Port Vale and Rochdale revived spirits, but the leeway was too much to make up, so the club had to be content with a satisfactory fifth position, their best since relegation from the Second Division.

Before the season came to an end Johnny Quinn was given a free transfer to herald the end of his Millmoor career which would have been even more illustrious if he hadn't had to miss about 18 months with an achilles tendon injury. For the second time in three years the United youngsters won the Breda Youth International Trophy in Holland, with a team which included several players who went on to become first team regulars.

Admission prices for the forthcoming season were increased by 10p, making it 60p to sit in the stand, while two free transfer players were acquired - Bruce Stowell from Bradford City and Paddy Buckley from Sheffield United, with the latter described as a "chunky" winger. Behind the scenes 23-year-old Alan Smith took over in charge of injury treatment in succession to Neil Falconer who had returned to his native Scotland.

The Football Association introduced a new penalty system for the 1972/73 season with each offence on the field carrying a fixed number of points from one to four, and there would be an automatic suspension when a player had collected 12 points in a season, and a three match suspension for a sending off.

Rotherham undertook a three match tour to Holland where they were beaten 4-1 by FC Bruges, drew 1-1 against Sparta Rotterdam and drew 2-2 with NAC Breda. That tour prepared the team for the start of the new League campaign, which got off to a winning start with Plymouth beaten at Millmoor by a single goal, and it was the same score-line four days later when a victory was obtained at Darlington in the League Cup.

After losing at Grimsby, Rotherham then thrashed Port Vale 7-0 and won at York, to top the table after the opening four games, a position which was to be a dim and distant memory by the time the season finished. The Vale slaughter was United's biggest win for 16 years and it was the first time Rother-

ham had topped their division since October 1964.

Brentford were beaten in the next round of the League Cup, and before they met Oldham Athletic on the last day of September, the Millers were still in the second position in the division, but things started to go wrong with a defeat at Boundary Park. Arsenal pulled off a comfortable 5-0 win at Highbury in the League Cup and two more defeats followed at the hands of Chesterfield - as usual - and Bournemouth. The game against the south coast team saw Rotherham beaten 7-2 but the scoreline fails to tell the full story. The visitors' Brian Clark finished with four goals, but he must have laid a claim for some sort of record for he scored his hat-trick against three different goalkeepers, while United's Carl Gilbert scored two goals and conceded three!

It was Rotherham United's biggest ever home defeat and the first time they had conceded seven goals in any peacetime game since the 8-2 defeat at Mansfield in 1936. The drama started in the 11th minute when keeper Jim McDonagh was concussed in a collision and he was replaced by Gilbert around 15 minutes later. Gilbert had actually given Rotherham the lead, but by half time they were trailing 3-1, before deciding to concentrate on all out attack. But Bournemouth exposed gaps at the back to add another goal at which stage Gilbert handed over the green jersey to Mick Leng. Rotherham received a round of sympathetic applause from their supporters at the end of the incident packed game, but the poor string of results continued despite the introduction of a new signature tune entitled "Let's work together".

When Scunthorpe were beaten at the end of October it was the first Rotherham victory for nine games and within the next few days two new recruits were brought in to try and halt the slide. Midfielder Billy Wilkinson moved from Hull City for £10,000, and he was quickly followed by Mike O'Grady from Wolves who cost £8,000.

Non-League South Shields were easily beaten in the first round of the F.A. Cup before Rotherham lost at home in the next round. But the League form still caused a lot of concern, although two wins and a draw at Christmas helped to lighten the darkening clouds. Along the way the Millers had lost at Bolton, where the Wanderers winning goal came in bizarre fashion. 'Keeper Jim McDonagh ran wide of his goal and stopped the ball with his foot before dribbling it out. As Bolton's Byrom came towards him, he put the ball on the edge of the six yard box and Byrom turned away. With McDonagh taking his time, referee Reynolds waved his arms, leaving the 'keeper under the impression he was being told to speed things up, so he turned and ran back ready to take the kick.

A horde of Bolton players descended on the ball, and Gary Jones pushed it into the net with the referee ignoring all the fervent Rotherham claims that the ball had gone out of play.

The holiday haul of points raised hopes of a Rotherham revival, but only one win from four matches didn't do too much to support that theory, although two of those games ended in draws. February was a real month of gloom with all five games ending in defeat, and after nurturing hopes of getting involved in the promotion race at the turn of the year, thoughts were now cast towards the other end of the table.

The dramatic slump was brought to a halt with a 1-0 win against Chesterfield, while Jim McDonagh went to Manchester United and Trevor Womble went to Halifax Town, both players on loan - and Trevor's handful

of goals were to save Town from relegation. Incoming was Ron Wigg, who moved from Watford for £10,000, and the Millers made it three wins out of four matches with victories against Brentford and Walsall, to ease the pressure.

It was all so close at the bottom end of the table, but Rotherham - one of five clubs locked on the same number of points - had played more games than all their rivals, so with six games left to play a mighty effort was needed to avoid relegation. It was produced with a win against promotion chasing Bolton Wanderers, and when the next two games both also saw 1-0 winning scorelines, safety seemed to be just round the corner. But two Easter defeats plunged the Millers back into the basement area and everything depended on the last game of the season, when fellow strugglers York City were the visitors to Millmoor. A draw would have been enough for United, but City won 2-1 to send Rotherham down into the Fourth Division for the first time in their history.

United occupied the last of the relegation places - fourth from the bottom - with four teams all finishing on the 41 points mark, but it was no consolation to learn that this total was the highest with which any club had previously been relegated from that division.

Deep depression centred on Millmoor and it was no real surprise when it was announced that Jim McAnearney had decided to relinquish his position as manager, to set off the guessing game concerning who the new boss would be. There was no doubt that the crowd's choice would by Johnny Quinn. Little time was lost in making the new appointment with Jim McGuigan accepting the post. He had been offered the Rotherham job in 1967 but decided to stay at Chesterfield where at the time he had only been for a couple of months, and had remained there ever since. He issued an early warning that players' reputations counted for nothing and he quickly made his first signing with experienced defender John Sjoberg joining from Leicester City.

Relegation proved to be a costly affair, for the club lost £63,000 for the year ending 31st May, but a much better season was anticipated with an immediate return to the Third Division uppermost in everyone's mind. The club got a rude awakening though on the opening day of season 1973/74, for they were beaten 3-1 at Northampton Town, but made amends by knocking Lincoln City out of the League Cup, and beating Swansea at Millmoor.

Then came an astonishing result at Crewe where Alexandra took a 21st minute lead only for Rotherham to forge in front by half time. The Millers went goal crazy in the second half and hit six more goals, to give them an 8-1 victory, with Trevor Phillips grabbing his first senior hat-trick. It equalled Rotherham's biggest ever away win - at Carlisle in December 1948 - in addition to levelling the team's highest tally, and it was Crewe's heaviest home defeat. To rub salt into Crewe's wounds, Rotherham vice-chairman Lewis Purshouse won their Golden Goal competition with the time of the first goal - which was scored by Crewe!

That runaway score was the last Rotherham victory for another five matches as they came back down to earth, and were well and truly despatched from the League Cup when Exeter City won 4-1 at Millmoor. The Millers gained quick revenge by beating City 4-0 in the League game at Millmoor three days later, leaving the manager demanding more consistency from his team. They rarely succeeded in providing it though, and after disposing of Southport in the first round of the F.A. Cup, they made

an exit from that competition in the next round at Wrexham.

Defensive problems had been prevalent throughout the season and in an attempt to rectify this, McGuigan bought Bob Delgado from Carlisle United for £7,000, and he went straight into the team which lost at Bury, but then beat Barnsley on Boxing Day. Four successive League defeats greeted 1974, and with gates touching an all-time low, hopes of making a quick return to a higher status were a long way from being fulfilled. The attendance was slightly higher than the 3,600 average, when 4,355 watched the first ever Sunday game at Millmoor on 20th January, but it was a poor game in which Jimmy Goodfellow, a £3,000 signing from Workington, made his debut.

The beginning of the month had seen chief coach Clive Baker dismissed, with Chesterfield's Charlie Bell coming in as his replacement, and McGuigan continued his team re-building by dismissing Eddie Ferguson for a breach of discipline, before placing six players on the transfer list.

Rotherham agreed a fee of £25,000 for the transfer of Trevor Hockey from Aston Villa, but the move fell through relating to the player's personal requirements, while Mike O'Grady became the second player within a few weeks to receive his cards, this time for an alleged breach of contract.

The long overdue win came in another Sunday game, at Doncaster, in early February, with the assistance of Trevor Swift's timely first goal of the season. That was followed by a Sabbath day draw against Newport County at Millmoor, but a return to the more accustomed Saturday followed as the Board felt that nothing had been gained from changing. A dismal performance against Darlington came before a slightly improved one at Barnsley, but both games ended in defeat, to leave the Millers in a precarious position.

Doncaster were anchored to the bottom with 21 points and Rotherham were the top of the next five clubs who all had 25 points - and the bottom four had to apply for re-election. But the team found some form by becoming the season's first team to win at leaders Colchester United, thanks to a Goodfellow goal, and in the next game another debutant - 18-year-old Thomas Rotherham College student Richard Finney - got on the scoresheet in a home draw against Brentford. The attendance was 2,259, the lowest of the season, and the outcome left United third from the bottom. But results gradually improved with the home win against Chester at the end of March, being the first at Millmoor since Boxing Day.

The club finally managed to climb up to a safe 15th position when the season ended, and manager McGuigan wasted no time in making his first summer signing when he took Nigel Davey on a free transfer from Leeds United. Yet another player sacking took place when Billy Wilkinson was given his cards after being convicted of a drink driving offence, but the club was ordered to reinstate him by the Football League after an appeal to them by the player. Further recruitment took place with the signing from Lincoln City of Tommy Spencer, and he went on to be probably the best ever Rotherham free transfer, while David Bentley went to Chesterfield for £9,000.

Announcing a loss of £56,191 for the year just ended, chairman Eric Purshouse called for all the players to pull their weight during the new season, and when he addressed the shareholders at the annual meeting, he supported Jim McGuigan who said that the younger players would be given their chance. Some dismal form in the pre-season friendlies quelled much of the promotion optimism, but the season couldn't have got off to a better start than with the 3-0 victory at Torquay.

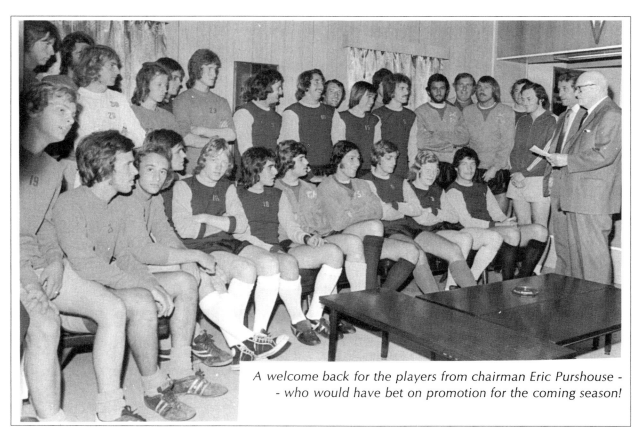

A welcome back for the players from chairman Eric Purshouse -
- who would have bet on promotion for the coming season!

It took three games to dispose of Lincoln City in the first round of the League Cup, and the League form produced three successive wins, to take Rotherham to the top of the table. The third of those wins came at Workington, and the long trip North had more rewards than the victory, for Bob Delgado and Jim McDonagh had success in an egg throwing competition! The pair visited a gala when they were staying at nearby Cockermouth on the Friday evening, and took first prize with Delgado hurling the egg 70 yards and McDonagh catching it without breaking the shell. As they were unable to take the first prize barrel of beer, they opted for the equivalent in cash instead, and bought a supply of cans to keep them refreshed on the journey home.

The season's first defeat came in the eighth game when the team lost 4-2 at Reading in the League Cup, and the first League setback came in the next game at Hartlepool. The following eight games saw just one defeat - at home to Northampton - with the first one being a remarkable 4-3 win at Brentford, who had just played eight successive home games without conceding a goal.

Meanwhile, railings were erected on the Millmoor Lane side of the ground to prevent spectators from moving from one end of the ground to the other, but they were happy to stay put as they watched their team climb to third place towards the end of October.

Goalkeeper Roy Tunks moved to Preston North End (managed by Bobby Charlton) for a tribunal fixed £7,500 fee, but the success continued on the field as the Millers were unbeaten in November, with the away form being particularly impressive.

Chester had just beaten Leeds in the League Cup when they clashed with Rotherham in the first round of the F.A. Cup, but the Millers knocked them out thanks to a Bob Delgado goal, and that led to a second round home game against Northampton Town, who had won the last nine meetings between the two teams. But Rotherham laid that bogey by winning 2-1. December was a poor month as far as League points were concerned, as only one was won from three matches, before United opened 1974 with a visit to non-League Stafford Rangers in the F.A. Cup. Much of the Millers' success up to this point had been due to a tightening up of the defence and in the previous 14 League and Cup games of the year, they had conceded just ten goals.

Stafford Rangers had expressed some disappointment when the Cup draw had been made, for after beating Halifax Town in the previous round, they had been hoping for a "big" team, but they were more than happy with a record crowd of over 8,500 who saw the home side hold their League opposition to a goalless draw. Anyone with the thought that the replay would be a foregone conclusion was quickly given a rude awakening, for Stafford went on to pull off a thoroughly deserved 2-0 win as the non-Leaguers completely outplayed United. The game attracted Rotherham's best crowd for nearly three years and it was the first time they had ever lost at home to a non-League team. United had so often in the past caused an embarrassment for bigger clubs in cup competitions, but this time, the tables were turned on them in a night of shame and humiliation.

However, the Cup defeat turned out to be not such a bad thing after all, for the team were able to concentrate on the League and the quest for promotion, and the last 23 League games produced just four defeats. Immediately after the Cup exit, United went nine games without defeat, starting that fine run with a single goal win at Chester who had been unbeaten at home for 14 months.

Ron Wigg was sold to Grimsby Town for £17,500 and he was immediately replaced by Reading's Dick Habbin, who cost £10,000, and he was a player who in the past had scored eight goals against Rotherham including two hat-tricks. He soon started to find the net for his new club who by the end of February were in fifth position, and Habbin was soon joined by another former Reading player when Barry Wagstaff moved to Millmoor for £10,000.

A defeat at promotion rivals Lincoln City left Rotherham clinging to fourth position - the last promotion place - but three wins out of three at Easter put them up into third, with a four point lead over Lincoln. A victory and a defeat kept the issue wide open, before two draws and a win against Rochdale saw Rotherham promoted. When Chester lost against Hartlepool, this set up a last day of the season celebratory trip to Southport. More than half of the 2,657 crowd (Southport's biggest of the season) were from Rotherham, but it was an anti-climax as the home team won 2-0, but it didn't really matter for their team was back in the Third Division.

It had indeed been a triumph for what was basically a young, inexperienced side, and they were given a civic reception and dinner by the Mayor of Rotherham, Councillor Jack Layden.

Behind the scenes sponsorship began to take on a new meaning for United, and a new, plush executive club, was planned for the start of the season, with several games already lined up for potential sponsors after only one match had received such treatment in the successful campaign just finished.

Nigel Davey was released without having made a first team appearance, while the admission charges were increased with the cost of a seat in the main stand raised to £1, compared to the previous 60p. The entrance fee to the ground would be either 60 or 65p depending on whatever the Football League were to set as the future minimum charge - quite unbelievable figures in modern day terms.

Surprisingly skipper Bob Delgado and Steve Derrett were put on the transfer list after they failed to agree new contract terms.

The leader of the Council - Jack Layden - congratulates skipper Bob Delgado at the civic reception promotion celebration.

Still in the limelight, the captain receives a celebratory kiss from Lyn Swift of sponsors Kirby Central.

They had only missed a handful of the previous season's games between them. The club could certainly do with any money which their sale might bring, for despite an increase of £10,000 in gate receipts and a transfer net gain of £20,000, there was a loss of £32,240 in the year ended 31 May. But Derrett settled his differences and re-signed.

In addition to the introduction of the executive club, a bright, new 12 page programme was launched, while the spectators could hear a new D.J./announcer, Jim Haigh, who is currently still doing the job.

Trevor Womble was sidelined for the opening of the season with knee ligament damage suffered in a pre-season game at Wigan, but there was a newcomer in the side for the first game at Brighton, with 17-year-old Paul Stancliffe taking his place in the centre of defence. It was a losing start to the 1975/76 season, with setbacks at Brighton in the League and against Nottingham Forest in the home League Cup game, and that was to set the stall for a season of struggle which

saw the team have to settle for a 16th position. This underlined the pre-season warning from manager McGuigan that it would be difficult to maintain the previous season's success. It was certainly a year when youngsters were given their chance, for in addition to Stancliffe, there were also debuts for 19-year-old goalkeeper Grahan Haslam, John Green (17), Mark Rhodes (18) and the youngest of them all, Kevin Eades. Eades was just 16 years and 207 days old when he played in a home defeat against Swindon Town at the beginning of October, but that was to be his one and only appearance of the season.

Delgado moved to Chester in November for £6,000 while there were rumours of more impending outgoings with the young players predictably attracting a lot of attention from other clubs.

The F.A. Cup produced a first round victory against Crewe, but United went out in the next stage at home to Bradford. But earlier they put on a super show at Hillsborough against Sheffield Wednesday to earn a point in a goalless draw. A Dick Habbin goal was enough to give the Millers a victory in the return game in March, when segregation was used, with the visitors even being allocated different coloured tickets.

Trevor Womble came back into the side for the game at Hillsborough as substitute, and he grabbed all the headlines again when he did the same in the next match against Chesterfield. This time, though, he had to take the place of goalkeeper Jim McDonagh who unfortunately broke his leg, and "Willie" turned on a super show to keep a clean sheet in a 2-0 victory.

Barry Watling was signed on loan from Hartlepool to stand in for McDonagh, and he played five games before Tom McAlister moved from Sheffield United. He initially came on loan as well, but he subsequently made the move permanent for a £15,000 fee, while Dave Gwyther was signed in March from Halifax Town for £17,000. McAlister's move prompted an immediate transfer request from McDonagh even though his leg was still in plaster.

Another highlight of the season - arguably the most memorable - was the home game against League leaders Crystal Palace at the beginning of February, when Malcolm Allison's team were beaten 4-1 with all the main action taking place in the second half. In addition to the five goals, there were two sendings off (Palace players), three more bookings (2-1 to Palace) and a player "sent off" after the final whistle - yet another Palace player.

Womble's unlucky season took another bitter twist when a bad tackle from Millwall's Barry Kitchener damaged his knee ligaments, which again ruled him out for the rest of the season, and he subsequently had to call it a day.

It was revealed during the summer that help had been sought from the club's bankers during the season to finance the transfers which were necessitated by the injury problems and that resulted in a massive £57,686 loss.

New signing David Pugh was in the team which started the 1976/77 with a 3-1 League Cup defeat at Chesterfield, but Trevor Phillips' goal was to prove vital as the Millers won the second leg at Millmoor 3-0 to progress into the second round. The winning goal came when Phillips collided in the penalty area with Chesterfield's Hunter who was penalised for using his hands, although to most onlookers it was Phillips who had handled the ball. That victory was the first of many in what proved to be a very successful season, with the first three League games all ending in victory, to put Rotherham at the top of the table.

Jim McGuigan was rewarded with the Bell's Third Division manager of the Month award for August, but September was in marked contrast as his team drew three and lost one of their four League games in addition to losing to Millwall in the League Cup.

McDonagh got his wish when he left the club to join Bolton Wanderers for a fee of just over £10,000, while the end of October saw the launch of Millers United, a social club for the young people who support Rotherham United, and it is pleasing to report that the club is still going strong to date.

At the same time, on the pitch, United ended the month with two draws, which launched an unbeaten run and stretched to 13 games, into the following February. The third game of that sequence was a magnificent 3-1 win at Hillsborough, where victory was achieved after Sheffield Wednesday had led at half time.

Another tip top away display ended with a 4-2 win at Swindon, and Altrincham's threats of causing an F.A. Cup upset were soon dispelled as they were soundly beaten 5-0 at Millmoor.

Further wins followed against Walsall and Gillingham, but it needed three games and extra time twice to dispose of York City in the second round of the F.A. Cup.

Jim McGuigan won his second gallon of whisky of the season when he was named Manager of the Month for November with five wins out of five. The year closed with Northampton Town being thumped 4-1 on their own ground, and an Alan Crawford penalty was enough to beat Chesterfield and put Rotherham once again at the top of the table.

1977 started with United frozen into inactivity so the year opened with a visit to Wolverhampton in the third round of the F.A. Cup, when the Millers did very well indeed against a team which finished the season as First Division champions. Wolves just managed a 3-2 victory, with Alan Crawford hitting both Rotherham's goals. While United were in cup action, Brighton took advantage to open up a two points gap at the top of the League but they had played two games more.

The next three games all ended in draws, although the team created a club record by going unchanged for 18 League and Cup games. A defeat at Mansfield, the first since the end of October, saw Rotherham slip down to sixth, but after drawing with League leaders Brighton, they pulled off five successive wins to move up to third position, two points behind Mansfield who by then had taken over the pole position.

It was Rotherham's turn to be number one when they won a Friday night game at

Tranmere, but their leadership lasted just 24 hours before Mansfield took over again, and the latest unbeaten run for the Millers reached ten games when they drew at home to Crystal Palace. Chesterfield broke that run by winning by the only goal of the game on Easter Saturday, before Northampton were beaten at Millmoor two days later. But the "big one" was the following day when Sheffield Wednesday were the visitors.

Special entertainment was provided for the spectators with a Military Band and the Penistone Drum Majorettes in action for the all-ticket game which attracted an attendance of 17,356. But it was a disappointing result for the out of touch Millers who could have no complaints about Wednesday winning the game, as they were the better side and with a corner count of 13 - 1 in their favour.

Two more defeats inside three days made it three setbacks on the trot with the 2-1 defeat at Wrexham throwing up a controversial incident. Mark Rhodes hit a stunning shot from 20 yards with such power it almost ripped the net off, but it was disallowed by a linesman who indicated that another Rotherham player was in an offside position. If the goal had counted it would have given the Millers a vital point, but the defeat at Portsmouth was to prove disastrous. Pompey won 5-1, but as things turned out, if they had only won 2-1 United would have gained promotion.

The rocking boat was steadied with a draw against Swindon and a victory at Walsall, to leave Rotherham with four matches left, but the odds were stacked against them gaining promotion. Those odds were not improved with the home defeat by Reading, but a miracle looked a little more of a possibility with wins at home to Gillingham and at Reading, where Trevor Phillips scored a hat-trick.

The last game of the season was at Port Vale - where promotion hopes had been dealt a severe blow in 1955 - with the Millers in fifth position.

Rotherham pulled off a fine 4-1 win, despite David Gwyther being sent off, to leave Palace grabbing the last promotion place with a slightly better goal difference. This brought the heavy defeat at Portsmouth into full perspective.

Six players - Tom McAlister, Paul Stancliffe, Tommy Spencer, Trevor Phillips, Alan Crawford and Davis Gwyther - were ever-present, and for Crawford it was a quite remarkable season. Together with John Breckin, he had been in dispute with the club regarding personal terms, but he eventually settled his differences, to go on and score 31 goals, including 13 from the penalty spot. It was the best individual haul since Ronnie Burke in 1953/54. Not for the first time in their history, the club was accused of not wanting to go up, but whoever it was making those suggestions, were guilty of some very muddled thinking.

There was a problem facing the club during the summer with the news that the Edgar Allen's ground would not be available for them to train on, and they had to utilise Thomas Rotherham College for the initial pre-season training. Tommy Young was signed from Tranmere Rovers for £10,000, while a sum of around £13,000 was spent on improving the floodlights - ironically a figure only just short of the original full installation costs. In addition to Young there was another new face in the line-up which kicked off the 1977/78, with Gerry Forrest making his debut, following his move from South Bank towards the end of the previous season. Gerry, of course, went on to become something of a cult hero at Millmoor, and he gave loyal service to the club in two different spells.

United staged a unique signing-on ceremony as the new season got underway, when 16 players - together with manager Jim McGuigan - all put their names to new, improved contracts, to underline the commitment the players had pledged to the club. It was to be a season in marked contrast to the one when promotion was missed by a whisker, with a very disappointing 20th position seeing the club miss relegation by only three points.

The campaign got off to a dramatic start when the first round of the League Cup against York City saw each team pull off a 3-0 win in the first two legs, to lead to a replay. The deadlock still had not been broken after extra time and it had to go to a penalty shoot out which the Millers won 6-5, but they were soundly beaten in the next round at West Bromwich Albion.

At the end of September, there had been little indication of the struggle ahead, but injuries began to bite hard and after beating Walsall in the first game in October, United moved into second place, but they had to endure the next 14 League games without being able to record a single victory. In the midst of that string of miserable results, the team made sure they would not become victims of potential giant-killers, by beating Mossley 3-0 and Spennymoor 6-0 in the first two rounds of the F.A. Cup.

Six of the League games ended in draws, but the year ended with three successive defeats, and Rotherham were the only team in Division Three not to gain a point at Christmas - and 1978 got off to the same kind of start with a 3-0 home defeat by Bury. The Millers went out of the F.A. Cup in a replay at Millwall after drawing at Millmoor in the first game, before the much overdue win finally arrived with a 2-0 victory against Oxford United. Shortly after, an informal meeting of shareholders were told that there would be no panic buying, despite the precarious League position, and the need to rear the club's own youngsters was emphasised again.

Results from then on to the end of the season were just good enough to keep them out of the bottom four, although they weren't helped by a 7-1 thrashing at Wrexham.

Would some re-building need to be done for the next season, was the question on many people's lips, with the supporters baffled that two seasons could have such widely differing outcomes. Off the pitch seats were installed under cover on the Millmoor Lane side to give a capacity of 800. It was hoped that this would become known as a family stand and the objective was achieved, for it is still known by that title.

John Flynn and Dave Smith were the two new faces when the players reported for training prior to a 1978/79 season which again was to be one of mainly struggle. The team finished in 17th position in the League, but they produced their best performances in the two Cup competitions.

Hartlepool were comfortably beaten in the first round over two legs of the League Cup, to see Rotherham rewarded with a plum home tie against Arsenal in the next round. It looked as if the game would follow the expected pattern when Malcolm Macdonald provided the opening for Frank Stapleton to give the Gunners a seventh minute lead. But the visitors were rocked when David Gwyther headed a 24th minute equaliser before John Green put the Millers in front two minutes later with another header.

With everyone expecting Arsenal to step up the pressure after the interval, it was United who surprised all the fans by producing some superb football. It was no less than they deserved when with 64 minutes gone,

Richard Finney scored with yet another header to send the Millmoor supporters into ecstasy.

MILLERS	3	ARSENAL	1
Tom McAlister	1	Pat Jennings	
Gerry Forrest	2	Pat Rice	
John Breckin	3	Sammy Nelson	
Mark Rhodes	4	David Price	
John Green	5	David O'Leary	
John Flynn	6	Willie Young	
Richard Finney	7	Liam Brady	
Trevor Phillips	8	Alan Sunderland	
Dave Gwyther	9	Malcolm MacDonald	
Alan Crawford	10	Frank Stapleton	
Dave Smith	11	Graham Rix	

Another star-studded opposition line-up, from the programme for the Arsenal match.

The reward for that great win was a home tie against Reading in which Rotherham looked to be heading for victory when they went two goals up. But Reading pulled level and gained a replay when David Gwyther missed a great scoring chance just before the end. The reward for the winners of the game at Elm Park was another "plum" with a home game against Southampton, but the honours went to the Berkshire outfit with their 1-0 win.

In the F.A. Cup the Millers disposed of Workington in the first round and had a very attractive game in the second with a visit to Barnsley, where an Alan Crawford goal in front of almost 15,500 brought the game back to Millmoor for a replay. Arctic weather conditions led to the replay being staged at the sixth attempt after previous postponements, with the Millers edging through to a tie at Maine Road against Manchester City in the third round. This game took place on a Monday night, and the Millers covered themselves in glory as they battled for a goalless draw which might have been a win if Dave Smith had not spurned a late scoring chance.

Trevor Phillips hits his 13th goal of the season but Rotherham were beaten 3-1 at Millmoor in March 1979.

The Blues came to Millmoor just two days later, and the near 14,000 crowd were treated to another action packed game, played in wet conditions. City were three up inside the first 15 minutes and the game seemed all over, but Rotherham came storming back and by the 58th minute they had pulled two goals back. This left the last half an hour with virtually one way traffic towards the City goal.

As often happens in such situations, the Manchester side grabbed another goal on the break with all the Rotherham players pushing forward, to give them a slightly flattering 4 - 2 win.

Following the re-arranging of the postponed League games, the Millers had the prospect of five successive home games from which success would lift them into the promotion race, but after winning the first two, the next three all ended in defeat, and at this point the season effectively came to an end.

There was a surprise in June when Trevor Phillips was sold to Hull City for £70,000, with half of the money immediately being spent on recruiting Rodney Fern from Chesterfield, and he was quickly joined by another newcomer, full back Ken Tiler who moved from Brighton.

The transfer activity continued with Billy McEwan signing from Peterborough United and Mick Gooding coming from Bishop Auckland, while going out was 'keeper Tom McAlister whose move to Blackpool swelled the Millmoor coffers by £45,000. More money was brought in with the sale of Alan Crawford to Chesterfield for the same fee that Fern had cost.

Before the 1979/80 season got underway chairman Eric Purshouse blasted the wage demands of players, who were likened to Dick Turpin, although he pointed out that a masked bandit usually left his victims with a few coppers!

The new signings for the 1979/80 season: Rodney Fern, Ken Tiler, Mick Gooding, Billy McEwan, with manager Jim McGuigan

Leicester City were beaten over two legs in the League Cup with Mick Gooding scoring in both games, and that took Rotherham into the second round, where, for the first time two legs would also be played. A victory at Ashton Gate by Bristol City by the game's only goal was enough to enable them to make further progress, as Rotherham were held to a 1-1 draw at Millmoor, but before then the League programme got underway, with a 5-1 crushing at Oxford.

That was the forerunner of what was to become a season of mediocrity, but it was activity behind the scenes that attracted most of the attention with the chairman and his son Lewis putting their shares up for sale after having to endure some personal abuse from supporters. Essex businessman Anton Johnson struck up a deal with them but the negotiations were postponed for an indefinite period until certain problems were sorted out.

Anton Johnson arrives on the scene.
Mr. Johnson is to the left.

Before they could be solved, the club had to contend with successive home games against the two Sheffield teams, and after a perimeter wall had collapsed at the United game, the same thing happened again when Wednesday were the visitors. But the blame was clearly laid at the fans who were said to be guilty of a deliberate act of vandalism, according to the chief superintendent of police who was in charge of the investigations.

All sorts of legalities were bandied about concerning the takeover, with Mr Johnson endeavouring to enforce the sale through the courts, and the situation had still not been settled by late November when manager Jim McGuigan left the club to take over at Stockport County.

Reserves and youth team coach Barry Claxton was put in temporary charge, getting off to a winning start with a 4-2 win against Brentford. Eventually the Millmoor shares deal went ahead in mid-December, after the Purshouses issued a 'pay-up-or-else' ultimatum, with Mr Johnson obtaining the control of the club for what must be the bargain of the century as far as football club sales has been concerned - £62,000.

Eric Purshouse may not have always endeared himself to the supporters with his blunt speaking, but he and his son left the club in a healthy financial state with assets, and cash in hand at the bank plus various stocks and shares totalling around £250,000 - how that situation was to change in the next couple of years.

The first task facing the new chairman was to appoint a new manager and a shortlist was drawn up, before the announcement was made on New Year's Eve 1979 that the Millers new boss would be 33-year-old Ian Porterfield. He had played 26 games for Sheffield Wednesday during the current season, but had been informed that he no longer figured as a regular so Rotherham obtained a potential player as well as a manager. His most important and immediate task was to ensure the club kept out of the relegation area, and he achieved that objective with his new charges eventually finishing in 13th position.

There were a handful of new players, with the first one being current chief executive Phil Henson, who made his debut in a 5-0 defeat at Hillsborough, and he was quickly followed in the line-up by Vic Halom and Graham Brown. Brown was to be a key figure for the rest of the season. His excellent goalkeeping helped the club to safety.

A new image for the club was planned with the ground being smartened up, the players kitted out in official club suits, and the supporters club was reformed at an exceptionally well attended June meeting.

Porterfield was on the look out for a striker and a midfield player and Rotherham were prepared to pay Reading £75,000 for their lanky striker Ollie Kearns, but nothing happened after he had visited Millmoor.

Mick Gooding (239 League appearances in total) in action - February 1980.

The club was about to enter an era of ups and downs both on and off the pitch and there certainly was never a dull moment with promotions, relegations, and almost extinction!

But they started with a never-to-be-forgotten championship winning season, the club's first for 30 years. After the too close for comfort flirtation with the wrong end of the table the previous season, something had to be done to prevent a re-occurrence, and the build-up to the start of the season was dominated by Rotherham's record bid for Fulham's Mexborough-born striker Peter Kitchen, with the Millers prepared to smash the £100,000 barrier. Terms were agreed between the two clubs and Kitchen spent the weekend in South Yorkshire mulling over the move which he eventually turned down, although there was compensation for that disappointment when Jimmy Mullen signed from Sheffield Wednesday for £25,000. The doughty defender was soon appointed skipper and he was to become a key figure in the success that lay ahead.

Towner and John Seasman from Millwall for a combined fee of £180,000. No official valuations were ever put to the pair but it is believed that Seasman was a "paperweight" in the deal at around £30,000 or £40,000, making Towner the club's record signing.

So the promises of chairman Anton Johnson that money would be spent had been fulfilled just as the doubters were beginning to gloat as he turned his words into action. He had promised ambition, and spending over £300,000 by far overshadowed anything United had even contemplated in the past.

None of the four newcomers had joined the club in time for the first game, a 3-1 home defeat in the League Cup against Bradford City. Three of the four, Mullen was the absentee, made their first appearance in the second leg at Valley Parade which ended in a goalless draw.

There was little indication of the form to come when the first four League games produced just three draws and one defeat,

His incoming did not prevent an unprecedented swoop in the transfer market, for Ronnie Moore was signed from Cardiff City for the £100,000 fee which had been offered for Kitchen, and he was quickly followed by the arrival of Tony

Three newcomers for the 1980/81 season: (from left) Ronnie Moore, Tony Towner and John Seasman.

and the opening victory was not achieved until Barnsley were beaten at Millmoor, where 'keeper Graham Brown saved a penalty. Ronnie Moore was carried off in the next game, a defeat at Swindon, and had to miss the away win at Walsall on an extremely wet Tuesday night when Tony "Tiger" Towner tormented the Saddlers' full back Kenny Mower to despair. That was the first of five wins on the trot, with one of them coming against Sheffield United at Bramall Lane, and the last one - against Exeter City - unfortunately saw Richard Finney suffer an injury which was eventually to end his career.

The customary defeat at Chesterfield was the only one in a 13 match spell but the darling of the terraces - Towner - had to miss 12 League and cup matches after suffering a cracked bone in his foot. But his absence did not halt progress, and Boston United were beaten in the F.A. Cup, but Barnsley won by the only goal of the game in the second round at Millmoor, the Oakwell outfit's first win there since 1938, apart from war-time games.

A pre-match circus provided the entertainment for the game which saw the return of Towner, who made visitors Brentford look the clowns as he ran them ragged to score two goals in the Millers' 4-1 win. Christmas saw wins against Hull City and Carlisle United, to leave United right up there with the division's leading bunch.

Much of the season's success so far had been the meanness of the defence, and the team went into 1981 with that very much to the fore as they launched a run which saw them concede just one goal in seven matches, that coming in a defeat at Huddersfield. Three successive home games gave a maximum points return and the middle one, against Swindon Town, led to the Millers taking over at the top of the table almost unnoticed, for they had spent most of the season hovering around fourth, fifth or sixth.

Before the third of that trio of wins - against Sheffield United - a midweek win by Charlton saw them leap-frog over the Millers, but

the Millmoor lads kept in touch with that special victory over the team from Bramall Lane. The visitors took a 27th minute lead through Mike Trusson - later to become a Miller - and it was not until the 70th minute that Towner scored a superb equaliser before Mooro headed the winner a minute from time, although he will probably admit, he didn't know all that much about it. It was the first ever double that Rotherham had recorded against Sheffield United, and it was their first win against them at Millmoor since 1952.

Tony Towner celebrates the equaliser, versus Sheffield United at Millmoor

The defence excelled themselves yet again by keeping six successive clean sheets, one of them in a 3-0 win against close rivals Charlton, which took the Millers back to the top and at the same time helped towards a new club record of six successive matches without conceding a goal. The sixth one was at Carlisle where a Rodney Fern goal gave the Millers a win. When results came in from the division's other games, promotion was confirmed.

Now there was the championship to play for, but a draw at home to Hull followed by defeats at Brentford and Barnsley left them still needing a point from the last game - at home to Plymouth Argyle. The tension was something to be experienced, and when news filtered through from Oakwell that Barnsley had hit the four goals with which they might pip the Millers for the title, it only increased. At that stage the Millers were being held at 1-1 by Argyle, but with ten minutes left there was bedlam, as Millmoor erupted over the goal which gave them the championship.

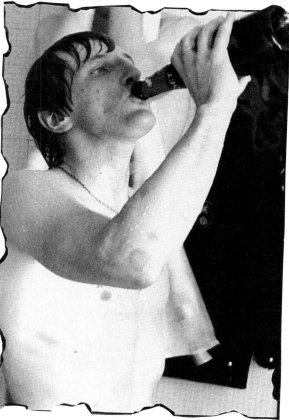

(Above) Ronnie Moore celebrates promotion at Carlisle
(Below) Relief for manager Ian Porterfield as his team clinches the Championship.

John Breckin's long ball found Rodney Fern, all alone and clear down the middle, as everyone in the ground held their breath. He seemed to take an age, but he knew what he was doing and the chance could not have fallen to a better person as he used all his experience in those long, vital seconds. Crudgington left his goal and defenders converged, before Rodney calmly lifted his shot wide of the 'keeper's right hand. The ball hit the net and Millmoor exploded.

The trophy was presented to the team a couple of days later at John Breckin's testimonial game but the celebrations went on for weeks. The team had kept a remarkable 26 clean sheets in 50 League and cup games, with Ronnie Moore hitting a total of 25 goals while Fern weighed in with 11 - a vital seven of them away from home.

But it was the way the team had played that had been so pleasing, with the home record being superb - they were unbeaten and let in a miserly eight goals.

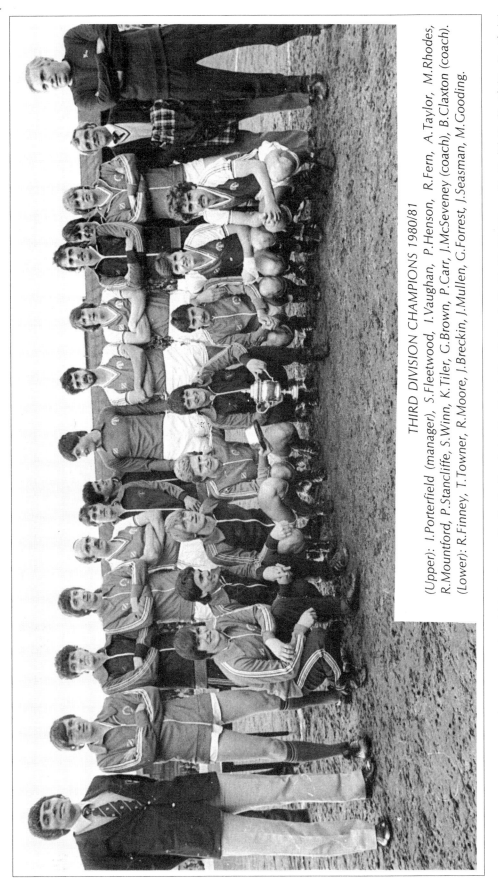

THIRD DIVISION CHAMPIONS 1980/81

(Upper): I.Porterfield (manager), S.Fleetwood, I.Vaughan, P.Henson, R.Fern, A.Taylor, M.Rhodes, R.Mountford, P.Stancliffe, S.Winn, K.Tiler, G.Brown, P.Carr, J.McSeveney (coach), B.Claxton (coach).
(Lower): R.Finney, T.Towner, R.Moore, J.Breckin, J.Mullen, G.Forrest, J.Seasman, M.Gooding.

Back in September the chairman had stated that he would guarantee promotion, after being asked about his sanity at the time, he now had justification in his big smile.

Before the euphoria had died down, the town was shocked to learn that manager Ian Porterfield was leaving to take over at Sheffield United, who on the same day that the Millers had clinched the title, slipped down into the Fourth Division. It was quite obviously sensational news, and with Rotherham asking for £250,000 compensation from Sheffield United, questions were asked as to how much effort had been made in trying to persuade Porterfield to stay. It was suggested in some quarters that this was a way of recovering the money which had been spent in the transfer market the previous August, and the players were far from happy with the situation .

However, it can now be revealed that Porterfield had been unhappy with certain things during the season and had in, fact, offered his resignation on two occasions, only to be persuaded to stay in charge.

An advertisement was placed in the national press to find the managerial replacement as the usual guessing game gathered momentum. It was hinted that a newcomer eager to prove himself on the managerial front - just as Porterfield had done - would take over and there were three names linked with the position. These were Emlyn Hughes, Bryan "Pop" Robson and none other than Nottingham Forest captain John McGovern, but it took the latter 13 more years to get the job, as it was the former England international Hughes who became the new boss.

Emlyn Hughes

Emlyn Hughes took over at an unusual time for it is not very often that a new manager has to be recruited at a successful club, being more usually very much a case of taking over at a losing outfit.

One of his first tasks was to tell his players that he would not stand for them getting into trouble for dissent, but he relied on the players from the championship winning squad to get the 1981/82 season off the ground with three points now at stake for a win.

It was, of course, the first time the Millers had played in that division for 13 years, and they started with a flourish as Norwich City, newly relegated from the First Division, were soundly beaten 4-1. It was down to earth with a bump for players and spectators alike when defeats were suffered at Cambridge and Sheffield Wednesday, before Ronnie Moore scored the only goal of the game against his old club Cardiff City.

After beating Bolton Wanderers at the end of September, when Emlyn Hughes made his playing debut, United then went six games without a win including an exit from the League Cup at the hands of Sunderland over two legs, but how the Millers came out of this spell. They thumped Chelsea 6-0, with Rodney Fern hitting a hat-trick to gain some reward for previous disappointing results, despite having played some good football.

Around the same time Hughes pulled off a master stroke in the transfer market when he plucked unknown 18-year-old goalkeeper Bobby Mimms from Halifax Town, and no one should need any reminding of what he went on to achieve at the very highest level, after Rotherham sold him for more than ten times the £15,000 fee they paid.

Hughes had intimated that the club had too many players and he started a clear out by releasing keeper Graham Brown, while Jimmy Mullen moved to Preston North End - managed by Tommy Docherty - on loan, with Ian Vaughan moving to Jim McGuigan at Stockport on a similar basis.

After beating Orient at Millmoor on the first Saturday in December, there was no further action for the team until the 1982 New Year, with ice and snow causing several postponements. There was some sad news, though, when it emerged that Richard Finney had lost his 14 month battle against injury, and he was to retire from the game, but he was not lost to the club as he was appointed as assistant secretary with a view to eventually taking over the main post.

The year 1982 started with a home draw against Sunderland in the third round of the F.A. Cup, but the next four games, including the cup replay at Sunderland, all ended in defeat, so Emlyn Hughes delved into the transfer market to sign Gerry Gow from Manchester City for £40,000 to add bite to the side.

Hughes maintained that his side was better than their League position suggested and he was true to his word as the team experienced a quite remarkable February. Following the re-arrangements of several games which had been postponed, they had no less than eight League games during the shortest month of the year, and they won them all. The bite Gow was expected to bring to the side was in too much evidence in February's first game, when he was booked against Derby County after just 55 seconds, and was then sent off after two minutes five seconds, to leave the Millers to battle with ten men.

It looked all over for them when Ronnie Moore missed a 53rd minute penalty, after County had taken the lead, but somehow the Millers clawed themselves back into the game thanks to an own goal, going on to win with - appropriately - thanks to a Moore goal.

Success just followed success and by the end of the month the team were taking the field expecting to win, and they had climbed from a position in the bottom three to fifth. And they hadn't finished, for the first game in March produced a 3-0 win at Oldham to take the run to nine successive victories - a club record. But it was oh so very nearly ten. The next game against Newcastle United (who had Imre Varadi in their side) finished goalless and Tony Towner missed a penalty in the first minute of injury time. But in the following game the undefeated run was broken by a defeat at Leicester.

So after looking prime candidates for relegation, Rotherham had transformed themselves into promotion possibilities which increased following wins at Chelsea and at home against Queens Park Rangers, when Moore was sent off. It proved impossible to maintain the momentum, and following a 3-0 defeat at Barnsley, the realistic hope of going up just about disappeared. Nevertheless, it was a splendid achievement to finish the first season back in the Second Division in seventh position due to that marvellous second half of the season.

There was an added bonus with the attendances, for the last two season had seen them shoot up by an incredible 58 per cent, and as a reward to the loyal fans, season tickets were made available for early purchase at 30 per cent discount. In addition arrangements were made with a credit company to spread the whole cost over a year, and the club claimed that this was the first time they had been made available in such a manner - but, of course, having read the earlier chapters, readers will know better!

An additional director was appointed to the Rotherham board in July, with the introduction of Alistair Ward who was described as a night club owner, and who numbered aviation companies and flying among his interests. There was also a newcomer in the playing ranks with winger Joe McBride coming from Everton for a fee of just under

£50,000. Meanwhile, speculation about chairman Johnson's future at Millmoor arose when he was linked with one of several business groups who were hoping to save financially ruined Wolves from extinction, and he was put on "standby" by the Receiver after tabling a £2m bid.

The 1982/83 season was to be one in marked contrast to the previous one and it was to see a managerial change followed by relegation. The first win of the season did not come until the fifth game with a victory at Burnley, and after being beaten 5-1 at home by Newcastle United, with Kevin Keegan hitting four of the goals, the Millers found themselves in the bottom half of the table.

Joe McBride nets for the Millers... meanwhile Newcastle score five...!

Anton Johnson was linked with another club, Derby County this time, but he once again pledged his future to Rotherham although he and his associates had had a bid accepted at the Derby end.

Some form was found with a 5-1 win at Charlton, but the team slipped down the table again until a 3-0 Christmas home victory against Grimsby was achieved, and which saw Phil Walker make a scoring debut.

Walker had just moved from Chesterfield with Mick Gooding going the other way, and that win was followed by two more, one of them against Sheffield Wednesday.

By early 1983, Rotherham had moved up to 11th place, but they failed to win any of the next 12 games as they slumped into the bottom three. Hopes of another fabulous February did not come to fruition and to add further problems, rumours that the club was the subject of a takeover bid were denied, although the chairman was missing from a shareholders meeting - not for the first time.

Following a 4-0 defeat at Queens Park Rangers, Emlyn Hughes was asked to resign, refused, and was sacked, with former Grimsby Town manager George Kerr taking over almost immediately. The town was divided in their opinions about Hughes's sacking, with many people feeling that he had broken up the championship winning side with Jimmy Mullen allowed to leave. John Breckin had also left the club around this time, after being "frozen out". Hughes could well have tried to utilise everything he had learned in his illustrious career at Liverpool, but he had not come to terms with the fact that he was dealing with players of a lesser ability. At the time of the sacking, the club had won just one of their earlier 11 games, but managers have survived spells like that in the past so perhaps the real reason for his dismissal was other than just results on the pitch....?

Kerr moved immediately to beat the transfer deadline by swopping Sheffield United's Kevin Arnott for Tony Towner on loan, and brought in Bobby Mitchell from Grimsby - the first of many signings from that club. Kerr failed to stop the rot and relegation was the United's fate, after just two seasons in a higher grade, but it was once again behind the scenes talk of takeovers that drew the attention.

John Seasman scores against Derby County, in the penultimate Second Division home game.

There was further speculation linking Sheffield United chairman Reg Brealey with Rotherham United, and its holding company Dexglade Ltd, with more rumours of Anton Johnson being involved with Bournemouth - although these stories were denied. Johnson was also to become involved with Southend United and Wigan Athletic, but it was a player, Tony Towner, who next attracted the attention, by moving to Wolves. Then came the news that Paul Stancliffe was moving to Sheffield United and the merry-go-round of players continued, as the season started with a draw at Southend. But that was to be the beginning of five years of struggle and more managerial upheavals.

At the end of September came the announcement that Anton Johnson would be leaving the club and his 52.33per cent majority shareholding in his company's name was put in proxy with new chairman Mick McGarry, a bookmaker and former vice-chairman of Grimsby Town. So ended the era of one of Rotherham's most colourful characters, but he left a legacy showing a loss of £285,000 with a bank overdraft of £129,000 and other liabilities of £131,000. When Johnson took over, the club showed £140,000 as current assets with no overdraft, and at the subsequent shareholders annual meeting, those present refused to vote to adopt the clubs financial accounts, in one of the stormiest ever meetings.

At a further meeting the following January, the shareholders again voted against accepting the accounts, but chairman McGarry administered a share poll which meant the accounts were accepted. At that meeting the members present were astonished at the admission that Rotherham United had lent

Derby County money to pay two weeks' wages, and further pertinent questions were asked about what had happened to the club's money in the last few years.

On the playing side the 1983/84 season was to be remembered mainly for its cup exploits with good runs in both the Milk Cup and the F.A. Cup. Hartlepool were disposed of in the first round of the Milk Cup - at which time crowd favourite Ronnie Moore moved to Charlton - and Rotherham seemed to be heading for their exit from the competition when they lost 3-2 at home to First Division Luton Town in the first leg of the second round.

Phil Walker pulled the Millers level at Kenilworth Road after 35 minutes and the tie went into extra time with Town still favourites to go through, for if the score remained the same they would win on the away goals rule. But Rotherham produced one of their all time great cup performances and snatched a late winner through Kevin Kilmore, to defy all the odds and go through to the next round, where they beat another First Division team, Southampton.

So into the fourth round where Wimbledon were beaten, but the trail came to an end with a fifth round home defeat at the hands of Walsall.

In the F.A. Cup, Hartlepool and Hull City were sent packing, but the Millers lost 3-0 at the Hawthorns against West Bromwich Albion, after holding them to a goalless draw at Millmoor.

The season ended on a high note, though, when the team won five of their last six matches to struggle up to 18th position, after they had spent some time in the bottom four.

But before the season drew to it's close there was a change in ownership yet again, with the club returning "home" in the hands of new chairman Syd Wood and his vice-chairman Graham Humphries, with the controlling 76 per cent interest now held in Bramwood Ltd, which was registered in Rotherham. However, with a massive £250,000 overdraft, the pair had a huge task in front of them.

Rotherham score the first goal in the League Cup match versus Southampton.

The last match of a season of turmoil saw Kevin Eley become the youngest ever Rotherham United player when he turned out at the tender age of 16 years 157 days - a record he still holds.

Summer renovations at the ground cost £60,000 and a further £50,000 was spent on relaying the pitch which had been in a poor condition the previous season. In addition, about £80,000 was spent on Tony Simmons' permanent move from Queens Park Rangers after he had had such a successful loan spell at the end of the previous season.

New chairman Syd Wood predicted that the team would gain promotion, but he saw them fail in that objective, although they did enjoy better times, finishing in 12th position. It could well have been much better, for the Millers had climbed up to second place following a 4-1 home win against York City just before Christmas.

The cart might well have come off the wheels when United were thrashed 7-0 at Burnley at the beginning of February, as Rotherham suffered their heaviest League defeat since the 8-0 defeat at West Ham in March 1958.

But they recovered to regain second position, although they only held that spot for a couple of games as they lost some form and the season ended with five successive defeats. The last home game against Cambridge United, who had only won three of their previous 44 games, attracted - if that is the word - an attendance of just 1,515 which was the lowest post-war League attendance at Millmoor.

In September of that 1984/85 season, Rotherham United was selected by the F.A. as one of its Centres of Excellence for budding young soccer talent, and it is refreshing to report that it is still in operation today.

There then came a programme made by Granada Television, which investigated the actions of former chairman Anton Johnson, who was put under the microscope for his dealings at seven different clubs, with the loan to Derby County using Rotherham United's money attracting particular attention. It also revealed that Mr Wood had requested a payment from him of £2,037, which was described as a benefit to Mr Johnson's nanny.

The subsequent annual shareholders meeting showed up some other unusual dealings, including loans to certain directors which the Football League instructed must be paid back to the club.

The following January, two more directors were appointed to the Board with the introduction of Ken Booth and John Harrison, further confirming that the club was now a "home town" club.

The shape of the ball was changed in March when Millmoor staged a Sheffield Eagles Rugby League game against Swinton, but it was only a temporary measure until the Eagles found a permanent home.

The end of the season also saw the end of George Kerr's managerial reign, for after discussions with the chairman and vice-chairman, he decided it was the right time to pass the job on to another manager. He had joined the club at a difficult time and to his credit did not squander money after Mr Wood took over, but he had not always endeared himself to the man on the terrace. Kerr upset some of the fans by coming out with statements such as, *I'm here for the next 15 years"*, but he invariably had the team's name in the news.

A large number of applicants for the vacant managerial chair was cut down to 20, with the applicants list understood to include Phil

Henson and Archie Gemmill, while among those keen to get back in the game was John McGovern. It was another well known name who got the vote, when Norman Hunter took over at a time when Bobby Mimms and Nigel Johnson had moved on to Everton and Manchester City respectively. The former England international had had past managerial experience at Barnsley, and for the previous 18 months he had been part of Johnny Giles' managerial team at West Bromwich Albion.

New manager - Norman Hunter

Hunter was soon active in the transfer market when he snapped up Stockport County's 22-year-old midfielder Dean Emerson for a fee of around £40,000. That signing was quickly followed by two more, with defender Kevan Smith coming from Darlington and prolific goalscorer Tommy Tynan who moved from Plymouth Argyle. Hunter's spending spree still wasn't over and the arrival of Daral Pugh from Huddersfield

Town preceded that of goalkeeper Kelham O'Hanlon from Middlesbrough.

Despite all the new recruits, 1985/86 was to be another average season with a final 14th position, although the team battled through to the F.A. Cup fourth round, only to be beaten 5-1 by Arsenal at Highbury. Along the way they beat Wolves 6-0 to equal their best ever Cup victory, although seven goals were scored at Darlington in the 1950/51 season.

After years of speculation about a possible move to a higher grade of football, Gerry Forrest eventually left the club in December 1985 with a £100,000 fee taking him to First Division Southampton - a move which he fully deserved, in order to be able to display his skills at the top level.

The following month the Mayday Club was launched with the hope of helping to reduce the massive £350,000 overdraft which had built up, with a weekly prize of £1,000 being a big attraction for the potential 1,500 members. The income that the new weekly draw would bring in was desperately needed as chairman Wood again stated that the debt-ridden club would not get back on its feet for a long, long time, for the bills kept coming in, such as £18,000 for the taxman and £1,000 had to be found quickly to prevent the electricity being cut off.

No sooner had the season ended than again the club was in the news when vice chairman Graham Humphries' own firm went out of business, and he, of course, was one of the people responsible for rescuing the club two years earlier. The miners' strike was blamed for the collapse of his engineering company, but it was not clear at that stage how this would affect the football club.

The club soldiered on and Norman Hunter began making his plans for the following

season by recruiting Colin Douglas from neighbouring Doncaster Rovers, while Andy Barnsley and Alan Birch moved to Sheffield United and Scunthorpe United respectively. Shortly after the departure of this pair, Mick Pickering rejected the offer of new terms and went to York City, so with his squad being somewhat depleted Hunter moved to sign defender Trevor Slack from Peterborough.

It was a smallish squad which faced the start of the 1986/87 season but they had the consolation of knowing that they could finish as low as fifth and still get promotion, for the play-off system was introduced. The First Division was to cut by two clubs, for each of the following two years.

The first three games all ended in draws and the playing staff received an early shuffle of the pack when Tommy Tynan and Tony Simmons moved out to be replaced by Winston Campbell and John McGinley. The team were to end in exactly the same position as the previous season - 14th - but this time there was to be no decent cup run apart from two good games against Coventry City in the Littlewoods Cup.

Doncaster Rovers had been beaten in the first round, and when Rotherham visited Highfield Road for the first leg of the second round, they did very well to lose by a narrow 3-2 margin. The second leg at Millmoor was something of a let down, though, as City won by the only goal of the game.

But in those games, Dean Emerson showed so much outstanding form that Coventry City signed him, with Rotherham getting Andy Williams and Gareth Evans in exchange. Williams scored the only goal of the game on his debut against Bolton Wanderers, while Evans netted 11 to become the club's leading scorer for the season.

The F.A. Cup saw the Millers pitted against Chester City, and they failed at the first hurdle, although it took City three games before they made further progress. Additionally United failed to go beyond the first round group games in the Freight Rover trophy.

The early season form had been depressing, as the team lost eight League and cup matches on the trot, and after losing 5-0 at Notts County they were firmly anchored to the bottom of the table. It was that Williams debut goal which stopped the rot, but it was not until late November that the team clambered off the bottom rung. However, they put together a good run starting just before Christmas, and after losing just one of the next eight games, they had climbed to a comfortable 13th mid-table position which they maintained to the end.

But the troubles on the field were nothing compared to those off it, as the club's debts rose to £500,000, and they were losing £3,000 per week, leading Wood to indicate that he would call it a day as chairman at the end of the season. Matters reached crisis level at the end of October with an urgent tax bill to meet, and it was only the Council stepping in with a £35,500 loan that prevented the club dropping even deeper into trouble, for the bailiffs turned up at the ground prepared to remove training equipment from the gymnasium.

The chairman asked the Council to buy the ground and lease it back to the club, but his pleas fell on deaf ears, and by mid-April the turmoil reached crisis level amid rumours that the club was on the edge of extinction due to the forever mounting financial difficulties. A week later an Administrator, David Stokes from Cork Gully, was appointed to take charge of the club's affairs, with the debts now having reached a massive £789,000.

David Stokes - Administrator

In the short term the future of the club was assured through the support of the club's bankers, National Westminster, and the decision by two firms, C.F.Booth Ltd and Rotherham Engineering Steels to guarantee wages until the end of the season. The main creditors were the Inland Revenue, the Gas Board ,the YEB, and the police, and Mr Stokes subsequently held a meeting of local businessmen and other interested parties at which he outlined the club's predicament and the ways in which it could be helped.

Wednesday, 13th May 1987 marked the day when the Millers came back from the brink, for scrap dealer Ken Booth, who had a spell as a director for 15 months in the past, stepped in to save the club, with a package that wiped off the debts of almost £800,000. He headed a new three man board that included son-in-law Ron Hull and Barry Peacock, managing director of a local car dealers. Outgoing directors Syd Wood and Graham Humphries agreed to waive £130,000 they were owed, and they were to receive only a partial payment. In addition, they transferred their majority shareholding of 75.9 per cent of the company's share capital to the new owners.

Advertiser

FRIDAY, MAY 15, 1987

20p

also Dalton, Thrybergh, Bramley, Braithwell, Tickhill, Hellaby, Stainton,
Ravenfield, Hooton Roberts, East Herringthorpe and Sunnyside

Millers back from the brink

Wealthy scrap dealer Ken Booth has stepped in to save Rotherham United with a package that wiped off the club's debts of almost £800,000.

Mr Booth (65), a life-long Millers' supporter, heads a new three-man board that includes son-in-law Ron Hull and Barry Peacock, managing director of Rotherham Toyota Centre.

The previous directors — chairman Syd Wood, Graham Humphries, Cliff Wright and Jack Layden — all resigned from the board to make way for Wednesday's takeover.

Mr Booth, owner of the C. F. Booth Ltd scrap empire which has property on two sides of Millmoor, and a director for 15 months until resigning in April last year, is "confident" the club's financial future is safe with him.

Outgoing directors Syd Wood and Graham Humphries agreed to waive £130,000 they were owed and will receive only a partial payment. In addition, they transferred their majority shareholding of 75.9 per cent of the company's share capital to the new owners.

■ Following the takeover South Yorkshire Police Authority is to press for national talks on the payments system for policing football matches.

The Authority has been forced to write off at least £16,000 owed by Rotherham United for policing home matches.

The authority voted to accept the rescue package on offer at the creditor's meeting, feeling it had no choice.

■ Full story — back page.

Millmoor saviours (from left), Barry Peacock, Ken Booth and Ron Hull

The club had some precarious times in the past with their lack of finances, but nothing so close to going out of business had ever been experienced before, so Mr Booth deserves the thanks he has probably never justly received.

With the club stabilised once more, Norman Hunter moved into the transfer market in July to re-sign Nigel Johnson from Manchester City, and a few hours later he had lined up former Barnsley striker Carl Airey, who had been with Belgian First Division Charleroi. Mike Trusson made way for them by accepting a move to Brighton, but there was a bombshell when Mick Gooding left to join Peterborough before the season could get underway. However, that disappointment was pushed into the background when Hunter swooped to sign Eire international Tony Grealish from Manchester City.

If thoughts were being formulated that success off the field would be followed by success on it, then they were quickly kicked into touch, for the season ended disastrously with relegation to the Fourth Division, and with yet another managerial change.

The season had opened with a defeat at Bristol Rovers, but there were better signs when Huddersfield Town were beaten on an aggregate 7-5 scoreline in the Littlewoods Cup. But by the time United visited Everton in the second round, the League position was an unhealthy sixth from the bottom.

Nigel Pepper scores at Goodison Park

The game at Goodison Park ended in a 3-2 defeat, with the home side scoring the winning goal two minutes before the end from the penalty spot, following an infringement - which only the referee saw! The highlight of a good Rotherham performance was undoubtedly the goal which Martin Scott scored - a thunderous free kick which 'keeper Neville Southall didn't even see. The second leg was a goalless draw, so the Millers made their exit from the competition, but they advanced in the F.A. Cup after beating Doncaster Rovers in a replay at Millmoor.

They suffered a 7-1 drubbing at Sunderland in the Freight Rover Trophy, but strangely still qualified for the next round, and they recovered to win at Aldershot in the following game, in the League. That took the team to eighth from the bottom, but it was to be Norman Hunter's last League game in charge, for he got 'the bullet', after a humiliating 4-0 F.A. Cup defeat at non-League Macclesfield.

So for the second time in the space of a few years, a manager with an illustrious international playing career behind him had failed to make the grade as a manager at Rotherham. John Breckin was made acting-manager, but he was only in charge for a couple of matches before Dave Cusack took over as player-manager, just three weeks after he had been replaced from a similar capacity - at Doncaster Rovers - by Dave Mackay.

The new boss got off to a winning start with three successive 1-0 wins over the Christmas and New Year holiday period, but he was soon brought down to earth as he saw his team go the next six matches without a win. February 1988 saw the team unbeaten, and after drawing with Wigan on 19 March, Rotherham seemed to be in a position of comparative safety, tenth from the bottom.

The net was cast wider than usual in the search for new players, with two young players from Iceland, Gretor Einarsson and Gestor Gylfason, paying their own fares to undergo trial periods at Millmoor, but a run out in the reserves was the best they could manage.

Then came another poor League run, with five successive defeats, which sent the team plummeting down five places, and it was also to cost Dave Cusack his job as he was sacked after just 126 days in office for probably the shortest spell of any Rotherham United boss.

Dave Cusack

His short reign in the role of player/manager saw him play only 18 League games for United.

There were only three matches left for the new manager, former player Billy McEwan, to keep the team out of the relegation zone, and he got off to a good start with wins against Aldershot and Gillingham. But a last game home defeat by runaway champions Sunderland and wins for other relegation candidates Chesterfield and Southend United, left the Millers in a relegation play-off position, at fourth from bottom.

The bottom three went down automatically, and this was the first time that relegation play-offs had been brought into use - and the last - with the Millers set to play the team who finished in sixth position in the Fourth Division, Swansea City.

To rub salt into their wounds, the last day of the season was the first time United had slipped as low as 21st position.

A single goal defeat at Vetch Field in the first leg gave United hope that they could avoid the drop, but they were held to a 1-1 draw, and so went down, with Billy McEwan planning a clear-out to pave the way for new players.

Four of the first team squad, Carl Airey, John Dungworth, Daral Pugh and Winston Campbell were released along with four youngsters, and McEwan replaced them by signing Des Hazel, Pat Heard, Bobby Williamson and Billy Russell. The latter three were on the scoresheet in the 1988/89 season's opening day 3-0 win against Doncaster Rovers. That victory was to mark a fine start to the season, with the first six games seeing the team unbeaten and sitting at the top of the table - a position which they were to occupy for a good proportion of the campaign.

Grimsby Town were disposed of in the Littlewoods Cup and that pitted the Millers against mighty Manchester United in the second round with the first leg ending goalless at Millmoor in front of just over 13,000 spectators.

Pre-season training at Wentworth Woodhouse - July 1988.

The return game at Old Trafford turned out to be a damp squib for the Millers, as they were beaten 5-0, but the good League form continued with Rotherham rarely out of the top two.

They beat Barrow in the first round of the F.A. Cup, but were then knocked out at Grimsby in early December in what was the fifth meeting of the season between the two clubs in four different competitions.

Crewe Alexandra had emerged as Rotherham's main rivals, and they leap-frogged to the top by pulling off a Boxing Day win at Millmoor, before two wins and a draw from the next three games put the Millers in the number one spot yet again. A dodgy little spell of one win, two draws and three defeats saw them slip down to fifth position - the lowest they reached at any stage - before they came back into form with a nine match unbeaten run. The climax of that sequence came against Crewe at Gresty Road, when Billy McEwan did his homework and preparations to perfection, to see his team pull off a superb 3-1 win with Bobby Williamson underlining his status as the crowd's favourite by hitting a hat-trick.

Hereford were thumped 6-0 for their heaviest ever League defeat, and a 3-1 away win at Stockport in the penultimate game, on a glorious sunny day, clinched promotion.

Many of the fans travelled in fancy dress in readiness of their celebrations, and even the problems they had on their journey due to road works did not dampen their spirits. Because of the fans' delay, the kick off was put back, and Rotherham did their job to perfection. The last game was a goalless draw against Cambridge at Millmoor, but the point was enough to give them the championship.

Manager Billy McEwan proudly parades with the Championship trophy.

Bobby Williamson underlined what a great free transfer he had been by hitting 27 League goals, with another one in the F.A. Cup for good measure, but the real key to success was the all-round teamwork, which led to the team bouncing back to the Third Division at the first time of asking.

In preparation for the new season, Ronnie Robinson was signed from West Bromwich Albion for a £40,000 fee, which was covered by the sale of Phil Crosby to Peterborough. Behind the scenes, a multi-thousand pounds redevelopment plan was outlined to improve the Millmoor facilities, with a training pitch behind the main stand being one of the proposals. Among others were the extending of the Family Stand to incorporate all the seating on the Millmoor Lane side, and the club intending to install seating in the central section of the Railway End for the away supporters.

The 1989/90 season got off to a promising start, including the defeat of Sheffield United over two legs in the Littlewoods Cup, and the team occupied fourth position after the opening five League games. They hit a purple spell, particularly at home where they three times rattled home five goals, which included two successive hat-tricks from Williamson. They were still fourth after 16 games in early November.

The last game of that month saw Rotherham in scoring form again as Shrewsbury Town were beaten 4-2, to take them into second place, just two points behind leaders Bristol Rovers which raised hopes that a second successive promotion was on the cards. An injection of some new blood was probably called for, but it was not forthcoming and results gradually began to tail away, although the team was still in fifth spot at the beginning of March. From then to the end of the season the Millers pulled off just three wins from 15 games, although they managed to hold on to ninth spot

In this, the first season after gaining promotion, that placing was quite respectable, but after the good start they had experienced it was somewhat disappointing.

The last two away games warrant a note in the history books, for they took place at Chester's Sealand Road ground and at Walsall's Fellows Park and they were the very last League matches played at both venues before the clubs concerned moved to new homes.

McEwan indicated that he would be asking for some money to splash out in the transfer market. He released Tony Grealish and Pat Heard and there was a change in personnel when Nigel Pepper went to York City with Steve Spooner coming to Millmoor. Two more defenders joined the Rotherham ranks with Nicky Law arriving from Notts County while former favourite Gerry Forrest made a return to the club after being released by Southampton.

What a season 1990/91 turned out to be for the Millers! After beating Wigan, for their first victory of the campaign in the fourth game, they were in 15th position, but that was to be the highest they occupied at any time and they were anchored on the bottom rung for the majority of the time.

Bobby Williamson was sold to Kilmarnock for £100,000 at the end of November, by which time McEwan was fending off speculation about his possible sacking, before another £200,000 was raked in with the sale of Martin Scott to Bristol City in early December establishing a club sale record.

Rotherham drew with Halifax Town at Millmoor in the F.A. Cup at Millmoor and won the replay at The Shay. At this time Billy McEwan revealed that he had offered to resign two weeks previously. He said he had been told his job was safe, but his tenure of the post was not improved when his team was beaten 5-0 at Swansea with four of the goals coming in a poor first half. That was on New Year's Day 1991 and the team had to visit the same venue in the F.A. Cup four days later, but McEwan was not among the party, with his absence explained that he was "away scouting".

It was revealed that assistant manager Phil Henson had picked the team which battled to earn a replay in a goalless draw, and McEwan was subsequently told to stay away from the ground to take what was described as a rest or a holiday. This farcical situation left his position untenable and he duly resigned shortly afterwards, to become the sixth manager to vacate the Millmoor hot seat in ten years. McEwan was quickly replaced by Phil Henson, but despite a valiant attempt which saw an improvement in results, the battle for safety was lost, and so the club was plunged back into the Fourth Division, just two seasons after they had left it.

Gerry Forrest was one of four players released, but Henson was under no illusions about the club's inability to delve into the transfer market as the overdraft had reached £520,000, and much dependence would be placed in the hands of the younger players. Goalkeeper Kelham O'Hanlon was another who departed to pastures new, but the Millers were boosted at the start of the 1991/92 season with the arrival of strikers Tony Cunningham and Don Page. They joined new full back Chris Hutchings in the side which beat Burnley in the season's opener, and lead the table after winning 4-0 at Halifax in the sixth match.

Three draws and a defeat were followed by a win at Aldershot, but all the records applicable to this game were expunged when the 'Shots' dropped out of the League later in the season. For a while United maintained a handy sixth position tucked nicely behind the leading few, before they met Scunthorpe United in the F.A. Cup, and drew 1-1 at Glanford Park. The replay put Rotherham in the competition's history books for ever, for they became the first team ever to win a place in the next round by means of a penalty shoot-out. It had been decided that ties must be settled after the second game, and at Millmoor the two sides were deadlocked at 3-3 after extra time.

After Scunthorpe missed with their first spot kick, Rotherham were heading for victory when their first three were all successful. But then Nicky Law and Don Page couldn't find the net. This left the situation still deadlocked at 3-3 after the first five kicks to each team, meaning that it would now revert to sudden death. With the visitors shooting first, their next three efforts were all successful. Therefore Barrick, Hutchings and Goater all had to score to keep matters even,

and they achieved their objective. Mercer then saved Helliwell's shot thereby leaving a 6-6 scoreline. A confident Pickering converted the 18th kick to give Rotherham a memorable 7-6 win.

That high drama was followed by two draws and two defeats, but a fine Boxing Day win at leaders Burnley boosted confidence, particularly in view of the fact that it was the home side's first defeat for 17 matches. After beating rivals Crewe in the first game of 1992, the Millers produced a poor performance to lose at home to Scarborough before their first ever visit to Barnet resulted in a convincing 5-2 victory, with the home side having two players sent off.

Things appeared to be falling apart when Cardiff recorded a well deserved win at Millmoor and Gillingham overcame an early Shaun Goater goal to inflict an unbelievable 5-1 defeat on the Millers, which included three goals in a nine minute spell. United's penalty shooting wasn't quite as good as it had been against Scunthorpe when Burnley won a shoot-out in the Autoglass Trophy quarter final. The team had slipped down to seventh position at the beginning of March before six successive wins took them storming up to fourth - just behind the promotion frame. A home win against Rochdale followed by a hard earned point from a goalless draw at Maidstone took them into that coveted third position, with seven matches left to play. A crowd of almost 9,000, then saw Rotherham beat third placed Blackpool at Millmoor to take over the runners-up spot. A most efficient display clinched a 3-0 win at Wrexham in the penultimate game, to leave the fans celebrating promotion in the last (home) game, although the Millers weren't able to lay the Chesterfield bogey as they were held to a 1-1 draw.

May 1992 - the last match of the season (at Millmoor), and happy supporters celebrate promotion.

Despite the season's success, there was some doubt about a renewed contract offer for manager Phil Henson, but after rejecting the original new deal he again pledged his immediate future to the club. Henson moved to make an early signing, with Ian Banks making the short journey from Barnsley, with no fee involved.

The formation of the Premier League meant that Rotherham went from the Fourth Division into the Second Division in one move, and they had the fillip of brand new training facilities, with the opening of a vast 32 acre site at Hooton Roberts to give them a set-up which was to become the envy of the majority of other clubs.

A new FIFA ruling prior to the 1992/93 season saw the goalkeepers forbidden to pick up back-passes, so plenty of pre-season work had to be done to come to terms with these new conditions. Meanwhile, off the pitch, Keith Walker was appointed as chief executive with a brief to improve the club's cash flow, but his stay was a comparatively short one.

There was a promising opening day 2-0 victory at Exeter, and Hull City were beaten on aggregate in the Coca Cola Cup, before defeats against Wigan and Port Vale saw the team in 13th position, the lowest they were

to occupy throughout the whole campaign. From then on there was a steady climb up the table, but at the back end of September all attention was turned to the Coca Cola with Premier League Everton coming to Millmoor for the first leg of the second round tie. And they were thankful that they went away having been beaten just 1-0, for the Millers played with such a verve and style that the Goodison Park manager Howard Kendall admitted that he was relieved the margin had not been much bigger.

Central defender Nicky Law excelled himself when he had to take over from the injured goalkeeper Billy Mercer in a win against Blackpool, as the team showed great determination to come back from being 2-1 down with only eight minutes left to play. The same two players were involved in the action again in the second leg against Everton, but this time Law had to take over after Mercer was shown the red card, and the ten men were unable to prevent a 3-0 defeat.

The club then had to do without the services of striker Shaun Goater, who returned to his homeland Bermuda for a lengthy World Cup stint. But the team hardly seemed to miss him as they moved up into second place before Christmas, to raise hopes of another promotion bid. Leaders Stoke City proved just too powerful, in front of over 21,000 spectators at the Victoria Ground, but the Millers had built up a three goal lead at half-time against Reading in the next match, only to concede two goals and struggle to hang on to win.

Shaun Goater playing for Bermuda

A Jonathan Howard last minute goal in the third round of the F.A. Cup at Northampton then gave Rotherham a home tie with Kevin Keegan's Newcastle United in the next round, with the game being played in front of a capacity crowd for the first time in many years. Although this was a much reduced figure due to the implications of the Taylor report, and there were 13,405 in the ground to see Nigel Johnson snatch the goal which gave Rotherham a replay in a 1-1 draw. The team put up a valiant display at St James Park but they went out 2-0, although they had the consolation of sharing the receipts of a sell-out attendance of almost 30,000.

A mid-January game at Blackpool ended in a 2-0 defeat and that match set the scene for a disappointing fade-out for the rest of the season, as the team slowly slid down the table with only five wins - including two in the last three matches - coming from the final 21 games. John Buckley returned to the club in February for his second spell, having left to join Partick Thistle in October 1990, but the move from Scunthorpe United was to be a far from happy one for him.

He was used as substitute on three occasions before starting his second game against Plymouth Argyle on 13th March, and unfortunately it was to be his last. The game was only seven minutes old when, under a challenge from defender Gary Poole, he hit the deck with a sickening thud. He spent several days in hospital on a life support machine suffering from a fractured skull. He made a valiant bid to return to action as he started summer training a few months later, but he sadly had to hang up his boots and is now working as part of the club's Football in the Community programme. At the end of the season Tony Cunningham, who had played such a vital part in the club's last successful promotion campaign was released, while Chris Hutchings moved into the backroom staff with coaching responsibilities.

A steady start to the 1993/94 season put Rotherham in sixth position after the first six games, but it was all downhill from then on with the majority of the rest of the season involving a battle to keep out of the relegation zone. Even the cup competitions brought scant reward, for after beating Wigan in the Coca Cola Cup, a poor display at Portsmouth saw the Millers on the end of a 5-0 drubbing in the second round. The F.A. Cup brought no joy either with Stockport winning at Millmoor after a Chris Wilder penalty had put United in front.

The team had been hovering just above the bottom four before an early April win against play-off spot chasing Bradford City saw them turn the corner, and a thumping 7-0 win against Hartlepool made the other struggling teams sit up. With injuries and suspensions biting hard into the club's resources, the youngsters were given their chance to shine with defenders Ian Breckin and Scott Smith showing the same admirable form that goalkeeper Matt Clarke had done in the second half of the season.

This season marked a particularly sad moment, for on 3rd September 1993, Derek Dalton passed away a week before his 46th birthday.

No one will surely need reminding that Derek was Rotherham United's number one fan, and he probably raised more money for the club than any other individual, which was quite remarkable as it had to be done from his wheelchair.

He contracted polio at the age of two, but despite his severe handicap he lived for Rotherham United,

Rotherham United's number one fan Derek Dalton meets the Queen.

and home and away he rarely missed a match, thanks to his party of willing helpers and most of all, his devoted mother, Hilda. Derek was known to every club throughout the whole country and he was a fine ambassador, not only for Rotherham, but also for football in general.

His home proudly displayed a host of photographs taken with well known celebrities with his proudest probably being one alongside the great Pele. Always full of cheerfulness and courage, Derek was a real example for everyone, and his coffin carried a token

of his dedication to the sport he loved, displaying a football pitch made of laurel leaves with a football in his favourite colours - red and white. There were also wreaths in the shape of the club badge as well as a wreath from the Professional Footballers' Association.

It is with justification that the vice-presidents' lounge - he was a long standing member of the club - was renamed the Derek Dalton lounge, and he can rest assured that his name will never be forgotten at Millmoor.

No sooner had the season ended than a degree of chaos prevailed, for the majority of players contracts' had expired, but to add further confusion as to who would stay and who would go, the manager himself was in doubt as to his own future. Yet again there was speculation suggesting he might move on, but he was eventually offered a one year extension to his contract. But he was left with little cash to recruit any new faces, and it was stories of a possible ground move for the club that attracted the summer headlines. The Football League Trust offered £1m towards the cost of renovating Millmoor, with the club having to find £250,000, but the offer was more than double that amount to re-locate.

The Council were approached regarding any possible suitable sites and the club favoured one in particular of the ones they viewed - off Bessemer Way near Ickles, and in sight of the present ground. It was proposed that the 40 acre site would be developed to include a multitude of other facilities, but unfortunately nothing came of the project.

Not for the first time Shaun Goodwin and Shaun Goater looked as if they might be on the move prior to the start of the season with both of them involved in talks with Port Vale. It made it difficult for Phil Henson to formulate his plans properly, but the pair eventually stayed at the club while other out-of-contract players gradually put pen to paper.

Goalkeeper Matt Clarke was the subject of pre-season gossip regarding a possible big money move to a higher club, and that story was given more fuel when he went to Spain to play in a friendly for Leeds United, but it was his rival for the 'keeper's job - Billy Mercer - who was subsequently to move on. He went to Sheffield United after playing for them during a summer tour to Australia, with the tribunal system coming down very much in the Bramall Lane outfit's favour when the fee was decided upon.

After the second half of the previous season and the lack of any major spending on new players, the 1994/95 season started with little optimism amongst the spectators. It started in a dreadful fashion with a home defeat at the hands of newly promoted Shrewsbury Town, which led to after-match crowd demonstrations with a demand for more transfer activity uppermost in their minds. Mr. Booth made an announcement that he was prepared to listen to offers from any potential buyers of the club, and contact was made by a so-called Essex business man on behalf of a three man consortium. The asking price was said to be £3.5m, but discussions did not advance very far as it was revealed that the person behind the threesome was believed to be something of a 'con' merchant with a shady background.

On the pitch, Third Division Carlisle United turned a first leg Coca Cola Cup deficit into victory over the Millers in the second leg, after Crewe had won with some ease in the League, and after six games, the Millers had taken just three points - all from a win against Bournemouth. Fortunately, three other clubs were in a worse position, but the pressure on the club was already having an effect when it was hinted that Archie Gemmill had been lined up to take over the managerial seat. Both he and John McGovern were in attendance at Millmoor to witness a battling performance to gain a draw against Birmingham City, and the pair were duly announced as joint managers the following day - 14th September 1994.

Henson was appointed chief executive to continue his long association with the club, and the new managerial pair - who had been told there would be no blank cheques for new players - made a winning start with a victory at Hull a few days later.

The behind the scenes upheaval took another twist when secretary Norman Darnill was sacked at the end of September, while on the pitch the new management duo hoped to solve one of the teams problems by taking left-sided midfielder Andy Roscoe on loan from Bolton Wanderers.

Gemmill and McGovern gradually introduced their own style into the team's play, which was built on the vast experience they had gained in illustrious playing careers, but it was still a long season's battle with 15th being the highest position they achieved, with a final 17th - and safety - the reward for their efforts.

Throughout the season there was a change of personnel in the team and the promised clear out at the end of the season came to fruition with several players released on free transfers.

The rebuilding for the 1995/96 season got underway with chairman Ken Booth authorising the biggest spending spree since the start of the 1980/81 season - and look what happened after that!

Mike Jeffrey was the first recruit at a cost of £100,000 from Newcastle United, and he has been followed by Darren Garner, Steve Farrelly, Gary Bowyer and Paul Blades who cost £110,000 from Wolves.

Whether this spending spree brings the success that is so keenly desired by the supporters remains to be seen - perhaps it can be the first chapter in the next edition of the club's history.

There can be no better way to sign off than repeat Derek Dalton's favourite three words:

"Up the Millers".

Gareth Farrelly scores the last Rotherham goal of the 1994/95 season, versus Stockport County

IN THE LEAGUE - THE RECORD

Rotherham Town/County/United: 1893/94 to 1994/95
(Town: 1893-1896. County: 1919-1925. United: 1925 to date)

Division	Season	Pl.	W.	D.	L.	F.	A.	Pts.	Pos	No.
2	1893-94	28	6	3	19	44	91	15	14	15
	1894-95	30	11	2	17	55	62	24	12	16
	1895-96*	30	7	3	20	34	97	17	15	16
	1919-20	42	13	8	21	51	83	34	17	22
	1920-21	42	12	12	18	37	53	36	19	22
	1921-22	42	14	11	17	32	43	39	16	22
	1922-23	42	13	9	20	44	63	35	21	22
3 (North)	1923-24	42	23	6	13	70	43	52	4	22
	1924-25	42	7	7	28	42	88	21	22	22
	1925-26	42	17	7	18	69	92	41	14	22
	1926-27	42	10	12	20	70	92	32	19	22
	1927-28	42	14	11	17	65	69	39	14	22
	1928-29	42	15	9	18	60	77	39	16	22
	1929-30	42	11	8	23	67	113	30	20	22
	1930-31	42	13	12	17	81	83	38	14	22
	1931-32**	40	14	4	22	63	72	32	19	21
	1932-33	42	14	6	22	60	84	34	17	22
	1933-34	42	10	8	24	53	91	28	21	22
	1934-35	42	19	7	16	86	73	45	9	22
	1935-36	42	16	9	17	69	66	41	11	22
	1936-37	42	14	7	21	78	91	35	17	22
	1937-38	42	20	10	12	68	56	50	6	22
	1938-39	42	17	8	17	64	64	42	11	22
	1939-40	3	1	1	1	5	6	3	11	22
	1946-47	42	29	6	7	114	53	64	2	22
	1947-48	42	25	9	8	95	49	59	2	22
	1948-49	42	28	6	8	90	46	62	2	22
	1949-50	42	19	10	13	80	59	48	6	22
	1950-51	46	31	9	6	103	41	71	1	24
2	1951-52	42	17	8	17	73	71	42	9	22
	1952-53	42	16	9	17	75	74	41	12	22
	1953-54	42	21	7	14	80	67	49	5	22
	1954-55	42	25	4	13	94	64	54	3	22
	1955-56	42	12	9	21	56	75	33	19	22
	1956-57	42	13	11	18	74	75	37	17	22
	1957-58	42	14	5	23	65	101	33	18	22
	1958-59	42	10	9	23	42	82	29	20	22
2	1959-60	42	17	13	12	61	60	47	8	22
	1960-61	42	12	13	17	65	64	37	15	22
	1961-62	42	16	9	17	70	76	41	9	22
	1962-63	42	17	6	19	67	74	40	14	22
	1963-64	42	19	7	16	90	78	45	7	22
	1964-65	42	14	12	16	70	69	40	14	22
	1965-66	42	16	14	12	75	74	46	7	22
	1966-67	42	13	10	19	61	70	36	18	22
	1967-68	42	10	11	21	42	76	31	21	22
3	1968-69	46	16	13	17	56	50	45	11	24
	1969-70	46	15	14	17	62	54	44	14	24
	1970-71	46	17	16	13	64	60	50	8	24
	1971-72	46	20	15	11	69	52	55	5	24
	1972-73	46	17	7	22	51	65	41	21	24
4	1973-74	46	15	13	18	56	58	43	15	24
	1974-75	46	22	15	9	71	41	59	3	24
3	1975-76	46	15	12	19	54	65	42	16	24
	1976-77	46	22	15	9	69	44	59	4	24
	1977-78	46	13	13	20	51	68	39	20	24
	1978-79	46	17	10	19	49	55	44	17	24
	1979-80	46	18	10	18	58	66	46	13	24
	1980-81	46	24	13	9	62	32	61	1	24
2	1981-82	42	20	7	15	66	54	67	7	22
	1982-83	42	10	15	17	45	68	45	20	22
3	1983-84	46	15	9	22	57	64	54	18	24
	1984-85	46	18	11	17	55	55	65	12	24
	1985-86	46	15	12	19	61	59	57	14	24
	1986-87	46	15	12	19	48	57	57	14	24
	1987-88	46	12	16	18	50	66	52	21	24
4	1988-89	46	22	16	8	76	35	82	1	24
3	1989-90	46	17	13	16	71	62	64	9	24
	1990-91	46	10	12	24	50	87	42	23	24
4	1991-92 #	42	22	11	9	70	37	77	2	22
2 ##	1992-93	46	17	14	15	60	60	65	11	24
	1993-94	46	15	13	18	63	60	58	15	24
	1994-95	46	14	14	18	57	61	56	17	24

TOTALS: 3085 1157 717 1210 4605 4779 3253

Totals do not include season 1939-40, which started but was halted by the war.
* Gainsborough Trinity, Blackpool and Walsall elected in place of Rotherham Town, Crewe Alexandra and Port Vale.
** Wigan Borough resigned October 1931. Their record was deleted, thus only 21 teams completed the season.
# Aldershot resigned March 1992, their record was deleted, thus only 22 teams completed the season.
Re-numbering of divisions. Division 3 became Division 2.

(Top) 1944-45; still war-time, and a flimsy single sheet programme had to suffice for Football League North matches.

(Middle) An amazing 7-2 away victory set the Millers on the way to a good F.A.Cup run.

(Bottom) (1950-51) The 2-0 victory at Sincil Bank was the clincher for promotion.

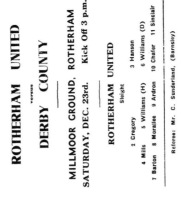

ROTHERHAM UNITED
versus
DERBY COUNTY

MILLMOOR GROUND, ROTHERHAM
SATURDAY, DEC. 23rd.   Kick Off 3 p.m.

ROTHERHAM UNITED

Sleight

2 Gregory   3 Hanson

4 Millis   5 Williams (H)   6 Williams (D)

7 Barton   8 Morallee   9 Ardron   10 Chafer   11 Sinclair

Referee: Mr. C. Sunderland, (Barnsley)

Our Reserve Team is needing Stockings very badly. Will any of our Supporters be kind enough to sell or give us Cycling or Golfing Stockings for which they have no immediate use.

Linesman : Cpl. A. R. Ellis and Mr. T. Waddams

11 Duncan   10 Carter   9 Lyman   8 Powell   7 Slack
              6 Musson   5 Leuty   4 Bullions
                   3 Trim   2 Parr
                      Savage

DERBY COUNTY

PROGRAMMES   —   ONE PENNY

Darlington F.C.

Programme Price 2d.

"Spirit Dispatch" Photo

Directors :—Chairman and Hon. Secretary : Mr. J. B. Smith, Messrs. E. Black, R. H. Black
H. Shaw, D. Jordan, Councillor J. Measham, W. Sewell, J. L. Sladford,
Team Manager : G. W. Irwin, Hon. Financial Secretary: Mr. J. B. Shaw

SATURDAY, 25th Nov., 1950 (F.A. CUP) v. ROTHERHAM U.

CLUB JOTTINGS :

LINCOLN CITY
VERSUS
ROTHERHAM UTD.

Saturday, April 28th
Kick-off 3-0 p.m.

OFFICIAL PROGRAM

No. 2936

(Top) An eagerly awaited local derby - in the Second Division. A 5-3 win before a crowd of nearly 55,000!

(Below) The Millers pulled off a shock 3-1 F.A.Cup victory over the holders.

(Right) A draw at Vale Park would have meant promotion to the First Division for the Millers - They lost 1-0.....

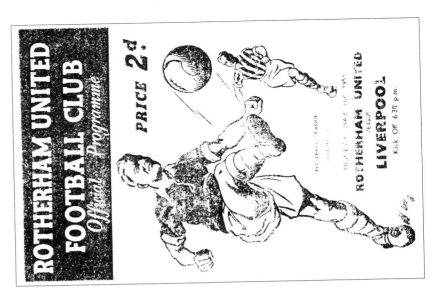

(Right)..... but the season finished with a 'bang', a thumping 6-1 victory over Liverpool (promotion could have been achieved if a 16-0 victory had resulted)!

(Right) Shock finalists in the first League Cup (1960-61 season) which was held over until the next season. A 2-0 home leg win .....

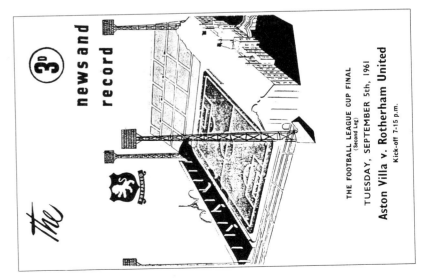

..... but this wasn't enough as the second leg was lost 3-0.

One season earlier the Cup highlight was without doubt a second replay win over the mighty Arsenal.

Memorable F.A. Cup matches against Manchester United.

(Above) The Championship contenders were held to a 0-0 draw at Old Trafford...

(Left) .... and the replay at Millmoor was only narrowly lost (1-0)

A near 42,000 Filbert Street crowd witnessed the end of the Millers F.A.Cup run in this 5th round replay.

Three years later the reigning League Champions were held to a scoreless draw at Millmoor.....

... In the replay the Third Division underdogs scored twice, but it wasn't enough as a 3-2 defeat was the final result.

In 1978, Arsenal were again the victims, this time by 3-1 in a League Cup match.

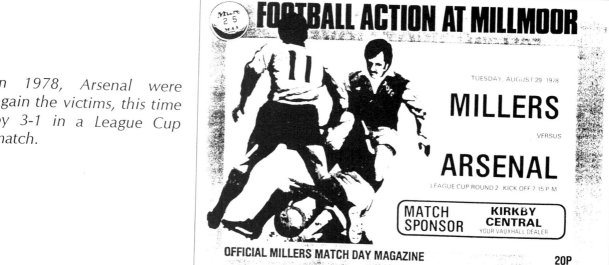

The last match in the 1980-81 season. A 2-1 home victory over Plymouth clinches the Third Division Championship for the Millers.

Two notable programmes from the 1991-92 season.
(Top) Rotherham entertain the eventual Fourth Division Champions
in the first League game of the season. (Below) A 1-1 draw with Chesterfield
in the last League match is enough to ensure the Millers promotion.

MILLERMEN: Seasons 1946/47 - 1994/95 Ainscow - Crawford

NAME	Born	Signed from:	Date	Played	Apps.	Sub.	Gls.
AINSCOW, Andrew P.	1/10/68	Wigan Athletic	8/89	1989	0	1	0
AIREY, Carl	6/2/65	Charleroi	8/87	1987	25	7	11
ALEXANDER, Ian	26/1/63	Glasgow Juv.	10/81	81-82	5	6	0
ALLEN, Derek	14/7/46	Juniors	11/65	1965	1	0	0
ARDRON, Walter	19/9/18	Denaby United	12/38	38-48	123	-	94
ARMITAGE, Louis C.	15/12/21		12/40	46-47	15	-	9
ARNOTT, Kevin W.	28/9/58	Sheffield United (Loan)	3/83	1982	9	0	2
ASH, Mark C.	22/1/68	Apprentice	1/86	86-88	14	6	0
ASHE, Norman J.	16/11/43	Aston Villa	3/63	1962	6	-	1
ATKINSON, Peter	14/12/49		5/69	1969	3	0	0
BADGER, Colin A.	16/6/30	Local	11/50	1950	2	-	0
BAMBRIDGE, Keith G.	1/9/35	Masborough St. Pauls	2/55	55-62	161	-	16
BANKS, Ian F.	9/1/61	Barnsley	7/92	92-93	76	0	7
BARNSLEY, Andrew	9/6/62	Denaby United	6/85	1985	28	0	0
		Sheffield United	12/88	88-90	77	6	3
BARRAS, Anthony	29/3/71	Stockport County (Loan)	2/94	1993	5	0	1
BARRICK, Dean	30/9/69	Sheffield Wednesday	2/91	90-92	96	3	7
BENNETT, Albert	16/7/44	Chester Moor Juniors	10/61	61-64	108	-	64
BENNETT, John	15/5/49	Apprentice	11/65	1965	1	0	0
BENTLEY, David A.	30/5/50	Apprentice	7/67	66-73	243	7	13
BETTANY, John W.	16/12/37	Barnsley	6/70	1970	16	0	1
BIRCH, Alan	12/8/56	Chesterfield	3/84	83-85	99	2	28
BLAIN, James D.	9/4/40	Southport	12/62	62-63	23	-	2
BLAKEMAN, Allan	2/11/37	Ashton United	5/58	1958	2	-	0
BOLTON, Ronald	1/9/21	Owen & Dyson	6/48	48-54	150	-	0
BOWER, Kenneth	18/3/26	Darlington	7/49	1949	27	-	11
BRADD, Leslie J.	6/11/47	Earl Sterndale	3/66	1967	3	0	0
BRECKIN, Ian	24/2/75	YTS	11/93	93-94	51	0	2
BRECKIN, John	27/7/53	Apprentice	11/71	71-82	405	4	8
BRIEN, Anthony J.	10/2/69	Chesterfield	10/93	93-94	41	2	2
BROADBENT, Albert H.	20/8/34	Sheffield Wednesday	12/57	57-58	48	-	13
BROGDEN, Lee	18/10/49	Ashley Road	12/67	67-71	79	8	16
BROWN, W. Dewis	4/6/19	Stockport County	8/50	1951	1	-	0
BROWN, Gordon A.	7/12/65	Apprentice	12/83	1983	1	0	0
BROWN, Graham C.	21/3/44	York City	2/80	79-80	31	0	0
BROWN, Robert	9/8/24	Barnsley	9/56	56-57	41	-	13
BUCKLEY, John W.	10/5/62	Leeds United	11/87	87-90	85	20	13
		Scunthorpe United	2/93	1992	2	2	0
BUCKLEY, Patrick M.	12/8/46	Sheffield United	6/72	1972	1	2	0
BUNCLARK, Cyril	27/3/31	Local	11/53	1954	2	-	1
BURGIN, Andrew	6/3/47	Sheffield Wednesday	8/67	1967	9	0	0
BURKE, Ronald S.	13/8/21	Huddersfield Town	3/53	52-54	73	-	54
BURNS, Barry	19/6/37	Dunscroft	10/54	1957	5	-	4
BUTLER, Ian	1/2/44	Apprentice	8/61	60-64	101	-	28
CALDWELL, David L.	7/5/32	Aberdeen	5/60	1960	1	-	0
CAMPBELL, David A.	2/6/65			1992	0	1	0
CAMPBELL, Winston R.	9/10/62	Barnsley	9/86	86-87	67	2	9
CARR, Peter	16/11/60	Apprentice	11/78	78-81	31	5	3
CARVER, David F.	16/4/44	Apprentice	1/62	61-64	83	-	0
CASH, Stuart P.	5/9/65	Nottingham Forest	3/90	1989	8	0	1
CASPER, Frank	9/12/44	Apprentice	7/62	62/66	101	1	26
CASSIDY, William P.	4/10/40	Glasgow Rangers	8/61	61-62	28	-	1
CHAMBERS, David M.	6/6/47	Apprentice	6/65	65-67	21	5	4
CHAPMAN, Roger A.	20/11/44	Local	7/65	1964	2	-	0
CHAPPELL, Leslie A.	6/2/47	Apprentice	2/65	65-67	109	2	36
CHURMS, Dennis J.	8/5/31	Spurley Hey	4/50	53-55	15	-	0
CLARKE, Matthew	3/11/73	YTS	7/92	92-94	83	1	0
CLISH, Colin	14/1/44	Newcastle United	12/63	63-67	130	0	4
CONROY, Steven H.	19/12/56	Sheffield United (N/C)	2/83	1982	5	0	0
COOPER, Douglas	18/10/36	Middlesbrough	1/59	1958	13	-	5
COWDRILL, Barry	3/1/57	West Brom. Alb. (Loan)	10/85	1985	2	0	0
CRAWFORD, Alan P.	30/10/53	Apprentice	10/71	73-78	233	4	49

MILLERMEN: 1946/47 - 1994/95   Crichton - Gregory

NAME	Born	Signed from:	Date	Played	Apps.	Sub.	Gls.
CRICHTON, Paul A.	3/10/65	Nottingham Forest (Loan)	3/88	1987	6	0	0
CRICKMORE, Charles A.	11/2/42	Gillingham	11/67	1967	7	1	1
CROSBY, Phillip A.	9/11/62	Grimsby Town	8/83	83-88	181	2	2
CULLEN, Anthony	30/9/69	Sunderland (Loan)	1/91	1990	3	0	1
CUNNINGHAM, Tony E.	12/11/59	Bolton Wanderers	8/91	91-92	65	4	24
CURRIE, David N.	27/11/62	Barnsley (Loan)	10/92	1992	5	0	2
CUSACK, David S.	6/6/56	Doncaster Rovers	12/87	1987	18	0	0
DARWIN, George H.	16/5/32	Derby County	10/60	1960	2	-	2
DAVISON, Robert	17/7/59	Sheffield United	10/94	1994	19	2	4
DAWSON, J.Reginald	4/10/14	Local	1/39	38-46	52	-	3
DAWSON, Richard	19/1/60	Apprentice	1/78	77-79	21	3	3
DELGADO, Robert A.	29/1/49	Carlisle United	12/73	73-75	69	1	5
DEMPSEY, Mark J.	14/1/64	Sheffield United	10/88	88-90	71	4	7
DERRETT, Stephen C.	16/10/47	Carlisle United	12/73	73-75	79	2	2
DIXON, Raymond	31/12/30	Denaby United	6/65	55-56	14	-	4
DOLBY, Christopher	4/9/74	YTS	8/93	93-94	0	3	0
DONOVAN, Terence C.	27/2/58	Burnley	9/83	83-84	9	4	0
DOUGLAS, Colin F.	9/9/62	Doncaster Rovers	7/86	86-87	82	1	4
DOWNES, Steven F.	2/12/49	Leeds M.D.B.C.	4/67	67-69	54	8	18
DUFFIELD, Peter	4/2/69	Sheffield United (loan)	3/91	1990	17	0	5
DUNGWORTH, John H.	30/3/55	Mansfield Town	2/84	83-87	177	11	16
DURHAM, Jonathan S.	12/6/65	Apprentice	6/83	1983	3	3	1
DURKIN, William	29/9/21	Bradford City	8/48	1948	2	-	0
EADES, Kevin M.	11/3/59	Apprentice	3/77	1975	1	0	0
EDWARDS, John F.	27/12/21	Manvers Main Colliery	9/44	46-53	296	-	9
ELEY, Kevin	4/3/68	Apprentice	3/86	83-86	3	10	0
EMERSON, Dean	27/12/62	Stockport County	7/85	85-86	55	0	8
EUSTACE, Peter	31/7/44	West Ham United (Loan)	3/72	1971	6	0	1
EVANS, Gareth J.	14/1/67	Coventry City	10/86	86-87	62	1	13
EVANS, Stewart J.	15/11/60	Plymouth Argyle	11/88	88-90	45	20	14
FANTHAM, John	6/2/39	Sheffield Wednesday	10/69	69-70	46	5	8
FARMER, Terence	11/5/31	Gainsborough Trinity	7/52	52-57	61	-	25
FARRELLY, Gareth	28/8/75	Aston Villa (Loan)	3/95	1994	9	1	2
FERGUSON, Edward B.	10/9/49	Dumbarton	2/71	70-73	64	3	5
FERN, Rodney A.	13/12/48	Chesterfield	6/79	79-82	98	7	34
FINNEY, Richard	14/3/56	Juniors	7/74	73-80	236	0	67
FLEETWOOD, Steven R.	27/2/62	Juniors	2/87	1986	0	1	0
FLOUNDERS, Andrew J.	13/12/63	Rochdale (Loan)	2/93	1992	6	0	2
FLYNN, John E.	20/3/48	Sheffield United	7/78	78-79	30	1	1
FLYNN, William	2/1/27	Maybold Juniors	7/49	1949	6	-	0
FORAN, Mark	30/10/73	Sheffield United (Loan)	8/94	1994	3	0	0
FORD, Stuart T.	20/7/71	YTS	7/89	89-91	5	0	0
FORREST, Gerald	21/1/57	South Bank	2/77	77-85	357	0	7
FOSTER, Robert J.	19/7/29	Preston N.E.	5/58	1958	1	-	0
FRIAR, J.Paul	6/6/63	Leicester City	2/83	82-83	20	0	0
FURNELL, James	23/11/37	Arsenal	9/68	68-69	76	0	0
GALLEY, John E.	7/5/44	Wolves	12/64	64-67	112	0	48
GEE, Alan A.	16/3/32	Amateur	8/52	1952	2	-	0
GIBSON, Alfred	9/9/19	Army	10/45	46-53	152	-	0
GILBERT, Carl G.	20/3/48	Bristol Rovers	3/71	70-73	78	16	37
GILLIVER, Alan H.	3/8/44	Blackburn Rovers	5/68	1968	23	3	2
GOATER, Shaun	25/2/70	Manchester United	10/89	89-94	125	40	52
GOODFELLOW, James	16/9/43	Workington	1/74	73-77	192	0	8
GOODING, Michael C.	12/4/59	Bishop Auckland	7/79	79-82	90	12	10
		Chesterfield	9/83	83-86	149	7	42
GOODWIN, Shaun	14/6/69	YTS	6/87	87-94	218	15	30
GOW, Gerald	29/5/52	Manchester City	1/82	81-82	58	0	4
GRAINGER, John (Jack)	3/4/24	Frickley Colliery	11/45	47-56	352	-	110
GREALISH, Anthony P.	21/9/56	Manchester City	8/87	87-89	105	5	7
GREEN, John R.	7/8/58	Apprentice	3/76	75-83	247	1	8
		Darlington	12/86	86-88	84	1	3
GREGORY, Charles F.			2/47	1946	1	-	0

MILLERMEN: 1946/47 - 1994/95

NAME	Born	Signed from:	Date	Played	Apps.	Sub.	Gls.
GRIDELET, Phillip R.	30/4/67	Barnsley (Loan)	3/93	1992	9	0	0
GRIFFIN, William	24/9/40	Workington	1/69	68-69	14	3	1
GUEST, Gladstone	26/6/17	Rawmarsh Welfare	12/39	46-55	356	-	130
GUNTHORPE, Kenneth	4/11/38		5/58	1958	2	-	0
GWYTHER, David J.A.	6/12/48	Halifax Town	2/76	75-79	162	0	45
HABBIN, Richard L.	6/1/49	Reading	1/75	74-77	79	5	19
HADDOCK, Andrew	5/5/46	Falkirk	12/66	1966	4	0	0
HAGUE, Neil	1/12/49	Apprentice	12/66	67-71	135	11	23
HAINSWORTH, Leonard	25/1/18	Local	3/39	38-47	32	-	8
HALOM, Victor L.	3/10/48	Oldham Athletic	2/80	79-80	19	1	2
HAM, Robert S.	29/3/42	Preston North End	10/71	71-72	67	1	24
HANSON, Frederick	23/5/15	Crystal Palace	3/36	35-46	106	-	28
HARDY, Robin	18/1/41	Sheffield Wednesday	2/65	64-65	41	0	2
HARGREAVES, Wilf O.	15/12/21	Rawmarsh Welfare	3/45	46-47	3	-	0
HARRITY, Michael D.	5/10/46	Local	10/65	65-68	36	3	0
HART, Harold	29/9/26	Local	12/45	1949	10	-	3
HASELDEN, John J.	3/8/43	Denaby United	2/62	61-68	100	2	0
HASLAM, Graham	29/4/56	Apprentice	4/74	1975	2	0	0
HATHAWAY, Ian A.	22/8/68	Mansfield Town	3/91	90-91	5	8	1
HAYCOCK, T.Paul	8/7/62	Burton Albion	8/86	86-89	77	20	22
HAYNES, Eric	18/6/36	Thorncliffe	4/56	1955	1	-	0
HAYWARD, Andrew	21/6/70	Frickley Athletic	8/94	1994	33	4	6
HAZEL, Desmond L.	15/7/67	Sheffield Wednesday	7/88	88-94	204	34	28
HEARD, T.Patrick	17/3/60	Hull City	7/88	88-89	41	3	7
HELLAWELL, John R.	20/12/43	Bradford City	1/65	64-65	5	1	2
HELLIWELL, Ian	7/11/62	Scunthorpe United	8/93	93-94	47	5	4
HENDERSON, Anthony	14/1/54	Apprentice	1/72	1973	5	1	0
HENDERSON, John S.P.	13/10/23	Third Lanark	11/53	53-54	47	-	7
HENSON, Phillip M.	30/3/53	Stockport County	2/80	79-83	87	5	7
HILL, Alan	3/11/43	Barnsley	6/66	66-68	82	0	0
HODGES, Mark	24/10/71	YTS	7/90	1990	3	1	0
HODGSON, William	9/7/35	Derby County	9/67	1967	9	0	0
HORNER, Phillip M.	10/11/66	Leicester City (Loan)	3/86	1985	3	1	0
HOUGHTON, Kenneth	18/10/39	Silverwood Colliery	5/60	60-64	148	-	56
HOUGHTON, William	20/2/39	Leicester City	1/70	69-73	139	0	1
HOWARD, Jonathan	7/10/71	YTS	7/90	90-93	25	11	5
HUDSON, Christopher B.	13/3/51	Apprentice	3/86	68-71	53	9	1
HUGHES, Emlyn W.	28/8/47	Wolves	9/81	81-82	55	1	6
HUGHES, Harold A.	12/8/37	Local	6/59	1959	1	-	0
HUNTER, John S.	26/5/34	Coltness United	6/56	1956	5	-	1
HURST, Paul	25/9/74	YTS	8/93	93-94	11	6	0
HUSSEY, Malcolm F.	11/9/33	Juniors	4/52	52-55	24	-	0
HUTCHINGS, Chris	5/7/57	Walsall	7/91	91-93	76	2	4
IBBOTSON, Dennis	4/12/20	Roth. Y.M.C.A. (Am.)	11/46	1946	4	-	0
IRONSIDE, Roy	28/5/35	Juniors	7/54	56-64	220	-	0
JACKSON, Brian	2/2/36	Maltby Main Colliery	9/54	55-64	131	-	6
JACKSON, Richard G.	13/12/32	York City	7/56	1956	1	-	0
JACOBS, Wayne G.	3/2/69	Hull City	8/93	1993	40	2	2
JAMES, Martin J.	18/5/71	Stockport County	8/94	1994	40	0	0
JENKINSON, Leigh	9/7/69	Hull City (Loan)	9/90	1990	5	2	0
JOHNSON, Nigel M.	23/6/64	Apprentice	6/82	82-84	89	0	1
		Manchester City	7/87	87-92	172	3	9
JOHNSON, Peter	31/7/31	Rawmarsh Welfare	3/53	53-57	153	-	23
JOHNSON, Rodney	8/1/45	Doncaster Rovers	12/70	70-73	108	2	8
JONES, Glyn	8/4/36	Sheffield United	12/57	57-58	22	-	6
JONES, Rodney E.	23/9/45	Ashton United	6/65	65-66	35	0	0
JORDAN, Brian A.	31/1/32	Denaby United	7/53	53-58	38	-	0
KETTLEBOROUGH, Keith F.	29/6/35	Rotherham Y.M.C.A.	12/55	55-60	119	-	20
KEYWORTH, Kenneth	24/2/34	Wolves	1/52	55-57	85	-	7
KILMORE, Kevin	11/11/59	Grimsby Town	8/83	83-84	82	2	20
KIRKMAN, Alan J.	21/6/36	Manchester City	3/59	58-63	143	-	58

NAME	Born	Signed from:	Date	Played	Apps.	Sub.	Gls.
KITE, Phillip D.	26/10/62	Sheffield United (Loan)	10/92	1992	1	0	0
KIWOMYA, Andrew D.	1/10/67	Dundee	8/93	1993	4	3	0
LAMBERT, Roy	16/7/33	Thorncliffe Colliery	7/54	56-64	306	-	6
LANCASTER, Raymond	17/8/41	Juniors	11/58	60-64	66	-	2
LAW, Nicholas	8/9/61	Notts County	7/90	90-93	126	2	3
LAYNE, David R.	29/7/39	Juniors	7/57	57-58	11	-	4
LEGGAT, Graham	20/6/34	Birmingham City	7/68	1968	13	3	7
LEIGH, Dennis	26/2/49	Doncaster Rovers	2/68	67-72	154	5	10
LENG, Michael	14/6/52	Apprentice	7/71	71-75	94	7	2
LEWIS, Michael	26/8/50	Apprentice	12/67	1967	0	1	0
LILL, David A.	17/2/47	Hull City	10/69	67-70	33	7	5
LODGE, Paul	13/2/61	Everton (Loan)	1/83	1982	4	0	0
LONGDEN, Colin	21/7/33	Juniors	8/50	1952	3	-	0
LOWDER, Thomas W.	17/10/24	Crystal Palace	8/47	1948	8	-	5
LYONS, Barry	14/3/45	Juniors	9/62	63-66	125	0	24
McALISTER, Thomas G.	10/12/52	Sheffield United	1/76	75-78	159	0	0
McBRIDE, Joseph	17/8/60	Everton	8/82	82-83	45	0	12
McCOLE, John	18/9/36	Bradford City	12/62	1962	14	-	5
McDONAGH, James M.	6/10/52	Apprentice	10/70	70-75	121	0	0
McEWAN, William J.M.	20/6/51	Peterborough United	7/79	79-83	86	9	10
McFADZEAN, John P.	2/4/66	Apprentice	6/82	1983	0	1	0
McGINLEY, John	11/6/59	Lincoln City	9/86	1986	1	2	0
McGLASHAN, John	3/6/67	Peterborough United	11/94	1994	27	0	3
McGOLDRICK, Thomas	20/9/29	Maltby	11/49	1951	5	-	2
McILMOYLE, Hugh	29/1/40	Leicester City	7/62	1962	12	-	4
McINNES, Ian	22/3/67	Apprentice	9/84	83-84	6	3	0
McKNIGHT, Allen D.	27/1/64	Stockport County (N/C)	10/91	1991	3	0	0
McLEAN, Stewart D.	30/8/23	Partick Thistle	5/46	46-47	35	-	18
McMAHON, Hugh	24/9/09	Hartlepool United	9/47	47-48	59	-	8
MADDEN, Peter	31/10/34	Thornton	10/55	55-56	308	2	7
MARGINSON, Karl	11/11/10	Ashton United	3/93	92-94	11	4	1
MARSDEN, James	10/4/28	Parkgate W.	8/52	52-54	12	-	2
MARSHALL, Frank	26/1/29	Scarborough	5/51	51-56	118	-	5
MARSHALL, John J.	12/2/49	Ross County	9/68	1968	4	0	0
MARSHALL, Scott	1/5/73	Arsenal (Loan)	12/93	1993	10	0	1
MARTIN, Michael P.	9/7/51	Peterborough United	8/85	1985	5	0	0
MASSEY, Roy	10/9/43	Local	7/64	64-66	15	1	6
MATTHEWS, Paul W.	30/9/46	Mansfield Town	10/77	1977	8	0	0
MEADOWS, Frank	27/6/33	Local	4/52	53-55	8	-	0
MEALAND, K.Barry	24/1/43	Fulham	8/68	68-69	44	1	0
MENDONCA, Clive P.	9/9/68	Sheffield United	3/88	87-90	71	13	27
MERCER, William	22/5/69	Liverpool	2/89	89-94	104	0	0
MIELCZAREK, Raymond	10/2/46	Huddersfield Town	1/71	70-73	114	1	7
MILLS, Henry	23/7/22	Sheffield United	3/48	1947	7	-	5
MIMMS, Robert A.	12/10/63	Halifax Town	11/81	81-84	83	0	0
MITCHELL, Robert	4/1/55	Carlisle United	3/83	82-84	86	9	2
MONINGTON, Mark D.	21/10/70	Burnley	11/94	1994	25	0	2
MOORE, Robert	14/12/32	Worksop Town	5/55	55-56	19	-	2
MOORE, Ronald D.	29/1/53	Cardiff City	8/80	80-83	124	1	51
MORGAN, Laurie (Lol).	5/5/31	Hudderfield Town	8/54	54-63	290	-	0
MORRIS, Andrew D.	17/11/67	Juniors	7/85	84-86	0	7	0
MORRITT, Gordon R.	8/2/42	Steel Peech & Tozer	6/61	61-65	77	0	0
MOSBY, Harold	25/6/26	Huddersfield Town	1/47	47-49	25	-	9
MOUNTFORD, Raymond	28/4/58	Manchester United	7/78	78-82	123	0	0
MULLEN, James	16/3/47	Charlton Athletic	2/69	68-73	173	3	24
MULLEN, James W.	8/11/52	Sheffield Wednesday	8/80	80-81	49	0	1
MURPHY, Paul	16/3/54	Ashington	2/72	1973	1	0	0
MYERSCOUGH, H.William	22/6/30	Aston Villa	7/59	1959	39	-	11
NEILSON, Stephen B.	25/4/31		7/55	1956	9	-	0
NEWCOMBE, Giles A.	9/7/68	YTS	6/87	1986	6	0	0

NAME	Born	Signed from:	Date	Played	Apps.	Sub.	Gls.
NIX, Peter	25/1/58	Juniors	8/76	77-79	22	0	2
NOBLE, Norman	8/823	Ransome & Marles	5/48	48-57	326	-	21
O'DELL, Andrew	2/1/63	Grimsby Town	8/83	83-84	16	2	0
O'GRADY, Michael	11/10/42	Wolves	11/72	72-73	24	0	2
O'HANLON, Kelham G.	16/5/62	Middlesbrough	8/85	85-90	248	0	0
O'HARA, Edward A.	28/10/35	Everton	2/60	59-60	20	-	3
OGDEN, Christopher J.	3/2/53	Swindon Town	11/79	1979	3	0	0
OWEN, Gordon	14/6/59	Sheffield Wed. (Loan)	3/80	1979	9	0	0
PAGE, Donald R.	18/1/64	Wigan Athletic	8/91	91-93	40	15	13
PARKER, Graham S.	23/5/46	Aston Villa	12/67	1967	3	1	0
PARTRIDGE, Cyril	12/10/31	Queens Park Rangers	8/57	1957	7	-	2
PEARSON, John S.	1/9/63	Leeds United (Loan)	3/91	1990	11	0	5
PEEL, Nathan J.	17/5/72	Burnley (Loan)	3/95	1994	9	0	4
PELL, Dennis	19/4/29	Methley	5/52	52-55	12	-	3
PEPPER, Nigel C.	25/4/68	Apprentice	4/86	85-89	35	10	1
PERRY, Arthur	15/10/32	Bradford Park Avenue	7/58	1958	2	-	0
PERRY, Peter	11/4/36	Treeton R.R.	7/56	57-61	97	-	12
PHILLIPS, Trevor	18/9/52	Apprentice	3/70	69-78	289	33	81
PHILISKIRK, Anthony	10/2/65	Sheffield United (Loan)	10/86	1986	6	0	1
PICKERING, Albert G.	22/6/67	Buxton	2/90	89-93	87	1	2
PICKERING, Michael J.	29/9/56	Sheffield Wednesday	1/84	83-85	102	0	1
PIKE, Martin R.	21/10/64	Fulham	8/94	1994	7	0	0
PILKINGTON, George	3/6/26	Great Houghton	11/48	1949	1	-	0
PRING, Keith D.	11/3/43	Newport County	10/64	64-67	80	2	6
PUGH, Daral J.	5/6/61	Huddersfield Town	7/85	85-87	106	6	6
PUGH, David	22/1/47	Halifax Town	7/76	76-78	57	1	0
QUAIRNEY, John	7/1/27	Girvan Juniors	7/48	48-59	260	-	0
QUINN, John D.	30/5/38	Sheffield Wednesday	11/67	67-71	114	0	7
RABJOHN, Christopher S.	10/3/45	Juniors	7/63	65-67	76	2	4
RADFORD, Arthur (Alf)	7/10/25	Local	5/47	47-49	44	-	0
RAWSON, Colin	12/11/26	Peterborough United	7/48	49-52	113	-	12
RAYNES, John	4/11/28	Sheffield United	3/49	1949	5	-	1
RAYNES, William	30/10/64	Heanor Town	9/83	83-84	17	3	2
REESON, M.Anthony	24/9/33	Juniors	11/53	1954	4	-	1
REGAN, James	7/12/27	Moorthorpe Colliery	8/49	51-52	12	-	0
RHODES, Mark N.	26/8/57	Apprentice	8/75	75-84	235	23	13
RICHARDSON, Ian P.	9/5/64	Watford (Loan)	2/85	1984	5	0	2
RICHARDSON, Neil T.	3/3/68	Brandon United	7/82	89-94	94	8	4
RICKETT, Walter	20/3/17	Sheffield Wednesday	9/52	1952	28	-	4
ROBERTS, Glyn	19/10/74	Norwich City	8/93	93-94	11	5	1
ROBINSON, Eric M.	1/7/35	West Bromwich Albion	1/59	58-59	14	-	1
ROBINSON, Frederick J.	29-12/54	Apprentice	1/73	1973	4	0	0
ROBINSON, Ronald	22/10/66	West Bromwich Albion	8/89	89-91	86	0	2
ROSCOE, Andrew	4/6/73	Bolton Wanderers	2/95	1994	31	0	4
RUDD, J.James	25-10-19	Leeds United	10/49	49-51	75	-	10
RUSSELL, William M.	19/9/59	Scunthorpe Unted	8/88	88-91	103	2	2
SANDERSON, Eric	10/11/21	Paramore	9/47	1947	2	-	1
SAWYER, Brian	28/1/38	Rawmarsh Welfare	1/58	57-62	92	-	31
SCOTT, Martin	7/1/68	Apprentice	1/86	84-90	93	1	3
SCRIVENS, Williams	26/5/36	Local	8/56	1956	3	-	0
SEASMAN, John	21/2/55	Millwall	8/80	80-83	93	7	25
SEDDON, Thomas	25/10/35	Local	3/54	1958	1	-	0
SELKIRK, John (Jack)	20/1/23	Edlington Colliery	10/44	46-56	427	-	12
SHAW, John S. (Jack)	10/4/24	Yorkshire Main Colliery	4/45	46-52	262	-	124
SHEFFIELD, Laurence J.	27/4/39	Norwich City	8/67	1967	19	0	7
SHEPHERD, John A.	20/9/45	Local	4/66	65-67	21	2	2
SILMAN, Roy	12/5/34	Edlington Colliery	4/52	52-59	105	-	1
SIMMONS, Anthony J.	9/2/65	Queens Park Rangers	3/84	83-86	85	11	27
SIMPSON, Kenneth	12/6/31	Ransome & Marles	9/55	55-57	7	-	0
SIMPSON, Owen	18/9/43		10/62	64-66	6	0	0

NAME	Born	Signed from:	Date	Played	Apps.	Sub.	Gls.
SJOBERG, John	12/6/41	Leicester City	6/73	1973	6	0	0
SLACK, Trevor C.	26/9/62	Peterborough United	8/86	1986	14	1	1
SLATER, J.Brian	20/10/32	Grimsby Town	9/55	1956	17	-	5
SMITH, E.Colin	3/3/36	Hull City	6/60	1960	9	-	3
SMITH, David	8/12/47	Lincoln City	7/78	78-79	32	1	3
SMITH, Ian R.	15/2/57	Tottenham Hotspur	6/76	1977	3	1	0
SMITH, Kevan	13/12/59	Darlington	7/85	85-86	59	0	4
SMITH, Scott	6/3/75	YTS	10/93	93-94	10	1	0
SNODIN, Glynn	14/2/60	Leeds United (Loan)	2/92	1991	3	0	0
SPENCER, Thomas H.	28/11/45	Lincoln City	7/74	74-77	137	1	10
SPOONER, Stephen A.	25/1/61	York City	7/90	1990	15	4	1
STANBRIDGE, George	28/3/20		11/38	46-48	36	-	1
STANCLIFFE, Paul I.	5/5/58	Apprentice	3/76	75-82	285	0	8
		Sheffield United (Loan)	9/90	1990	5	0	0
STEPHENS, Malcolm K.	17/2/30	Brighton & Hove Albion	7/57	1957	12	-	3
STEPHENSON, Roy A.	27/5/32	Burnley	9/56	56-57	43	-	14
STEVENSON, Alan	6/11/50	Burnley	8/83	1983	24	0	0
STONE, John G.	3/3/53	Grimsby Town	9/83	1983	10	0	1
STORRIE, James	31/3/40	Aberdeen	12/67	67-69	70	1	19
STOWELL, Bruce	20/9/41	Bradford City	7/72	1972	14	2	0
STREET, John	30/5/28	Liverpool (AM)	7/47	1947	2	-	0
SURMAN, Leslie	23/11/47	Charlton Athletic	6/66	1966	1	0	0
SWANN, Gordon	7/12/37	Local	7/57	58-60	10	-	2
SWIFT, Trevor	14/9/48	Juniors	9/65	67-74	283	4	21
TAYLOR, Andrew	19/1/73	YTS	6/91	90-92	17	1	0
TAYLOR, Ashley	11/12/59	Apprentice	12/77	79-81	21	1	0
TAYLOR, Brian J.	24/3/37	Birmingham City	10/61	61-62	44	-	5
THOMPSON, Ronald	24/12/21	Sheffield Wednesday	5/47	47-48	30	-	11
THOMPSON, Simon L.	27/2/70	YTS	6/88	88-90	12	16	0
THOMPSON, William	5/1/40	Newcastle United	6/67	1967	8	0	0
TILER, Brian	15/3/43	Local	7/62	62-68	212	0	27
TILER, Kenneth D.	23/5/50	Brighton & Hove Albion	7/79	79-80	45	1	1
TODD, Mark K.	4/12/67	Sheffield United	9/91	91-94	92	4	9
TODD, Robert C.	11/9/49	Liverpool	3/68	1968	2	4	0
TOMLINSON, Charles C.	2/12/19	Sheffield Wednesday	3/51	50-51	32	-	12
TOMLINSON, David I.	13/12/68	Sheffield Wednesday	8/87	1987	6	3	0
TOWNER, Anthony J.	2/5/55	Millwall	8/80	80-82	108	0	12
TRUSSON, Michael S.	26/5/59	Sheffield United	12/83	83-86	124	0	19
TUNKS, Roy W.	21/1/51	Apprentice	3/68	67-73	138	0	0
TWIDLE, Kenneth G.	10/10/31	Retford Town	12/57	57-58	24	-	6
TYNAN, Thomas E.	17/11/55	Plymouth Argyle	7/85	85-86	32	0	13
VARADI, Imre	8/7/59	Leeds United	3/93	92-94	55	12	25
VAUGHAN, Ian	3/7/61	Apprentice	7/79	79-80	5	0	0
WAGSTAFF, Barry	28/11/45	Reading	3/75	74-76	42	3	1
WALKER, Phillip A.	27/1/57	Chesterfield	12/82	82-83	20	5	3
WARBURTON, Raymond	7/10/67	Apprentice	10/85	84-86	3	1	0
WARNER, Dennis P.A.	6/12/30	Spurley Hey O.B.	3/50	52-56	64	-	0
WARNES, George	4/12/25	Dinnington	12/44	46-49	98	-	0
WARNOCK, Neil	1/12/48	Chesterfield	6/69	69-70	46	8	5
WATERHOUSE, Kenneth	23/1/30	Preston North End	5/58	58-62	115	-	11
WATLING, Barry J.	16/7/46	Hartlepool United (Loan)	12/75	1975	5	0	0
WATSON, David V.	5/10/46	Notts County	1/68	67-79	121	0	20
WATSON, Graham S.	3/8/49	Doncaster Rovers	2/68	67-68	13	0	0
WATTS, Julian D.	17/3/71	Frecheville C.A.	7/90	90-91	17	3	1
WEAKLEY, Bernard	20/12/32	Local	8/55	1955	2	-	1
WEBSTER, J.Barry	3/3/35	Gainsborough Trinity	5/56	56-61	180	-	37
WESTON, Donald P.	6/3/36	Birmingham City	12/60	60-62	76	-	21
WHITE, Leonard R.	23/3/30	Upton Colliery	5/48	50-52	43	-	14
WHITEHEAD, Norman J.	22/4/48	Rochdale	3/72	71/72	29	4	2
WHITTAM, Ernest A.	7/1/11	Reading	4/45	1946	1	-	0
WHITWORTH, Neil	12/4/72	Manchester United (Loan)	10/93	1993	8	0	1

MILLERMEN: 1946/47 - 1994/95

NAME	Born	Signed from:	Date	Played	Apps.	Sub.	Gls.
WIGG, Ronald G.	18/5/49	Watford	3/73	72-74	65	0	22
WILCOCKSON, Harold	23/7/43		7/63	64-67	108	0	3
WILCOX, George E.	23/8/17	Derby County	8/48	1948	1	-	0
WILDER, Christopher	23/9/67	Sheffield United	7/92	92-94	111	3	11
WILKINSON, William	24/3/43	Hull City	11/72	72-73	25	1	0
WILLIAMS, Andrew	29/7/62	Coventry City	10/86	86-88	87	0	13
		Notts County	10/93	93-94	51	0	2
WILLIAMS, Carey			8/94	1994	0	2	0
WILLIAMS, Daniel T.	20/11/24	Silverwood Colliery	10/43	46-59	459	-	19
WILLIAMS, Horace O.	4/10/21	Thurcroft Colliery	1/43	46-53	210	-	12
WILLIAMS, Kenneth	7/1/27	Local	9/48	1949	3	-	0
WILLIAMS, G.Robert	18/11/32	Juniors	7/50	1953	4	-	2
WILLIAMS, Robert G.	17/2/40	Bristol City	2/65	64-66	47	0	12
WILLIAMSON, Robert	13/8/61	West Bromwich Albion	7/88	88-90	91	2	49
WILSON, Albert	28/1/15	Mansfield Town	6/46	1946	38	-	19
WILSON, Alexander	3/7/38	Clyde	7/61	1961	5	-	0
WILSON, Andrew P.	13/10/47	Local	6/67	1967	12	4	3
WILSON, John G. (Ian)	11/2/23	Chesterfield	5/53	53-55	108	-	44
WILSON, Robert I.	5/6/61	Huddersfield T.	9/91	1991	11	3	3
WINN, Stephen	16/9/59		3/78	78-80	17	7	3
WOMBLE, Trevor	7/6/51	Apprentice	10/68	68-77	185	28	39
WOODALL, John B.	16/1/49	Gainsborough Trinity	3/74	73-74	25	1	6
WRAGG, Peter	12/1/31	Juniors	5/48	48-52	31	-	4
WREN, John	26/4/36	Hibernian	8/60	1960	1	-	0
WRIGHT, Patrick D.J.	17/11/40	Derby County	9/70	1970	1	0	0
WYLDE, Rodger J.	8/3/54	Barnsley (Loan)	3/88	1987	6	0	1
YOUNG, Thomas	24/12/47	Tranmere Rovers	7/77	77-78	11	4	1

KEY

Played: The year shown is the first year of the season played. Thus, 1979 indicates the season 1970-80, "79-85" means that the player made his debut in 1979-80 and his last appearance in 1985-86, but does not mean necessarily that he played in every intervening season.

Loan: The player was signed on loan from the club in brackets.

N/C: The player was a non-contract signing.

Junior: Junior players signed from school/college, without serving an apprenticeship or trainee period.

Apprentice: Apprentice signing prior to 1986.

YTS: Trainee. This rank was introduced in 1986 and indicates players sponsored by the Government's Youth Training Scheme.

These records relate to Football League games only.

STATISTICAL NOTES

The seasonal statistical pages that follow have been designed for easy reference, and are generally self explanatory, however the following notes are added to avoid confusion:

Left hand (first) column: Signifies the League match number, or the round number in a Cup Competition (Q = qualifying round, R = round proper - e.g. 1R = 1st round proper, Rr = round replay - e.g. 2Rr = 2nd round replay, 2R2r = 2nd round 2nd replay, L = Leg - e.g. 1R1L = 1st round first leg, SF = Semi-final, F = Final). Second column: Provides the date (Months abbreviated). Third column: Provides the opposition ('Home' matches in upper case - capital letters). Fourth column: ('Res.') Is the final score. Fifth column: ('Att.') The attendance (where known). Sixth column: The goalscorers (where known). O.G. indicates a goal scored by an opposition player.

The numbers used in the charts refer to the normally accepted position for that period - 'X' indicates a team member, but position unknown (numbered shirts did not appear until the 1939-40 season), e.g. 1 = goalkeeper, 2 = right-back ...., 11 = left-winger, etc. Substitutes are included, i.e. 12 and/or 14. Where used, 12 replaced the asterisk suffixed player (e.g. 4*), and 14 replaced the 'hash' suffixed player (e.g. 6#).

SEASON 1893/94
DIVISION TWO (ROTHERHAM TOWN)

Players (columns): McKay H., Watson P., Thickett H., Barr J., Brown H., Broadhead W., Pickering A., McCormick J.J., Leatherbarrow C., Cutts E., Longden W., Williamson J., Allen W., Turner F. (Snr.), Heppenstall F., Wharton A., Wheatcroft E., Macbeth I., Dawson F., Rae F., Smith J., Simmonite H., Rodgers A., Simpson F., Turner F. (Jun.), Hobson W., Bartlett A.E., Hill W., Sylvester W., Fairburn A., Ledger R., Nesbitt J., McLean D., Leather R., Hawke W.

No.	Date	Opposition	Res.	Att.	Goalscorers
1	2 Sep	Lincoln City	1-1	2500	?
2	4	Small Heath	3-4		McCormick(2), Cutts
3	9	GRIMSBY TOWN	4-3		Cutts(2), Allen, Leatherbarrow
4	16	NOTTS COUNTY	0-2		
5	26	Walsall	0-3		
6	30	Burton Swifts	1-4		McCormick
7	21 Oct	Port Vale	3-2		Cutts, Dawson, Leatherbarrow
8	28	PORT VALE	0-1		
9	11 Nov	BURTON SWIFTS	2-4		Leatherbarrow, Longden
10	13	Arsenal	0-3		
11	2 Dec	LINCOLN CITY	2-8		Cutts, Rodgers
12	9	Middlesbrough I.	1-6	*	Turner Jnr.
13	26	Ardwick	2-3		Fairburn, Sylvester
14	30	NORTHWICH VIC.	5-4		Cutts(2), McCormick, Rae, ?
15	6 Jan	LIVERPOOL	1-4		Turner Jnr.
16	11	Notts County	2-4		McCormick, Rae
17	13	Liverpool	1-5		Turner Jnr.
18	20	NEWCASTLE U.	2-1		Fairburn, McCormick
19	27	Crewe Alex.	0-2		
20	3 Feb	WALSALL	3-2		Broadhead, Fairburn, Rae
21	6	ARSENAL	1-1		Barr
22	10	Grimsby Town	1-7		?
23	17	Newcastle U.	0-4		
24	23	BIRMINGHAM	2-3		Rae, Wheatcroft
25	26	ARDWICK	1-3		Broadhead
26	31	Northwich Vic.	1-1		Leather
27	9 Apr	CREWE ALEX.	1-4		?
28	14	MIDDLESBROUGH I.	4-1		?

Apps: 7 8 10 28 11 26 7 15 10 22 19 2 1 16 1 20 5 2 6 19 1 15 8 1 6 15 4 1 6 10 1 10 2 3 1
Goals: 1 2 6 3 7 1 1 1 1 4 1 1 3 1 3 1

* Played with 10 men.

SEASON 1894/95
DIVISION TWO (ROTHERHAM TOWN)

Players (columns): Lilley J.W., Porteous T., Broadhead W., Longden W., Brown H., Manson D.G., Cutts E., Bryant W., McCormick J., Walker W., Clements J.E., Hobson W., Cross E., Croxon W., Ackroyd W., Nixon A., Porteous D., Widdowson F., Coupar J., Turner F., Reid W., Parkinson R., Wheatcroft E., Wilkinson W.

No.	Date	Opposition	Res.	Att.	Goalscorers
1	1 Sep	BURTON WANDERERS	1-3	3000	McCormick
2	8	Leicester Fosse	2-4		Bryant, McCormick
3	15	LINCOLN CITY	5-2	2000	McCrmck(2), Ackryd, Clemnts, Croxn
4	18	Bury	1-2	2000	Ackroyd
5	22	Crewe Alexandra	1-2		Longden
6	24	Walsall	2-1		McCormick(2)
7	1 Oct	MANCHESTER CITY	3-2		McCormick(2), Manson
8	6	Burton Wanderers	0-4		
9	20	Arsenal	1-2		McCormick
10	27	Grimsby Town	1-4		D.Porteous
11	5 Nov	NOTTS COUNTY	1-2		Manson
12	6	BURY	2-3		Coupar, McCormick
13	10	Newton Heath	2-3		Coupar, McCormick
14	17	WALSALL	6-1		Brynt(2), Coupr, Clemnts, Mson, D.Prteous
15	15 Dec	Newcastle United	2-5		Bryant(2)
16	25	Lincoln City	0-2		
17	26	NEWCASTLE UNITED	1-0		?
18	29	BURTON SWIFTS	4-1		Coupar(2), Parkinson, Reid
19	1 Jan	Manchester City	0-1		
20	7	GRIMSBY TOWN	3-2		Coupar, McCormick, Parkinson
21	12	NEWTON HEATH	2-1	1500	Coupar, Reid
22	26	LEICESTER FOSSE	0-1		
23	9 Feb	Arsenal	1-1	2000	Manson
24	16	Port Vale	1-1		Bryant
25	2 Mar	PORT VALE	2-1	1000	Bryant(2)
26	9	Darwen	3-4	2000	Clements, Coupar, D.Porteous
27	16	Notts County	2-4	2000	Ackroyd, Bryant
28	30	Burton Swifts	0-2	2000	
29	13 Apr	DARWEN	4-1		Parkinson(2), Bryant, Coupar
30	15	CREWE ALEXANDRA	2-0		?

Apps: 9 30 7 29 5 19 2 28 22 1 27 6 2 9 16 20 21 24 20 1 16 13 2 1
Goals: 1 4 10 12 3 1 3 3 9 2 4

Final League Table 1893/94

Pl		Home W	D	L	F	A	Away W	D	L	F	A	F.	A.	Pts
1	Liverpool	28 14	0	0	46	8	8	6	0	31	12	77	18	50
2	Small Heath	28 12	0	2	68	19	9	0	5	35	25	103	44	42
3	Notts County	28 12	1	1	55	14	6	2	6	15	17	70	31	39
4	Newcastle United	28 12	1	1	44	10	3	5	6	22	29	66	39	36
5	Grimsby Town	28 11	1	2	47	16	4	1	9	24	42	71	58	32
6	Burton Swifts	28 9	1	4	52	26	5	2	7	27	35	79	61	31
7	Burslem Port Vale	28 10	2	2	43	20	3	2	9	23	44	66	64	30
8	Lincoln City	28 5	4	5	31	22	6	2	6	28	36	59	58	28
9	Woolwich Arsenal	28 9	1	4	33	19	3	3	8	19	36	52	55	28
10	Walsall Town Swifts	28 8	1	5	36	22	2	1	10	15	38	51	61	22
11	Middlesbro Ironopolis	28 7	4	3	27	20	1	0	13	10	52	37	72	20
12	Crewe Alexandra	28 3	3	4	27	23	3	0	11	20	51	47	71	18
13	Ardwick	28 6	1	7	32	20	2	1	11	15	51	47	71	18
14	Rotherham Town	28 5	1	8	28	42	1	2	11	16	49	44	91	15
15	Northwich Victoria	28 3	3	11	17	34	0	0	14	13	64	30	98	9

Final League Table 1894/95

Pl		Home W	D	L	F	A	Away W	D	L	F	A	F.	A.	Pts
1	Bury	30 15	0	0	48	11	8	2	5	30	22	78	33	48
2	Notts County	30 12	1	2	50	15	5	5	5	25	30	75	45	39
3	Newton Heath	30 9	6	0	52	18	6	2	7	26	26	78	44	38
4	Leicester Fosse	30 11	2	2	45	20	4	6	5	27	33	72	53	38
5	Grimsby Town	30 14	0	1	51	16	4	1	10	28	36	79	52	37
6	Darwen	30 13	1	1	53	10	3	3	9	21	38	74	43	36
7	Burton Wanderers	30 10	3	2	49	9	4	4	7	18	30	67	39	35
8	Woolwich Arsenal	30 11	3	1	54	20	3	2	10	21	38	75	58	34
9	Manchester City	30 11	3	1	56	28	3	0	12	26	44	82	72	31
10	Newcastle United	30 11	1	3	51	28	1	2	12	21	56	72	84	27
11	Burton Swifts	30 10	0	5	37	22	1	2	12	18	54	55	62	24
12	Rotherham Town	30 10	0	5	37	32	1	2	12	18	40	55	62	24
13	Lincoln City	30 8	0	7	32	27	2	0	13	12	67	47	92	20
14	Walsall Town Swfts	30 8	3	4	35	25	2	0	13	12	67	47	92	20
15	Burslem Port Vale	30 6	3	6	30	23	1	1	13	9	54	39	77	18
16	Crewe Alexandra	30 6	3	6	28	34	0	4	11	18	69	26	103	10

Final League Table 1895/96

Pl		Home W	D	L	F	A	Away W	D	L	F	A	F.	A.	Pts
1	Liverpool	30 14	1	0	65	11	8	1	6	41	21	106	32	46
2	Manchester City	30 12	3	0	37	9	9	1	5	26	29	63	38	46
3	Grimsby Town	30 14	0	1	51	9	6	1	8	31	29	82	38	42
4	Burton Wanderers	30 12	1	2	43	15	7	3	5	26	35	69	40	42
5	Newcastle United	30 14	0	1	57	14	2	1	11	16	42	66	57	33
6	Newton Heath	30 12	2	1	48	15	3	1	11	18	42	66	57	33
7	Woolwich Arsenal	30 11	1	3	42	11	3	3	9	16	31	58	42	32
8	Leicester Fosse	30 10	0	5	40	16	4	4	7	17	28	57	44	32
9	Darwen	30 11	2	2	55	23	2	0	13	17	45	72	67	30
10	Notts County	30 8	1	6	41	22	4	1	10	16	32	57	54	26
11	Burton Swifts	30 7	3	5	32	25	2	1	11	8	41	40	66	23
12	Loughborough	30 7	1	7	36	24	2	3	10	15	53	51	75	22
13	Lincoln City	30 8	4	3	33	14	1	0	14	20	56	53	70	22
14	Burslem Port Vale	30 6	4	5	25	11	0	14	18	66	43	77	18	
15	Rotherham Town	30 7	2	6	27	26	0	1	14	7	67	34	97	17
16	Crewe Alexandra	30 5	2	8	22	28	0	1	14	8	67	30	95	13

Rotherham Town
Midland League
Champions 1891/92

Standing: William Vickers, Harry Thickett, Arthur Wharton, Fred Turner, Gerry Steer (trainer).
Seated: George Gummer, Billy Cutts, Albert Pye, Albert Rodgers, Ted Cross, Bob Herrod, Johnny Walker.
Front: Billy Longden, Bob Leather, Johnny McCormick.

SEASON 1895/96

DIVISION TWO (ROTHERHAM TOWN)

No.	Date	Opposition	Res.	Att.	Goalscorers	Wharton A.	Porteous T.	Boylan E.	Longden W.	Porteous D.	Broadhead W.	Bryant W.	McGee J.	Poole R.	Reid W.	McCabe A.	Stewart H.A.	McCormick J.	Simmonite H.	Hargreaves J.J.	Webster	Cutts A.	McArdle J.	Wheatcroft E.	Wilkinson W.	Nixon A.	Daughtrey J.T.	Mathieson W.	Fisher	Widdowson F.	Hobson M.
1	7 Sep	PORT VALE	0-2	1500		1	X	X	X	X	X	X	X	X	X	X															
2	9	Manchester City	0-2	3000		1	X	X	X	X	X	X	X	X	X	X															
3	14	Burton Swifts	0-2	5000		1	X	X	X	X	X	X	X	X	X	X															
4	21	CREWE ALEXANDRA	4-0		Bryant(2), D.Porteous, Reid	1	X	X	X	X		X	X		X	X	X	X													
5	23	BURTON SWIFTS	1-4		Bryant	1	X	X	X	X		X	X		X	X	X	X													
6	28	NEWCASTLE UNITED	1-1		Hargreaves	1	X	X	X	X		X	X		X			X	X	X											
7	5 Oct	Arsenal	0-5	6000		1	X	X	X	X		X	X		X	X		X		X											
8	26	ARSENAL	3-0	1500	McCabe(2), Broadhead	1	X		X	X	X	X			X	X		X				X		X							
9	4 Nov	MANCHESTER CITY	2-3		Bryant, McCormick	1	X		X	X	X	X			X	X		X				X		X							
10	9	Crewe Alexandra	2-3		Bryant, Reid	1	X		X	X	X	X			X	X		X				X		X							
11	16	NOTTS COUNTY	1-0		Bryant	1	X		X	X		X			X	X		X				X	X	X							
12	30	Notts County	0-0			1	X		X	X		X			X	X		X				X	X	X							
13	7 Dec	BURTON WANDERERS	1-6		McCormick	1	X		X	X					X	X		X			X	X	X	X							
14	21	Newcastle United	1-6		Bryant	1	X		X	X		X			X	X		X			X		X	X							
15	26	DARWEN	3-0		McCabe, Wheatcroft, ?	1	X		X	X	X	X				X		X			X		X	X							
16	4 Jan	LIVERPOOL	0-5				X		X	X	X	X				X		X			X		X	X	1						
17	11	Newton Heath	0-3				X		X	X	X	X				X		X			X		X	X		1					
18	13	Darwen	2-10		Bryant, Webster		X		X	X	X	X				X					X			X		1	X	X			
19	18	LEICESTER FOSSE	2-0		McCabe, Wheatcroft		X		X	X	X	X				X		X			X			X		1	X				
20	25	Port Vale *	0-4						X	X	X	X										X		X			X				
21	1 Feb	Lincoln City +	0-5	1500					X	X	X	X						X			X	X		X		1	X	X	X		
22	8	GRIMSBY TOWN	1-0						X	X	X	X						X			X	X		X	1		X			X	
23	18	Liverpool #	1-10		?				X	X	X	X						X			X	X			1		X			X	
24	3 Mar	Grimsby Town #	0-4						X	X	X	X						X			X	X			1		X			X	
25	7	Newton Heath	2-3	1500	Cutts, McCormick				X	X	X	X						X			X	X		X	1		X			X	
26	14	LOUGHBOROUGH ~	4-0		?				X	X	X	X						X			X				1		X			X	
27	16	LINCOLN CITY ^	2-2	300	?				X	X	X	X						X			X				1					X	
28	21	Burton Wanderers	1-6		?				X	X	X	X						X			X	X			1		X		X	X	
29	3 Apr	Leicester Fosse #	0-8						X	X	X							X			X	X		X			X		X		X
30	6	Loughborough #	0-3						X	X	X							X			X	X		X	1		X				X
		Apps.				15	19	7	30	30	22	27	7	3	14	18	2	25	1	2	17	15	7	18	9	4	12	2	3	7	2
		Goals								1	1	8			2	3		4		1	1	1		2							

* These 7 players registered with Football League, but according to 'Advertiser' records, Nixon, Simmonite, Webster, McCormick played; Wheatcorft & Cutts did not.
+ 12 players registered with Football League. # Played with 10 men. ~ Played with 9 men. ^ Played with 8 men.

Rotherham Town 1900-01: Charity Cup Winners.
(Back): Beevers, Bramhill, Baker, Cooper, Kenway, Bob Leather (Trainer)
(Seated): Cullumbine, Merryweather, Dr. Selby, Binny Parkinson, Horace Parkinson. (Front): Parkin

ROTHERHAM COUNTY
SEASON 1919/20

DIVISION TWO

No.	Date	Opposition	Res.	Att.	Goalscorers	Branston J.H.	Alton C.	Baines F.	Bailey H.	Coe F.	Stanton W.	Lee F.	Cawley T.	Glennon E.	Lees J.	Lamb S.	Harrison J.	Lloyd H.	Archer F.	Hopkinson S.	Manning J.	McKenzie F.	Simmonite W.	Foxall J.	Marshall W.	Millership H.	Lounds H.	Bratley H.	Chambers W.A.	Pape A.A.	Harrison E.	Haddon P.	Wallace J.	Frith W.	Darby A.	Ackroyd
1	30 Aug	NOTTINGHAM FOREST	2-0	10000	Cawley, Lee	1	2	3	4	5	6	7	8	9	10	11																				
2	1 Sep	Stockport County	1-4		Glennon	1	2	3	4	5	6	7	8	9	10	11																				
3	6	Nottingham Forest	1-4		Glennon	1	2	3	4	5	6	7	8	9	10	11																				
4	8	STOCKPORT COUNTY	1-0	5000	Archer	1	2	3	4		6	7			10	11	5		8	9																
5	13	WEST HAM UNITED	0-1			1	2	3	4		6		8	9		11		10	5	7																
6	20	West Ham United	1-2		Lees	1		3		4	5	6			9	10	11		8					7	2											
7	27	BARNSLEY	1-0	10000	Coe	1		3		4	5	6	7	8	9	10	11								2											
8	29	Fulham	0-3			1		3		4	5	6			9	10	11		8					7	2											
9	4 Oct	Barnsley	0-4			1		3		4	5	6			9	10	11		8					7	2											
10	11	BRISTOL CITY	2-2	10000	Cawley, Lees	1		3				6		7	9	8		5							2	4	10	11								
11	18	Bristol City	1-2		Lees	1		3		4	5			7	9	8		6							2		10	11								
12	25	Stoke City	0-3			1		3		4	5	6	7		9										10	11	2	8								
13	1 Nov	STOKE CITY	1-3		Lees	1		3		4	5	6	7		9	10	11										2	8								
14	8	Grimsby Town	1-0		Lees	1		3		4	5	6		8	9	10	11									2	7									
15	15	GRIMSBY TOWN	3-1		Lees(2), Lounds	1		3		4	5	6		8	9	10	11									2	7									
16	22	Birmingham City	2-2		Cawley, Glennon	1		3		4		6		8	9	10	11	5								2	7									
17	29	BIRMINGHAM CITY	0-3			1		3		4	5	6		8	9	10	11									2	7									
18	6 Dec	Leicester	1-1	10000	Glennon	1		3		4		6		8	9	10	11	5								2	7									
19	13	LEICESTER	1-0		Millership	1		3		4		6		8	9	10	11	5								2	7									
20	25	Huddersfield Town	1-7		Lees	1		3		4					9	10	11	5	8							2	7									6
21	26	HUDDERSFIELD TOWN	1-3	12000	Coe	1		3		4	5	8			9		11	6								2	7	10								
22	27	FULHAM	1-1		O.G.	1		3		4	5	8			9	11		6						10		2	7									
23	1 Jan	Blackpool	1-5		Stanton	1		3		4	5	9			8	11		6						10		2	7									
24	3	Coventry City	1-1	17000	Glennon	1		3		4		6		8	9	10		5								2	7		11							
25	17	COVENTRY CITY	4-3		Glennon, Lamb, Lounds, Pape	1		3			5	6			10	11		4								2	7			9	8					
26	24	LINCOLN CITY	3-0	8000	Coe, Glennon, E.Harrison	1		3			5	6			10		11	4								2	7		4	9	8					
27	31	Lincoln City	0-0			1		3		4	5	6			10		11									2	7			9	8					
28	7 Feb	BURY	1-2		E.Harrison	1		3		4	5	6			10		11									2	7			8		9				
29	14	Bury	1-4		?	1			2		5	6			10		11	4									7			9		8				
30	21	PORT VALE	2-2		Glennon, E.Harrison	1			3	6	5				10		11	4								2	7			9	8					
31	28	Port Vale	2-4		Lees(2)	1		3		6	5				10	8	11	4								2	7			9						
32	6 Mar	Orient	2-1		?	1		3		6					10	8	11	4								2	7			9			5			
33	13	ORIENT	3-1		Glennon, Lamb, Millership	1		3		6					10	8	11	4								2	7			9			5			
34	20	Tottenham Hotspur	0-2			1		3		6					10	8	11	4						2			7			9			5			
35	27	TOTTENHAM HOTSPUR	1-1	18000	Lees	1		3		6					10	8	11	4								2	7			9			5			
36	3 Apr	South Shields	2-6		Glennon, Lees	1		3		6					10	8	11	4								2	7			9			5			
37	5	BLACKPOOL	1-2		Pape	1		3		6					10	8	11	4								2	7			9			5			
38	10	SOUTH SHIELDS	1-0		Glennon	1		3		6					10	8	11	4								2	7			9			5			
39	17	Wolverhampton Wanderers	1-0		Lounds	1		3		6					10	8	11	4								2	7			9			5			
40	24	WOLVERHAMPTON WANDS.	2-0		E.Harrison, Pape	1		3		6					10		11									2	7	4		9	8		5			
41	26	Hull City	0-1			1		3		6					10		11					7				2		4	9		8	5			
42	1 May	HULL CITY	1-2		Alton	1		3		6					10	8				5						2		4	9							11
				Apps.		42	40	7	38	23	27	7	14	40	32	35	12	17	2	1	5	13	1	6	3	22	30	2	4	17	6	1	3	10	1	1
				Goals			1			3	1	1	3	11	12	2			1							2	3			3	4					

F.A. CUP

	Date		Res.	Att.		Branston J.H.		Baines F.	Bailey H.		Stanton W.			Glennon E.	Lees J.	Lamb S.	Harrison J.	Lloyd H.								Millership H.	Lounds H.									
QR	20 Dec	West Stanley	0-1	7000		1		3	4		6			9	10	11	8	5								2	7									

Final League Table

		Pl.	Home					Away					F.	A.	Pts
			W	D	L	F	A	W	D	L	F	A			
1	Tottenham Hotspur	42	19	2	0	60	11	13	4	4	42	21	102	32	70
2	Huddersfield Town	42	16	4	1	58	13	12	4	5	39	25	97	38	64
3	Birmingham	42	14	3	4	54	16	10	5	6	31	18	85	34	56
4	Blackpool	42	13	4	4	40	18	8	6	7	25	29	65	47	52
5	Bury	42	14	4	3	35	15	6	4	11	25	29	60	44	48
6	Fulham	42	11	6	4	36	18	8	3	10	25	32	61	50	47
7	West Ham United	42	14	3	4	34	14	5	6	10	13	26	47	40	47
8	Bristol City	42	9	9	3	30	18	4	8	9	16	25	46	43	43
9	South Shields	42	13	5	3	47	18	2	7	12	11	30	58	48	42
10	Stoke	42	13	3	5	37	15	5	3	13	23	39	60	54	42
11	Hull City	42	13	4	4	53	23	5	2	14	25	49	78	72	42
12	Barnsley	42	9	5	7	41	28	6	5	10	20	27	61	55	40
13	Port Vale	42	11	3	7	35	27	5	5	11	24	35	59	62	40
14	Leicester City	42	8	6	7	26	29	7	4	10	15	32	41	61	40
15	Clapton Orient	42	14	3	4	34	17	2	3	16	17	42	51	59	38
16	Stockport County	42	11	4	6	34	24	3	5	13	18	37	52	61	37
17	Rotherham County	42	10	4	7	32	27	3	4	14	19	56	51	83	34
18	Nottingham Forest	42	9	4	8	23	22	5	1	15	20	51	43	73	31
19	Wolverhampton W.	42	8	4	9	41	32	2	6	13	14	48	55	80	30
20	Coventry City	42	7	7	7	20	26	2	4	15	15	47	35	73	29
21	Lincoln City	42	8	6	7	27	30	1	3	17	17	71	44	101	27
22	Grimsby Town	42	8	4	9	23	24	2	1	18	11	51	34	75	25

ROTHERHAM COUNTY
SEASON 1920/21
DIVISION TWO

No.	Date	Opposition	Res.	Att.	Goalscorers
1	28 Aug	COVENTRY CITY	2-3	12000	Glennon, Lees
2	30	Stoke City	0-2		
3	4 Sep	Coventry City	1-0		Lees
4	6	STOKE CITY	1-1	10000	Millership
5	11	Port Vale	1-1		Millership
6	18	PORT VALE	1-1		Cawley
7	20	BRISTOL CITY	0-0		
8	25	South Shields	0-1		
9	2 Oct	SOUTH SHIELDS	5-4	16000	Lees(2), Clarkson, Glennon, Millership
10	9	Hull City	1-1		Clarkson
11	16	HULL CITY	1-1		Lees
12	23	Wolverhampton Wanderers	0-3		
13	30	WOLVERHAMPTON WANDS.	1-0	12000	Lees
14	1 Nov	SHEFFIELD WEDNESDAY	2-0	21000	Pape(2)
15	6	Stockport County	1-0		Kitchen
16	13	STOCKPORT COUNTY	1-0		Pape
17	20	LEYTON ORIENT	0-2		
18	27	Leyton Orient	0-0		
19	4 Dec	Bury	0-1	10000	
20	11	BURY	0-5		
21	25	Nottingham Forest	1-6		Wallace
22	27	NOTTINGHAM FOREST	0-0		
23	1 Jan	Bristol City	4-2		Wallace(2), Glennon, Lounds
24	8	Leeds United	0-1		
25	15	NOTTS COUNTY	0-0		
26	22	Notts County	0-1		
27	29	Barnsley	1-2		Pape
28	5 Feb	BARNSLEY	1-0		Cawley
29	12	BLACKPOOL	0-2		
30	19	Blackpool	1-0		Glennon
31	26	LEICESTER	1-1		Glennon
32	5 Mar	Leicester	1-1	17000	Glennon
33	12	CARDIFF CITY	2-0		Millership(2)
34	26	Fulham	0-1		
35	28	Sheffield Wednesday	0-2	25000	
36	2 Apr	FULHAM	2-0		Lloyd(2)
37	9	West Ham United	0-1		
38	11	Cardiff City	0-1	35000	
39	16	WEST HAM UNITED	2-0		Cawley, Pape
40	23	Birmingham City	2-3		Chambers, Lees
41	30	BIRMINGHAM CITY	1-1	15000	Chambers
42	7 May	LEEDS UNITED	0-2		

Appearances and goals (players in column order):

Player	Apps	Goals
Branston J.	41	
Millership H.	37	5
Alton C.	15	
Emmett H.	5	
Frith W.	11	
Bailey H.	35	
Lees J.	21	7
Kitchen J.	18	1
Glennon E.	25	6
Clarkson W.	41	2
Chambers W.A.	39	2
Shaw R.	12	
Cawley T.	12	3
Hargreaves C.	31	
Sutcliffe C.	1	
Lounds H.	27	1
Pape A.A.	29	5
Wallace J.	20	3
Harrison E.	1	
Bratley H.	8	
Simmonite W.	7	
Coe F.	1	
McKenzie F.	5	
Wheatley E.	15	
Redfearn A.	2	2
Lloyd H.	3	
Pickin W.	1	

F.A. CUP

	Date		Res.		Goalscorers
QR	17 Dec	LUTON TOWN	1-3		Shaw

The programme (cover), for one of the County's matches in their second Football League season.

Wolves were beaten 1-0 on 30th October 1920

Final League Table

		Pl	Home W	D	L	F	A	Away W	D	L	F	A	F.	A.	Pts
1	Birmingham	42	16	4	1	55	13	8	6	7	24	25	79	38	58
2	Cardiff City	42	13	5	3	27	9	11	5	5	32	23	59	32	58
3	Bristol City	42	14	3	4	35	12	5	10	6	14	17	49	29	51
4	Blackpool	42	12	3	6	32	19	8	7	6	22	23	54	42	50
5	West Ham United	42	12	3	6	38	11	6	5	10	13	19	51	30	48
6	Notts County	42	12	5	4	36	17	6	6	9	19	23	55	40	47
7	Clapton Orient	42	14	4	3	38	19	2	5	14	16	36	45	49	41
8	South Shields	42	13	4	4	41	16	4	11	20	30	61	46	44
9	Fulham	42	14	4	3	33	12	2	6	13	10	35	42	48	42
10	Sheffield Wed.	42	14	4	3	33	12	4	1	17	34	48	48	41
11	Bury	42	10	8	3	29	13	5	2	14	16	36	45	49	40
12	Leicester City	42	10	8	3	26	11	2	8	11	13	35	39	46	40
13	Hull City	42	7	10	4	24	18	3	10	8	19	35	43	53	40
14	Leeds United	42	10	8	3	25	14	4	5	12	15	31	40	45	38
15	Wolverhampton W.	42	11	4	6	34	24	5	2	14	15	42	49	66	38
16	Barnsley	42	9	6	6	37	26	3	6	12	11	29	48	50	36
17	Port Vale	42	8	8	5	28	19	4	4	15	15	30	43	49	36
18	Nottingham Forest	42	10	7	4	33	22	2	5	14	15	33	48	55	36
19	Rotherham County	42	8	9	4	23	21	4	3	14	14	32	37	53	36
20	Stoke	42	9	5	7	26	16	3	6	12	20	40	46	56	35
21	Coventry City	42	8	6	7	24	25	4	5	12	15	45	39	70	35
22	Stockport County	42	8	6	7	30	24	1	6	14	12	51	42	75	30

ROTHERHAM COUNTY
SEASON 1921/22
DIVISION TWO

No.	Date	Opposition	Res.	Att.	Goalscorers
1	27 Aug	WOLVERHAMPTON WANDS.	1-0	14000	Pape
2	29	Coventry City	0-4		
3	3 Sep	Wolverhampton Wanderers	1-3		Cameron
4	5	COVENTRY CITY	0-0		
5	10	Crystal Palace	0-2		
6	17	CRYSTAL PALACE	1-1		Pape
7	24	Bradford	2-4		Lounds, Wheatley
8	1 Oct	BRADFORD	2-0	12000	Chambers, Shaw
9	8	Sheffield Wednesday	0-1		
10	15	SHEFFIELD WEDNESDAY	0-0	17000	
11	22	Fulham	0-4	20000	
12	29	FULHAM	1-0		Wallace
13	5 Nov	BLACKPOOL	0-1		
14	7	BARNSLEY	0-0	17000	
15	12	Blackpool	1-3		Wallace
16	19	Leyton Orient	2-1	12000	Pape, Wallace
17	26	LEYTON ORIENT	2-0		Chambers, Pape
18	10 Dec	Barnsley	1-0	12000	Pape
19	17	STOKE CITY	0-0		
20	24	Stoke City	1-1		Dobson
21	26	Hull City	1-0	16000	Shaw
22	27	HULL CITY	2-0	15500	Chambers, Pape
23	31	Leeds United	2-0		Chambers, Williams
24	14 Jan	LEEDS UNITED	1-0		Pape
25	21	NOTTINGHAM FOREST	0-1		
26	28	South Shields	0-2		
27	8 Feb	Nottingham Forest	0-1		
28	11	Bristol City	2-1		Elliott, Hirst
29	18	SOUTH SHIELDS	1-1		Williams
30	20	BRISTOL CITY	0-0		
31	4 Mar	PORT VALE	0-1		
32	11	Port Vale	0-1		
33	18	West Ham United	2-1		Chambers, Bell
34	25	WEST HAM UNITED	0-1		
35	1 Apr	Bury	0-0		
36	8	BURY	1-1		Lounds
37	14	Notts County	0-2		
38	15	Leicester	0-1		
39	17	NOTTS COUNTY	3-0		Pape(3)
40	22	LEICESTER	0-0		
41	29	Derby County	0-4		
42	6 May	DERBY COUNTY	2-0		Bell, Pape

Player appearances/goals totals

Player	Apps	Goals
Branston J.	28	
Millership H.	22	
Wheatley E.	12	1
Thompson G.	30	
Hargreaves C.	11	
Chambers W.	33	5
Lounds H.	21	2
Murphy J.	2	
Pape A.A.	30	11
Cameron D.	5	1
Clarkson W.	22	
Pickin W.	30	
Lloyd R.	4	
Cawley T.	10	
Bailey H.	37	
Wallace J.	9	3
Emmett H.	29	
Shaw R.	17	2
McKenzie F.	31	
Williams J.	21	2
Dallinson A.	2	
Dobson G.	17	1
Breckin C.	1	
Sutcliffe C.	14	
Elliott C.	5	1
Hirst H.	2	1
Moiser G.	1	
Bell J.	12	2
Humphries H.	4	

F.A. CUP

Round	Date	Opposition	Res.	Att.	Goalscorers
QR	3 Dec	COVENTRY CITY	1-1		Thompson
QRr	8	Coventry City	0-1	7814	

ROTHERHAM COUNTY c.1920

Final League Table

		Pl	Home W	D	L	F	A	Away W	D	L	F	A	F.	A.	Pts
1	Nottingham Forest	42	13	7	1	29	9	9	5	7	22	21	51	30	56
2	Stoke	42	9	11	1	31	11	9	5	7	29	33	60	44	52
3	Barnsley	42	14	5	2	43	18	8	3	10	24	34	67	52	52
4	West Ham United	42	15	3	3	39	13	5	11	13	26	52	39	48
5	Hull City	42	13	5	3	36	13	6	5	10	15	28	51	41	48
6	South Shields	42	11	7	3	25	13	6	5	10	18	25	43	38	46
7	Fulham	42	14	5	2	41	8	4	4	13	16	30	57	38	45
8	Leeds United	42	10	8	3	31	12	6	5	10	17	26	48	38	45
9	Leicester City	42	11	6	4	30	16	3	11	7	9	18	39	34	45
10	Sheffield Wed.	42	12	4	5	31	24	3	10	8	16	26	47	50	44
11	Bury	42	11	3	7	35	19	4	7	10	19	36	54	55	40
12	Derby County	42	11	3	7	34	22	4	6	11	26	42	60	64	39
13	Notts County	42	10	7	4	34	18	2	8	11	13	33	47	51	39
14	Crystal Palace	42	9	6	6	28	20	4	7	10	17	31	45	51	39
15	Clapton Orient	42	12	4	5	33	18	3	5	13	10	32	43	50	39
16	Rotherham County	42	8	9	4	17	7	6	2	13	15	36	32	43	39
17	Wolverhampton W.	42	8	7	6	28	19	5	2	16	16	30	44	49	37
18	Port Vale	42	10	5	6	28	19	4	3	14	15	38	43	57	36
19	Blackpool	42	11	1	9	33	27	4	4	13	11	30	44	57	35
20	Coventry City	42	8	5	8	31	21	4	5	12	20	39	51	60	34
21	Bradford Park Ave.	42	10	4	6	32	22	2	4	15	14	40	46	62	33
22	Bristol City	42	10	3	8	25	18	2	6	13	12	40	37	58	33

ROTHERHAM COUNTY
SEASON 1922/23

DIVISION TWO

No.	Date	Opposition	Res.	Att.	Goalscorers	Sutcliffe C.	Thompson G.	McKenzie F.	Emmett H.	Pickin W.	Bailey H.	Lounds H.	Cook G.	Procter N.	Humphries N.	Bell J.	Jackson R.	Evans T.	Chambers W.	Crichton W.	Pape A.A.	Williams J.	Chappell T.	Harris B.	Pearson R.	Crate C.	Neal S.	Dobson G.	Hirst H.	Lofthouse J.	Lambert J.
1	26 Aug	SHEFFIELD WEDNESDAY	1-2	19000	Cook	1	2	3	4	5	6	7	8	9	10	11															
2	28	Leicester	0-3			1		3	4	5		7	8	9			2	6	10	11											
3	2 Sep	Sheffield Wednesday	0-1			1		3	4	5		7	8	10			2	6		11	9										
4	4	LEICESTER	0-0			1		3	4	5			8	10			2	6		11	9	7									
5	9	West Ham United	0-4			1		3	4	5	6	7	8	10			2			11	9										
6	16	WEST HAM UNITED	2-2		Pape, Procter	1			4	5	6	7	8	10			2			11	9		3								
7	23	South Shields	0-2			1			4	5	6	7	8	10			2		11		9		3								
8	30	SOUTH SHIELDS	2-1		Pape(2)	1			4	5	6	7	8	10			2		11		9										
9	7 Oct	Wolverhampton Wanderers	2-3		Cook(2)	1			4	5	6	7	8	10			2		11		9			3							
10	14	WOLVERHAMPTON WANDS.	3-2		Pearson(2), Cook	1	3			5	6	7	8	10			2		11						9	4					
11	21	HULL CITY	0-1			1			4	5	6	7	8	10			2		11					3							
12	28	Hull City	3-2		Pape(3)	1			4	5	6		8	10			2				9	7		3							
13	4 Nov	COVENTRY CITY	2-0		Jackson, Pearson	1			4	5	6		8	11			2		10			7		3	9						
14	6	CRYSTAL PALACE	4-1		Pape(2), Cook, Pearson	1			4	5	6		8	11			2				9	7		3	10						
15	11	Coventry City	1-2		Pape	1				5	6		8	11			2		4		9	7		3	10						
16	18	PORT VALE	3-1		Pape(2), Pearson	1				5	6		8	11			2		4		9	7		3	10		11				
17	25	Port Vale	0-0			1	2			5	6		8						4		9	7		3	10		11				
18	2 Dec	Manchester United	0-3			1			4	5	6		8				2				9	7		3	10		11				
19	9	MANCHESTER UNITED	1-1	12000	Pearson	1			4	5	6		8				2		11		9	7		3	10						
20	16	Bury	0-1			1			4	5	6		8				2		11		9	7		3	10						
21	23	BURY	0-0	9500		1			4	5	6		8				2			11	9	7		3	10						
22	25	BARNSLEY	1-1	14500	Pape	1			4	5	6		8				2			11	9	7		3	10						
23	26	Barnsley	2-2		Cook, Pape	1			4	5			8				2	6			9	7		3	10						
24	30	Leyton Orient	1-5		Pearson	1		3	4	5			8				2	6			9	7			10						
25	6 Jan	LEYTON ORIENT	0-0			1	5		4		6		8	11			2				9	7		3	10						
26	20	Stockport County	0-1			1			4	5	6		8	11			2		10		9	7		3							
27	27	STOCKPORT COUNTY	2-1		Pape(2)	1			4	5	6		8	11			2		10		9	7		3							
28	10 Feb	Crystal Palace	0-4			1	10		4	5	6		8				2				9	7		3			11				
29	17	FULHAM	1-3		Humphries	1			4	5	6		8	11	10		2					7		3	9						
30	24	Fulham	2-1		Chambers, Pape	1	3		4	5	6		8	11			2		10		9	7									
31	3 Mar	NOTTS COUNTY	1-0		Williams	1	3			5	6		8	11			2		10		9	7							4		
32	10	Notts County	0-2			1	3			5	6		8				2		10		9	7								11	
33	17	Derby County	0-1			1		2	4	5	6		8						10		9	7		3						11	
34	26	DERBY COUNTY	3-0		Lofthouse(2), Cook	1		2	4	5	6		8		10						9	7		3						11	
35	30	Leeds United	0-2	10000		1		2	4	5	6		8		10						9	7		3						11	
36	31	Southampton	2-4		Cook, Williams	1		2	4	5	6		8		10	3					9	7								11	
37	2 Apr	LEEDS UNITED	3-1		Pape(2), Williams	1		2		5	6		8						4		9	7		3	10					11	
38	7	SOUTHAMPTON	0-0			1		2	4	5	6		8						10		9	7		3						11	
39	14	Bradford City	1-0		Lambert	1		2	4	5	6		10								9	7		3						11	8
40	21	BRADFORD CITY	0-2	8000		1		2	4	5	6		8						10		9	7		3						11	
41	28	Blackpool	0-1			1		2	4	5	6		8						10		9	7		3						11	
42	5 May	BLACKPOOL	1-0		Pape	1	5	2	4		6		8								9	7		3	10					11	
		Apps.				42	6	18	36	40	37	10	42	22	6	3	31	4	20	7	37	32	2	30	18	1	3	2	1	11	1
		Goals											8	1	1		1		1		19	3			7					2	1

F.A. CUP

No.	Date	Opposition	Res.	Att.	Goalscorers	Sutcliffe C.	Thompson G.	McKenzie F.	Emmett H.	Pickin W.	Bailey H.	Lounds H.	Cook G.	Procter N.	Humphries N.	Bell J.	Jackson R.	Evans T.	Chambers W.	Crichton W.	Pape A.A.	Williams J.	Chappell T.	Harris B.	Pearson R.
1R	13 Jan	Chelsea	0-1	34500		1			4	5	6		8	11			2				9	7		3	10

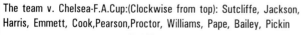

The team v. Chelsea-F.A.Cup:(Clockwise from top): Sutcliffe, Jackson, Harris, Emmett, Cook, Pearson, Proctor, Williams, Pape, Bailey, Pickin

Final League Table

		Pl.	Home W	D	L	F	A	Away W	D	L	F	A	F.	A.	Pts
1	Notts County	42	16	1	4	29	15	7	6	8	17	19	46	34	53
2	West Ham United	42	9	8	4	21	11	11	3	7	42	27	63	38	51
3	Leicester City	42	14	2	5	42	19	7	7	7	23	25	65	44	51
4	Manchester United	42	10	6	5	25	17	7	8	6	26	19	51	36	48
5	Blackpool	42	12	4	5	37	14	6	7	8	23	29	60	43	47
6	Bury	42	14	5	2	41	16	4	6	11	14	30	55	46	47
7	Leeds United	42	11	8	2	26	10	7	3	11	17	26	43	36	47
8	Sheffield Wed.	42	14	3	4	36	16	3	9	9	18	31	54	47	46
9	Barnsley	42	14	4	5	42	21	5	7	9	20	30	62	51	45
10	Fulham	42	12	7	2	35	21	5	1	15	11	34	46	55	42
11	Southampton	42	10	5	6	28	21	4	9	8	12	19	40	40	42
12	Hull City	42	10	7	3	26	12	5	6	10	14	23	43	35	42
13	South Shields	42	11	7	3	26	14	3	9	9	14	32	35	44	40
14	Derby County	42	9	5	7	25	16	5	6	10	21	34	46	50	39
15	Bradford City	42	8	7	6	27	18	4	6	11	14	27	41	45	37
16	Crystal Palace	42	10	7	4	33	16	3	4	14	21	46	54	62	37
17	Port Vale	42	8	6	7	23	18	6	3	12	16	33	39	51	37
18	Coventry City	42	12	2	7	35	21	3	5	13	11	42	46	63	37
19	Clapton Orient	42	9	6	6	26	17	3	6	12	14	33	40	50	36
20	Stockport County	42	10	6	5	32	24	4	2	15	11	34	43	58	36
21	Rotherham County	42	10	7	4	30	19	3	2	16	14	44	44	63	35
22	Wolverhampton W.	42	9	4	8	32	26	0	5	16	10	51	42	77	27

ROTHERHAM COUNTY
SEASON 1923/24
DIVISION THREE (NORTH)

No.	Date	Opposition	Res.	Att.	Goalscorers	Sutcliffe C.	Jackson R.	Emmett H.	Burnip G.	Bailey H.	Williams J.	Chambers W.	Whittaker M.	Easton W.	Lofthouse J.	McKenzie F.	Pearson R.	Finnigan F.	Hammerton J.D.	Turner J.	Hodgson F.	Boulton R.	Gibson A.	Scott J.	Brown R.	Barton J.	Hanwell J.	Windle E.
1	25 Aug	WALSALL	0-2			1	2	4	5	6	7	8	9	10	11	3												
2	27	Wolverhampton Wanderers.	0-3	15000		1	2	4	5	6	7	8		10	11	3	9											
3	1 Sep	Walsall	1-1		Lofthouse	1	2	4	5	6	7				11	3	10	8	9									
4	3	WOLVERHAMPTON WANDS.	1-1	7000	Chambers	1	2	4		6	7	5			11	3	10	8	9									
5	8	WREXHAM	2-1	8000	Pearson, Williams	1	2	4		6	7	5			11	3	10	8	9									
6	15	Wrexham	0-1			1	2	4		6	7	5			11	3	10	8	9									
7	22	DONCASTER ROVERS	3-0	9000	Bailey, Hammerton, Lofthouse	1	2	4		6	7	5			11	3	10	8	9									
8	29	Doncaster Rovers	1-0		Pearson	1	2			6	7	5			11	3	10	8	9	4								
9	6 Oct	ROCHDALE	0-0	7000		1	2	4		6	7	5			11	3	10	8	9									
10	13	Rochdale	0-1			1	2	4		6	7	5			11		10		8		3		9					
11	20	Southport	0-0			1	2	4		6	7	5			11		10		8		3		9					
12	27	SOUTHPORT	1-1	6000	Hammerton	1	2	4		6	7	5			11		10		9		3		8					
13	3 Nov	BARROW	2-0	5000	Lofthouse(2)	1		4		6	7	5		10	11	2	9				3		8					
14	10	Barrow	2-1		Hammerton, O.G.	1	2	4		6	7	5			11		10		9		3		8					
15	17	CREWE ALEXANDRA	1-0		Lofthouse	1	2	4		6	7	5			11		10		9		3		8					
16	24	Ashington	2-1		Chambers, O.G.	1	2	4		6	7	5			11		10		9		3		8					
17	8 Dec	Lincoln City	1-2		Pearson	1	2	4		6	7	5					10		9		3		8	11				
18	22	Tranmere Rovers	1-0		Scott	1	2	4		6	7	5					10				3			11	9	8		
19	25	Chesterfield	1-3	8521	McKenzie	1	2	4		6	7	5				8	9		10		3			11				
20	26	CHESTERFIELD	1-2	10000	McKenzie	1	2				7	5				8	9		10		3			11			4	6
21	1 Jan	Darlington	0-1	7000		1	2	4			7	5					9		10		3			11			8	6
22	5	Bradford	0-2	7000		1	2	4		6	7	5					10		9		3			11			8	
23	12	TRANMERE ROVERS	5-1		Hammerton(3), Hodgson(2)	1	2	4		6	7	5					10		9		3			11			8	
24	19	NEW BRIGHTON	3-1	7000	Hanwell(2), Pearson	1	2	4		6	7	5					10		9		3			11			8	
25	26	New Brighton	2-1		Hammerton, Pearson	1	2	4		6	7	5					10		9		3			11			8	
26	2 Feb	GRIMSBY TOWN	2-1		Hanwell, Pearson	1	2	4		6	7	5					10		9		3			11			8	
27	9	Grimsby Town	1-1		Hanwell	1	2	4		6	7	5					10		9		3			11			8	
28	16	HALIFAX TOWN	3-2	8000	Hammerton(2), Hanwell	1	2	4		6	7	5					10		9		3			11			8	
29	23	Halifax Town	2-0		Hammerton, Pearson	1	2	4		6	7	5					10		9		3			11			8	
30	1 Mar	HARTLEPOOLS UNITED	5-0		Bailey, Hmmertn, Pearsn, Sctt, Wlliams	1	2	4		6	7	5					10		9		3			11			8	
31	8	Hartlepools United	5-2		Hammerton(3), Hanwell, Scott	1	2	4		6	7	5					10		9		3			11			8	
32	15	Accrington Stanley	2-3		Hammerton, Scott	1	2	4		6	7	5					10		9		3			11			8	
33	17	ASHINGTON	1-0		Hammerton	1	2	4		6	7	5					10		9		3			11			8	
34	22	ACCRINGTON STANLEY	2-0	8000	Bailey, Hammerton	1	2	4		6	7	5					10		9		3			11			8	
35	24	BRADFORD	1-0		Scott	1	2	4		6	7	5					10		9			3		11			8	
36	29	Crewe Alexandra	0-1			1	2	4		6	7	5					10		9		3			11			8	
37	12 Apr	Durham	2-2		Pearson, Scott	1	2	4		6	7	5					10		9		3			11			8	
38	19	DURHAM	5-1		Hammerton(2), Bailey, Scott, Wlliams	1	2			6	7	5					10		9	4	3			11			8	
39	21	DARLINGTON	2-0		Hammerton(2)	1	2			6	7	5					10		9	4	3			11			8	
40	22	LINCOLN CITY	2-0		Easton, McKenzie	1	2			6	7	5		8		4	10		9		3			11				
41	26	Wigan Borough	1-3		Hammerton	1	2	4		6	7	5		8			10		9		3			11				
42	3 May	WIGAN BOROUGH	4-0		Hammerton(2), McKenzie, Scott	1	2			6	7	5		8		4	10		9		3			11				
					Apps.	42	41	38	3	40	42	41	1	6	16	17	41	6	35	4	32	1	7	26	1	1	19	2
					Goals					4	3	2		1	5	4	9		24		2			8			6	

F.A. CUP

Rd.	Date	Opposition	Res.	Goalscorers	Sutcliffe C.	Jackson R.	Emmett H.	Burnip G.	Bailey H.	Williams J.	Chambers W.	Whittaker M.	Easton W.	Lofthouse J.	McKenzie F.	Pearson R.	Finnigan F.	Hammerton J.D.	Turner J.	Hodgson F.	Boulton R.	Gibson A.	Scott J.	Brown R.	Barton J.	Hanwell J.	Windle E.
QR	1 Dec	Scuthorpe United	1-1	Hammerton	1	2	4		6	7	5					10		9		3		8	11				
QRr	6	SCUNTHORPE UNITED	2-0	Chambers, Williams	1	2	4		6	7	5					10		9		3		8	11				
QR	15	Halifax Town	0-1		1	2	4		6	7	5					10				3		8	11			9	

Front row (left to right):—J. M. Watt (director), Dungworth, Ellerby, Ingham, Boulton, Pearson, Bailey, Jackson, J. Briggs (secretary). Middle row:—W. Heald (assistant sec.), Brown, Hodgson, Ellison, Hanwell, Sutcliffe, Robinson, Chambers, F. Coe (trainer). Back row:—T. Hakin (assistant trainer), Scott, Easton, McKenzie, Lofthouse, Burnip.

Final League Table

		Pl.	Home					Away					F.	A.	Pts
			W	D	L	F	A	W	D	L	F	A			
1	Wolverhampton W.	42	18	3	0	51	10	6	12	3	25	17	76	27	63
2	Rochdale	42	17	4	0	40	8	8	5	20	18	60	26	62
3	Chesterfield	42	16	4	1	54	15	6	6	9	16	24	70	39	54
4	Rotherham County	42	16	3	2	46	13	7	3	11	24	30	70	43	52
5	Bradford Park Ave.	42	17	3	1	50	12	4	7	10	19	31	69	43	52
6	Darlington	42	16	5	0	51	19	4	3	14	19	34	70	53	48
7	Southport	42	13	7	1	30	10	3	7	11	14	32	44	42	46
8	Ashington	42	14	3	4	31	21	4	4	13	18	40	59	61	44
9	Doncaster Rovers	42	13	4	4	41	17	2	8	11	18	36	59	53	42
10	Wigan Borough	42	12	5	4	39	15	2	9	10	16	38	55	53	42
11	Grimsby Town	42	11	9	1	30	7	3	4	14	19	40	49	47	41
12	Tranmere Rovers	42	11	5	5	32	21	2	10	9	19	39	51	60	41
13	Accrington Stanley	42	12	5	4	35	21	4	3	14	13	40	48	61	40
14	Halifax Town	42	11	4	6	26	17	4	6	11	16	42	42	59	40
15	Durham City	42	12	5	4	40	23	3	4	14	19	37	59	60	39
16	Wrexham	42	8	11	2	24	12	2	7	12	13	32	37	44	38
17	Walsall	42	10	5	6	31	20	4	3	14	13	39	44	59	36
18	New Brighton	42	9	9	3	28	10	2	4	15	12	43	40	53	35
19	Lincoln City	42	8	5	5	29	22	2	4	15	19	37	48	59	32
20	Crewe Alexandra	42	6	7	8	20	24	1	6	14	12	34	32	58	27
21	Hartlepools United	42	7	9	5	22	24	2	4	15	11	46	33	70	25
22	Barrow	42	7	7	7	25	24	1	2	18	10	56	35	80	25

ROTHERHAM COUNTY
SEASON 1924/25
DIVISION THREE (NORTH)

No.	Date	Opposition	Res.	Att.	Goalscorers	Sutcliffe C.	Jackson R.	Hodgson F.	Emmett H.	Chambers R.	Bailey H.	Etherington R.D.	Chambers W.A.	Hammerton J.D.	Pearson R.	Scott T.	Hopkins G.	Marshall J.H.	Turner J.	Johnson J.M.	Boulton R.	Broadhead W.	Bramley C.	Beever L.	Bertram G.	Yates H.	Rhodes C.	Bramley J.	Wilks S.	Foster C.	Pye R.	Roe A.	Millsom L.	Kent E.	Reid G.	Mehaffy J.	Lilly E.	Hamilton H.	Miller E.	Bestall J.
1	30 Aug	Accrington Stanley	0-2			1	2	3	4	5	6	7	8	9	10	11																								
2	1 Sep	TRANMERE ROVERS	2-0	7000	R.Chambers, Hammerton	1	2	3	4	5	6	7	8	9	10	11																								
3	6	HALIFAX TOWN	0-0			1	2	3	4	5	6	7	8	9	10	11																								
4	9	Southport	0-2				2	3	4	5	6	7		9	10	11	1	8																					
5	13	New Brighton	1-3		Pearson		2	3		5	6	7		8	10	11	1		4	9																				
6	20	GRIMSBY TOWN	3-0	6000	Pearson, Hammerton, O.G.		2	3	4	5	6			9	10	11	1				7	8																			
7	27	Hartlepools United	0-0				2	3	4	5	6			9	10	11	1				7	8																	
8	4 Oct	ROCHDALE	1-3		Hammerton		2	3	4	5	6			9	10	11	1				8	7																		
9	11	Darlington	0-4				2	3	4	5				9	10	11	1				8	6		7														
10	18	BRADFORD	1-1	7000	Pearson		2	3	4	5				9	10	11	1				8			7	6															
11	25	Doncaster Rovers	1-4		Hammerton		2		4		5			9	10	11	1							7	6	8														
12	1 Nov	DURHAM	1-2		Hammerton		2	3	4	5	6			8	10	11	1		3		9			7																
13	8	Crewe Alexandra	1-3		Bailey		2		4	5	6			9	10	11	1				8			7																
14	15	WIGAN BOROUGH	3-4		Hammerton(2), Scott		2						8	9		7	1									3														
15	22	Walsall	1-0		O.G.		2			4				9	8	7	1								6	3		4	5	10	11										
16	6 Dec	Lincoln City	1-3		Pearson				4	6				9	8	7	1								6	3			5	10	11										
17	13	LINCOLN CITY	1-1		Wilks					4				8	11	1		2			9			7	6	3			5	10											
18	20	Nelson	1-4		Roe				4	8					11	1		2						7	6	3			5	10		2									
19	25	ASHINGTON	1-4		Etherington				4	8			7		11	1		2						7	6	3			5	10			9								
20	27	ACCRINGTON STANLEY	1-1	3000	Roe				5	4	8				2						11			7	6	3				10			9	1						
21	1 Jan	Ashington	1-3		Roe				5	4	8				2						11			7		3				10			9	1						
22	3	Halifax Town	0-4				4	5	6	8				10							7					3							9	1	2				
23	17	NEW BRIGHTON	2-1	7000	Scott, Pearson		4	5	6					8	11			2	7							3				10			9	1						
24	24	Grimsby Town	1-3		R.Chambers		4	5	6					8	11			2	7							3				10			9	1						
25	31	HARTLEPOOLS UNITED	1-2		Reid		4	5	6					8	11			2								3				10			9	1						
26	7 Feb	Rochdale	1-4		Scott			5	6		4			8	11			2	7							3				10			9	1						
27	14	DARLINGTON	1-1	7000	Bailey			5	4	7				10	11			2								3							9	1						
28	21	Bradford	0-3					5	4					8	11			2											8			9	1						
29	28	DONCASTER ROVERS	3-0		Johnston, Reid, Scott			4	5	6				8	11			2							7	6	3				10			9	1						
30	7 Mar	Durham	1-1	9000	Pearson			4	5	6				8	11			2	9							3								10	1					
31	14	CREWE ALEXANDRA	1-3	7000	Reid			4	5	6				8	11			2							7		3		2				1	10						
32	16	BARROW	0-1					4	5	6				8	11			2							7								10	1	2	9		
33	21	Wigan Borough	1-4		Reid			4	5	6				8	11			2	9							3		2						10	1			7		
34	28	WALSALL	2-0	4000	Pearson, Scott			4	5	6				8	11			2								3		2		9				10	1			7		
35	30	Chesterfield	2-3		Bailey, Scott			4	5	6				8	9	11		2								3		2		10					1			7		
36	4 Apr	Tranmere Rovers	0-1					4	5	6				8	9	11										3		2		10				1					
37	10	Wrexham	1-3		W.Chambers			4	5	6	7		8	9	11			3										2		10				1						
38	13	WREXHAM	0-1					4	5	6	7		8	9	11			3										2		10				1						
39	14	SOUTHPORT	1-3		Pearson			4	5	6			9		10	11										2							10	1		8	11	
40	18	Barrow	1-3		Hamilton			4	5	6				10	11			2	9							7		3						1		8			
41	25	NELSON	1-0		Hamilton			4	5	6				10	11											7		3		2				1		9		8	
42	2 May	CHESTERFIELD	1-3		Hamilton			4	5						10											7	6	3				11			1		9		8	11
			Apps.			3	15	11	31	37	37	14	9	17	38	37	16	1	17	15	4	3	20	12	1	24	1	18	17	5	1	7	5	1	12	18	1	9	2	2
			Goals						2	3	1	1	7	8	6				1											1			3	3		4			3	

F.A. CUP

	Date	Opposition	Res.	Att.	Goalscorers																																					
QR	29 Nov	DONCASTER ROVERS	2-3	15000	Hammerton, Scott				6	4				9	8	7	1		2							3			5	10	11									

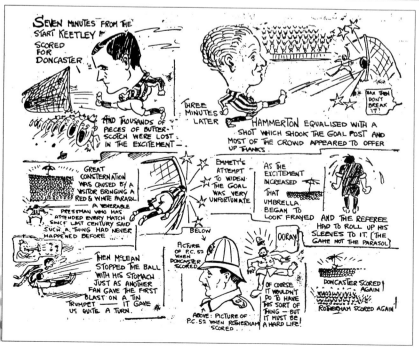

SEVEN MINUTES FROM THE START KEETLEY SCORED FOR DONCASTER

THREE MINUTES LATER HAMMERTON EQUALISED WITH A SHOT WHICH SHOOK THE GOAL POST AND MOST OF THE CROWD APPEARED TO OFFER UP THANKS

NAH THEN DON'T BREAK IT!

AND THOUSANDS OF PIECES OF BUTTER-SCOTCH WERE LOST IN THE EXCITEMENT —

GREAT CONSTERNATION WAS CAUSED BY A VISITOR BRINGING A RED & WHITE PARASOL

A VENERABLE PRESSMAN WHO HAS ATTENDED EVERY MATCH SINCE LAST CENTURY SAID SUCH A THING HAD NEVER HAPPENED BEFORE

EMMETT'S ATTEMPT TO WIDEN THE GOAL WAS VERY UNFORTUNATE

AS THE EXCITEMENT INCREASED THAT UMBRELLA BEGAN TO LOOK FRAYED AND THE REFEREE HAD TO ROLL UP HIS SLEEVES TO IT. (THE GAME NOT THE PARASOL)

BELOW

PICTURE OF P.C. 52 WHEN DONCASTER SCORED

OORAY

THEN McLEAN STOPPED THE BALL WITH HIS STOMACH JUST AS ANOTHER FAN GAVE THE FIRST BLAST ON A TIN TRUMPET — IT GAVE US QUITE A TURN.

ABOVE: PICTURE OF P.C. 52 WHEN ROTHERHAM SCORED.

OF COURSE IT WOULDN'T DO TO HAVE THIS SORT OF THING — BUT IT MUST BE A HARD LIFE!

DONCASTER SCORED AGAIN

ROTHERHAM SCORED AGAIN!

How cartoonist George Middleton of the 'Sheffield Mail' saw the F.A.Cup-tie v. Doncaster.

Final League Table

		Pl.	Home					Away					F.	A.	Pts
			W	D	L	F	A	W	D	L	F	A			
1	Darlington	42	16	4	1	50	14	8	6	7	28	19	78	33	58
2	Nelson	42	18	2	1	58	14	5	5	11	21	36	79	50	53
3	New Brighton	42	17	3	1	56	16	6	4	11	19	34	75	50	53
4	Southport	42	17	2	2	41	7	5	5	11	18	30	59	37	51
5	Bradford Park Ave.	42	15	5	1	59	13	4	7	10	25	29	84	42	50
6	Rochdale	42	17	2	2	53	16	4	5	12	22	37	75	53	49
7	Chesterfield	42	14	3	4	42	15	3	8	10	18	29	60	44	45
8	Lincoln City	42	13	4	4	39	19	5	4	12	14	33	53	58	44
9	Halifax Town	42	11	5	5	36	22	5	6	10	20	30	56	52	43
10	Ashington	42	13	4	4	41	24	3	6	12	27	52	68	76	42
11	Wigan Borough	42	10	7	4	39	16	5	4	12	23	49	62	65	41
12	Grimsby Town	42	10	6	5	38	21	5	3	13	22	39	60	60	39
13	Durham City	42	11	6	4	38	17	2	7	12	12	51	50	68	39
14	Barrow	42	14	4	3	39	22	2	3	16	12	52	51	74	39
15	Crewe Alexandra	42	11	7	3	35	24	2	6	13	18	54	53	78	39
16	Wrexham	42	11	5	5	37	21	4	3	14	16	40	53	61	38
17	Accrington Stanley	42	12	5	4	43	23	3	1	17	49	60	72	38
18	Doncaster Rovers	42	12	5	4	36	17	2	5	14	18	48	54	65	38
19	Walsall	42	10	6	5	27	16	3	5	13	17	44	53	37
20	Hartlepools United	42	9	8	4	28	21	3	3	15	17	42	45	63	35
21	Tranmere Rovers	42	11	3	7	40	29	3	1	17	19	49	59	78	32
22	Rotherham County	42	6	5	10	27	31	1	2	18	15	57	42	88	21

ROTHERHAM UNITED
SEASON 1925/26
DIVISION THREE (NORTH)

No.	Date	Opposition	Res.	Att.	Goalscorers
1	29 Aug	Bradford	1-6	1129	Hammerton
2	31	TRANMERE ROVERS	2-0	5422	Bestall, Hammerton
3	5 Sep	GRIMSBY TOWN	2-1	5388	Bestall, Scott
4	8	Rochdale	2-2	5643	Harrison, Lievesley
5	12	Wrexham	2-2	7610	Chambers, Scott
6	19	Halifax Town	1-5	2537	Scott
7	26	ACCRINGTON STANLEY	3-1	6405	Bestall, Hammerton, Scott
8	3 Oct	Durham City	1-5	3368	Hammerton
9	10	HARTLEPOOLS UNITED	1-0	6015	Lievesley
10	17	DONCASTER ROVERS	1-1	10187	Scott
11	24	Southport	1-1	4016	Scott
12	31	NELSON	1-3	7360	Scott
13	2 Nov	ROCHDALE	0-4	5363	
14	7	Coventry City	0-7	10160	
15	14	NEW BRIGHTON	1-0	4526	Lievesley
16	21	Wigan Borough	1-0	5110	Brelsford
17	5 Dec	Barrow	2-1	2338	Bestall, Chambers
18	19	Crewe Alexandra	1-3	4085	Scott
19	25	CHESTERFIELD	0-1	10571	
20	26	Chesterfield	1-6	9404	Lee
21	1 Jan	Tranmere Rovers	1-3	3330	Scott
22	2	BRADFORD	2-3	6624	Bestall, Scott
23	16	Grimsby Town	0-3	7059	
24	23	WREXHAM	6-2	3770	Yates(3), Bestall(2), Scott
25	30	HALIFAX TOWN	1-1	5310	Yates
26	6 Feb	Accrington Stanley	3-2	3947	Yates(2), Lee
27	13	DURHAM CITY	2-0	5994	Bestall, Scott
28	20	Hartlepools United	1-2	4408	Scott
29	22	ASHINGTON	5-1	3432	Bestall(2), Hemmingway(2), Yates
30	27	Doncaster Rovers	0-0	7198	
31	6 Mar	SOUTHPORT	5-2	5420	Yates(3), Hemmingway, Ramsden
32	13	Nelson	0-3	4451	
33	20	COVENTRY CITY	2-1	5749	Ramsden, Scott
34	27	New Brighton	1-5	3889	Bestall
35	3 Apr	WIGAN BOROUGH	1-0	5327	Ramsden
36	5	Walsall	1-4	5670	Hemingway
37	6	WALSALL	4-1	3809	Hardy, Harrison, Hemmingwy, Picken
38	10	Ashington	2-4	2793	Hemingway, Smith
39	17	BARROW	2-1	2680	Brelsford, Higginbottom
40	19	LINCOLN CITY	1-3	2458	Bestall
41	24	Lincoln City	3-0	4883	Hardy, Hemingway, Lievesley
42	1 May	CREWE ALEXANDRA	2-2	1928	Ramsden(2)

Player appearances (shirt numbers worn per match):

No.	McHaffy J.W.	Jackson R.	Yates H.	Brelsford T.	Chambers B.	Emmett B.	Glew J.	Bestall J.	Hammerton J.	Hodgetts A.	Scott J.	Lievesley F.	Bailey H.	Harrison J.T.	Julian E.	Lee J.	Boulton R.	Goldthorpe E.	Heald J.	Pickin W.	Turner J.	Ramsden C.W.	Bramley J.	Hemingway C.	Snee J.	Bentley R.	Higginbottom E.	Hardy R.	Smith N.H.	Lee W.
1	1	2	3	4	5	6	7	8	9	10	11																			
2	1	2	3	6	5	4	7	8	9		11	10																		
3	1	2	3	6	5	4		8	9		11	10		7																
4	1	2	3	6	5	4		8			11	10		7	9															
5	1	2	3	6	5	4	7	8			11	10			9															
6	1	2	3	6	5	4		8			11	10		7		9														
7	1	2	3	6	5	4		8	9		11			7																10
8	1	2	3	6	5	4		8	9	10	11			7																
9	1	2	3	5	4		7	8	9		11	10	6																	
10	1	2	3	5	4		7	8			11	10	6																	9
11	1	2	3	5	4		7	8			11	10	6																	
12	1	2	3	5	4		7	8			11	10	6				9													
13	1	2	3	5		4		8			11	10	6				9		7											
14	1	2	3	10	4		7				11		6				9			5										
15	1	2					7	8			11	10	6				9			5	3									
16	1	2	10	4				8	9		11		6							5	3	7								
17	1	2		4	9			8			11					10	7			5	3									
18	1	2		4	9		7	8			11					10	5				3									
19	1	2		4	9			8			11		6			10	7			5	3									
20	1	2		4	9			8			11		6			10				5	3									
21	1	2		4			7	8	9		11					10					3		5							
22	1	2		4		6		8	9		11					10				5			7	3						
23	1		3	4				8	9		11		6			10				5		2		7						
24	1	2	9	4				8			11		6			10				5			3	7						
25	1	2	9	5	4			8			11		6			10					7		3							
26	1	2	9	4			7	8			11		6			10				5			3							
27	1	2	9	4			7	8			11		6			10				5			3							
28	1	2	9	4			7	8			11		6			10				5			3							
29	1	2	9	4				8			11		6							5			3	7			10			
30	1	2	9	4	5			8			11		6										3	7			10			
31	1	2	9	4				8			11		6							5			3	7			10			
32	1	2	9	4				8			11		6							5			3	7			10			
33	1	2	9	4				8			11		6							5			3	7			10			
34	1	3		6	5			10			7		4				9						2	11			8			
35	1	2	9			5		8			11		6				7					3		10	4	9				
36	1	2	9			5		8			11		6				7					3		10			4			
37	1	2		3	4			8					6	9			7			5				10				11		
38	1	2		5	4			8					6				7					3		10			3	11	9	
39	1		9	5				8					6							2	7			10	4		3	11		
40	1	3	4	5				8					6				7			2				10	9			11		
41	1	2						8				9	6							3	7	5		10	4			11		
42	1	2						8				9	6							3	7	5		10	4			11		
Apps	42	39	29	36	22	21	4	42	15	2	36	13	38	3	1	17	6	2	1	17	24	15	5	14	4	1	4	6	1	2
Goals			10	2	2			12	4		13	4		2		2	1			1		5		7			1	2	1	

F.A. CUP

Rnd	Date	Opposition	Res	Att	Goalscorers	McHaffy	Jackson	Brelsford	Chambers	Bestall	Hammerton	Scott	Bailey	Lee J.	Boulton	Pickin	Turner	Emmett
1R	28 Nov	Halifax Town	3-0		Boulton(2), Lee	1	2	4	9	8		11	6	10	7	5	3	
2R	12 Dec	Doncaster Rovers	2-0		Lee, Picken	1	2	4	9	8		11	6	10	7	5	3	
3R	9 Jan	BURY	2-3	16442	Emmett, Hammerton	1	2	4		8	9	11	6	10		5	3	7

An un-named team group of the period (exact season unknown)

Final League Table

		Pl.	Home W	D	L	F	A	Away W	D	L	F	A	F.A.	A.	Pts
1	Grimsby Town	42	20	1	0	61	8	6	8	7	30	32	91	40	61
2	Bradford Park Ave.	42	18	2	1	65	10	8	6	7	36	33	101	43	60
3	Rochdale	42	16	1	4	55	25	11	4	6	49	33	104	58	59
4	Chesterfield	42	18	2	1	70	19	7	3	11	30	35	100	54	55
5	Halifax Town	42	12	5	4	34	19	5	6	10	19	31	53	50	45
6	Hartlepools United	42	15	5	1	59	23	3	3	15	23	50	82	73	44
7	Tranmere Rovers	42	15	2	4	45	27	4	4	13	28	56	73	83	44
8	Nelson	42	12	8	1	67	29	4	3	14	22	42	89	71	43
9	Ashington	42	11	6	4	44	23	5	5	11	26	39	70	62	43
10	Doncaster Rovers	42	11	7	3	52	25	5	4	12	28	47	80	72	43
11	Crewe Alexandra	42	14	4	3	43	23	3	6	12	20	38	63	61	43
12	New Brighton	42	13	4	4	51	29	4	4	13	18	38	69	67	42
13	Durham City	42	14	5	2	45	19	4	1	16	18	51	63	70	42
14	Rotherham United	42	13	3	5	44	28	4	4	13	25	64	69	92	41
15	Lincoln City	42	14	2	5	42	28	3	3	15	24	54	66	82	39
16	Coventry City	42	13	6	2	47	19	3	0	18	26	63	73	82	38
17	Wigan Borough	42	12	5	4	53	22	1	6	14	15	52	68	74	37
18	Accrington Stanley	42	14	0	7	49	34	3	3	15	32	71	81	105	37
19	Wrexham	42	9	6	6	39	31	2	4	15	24	61	63	92	32
20	Southport	42	9	6	6	37	34	2	4	15	25	58	62	92	32
21	Walsall	42	9	4	8	40	34	1	2	18	18	73	58	107	26
22	Barrow	42	4	2	15	28	49	3	2	16	22	49	50	98	18

SEASON 1926/27
DIVISION THREE (NORTH)

No.	Date	Opposition	Res.	Att.	Goalscorers
1	28 Aug	CREWE ALEXANDRA	2-1	5814	Bestall, Hemmingway
2	30	WREXHAM	2-0	4937	Oakton(2)
3	4 Sep	Bradford	2-2	13060	Hemmingway(2)
4	8	Wrexham	0-3	5653	
5	11	WALSALL	4-1	6200	Higginbottom(2), Bestall, Oakton
6	18	Nelson	3-5	6395	Fergusson, Hemmingway, Scott
7	25	CHESTERFIELD	0-4	7510	
8	2 Oct	Ashington	4-4	2022	Scott(3), Higginbottom
9	9	NEW BRIGHTON	0-0	3624	
10	16	HALIFAX TOWN	2-4	4597	Bentley, Ramsden
11	23	Barrow	2-2	4667	Bentley, Ramsden
12	30	HARTLEPOOLS UNITED	5-3	3013	Bestall(2), Higginbottom(2), Ramsdn
13	1 Nov	WIGAN BOROUGH	2-0	2990	Fergusson, Hardy
14	6	Stockport County	1-3	7998	Ramsden
15	13	SOUTHPORT	1-2	2925	Yates
16	20	Rochdale	1-2	4795	Higginbottom
17	4 Dec	Durham City	1-0	1471	Yates
18	11	ROCHDALE	1-1	3296	Scott
19	18	Lincoln City	2-1	3723	Ramsden, Scott
20	25	Stoke City	1-4	13530	Chilton
21	27	STOKE CITY	2-2	9105	Hardy, Ramsden
22	1 Jan	DONCASTER ROVERS	1-3	8159	Ramsden
23	8	TRANMERE ROVERS	2-2	2553	Chilton(2)
24	15	Crewe Alexandra	2-2	4123	Chilton, Hemingway
25	22	BRADFORD	1-1	4023	Hemingway
26	24	ACCRINGTON STANLEY	1-1	1631	Chilton
27	29	Walsall	2-3	4212	Chilton(2)
28	5 Feb	NELSON	2-3	4345	Hemingway, Ramsden
29	12	Chesterfield	2-5	3892	Lievesley, Snee
30	19	ASHINGTON	5-0	3543	Bailey(2), Ramsden(2), Parkin
31	26	New Brighton	0-3	4298	
32	5 Mar	Halifax Town	2-4	6220	Bailey, Hemingway
33	12	BARROW	2-0	3146	Hemingway, Lievesley
34	19	Hartlepools United	1-3	2766	Parkin
35	26	STOCKPORT COUNTY	1-2	4176	Scott
36	2 Apr	Southport	0-2	2358	
37	16	Tranmere Rovers	0-4	5321	
38	18	Wigan Borough	0-0	4943	
39	19	Doncaster Rovers	2-2	5611	Chilton, Scott
40	23	DURHAM CITY	3-1	2389	Chilton, Harrison, Scott
41	30	Accrington Stanley	1-3	2991	Chilton
42	7 May	LINCOLN CITY	2-4	2155	Hemingway(2)

Player appearances grid

No.	McHaffy J.W.	Jackson R.	Turner J.	Pantling H.	Chambers B.	Bailey H.	Oakton A.	Bestall J.	Fergusson W.	Hemingway C.	Scott J.	Lievesley F.	Higginbottom E.	Emmett B.	Capley C.H.	Ramsden C.	Bentley R.	Yates H.	Steele P.H.	Hardy E.	Atter J.	Chilton C.	Harrison J.T.	Snee J.	Parkin A.	Saville W.	Marsden L.
1	1	2	3	4	5	6	7	8	9	10	11																
2	1	2	3	4		6	7	8	9	10	11	5															
3	1	2	3	4	5	6	7	8	9	10	11																
4	1	2	3	4	5	6	7	8	9	10	11																
5	1	2	3	4	5	6	7	8	9		11		10														
6	1	2	3	4	5	6	7	8	9	10	11																
7	1	2	3	4	5	6	7	8	9		11		10														
8	1	2	3	4	5	6		8			11		10														
9	1	2	3		5	6		8		10	11			4		7			9								
10	1	2	3		5	6		8		10	11			4		7	9										
11	1	2			5			8		10				4	11	7	9		3	6							
12	1	2	3		5			8	9				10	4		7				6		11					
13	1	2	3		5			8	9				10	4		7				6		11					
14	1	2	3		5			8	9				10	4	11	7				6							
15	1	2	3		5			8			11		10	4		7		9		6							
16	1	2	3		5			8	9		11		10	4		7				6							
17		2	3	4	5			8		10	11					7		9		6	1						
18		2	3	4	5			8		10	11					7				6	1	9					
19		2	3	4	5				8	10	11					7				6	1	9					
20		2	3	4	5			8			11					7				6	1	9	10				
21			3		5	4			9	10	11					7			3	6	1	8					
22		2	3		5	4			9	10	11					7				6	1	8					
23		2	3		5	6		8			11	10				7					1	9			4		
24		2	3		5	6		8			11					7					1	9			4		
25		2	3		5	6				10	11	8				7					1	9			4		
26		2	3		5	6		8		10	11					7					1	9			4		
27		2	3		5	6				10	11	8				7					1	9			4		
28		2	3		5	6				10	11	8				7					1	9			4		
29		2	3		5	6				10	11	8				7					1	9			4		
30		2	3		5	6				10		8		11		7					1				4	9	
31		2	3		5	6				10	11	8				7					1				4	9	
32		2			5	6		9		10	11	8			3	7					1				4		
33		2	3		5	6				10	11	8				7					1				4	9	
34		2	3		5	6				10	11	8				7					1				4	9	
35		2	3			6				10	11	8			5	7					1				4	9	
36		2	3		5	6				10	11	8				7					1				4	9	
37		2	3			6				10	11	8				7		4			1					9	
38	1	2	3			6				10	11	5				7		4			1	8	9				
39	1	2	3			6				10	11	5				7		4				9	8				
40	1	2	3			6				10	11					7		5				9	8		4		
41		2	3			6					11	8				7					1	9	10	4		5	
42		2	3			6				10	11	5				7					1	9				6	8
Apps.	19	40	41	12	34	32	7	17	19	30	37	18	10	8	2	35	3	6	16	5	23	15	7	15	7	3	1
Goals						3	3	4	2	11	9	2	6			10	2	2		2		10	1	1	2		

F.A. CUP

	Date	Opposition	Res.	Att.	Goalscorers
1R	27 Nov	Lincoln City	0-2	7394	

F.A. Cup line-up: McHaffy 1, Jackson 2, Turner 3, Pantling 4, Chambers 5, Fergusson 8, Scott 11, Hemingway 9, Higginbottom 10, Ramsden 7, Hardy 6

Final League Table

		Pl.	Home					Away					F.	A.	Pts
			W	D	L	F	A	W	D	L	F	A			
1	Stoke City	42	17	3	1	57	11	10	6	5	35	29	92	40	63
2	Rochdale	42	18	2	1	72	22	8	4	9	33	43	105	65	58
3	Bradford Park Ave.	42	18	3	0	74	21	6	4	11	27	38	101	59	55
4	Halifax Town	42	13	6	2	46	23	8	5	8	24	30	70	53	53
5	Nelson	42	16	2	3	64	20	6	5	10	40	55	104	75	51
6	Stockport County	42	13	4	4	60	31	9	3	9	33	38	93	69	49
7	Chesterfield	42	15	4	2	65	24	6	1	14	27	44	92	68	47
8	Doncaster Rovers	42	13	4	4	58	27	5	7	9	23	38	81	65	47
9	Tranmere Rovers	42	13	5	3	54	22	6	3	12	31	45	85	67	46
10	New Brighton	42	14	2	5	49	21	4	8	9	30	46	79	67	46
11	Lincoln City	42	9	5	7	50	33	6	7	8	40	45	90	78	42
12	Southport	42	11	5	5	54	32	4	4	13	26	53	80	85	39
13	Wrexham	42	10	5	6	41	26	4	5	12	24	47	65	73	38
14	Walsall	42	10	4	7	35	22	4	6	11	33	59	68	81	38
15	Crewe Alexandra	42	11	5	5	46	28	3	4	14	25	53	71	81	37
16	Ashington	42	9	8	4	42	30	3	4	14	18	60	60	90	36
17	Hartlepools United	42	11	4	6	43	26	3	2	16	23	55	66	81	34
18	Wigan Borough	42	10	6	5	44	28	1	4	16	22	55	66	83	32
19	Rotherham United	42	8	6	7	41	35	2	6	13	29	57	70	92	32
20	Durham City	42	9	4	8	35	35	3	2	16	23	70	58	105	30
21	Accrington Stanley	42	9	3	9	45	38	1	4	16	17	60	62	98	27
22	Barrow	42	5	6	10	22	40	2	2	17	12	77	34	117	22

SEASON 1927/28
DIVISION THREE (NORTH)

No.	Date	Opposition	Res	Att	Goalscorers	Alter J.	Jackson R.	Turner J.	Bailey H.	Reed E.	Higginbottom E.	Phillips W.	Clayton J.	Chilton C.	Hemingway C.	Scott J.	Saville W.	Parkin A.	Taylor A.	Lievesley F.	Snee J.	Hall T.	Mountney C.	Dransfield E.	Sellars W.	Best J.	Webb G.	Jackson R.	Davies A.
1	27 Aug	Stockport County	0-2	11546		1	2	3	4	5	6	7	8	9	10	11													
2	29	TRANMERE ROVERS	2-1	4200	Clayton, Scott	1	2	3	4	5	6	7	8	9	10	11													
3	3 Sep	BARROW	3-0	4227	Bailey, Chilton, Phillips	1	2	3	4	5	6	7	8	9	10	11													
4	10	Nelson	1-6	4881	Scott	1	2	3	4	5	6	7	8	9	10	11													
5	17	ROCHDALE	3-1	4911	Scott(2), Parkin	1	2	3	6	5		7	8		10	11	4	9											
6	24	Doncaster Rovers	0-2	7764		1	2	3	6	5		7	8		10	11	4	9											
7	1 Oct	Southport	1-1	2977	Scott	1	2	3	6	5			8	9		11	4		7	10									
8	8	DURHAM CITY	1-1	4520	Scott	1	2	3	6	5			8			11	4	9	7	10									
9	15	Wrexham	2-3	7139	Clayton, Phillips	1	2	3	6	5		7	8		9	11				10	4								
10	22	HARTLEPOOLS UNITED	5-0	2395	Clayton(3), Phillips, Scott	1	2	3	6	5	9	7	8			11				10	4								
11	29	Accrington Stanley	1-3	4930	Scott	1	2	3	6	5	9	7	8			11				10	4								
12	5 Nov	WIGAN BOROUGH	6-0	3819	Hall(4), Hemmingway, Lievesley	1	2	6		5	3		8		7	11				10	4	9							
13	12	Lincoln City	1-4	5819	Lievesley	1	2		6	5	3		8		7	11				10	4	9							
14	19	NEW BRIGHTON	0-0	4135		1	2	3		5		7	8	6		11				10	4	9							
15	3 Dec	HALIFAX TOWN	0-0	4965		1	2	3		6			8			11			7	10	4	9	5						
16	17	ASHINGTON	1-1	4420	Scott	1		3	6	5		7	8			11				10	4	9		2					
17	24	Darlington	1-4	3409	Lievesley	1		3	6	5		7	8			11				10	4	9		2					
18	26	CHESTERFIELD	1-2	6748	Hall	1		3	6	5		7	8			11				10	4	9		2					
19	27	Chesterfield	5-2	5227	Phillips, Scott, Lievesley(2), Hall	1		3	6	5		7	8			11				10	4	9		2					
20	31	STOCKPORT COUNTY	0-1	3625		1		3	6	5			8			11				10	4	9		2	7				
21	2 Jan	Tranmere Rovers	0-2	5576		1		3	6	5			8		10	11				4	9			2	7				
22	7	Barrow	1-1	2804	Hemmingway	1	2	3	6	5			8		9	11				10	4				7				
23	21	NELSON	4-3	4505	Higginbottm, Claytn, Scott, Lievesley	1	2	3	6	5	9		8			11				10	4				7				
24	4 Feb	DONCASTER ROVERS	2-1	11530	Bailey, Clayton	1	2	3	6	5			8			11		9		10	4				7				
25	8	Crewe Alexandra	2-3	2169	Hemmingway, Scott	1	2	3	6	5			8		9	11				10	4				7				
26	11	SOUTHPORT	1-1	4155	Higginbottom	1	2	3	6	5	9		8			11				10	4				7				
27	18	Durham City	4-1	2037	Scott(2), Parkin, Lievesley		2	3	6	5			8			11		9		10	4				7	1			
28	25	WREXHAM	0-1	5665			2	3	6	5	11		8		10	10		9			4				7	1			
29	28	Rochdale	1-2	1885	Scott		2	3	6	5			8	10	8	11		9			4				7	1			
30	3 Mar	Hartlepools United	3-1	4190	Scott, Parkin(2)	1	2	3	6	5			8	10	4	11		9			8				7				
31	10	ACCRINGTON STANLEY	2-1	3763	Chilton, Scott	1	2	3	6	5			8	10	8	11		9			4				7				
32	14	Bradford City	1-3	3821	Scott	1	2	3	6	5			8	10	8	11				10	4				7				
33	17	Wigan Borough	0-0	3281		1	2	3	6	5			8			11		9		10	4				7				
34	24	LINCOLN CITY	2-4	4339	Clayton, Lievesley	1	2	3	6	5			8	4						10		9			7			11	
35	31	New Brighton	1-1	3240	Lievesley	1	2	3	6	5			8							10	4	9			7			11	
36	7 Apr	CREWE ALEXANDRA	2-0	3625	Phillips, Lievesley	1	2	3	6	5		7	8			11				10	4	9							
37	9	BRADFORD PARK AVENUE	1-0	6288	Clayton	1	2	3	6	5		7	8			11				10	4	9							
38	10	Bradford Park Avenue	1-3	14311	Phillips	1	2	3	6	5		7	8			11				10	4	9							
39	14	Halifax Town	0-0	3171		1		3	6	5		7	8			11				10	4						9		
40	21	BRADFORD CITY	0-0	2775		1	2	3	6	5			8			11				9	4				7				10
41	28	Ashington	0-6	1464		1	2	3	6				8			11		9			4				5	7			10
42	5 May	DARLINGTON	3-1	2058	Hemingway, Parkin, Sellars	1	2	3	6	5			8			11		9			4				7				10
		Apps.				39	35	40	40	40	12	19	42	10	23	31	4	11	2	29	32	16	2	7	19	3	2	1	3
		Goals							2		2	6	9	2	4	18		5		10		6			1				

F.A. CUP

	Date	Opposition	Res		Goalscorers	Alter J.	Jackson R.	Turner J.	Bailey H.	Reed E.	Higginbottom E.	Phillips W.	Clayton J.	Chilton C.	Hemingway C.	Scott J.	Saville W.	Parkin A.	Taylor A.	Lievesley F.	Snee J.	Hall T.	Mountney C.	Dransfield E.	Sellars W.	Best J.	Webb G.	Jackson R.	Davies A.
1R	26 Nov	Spennymoor United	1-1		Scott	1	2	3		5	6	7	8			11				10	4	9							
1Rr	1 Dec	SPENNYMOOR UNITED	4-2		Lievesley(2), Phillips, Hall	1	2	3	6	5		7	8			11				10	4	9							
2R	10	Bradford City	3-2		Phillips, Clayton, Lievesley	1		3	6	5		7	8			11				10	4	9							
3R	14 Jan	EXETER CITY	3-3		Scott(2), Hemingway	1	2	3	6	5			8		9	11				10	4				7				
3Rr	18	Exeter City	1-3		Hall	1	2	3	6	5			8			11				10	4	9			7				

A section of the crowd present at the Exeter Cup match

Final League Table

		Pl.	Home					Away					F.	A.	Pts
			W	D	L	F	A	W	D	L	F	A			
1	Bradford Park Ave.	42	18	2	1	68	22	9	7	5	33	23	101	45	63
2	Lincoln City	42	15	4	2	53	20	9	3	9	38	44	91	64	55
3	Stockport County	42	16	5	0	62	14	7	3	11	27	37	89	51	54
4	Doncaster Rovers	42	15	4	2	59	18	8	3	10	21	26	80	44	53
5	Tranmere Rovers	42	14	6	1	68	28	8	3	10	37	44	105	72	53
6	Bradford City	42	15	4	2	59	19	3	8	10	26	41	85	60	48
7	Darlington	42	15	1	5	63	28	6	4	11	26	46	89	74	47
8	Southport	42	15	2	4	55	24	5	3	13	24	46	79	70	45
9	Accrington Stanley	42	14	3	4	49	22	5	3	13	27	45	76	67	44
10	New Brighton	42	10	7	4	45	22	4	7	10	27	40	72	62	42
11	Wrexham	42	15	1	5	48	19	3	5	13	16	48	64	67	42
12	Halifax Town	42	11	7	3	47	24	2	8	11	26	47	73	71	41
13	Rochdale	42	13	4	4	45	24	4	3	14	29	53	74	77	41
14	Rotherham United	42	11	6	4	39	19	3	5	13	26	50	65	69	39
15	Hartlepools United	42	10	3	8	41	35	6	3	12	28	46	69	81	38
16	Chesterfield	42	10	4	7	46	29	3	6	12	25	49	71	78	36
17	Ashington	42	10	6	5	51	28	2	4	15	26	58	77	86	34
18	Crewe Alexandra	42	10	5	6	54	36	1	6	14	23	67	77	103	33
19	Barrow	42	10	8	3	41	24	0	3	18	13	78	54	102	31
20	Wigan Borough	42	8	5	8	30	32	2	5	14	26	65	56	97	30
21	Durham City	42	10	5	6	37	30	1	2	18	16	70	53	100	29
22	Nelson	42	8	4	9	50	49	2	2	17	26	87	76	136	26

SEASON 1928/29
DIVISION THREE (NORTH)

No.	Date	Opposition	Res.	Att.	Goalscorers	Atter J.	Jackson R.	Turner J.	Gallyer R.	Reed E.	Snee J.	Sellars W.	Clayton J.	Bottrill W.G.	Lievesley F.	Pears J.	Best J.	Hastings J.	Davies A.	Orr A.	Cooper W.T.	Atkinson R.	Parkin A.	Portman J.	Dransfield E.	Coleman A.	Colley W.	Sharp J.
1	25 Aug	Bradford City	1-11	12356	Pears	1	2	3	4	5	6	7	8	9	10	11												
2	27	LINCOLN CITY	3-2	3640	Bottrill(3)	1	2	3	6	5	4	7	8	9	10	11												
3	1 Sep	ACCRINGTON STANLEY	2-1	5652	Bottrill, Lievesley	1	2	3	6	5	4	7	8	9	10	11												
4	3	Lincoln City	1-1	5943	Lievesley	1	2	3	6	5	4	7	8	9	10	11												
5	8	Hartlepools United	1-1	4867	Bottrill	1	2	3	6	5	4	7	8	9	10	11												
6	15	CARLISLE UNITED	4-0	8075	Lievesley(2), Clayton, Pears	1	2	3	6	5	4	7	8	9	10	11												
7	22	Southport	0-2	4044		1	2	3	6	5	4	7	8	9	10	11												
8	29	Wigan Borough	0-1	6331		1	2	3	6	5	4	7	8	9				11	8	10									
9	6 Oct	CREWE ALEXANDRA	1-2	6240	Davies	1	2	3	6	5	4	7	8	9					10			11							
10	13	Tranmere Rovers	0-3	4766		1	2	3	6	5	4	7	10	9						8	11								
11	20	DARLINGTON	2-0	4369	Gallyer, Parkin	1	2	3	6	5	4	7		8				11		10			9						
12	27	Nelson	2-4	3795	Bottrill, Orr	1	2	3		5	4	7	10	8				11	6	9									
13	3 Nov	SOUTH SHIELDS	1-1	5167	Sellars	1	2	3		5	4	7	10	8					6	9		11							
14	10	Ashington	1-0	1626	Bottrill	1	2	3	4			7	10	8					6	9		11		5					
15	17	DONCASTER ROVERS	1-2	7347	Clayton	1		3		5		7	10	8					6	9		11			2	4			
16	1 Dec	CHESTERFIELD	2-0	5795	Atkinson(2)		2	3			4		8	9	10		1		6	7		11	5					
17	8	Wrexham	0-2	5224			2	3			4	7	10	9			1		6	8		11	5					
18	15	NEW BRIGHTON	3-1	3620	Sellars, Parkin(2)		2	3			4	8			10		1		6	7		11	9	5				
19	22	Rochdale	1-2	2120	Atkinson		2	3			8	4			10		1		6	7		11	9	5				
20	25	Stockport County	0-1	14238				3			8	4	9		10		1		6	7		11	5	2				
21	26	STOCKPORT COUNTY	3-3	8627	Bottrill, Orr(2)						4	8		10	5		1		6	7		11	9	3	2			
22	29	BRADFORD CITY	2-2	6239	Sellars(2)	2					4	8		10	9	1			6	7		11	5	3				
23	5 Jan	Accrington Stanley	3-1	3319	Pears(2), Orr	2	3				8	4		10	9	1			6	7		11	5					
24	12	Barrow	0-4	5115		2	3				8	4		10	9	1			6	7		11	5					
25	19	HARTLEPOOLS UNITED	3-2	4339	Sellars, Pears, Orr	2					8	4		10	11	1			6	7			9	5	3			
26	26	Carlisle United	1-1	6251	Parkin	2					8	4		10	11	1			6	7			9	5	3			
27	2 Feb	SOUTHPORT	0-2	2965		2					4	8		10	11	1			6	7			9	5	3			
28	9	WIGAN BOROUGH	4-2	4034	Sellars, Lievesley, Parkin(2)	2	3				8	4		10		1			6	7	11		9	5				
29	23	TRANMERE ROVERS	0-1	3829		2					8	4		10		1			6	7	11		9	3	5			
30	2 Mar	Darlington	1-2	2874	Pears	2	3		6		7	4	8	10	9	1					11			5				
31	9	NELSON	4-0	3939	Sellars(3), Orr	2	3		6		7	4	8	10	9	1					11			5				
32	16	South Shields	1-10	3134	Pears	2	3		5		8	4	7	10	9	1			6		11			5				
33	23	ASHINGTON	0-0	3078		2	3				8	4	7	10	9	1			6		11							
34	30	Doncaster Rovers	0-1	7891		2	3				7	4	8	10		1			6		11			5				
35	1 Apr	HALIFAX TOWN	0-0	2679		2	3		6		8	4	7	10	9	1					11			5				
36	2	Halifax Town	1-3	3112	Bottrill	5	3		6		8	4	7	10	9	1					11			2				
37	6	BARROW	2-1	2196	Lievesley, Orr	5	3				8	10		9		1	6				11			2	7	4		
38	13	Chesterfield	2-1	2545	Hastings, Sharp	1	2	3			7	8		10			6				11		9			4	5	
39	17	Crewe Alexandra	0-3	1373		1	2	3			7	8		10			6				11		9			4	5	
40	20	WREXHAM	2-1	3187	Orr, Parkin	1	2	3			7	6	8					10	11		11		9	5		4		
41	27	New Brighton	0-0	2239		1	2	3			7	4	8				6	10	11		11		9			4		5
42	4 May	ROCHDALE	5-0	2899	Bottrill(2), Parkin(2), Orr	1	2	3			7	4	8				6	10	11		11		9					5
		Apps.				20	39	36	12	19	18	40	37	30	30	21	22	27	5	32	4	14	15	18	13	2	4	4
		Goals						1				9	2	11	6	7		1	1	9			3	9				

F.A. CUP

						Atter J.	Jackson R.	Turner J.	Gallyer R.	Reed E.	Snee J.	Sellars W.	Clayton J.	Bottrill W.G.	Lievesley F.	Pears J.	Best J.	Hastings J.	Davies A.	Orr A.	Cooper W.T.	Atkinson R.	Parkin A.	Portman J.	Dransfield E.	Coleman A.	Colley W.	Sharp J.
1R	24 Nov	Tranmere Rovers	1-2		Orr		2	3			4	7	10	8				11	1	6		9	5					

Final League Table

		Pl.	Home					Away					F.	A.	Pts
			W	D	L	F	A	W	D	L	F	A			
1	Bradford City	42	17	2	2	82	18	10	7	4	46	25	128	43	63
2	Stockport County	42	19	2	0	77	23	9	4	8	34	35	111	58	62
3	Wrexham	42	17	2	2	59	25	4	8	9	32	44	91	69	52
4	Wigan Borough	42	16	4	1	55	16	5	5	11	27	33	82	49	51
5	Doncaster Rovers	42	14	3	4	39	20	6	7	8	37	46	76	66	50
6	Lincoln City	42	15	3	3	58	18	6	3	12	33	49	91	67	48
7	Tranmere Rovers	42	15	3	3	55	21	7	0	14	24	56	79	77	47
8	Carlisle United	42	15	3	3	61	27	4	5	12	25	50	86	77	46
9	Crewe Alexandra	42	11	6	4	47	23	7	2	12	33	45	80	68	44
10	South Shields	42	13	5	3	57	24	5	3	13	26	50	83	74	44
11	Chesterfield	42	13	2	6	46	28	5	3	13	25	49	71	77	41
12	Southport	42	13	5	3	52	27	3	3	15	23	58	75	85	40
13	Halifax Town	42	11	7	3	42	24	2	6	13	21	38	63	62	39
14	New Brighton	42	11	3	7	40	28	4	6	11	24	43	64	71	39
15	Nelson	42	14	1	6	48	28	3	4	14	29	62	77	90	39
16	Rotherham United	42	12	5	4	44	23	3	4	14	16	54	60	77	39
17	Rochdale	42	12	4	5	55	34	1	6	14	24	62	79	96	36
18	Accrington Stanley	42	11	5	5	42	22	2	3	16	26	60	68	82	34
19	Darlington	42	12	6	3	47	26	1	1	19	17	62	64	88	33
20	Barrow	42	7	6	8	42	37	3	2	16	22	56	64	93	28
21	Hartlepools United	42	9	4	8	35	38	1	2	18	24	74	59	112	26
22	Ashington	42	6	5	10	31	52	2	2	17	14	63	45	115	23

SEASON 1929-30
DIVISION THREE (NORTH)

No.	Date	Opposition	Res.	Att.	Goalscorers	Emery A.	Jackson R.	Turner J.	Pattison E.	Sharp J.	Hastings J.	Sellars W.	Clayton J.	Wright V.	Lievesley F.	Little J.	Atter J.	Smailes A.	Harris T.	Murden G.	Bratley G.	Lowe J.	Orr A.	Liddle J.F.	Waring W.	Davies S.	Dransfield E.	Robinson C.	Parkin A.	Turner A.	Portman T.	Wheeler F.
1	31 Aug	Tranmere Rovers	4-5	5960	J.Turner, Wright, Lievesley, Little	1	2	3	4	5	6	7	8	9	10	11																
2	2 Sep	LINCOLN CITY	1-0	6605	Wright		2	3	4	5	6	7		9	10	11	1		8													
3	7	HALIFAX TOWN	2-0	6524	Wright, Lievesley		2	3	4		6	7		9	10	11	1	5	8													
4	9	Lincoln City	1-1	5739	Wright		2	3	4		6	7		9	10	11	1	5	8	10												
5	14	Barrow	1-5	6066	Harris		2	3	4		6	7		9	10	11	1	5	8													
6	21	Rochdale	2-1	4700	Smailes, Murden		2	3	4					9			1	6	8	10	5		7		11							
7	28	SOUTH SHIELDS	0-1	7054			2	3	4					9			1	6	8	10	5		11									
8	5 Oct	Accrington Stanley	0-2	5183			2	3	4			7	8	9			1	6		10	5		11									
9	12	DARLINGTON	1-4	5785	Murden		2	3	4				8	9			1	6		10	5		11	7								
10	19	PORT VALE	2-2	6583	Sellars, Murden		2	3	4		6	8			10	11	1	5		9			7									
11	26	New Brighton	2-2	3051	Lievesley, Murden		2		4		6	8			10	11	1	5		9			7					3				
12	2 Nov	STOCKPORT COUNTY	2-2	5622	Murden(2)		2	3	6			8	4		10	11	1	5		9			7									
13	9	York City	0-3	3715			2	3	6			8	4		10	11	1	5		9			7									
14	16	CREWE ALEXANDRA	2-1	3717	Murden, Waring		2	3	6			8	4		10		1	5		9			7		11							
15	23	Southport	1-7	2648	Murden		2	3	6			8	4		10		1	5		9			7		11							
16	7 Dec	Carlisle United	1-3	4820	Parkin		2	3	6			7				8	1	5		10			11						4	9		
17	21	Wrexham	0-1	3735			2	3	6			7			8	10	1			9	5		11						4			
18	25	CHESTERFIELD	1-1	5645	Murden		2				6	7	8				1			10	5		11		9			3	4			
19	26	Chesterfield	1-2	8484	Sellars		2				6	7		8						10	5		11					3	4	9	1	
20	28	TRANMERE ROVERS	5-0	4528	Sellars, Wright, Murden(3)			3			6	7		8						10	5		11					2	4	9	1	
21	1 Jan	Hartlepools United	1-5	4756	Wright			3			6	7		8						10	5		11					2	4	9	1	
22	4	Halifax Town	1-1	4501	Murden	1	2	3	6			7		8	10					9	5		11						4			
23	18	BARROW	7-0	3977	Sellars, Murden(4), Orr, Parkin		2		4			7		8			1			10	5		11					3	9			
24	25	ROCHDALE	0-4	5915			2		6			7		8			1			10	5		11					3	4	9		
25	15 Feb	South Shields	0-5	1239		1	2				6	7		8		10				9	5		11					4			3	
26	8	ACCRINGTON STANLEY	2-4	4096	Wright, Lievesley		2	3			6	7		9	8			5		10			11						4	1		
27	15	Darlington	1-8	2382	Wright		2	3			6	7	4	8				5		11			10						9			
28	22	Port Vale	1-7	7989	Wright		2	3	6			7		8	10		1	5		9			11						4			
29	24	WIGAN BOROUGH	4-1	1664	Sellars(2), Wright, Lievesley		2	3	4		6	7		8	10		1	5					11						9			
30	1 Mar	NEW BRIGHTON	2-2	4024	Lievesley(2)		2	3	4			7		8	10	6	1	5			9	11										
31	8	Stockport County	1-6	9544	Sellars		2		4			7			8	6	1	5			9	11					3					
32	15	YORK CITY	2-5	2259	Wright, Orr		2					7	8		6	1		5			9	11						4	9		3	
33	22	Crewe Alexandra	1-6	3967	Orr		2	3				7	4	8	6		1			10	5		9	11								
34	24	NELSON	1-2	1831	Orr	1	2	3				7	4	8	6					10	5		9	11								
35	29	SOUTHPORT	6-3	3274	Sellars, Wright, Murden(2), Orr(2)	1	2	3				7	4	8	6					10	5		9	11								
36	5 Apr	Nelson	1-0	2280	Orr	1	2	3				7	4	8	6					10	5		9	11								
37	12	CARLISLE UNITED	4-1	4140	Sellars, Murden(2), Orr	1	2	3				7	4	8	6					10	5		9	11								
38	18	Doncaster Rovers	0-2	9451		1	2	3				7	4	8	6					10	5		9	11								
39	19	Wigan Borough	1-1	2106	Orr	1	2	3				7	4	8	6					10			9	11				5				
40	21	DONCASTER ROVERS	1-0	6749	Orr	1	2	3				7	4	8	6					10			9	11				5				
41	26	WREXHAM	1-3	3415	Sellars	1	2	3				7	4	8	6					10	5		9									11
42	3 May	HARTLEPOOLS UNITED	0-4	3477				3				7	4	8	10	6					5		9				2				1	11
				Apps.		11	39	34	24	2	16	40	19	33	18	24	26	20	6	33	22	1	33	13	6	1	11	12	9	5	2	2
				Goals			1					10		12	6	1		1	1	22			10				1		2			

F.A. CUP

	Date	Opposition	Res.	Att.	Goalscorers	Emery A.	Jackson R.	Turner J.	Pattison E.	Sharp J.	Hastings J.	Sellars W.	Clayton J.	Wright V.	Lievesley F.	Little J.	Atter J.	Smailes A.	Harris T.	Murden G.	Bratley G.	Lowe J.	Orr A.	Liddle J.F.	Waring W.	Davies S.	Dransfield E.	Robinson C.	Parkin A.	Turner A.	Portman T.	Wheeler F.
1R	30 Nov	ASHINGTON	3-0	6537	Sellars(2), Davies		2	3	6			7					1	5		10			11			8			4	9		
2R	14 Dec	Scunthorpe United	3-3		Pattison, Davies(2)		2	3	6			7			10		1	5					11			8			4	9		
2Rr	19	SCUNTHOPRE UNITED	5-4		Sellars, Lievesley(2), Orr		2	3	6			7			10		1	5			9		11			8			4			
3R	11 Jan	NOTTINGHAM FOREST	0-5	15862		1	2	3	6			7		8				5			9		11						8	4		

April 1930: Past and present Rotherham United players stage a match in aid of the Rotherham Hospital Reconstruction Scheme. The players of both sides plus the Mayor and Mayoress are pictured above.

Final League Table

		Pl.	Home					Away					F.	A.	Pts
			W	D	L	F	A	W	D	L	F	A			
1	Port Vale	42	17	2	2	64	18	13	5	3	39	19	103	37	67
2	Stockport County	42	15	3	3	67	20	13	4	4	39	24	106	44	63
3	Darlington	42	14	2	5	71	29	8	4	9	37	44	108	73	50
4	Chesterfield	42	18	1	2	53	15	4	5	12	23	41	76	56	50
5	Lincoln City	42	12	8	1	54	23	5	6	10	29	38	83	61	48
6	York City	42	11	7	3	43	20	4	9	8	34	44	77	64	46
7	South Shields	42	11	6	4	49	32	7	4	10	28	42	77	74	46
8	Hartlepools United	42	13	4	4	50	24	4	7	10	31	50	81	74	45
9	Southport	42	11	5	5	49	31	4	8	9	32	43	81	74	43
10	Rochdale	42	14	3	4	57	30	4	4	13	32	61	89	91	43
11	Crewe Alexandra	42	12	5	4	55	28	5	3	13	27	43	82	71	42
12	Tranmere Rovers	42	12	4	5	57	35	4	5	12	26	51	83	86	41
13	New Brighton	42	13	4	4	48	22	3	4	14	21	57	69	79	40
14	Doncaster Rovers	42	13	5	3	39	22	2	4	15	23	47	62	69	39
15	Carlisle United	42	13	4	4	63	34	3	3	15	27	67	90	101	39
16	Accrington Stanley	42	11	4	6	55	30	3	5	13	29	51	84	81	37
17	Wrexham	42	10	5	6	42	28	3	3	15	25	60	67	88	34
18	Wigan Borough	42	12	4	5	44	26	1	3	17	16	62	60	88	33
19	Nelson	42	9	4	8	31	25	4	3	14	20	55	51	80	33
20	Rotherham United	42	9	4	8	46	40	2	4	15	21	73	67	113	30
21	Halifax Town	42	7	7	7	26	23	1	1	17	17	53	43	79	28
22	Barrow	42	9	4	8	31	28	2	1	18	10	70	41	98	27

SEASON 1930-31
DIVISION THREE (NORTH)

No.	Date	Opposition	Res.	Att.	Goalscorers	Emery A.	Jackson R.	Turner J.	Skull F.	Bratley G.	Whitworth E.	Sellars W.	Wright V.	Cooke E.	Gray R.	Orr A.	Wheeler F.C.	Freeman R.	Parkin A.	Murden G.	Harris J.	Hick W.	Ward A.	Johnson J.	Hackford G.	Stewart J.	Beynon J.	Cockroft J.	Smailes A.	McCormick J.
1	30 Aug	YORK CITY	2-1	6354	Wright(2)	1	2	3	4	5	6	7	8	9	10	11														
2	1 Sep	Crewe Alexandra	3-2	3828	Skull, Wright, Orr	1	2	3	4	5	6	7	8	9	10	11														
3	6	Doncaster Rovers	3-3	6660	Bratley, Sellars, Wright	1	2	3	4	5	6	7	8		10	9	11													
4	8	WREXHAM	1-4	7513	Bratley	1	2		4	5	6	7	8		10	9	11	3												
5	13	Chesterfield	1-2	6777	Sellars	1	2		4	5	6	7	8		10	9	11	3												
6	17	Wrexham	2-3	4350	Sellars, Gray	1	2		4	5	6	7			8	9	11		3	9	10									
7	20	BARROW	6-0	7136	Wheeler(2), Murden, Hick(3)		2		4	5	6	7			8			11	3		10	1	9							
8	27	Southport	1-4	2676	Hick		2		4	5	6	7			8			11	3		10	1	9							
9	4 Oct	ACCRINGTON STANLEY	8-1	7070	Wright(4), Gray, Hick(3)		2		4	5	6	7	10		8			11	3			1	9							
10	11	Rochdale	1-6	3480	Hick		2		4	5	6	7	10		8	11			3			1	9							
11	18	GATESHEAD	1-1	7013	Hick		2		4	5	6	7			8			11	3		10	1	9							
12	25	Hull City	2-2	5805	Bratley, Gray		2		4	5	6	7			8			11	3		10	1	9							
13	1 Nov	NEW BRIGHTON	2-0	6135	Sellars, Hick		2		4	5	6	7			8			11	3		10	1	9							
14	8	Halifax Town	1-0	6045	Murden		2		4	5	6	7			8			11	3		10	1	9							
15	15	DARLINGTON	0-2	5491			2		4	5	6	7			8			11	3		10	1	9							
16	22	Nelson	0-0	1606			2		4	5	6	7			8	10			3		11	1	9							
17	6 Dec	Hartlepools United	2-4	3020	Sellars, Murden		2		4	5	6	7				8	11	3			10		9	1						
18	15	LINCOLN CITY	2-2	2668	Gray, Orr		2		4	5	6	7			10	11		3				9	1	8						
19	20	Stockport County	2-5	5713	Orr, Johnson		2		4	5	6	7			10	9		11	3				1	8						
20	25	TRANMERE ROVERS	4-6	7328	Sellars, Orr, Hick(2)		2		4	5	6	7				10	11	3				9	1	8						
21	26	Tranmere Rovers	2-1	8469	Hick, Johnson	1	2		4	5	6	7			10			3				9		8	11					
22	27	York City	1-1	4352	Hick		2		4	5	6	7			10			3				9	1	8	11					
23	3 Jan	DONCASTER ROVERS	3-0	4132	Hick(3)	1		2	4	5	6	7			10			11	3			9		8						
24	10	WIGAN BOROUGH	5-2	5289	Sellars(2), Hick(3)	1	2		4	5	6	7			10			11	3			9		8						
25	17	CHESTERFIELD	0-1	9690		1	2		4	5	6	7			10			11	3			9		8						
26	24	Barrow	0-1	4385		1	2		4	5	6	7			10	11		3				9		8						
27	31	SOUTHPORT	3-3	5446	Orr, Hick(2)	1	2		4	5	6	7				10	11	3				9		8						
28	7 Feb	Accrington Stanley	2-3	2396	Sellars, Hick	1	2		4	5	6	7			8	10	11	3				9								
29	14	ROCHDALE	1-3	5047	Hick	1		2	4	5	6	7			10	8	11	3				9								
30	21	Gateshead	0-2	4383		1	2			5	6	7			10			3				9		8		4	11			
31	7 Mar	New Brighton	1-3	1742	Gray	1	2			5	6	7			8	11		3				9				4	10			
32	14	HALIFAX TOWN	2-1	4045	Parkin(2)	1	2		4		6	7			8	10		3	9							5	11			
33	21	Darlington	2-2	2503	Sellars, Gray	1	2	3	4		6	7			8				9		10					5	11			
34	28	NELSON	3-0	3442	Parkin, Johnson, Beynon	1	2	3		5	6	7			10				9					8		4	11			
35	3 Apr	Carlisle United	2-1	5190	Gray, Beynon	1	2	3		5	6	7			10	8			9					4			11			
36	4	Wigan Borough	0-0	3891		1	2	3		5	6	7			10				9					10		4	11			
37	6	CARLISLE UNITED	1-0	4814	Beynon	1	2	3		5	6	7			10	8					9			4			11			
38	11	HARTLEPOOLS UNITED	1-1	4182	Cockroft	1	2	3		5	6	7			10						9			4			11	8		
39	18	Lincoln City	3-1	7857	Hick(3)	1	2	3		5	6	7			10	8					9			4			11			
40	25	STOCKPORT COUNTY	3-4	2813	Gray, Hick, Beynon	1	2	3	5		6	7			10	8					9			4			11			
41	27	HULL CITY	1-1	2776	Hick		2	3	5		6	7			10	8					9	1		4			11			
42	4 May	CREWE ALEXANDRA	1-1	3380	Hick		2	3	6						10						9	1		4			11	8	5	7
		Apps.				25	40	15	34	37	41	41	7	2	38	24	20	29	6	10	10	31	7	20	2	6	13	2	1	1
		Goals							1	3		10	8		8	5	2		3		30	3					4	1		

F.A. CUP

						Emery A.	Jackson R.	Turner J.	Skull F.	Bratley G.	Whitworth E.	Sellars W.	Wright V.	Cooke E.	Gray R.	Orr A.	Wheeler F.C.	Freeman R.	Parkin A.	Murden G.	Harris J.	Hick W.	Ward A.	Johnson J.	Hackford G.	Stewart J.	Beynon J.	Cockroft J.	Smailes A.	McCormick J.
1R	29 Nov	Newark Town	1-2		Murden		2		4	5	6	7			8			11	3		10	1	9							

A Parkgate Cartoonist's impression of United's 1-1 draw against Gateshead. October 1930.

Final League Table

		Pl.	Home				Away					F.	A.	Pts
			W	D	L	F	A	W	D	L	F	A			
1	Chesterfield	42	19	1	1	66	22	7	5	9	36	35	102	57	58
2	Lincoln City	42	16	3	2	60	19	9	4	8	42	40	102	59	57
3	Wrexham	42	16	4	1	61	25	5	8	8	33	37	94	62	54
4	Tranmere Rovers	42	16	3	2	73	26	8	3	10	38	48	111	74	54
5	Southport	42	15	3	3	52	19	7	6	8	36	37	88	56	53
6	Hull City	42	12	7	2	64	20	8	3	10	35	35	99	55	50
7	Stockport County	42	15	5	1	54	19	5	4	12	23	42	77	61	49
8	Carlisle United	42	13	4	4	68	32	7	1	13	30	49	98	81	45
9	Gateshead	42	14	3	4	46	22	2	9	10	25	51	71	73	45
10	Wigan Borough	42	14	4	3	48	25	5	1	15	28	61	76	86	43
11	Darlington	42	9	6	6	44	30	7	4	10	27	29	71	59	42
12	York City	42	15	3	3	59	30	3	3	15	26	52	85	82	42
13	Accrington Stanley	42	14	2	5	51	31	1	7	13	33	77	84	108	39
14	Rotherham United	42	9	6	6	50	34	4	6	11	31	49	81	83	38
15	Doncaster Rovers	42	9	8	4	40	18	4	3	14	25	47	65	65	37
16	Barrow	42	13	4	4	45	23	2	3	16	26	68	89	37
17	Halifax Town	42	11	6	4	30	16	2	3	16	25	73	55	89	35
18	Crewe Alexandra	42	13	2	6	52	35	1	4	16	14	58	66	93	34
19	New Brighton	42	12	4	5	36	25	1	3	17	13	51	49	76	33
20	Hartlepools United	42	10	2	9	47	37	2	4	15	22	67	86	30
21	Rochdale	42	9	1	11	42	50	3	5	13	20	57	62	107	30
22	Nelson	42	6	7	8	28	40	0	0	21	15	73	43	113	19

SEASON 1931/32
DIVISION THREE (NORTH)

No.	Date	Opposition	Res.	Att.	Goalscorers
1	29 Aug	Southport	2-3	6510	Hick, Beynon
2	31	ROCHDALE	5-1	6431	Sellars, Hick(2), Spicer(2)
3	5 Sep	YORK CITY	0-1	6685	
4	12	Tranmere Rovers	1-6	3887	Hick
5	14	DONCASTER ROVERS	6-3	4717	Sellars(2), Gray, Hick, Roscoe(2)
6	19	BARROW	0-2	4861	
7	21	Doncaster Rovers	0-2	2570	
8	28	STOCKPORT COUNTY	1-1	4044	Roscoe
9	3 Oct	Accrington Stanley	2-5	3983	Spicer, Beynon
10	10	WREXHAM	0-0	3763	
11	17	Hull City	1-0	6645	Gray
12	24	LINCOLN CITY	0-1	4714	
13	31	Chester	1-2	6704	Gray
14	7 Nov	HARTLEPOOLS UNITED	1-2	3294	Parkin
15	21	DARLINGTON	2-4	3248	Sellars, Spicer
16	5 Dec	WALSALL	3-0	2359	Hick, Spicer, McCormick
17	16	Gateshead	1-4	2824	Turner
18	19	NEW BRIGHTON	2-2	2240	Spicer, McCormick
19	25	Crewe Alexandra	0-5	6154	
20	26	CREWE ALEXANDRA	0-2	5217	
21	2 Jan	SOUTHPORT	2-0	3278	Spicer, Parkin
22	11	Halifax Town	1-1	1430	Beynon
23	16	York City	0-2	3692	
24	23	TRANMERE ROVERS	1-0	4015	Nock
25	30	Barrow	0-3	6725	
26	6 Feb	Stockport County	0-1	6042	
27	13	ACCRINGTON STANLEY	2-3	2672	Nock(2)
28	20	Wrexham	0-2	3051	
29	27	HULL CITY	2-0	4039	Beynon, Nock
30	5 Mar	Lincoln City	1-3	7997	Nock
31	12	CHESTER	3-0	4023	Spicer, Parkin(2)
32	19	Hartlepools United	4-1	2967	Freeman, Spicer, Parkin(2)
33	25	Carlisle United	2-1	4962	Gray, Parkin
34	28	CARLISLE UNITED	4-1	4645	Sellars(2), Spicer, Parkin
35	2 Apr	Darlington	1-2	1939	Parkin
36	9	HALIFAX TOWN	5-0	2951	Freeman, Sellars, Parkin(2), O.G.
37	16	Walsall	0-3	2079	
38	23	GATESHEAD	2-1	4091	Parkin(2)
39	30	New Brighton	1-3	1923	Beynon
40	7 May	Rochdale	4-1	1724	Gray, Beynon, Parkin(2)

Appearances and goals

	Soutar H.W.	Jackson R.	Freeman R.	Johnson J.	Davis G.	Whitworth E.	Sellars W.	Gray R.	Hick W.	Spicer W.	Beynon J.	Tordoff H.	Turner J.	Skull F.	Roscoe J.	Crawford R.	Bradbury N.	Cockroft J.	Fantham J.T.	Bratley G.	Gowland N.	Parkin A.	Smailes A.	McCormick J.	Nock J.E.	Birkhead A.	Rowbotham S.	Bembridge C.W.
Apps	23	26	24	38	32	23	25	31	16	30	37	2	33	5	5	3	1	1	20	1	5	14	5	18	8	12	1	1
Goals		2					7	5	6	10	6		1		3							15		2	5			

F.A. CUP

	Date	Opposition	Res.	Att.	Goalscorers
1R	28 Nov	ACCRINGTON STANLEY	0-0	6118	
1Rr	2 Dec	Accrington Stanley	0-5		

(Back): Jackson (Capt.), Johnson, Soutar, Tordoff, Freeman, Davies.
(Front): Sellers, Gray, Hick, Spicer, Beynon.

Final League Table

		Pl.	Home W	D	L	F	A	Away W	D	L	F	A	F.	A.	Pts
1	Lincoln City	40	16	2	2	65	13	10	3	7	41	34	106	47	57
2	Gateshead	40	15	3	2	59	20	10	4	6	35	28	94	48	57
3	Chester	40	16	2	2	54	22	5	6	9	24	38	78	60	50
4	Tranmere Rovers	40	15	4	1	76	23	4	7	9	31	35	107	58	49
5	Barrow	40	16	1	3	59	23	8	0	12	27	36	86	59	49
6	Crewe Alexandra	40	15	3	2	64	24	6	3	11	31	42	95	66	48
7	Southport	40	14	5	1	44	15	4	5	11	14	38	58	53	46
8	Hull City	40	14	1	5	52	21	6	4	10	30	32	82	53	45
9	York City	40	13	3	4	49	24	4	4	12	27	57	76	81	43
10	Wrexham	40	14	2	4	42	25	4	5	11	22	44	64	69	43
11	Darlington	40	12	1	7	41	27	5	3	12	25	42	66	69	38
12	Stockport County	40	12	3	5	41	15	1	8	11	24	38	55	53	37
13	Hartlepools United	40	10	4	6	47	36	7	1	13	31	63	78	100	37
14	Accrington Stanley	40	14	4	2	56	20	1	2	17	19	60	75	80	36
15	Doncaster Rovers	40	12	3	5	38	27	4	1	15	21	53	59	80	36
16	Walsall	40	12	3	5	42	30	4	0	16	15	55	57	85	35
17	Halifax Town	40	11	6	3	36	18	2	2	16	25	69	61	87	34
18	Carlisle United	40	9	7	4	40	23	2	4	14	24	56	64	79	33
19	Rotherham United	40	10	3	7	41	23	1	5	14	22	49	63	72	32
20	New Brighton	40	8	5	7	25	23	3	0	17	13	53	38	76	27
21	Rochdale	40	4	2	14	33	63	0	1	19	15	72	48	135	11

SEASON 1932-33
DIVISION THREE (NORTH)

No.	Date	Opposition	Res.	Att.	Goalscorers	Birkhead A.	Freeman R.	Turner J.	Johnson J.	Davies G.	Fantham J.	Briggs F.	Spicer W.	Parkin A.	Pynegar A.	Wheeler F.C.	Bratley G.	Jones L.	Nock J.	Staniforth H.	Smelt T.	Hackford G.	Sykes R.	Rodgers W.R.	Rowbotham S.	Hardy R.	Bembridge C.	Anderson T.	Wright V.	Ford S.	Bell E.	Blackwell W.
1	27 Aug	NEW BRIGHTON	1-0	4941	Parkin	1	2	3	4	5	6	7	8	9	10	11																
2	29	Accrington Stanley	1-5	3402	O.G.	1	2	3	4		6	7	8	9	10	11																
3	3 Sep	Chester City	0-1	7657		1	2	3	4		6	7	9	8		11	5	10														
4	5	ACCRINGTON STANLEY	2-3	3064	Parkin, Pynegar	1	2	3	4		6	7	8	9	10		5			11												
5	10	BARROW	1-0	3514	Staniforth	1	2	3	4		6	7	9		10		5			11	8											
6	17	Carlisle United	0-0	6286		1	2	3	4		6	7	10				5			9	11	8										
7	24	YORK CITY	1-0	4130	Pynegar	1	2	3	4		6	9	8		10	11	5			7												
8	1 Oct	Crewe Alexandra	0-8	4204		1	2	3	4		6		8	9	10	11	5			7												
9	8	ROCHDALE	2-0	2555	Pynegar, Staniforth	1	2	3	4		6	8	10		9		5			7	11											
10	15	Southport	0-2	4411		1	2	3	4		6	8	10				5		9	7	11											
11	23	BARNSLEY	0-0	7347		1	2	3	4	6	8		10	7	9	11	5															
12	29	Hull City	2-4	7997	Parkin, Bratley	1	2	3	7	4	6		8	9	10	11	5															
13	5 Nov	DONCASTER ROVERS	1-1	6740	Wheeler	1	2	3	7	4	6		8	9	10	11	5															
14	12	Darlington	1-4	2475	Spicer	1	2	3	7	4	6	10	8	9		11	5															
15	19	STOCKPORT COUNTY	2-1	3618	Spicer, O.G.	1	2	3	7	4	6	8		10	11	5			9													
16	3 Dec	WALSALL	4-1	2944	Bratley, Nock(3)	1	2	3	7	4	6	8				11	5		10	9												
17	17	TRANMERE ROVERS	2-0	2834	Wheeler, Jones	1		3	2	7	4	6	8			11	5	10	9													
18	25	Halifax Town	1-2	5332	Bratley	1		3	2	4	6	7	8			11	5	10	9													
19	27	MANSFIELD TOWN	3-0	5580	Spicer, Wheeler, O.G.	1		3	2	4	6	7	8		10	11	5		9													
20	28	Mansfield Town	2-9	7192	Wheeler, Bratley	1		3	2	4	6	7	8	9		11	5	10														
21	31	New Brighton	2-5	1855	Rowbotham, O.G.	1		3	2	4	6	7	8			11	5								4		10					
22	7 Jan	CHESTER CITY	0-5	4724		1	2	3	4		6		8	9		11	5							7	10							
23	21	Barrow	1-2	2474	Bratley	1		3	4		6		10	9	8		5	11						7	10							
24	25	Gateshead	1-1	1821	Parkin	1		3	4		6		8		9		5	11					10				2	7				
25	28	CARLISLE UNITED	1-0	2738	Nock	1		3	4		6	8		9			5	11									7	2				
26	4 Feb	York City	3-4	3237	Parkin, Bratley, Sykes	1		3	4		6	8		9		11	5						10	7				2				
27	11	CREWE ALEXANDRA	5-0	3649	Wheeler, Nock(3), Wright	1	2	3	4		6		5			11			9				10	7				2	8			
28	18	Rochdale	2-2	1932	Briggs, Wright	1	2	3	4		6	7	5			11			9				10						8			
29	25	Wrexham	1-5	4701	Nock	1	2	3	4		6	7	5			11			9				10						8			
30	4 Mar	Barnsley	1-3	6243	Briggs	1	2	3	4		6	9	5			11							10	7					8			
31	11	HULL CITY	3-2	6861	Spicer, Nock, Wright	1	2	3	4		6		5			11			9				10	7					8			
32	18	Doncaster Rovers	0-1	6565		1	2	3	4		6		5			11			9				10	7					8			
33	25	DARLINGTON	3-1	3894	Spicer, Wheeler, Wright	1	2	3		4	6	7	5			11							10	7					8			
34	1 Apr	Stockport County	0-1	5087		1	2	3			6	7	5	9		11							10					4	8			
35	8	GATESHEAD	1-2	3456	Parkin	1	2	3			6	7	10	9		11												4	8			
36	14	Hartlepools United	0-2	3682		1	2	3		5	6					11							10					4	8	5		
37	15	Walsall	0-1	4438		1	2	3			6	9				11							10	5				4	8		4	7
38	17	HARTLEPOOLS UNITED	1-1	2659	Wheeler	1	2	3		5		7				11							10	4				4	8		6	
39	18	SOUTHPORT	3-1	2223	Parkin(2), Rodgers	1	2	3		5	6			10	9	11							7						8		4	
40	22	WREXHAM	0-2	3492		1	2	3		5	6			10	9	11							7					4	8			
41	29	Tranmere Rovers	0-1	1344		1	2	3		5	6	7		10	9	11												4	8			
42	6 May	HALIFAX TOWN	6-1	1588	Briggs(2),Wheeler,Nock,Wright(2)	1	2	3			6	7	5			11			9									4	8			
					Apps.	42	33	42	32	17	41	28	33	21	17	35	25	7	17	6	2	2	15	9	2	10	4	1	16	1	3	1
					Goals							4	5	8	3	8	6	1	10	2			1	1	1				6			

F.A. CUP

Round	Date	Opposition	Res.	Goalscorers	Birkhead A.	Freeman R.	Turner J.	Johnson J.	Davies G.	Fantham J.	Briggs F.	Spicer W.	Parkin A.	Pynegar A.	Wheeler F.C.	Bratley G.	Jones L.	Nock J.
1R	26 Nov	Chester City	0-4		1	2	3	7	4	6	10	8			11	5		9

Final League Table

		Pl.	Home					Away					F.	A.	Pts
			W	D	L	F	A	W	D	L	F	A			
1	Hull City	42	18	3	0	69	14	8	4	9	31	31	100	45	59
2	Wrexham	42	18	2	1	75	15	6	7	8	31	36	106	51	57
3	Stockport County	42	16	2	3	69	30	5	10	6	30	28	99	58	54
4	Chester	42	15	4	2	57	25	7	4	10	37	41	94	66	52
5	Walsall	42	16	4	1	53	15	3	6	12	22	43	75	58	48
6	Doncaster Rovers	42	13	8	0	52	26	4	6	11	25	53	77	79	48
7	Gateshead	42	12	5	4	45	25	7	4	10	33	42	78	67	47
8	Barnsley	42	14	3	4	60	31	5	5	11	32	49	92	80	46
9	Barrow	42	12	3	6	41	24	6	4	11	19	36	60	60	43
10	Crewe Alexandra	42	16	3	2	57	16	4	0	17	23	68	80	84	43
11	Tranmere Rovers	42	11	4	6	49	31	6	4	11	21	35	70	66	42
12	Southport	42	15	3	3	54	20	2	4	15	16	47	70	67	41
13	Accrington Stanley	42	12	4	5	55	29	3	6	12	23	47	78	76	40
14	Hartlepools United	42	15	3	3	56	29	1	4	16	31	87	87	116	39
15	Halifax Town	42	12	4	5	39	23	3	4	14	32	67	71	90	38
16	Mansfield Town	42	13	4	4	57	22	1	3	17	27	78	84	100	35
17	Rotherham United	42	14	3	4	42	21	0	3	18	18	63	60	84	34
18	Rochdale	42	9	4	8	32	33	4	3	14	26	47	58	80	33
19	Carlisle United	42	8	7	6	34	25	5	0	16	17	50	51	75	33
20	York City	42	10	4	7	51	38	3	2	16	21	54	72	92	32
21	New Brighton	42	8	6	7	42	36	3	4	14	21	52	63	88	32
22	Darlington	42	9	6	6	42	32	1	2	18	24	77	66	109	28

SEASON 1933-34
DIVISION THREE (NORTH)

No.	Date	Opposition	Res.	Att.	Goalscorers	Turner G.	Turner J.	Smith W.	Hardy R.	Spicer W.	Fantham J.T.	Raynor G.	Wright V.	Wright J.E.	Burkinshaw W.	Wheeler F.C.	Davis G.	Johnson W.H.	Freeman R.	Wilson W.R.	Briggs F.	Ford S.	McConnell J.	Sturgess A.	Birkhead A.	Curry R.	Millington M.	Sykes R.	Hick G.	Pale E.	Bembridge C.	Bratley G.	Lewis J.	Cuthbert W.
1	26 Aug	Chester	1-5	9616	Raynor	1	2	3	4	5	6	7	8	9	10	11																		
2	28	BARNSLEY	0-2	6691		1	2	3	4		6	7	8		10	11	5	9																
3	2 Sep	DONCASTER ROVERS	0-0	4882		1	2	3	10			7		9		11	4		5	6	8													
4	9	Barrow	1-4	4987	V.Wright	1	2	3				7	8			11	4			6		5	9	10										
5	16	CARLISLE UNITED	0-1	3258				3			6	7	8		11					2	10	5	9		1									
6	23	Stockport County	1-3	4763	Sturgess			3			6	7	8		11		4			2	9	5		10	1									
7	30	HALIFAX TOWN	1-2	3122	Raynor	1	3	2			6	7	8		10	11			5		9													
8	7 Oct	Crewe Alexandra	2-0	3425	V.Wright, McConnell	1	3	2			6	7	8		11						9		10			4		5						
9	14	NEW BRIGHTON	2-2	3297	Raynor, Wright	1	3	2			6	7	8		11						9		10			4		5						
10	21	TRANMERE ROVERS	2-2	3912	Raynor(2)	1	3	2			6	7	8		11						9		10			4		5						
11	28	Rochdale	2-0	4322	Raynor(2)	1	3	2			6	7	8			11					9		10			4		5						
12	4 Nov	CHESTERFIELD	1-3	13732	Raynor	1	3	2			6	7	8								9		10			4		5	11					
13	11	Accrington Stanley	2-2	3020	V.Wright, Pale		3	2			6		8		10						9				1	4		5	11	7				
14	18	GATESHEAD	3-2	3574	McConnell(2), Hick		3				6		8		10						9				1	4		5	11	7	2			
15	2 Dec	SOUTHPORT	0-1	3315			3	2			6	7	8		10						9				1	4		5	11					
16	16	HARTLEPOOLS UNITED	4-2	3148	Raynor, V.Wright, Briggs, McConnell		3				6	7	8							2	9		10		1	4		5	11					
17	23	Mansfield Town	0-3	3818			3				6	7	8							2	9		10		1	4		5	11					
18	25	York City	1-0	3641	Hicks		3				6	7	8							2	9		10		1	4		5	11					
19	26	YORK CITY	3-2	6783	Fantham, V.Wright, McConnell		3				6	7	8							2	9		10		1	4		5	11					
20	30	CHESTER	0-3	5132			3				6	7	8							2	9		10		1	4		5	11					
21	1 Jan	Barnsley	1-5	9036	V.Wright	1	3				6	7	8							2	9		10			4		5	11					
22	6	Doncaster Rovers	1-2	5038	V.Wright		3		7		6		8	1						2	10		9			4		5	11					
23	20	BARROW	1-1	3711	Briggs		3				6	7	8	1	10						9	2				4		5	11					
24	24	Darlington	1-4	1587	Briggs		3					10	8	1					6	7	9	2				4		5	11					
25	27	Carlisle United	1-0	3828	V.Wright		3	2			6		8	1						7						4		5	11			9		
26	3 Feb	STOCKPORT COUNTY	1-1	5284	Curry		3	2			6	7	8	1		11			4		9					10		5						
27	10	Halifax Town	2-3	5218	V.Wright, Briggs		3	2			6	7	8	1							9					4		5	11			10		
28	17	CREWE ALEXANDRA	3-4	3425	Sykes, Bratley(2)		3	2			6	7	8	1									10			4		5	11			9		
29	24	New Brighton	1-3	2929	V.Wright		3	2			6	7	8	1		11							10			4		5				9		
30	3 Mar	Tranmere Rovers	2-1	2701	Briggs, Hick		3	2			6	7	8	1							9					4		5	11			10		
31	7	Wrexham	0-4	2059			3	2			6	7	8	1							9					4		5	11			10		
32	10	ROCHDALE	4-0	2227	V.Wright, Briggs(2), Hick	1	3	2			6	7	8								9					4		5	11			10		
33	17	Chesterfield	1-2	8784	Hick	1	3	2			6	7							4		9				8			5	11			10		
34	24	ACCRINGTON STANLEY	3-1	2866	Briggs, Hick, Bratley	1	3	2			6	7							4		9				8			5	11			10		
35	30	Walsall	1-3	6284	Briggs	1	3	2			6	7							4		9				8			5	11			10		
36	31	Gateshead	1-4	1795	Briggs	1	3				6	7				10					9	5	8			4		5	11					
37	2 Apr	WALSALL	1-1	3806	Briggs	1	3				6	7				10					9	2				4		5	11			10		
38	7	DARLINGTON	0-0	2725		1	3				6	7				10					9	2				4		5	11			8		
39	14	Southport	0-4	1721		1	3					7							4		10	2	9		8			5	11	6				
40	21	WREXHAM	1-3	2249	Fantham	1	3				11	7							6		9	2				4		5				10	8	
41	28	Hartlepools United	0-4	1083		1	3				8	7			10						9	2				4		5	11					
42	5 May	MANSFIELD TOWN	1-2	1324	Lewis	1	2				6	7			10						9					4		5	11				8	3
		Apps.				22	40	26	2	3	39	37	32	11	11	12	6	1	9	11	37	12	21	2	10	35	2	33	28	2	1	14	2	1
		Goals									2	9	12							1	11		4		1	1		1	6	1		3	1	

F.A. CUP

	Date		Res.	Att.	Goalscorers	Turner J.	Smith W.	Fantham	Raynor	Wright V.	Wright J.E.	Freeman	Wilson	Briggs	Ford	McConnell	Birkhead	Curry	Sykes	Hick
1R	25 Nov	SOUTH BANK ST.PETER'S	3-2	5775	Raynor, Hicks(2)	3	2	6	7	8				9		10	1	4	5	11
2R	9 Dec	COVENTRY CITY	2-1		Raynor, McConnell	3		6	7	8			2	9		10	1	4	5	11
3R	19 Jan	Sheffield Wednesday	0-3	20000		3		6	7	8	1	6		9	2	10		4	5	11

NORTH SECTION CUP

	Date		Res.	Att.	Goalscorers	Turner J.	Smith W.	Fantham	Raynor	Wright V.	Wright J.E.	Freeman	Briggs	Curry	Sykes	Hick	Bratley
1R	29 Jan	BARNSLEY	2-1	1845	V.Wright, Briggs	3	2	6	7	8	1	4	9	10	5	11	
2R	14 Feb	Chesterfield	1-4		Hick	3	2	6	7	8	1		9		5	11	10

Players and Directors at the Dinner at the Crown Hotel, following the Wednesday Cup-tie.

Final League Table

		Pl.	Home					Away					F.	A.	Pts
			W	D	L	F	A	W	D	L	F	A			
1	Barnsley	42	18	3	0	64	18	9	5	7	54	43	118	61	62
2	Chesterfield	42	18	1	2	56	17	9	6	6	30	26	86	43	61
3	Stockport County	42	18	3	0	84	23	6	8	7	31	29	115	52	59
4	Walsall	42	18	2	1	66	18	5	5	11	31	42	97	60	53
5	Doncaster Rovers	42	17	1	3	58	24	5	8	8	25	37	83	61	53
6	Wrexham	42	14	1	6	68	35	9	4	8	34	38	102	73	51
7	Tranmere Rovers	42	16	2	3	57	21	4	5	12	27	42	84	63	47
8	Barrow	42	12	5	4	78	45	7	4	10	38	49	116	94	47
9	Halifax Town	42	15	2	4	57	30	5	2	14	23	61	80	91	44
10	Chester	42	11	6	4	59	26	6	0	15	30	60	89	86	40
11	Hartlepools United	42	14	3	4	54	24	2	4	15	35	69	89	93	39
12	York City	42	11	5	5	44	28	4	3	14	27	46	71	74	38
13	Carlisle United	42	11	6	4	43	23	4	2	15	23	58	66	81	38
14	Crewe Alexandra	42	12	3	6	54	38	3	3	15	27	59	81	97	36
15	New Brighton	42	13	3	5	41	25	1	5	15	21	62	62	87	36
16	Darlington	42	11	4	6	47	35	2	5	14	23	66	70	101	35
17	Mansfield Town	42	9	7	5	49	29	2	5	14	32	59	81	88	34
18	Southport	42	8	6	7	49	29	2	5	14	26	61	75	90	33
19	Gateshead	42	10	3	8	46	40	2	6	13	30	70	76	110	33
20	Accrington Stanley	42	10	6	5	44	38	1	7	13	31	63	65	101	33
21	Rotherham United	42	5	7	9	31	35	5	1	15	22	56	53	91	28
22	Rochdale	42	7	5	9	34	30	2	1	18	19	73	53	103	24

SEASON 1934/35

DIVISION THREE (NORTH)

No.	Date	Opposition	Res.	Att.	Goalscorers	Clough J.	Turner J.	Birkett W.	Duckworth R.	Sykes R.	Heelbeck L.	Raynor G.	Fenoughty T.	Briggs F.	Dickenson W.	Reid J.	Ford S.	Bastow R.	Curry R.	Hawkins J.	Roberts H.	Cuthbert W.	Miller J.	Lewis J.	Woodward B.
1	25 Aug	CHESTERFIELD	2-2	8041	Dickenson, Heelbeck	1	2	3	4	5	6	7	8	9	10	11									
2	27	HALIFAX TOWN	2-2	7090	Briggs, Raynor	1	2	3	4	5	6	7	8	9	10	11									
3	1 Sep	Mansfield Town	1-2	6588	Dickenson	1	2	3	4	5	6	7	8	9	10	11									
4	3	Halifax Town	1-2	7710	Bastow	1		3	4	5	6		8	7	10	11	2	9							
5	8	BARROW	0-0	6419		1		3	4	5	6		8	7	10	11	2	9							
6	15	Carlisle United	1-2	5145	Fenoughty	1		3	4	5	6	7	8	9	10	11	2								
7	22	ROCHDALE	4-0	3807	Bastow(2), Dickenson, Fenoughty	1		3			6	7	8		10	11	2	9	4	5					
8	29	Lincoln City	0-4	5249		1		3			6	7	8		10	11	2	9	4	5					
9	6 Oct	TRANMERE ROVERS	3-1	5197	Bastow(2), Raynor	1		3	5		6	7	8		10	11	2	9	4						
10	13	Wrexham	1-0	5326	Dickenson	1		3	5		6	7	8		10	11	2	9	4						
11	20	SOUTHPORT	4-2	7211	Bastow(2), Fenoughty(2)	1		3	5		6	7	8		10	11	2	9	4						
12	27	Chester	1-4	5889	Dickenson	1	3		5		6	7	8		10	11	2	9	4						
13	3 Nov	NEW BRIGHTON	1-2	6491	Roberts	1	3		5		6	7	8			11	2	9	4		10				
14	10	York City	0-5	3992		1			5		6	7	8			11	2	9	4		10	3			
15	17	DARLINGTON	2-1	5306	Fenoughty(2)	1	3		5		6	7	8		10	11	2	9	4						
16	1 Dec	GATESHEAD	3-0	4723	Raynor(2), Dickenson	1	3		5		6	7	8		10	11	2	9	4						
17	15	CREWE ALEXANDRA	2-2	3479	Briggs, Dickenson	1	3		5		6	7	8	9	10	11	2		4						
18	25	Walsall	2-5	8449	Fenoughty(2)	1		3	5		6	7	8	9	10	11	2		4						
19	26	WALSALL	4-2	6370	Raynor(2), Dickenson, Fenoughty	1	3		5		6	7	8		10	11	2	9	4						
20	29	Chesterfield	1-2	5464	Fenoughty	1	3		5		6	7	8		10	11	2	9	4						
21	1 Jan	Stockport County	0-4	4661		1	3		5		6	7	8		10	11	2	9	4						
22	5	MANSFIELD TOWN	3-0	5740	Bastow(2), Fenoughty	1	3				6	7	8		10	11	2	9	4	5					
23	12	Accrington Stanley	3-2	2518	Bastow(2), Reid	1	3				6	7	8		10	11	2	9	4	5					
24	19	Barrow	1-2	3113	Dickenson	1	3				6	7	8		10	11	2	9	4	5					
25	26	CARLISLE UNITED	4-1	3626	Dickenson, Fenoughty, Raynor, O.G.	1	3				6	7	8		10	11	2	9	4	5					
26	2 Feb	Rochdale	3-1	4212	Bastow, Dickenson, Raynor	1	3				6	7	8		10	11	2	9	4	5					
27	9	LINCOLN CITY	5-0	6371	Reid(2), Dickensn, Fnoughty, Heelbck	1	3				6		8		10	7	2	9	4	5			11		
28	16	Tranmere Rovers	3-3	5297	Bastow(2), Fenoughty	1	3				6		8		10	7	2	9	4	5			11		
29	23	WREXHAM	2-0	8055	Bastow(2)	1	3				6		8		10	7	2	9	4	5			11		
30	2 Mar	Southport	3-0	1933	Dickenson, Fenoughty, O.G.	1	3				6		8		10	7	2	9	4	5			11		
31	6	Hartlepools United	1-3	2211	Dickenson	1	3				6		8		10	7	2	9	4	5			11		
32	9	CHESTER	6-1	8182	Dickensn(2), Rberts(2), Curry, Heelbck	1	3				6				10	7	2	9	4	5	8		11		
33	16	New Brighton	2-3	2834	Dickenson, Roberts	1	3				6				10	7	2	9	4	5	8		11		
34	23	YORK CITY	4-1	5302	Dickenson(2), Reid, Roberts	1	3				6				10	7	2	9	4	5	8		11		
35	30	Darlington	0-4	3044		1	3				6				10	7	2	9	4	5	8		11		
36	6 Apr	ACCRINGTON STANLEY	2-0	5126	Dickenson(2)	1	3				6				10	7	2	9	4	5	8		11		
37	13	Gateshead	1-1	2232	Dickenson	1	3				6				10	7	2	9	4	5			11	8	
38	19	Doncaster Rovers	5-3	27554	Dickenson(2), Miller(2), Fenoughty	1	3				6		8		10	7	2	9	4	5			11		
39	22	DONCASTER ROVERS	1-3	20357	Dickenson	1	3				6		8		10	7	2	9	4	5			11		
40	25	STOCKPORT COUNTY	2-0	3881	Bastow(2)	1	3				6		8		10	7	2	9	4	5					11
41	27	Crewe Alexandra	0-0	2218		1	3	2			6		8		10	7		9	4	5			11		
42	4 May	HARTLEPOOLS UNITED	0-1	3231		1	3				6		8		10	7	2	9	4	5			11		
					Apps.	42	11	15	38	6	42	22	36	9	42	39	38	36	36	23	9	1	15	1	1
					Goals						3	8	16	2	25	4		18	1		5		2		

F.A. CUP

No.	Date	Opposition	Res.	Att.	Goalscorers	Clough J.	Turner J.	Birkett W.	Duckworth R.	Sykes R.	Heelbeck L.	Raynor G.	Fenoughty T.	Briggs F.	Dickenson W.	Reid J.	Ford S.	Bastow R.	Curry R.	Hawkins J.	Roberts H.
1R	24 Nov	SPENNYMOOR UNITED	2-0	7493	Briggs, Dickenson	1	3		5		6	7	8	9	10	11	2		4		
2R	8 Dec	BRISTOL CITY	1-2		Fenoughty	1	3		5		6	7	8	9		11	2		4	10	

NORTH SECTION CUP

No.	Date	Opposition	Res.	Goalscorers	Clough J.	Turner J.	Heelbeck L.	Raynor G.	Fenoughty T.	Dickenson W.	Reid J.	Ford S.	Bastow R.	Curry R.	Hawkins J.	Miller J.
1R	28 Jan	Doncaster Rovers	4-3	Fenoughty(2), Bastow, Raynor	1	3	6	7	8	10	11	2	9	4	5	
2R	13 Feb	Chesterfield	0-3		1	3	6		8	10	7	2	9	4	5	11

(Back): Smith, Curry, Ford, Clough, Birkett, Jolly, Smailes (Trainer).

(Front): Reid, Hardy, Bastow, Fenoughty, Miller, Hawkins.

Final League Table

		Pl.	Home					Away					F.	A.	Pts
			W	D	L	F	A	W	D	L	F	A			
1	Doncaster Rovers	42	16	0	5	53	21	10	5	6	34	23	87	44	57
2	Halifax Town	42	17	2	2	50	24	8	3	10	26	43	76	67	55
3	Chester	42	14	4	3	62	27	6	10	5	29	31	91	58	54
4	Lincoln City	42	14	3	4	55	21	8	4	9	32	37	87	58	51
5	Darlington	42	15	5	1	50	15	6	4	11	30	44	80	59	51
6	Tranmere Rovers	42	15	4	2	53	20	5	7	9	21	35	74	55	51
7	Stockport County	42	15	2	4	57	22	7	1	13	33	50	90	72	47
8	Mansfield Town	42	16	3	2	55	25	3	6	12	20	37	75	62	47
9	Rotherham United	42	14	4	3	56	21	5	3	13	30	52	86	73	45
10	Chesterfield	42	13	4	4	46	21	4	6	11	25	31	71	52	44
11	Wrexham	42	12	5	4	47	25	4	6	11	29	44	76	69	43
12	Hartlepools United	42	12	4	5	52	34	5	3	13	28	44	80	78	41
13	Crewe Alexandra	42	12	6	3	41	25	2	5	14	25	61	66	86	39
14	Walsall	42	11	7	3	51	18	2	3	16	30	54	81	72	36
15	York City	42	12	5	4	50	20	3	1	17	26	62	76	82	36
16	New Brighton	42	9	6	6	32	25	5	2	14	27	51	59	76	36
17	Barrow	42	11	5	5	37	31	2	4	15	21	56	58	87	35
18	Accrington Stanley	42	11	5	5	44	36	1	5	15	19	53	63	89	34
19	Gateshead	42	12	4	5	36	28	1	4	16	22	68	58	96	34
20	Rochdale	42	9	5	7	39	35	2	6	13	14	36	53	71	33
21	Southport	42	6	6	9	27	36	4	6	11	28	49	55	85	32
22	Carlisle United	42	7	6	8	34	36	1	1	19	17	66	51	102	23

SEASON 1935/36
DIVISION THREE (NORTH)

No.	Date	Opposition	Res.	Att.	Goalscorers	Clough J.	Ford S.	Birkett W.	Curry R.	Hawkins J.	Heelbeck L.	Reid J.	Fenoughty T.	Bastow R.	Dickenson W.	Lovett A.	Smith E.	Duckworth R.	Deacon H.	Dobson G.	Hardy R.	Black R.	Jolly H.	Armeson L.	Rushforth S.	Woodward B.	Miller P.	Senior W.	Greaves G.	Roberts H.
1	31 Aug	WREXHAM	1-2	8937	Bastow	1	2	3	4	5	6	7	8	9	10	11														
2	3 Sep	Southport	1-2	4314	Dickenson	1	2	3	4	5	6	7	8	9	10	11														
3	7	Oldham Athletic	1-4	7437	Dickenson	1	2	3	4	5	6	7		9	10	11	8													
4	9	SOUTHPORT	5-0	5020	Dickenson(3), Dobson, Smith	1	2	3	4	5		7			10		9	6	8	11										
5	14	HALIFAX TOWN	2-0	7300	Dickenson(2)	1	2	3	4	5		7			10		9	6	8	11										
6	16	MANSFIELD TOWN	2-1	6299	Dickenson(2)	1	2	3	4	5		7			10		9	6	8	11										
7	21	Darlington	1-3	4112	Smith	1	2	3	4	5		7			10		9	6	8	11										
8	28	GATESHEAD	3-0	6541	Bastow, Dickenson, Dobson	1	2	3	4	5	6	7		9	10		8			11										
9	5 Oct	Tranmere Rovers	2-2	7805	Dickenson(2)	1	2	3	4	5	6	7	10	9			8			11										
10	12	WALSALL	2-0	7363	Dickenson, Smith	1	2	3	4	5	6	7	10	9			8			11										
11	19	Chester	0-0	5187		1	2	3	4	5	6				10	9	11		8			7								
12	26	LINCOLN CITY	1-1	9360	Fenoughty	1	2	3	4	5	6	7	10				8			11	9									
13	2 Nov	Rochdale	1-1	5786	Smith	1	2	3		5	6	7	10				8	4		11					9					
14	9	YORK CITY	5-1	7153	Bastow(4), Fenoughty	1	2	3	4	5	6	7	10				8			11										
15	16	Barrow	0-3	4606		1	2	3	4	5	6	7	10	9			8			11										
16	23	NEW BRIGHTON	5-0	6230	Dickensn(2), Bastw, Heelbck, Fnoughty	1	2	3	4	5	6	7	8	9	10		11													
17	7 Dec	STOCKPORT COUNTY	1-1	5938	Dobson	1	2	3	4	5	6		8	9	10					11						7				
18	21	ACCRINGTON STANLEY	1-3	4035	Smith	1	2	3		11		7			9		10	6	8				5							
19	26	CARLISLE UNITED	4-0	4497	Bastow(2), Dickenson, Fenoughty	1	2	3	4	5	6	7	8	9	10					11										
20	28	Wrexham	0-2	3447		1	2	3	4	5	6	7	8		10					11				9						
21	1 Jan	Carlisle United	1-1	8456	Fenoughty	1	2	3	4	5	6	7	8	9	10					11										
22	4	OLDHAM ATHLETIC	1-0	6024	Dobson	1	2	3	4	5	6	7	8	9	10					11										
23	11	Chesterfield	0-5	9945		1	2	3	4	5	6	7		9	10		8			11										
24	18	Halifax Town	0-1	4103		1	2	3	4	5	6	7	8		9					11	10									
25	25	DARLINGTON	4-0	3616	Hardy(2), Dickenson, Miller	1	2	3	4		6	7			10						8	5		9			11			
26	1 Feb	Gateshead	1-1	2843	Reid	1	2	3	4	5	6	7			10						8			9			11			
27	8	TRANMERE ROVERS	1-2	8683	Bastow	1	2	3	4	5		7		9	10						8	6					11			
28	15	Walsall	1-0	6968	Hardy	1	2	3	4	5		7	10	9							8	6					11			
29	22	CHESTER	1-2	5300	Bastow	1	2	3	4	5		7	10	9							8	6					11			
30	29	York City	1-2	1811	Hardy	1	2	3	4	5		7		9	10			6			8							11		
31	7 Mar	ROCHDALE	6-0	2957	Bastow(4), Dickenson, Hardy	1		3	4	5		7		9		11		2			8		6					10		
32	14	Lincoln City	0-4	4087			2	3	4	5		7		9	10						8		6					11		1
33	21	BARROW	1-0	3924	Miller		2	3	4		6				10	7					9			5				11		1
34	28	New Brighton	0-3	2092			2	3	4		6				10	7					9			5				11		1
35	4 Apr	CHESTERFIELD	0-0	7139			2	3	4	5		7	6	9						11	8							10		1
36	10	Hartlepools United	1-5	4051	Bastow		2	3	4	5		7	6	9				10		11	8									1
37	11	Stockport County	2-1	5231	Dobson, Smith		2	3	4	5		7	10		9					11	8								1	6
38	13	HARTLEPOOLS UNITED	3-0	4539	Fenoughty, Hardy, Smith		2	3	4	5		7	10		9					11	8								1	6
39	18	CREWE ALEXANDRA	3-1	3539	Smith(2), Ford		2	3	4	5		7	10		9					11	8									6
40	22	Accrington Stanley	1-1	2154	Reid		2	3	4	5		7			9					11	8							10	1	6
41	27	Crewe Alexandra	1-4	1399	Smith		2	3	4	5		7	10		9					11	8									6
42	2 May	Mansfield Town	2-8	3264	Smith(2)	1	2	3	4	5		7	10		9					11	8									6
					Apps.	33	41	42	41	40	22	37	28	20	28	4	24	8	6	26	21	7	2	4	1	11	1	11	9	6
					Goals		1				1	2	6	16	18		12			5	6						2			

F.A. CUP

No.	Date	Opposition	Res.	Att.	Goalscorers	Clough J.	Ford S.	Birkett W.	Curry R.	Hawkins J.	Heelbeck L.	Reid J.	Fenoughty T.	Bastow R.	Dickenson W.	Lovett A.	Smith E.	Duckworth R.	Deacon H.	Dobson G.
1R	30 Nov	Wigan	2-1	15500	Bastow, Dickenson	1	2	3	4	5	6	7	8	9	10					11
2R	14 Dec	WATFORD	1-1	12700	Dickenson	1	2	3	4	5	6	7	8	9	10					11
2Rr	18	Watford	0-1			1	2	3	4	6	11	7	8	9		10				5

NORTH SECTION CUP

No.	Date	Opposition	Res.	Att.	Goalscorers	Ford S.	Birkett W.	Reid J.	Fenoughty T.	Duckworth R.	Dobson G.	Hardy R.	Jolly H.	Rushforth S.	Woodward B.	Miller P.
1R	30 Nov	Lincoln City	1-2	1745	Rushforth	2	3	7	10	4	11	8	1	5	6	9

Millmoor as it looked from the air in 1935.

Final League Table

		Pl.	Home					Away					F.	A.	Pts
			W	D	L	F	A	W	D	L	F	A			
1	Chesterfield	42	15	3	3	60	14	9	9	3	32	25	92	39	60
2	Chester	42	14	5	2	69	18	8	6	7	31	27	100	45	55
3	Tranmere Rovers	42	17	2	2	75	28	5	9	7	18	30	93	58	55
4	Lincoln City	42	18	1	2	64	14	4	8	9	27	37	91	51	53
5	Stockport County	42	15	2	4	45	18	5	6	10	20	31	65	49	48
6	Crewe Alexandra	42	14	3	4	55	31	5	5	11	25	45	80	76	47
7	Oldham Athletic	42	13	5	3	60	25	5	4	12	26	48	86	73	45
8	Hartlepools United	42	13	6	2	41	18	6	2	13	16	43	57	61	46
9	Accrington Stanley	42	12	5	4	43	24	5	3	13	20	48	63	72	42
10	Walsall	42	15	2	4	58	13	1	7	13	21	46	79	59	41
11	Rotherham United	42	14	3	4	52	13	2	6	13	17	53	69	66	41
12	Darlington	42	16	3	2	60	26	1	3	17	14	53	74	79	40
13	Carlisle United	42	13	5	3	44	19	1	7	13	12	43	56	62	40
14	Gateshead	42	11	10	0	37	18	2	4	15	19	58	56	76	40
15	Barrow	42	9	9	3	33	16	4	3	14	25	49	58	65	38
16	York City	42	10	8	3	41	28	3	4	14	21	67	62	95	38
17	Halifax Town	42	12	3	6	34	22	3	4	14	23	39	57	61	37
18	Wrexham	42	12	3	6	39	18	3	4	14	27	57	66	75	37
19	Mansfield Town	42	13	5	3	55	25	1	4	16	25	66	80	91	37
20	Rochdale	42	8	10	3	35	26	2	3	16	23	62	58	88	33
21	Southport	42	9	8	4	41	26	2	1	18	17	64	48	90	31
22	New Brighton	42	8	5	8	29	33	1	1	19	14	69	43	102	24

SEASON 1936/37
DIVISION THREE (NORTH)

No.	Date	Opposition	Res.	Att.	Goalscorers
1	29 Aug	GATESHEAD	3-0	6227	Bastow(2), Wynn
2	31	Hull City	1-2	9267	Hardy
3	5 Sep	Darlington	3-6	5855	Hawkins, Heelbeck, Pedwell
4	7	HULL CITY	0-0	5277	
5	12	WREXHAM	2-2	3590	Pedwell(2)
6	19	Stockport County	2-4	10630	Bastow, Hardy
7	26	BARROW	4-1	5005	Bastow, Heelbeck, Pedwell, Reid
8	3 Oct	PORT VALE	2-0	7032	Bastow, O.G.
9	10	Oldham Athletic	1-4	5006	Bastow
10	17	York City	3-4	3804	Bastow(2), Pedwell
11	24	CARLISLE UNITED	0-1	5916	
12	31	Hartlepools United	2-0	5892	Pedwell, Smith
13	7 Nov	SOUTHPORT	3-0	4781	Brown, Pedwell, Smith
14	14	Tranmere Rovers	2-1	5410	Hardy, Smith
15	21	HALIFAX TOWN	6-0	5918	Brown(3), Hardy, Pedwell, Smith
16	5 Dec	CREWE ALEXANDRA	3-2	3812	Pedwell(2), Bastow
17	12	Chester	1-2	4076	Smith
18	19	ROCHDALE	1-1	4043	Smith
19	25	Lincoln City	0-3	9425	
20	26	Gateshead	1-2	3825	Hanson
21	28	LINCOLN CITY	3-1	3308	Smith(2), Bramham
22	1 Jan	Accrington Stanley	0-3	4924	
23	2	DARLINGTON	2-4	3973	Hardy, Smith
24	9	Wrexham	2-4	3950	Smith(2)
25	16	Mansfield Town	1-4	4137	Smith
26	23	STOCKPORT COUNTY	1-1	2294	Smith
27	30	Barrow	1-5	1299	Pedwell
28	6 Feb	Port Vale	1-2	7440	Brown
29	13	OLDHAM ATHLETIC	4-4	3539	Smith(2), Brown, Pedwell
30	20	YORK CITY	2-2	4035	Pedwell, Smith
31	27	Carlisle United	1-4	2982	Smith
32	6 Mar	HARTLEPOOLS UNITED	2-4	2601	Rhodes, Smith
33	13	Southport	1-4	5018	Smith
34	20	TRANMERE ROVERS	3-1	3816	Pedwell(2), Smith
35	26	New Brighton	0-4	4420	
36	27	Halifax Town	1-4	5820	Brown
37	29	NEW BRIGHTON	3-0	4148	Bastow, Dyson, Pedwell
38	3 Apr	MANSFIELD TOWN	4-1	4890	Pedwell(2), Bastow, Dyson
39	10	Crewe Alexandra	2-0	2746	Pedwell, Smith
40	17	CHESTER	2-1	4054	Bastow, Pedwell
41	24	Rochdale	0-1	4243	
42	1 May	ACCRINGTON STANLEY	2-2	3152	Dyson, Smith

Player appearances / goals

	Clough J.	Ford S.	Birkett W.	Roberts H.	Hawkins J.	Heelbeck L.	Reid J.	Hardy R.	Bastow R.	Wynn J.	Pedwell R.	Brown W.	Haigh K.	Kilsby R.	Bramham R.	Curry R.	Smith E.	Greaves J.	Courts F.	Garton H.	Hartley G.	Hanson F.	Fieldsend G.	Rhodes I.	Dyson S.
Apps.	16	24	40	3	39	38	41	25	22	5	36	16	28	1	8	28	34	26	5		3	13	1	2	8
Goals					1	2	1	5	12	1	20	7			1		22					1		1	3

F.A. CUP

| 1R | 28 Nov | HARTLEPOOLS UNITED | 4-4 | 11552 | Brown(3), Pedwell |
| 1Rr | 2 Dec | Hartlepools United | 0-2 | 8000 | |

NORTH SECTION CUP

| 1R | 2 Nov | HALIFAX TOWN | 1-0 | | Ford |
| 2R | 8 Mar | Port Vale | 0-1 | | |

Un-named team group of c. 1936.

Final League Table

		Pl.	Home					Away					F.	A.	Pts
			W	D	L	F	A	W	D	L	F	A			
1	Stockport County	42	17	3	1	59	18	6	11	4	25	21	84	39	60
2	Lincoln City	42	18	1	2	65	20	7	6	8	38	37	103	57	57
3	Chester	42	15	5	1	68	21	7	4	10	19	36	87	57	53
4	Oldham Athletic	42	13	7	1	49	25	7	4	10	28	34	77	59	51
5	Hull City	42	13	6	2	39	22	4	6	11	29	47	68	69	46
6	Hartlepools United	42	16	1	4	53	21	3	6	12	22	48	75	69	45
7	Halifax Town	42	12	4	5	40	20	6	5	10	28	43	68	63	45
8	Wrexham	42	12	3	6	41	21	4	9	8	30	36	71	57	44
9	Mansfield Town	42	13	1	7	64	35	5	7	9	27	41	91	76	44
10	Carlisle United	42	13	6	2	42	19	5	2	14	23	49	65	68	44
11	Port Vale	42	12	6	3	39	23	5	4	12	19	41	58	64	44
12	York City	42	13	5	5	54	27	3	8	10	25	43	79	70	43
13	Accrington Stanley	42	14	2	5	51	26	2	7	12	25	43	76	69	41
14	Southport	42	10	8	3	39	28	2	5	14	34	59	73	87	37
15	New Brighton	42	10	8	3	36	16	3	3	15	19	54	55	70	37
16	Barrow	42	11	5	5	42	25	2	5	14	28	61	70	86	36
17	Rotherham United	42	11	7	3	52	28	3	0	18	26	63	78	91	35
18	Rochdale	42	12	3	6	44	27	1	6	14	25	59	69	86	35
19	Tranmere Rovers	42	10	8	3	52	30	2	1	18	19	58	71	88	33
20	Crewe Alexandra	42	6	8	7	31	31	4	4	13	24	52	55	83	32
21	Gateshead	42	9	8	4	40	31	2	2	17	23	67	63	98	32
22	Darlington	42	6	8	7	42	46	2	6	13	24	50	66	96	30

SEASON 1937/38
DIVISION THREE (NORTH)

No.	Date	Opposition	Res.	Att.	Goalscorers	Sleight H.	Haigh K.	Birkett W.	Curry R.	Hawkins J.	Lynch J.	Reid J.	Humphrey E.	Bastow R.	Smith E.	Hanson F.	Hartley G.	Mills J.	Courts F.	Bramham A.	Knowles H.	Wilkinson C.	Bradley G.	Brown W.D.	Clarke J.	Lister A.
1	28 Aug	TRANMERE ROVERS	2-1	5795	Bastow, Hawkins	1	2	3	4	5	6	7	8	9	10	11										
2	30	Halifax Town	3-1	7666	Bastow, Hanson, Humphrey	1	2	3		5	6	7	8	9	10	11	4									
3	4 Sep	York City	1-4	7395	Hanson	1	2	3		5	6	7	8	9	10	11	4									
4	6	HALIFAX TOWN	4-1	6010	Bramham, Hanson, Humphrey, Mills	1	2	3			6	7	8		10	11		4	5	9						
5	11	BRADFORD CITY	2-1	8220	Reid(2)	1	2	3		5	6	7	8		10	11		4		9						
6	13	CARLISLE UNITED	0-1	6393		1	2	3		5	6	7	8		10	11		4		9						
7	18	Southport	3-0	5820	Bramham(3)	1	2	3	4			7			10	11		6		9	8					
8	25	DONCASTER ROVERS	2-2	17744	Smith, Reid	1	2	3	4	5		7			10	11		6		9	8					
9	2 Oct	Rochdale	0-2	5019			2	3	4	5		7		8	10	11		6		9		1				
10	9	BARROW	3-0	6744	Bastow, Hanson, Smith		2	3	4	5		7		8	10	11		6		9		1				
11	16	Wrexham	0-2	4167			2	3	4	5		7		8	10	11		6		9		1				
12	23	HARTLEPOOLS UNITED	3-1	4700	Braham, Hanson, Knowles		2	3		5	4	7			10	11		6		9	8	1				
13	30	Lincoln City	0-5	8054			2	3		5		7			10	11		6		9	8	1	4			
14	6 Nov	HULL CITY	2-2	5371			2	3	4	5	6	7			10	11		6		9		1				
15	13	New Brighton	3-2	4495	Hanson, Mills, Smith	1	2	3	4			7			10	11		6	5	9	8					
16	20	GATESHEAD	1-1	8251	Smith	1	2	3	4	5		7			10	11		6		9	8					
17	4 Dec	DARLINGTON	4-2	3353	Bramham, Hanson, Reid, Smith	1	2	3	4	5		7			10	11				9	8		6			
18	18	CREWE ALEXANDRA	1-0	4471	Bramham	1	2	3	4	5		7		9	10	11		6		8						
19	25	Chester	3-2	6105	Clarke, Mills, Smith	1	2	3	4	5		11			10	8		6		9					7	
20	26	CHESTER	4-1	11394	Bramham, Clarke, Hanson, Reid	1	2	3	4	5		11			10	8		6		9					7	
21	1 Jan	Tranmere Rovers	2-0	13614	Bramham, Clarke	1	2	3	4	5		11			10	8		6		9					7	
22	3	Port Vale	0-0	3604		1	2	3	4		6	11			10	8			5	9					7	
23	8	Oldham Athletic	1-3	17175	Clarke	1	2	3	4	5	6	11			10	8				9					7	
24	15	YORK CITY	3-0	6117	Clarke, Bramham, Smith		2	3		5	4	11			10	8		6		9		1			7	
25	22	Bradford City	2-3	6916	Clarke, Smith	1	2	3		5	4	11			10	8		6		9					7	
26	29	SOUTHPORT	1-1	6042	Bramham	1	2	3	4		6	11			10	8			5	9					7	
27	5 Feb	Doncaster Rovers	1-0	20618	Clarke	1	2			5	4	11			10	8		6	3	9					7	
28	12	ROCHDALE	1-0	9282	Smith	1	2			5	4	11			10	8		6	3	9					7	
29	19	Barrow	0-1	4946		1	2	3							10	8				9				6	7	11
30	26	WREXHAM	1-1	8096	Bramham	1	2	3		5	4	11			10	8				9				6	7	
31	5 Mar	Hartlepools United	0-4	5639		1	2	3		5	4	7			10	11				9				6	8	
32	12	LINCOLN CITY	4-0	10443	Bramham(2), Hanson, Mills	1		3	4						10	11		8	2	9				6	7	
33	19	Hull City	1-1	15687	Bramham	1		3	4	5					10	11		8	2	9				6	7	
34	26	NEW BRIGHTON	1-2	9179	Bramham	1		3	4	5					10	11		8	2	9				6	7	
35	2 Apr	Gateshead	0-0	8796		1		3	4	5				8	10	11			2	9				6	7	
36	9	OLDHAM ATHLETIC	2-1	9873	Bramham, Clarke	1	2	3	4	5				8	10	11				9				6	7	
37	15	Accrington Stanley	0-0	3831		1	2	3	4	5				8	10	11				9				6	7	
38	16	Darlington	1-2	4932	Bramham	1	2	3	4	5				8	10	11				9				6	7	
39	18	ACCRINGTON STANLEY	1-1	7187	Smith	1	2	3	4	5				8	10	11		6		9					7	
40	23	PORT VALE	3-2	5346	Bramham(2), Clarke	1	2	3	4	5				8	10	11			4	9				6	7	
41	30	Crewe Alexandra	1-3	3107	Bramham		2	3	4	5				8	10	11				9		1		6	7	
42	7 May	Carlisle United	1-0	3748	Hanson	1	2	3	4			6		8	10	11				9				5	7	
					Apps.	34	38	40	27	37	18	31	6	15	42	42	2	24	12	39	7	8		15	24	1
					Goals					1		5	2	3	10	11		4		22	1				9	

F.A. CUP

No.	Date	Opposition	Res.	Att.	Goalscorers	Sleight H.	Haigh K.	Birkett W.	Curry R.	Hawkins J.	Lynch J.	Reid J.	Humphrey E.	Bastow R.	Smith E.	Hanson F.	Hartley G.	Mills J.	Courts F.	Bramham A.	Knowles H.	Wilkinson C.	Bradley G.	Brown W.D.	Clarke J.	Lister A.
1R	27 Nov	Burton Town	1-1	6000	Smith	1	2	3	4	5		7			10	11		6		9	8					
1Rr	29	BURTON TOWN	3-0	4544	Bramham(2), Hawkins	1	2	3	4	5		7			10	11				9	8		6			
2R	11 Dec	ALDERSHOT	0-3	11200		1	2	3	4	5		7			10	11				9	8		6			

NORTH SECTION CUP

No.	Date	Opposition	Res.	Att.	Goalscorers	Sleight H.	Haigh K.	Birkett W.	Curry R.	Hawkins J.	Lynch J.	Reid J.	Humphrey E.	Bastow R.	Smith E.	Hanson F.	Hartley G.	Mills J.	Courts F.	Bramham A.	Knowles H.	Wilkinson C.	Bradley G.	Brown W.D.	Clarke J.	Lister A.
1R	1 Nov	GATESHEAD	0-1				2	3		5		7	8		10	11		6		9				1	4	

Final League Table

		Pl.	Home					Away					F.	A.	Pts
			W	D	L	F	A	W	D	L	F	A			
1	Tranmere Rovers	42	15	4	2	57	21	8	6	7	24	20	81	41	56
2	Doncaster Rovers	42	15	4	2	48	16	6	8	7	26	33	74	49	54
3	Hull City	42	11	8	2	51	19	9	5	7	29	24	80	43	53
4	Oldham Athletic	42	16	4	1	48	18	3	9	9	19	28	67	46	51
5	Gateshead	42	15	5	1	53	20	5	6	10	31	39	84	59	51
6	Rotherham United	42	13	6	2	45	21	7	4	10	23	35	68	56	50
7	Lincoln City	42	14	3	4	48	17	5	5	11	18	33	66	50	46
8	Crewe Alexandra	42	14	3	4	47	17	4	6	11	24	36	71	53	45
9	Chester	42	13	4	4	54	31	3	8	10	23	41	77	72	44
10	Wrexham	42	14	4	3	37	15	2	7	12	21	48	58	63	43
11	York City	42	11	4	6	40	25	5	6	10	30	43	70	68	42
12	Carlisle United	42	11	5	5	35	19	4	4	13	22	48	57	67	39
13	New Brighton	42	12	5	4	43	18	3	3	15	17	43	60	61	38
14	Bradford City	42	12	6	3	46	21	2	4	15	20	48	66	69	38
15	Port Vale	42	11	8	2	45	27	1	6	14	20	46	65	73	38
16	Southport	42	8	8	5	30	26	4	6	11	23	56	53	82	38
17	Rochdale	42	7	10	4	38	27	6	1	14	29	51	67	78	37
18	Halifax Town	42	9	7	5	24	19	3	5	13	20	47	44	66	36
19	Darlington	42	10	4	7	37	31	1	6	14	17	48	54	79	32
20	Hartlepools United	42	10	8	3	36	20	0	4	17	17	60	53	80	32
21	Barrow	42	9	6	6	28	20	2	4	15	13	51	41	71	32
22	Accrington Stanley	42	9	2	10	31	32	2	5	14	14	43	45	75	29

(Back): Freeman (Manager), Haigh, Curry, Hawkins, Sleight, Mills, Birkett, Heald (Sec.), Smailes (Trainer).
(Front): Clarke, Hanson, Bramham, Smith, Reid.

- 1937-38 -

Back Row (left to right): Reid, Haigh, Courts, Birkett, Quinton, Westley.
Second Row: Mills, Curry, Wilkinson, Sleight, Hawkins, Bradley, Lynch.
Third Row (seated): Mr. R. V. Freeman (manager), Clarke, Bastow, Bramham, Bodle, Hanson, A. Smailes (trainer).
Seated in front: Smith, Murray.

-1938-39 -

SEASON 1938/39
DIVISION THREE (NORTH)

Player columns (left to right): Sleight H. | Haigh K. | Birkett W. | Curry R. | Hawkins J. | Bradley G. | Clarke J. | Bastow R. | Bramham A. | Bodle H. | Hanson F. | Smith E. | Anderson J. | Mills J. | Reid J. | Quinton W. | Wilkinson C. | Courts F. | Wadsworth C.E. | Murray W. | Dawson J.R. | Herdman H. | Newton H. | Hainsworth L. | Westley C. | Charnley J. | Lynch | Brown | Priestley

No.	Date	Opposition	Res.	Att.	Goalscorers	Sle	Hai	Bir	Cur	Haw	Bra	Cla	Bas	Brm	Bod	Han	Smi	And	Mil	Rei	Qui	Wil	Cou	Wad	Mur	Daw	Her	New	Hns	Wes	Chr	Lyn	Brn	Pri
1	27 Aug	ROCHDALE	7-1	7438	Bramham(4),Bastow,Clarke,Hanson	1	2	3	4	5	6	7	8	9	10	11																		
2	29	CREWE ALEXANDRA	4-1	7367	Bramham(2), Bastow, Hanson	1	2	3	4	5	6	7	8	9	10	11																		
3	3 Sep	York City	1-0	5310	Bramham	1	2	3	4	5	6	7		9	10	11	8																	
4	5	Barnsley	0-2	17613		1	2	3	4	5	6	7		9	10	11	8																	
5	10	WREXHAM	3-0	10419	Hanson(2), Bramham	1	2	3	4	5	6	7		9	10	11		8																
6	12	BARNSLEY	0-1	20144		1	2	3	4	5	6	7		9	10	11			8															
7	17	Gateshead	1-7	12470	Hanson	1	2	3	4	5	6	7		9	10	11			8															
8	24	HARTLEPOOLS UNITED	5-1	7698	Bastow(2), Hanson(2), Bramham	1	2	3	4	5	6	7	8	9		11			10															
9	1 Oct	Darlington	1-3	4210	Bramham	1	2	3	4	5	6		8	9		11			10		7													
10	8	CARLISLE UNITED	4-0	7110	Bramham(2), Hanson(2)	1		3	4	5	6	7	8	9		11			10			2												
11	15	Oldham Athletic	0-2	10555		1		3	4	5	6	7	8	9		11			10			2												
12	22	HALIFAX TOWN	0-1	7611		1		3	4	5	6	7	8	9		11			10			2												
13	29	New Brighton	0-3	5126		1		3	4	5	6	7	8	9		11			10			2												
14	5 Nov	BARROW	1-2	5828	Bramham	1		3	4	5		7	8	9		11			10			2												
15	12	Chester	4-1	7082	Bramham(2), Clarke, Hanson	1		3	4			7	8	9	10	11					6	2		5										
16	19	BRADFORD CITY	2-0	7177	Bastow(2)	1		3	4			7	8	9	10	11					6	2		5										
17	3 Dec	LINCOLN CITY	1-3	5607	Hanson	1		3	4					9		11		8	6	7		2		5	10									
18	10	Barrow	1-4	6075	Hanson			3	4					9		11		8		7	6	2	1	5	10									
19	17	ACCRINGTON STANLEY	2-1	2654	Bramham, Clarke		4	3				7	8	9		11					6	2	1	5	10									
20	24	Rochdale	1-0	5811	Wadsworth		4	3				7	8	9		11					6	2	1	5	10									
21	26	Doncaster Rovers	1-1	17868	Wadsworth		4	3				7	8	9		10					6	2	1	5			11							
22	27	DONCASTER ROVERS	0-0	17042			2	3	4			7	8	9		10					6		1	5			11							
23	31	YORK CITY	2-0	6615	Hanson, Reid		4	3				7		9		10				8	6	2	1	5			11							
24	2 Jan	Stockport County	0-5	10044			4	3				7	8	9		10					6	2	1	5			11							
25	14	Wrexham	0-2	2778			4	3				7	8	9		6				5	11	2	1		10									
26	21	GATESHEAD	2-2	4133	Bramham(2)		4	3				7	8	9		11				5	6	2	1		10									
27	28	Hartlepools United	1-1	2604	Bastow		4	3				7	8	9		11				5	6	2	1		10									
28	4 Feb	DARLINGTON	3-3	4822	Hanson(2), Dawson			3				7		9		8		4	5	6		2	1		10	11								
29	11	Carlisle United	1-3	3027			8	3	4			7		9		11			5	6		2	1		10									
30	18	OLDHAM ATHLETIC	3-1	6071	Bastow, Bramham, Hanson		4	3				7	8	9		11					6	2	1		10			5						
31	25	Halifax Town	1-1	4950	Murray		4	3				7	8	9		11					6	2	1		10			5						
32	4 Mar	NEW BRIGHTON	0-0	4620			4	3					8	9		11					6	2	1		10		5	7						
33	9	Hull City	2-0	4040	Bramham, Newton		4	3					8	9		11					6	2	1		10		5	7						
34	18	CHESTER	2-0	5317	Bramham(2)		4	3					8	9		11					6	2	1		10		5	7						
35	25	Bradford City	2-5	5679	Bramham(2)		4	3					8	9		11					6	2	1	5	10			7						
36	1 Apr	HULL CITY	0-2	5470				3	4					9		11					6	7	2	1	3	10			8				
37	7	Southport	0-1	6420			4							9		11					6	7	2	1	3	10		5					
38	8	Lincoln City	1-0	5192	Bramham		4							9		8					6	7	2	1	3	10	11	5					
39	10	SOUTHPORT	1-0	5308	Hanson		4							9		8		10			6	7	2	1	3		11	5					
40	15	STOCKPORT COUNTY	3-0	4054	Bramham(3)		4							9		8					6	7	2	1	3	10	11	5					
41	22	Accrington Stanley	1-2	2059	Clarke							7		9		8					6	4	2	1	3	10	11	5					
42	29	Crewe Alexandra	0-0	1713			4					7		9		8					6	11	2	1	3	10		5					
					Apps.	17	30	36	22	14	13	30	20	42	9	42	7	8	30	21	32	25	17	7	18	6	11	4	1					
					Goals							4	8	29		17				1				2	1	1		1						

F.A. CUP

No.	Date	Opposition	Res.	Goalscorers	Sle	Bir	Cur	Cla	Bas	Brm	Bod	Han	Qui	Wil	Wad
1R	26 Nov	Hull City	1-4	Bramham	1	3	4	7	8	9	10	11	6	2	5

NORTH SECTION CUP

No.	Date	Opposition	Res.	Goalscorers	Hai	Bir	Cur	Cla	Bas	Brm	Han	Rei	Qui	Wil	Cou	Mur	Wes	Chr	Lyn	Brn	Pri
1R	30 Jan	BRADFORD CITY	0-0		4	3		7	8	9	11	5	6		1	10	2				
1Rr	8 Feb	Bradford City	0-1			3	4	7			11	10		2	1			5	6	8	9

Final League Table

		Pl.	Home W	D	L	F	A	Away W	D	L	F	A	F.	A.	Pts
1	Barnsley	42	18	2	1	60	12	12	5	4	34	22	94	34	67
2	Doncaster Rovers	42	12	5	4	47	21	9	9	3	40	26	87	47	56
3	Bradford City	42	16	2	3	59	21	6	6	9	30	35	89	56	52
4	Southport	42	14	5	2	47	16	6	5	10	28	38	75	54	50
5	Oldham Athletic	42	16	1	4	51	21	4	4	11	25	38	76	59	49
6	Chester	42	12	5	4	54	31	8	4	9	34	39	88	70	49
7	Hull City	42	13	5	3	57	25	5	5	11	26	49	83	74	46
8	Crewe Alexandra	42	12	5	4	54	23	7	1	13	28	47	82	70	44
9	Stockport County	42	13	6	2	57	24	4	3	14	34	53	91	77	43
10	Gateshead	42	11	6	4	45	24	3	8	10	29	43	74	67	42
11	Rotherham United	42	12	4	5	45	21	5	4	12	19	43	64	64	42
12	Halifax Town	42	9	10	2	33	22	4	6	11	19	32	52	54	42
13	Barrow	42	11	5	5	46	22	5	4	12	20	43	66	65	41
14	Wrexham	42	15	2	4	46	28	2	5	14	20	51	66	79	41
15	Rochdale	42	10	5	6	58	29	5	4	12	34	53	92	82	39
16	New Brighton	42	11	2	8	46	32	4	7	10	22	41	68	73	39
17	Lincoln City	42	9	6	6	40	33	3	3	15	26	59	66	92	33
18	Darlington	42	12	2	7	43	30	1	5	15	19	62	62	92	33
19	Carlisle United	42	10	5	6	44	33	3	2	16	22	78	66	111	33
20	York City	42	8	5	8	37	34	4	3	14	27	58	64	92	32
21	Hartlepools United	42	10	4	7	36	33	2	3	16	19	61	55	94	31
22	Accrington Stanley	42	6	5	10	30	39	1	1	19	19	64	49	103	20

SEASON 1939/40
East Midlands Regional League

No.	Date	Opposition	Res.	Goalscorer
1	21 Oct	Notts County	0-2	
2	28	CHESTERFIELD	1-1	Hooper
3	11 Nov	Barnsley	2-2	Bramham, Hanson
4	18	GRIMSBY TOWN	2-1	Bastow, Bramham
5	25	Sheffield United	0-5	
6	2 Dec	NOTTINGHAM FOREST	1-0	Bastow
7	9	Mansfield Town	1-1	Bramham
8	6 Jan	Lincoln City	1-0	Bastow
9	13	Sheffield Wednesday	1-0	Bramham
10	2 Mar	SHEFFIELD WEDNESDAY	1-1	Hanson
11	9	BARNSLEY	0-4	
12	16	Grimsby Town	1-3	Hanson
13	23	SHEFFIELD UNITED	0-4	
14	25	NOTTS COUNTY	3-2	Hooper, Hainsworth, Brotherton
15	26	DONCASTER ROVERS	3-1	Wadsworth(2), Mills
16	30	Nottingham Forest	1-4	Brotherton
17	6 Apr	MANSFIELD TOWN	1-2	Hanson
18	4 May	Chesterfield	1-6	Hainsworth
19	11	LINCOLN CITY	3-1	Bramham(2), Barlow
20	18	Doncaster Rovers	1-2	Armitage

War Cup

No.	Date	Opposition	Res.	Goalscorer
1R	13	Doncaster Rovers	0-0	
1Rr	15	DONCASTER ROVERS	1-0	Brotherton
2R	20	Sheffield United	0-0	
2Rr	27	SHEFFIELD UNITED	0-3	

SEASON 1940/41
North Regional League

No.	Date	Opposition	Res.	Goalscorer
1	31 Aug	SHEFFIELD UNITED	3-3	Westwood(3)
2	14 Sep	GRIMSBY TOWN	1-0	Bramham
3	21	YORK CITY	3-0	Bramham(2), Westwood
4	28	Lincoln City	2-2	Bramham, Westwood
5	5 Oct	Hull City	2-0	Purdy, Westwood
6	12	LEEDS UNITED	0-0	
7	19	York City	1-3	Purdy
8	26	GRIMSBY TOWN	3-2	Bramham(2), Armitage
9	9 Nov	HUDDERSFIELD TOWN	1-0	Westwood
10	16	Sheffield Wednesday	1-1	Bramham
11	23	LINCOLN CITY	0-3	
12	30	Bradford City	2-1	Bramham, Westwood
13	7 Dec	SHEFFIELD WEDNESDAY	1-0	Brotherton
14	21	CHESTERFIELD	0-3	
15	25	BARNSLEY	0-3	
16	25	Barnsley	3-3	Bramham, Hanson, Wadsworth
17	28	SHEFFIELD UNITED	2-0	Bramham, Mills
18	4 Jan	Sheffield Wednesday	2-4	Hanson, Westwood
19	11	BARNSLEY	4-3	Bramham(2), Hanson, Mills
20	8 Feb	Doncaster Rovers	2-3	Stamps(2)
21	1 Mar	BRADFORD CITY	1-2	Stamps
22	8	DONCASTER ROVERS	1-2	Hanson
23	5 Apr	Barnsley	1-5	O.G.
24	12	Mansfield Town	1-0	Wadsworth
25	14	HUDDERSFIELD TOWN	3-1	Carr, Myers, Wadsworth
26	19	Grimsby Town	3-5	Myers, Newman, Westwood
27	26	BRADFORD PARK AVENUE	2-0	Stamps, ?
28	3 May	BRADFORD PARK AVENUE	1-5	Wadsworth

War Cup

No.	Date	Opposition	Res.	Goalscorer
1R	15 Feb	Sheffield United	3-2	Bramham(2), Hanson
1R	22	SHEFFIELD UNITED	0-3	

SEASON 1941/42
North Regional League

No.	Date	Opposition	Res.	Goalscorer
1	30 Aug	Sheffield Wednesday	0-1	
2	6 Sep	SHEFFIELD WEDNESDAY	4-1	Wadsworth(2), Carr, Clarke
3	13	Bradford City	2-0	Hooper, Wadsworth
4	20	BRADFORD CITY	3-1	Hanson, Hooper, Myers
5	27	GRIMSBY TOWN	2-3	Myers, Wadsworth
6	4 Oct	Grimsby Town	2-6	Carr, Myers
7	11	Lincoln City	0-3	
8	18	LINCOLN CITY	2-3	Hanson, Mills
9	25	DONCASTER ROVERS	2-1	Hanson, Stamps
10	1 Nov	Doncaster Rovers	1-5	Carr
11	8	Sheffield United	1-5	Myers
12	15	SHEFFIELD UNITED	1-1	Brown
13	22	MANSFIELD TOWN	4-0	Hainsworth, Hanson, Stamps, O.G.
14	29	Mansfield Town	1-4	Hainsworth
15	6 Dec	Chesterfield	1-2	Ardron
16	13	CHESTERFIELD	3-1	Ardron(2), Hanson
17	20	BARNSLEY	3-3	Ardron, Hanson, Mills
18	28	HUDDERSFIELD TOWN	1-3	Ardron

War Cup

No.	Date	Opposition	Res.	Goalscorer
Pre	27 Dec	LEEDS UNITED	3-1	Hainsworth(2), Hanson
Pre	3 Jan	Halifax Town	0-1	
Pre	17	HALIFAX TOWN	2-0	Clarke, ?
Pre	31	Bradford Park Avenue	5-5	Clarke, Hainswoth(2), Stamps, ?
Pre	7 Feb	NEWCASTLE UNITED	2-1	Clarke, Stamps
Pre	14	Newcastle United	3-1	Ardron, Myers
Pre	21	LINCOLN CITY	0-1	
Pre	28	Lincoln City	2-4	Ardron(2)
Pre	21 Mar	BRADFORD PARK AVENUE	3-1	Ardron(2), Clarke
1R	4 Apr	SHEFFIELD UNITED	2-5	Ardron(2)
1R	6	Sheffield United	3-3	Ardron(2), Haigh

SEASON 1942/43
North Regional League

No.	Date	Opposition	Res.	Goalscorer
1	29 Aug	Mansfield Town	3-4	Carr, Clarke, Haigh
2	5 Sep	MANSFIELD TOWN	0-0	
3	12	Sheffield Wednesday	1-4	Ardron
4	19	SHEFFIELD WEDNESDAY	2-2	Hanson, Mills
5	26	SHEFFIELD UNITED	1-1	Carr
6	3 Oct	Sheffield United	2-4	Clarke, Hooper
7	10	CHESTERFIELD	3-3	Hainsworth(2), Clarke
8	17	Chesterfield	1-0	Carr
9	24	Halifax Town	0-4	
10	31	HALIFAX TOWN	1-4	Ardron
11	7 Nov	Barnsley	3-2	Ardron, Carr, Hainsworth
12	14	BARNSLEY	1-5	Ardron
13	21	Lincoln City	1-1	Hanson
14	28	LINCOLN CITY	3-0	Ardron(2), Clarke
15	5 Dec	GRIMSBY TOWN	1-6	Hainsworth
16	12	Grimsby Town	1-4	Ardron
17	19	York City	1-2	Ardron
18	25	YORK CITY	3-2	Ardron(3)
19	10 Apr	STOCKPORT COUNTY	2-0	Ardron, Mills
20	17	Doncaster Rovers	1-3	?
21	24	DONCASTER ROVERS	5-1	Raynor(3), Clarke, Owen
22	1 May	Barnsley	1-7	O.G.
23	15	BARNSLEY	5-3	Mills(3), Ford, Mills

War Cup

No.	Date	Opposition	Res.	Goalscorer
Pre	26 Dec	Chesterfield	0-3	
Pre	2 Jan	CHESTERFIELD	1-2	Clarke
Pre	9	GRIMSBY TOWN	1-3	Hanson
Pre	16	Grimsby Town	3-3	Ardron, Haigh, O.G.
Pre	23	Sheffield Wednesday	2-3	Mills, Tomlinson
Pre	30	SHEFFIELD WEDNESDAY	1-1	Carr
Pre	6 Feb	HALIFAX TOWN	2-3	Hainsworth(2)
Pre	13	Halifax Town	0-5	
Pre	20	Notts County	0-4	
Pre	27	NOTTS COUNTY	2-2	Hainsworth(2)
Pre	6 Mar	Doncaster Rovers	1-1	Ardron
Pre	13	DONCASTER ROVERS	3-0	Ardron, Burke, Mills

SEASON 1943/44

North Regional League

No.	Date	Opposition	Res.	Goalscorer
1	28 Aug	HALIFAX TOWN	3-0	Bastow, Moralee, Tomlinson
2	4 Sep	Halifax Town	1-2	Ardron
3	11	MANSFIELD TOWN	3-1	Ardron, Moralee, Tomlinson
4	18	Mansfield Town	2-3	Moralee, Tomlinson
5	25	Sheffield United	1-3	Ardron
6	2 Oct	SHEFFILED UNITED	2-3	Ardron(2)
7	9	SHEFFIELD WEDNESDAY	5-1	Ardron(2), Tomlinson, Waller, O.G.
8	16	Sheffield Wednesday	1-1	Tomlinson
9	23	Chesterfield	1-7	Tomlinson
10	30	CHESTERFIELD	2-0	Nightingale, Tomlinson
11	6 Nov	BARNSLEY	3-1	Moralee(2), Ardron
12	13	Barnsley	3-3	Waller(2), Ardron
13	20	LINCOLN CITY	1-2	Ardron
14	27	Lincoln City	1-5	Nightingale
15	4 Dec	Grimsby Town	1-4	Mills
16	11	GRIMSBY TOWN	4-3	Wilson(2), Moralee, Tomlinson
17	18	YORK CITY	3-1	Ardron, Moralee, Tomlinson
18	25	York City	1-2	Ardron
19	1 Apr	Barnsley	4-1	Ardron(4)
20	8	BARNSLEY	3-0	Barton(2), Tomlinson
21	10	LEEDS UNITED	5-3	Ardron, Barton, Hanson, Mills, Tomlinson
22	15	DERBY COUNTY	0-2	
23	22	Derby County	0-0	

War Cup

No.	Date	Opposition	Res.	Goalscorer
QR	26 Dec	Sheffield United	1-4	Moralee
QR	1 Jan	SHEFFIELD UNITED	7-2	Ardron(3), McDonald(2), Moralee, Tmlinson
QR	8	CHESTERFIELD	1-1	Barton
QR	15	Chesterfield	2-1	Tomlinson, Waller
QR	22	Doncaster Rovers	2-1	Ardron(2)
QR	29	DONCASTER ROVERS	2-2	Ardron, Moralee
QR	5 Feb	Grimsby Town	1-2	Tomlinson
QR	12	GRIMSBY TOWN	6-1	Ardron(3), Mills, Moralee, Wilson
QR	19	Lincoln City	4-2	Ardron(2), Austin, Barton
QR	26	LINCOLN CITY	6-1	Ardron(3), Barton, Moralee, Tomlinson
1R	4 Mar	GRIMSBY TOWN	2-2	Moralee, Williams
1R	11	Grimsby Town	1-2	Ardron

SEASON 1944/45

North Regional League

No.	Date	Opposition	Res.	Goalscorer
1	26 Aug	CHESTERFIELD	3-2	Ardron, Austin, Moralee
2	2 Sep	Chesterfield	0-0	
3	9	Mansfield Town	2-1	Barton, Moralee
4	16	MANSFIELD TOWN	0-0	
5	23	Grimsby Town	1-1	Ardron
6	30	GRIMSBY TOWN	2-0	Ardron(2)
7	7 Oct	LINCOLN CITY	1-0	Ardron
8	14	Lincoln City	6-2	Hanson(3), Ardron(2), Sinclair
9	21	Sheffield Wednesday	0-1	
10	28	SHEFFIELD WEDNESDAY	3-3	Hanson, Moralee, Sinclair
11	4 Nov	NOTTINGHAM FOREST	1-2	Barton
12	11	Nottingham Forest	2-1	Ardron, Chafer
13	18	Barnsley	5-6	Barton(3), Ardron, Chafer
14	25	BARNSLEY	1-0	Barton
15	2 Dec	Notts County	2-0	Ardron(2)
16	9	NOTTS COUNTY	2-1	Ardron, Chafer
17	16	Derby County	0-4	
18	23	DERBY COUNTY	0-1	
19	3 Mar	Bradford City	3-5	Barton, Kearney, Lennon
20	17	BRADFORD CITY	2-0	Barton, Smith
21	7 Apr	Sheffield United	1-6	Ardron
22	14	SHEFFIELD UNITED	1-0	Shaw
23	21	Hull City	8-2	Ardron(4), Shaw(2), Cowles, Hanson
24	28	HULL CITY	1-2	Ardron
25	5 May	BURY	5-1	Ardron(2), Shaw(2), Kearney

War Cup

No.	Date	Opposition	Res.	Goalscorer
QR	26 Dec	Doncaster Rovers	0-0	
QR	30	DONCASTER ROVERS	3-0	Barton(2), Ardron
QR	6 Jan	Sheffield United	1-0	Barton
QR	13	SHEFFIELD UNITED	1-3	Ardron
QR	20	Sheffield Wednesday	4-1	Ardron, Barton, Carr, Gregory
QR	27	SHEFFIELD WEDNESDAY	1-1	Ardron
QR	3 Feb	LINCOLN CITY	3-2	Ardron(3)
QR	10	Lincoln City	2-2	Carr, Chafer
QR	17	Grimsby Town	0-5	
QR	24	GRIMSBY TOWN	3-0	Barton, Mills, Smith
1R1L	24 Mar	BARNSLEY	2-1	Ardron, Sinclair
1R2L	31	Barnsley	0-3	

SEASON 1945/46

Third Division (East)

No.	Date	Opposition	Res.	Goalscorer
1	25 Aug	Lincoln City	1-1	Ardron
2	1 Sep	LINCOLN CITY	3-0	Ardron, Kearney, J.Shaw
3	8	HARTLEPOOLS UNITED	3-0	Mills, J.Shaw, O.G.
4	15	Hartlepools United	4-2	Ardron(2), Kearney, Nightingale
5	22	Doncaster Rovers	3-0	D.Williams(2), Ardron
6	29	DONCASTER ROVERS	7-1	Ardron(3), Kearney(3), D.Williams
7	6 Oct	DARLINGTON	1-2	Ardron
8	13	Darlington	1-6	Ardron
9	20	BRADFORD CITY	4-1	Ardron, Kearney, Mills, J.Shaw
10	27	Bradford City	4-0	D.Williams(2), Ardron, J.Shaw
11	3 Nov	Carlisle United	2-3	Kearney, Mills
12	10	CARLISLE UNITED	5-0	Ardron(2), D.Williams(2), Nightingale
13	1 Dec	Gateshead	1-4	J.Shaw
14	22	YORK CITY	3-2	Ardron, Nightingale, R.Shaw
15	25	Halifax Town	4-1	Ardron(4)
16	26	HALIFAX TOWN	6-3	J.Shaw(3), Ardron(2), Dawson
17	1 Jan	GATESHEAD	3-1	Burke, J.Shaw, D.Williams
18	20 Feb	York City	1-1	R.Shaw

Third Division Cup

No.	Date	Opposition	Res.	Goalscorer
QR	12 Jan	HARTLEPOOLS UNITED	1-1	Hooper
QR	19	Hartlepools United	3-2	Ardron(2), R.Shaw
QR	2 Feb	Gateshead	4-6	Burke(2), Dawson, Nightingale
QR	9	Lincoln City	5-1	Ardron(2), Burke(2), R.Shaw
QR	16	LINCOLN CITY	6-1	Ardron(2), Dawson(2), Burke, Guest
QR	27	Doncaster Rovers	0-0	
QR	2 Mar	DONCASTER ROVERS	1-3	Mills
QR	7	BRADFORD CITY	2-4	Ardron(2)
QR	9	Bradford City	1-5	R.Shaw
QR	16	GATESHEAD	1-3	Nightingale
1R1L	23	WREXHAM	4-0	Burke(2), Mills, J.Shaw
1R2L	30	Wrexham	2-0	Nightingale, J.Shaw
2R1L	6 Apr	Doncaster Rovers	0-0	
2R2L	13	DONCASTER ROVERS	2-0	Burke, J.Shaw
SF1L	19	Gateshead	2-2	Burke(2)
SF2L	21	GATESHEAD	3-1	Burke, Hainsworth, J.Shaw
F1L	27	CHESTER	2-2	J.Shaw
F2L	4 May	Chester	3-2	Burke, Dawson, J.Shaw

F.A. Cup (Two legs each round)

No.	Date	Opposition	Res.	Goalscorer
1L	17 Nov	Doncaster Rovers	1-0	Ardron
2L	24	DONCASTER ROVERS	2-1	Nightingale, Kearney
1L	8 Dec	LINCOLN CITY	2-1	Nightingale, J.Shaw
2L	15	Lincoln City	1-1	Ardron
1L	5 Jan	GATESHEAD	2-2	Dawson, J.Shaw
2L	9	Gateshead	2-0	Ardron(2)
1L	26	Barnsley	0-3	
2L	31	BARNSLEY	2-1	R.Shaw, O.G.

Triumphant players and officials display the Third Division Cup and the Third Division (East) trophies, after the Chester match. (Back): Freeman (manager), Smailes (trainer), Directors - Messrs. Parkin, Smart & Mills; Ardron, Selkirk, Warnes, Mr.Watt (Dir.), H.Williams, D.Williams, Edwards, Wilson, Curry (former player) and Mr. Fergusson (Dir.) Front: Guest, Shaw, Hanson, Mills, Burke, and Dawson.

Rotherham United 1945-46:
(Back): Mills, H.Williams, Selkirk, Warnes, Hanson, D.Williams.
(Front): R.Shaw, Guest, Ardron, Burke, Kearney

- December 1946 -
(Back): Selkirk, D.Williams, Warnes, Edwards, H.Williams, Stanbridge.
(Front): J.Shaw, Ardron, Wilson, McLean, Dawson.

SEASON 1946/47
DIVISION THREE (NORTH)

No.	Date	Opposition	Res.	Att.	Goalscorers	Warnes G.	Selkirk J.	Hanson F.	Edwards J.	Williams H.	Williams D.	Wilson A.	Guest G.	Ardron W.	McLean S.	Dawson J.	Stanbridge G.	Shaw J.	Whittam E.	Armitage L.	Hainsworth L.	Ibbotson D.	Gibson A.	Gregory F.	Grainger J.	Hargreaves D.	Thompson R.
1	31 Aug	Tranmere Rovers	4-1	8372	Wilson, Guest, Ardron, McLean	1	2	3	4	5	6	7	8	9	10	11											
2	4 Sep	York City	3-2	5229	Ardron(2), Wilson	1	2	3	4	5	6	7	8	9	10	11											
3	7	DARLINGTON	4-1	14887	Guest(2), Ardron, Wilson	1	2	3	4	5	6	7	8	9	10	11											
4	11	Wrexham	1-1	10549	McLean	1		3	4	5	6	11	8	9	10		2	7									
5	14	Hull City	2-0	22187	Wilson(2)	1		3	4	5	6	11	8	9	10	11	2										
6	21	GATESHEAD	4-0	13956	Edwards, Guest, McLean, Dawson	1		3	4	5	6	7	8	9	10	11	2										
7	28	Hartlepools United	1-2	12500	McLean	1	2	3	4	5	6	7		9	10	11											
8	5 Oct	CREWE ALEXANDRA	5-1	13195	Ardron(4), Guest	1	2	3	4	5	6	7	8	9		11		10									
9	12	Lincoln City	0-4	9653		1	2	3	4	5	6	7	8	9	23	11		10									
10	19	STOCKPORT COUNTY	2-1	13037	Wilson, Ardron	1	2		4	5	6	7	8	9		11		10	3								
11	26	Oldham Athletic	1-0	17121		1	2		4	5	6	7	8	9		11	3	10									
12	2 Nov	BRADFORD CITY	2-1	15195	Guest, Shaw	1	2		4	5	6	7	10	9		11	3	8									
13	9	Barrow	3-2	8202	Ardron(2), Shaw	1	2		4	5	6	7	10	9		11	3	8									
14	16	ACCRINGTON STANLEY	4-1	12032	Shaw(2), McLean, Wilson	1	2		4	5	6	7		9	10	11	3	8									
15	23	Carlisle United	1-1	14816	Shaw	1	2		4	5	6	7		9	10	11	3	8									
16	21 Dec	Doncaster Rovers	1-1	21297	Shaw	1	2		4	5	6	7		9	10	11	3	8									
17	25	Chester	2-2	9096	Wilson, McLean	1	2		4	5	6	7		9	10	11	3	8									
18	26	CHESTER	3-1	18000	Ardron(3)	1	2		4	5	6	7		9	10	11	3	8									
19	28	TRANMERE ROVERS	6-0	16000	Guest(2),Shaw(2),Ardron,McLean	1	2		4	5	6	11	7	9	10		3	8									
20	1 Jan	YORK CITY	6-1	14947	Wilson(2), Guest(2), Ardron, McLean	1	2		4	5	6	7		9	10	11	3	8									
21	4	Darlington	3-4	7811	McLean(2), Wilson	1	2		4	5	6	11	7		10		3	8		9							
22	13	HALIFAX TOWN	6-1	8001	Ardron(2), McLean(2), Shaw(2)	1	2		4	5	6		7	9	10	11	3	8									
23	18	HULL CITY	2-0	16971	Ardron, McLean	1	2		4	5	6	7		9	10	11	3	8									
24	25	Gateshead	0-2	5673		1	2		4	5	6	7		9	10	11	3	8									
25	1 Feb	HARTLEPOOLS UNITED	4-0	9354	Ardron(2), McLean, Guest	1		4	5	6	7	8	9	10	11					2	3						
26	8	Crewe Alexandra	2-1	2537	Wilson(2)	1	2		5	6	7		9	10		3	8			11	4						
27	22	Stockport County	2-1	7894	Hainsworth, Wilson	1	2		4	5	6	7		9	10		3	8			11						
28	22 Mar	Accrington Stanley	3-2	4840	Ardron(2), McLean	1	2		4	5	6	11	7	9	10			3									
29	29	CARLISLE UNITED	4-0	10180	Ardron(2), McLean, Wilson	1	2		4	5	6	11		9	10			8		7			3				
30	4 Apr	Southport	0-2	7407		1	2		4	5	6	11		9	10			8		7							
31	5	Halifax Town	3-2	4355	Ardron, Wilson, O.G.	1	2		4	5	6	7		9	10	11	3	8									
32	7	SOUTHPORT	2-1	7407	Ardron, Shaw	1	2		4	5	6	7		9	10	11	3	8									
33	12	NEW BRIGHTON	3-0	11558	Ardron(2), McLean	1	2		4	5	6	7		9	10	11	3	8									
34	19	Rochdale	1-1	11908	McLean	1	2		4	5	6	7		9	10	11	3	8									
35	26	DONCASTER ROVERS	3-2	20247	Hainsworth, McLean, Shaw	1	2		4	5	6		8	9	10		3	7			11						
36	3 May	WREXHAM	3-2	12035	Hainsworth(2), Ardron	1	2		4	5	6	7		9	10		3	8			11						
37	10	LINCOLN CITY	3-0	11667	Ardron(3)	1	2		4	5	6	7		9			3	8			11						
38	24	BARROW	4-3	9974	Ardron(2), Guest, D.Williams	1	2		4	5	6	7	10	9				8			11	3					
39	26	OLDHAM ATHLETIC	8-0	10398	Ardrn(3),Wilsn(2),Guest,Shaw,Hainswrth	1	2		4	5	6	7	10	9				8			11	3					
40	31	Bradford City	0-2	11343		1	2			5	6	7	10	9				8			11	3			4		
41	7 Jun	ROCHDALE	3-3	10375	Guest, Hainsworth, Wilson	1	2		4	5	6	7	10	9			3	8			11						
42	14	New Brighton	0-1	3426		1	2		4	5	6	7	8				11	3					9	10			
		Apps.				42	38	9	40	42	42	38	27	40	30	26	29	35	1	2	14	4	1	1	1		
		Goals							1		1	19	15	38	19	1		13			6						

F.A. CUP

No.	Date	Opposition	Res.	Att.	Goalscorers	Warnes G.	Selkirk J.	Hanson F.	Edwards J.	Williams H.	Williams D.	Wilson A.	Guest G.	Ardron W.	McLean S.	Dawson J.	Stanbridge G.	Shaw J.	Whittam E.	Armitage L.
1R	30 Nov	CREWE ALEXANDRA	2-0	15151	Wilson, Armitage	1	2		4	5	6	7			10	11	3	8		9
2R	14 Dec	SCUNTHORPE UNITED	4-1	14584	Ardron(2), Wilson, Shaw	1	2		4	5	6	7		9	10	11	3	8		
3R	11 Jan	Wolverhampton W.	0-3	43119		1	2		4	5	6	7		9	10	11	3	8		

Final League Table

		Pl.	Home W	D	L	F	A	Away W	D	L	F	A	F.	A.	Pts
1	Doncaster Rovers	42	15	5	1	67	16	18	1	2	56	24	123	40	72
2	Rotherham United	42	20	1	0	81	19	9	5	7	33	34	114	53	64
3	Chester	42	17	2	2	53	13	8	4	9	42	38	95	51	56
4	Stockport County	42	17	0	4	50	19	7	2	12	28	34	78	53	50
5	Bradford City	42	12	5	4	40	20	8	5	8	22	27	62	47	50
6	Rochdale	42	9	5	7	39	25	10	5	6	41	39	80	64	48
7	Wrexham	42	13	5	3	43	21	4	7	10	22	30	65	51	46
8	Crewe Alexandra	42	12	4	5	39	26	5	5	11	31	48	70	74	43
9	Barrow	42	10	2	9	28	24	7	5	9	26	38	54	62	41
10	Tranmere Rovers	42	11	5	5	43	33	6	2	13	23	44	66	77	41
11	Hull City	42	9	5	7	25	19	7	3	11	24	34	49	53	40
12	Lincoln City	42	12	3	6	52	32	5	2	14	34	55	86	87	39
13	Hartlepools United	42	10	5	6	36	26	5	4	12	28	47	64	73	39
14	Gateshead	42	10	3	8	49	33	6	3	12	23	39	72	72	38
15	York City	42	6	4	11	35	42	8	5	8	32	39	67	81	37
16	Carlisle United	42	10	5	6	45	38	4	4	13	25	55	70	93	37
17	Darlington	42	12	4	5	48	26	3	2	16	20	54	68	80	36
18	New Brighton	42	11	3	7	37	30	3	5	13	20	47	57	77	36
19	Oldham Athletic	42	6	5	10	29	31	6	3	12	26	49	55	80	32
20	Accrington Stanley	42	8	3	10	37	38	6	1	14	19	54	56	92	32
21	Southport	42	6	5	10	35	41	1	6	14	18	44	53	85	25
22	Halifax Town	42	6	3	12	28	36	2	3	16	15	56	43	92	22

SEASON 1947/48
DIVISION THREE (NORTH)

No.	Date	Opposition	Res.	Att.	Goalscorers	Warnes G.	Selkirk J.	Stanbridge G.	Edwards J.	Williams H.	Williams D.	Thompson R.	Shaw J.	Ardron W.	McLean S.	Hainsworth L.	Armitage L.	Guest G.	McMahon H.	Hargreaves O.	Mosby H.	Gibson A.	Sanderson E.	Street J.	Radford A.	Grainger J.	Mills H.
1	23 Aug	GATESHEAD	0-0	12205		1	2	3	4	5	6	7	8	9	10	11											
2	26	Oldham Athletic	5-1	19149	Ardrn,Hainswrth,Stanbrdge,D.Wlliams,Shaw	1	2	3	4	5	6	7	8	9	10	11											
3	30	Hartlepools United	2-2	9133	Thompson, McMahon	1	2	3	4	5	6	7	8	9	10	11											
4	1 Sep	OLDHAM ATHLETIC	4-1	12572	Ardron(3), Armitage	1	2	3	4	5	6		8	9			11	10	7								
5	6	HULL CITY	0-0	15205		1	2	3	4	5	6		8	9		11		10	7								
6	10	York City	0-2	13684		1	2		4	5	6		8	9		3		10	7		11						
7	13	CARLISLE UNITED	7-2	11631	Ardron(4), Shaw(2), Guest	1	2		4	5	6		10	9		3		7	8		11						
8	16	SOUTHPORT	0-2	12453		1	2		4	5			10	9		3		7	8		11	6					
9	20	Crewe Alexandra	3-3	9596	Ardron, Guest, Shaw	1	2		4	5	6		10	9		3		7	8		11						
10	22	ACCRINGTON STANLEY	1-0	10630	Ardron	1	2		4	5	6		10	9		3		7	8		11						
11	27	CHESTER	2-1	14262	Ardron, Mosby	1	2		4	5	6		10	9		3		7	8		11						
12	4 Oct	Mansfield Town	1-2	13886	Ardron	1	2		4	5	6		10	9		3		7	8		11						
13	11	Stockport County	2-2	11576	Armitage, Mosby	1	2		4	5	6		10	9		3	8		7		11						
14	18	BRADFORD CITY	4-1	13449	Armitage(2), Ardron, Mosby	1	2		4	5	6		10	9		3	8		7		11						
15	25	Barrow	3-1	11428	D.Williams, Armitage(2)	1	2		4	5	6		10	9		3	8		7		11						
16	1 Nov	WREXHAM	6-0	16702	Armitge(2),McMhon(2),Guest,Ardrn	1	2		4	5	6		10	9		3	8		7		11						
17	8	Halifax Town	1-2	12078	Mosby	1	2		4	5	6		10	9		3	8		7		11						
18	15	ROCHDALE	4-1	13141	Ardron(2), Armitage, Mosby	1	2		4	5	6		10	9		3	8		7		11						
19	22	New Brighton	2-1	5231	D.Williams, Sanderson		2		4	5	6		10	9		3	8				11		7	1			
20	6 Dec	Lincoln City	1-3	13320	Shaw		2		4	5	6		10	9				8	11					1	3	7	
21	20	Gateshead	1-1	5200	Ardron	1	2		4	5	6		10	9				8	11						3	7	
22	25	Darlington	1-1	10730	Ardron	1	2		4	5	6		10	9				8	11						3	7	
23	27	DARLINGTON	0-0	10811		1	2		4	5	6		10	9				8	11						3	7	
24	1 Jan	YORK CITY	3-2	16973	Ardron, Guest, Thompson	1	2		4	5	6	10		9				8	11						3	7	
25	3	HARTLEPOOLS UNITED	3-2	13765	Thompson(2), Ardron	1	2		4	5	6	10	7	9				8	11						3		
26	17	Hull City	3-5	29821	Guest(2), D.Williams	1	2		4	5	6	10	7	9				8	11						3		
27	31	Carlisle United	3-0	14344	Shaw(2), McMahon	1	2		4	3	6	10	7	9				8	11			5					
28	7 Feb	CREWE ALEXANDRA	5-1	12503	Shaw(2), Thompson(2), Ardron	1	2		4	3	6	10	7	9				8	11			5					
29	14	Chester	3-2	9994	Ardron, Shaw, Thompson	1	2		4	3	6	10	7	9				8	11			5					
30	28	STOCKPORT COUNTY	4-1	13339	Ardron(2), Thompson	1	2		4	3	6	10	7	9				8	11			5					
31	6 Mar	Bradford City	1-0	13394	Shaw	1	2		4	3	6	10	7	9				8	11			5					
32	13	BARROW	0-0	15710		1	2		4	3	6	10	7		9			8	11			5					
33	20	Wrexham	3-1	12822	Ardron(2), Guest	1	2		4	3	6	10	7	9				8	11			5					
34	26	TRANMERE ROVERS	2-0	15420	Ardron, Guest	1	2		4	3	6	10	7	9				8	11			5					
35	27	HALIFAX TOWN	3-0	15792	Grainger, Mills, Thompson	1	2		4	3	6	10	7					8				5				11	9
36	29	Tranmere Rovers	1-0	10927	Selkirk	1	2		4	3		10	7	9					11	6		5					8
37	3 Apr	Rochdale	0-1	7314		1	2		4	3		10	7	9					11	6		5					8
38	10	NEW BRIGHTON	6-0	13669	Guest(2),Mills,McMhon,Thmpsn,Slkrk	1	2		4	3	6	10		9				7	11			5					8
39	12	MANSFIELD TOWN	2-1	20522	Ardron, Mills	1	2		4	3	6	10		9				7	11			5					8
40	17	Southport	2-1	12829	Ardron, McMahon	1	2		4	3	6	10		9				7	11			5					8
41	24	LINCOLN CITY	0-2	20177		1	2		4	3	6	10		9				7	11			5					8
42	1 May	Accrington Stanley	1-0	6545	Ardron	1	2		4		6	10	7	9				8	11			5			3		
					Apps.	40	42	5	42	41	34	21	37	40	5	18	13	31	36	2	14	17	2	2	8	6	6
					Goals			1			5	10	10	30		1	9	10	5		5	5	1			1	3

F.A. CUP

Rd	Date	Opposition	Res.	Att.	Goalscorers	Warnes G.	Selkirk J.	Stanbridge G.	Edwards J.	Williams H.	Williams D.	Thompson R.	Shaw J.	Ardron W.	McLean S.	Hainsworth L.	Armitage L.	Guest G.	McMahon H.	Hargreaves O.	Mosby H.	Gibson A.	Sanderson E.	Street J.	Radford A.	Grainger J.	Mills H.
3R	10 Jan	BRENTFORD	0-3	22000		1	2		4	5	6		10	9				8	7						3	11	

Final League Table

		Pl.	Home					Away					F.	A.	Pts
			W	D	L	F	A	W	D	L	F	A			
1	Lincoln City	42	14	3	4	47	18	12	5	4	34	22	81	40	60
2	Rotherham United	42	15	4	2	56	18	10	5	6	39	31	95	49	59
3	Wrexham	42	14	3	4	49	23	7	5	10	25	31	74	54	50
4	Gateshead	42	11	5	5	48	28	8	6	7	27	29	75	57	49
5	Hull City	42	12	5	4	38	21	6	6	9	21	27	59	48	47
6	Accrington Stanley	42	13	1	7	36	24	7	5	9	26	35	62	59	46
7	Barrow	42	9	4	8	24	19	7	9	5	25	21	49	40	45
8	Mansfield Town	42	11	4	6	37	24	6	7	8	20	27	57	51	45
9	Carlisle United	42	10	4	7	50	35	8	3	10	38	42	88	77	43
10	Crewe Alexandra	42	12	4	5	41	24	6	3	12	20	39	61	63	43
11	Oldham Athletic	42	6	10	5	25	25	8	3	10	38	39	63	64	41
12	Rochdale	42	12	4	5	32	23	3	7	11	16	49	48	72	41
13	York City	42	8	7	6	38	25	5	7	9	27	35	65	60	40
14	Bradford City	42	10	4	7	38	27	5	6	10	27	39	65	66	40
15	Southport	42	10	4	7	34	27	4	7	10	26	36	60	63	39
16	Darlington	42	7	8	6	30	31	6	5	10	24	39	54	70	39
17	Stockport County	42	9	6	6	42	28	4	6	11	21	39	63	67	38
18	Tranmere Rovers	42	10	1	10	30	28	6	3	12	24	44	54	72	36
19	Hartlepools United	42	10	6	5	34	23	4	2	15	17	50	51	73	36
20	Chester	42	11	6	4	44	25	2	3	16	20	42	64	67	35
21	Halifax Town	42	4	10	7	25	27	3	3	15	18	49	43	76	27
22	New Brighton	42	5	6	10	20	28	3	3	15	18	53	38	81	25

1947-48: (Back): Smailes (Trainer), Selkirk, Edwards, Warnes, Gibson, H.Williams, D.Williams, Freeman (Manager). (Front): Shaw, Guest, Ardron, Thompson, McMahon.

1948-49: (Back): Selkirk, Bolton, Radford, Edwards, Warnes, H.Williams, D.Williams. (Front): Grainger, Guest, Ardron, Shaw, McMahon.

SEASON 1948/49
DIVISION THREE (NORTH)

No.	Date	Opposition	Res.	Att.	Goalscorers	Warnes G.	Selkirk J.	Williams H.	Edwards J.	Gibson A.	Williams D.	Shaw J.	Guest G.	Ardron W.	Thompson R.	McMahon H.	Radford A.	Grainger J.	Bolton D.	Williams K.	Durkin B.	Lowder T.	Mosby H.	Noble N.	Quaimey J.	Wilcox G.	Stanbridge G.	Wragg P.	Pilkington G.	Rawson C.
1	21 Aug	Oldham Athletic	3-1	15144	Guet(2), Shaw	1	2	3	4	5	6	7	8	9	10	11														
2	25	Accrington Stanley	3-2	7681	Edwards, Ardron(2)	1	2	3	4	5	6	7	8	9	10	11														
3	28	TRANMERE ROVERS	7-0	15571	Ardrn(2),Guest(2),Shaw(2),Thmpsn	1	2	3	4	5	6	7	8	9	10	11														
4	30	ACCRINGTON STANLEY	1-0	15249	Ardron	1	2	3	4	5	6	7	8	9	10	11														
5	4 Sep	Mansfield Town	2-1	16224	Selkirk(2)	1	2	3	4	5	6	7	8	9	10	11														
6	6	HARTLEPOOLS UNITED	2-1	15468	McMahon, Shaw	1	2	3	4	5	6	7	8	9	10	11														
7	11	BARROW	2-2	15757	Guest, Selkirk	1	2	3	4	5	6	7	8	9	10	11														
8	13	Hartlepools United	4-1	12777	Ardron(4)	1	2	5	4		6		10	8		9	11	3	7											
9	18	Wrexham	4-0	17680	Ardron(2), Guest(2)		2	5	4		6		10	8		9	11	3	7	1										
10	25	HALIFAX TOWN	4-1	16023	Ardron(2), Guest(2)		2	5	4		6		10	8		9	11	3	7	1										
11	2 Oct	Bradford City	2-1	18034	Ardron, Grainger		2	5	4		6		10	8		9	11	3	7	1										
12	9	Darlington	0-2	14560			2	5	4		6		10	8		9	11	3	7	1										
13	16	ROCHDALE	3-0	16750	Grainger, Guest, Shaw		2	5	4		6		10	8		9		3	7	1	11									
14	23	New Brighton	1-0	7052	Ardron		2	5	4		6		10	8		9	11	3	7	1										
15	30	CHESTER	2-1	15080	Guest, Grainger		2	5	4		6		10	8		9	11	3	7	1										
16	6 Nov	Southport	3-1	9716	Ardron, McMahon, Shaw		2	5	4		6		10	8		9	11	3	7	1										
17	13	CREWE ALEXANDRA	6-1	12660	Ardron(3), Shaw(2), McMahon		2	5	4		6		10	8		9	11	3	7	1										
18	20	York City	1-6	19271	Ardron		2	5	4		6		10	8		9	11	3	7	1										
19	4 Dec	Carlisle United	8-1	14639	Ardron(3),Lowdr(3),Graingr,Edwrds		2	5	4		6		10	8		9		3	7	1		11								
20	18	GATESHEAD	1-0	12716	Ardron		2	5	4		6		10	8		9		3	7	1		11								
21	25	Hull City	2-3	54652	Shaw, Lowder		2	5	4		6		10	8		9		3	7	1		11								
22	26	HULL CITY	0-0	22159			2	5	4		6		10	8		9		3	7	1		11								
23	1 Jan	Tranmere Rovers	1-2	9562	Grainger		2	5	4		6		10	8		9		3	7	1		11								
24	15	MANSFIELD TOWN	1-0	16841	Grainger		2	5	4		6			8		9		3	7	1		11								
25	22	Barrow	2-0	9326	Shaw(2)		2	5	4		6		10	8		9	11	3	7	1										
26	5 Feb	WREXHAM	1-3	13934	Ardron		2	5			6			8	9	10	11	3	7	1							4			
27	12	STOCKPORT COUNTY	2-1	12495	Grainger, Lowder	1	2	5	4		6			8	9		3	11				10	7							
28	19	Halifax Town	0-2	9286			2	5	4		6		10	8		9		3	7	1		11								
29	26	BRADFORD CITY	2-0	10454	Ardron, Mosby		2		4	5	6		8	10	9		3	7	1				11							
30	5 Mar	DARLINGTON	4-3	9150	Guest(2), Ardron, Grainger		2	3		5	6		8	10	9			7	1				11	4						
31	12	Rochdale	0-2	9840			2	3	4	5	6		8	10	9			7		1			11		1					
32	19	NEW BRIGHTON	1-1	9380	Guest		2	4		5	6		8	10	9			7	1				11		3					
33	26	Chester	1-1	6431	Ardron		2		4	5	6		8	10	9				1				11				3	7		
34	2 Apr	SOUTHPORT	1-0	8681	Edwards		2		4	5	6	7	8	10	9		3		1				11					8		
35	4	OLDHAM ATHLETIC	2-1	8341	Grainger, Mosby		2		4	5	6		8	10	9		3	11	1				7							
36	9	Crewe Alexandra	3-0	6889	Selkirk, Guest, Ardron		2	5	4		6		8	10	9		3	11	1										7	
37	15	Doncaster Rovers	0-0	32322			2	5	4		6		8	10	9		11		3				1						7	
38	16	YORK CITY	2-1	14229	Shaw, Wragg		2	5	4		6		8	10	9		11		1									3	7	
39	18	DONCASTER ROVERS	2-0	14337	Guest, Shaw			5	4		6		8	10	9		3	11	1				7	2						
40	23	Stockport County	1-0	14278	Wragg			5	4		6		8	10	9			11	1				2						7	
41	30	CARLISLE UNITED	1-1	9085	Shaw			5	4		6		8	10	9	11		3	1				2						7	
42	7 May	Gateshead	2-3	6586	Ardron(2)		2	5	4		6		8	10	9		3	11	1										7	
		Apps.				9	38	38	40	14	42	39	42	42	9	23	30	29	32	1	8	9	5	1	1	2	8			
		Goals					4		3			14	17	30		3		9				5	2					2		

F.A. CUP

Round	Date	Opposition	Res.	Att.	Goalscorers	Warnes G.	Selkirk J.	Williams H.	Edwards J.	Gibson A.	Williams D.	Shaw J.	Guest G.	Ardron W.	Thompson R.	McMahon H.	Radford A.	Grainger J.	Bolton D.	Williams K.	Durkin B.	Lowder T.	Mosby H.	Noble N.	Quaimey J.	Wilcox G.	Stanbridge G.	Wragg P.	Pilkington G.	Rawson C.
3R	8 Jan	DARLINGTON	4-2	18370	Ardron(2), Grainger, Noble		2	5			6		10	8			3	7	1			11		4						
4R	29	BURNLEY	0-1	22000			2	5	4		6		10	8			11	3	7	1										

Final League Table

		Pl.	Home					Away					F.	A.	Pts
			W	D	L	F	A	W	D	L	F	A			
1	Hull City	42	17	1	3	65	14	10	10	1	28	14	93	28	65
2	Rotherham United	42	16	4	1	47	17	12	2	7	43	29	90	46	62
3	Doncaster Rovers	42	10	8	3	26	12	10	2	9	27	28	53	40	50
4	Darlington	42	10	3	8	42	36	10	3	8	41	38	83	74	46
5	Gateshead	42	10	6	5	41	28	6	7	8	28	30	69	58	45
6	Oldham Athletic	42	12	4	5	49	28	6	5	10	26	39	75	67	45
7	Rochdale	42	14	3	4	37	16	4	6	11	18	37	55	53	45
8	Stockport County	42	13	5	3	44	16	3	6	12	17	40	61	56	43
9	Wrexham	42	12	6	3	35	22	5	3	13	21	40	56	62	43
10	Mansfield Town	42	13	6	2	39	15	1	8	12	13	33	52	48	42
11	Tranmere Rovers	42	8	9	4	23	19	5	6	10	23	38	46	57	41
12	Crewe Alexandra	42	13	4	4	31	18	3	5	13	21	56	52	74	41
13	Barrow	42	10	8	3	27	13	4	4	13	14	35	41	48	40
14	York City	42	11	3	7	49	28	4	6	11	25	46	74	74	39
15	Carlisle United	42	12	7	2	46	32	2	4	15	14	45	60	77	39
16	Hartlepools United	42	10	5	6	34	25	4	5	12	11	33	45	58	38
17	New Brighton	42	10	4	7	25	19	4	4	13	21	39	46	58	36
18	Chester	42	10	7	4	36	19	1	6	14	21	37	57	56	35
19	Halifax Town	42	8	4	9	26	27	4	7	10	19	35	45	62	35
20	Accrington Stanley	42	11	4	6	39	23	1	6	14	16	41	55	64	34
21	Southport	42	6	5	10	24	29	5	4	12	21	35	45	64	31
22	Bradford City	42	7	6	8	29	31	3	3	15	19	46	48	77	29

SEASON 1949/50
DIVISION THREE (NORTH)

No.	Date	Opposition	Res.	Att.	Goalscorers	Bolton D.	Selkirk J.	Gibson A.	Edwards J.	Williams H.	Williams D.	Grainger J.	Shaw J.	Bower K.	Guest G.	Flynn W.	Hart H.	Noble N.	Wragg P.	Quairney J.	Radford A.	Pilkington G.	Raynes J.	Williams K.	Rudd J.	Rawson C.	Warnes G.	Mosby H.
1	20 Aug	WREXHAM	2-2	13519	Bower, Shaw	1	2	3	4	5	6	7	8	9	10	11												
2	22	Oldham Athletic	2-2	25788	Grainger, Guest	1	2	3	4	5	6	7	8	9	10	11												
3	27	Accrington Stanley	4-1	8302	Guest(2), Shaw(2)	1	2	3	4	5	6	7	8	9	10	11												
4	29	OLDHAM ATHLETIC	0-1	14331		1	2	3	4	5	6	7		9	11	10	8											
5	3 Sep	MANSFIELD TOWN	2-2	14794	Grainger(2)	1	2	3		5	6	7		9	10	11		4	8									
6	5	Crewe Alexandra	1-4	10693	Bower		2			5	6	7	8	9	10	11		4			1		3					
7	10	Carlisle United	1-3	14621	Bower		2			5	6	7	8	9	10	11		4			1		3					
8	17	DONCASTER ROVERS	0-2	15217			2		4	5	6	7	8	9	10						1		3	11				
9	19	Chester	3-2	8421	Bower, Guest, Raynes		2		4	5	6	7	8	9	10						1		3	11				
10	24	LINCOLN CITY	1-3	11096	Hart		2		4	5	6	7		9	10		8				1		3	11				
11	26	STOCKPORT COUNTY	2-1	8768	Hart, Shaw		2	3	4	5	6		8	9	10		7				1			11				
12	1 Oct	Barrow	1-1	7145	Shaw		2	3	4	5	6		8	9	10		7			1				11				
13	8	Gateshead	2-2	10943	Grainger, Shaw		2		4	5	6	7	8	9	10			3		1					11			
14	15	HARTLEPOOLS UNITED	5-1	10721	Guest(3), Bower, Shaw		2		4	5	6	7	8	9	10			3		1					11			
15	22	Darlington	1-2	9704	Guest		2		4	5	6	7	8	9	10			3		1					11			
16	29	NEW BRIGHTON	3-0	10492	Guest, Rudd, Noble	1	2		4	5	6	7	8	9	10			3							11			
17	5 Nov	Halifax Town	3-4	6760	Grainger(2), Guest	1	2		4	5	6	7	8	9	10			3							11			
18	12	ROCHDALE	4-3	9113	Bower, Guest, Shaw, Rudd	1	2		4	5	6	7	8	9	10			3							11			
19	19	Bradford City	2-1	13695	Bower, Rudd	1	2		4	5	6	7	8	9	10			3							11			
20	3 Dec	Southport	0-4	6434		1	2		4	5	6	7	8	9	10			3							11			
21	17	Wrexham	1-0	5459	Hart		2		4	5	6	7	8		10		9	3		1					11			
22	24	ACCRINGTON STANLEY	6-0	9448	Bower(3), Grainger, Shaw, Rudd		2		4	5	6	7	8	9	10			3		1					11			
23	26	TRANMERE ROVERS	1-1	14476	Edwards		2		4	5	6	7	8	9	10			3		1					11			
24	27	Tranmere Rovers	2-0	15670	Guest, Noble		2		4	5	6	7	8	9	10			3		1					11			
25	31	Mansfield Town	2-0	15352	Shaw(2)		2		4	5	6	7	8	9	10			3		1					11			
26	14 Jan	CARLISLE UNITED	1-1	12893	Edwards		2		4	5	6	7	8	9	10			3		1					11			
27	21	Doncaster Rovers	0-1	30893			2		4	5	6	7	8	9	10			3				1			11			
28	4 Feb	Lincoln City	0-0	13329		1	2		4	5	6	7	8	9	10			3							11			
29	18	BARROW	1-2	10147	Edwards	1	2		4	5	6	7	8	9				3							11	10		
30	25	BRADFORD CITY	5-2	6086	Guest(2), Grainger, Hart, Shaw	1	2		4	5	6	7	8		10		9	3							11			
31	4 Mar	Chester	2-4	6533	Guest, O.G.	1	2		4	5	6	7	8		10		9	3							11			
32	11	DARLINGTON	1-1	7436	Grainger	1	2		4	5	6	7	8	9	10			3							11			
33	18	New Brighton	3-0	4229	Rudd, Shaw, H.Williams	1	2	5	4	9	6	7	8		10			3							11			
34	25	HALIFAX TOWN	2-1	7549	Rudd, H.Williams	1	2	5	4	9	6	7	8		10			3							11			
35	1 Apr	Rochdale	0-1	7653		1	2	5	4	9	6	7	8		10			3							11			
36	7	York City	3-0	12382	Guest(2), H.Williams	1	2	5	4	9		7	8		10			3							11		6	
37	8	GATESHEAD	1-2	8405	H.Williams	1	2	5	4	9		7	8		10			3							11		6	
38	10	YORK CITY	2-1	6367	Mosby, H.Williams	1	2	5	4	9			8		10			3							11		6	7
39	15	Hartlepools United	2-1	5951	Mosby, Noble	1	2	5	4	9			8		10			3							11		6	7
40	22	SOUTHPORT	4-0	8055	Guest, Shaw, Rudd, H.Williams	1	2	5	4	9			8		10			3							11		6	7
41	29	Stockport County	2-0	3385	Shaw, H.Williams	1	2	5	4	9		7	8		10			3							11		6	
42	6 May	CREWE ALEXANDRA	0-0	6022		1	2	5	4	9		7	8		10			3							11		6	
Apps.						25	41	17	39	40	35	36	37	27	42	6	10	33	4	10	6	1	5	3	29	6	7	3
Goals									3	7		9	15	10	18		4	3					1		7			2

F.A. CUP

No.	Date	Opposition	Res.	Att.	Goalscorers	Bolton D.	Selkirk J.	Gibson A.	Edwards J.	Williams H.	Williams D.	Grainger J.	Shaw J.	Bower K.	Guest G.	Flynn W.	Hart H.	Noble N.	Wragg P.	Quairney J.	Radford A.	Pilkington G.	Raynes J.	Williams K.	Rudd J.	Rawson C.	Warnes G.	Mosby H.
3R	7 Jan	Bury	4-5	23308	Bower, Noble, Shaw, Rudd		2		4	5	6	7	8	9	10			3							11	1		

Final League Table

		Pl.	Home					Away					F.	A.	Pts
			W	D	L	F	A	W	D	L	F	A			
1	Doncaster Rovers	42	9	9	3	30	15	10	8	3	36	23	66	38	55
2	Gateshead	42	13	5	3	51	23	10	2	9	36	31	87	54	53
3	Rochdale	42	15	3	3	42	13	6	6	9	26	28	68	41	51
4	Lincoln City	42	14	5	2	35	9	7	4	10	25	30	60	39	51
5	Tranmere Rovers	42	15	3	3	35	21	4	8	9	16	27	51	48	49
6	Rotherham United	42	10	6	5	46	28	9	4	8	34	31	80	59	48
7	Crewe Alexandra	42	10	6	5	38	27	7	8	6	30	28	68	55	48
8	Mansfield Town	42	12	4	5	37	20	6	8	7	29	34	66	54	48
9	Carlisle United	42	12	6	3	39	20	4	9	8	29	31	68	51	47
10	Stockport County	42	14	2	5	33	21	5	5	11	22	31	55	52	45
11	Oldham Athletic	42	10	4	7	32	31	6	7	8	26	32	58	63	43
12	Chester	42	12	3	6	47	33	5	3	13	23	46	70	79	40
13	Accrington Stanley	42	12	5	4	41	21	4	2	15	16	41	57	62	39
14	New Brighton	42	10	5	6	27	25	4	5	12	18	38	45	63	38
15	Barrow	42	9	6	6	27	20	5	3	13	20	33	47	53	37
16	Southport	42	7	10	4	29	26	5	3	13	22	45	51	71	37
17	Darlington	42	9	8	4	35	27	2	5	14	21	42	56	69	35
18	Hartlepools United	42	10	3	8	37	35	4	2	15	15	44	52	79	33
19	Bradford City	42	11	1	9	38	32	1	7	13	23	44	61	76	32
20	Wrexham	42	8	7	6	24	17	2	5	14	15	37	39	54	32
21	Halifax Town	42	9	5	7	35	31	3	3	15	23	54	58	85	32
22	York City	42	6	7	8	29	33	3	6	12	23	37	52	70	31

1949-50: *(Back): Selkirk, Edwards, Bolton, Gibson, D.Williams*
(Front): Grainger, Shaw, H.Williams, Bower, Guest, Flynn.

1950-51: (Back): Selkirk, Gibson, Noble, Bolton, Edwards, Rawson.
(Front): Grainger, D.Williams, Shaw, Guest, Tomlinson, Rudd

SEASON 1950/51
DIVISION THREE (NORTH)

No.	Date	Opposition	Res.	Att.	Goalscorers	Bolton D.	Selkirk J.	Noble N.	Edwards J.	Gibson A.	Rawson C.	Grainger J.	Shaw J.	Williams H.	Guest G.	Rudd J.	White L.	Williams D.	Quairney J.	Wragg P.	Badger C.	Tomlinson C.
1	19 Aug	Oldham Athletic	5-4	19182	Guest(2), Grainger, Shaw, H.Williams	1	2	3	4	5	6	7	8	9	10	11						
2	21	STOCKPORT COUNTY	0-0	12235		1	2	3	4	5	6	7	8	9	10	11						
3	26	WREXHAM	5-0	9565	Rudd(2), Guest, White, H.Williams	1	2	3	4	5	6		8	9	10	11	7					
4	28	Stockport County	3-1	14937	Guest(2), Shaw	1	2	3	4	5	6		8	9	10	11	7					
5	2 Sep	Scunthorpe United	0-0	14656		1	2	3	4	5	6	7	8	9	10	11						
6	4	TRANMERE ROVERS	1-2	13308	Guest	1	2	3	4	5	6	7	8	9	10	11						
7	9	MANSFIELD TOWN	3-0	13133	Guest, Shaw, D.Williams	1	2	3	4	5	6	7	9		10	11		8				
8	12	Tranmere Rovers	1-2	10910	Shaw	1	2	3	4	5	6	7	9		10	11		8				
9	16	DARLINGTON	0-1	10851		1	2	3	4	5	6	7	9		10	11		8				
10	23	Barrow	2-0	7174	Rudd, Shaw	1	2	3	4	5	6	7	9		10	11		8				
11	30	YORK CITY	3-1	6807	Guest(2), Noble	1	2	3	4	5	6	7	9		10	11		8				
12	7 Oct	New Brighton	4-2	4419	Shaw(3), Guest	1	2	3	4	5	6	7	9		10	11		8				
13	14	BRADFORD CITY	1-0	11745	Shaw	1	2	3	4	5	6	7	9		10	11		8				
14	21	Gateshead	3-0	14039	Shaw(2), Rudd	1	2	3	4	5	6	7	9		10	11		8				
15	28	CREWE ALEXANDRA	2-3	11179	Guest, Shaw	1	2	3	4	5	6	7	9		10	11		8				
16	4 Nov	Halifax Town	2-1	9175	Shaw(2)	1	2	3	4	5	6	7	9		10	11		8				
17	11	HARTLEPOOLS UNITED	2-1	10440	Shaw, D.Williams	1	2	3	4	5	6	7	9		10	11		8				
18	18	Rochdale	2-0	7986	Grainger, Guest	1	2	3	4	5	6	7	9		10	11		8				
19	2 Dec	Shrewsbury Town	2-1	10317	Shaw, D.Williams	1	2	3	4	5	6	7	9		10	11		8				
20	23	Wrexham	0-0	8323		1	2	3	4	5	6	7	9		10	11		8				
21	25	Bradford P.A.	4-0	23195	Guest, Shaw, White, D.Williams	1	2	3	4	5	6		9		10	11	7	8				
22	26	BRADFORD P.A.	2-1	17888	Shaw, O.G.		2	3	4	5	6		9		10	11	7	8	1			
23	30	SCUNTHORPE UNITED	4-1	10169	Shaw(2), Grainger, Guest	1	2	3	4	5	6	7	9		10	11		8				
24	1 Jan	Accrington Stanley	2-1	5004	Grainger, Shaw	1	2	3	4	5	6	7	9		10	11		8				
25	10	Southport	1-0	2892	Grainger	1	2	3	4	5	6	7	9		10	11		8				
26	17	Mansfield Town	1-1	18241	Grainger	1	2	3	4	5	6	7	9		10	11		8				
27	20	Darlington	2-2	8421	Noble, Shaw	1	2	3	4	5	6	7	9		10	11		8				
28	30	SOUTHPORT	1-1	7359	White	1	2	3	4	5	6	7	9		10	11		8				
29	3 Feb	BARROW	3-0	12420	Grainger, Guest, Noble	1	2	3	4	5	6	7	9		10		7	8		11		
30	10	ACCRINGTON STANLEY	6-2	14504	Shaw(3), Grainger(2), Noble	1	2	3	4			7	9	5			11	8		11	10	
31	17	York City	3-3	9184	Grainger, Guest, Shaw	1	2	3	4	5	6	7	9		10	11		8				
32	24	NEW BRIGHTON	5-0	13386	Shaw(3), Noble, D.Williams	1	2	3	4	5	6	7	9		10	11		8				
33	3 Mar	Bradford City	4-3	19229	Guest, Shaw, White, D.Williams	1	2	3	4	5	6		9		10	11	7	8				
34	10	GATESHEAD	0-1	14655		1	2	3	4	5	6	7	9		10	11		8				
35	17	Crewe Alexandra	2-1	7322	Shaw, D.Williams	1	2	3	4	5	6	7	9		10	11		8				
36	23	Carlisle United	0-0	20454		1	2	3	4	5	6	7	9		10	11		8				
37	24	HALIFAX TOWN	2-0	14195	Noble, Shaw	1	2	3	4	5	6		9		10	11	7	8				
38	26	CARLISLE UNITED	3-0	17309	Shaw(2), Grainger	1	2	3	4	5	6	7	9		10	11		8				
39	31	Hartlepools United	1-3	8706	Shaw	1	2	3	4	5	6	7	9		10	11		8				
40	7 Apr	ROCHDALE	3-0	14202	Grainger, Guest, D.Williams	1	2	3	4	5	6	7	9		10	11		8				
41	14	Chester	2-1	7760	Guest, D.Williams	1	2	3	4	5	6	7	9		10	11		8				
42	16	CHESTER	0-0	18481		1	2	3	4	5	6	7	9		10	11		8				
43	21	SHREWSBURY TOWN	2-0	15906	Guest, Tomlinson	1	2	3	4	5	6	7	9		10			8				11
44	28	Lincoln City	2-0	14714	Guest(2)	1	2	3	4	5	6		9		10			8				11
45	30	LINCOLN CITY	3-0	15396	Edwards, Guest, White	1	2	3	4	5	6		9		10		7	8				11
46	5 May	OLDHAM ATHLETIC	3-1	12868	Grainger, Selkirk, Shaw	1	2	3	4	5	6	7	9		10	11		8				
				Apps.		45	46	46	46	45	46	37	46	7	45	41	10	40	1		2	3
				Goals			1	6	1			13	37	2	23	4	5	9				1

F.A. CUP

	Date	Opposition	Res.	Att.	Goalscorers	Bolton D.	Selkirk J.	Noble N.	Edwards J.	Gibson A.	Rawson C.	Grainger J.	Shaw J.	Williams H.	Guest G.	Rudd J.	White L.	Williams D.	Quairney J.	Wragg P.	Badger C.	Tomlinson C.
1R	25 Nov	Darlington	7-2	10616	Shaw(5), Guest, D.Williams	1	2	3	4	5	6	7	9		10	11		8				
2R	9 Dec	NOTTINGHAM FOREST	3-1	22000	Shaw(3)	1	2	3	4	5	6	7	9		10	11		8				
3R	6 Jan	DONCASTER ROVERS	2-1	22000	Shaw, D.Williams	1	2	3	4	5	6	7	9			11		8		10		
4R	27	Hull City	0-2	50040		1	2	3	4	5	6	7	9		10		11	8				

Final League Table

		Pl.	Home				Away				F.	A.	Pts
			W	D	L	F	A	W	D	L	F	A			
1	Rotherham United	46	16	3	4	55	16	15	6	2	48	25	103	41	71
2	Mansfield Town	46	17	6	0	54	19	9	6	8	24	29	78	48	64
3	Carlisle United	46	18	4	1	44	17	7	8	8	35	33	79	50	62
4	Tranmere Rovers	46	15	5	3	51	26	9	6	8	32	36	83	62	59
5	Lincoln City	46	18	1	4	62	23	7	7	9	27	35	89	58	58
6	Bradford Park Ave.	46	15	3	5	46	23	8	5	10	44	49	90	72	54
7	Bradford City	46	13	4	6	55	30	8	6	9	35	33	90	63	52
8	Gateshead	46	17	1	5	60	21	4	7	12	24	41	84	62	50
9	Crewe Alexandra	46	11	5	7	38	26	8	5	10	23	34	61	60	48
10	Stockport County	46	15	3	5	45	26	5	5	13	18	37	63	63	48
11	Rochdale	46	11	6	6	38	18	6	5	12	31	44	69	62	45
12	Scunthorpe United	46	10	12	1	32	9	3	6	14	26	48	58	57	44
13	Chester	46	11	6	6	42	30	6	3	14	20	34	62	64	43
14	Wrexham	46	12	6	5	37	28	3	6	14	18	43	55	71	42
15	Oldham Athletic	46	10	5	8	47	36	6	3	14	26	37	73	73	40
16	Hartlepools United	46	14	5	4	55	26	2	2	19	9	40	64	66	39
17	York City	46	7	12	4	37	24	5	3	15	29	53	66	77	39
18	Darlington	46	10	8	5	35	29	3	5	15	24	48	59	77	39
19	Barrow	46	16	3	8	38	27	4	3	16	13	49	51	76	38
20	Shrewsbury Town	46	11	3	9	28	30	4	4	15	15	44	43	74	37
21	Southport	46	9	4	10	29	25	4	6	13	27	47	56	72	36
22	Halifax Town	46	11	6	6	36	24	0	6	17	14	45	50	69	34
23	Accrington Stanley	46	10	4	9	28	29	1	6	16	14	72	42	101	32
24	New Brighton	46	7	6	10	22	32	4	2	17	18	58	40	90	30

SEASON 1951/52

DIVISION TWO

No.	Date	Opposition	Res.	Att.	Goalscorers	Bolton D.	Selkirk J.	Noble N.	Edwards J.	Gibson A.	Rawson C.	Grainger J.	Williams D.	Shaw J.	Guest G.	Rudd J.	Tomlinson C.	White L.	Wragg P.	Regan J.	Williams H.	McGoldrick T.	Brown D.	Quairney J.	Marshall F.
1	18 Aug	NOTTINGHAM FOREST	1-2	18463	Noble	1	2	3	4	5	6	7	8	9	10	11									
2	20	Cardiff City	4-2	32442	Shaw(2), Grainger, D.Williams	1	2	3	4	5	6	7	8	9	10		11								
3	25	Brentford	0-2	24904		1	2	3	4	5	6	7	8	9			11	10							
4	27	CARDIFF CITY	2-0	17062	Noble, Tomlinson	1	2	3	4	5	6	7	8	9		11	10								
5	1 Sep	DONCASTER ROVERS	2-0	21252	Guest, Shaw	1	2	3	4	5	6	7	8	9	10	11									
6	3	Coventry City	1-2	20884	Grainger	1	2	3	4	5	6	7	8	9		11	10								
7	8	Everton	3-3	44838	Edwards, Guest, Shaw	1	2	3	4	5	6	7	8	9	10	11									
8	15	SOUTHAMPTON	4-1	16342	Tomlinson(2), Grainger, Guest	1	2	3	4	5	6	7		9	10		11		8						
9	22	Sheffield Wednesday	5-3	54846	Shaw(2), Grainger, Tomlinson, Wragg	1	2	3	4	5		7	6	9	10		11		8						
10	29	LEEDS UNITED	4-2	21352	Shaw(2), Guest, Tomlinson	1	2	3	4	5		7	6	9	10		11		8						
11	6 Oct	WEST HAM UNITED	2-1	19998	Guest, Tomlinson	1	2	3	4	5		7		9	10		11		8	6					
12	13	Sheffield United	0-1	52199		1	2	3	4	5		7	6	9			11		8						
13	20	BARNSLEY	4-0	22320	Shaw(3), Tomlinson	1	2	3	4	5		7		9	10		11		8	6					
14	27	Hull City	3-3	31369	Shaw(3)	1	2	3	4	5		7		9	10		11		8	6					
15	3 Nov	BLACKBURN ROVERS	3-0	18254	Shaw(2), Tomlinson	1	2	3	4	5		7		9	10		11		8	6					
16	10	Queens Park Rangers	3-2	19072	Selkirk, Shaw, Wragg	1	2	3	4	5		7		9	10		11		8	6					
17	17	NOTTS COUNTY	2-0	20961	Noble, Shaw	1		3	4	5		7		9	10		11		8	6		2			
18	24	Luton Town	1-1	23565	O.G.	1		3	4	5		7		9	10		11		8	6		2			
19	1 Dec	BURY	4-3	18888	Grainger, Guest, Shaw, Tomlinson	1	2	3	4	5	6	7		9	10		11		8						
20	8	Swansea Town	0-5	11425		1	2	3	4	5	6	7			10		11	8	9						
21	15	Nottingham Forest	2-4	31091	McGoldrick, Tomlinson	1	2	3	4	5	6	7		8	10		11					9			
22	22	BRENTFORD	1-1	14809	Tomlinson	1	2		4	5	6	7		8	10		11				3				
23	25	Birmingham City	0-4	27531		1	2		4	5	6		10	9			11				3	8			
24	26	BIRMINGHAM CITY	1-2	22371	McGoldrick	1	2		4	5	6	7		9			11				3	8	10		
25	29	Doncaster Rovers	3-0	29267	Shaw(2), Grainger		2		4	5	6	7	10	9	8		11				3			1	
26	5 Jan	EVERTON	1-1	17754	Guest		2		4	5	6		11	9	8	7					3	8		1	
27	19	Southampton	1-3	16674	Shaw		2		4	5	6	7	8	9	10		11				3			1	
28	26	SHEFFIELD WEDNESDAY	3-3	25149	Guest, Shaw, H.Williams		2		4	5	6	7		9	10		11		8		3			1	
29	9 Feb	Leeds United	0-3	47985		1	2	3	4	5	6	7	8	9	10		11								
30	16	West Ham United	1-2	19357	Selkirk	1	2		4	5	6	7		9	10		11				3				8
31	23	COVENTRY CITY	0-1	18132		1	2		4	5	6	7		9	10		11				3				8
32	1 Mar	SHEFFIELD UNITED	3-1	25137	Guest(2), Grainger	1	2		4	5	6	7		9	10			11			3				8
33	8	Barnsley	1-0	26922	Rawson	1	2		4	5	6	7		9	10			11			3				8
34	15	HULL CITY	1-1	19069	Grainger	1	2		4	5	6	7		9	10			11			3				8
35	22	Blackburn Rovers	1-1	25833	Grainger	1	2		4	5	6	7		9	10			11			3				8
36	29	QUEENS PARK RANGERS	1-0	9311	Grainger	1	2		4	5	6	7		9	10			11			3				8
37	5 Apr	Notts County	3-1	13161	Marshall, Shaw, White	1	2		4	5	6	7		9	10			11			3				8
38	12	LUTON TOWN	0-1	17309		1	2		4	5	6	7		9	10			11			3				
39	14	LEICESTER CITY	0-2	16171			2		4	5	6	7		9	10		11	8			3			1	
40	15	Leicester City	0-2	27875			2			5	6	7		9	10		11			4	3			1	8
41	19	Bury	1-3	13620	Grainger	1	2		4	5	6	7		9	10		11	8			3				8
42	26	SWANSEA TOWN	1-3	14074	Wragg	1	2		4	5	6			9	10		11	7	8		3				
		Apps.				36	40	22	41	42	32	41	13	41	38	5	29	13	17	9	21	5	1	6	10
		Goals					2	3	1		1	11	1	24	10		11	1	3		1	2			1

F.A. CUP

No.	Date	Opposition	Res.	Att.	Goalscorers	Bolton D.	Selkirk J.	Noble N.	Edwards J.	Gibson A.	Rawson C.	Grainger J.	Williams D.	Shaw J.	Guest G.	Rudd J.	Tomlinson C.	White L.	Wragg P.	Regan J.	Williams H.	McGoldrick T.	Brown D.	Quairney J.	Marshall F.
3R	12 Jan	BURY	2-1	22000	Guest, Shaw		2	11	4	5	6	7	8	9	10						3			1	
4R	2 Feb	Swansea Town	0-3	22572			2		4	5	6	7	8	9	10		11				3			1	

Final League Table

		Pl.	Home					Away					F.	A.	Pts
			W	D	L	F	A	W	D	L	F	A			
1	Sheffield Wed.	42	14	4	3	54	23	7	7	7	46	43	100	66	53
2	Cardiff City	42	18	2	1	52	15	2	9	10	20	39	72	54	51
3	Birmingham City	42	11	6	4	36	21	10	3	8	31	35	67	56	51
4	Nottingham Forest	42	12	6	3	41	22	6	7	8	36	40	77	62	49
5	Leicester City	42	12	6	3	48	24	7	3	11	30	40	78	64	47
6	Leeds United	42	13	7	1	35	15	5	4	12	24	42	59	57	47
7	Everton	42	12	5	4	42	25	5	5	11	22	33	64	58	44
8	Luton Town	42	9	7	5	46	35	7	5	9	31	43	77	78	44
9	Rotherham United	42	11	4	6	40	25	6	4	11	33	46	73	71	42
10	Brentford	42	11	7	3	34	20	4	5	12	20	35	54	55	42
11	Sheffield United	42	13	2	6	57	28	5	3	13	33	48	90	76	41
12	West Ham United	42	13	5	3	48	29	2	6	13	19	48	67	77	41
13	Southampton	42	11	6	4	40	25	4	5	12	21	48	61	73	41
14	Blackburn Rovers	42	11	3	7	35	30	6	3	12	19	33	54	63	40
15	Notts County	42	11	5	5	45	27	5	2	14	26	41	71	68	39
16	Doncaster Rovers	42	9	4	8	29	28	4	8	9	26	32	55	60	38
17	Bury	42	13	2	6	43	22	2	5	14	24	47	67	69	37
18	Hull City	42	11	5	5	44	23	2	6	13	16	47	60	70	37
19	Swansea Town	42	10	4	7	45	26	2	8	11	27	50	72	76	36
20	Barnsley	42	8	7	6	39	33	3	7	11	20	39	59	72	36
21	Coventry City	42	9	5	7	36	33	5	1	15	23	49	59	82	34
22	Queen's Park Rgs.	42	8	8	5	35	35	3	4	14	17	46	52	81	34

1951-52: (Back): Brown, Cox, Regan, McGoldrick, Balding, Pilkington,
(Middle): Hooper (Trainer), Selkirk, Rawson, Gibson, Bolton, Edwards, Noble, Tomlinson, H.Williams, Quairney.
(Front):Freeman(Man.), Grainger, D.Williams, Guest, Watt(Chair.), Shaw, Rudd, Fergusson(Dir.),Smailes (Train.).

1952-53: (Back): Selkirk, Edwards, Quairney, Gibson, H.Williams, D.Williams.
(Front): White, Guest, Grainger, Rawson, Rickett.

SEASON 1952/53

DIVISION TWO

Player columns (left→right): Bolton D. · Selkirk J. · Williams H. · Edwards J. · Noble N. · Rawson C. · White L. · Marsden J. · Grainger J. · Marshall F. · Williams D. · Regan J. · Farmer T. · Guest G. · Wragg P. · Shaw J. · Longden C. · Quairney J. · Warner D. · Gee D. · Rickett W. · Hussey M. · Gibson A. · Silman R. · Burke R. · Pell D.

No.	Date	Opposition	Res.	Att.	Goalscorers	Bol	Sel	WiH	Edw	Nob	Raw	Whi	Mar	Gra	MaF	WiD	Reg	Far	Gue	Wra	Sha	Lon	Qua	War	Gee	Ric	Hus	Gib	Sil	Bur	Pel
1	23 Aug	BIRMINGHAM	1-1	15206	Marshall	1	2	3	4	5	6	7	8	9	10	11															
2	28	Notts County	1-2	23216	Marsden	1	2		4	3	6	11	8	7					5	9	10										
3	30	Luton Town	1-2	14427	Marsden	1	2		4	3		11	8	7		6			5	9	10										
4	1 Sep	NOTTS COUNTY	2-3	17043	Guest, Wragg	1	2		4	3				7		6	5		10	8	9	11									
5	6	LEEDS UNITED	3-1	14906	Grainger, Noble, White		2		4	5		7		9		6			8		10		1			3		11			
6	11	Southampton	3-2	14313	White(2), Grainger		2		4	5	10	7		9		6			8				1			3		11			
7	13	Plymouth Argyle	3-4	28820	Rawson(2), Guest		2		4	5	10	7		9		6			8				1			3		11			
8	15	SOUTHAMPTON	2-2	16032	Grainger, White		2	3	4	5	10	7		9		6			8				1					11			
9	20	BARNSLEY	3-1	16327	Grainger, Guest, Rawson		2	3	4	5	10	7		9		6			8				1					11			
10	27	FULHAM	1-0	16692	Rawson		2		4	5	10	7	8	9		6							1			3		11			
11	4 Oct	West Ham United	4-2	21895	White(2), Grainger, Rickett		2		4		10	7		9		6			8				1			3	5	11			
12	11	Lincoln City	3-1	19626	Guest, White, Rickett		2		4		10	7		9		6			8				1			3	5	11			
13	18	HULL CITY	2-1	19929	Grainger(2)		2		4		10	7		9		6			8				1			3	5	11			
14	25	Blackburn Rovers	1-0	24890	Grainger		2	3	4		10	7		9		6					8		1				5	11			
15	1 Nov	NOTTINGHAM FOREST	2-3	19488	Grainger(2)		2	3	4	5	10	7		9		6			8				1					11			
16	8	Everton	1-0	38808	Shaw		2	3		5	10	7		9		6					8		1				4	11			
17	15	BRENTFORD	4-1	15427	Grainger(3), Rickett		2			5	10	7		9		6					8		1			3	4	11			
18	22	Doncaster Rovers	1-2	21561	Shaw		2	3		5	10	7		9		6					8		1				4	11			
19	29	SWANSEA TOWN	2-1	12019	Rawson(2)		2	3	4		10	7		9		6			8				1				5	11			
20	6 Dec	Huddersfield Town	0-1	31312			2	3	4		10	7		9		6			8				1				5	11			
21	13	SHEFFIELD UNITED	0-2	25170			2		4	3	10	7		9		6			8				1					11	5		
22	20	Birmingham City	0-4	11978			2		4	3	10			7		6			8		9		1					11	5		
23	26	BURY	6-1	16718	Grainger(2), Guest(2), Rawson, Shaw		2		4	3	10			7		6			8		9		1					11	5		
24	27	Bury	0-2	14420			2		4	3	10			7		6			8		9		1					11	5		
25	1 Jan	Sheffield United	4-1	36164	Guest(2), Rawson, Shaw		2		4	3	10			7		6			8		9		1					11	5		
26	3	LUTON TOWN	1-3	16850	Rawson		2		4	3	10			7		6			8		9		1					11	5		
27	17	Leeds United	0-4	24048			2	5	4		10			7		6			8		9		1	3				11			
28	24	PLYMOUTH ARGYLE	2-3	14907	Guest, Rawson		2	3	4	5	10			7		6			8		9		1					11			
29	7 Feb	Barnsley	3-2	16542	Guest, Noble, White		2		4	5	10	7				6			8		9		1					11	5		
30	18	Fulham	1-4	9482	White		2		4	5		7		9		6			8		10		1			3		11			
31	21	WEST HAM UNITED	1-1	14861	Shaw		2		4	5		7				6			9		10		1	8				11		3	
32	28	LINCOLN CITY	3-2	16751	Guest, Shaw, H.Williams		2	3	4	5		7		9		6			8		10		1					11			
33	7 Mar	Hull City	2-3	25215	Rawson, Rickett		2	3	4		10			7		6			8		9		1					11			
34	14	BLACKBURN ROVERS	0-0	14439			2	3		5	10			7		6			8		9		1				4	11			
35	21	Nottingham Forest	3-4	18225	Burke, Grainger, Guest		2	3		5				7		6			8		10		1				4	11		9	
36	28	EVERTON	2-2	12633	Rawson, Shaw		2	3		5	10			7		6			8		9		1					11		9	
37	4 Apr	Brentford	1-1	14411	Burke		2		4	3				7		6			8		10	11	1						5	9	
38	6	LEICESTER CITY	0-0	14330					4	3				7		6		8			10		1	2				11		5	9
39	7	Leicester City	2-3	24809	Burke, Shaw		2		4					7		6			8		10		1	2				11	5	9	11
40	11	DONCASTER ROVERS	4-2	14574	Burke(2), Pell, Shaw				4	3				7		6			8		10		1					11	5	9	11
41	18	Swansea Town	0-0	21116					4	3				7		6			8		10		1					11	5	9	11
42	25	HUDDERSFIELD TOWN	0-0	19777					4	3				7		6			8	9	10		1	2					5		11
				Apps		4	37	17	36	36	27	20	7	41	5	40	3	4	34	2	27	3	38	13	2	28	11	12	2	7	4
				Goals				1		2	11	9	2	16	1				12	1	9					4				6	1

F.A. CUP

Round	Date	Opposition	Res.	Att.	Goalscorers	Bol	Sel	WiH	Edw	Nob	Raw	Whi	Mar	Gra	MaF	WiD	Reg	Far	Gue	Wra	Sha	Lon	Qua	War	Gee	Ric	Hus	Gib	Sil	Bur	Pel
3R	10 Jan	COLCHESTER UNITED	2-2	16547	Shaw(2)		2		4	3	10			7		6			8		9		1					11	5		
3Rr	14	Colchester United	2-0	8991	Rawson, Shaw		2	5	4	3	10			7		6			8		9		1					11			
4R	31	NEWCASTLE UNITED	3-1	54356	Grainger(2), Rickett		2		4	5	10			7		6			8		9		1			3		11			
5R	14 Feb	ASTON VILLA	1-3	25000	Shaw		2		4	5	10	11		7		6			8		9		1			3					

Final League Table

	Team	Pl.	Home W	D	L	F	A	Away W	D	L	F	A	F.	A.	Pts
1	Sheffield United	42	15	3	3	60	27	10	7	4	37	28	97	55	60
2	Huddersfield Town	42	14	4	3	51	14	10	6	5	33	19	84	33	58
3	Luton Town	42	15	1	5	53	17	7	7	7	31	32	84	49	52
4	Plymouth Argyle	42	12	5	4	37	24	8	4	9	28	36	65	60	49
5	Leicester City	42	13	6	2	55	29	5	6	10	34	45	89	74	48
6	Birmingham City	42	11	3	7	44	38	8	7	6	27	28	71	66	48
7	Nottingham Forest	42	11	5	5	46	32	7	3	11	31	35	77	67	44
8	Fulham	42	14	1	6	52	28	3	9	9	29	43	81	71	44
9	Blackburn Rovers	42	12	4	5	40	20	6	4	11	28	45	68	65	44
10	Leeds United	42	13	4	4	42	24	1	11	9	29	39	71	63	43
11	Swansea Town	42	10	9	2	45	26	5	3	13	33	55	78	81	42
12	Rotherham United	42	9	7	5	41	30	7	2	12	34	44	75	74	41
13	Doncaster Rovers	42	9	9	3	26	17	3	7	11	32	47	58	64	40
14	West Ham United	42	9	5	7	38	28	4	8	9	20	32	58	60	39
15	Lincoln City	42	9	9	3	41	26	2	8	11	23	45	64	71	39
16	Everton	42	9	8	4	38	23	3	6	12	33	52	71	75	38
17	Brentford	42	8	8	5	38	29	5	3	13	21	47	59	76	37
18	Hull City	42	11	6	4	36	19	3	2	16	21	50	57	69	36
19	Notts County	42	11	5	5	41	31	3	3	15	19	57	60	88	36
20	Bury	42	10	6	5	33	30	3	3	15	20	51	53	81	35
21	Southampton	42	5	7	9	45	44	5	6	10	23	41	68	85	33
22	Barnsley	42	4	4	13	31	46	1	4	16	16	62	47	108	18

SEASON 1953/54
DIVISION TWO

No.	Date	Opposition	Res.	Att.	Goalscorers	Quairmey J.	Warner D.	Noble N.	Edwards J.	Gibson A.	Williams D.	Grainger J.	Marsden J.	Burke R.	Meadows F.	Wilson I.	Marshall F.	Guest G.	Hussey M.	Williams R.	Selkirk J.	Farmer T.	Johnson P.	Silman R.	Bolton D.	Jordan B.	Henderson J.	Churns D.	Pell D.
1	20 Aug	BLACKBURN ROVERS	1-4	17834	Burke	1	2	3	4	5	6	7	8	9	10	11													
2	22	Leeds United	2-4	24309	Burke, Wilson	1	2	3		5	6	7	10	9		11	4	8											
3	24	WEST HAM UNITED	5-0	12895	Burke(2), Wilson(2), R.Williams	1	2	3			6	7		9		11	4	10	5	8									
4	29	BIRMINGHAM CITY	1-0	12670	Burke	1	2	3			6	7		9		11	4	10	5	8									
5	31	West Ham United	0-3	22089		1	2	3			6	7		9		11	4	10	5	8									
6	5 Sep	Nottingham Forest	1-4	22502	R.Williams	1	2	3		5	6		7	9		11	4	10			8								
7	7	FULHAM	3-2	14427	Burke(2), Wilson	1		3			6	7		9		11	4	8	5		2	10							
8	12	LUTON TOWN	2-1	15726	Grainger, Guest	1	3	5	4		6	7		9		11	8	10			2								
9	16	Fulham	4-2	11857	Burke, Grainger, Guest, Marshall	1	3	5	4		6	7		9		11	8	10			2								
10	19	Plymouth Argyle	2-2	21512	Burke(2)	1	3	5	4		6	7		9		11	8	10			2								
11	21	STOKE CITY	2-0	13346	Burke(2)	1	3	5	4		6	7		9		11	8	10			2								
12	26	SWANSEA TOWN	2-1	16280	Grainger, Wilson	1	3	5	4		6	7		9		11		10	8		2								
13	3 Oct	Doncaster Rovers	2-1	29380	Wilson(2)	1	3	5	4		6	7		9		11		10			2		8						
14	10	BURY	1-0	16888	Burke	1		5	4		6	7		9		11		10			2		8	3					
15	17	Oldham Athletic	3-2	22872	Burke(2), Johnson	1	3	5	4		6	7		9		11		10			2		8						
16	24	EVERTON	1-2	18860	Burke	1	3	5	4	5	6	7		9		11		10			2		8						
17	31	Hull City	0-1	24831		1	3	5	4			7				11	8	10	6		2								
18	7 Nov	NOTTS COUNTY	0-1	12189			3		4			7				11	6	8			2		10	1	5				
19	14	Lincoln City	3-4	15460	Guest, Johnson, Wilson	1	3	5			6	7		9		11	4	8			2		10						
20	21	BRISTOL ROVERS	1-1	13210	Burke	1	3	5			6	7		9	4	11		8			2		10						
21	28	Brentford	1-0	16740	Burke	1	3	5			6	7		9	4	11		10			2					8			
22	5 Dec	DERBY COUNTY	5-2	14208	Burke(2), Grainger, Guest, Wilson	1	3	5			6	7		9	4	11		10			2					8			
23	12	Blackburn Rovers	0-3	17248		1	3	5			6	7		9	4	11		10			2					8			
24	19	LEEDS UNITED	2-4	13145	Burke, Henderson	1		5			6	7		9	4	11		10			2			3		8			
25	25	Leicester City	1-4	30902	Guest	1		5			6	7		9	4	11		10			2			3		8			
26	26	LEICESTER CITY	1-1	16757	Wilson	1	3				6	7		9	4	11		10	5		2					8			
27	2 Jan	Birmingham City	3-2	16768	Burke, Grainger, Wilson	1	3	5			6	7		9		11	4	10			2					8			
28	16	NOTTINGHAM FOREST	3-0	14325	Burke, Grainger, O.G.	1		5			6	7		9		11	4				2			3		8			
29	23	Luton Town	1-1	17300	Burke	1		5			6	7		9		11	4				2			3		8	10		
30	6 Feb	PLYMOUTH ARGYLE	2-1	12284	Farmer, Guest	1		5			6	7				11	4	10			2	9		3		8	10		
31	13	Swansea Town	2-0	14347	Burke, Noble	1		5			6	7		9		11	4	10			2			3		8			
32	27	Bury	0-3	13929		1		5			6	7		9		11	4				2	10		3		8			
33	6 Mar	OLDHAM ATHLETIC	7-0	11686	Burke(3), Grainger, Noble, Wilsn, O.G.	1		5			6	7		9		11	4				2			3		8			
34	13	Everton	0-3	52302		1		5			6	7		9		11	4				2			3		8			10
35	20	HULL CITY	3-2	13037	Burke(2), Guest	1		5			6	7		9		11	4	10			2			3		8			
36	27	Bristol Rovers	0-1	19638		1		5			6	7		9		11	4	10			2			3		8			
37	3 Apr	BRENTFORD	1-1	9198	Guest	1	3	5			6	7		9		11	4	10			2					8			
38	10	Notts County	2-1	11894	Grainger, Guest	1	2	5			6	7				11	4	10						3	9	8			
39	17	LINCOLN CITY	4-1	12213	Burke, Grainger, Noble, Wilson	1		5			6	7		9		11	4	10			2			3		8			
40	19	Stoke City	1-1	13953	Henderson	1		5			6	7		9		11	4	10			2			3		8			
41	24	Derby County	1-1	12689	Burke	1		5			6	7		9		11	4	10			2			3		8			
42	29	DONCASTER ROVERS	4-0	13017	Burke, Grainger, Noble, Wilson	1		5			6	7		9		11	4	10			2			3		8			
		Apps.				42	25	39	12	4	40	41	3	40	7	42	30	37	7	4	35	4	23	1	1	22	2	1	
		Goals						4				10		33		14	1	9		2		1	2				2		

F.A. CUP

	Date		Res.	Att.	Goalscorers	Quairmey J.	Warner D.	Noble N.	Edwards J.	Gibson A.	Williams D.	Grainger J.	Marsden J.	Burke R.	Meadows F.	Wilson I.	Marshall F.	Guest G.	Hussey M.	Williams R.	Selkirk J.	Farmer T.	Johnson P.	Silman R.	Bolton D.	Jordan B.	Henderson J.	Churns D.	Pell D.
3R	9 Jan	Britol City	3-1	29216	Grainger(3)	1	3	5			6	7		9		11	4	10			2					8			
4Rr	30	West Bromwich Albion	0-4	48242		1		5			6	7		9		11	4	10			2	3				8			

Final League Table

		Pl.	Home					Away					F.	A.	Pts
			W	D	L	F	A	W	D	L	F	A			
1	Leicester City	42	15	4	2	63	23	8	6	7	34	37	97	60	56
2	Everton	42	13	6	2	55	27	7	10	4	37	31	92	58	56
3	Blackburn Rovers	42	15	4	2	54	16	8	5	8	32	34	86	50	55
4	Nottingham Forest	42	15	5	1	61	27	5	7	9	25	32	86	59	52
5	Rotherham United	42	13	4	4	51	26	8	3	10	29	41	80	67	49
6	Luton Town	42	11	7	3	36	23	7	5	9	28	36	64	59	48
7	Birmingham City	42	12	6	3	49	18	6	5	10	29	40	78	58	47
8	Fulham	42	12	3	6	62	39	5	7	9	36	46	98	85	44
9	Bristol Rovers	42	10	7	4	32	19	4	9	8	32	39	64	58	44
10	Leeds United	42	12	5	4	56	30	3	8	10	33	51	89	81	43
11	Stoke City	42	8	8	5	43	28	4	9	8	28	32	71	60	41
12	Doncaster Rovers	42	9	5	7	32	28	7	4	10	27	35	59	63	41
13	West Ham United	42	11	6	4	44	20	4	3	14	23	49	67	69	39
14	Notts County	42	8	6	7	26	29	5	7	9	28	45	54	74	39
15	Hull City	42	14	1	6	47	22	2	5	14	17	44	64	66	38
16	Lincoln City	42	11	6	4	46	23	3	3	15	19	60	65	83	37
17	Bury	42	9	7	5	39	32	2	7	12	15	40	54	72	36
18	Derby County	42	9	5	7	38	35	3	6	12	26	47	64	82	35
19	Plymouth Argyle	42	6	12	3	38	31	3	4	14	27	51	65	82	34
20	Swansea Town	42	11	5	5	34	25	2	3	16	24	57	58	82	34
21	Brentford	42	9	5	7	25	26	1	6	14	15	52	40	78	31
22	Oldham Athletic	42	6	7	8	26	31	2	2	17	14	58	40	89	25

ALF GIBSON

NORMAN NOBLE

JACK SELKIRK

(1953-54) Three stalwarts of the period

Jock Quairney punches the ball away from Frank Marshall, during a 1955 training session.

SEASON 1954/55
DIVISION TWO

No.	Date	Opposition	Res.	Att.	Goalscorers
1	21 Aug	IPSWICH TOWN	3-2	14594	Grainger(2), Burke
2	25	Leeds United	4-2	25021	Wilson(2), Burke, Henderson
3	28	Birmingham City	1-3	27260	Guest
4	30	LEEDS UNITED	3-0	17799	Grainger, Noble, Wilson
5	4 Sep	MIDDLESBROUGH	3-0	17022	Burke, Guest, Wilson
6	6	BURY	4-2	15235	Burke(4)
7	11	Stoke City	2-1	27272	Burke, Guest
8	18	DONCASTER ROVERS	2-3	20207	Burke, Guest
9	20	Bury	2-2	11900	Williams, O.G.
10	25	LUTON TOWN	2-0	17114	Grainger(2)
11	2 Oct	Hull City	2-1	31814	Bunclark, Henderson
12	9	Liverpool	1-3	45868	Burke
13	16	BRISTOL ROVERS	6-2	17660	Graingr(2), Brke, Gust, Hndersn, Wilsn
14	23	Blackburn Rovers	1-4	28605	Burke
15	30	FULHAM	2-3	19316	Burke, Grainger
16	6 Nov	Swansea Town	1-2	21955	Wilson
17	13	NOTTS COUNTY	2-0	11740	Guest, Wilson
18	20	Derby County	3-2	15073	Burke(2), Henderson
19	27	WEST HAM UNITED	2-2	13501	Williams, Wilson
20	4 Dec	Plymouth Argyle	1-2	15427	Wilson
21	11	PORT VALE	3-0	12850	Grainger(2), Guest
22	18	Ipswich Town	2-2	11371	Burke, Wilson
23	25	LINCOLN CITY	3-0	14990	Grainger, Burke, Guest
24	27	Lincoln City	3-2	18897	Guest, Henderson, Wilson
25	1 Jan	BIRMINGHAM CITY	0-2	17166	
26	15	Middlesbrough	1-5	12320	Guest
27	5 Feb	Doncaster Rovers	4-0	16580	Grainger(2), Guest, Reeson
28	12	Luton Town	0-4	18450	
29	19	HULL CITY	2-0	11447	O.G.(2)
30	5 Mar	Bristol Rovers	0-1	19739	
31	12	BLACKBURN ROVERS	5-1	16110	Farmer(3), Grainger, Wilson
32	19	Fulham	1-1	16450	Wilson
33	2 Apr	Notts County	2-3	15812	Grainger(2)
34	8	Nottingham Forest	2-0	12837	Guest, Grainger
35	9	DERBY COUNTY	2-1	14761	Guest, Pell
36	11	NOTTINGHAM FOREST	3-2	14995	Farmer, Johnson, Selkirk
37	16	West Ham United	2-1	24056	Farmer(2)
38	18	STOKE CITY	2-1	20112	Johnson, Noble
39	23	PLYMOUTH ARGYLE	2-0	16847	Farmer, Grainger
40	25	SWANSEA TOWN	2-0	22033	Farmer, Guest
41	30	Port Vale	0-1	25271	
42	2 May	LIVERPOOL	6-1	17907	Wilson(4), Grainger, Pell

Appearances (shirt numbers)

No.	Quairney J.	Selkirk J.	Johnson P.	Marshall F.	Noble N.	Williams D.	Grainger J.	Henderson J.	Burke R.	Guest G.	Wilson I.	Silman R.	Reeson A.	Marsden J.	Bunclark C.	Morgan L.	Churms D.	Pell D.	Bolton D.	Farmer T.	Jordan B.	Warner D.	Hussey M.
1	1	2	3	4	5	6	7	8	9	10	11												
2	1	2		4	5	6	7	8	9	10	11	3											
3	1	2	3	4	5	6	7	8	9	10	11												
4	1	2	3	4	5	6	7	8	9	10	11												
5	1	2	3	4	5	6	7	8	9	10	11												
6	1	2	3	4	5	6	7	8	9	10	11												
7	1	2	3	4	5	6	7	8	9	10					11								
8	1	2	3	4	5	6	7	8	9	10	11												
9	1	2	3	4	5	6	7		9	10			11	8									
10	1	2	3	4	5	6	7	8	9	10			11										
11	1	2	3	4	5	6		8	9	10	11				7								
12	1	2	3	4	5	6		8	9	10	11		7										
13	1	2	3	4	5	6	7	8	9	10	11												
14	1	2	3	4	5	6	7	8	9	10	11												
15	1	2	3	4	5	6	7	8	9	10	11												
16	1	2	3	4	5	6	7	8	9	10	11												
17	1	2	3	4	5	6	7	8	9	10	11												
18	1	2	3	4	5	6	7	8	9	10	11												
19	1	2	3	4	5	6	7	8	9	10	11												
20	1	2	3	4	5	6	7	8	9	10	11												
21	1	2	3	4	5		7	8	9	10	11					6							
22	1	2	3	4	5	6	7	8	9	10	11												
23	1	2	3	4	5	6	7	8	9	10	11												
24	1	2	3	4	5	6	7	8	9	10	11												
25	1	2	3	4	5		7	8	9	10						6		11					
26	1	2	3	4	5	6	7	8	9	10	11												
27		2	3	4	5	6	7			10			11				8		1	9			
28		2	3	4	5	6	7			10	11						8		1	9			
29		2	3	4	5	6	7			10	11						8		1	9			
30		2	3	4		6	7			10	11						8		1	9	5		
31		2	3	4	5	6	7			10	11						8		1	9			
32		2	3	4	5	6	7			10	11						8		1	9			
33		2	3	4	5	6	7			10	11						8		1	9			
34		2	3	4	5	6	7			10							8	11	1	9			
35	1	2	3	4	5	6	7			10							8	11		9			
36	1	2	8	4		6	7			10	11									9		3	5
37	1	2	8	4		6	7			10	11									9		3	
38	1	2	8	4	5	6	7			10	11									9		3	
39	1	2	8	4	5	6	7			10	11									9		3	
40	1	2		4	5	6	7			10	11						8			9		3	
41	1	2	8	4	5	6	7			10	11									9		3	
42	1	2		4		6	7				11							8		9	5	3	
Apps.	34	41	40	42	39	40	40	25	26	42	34	1	4	1	2	2	11	4	8	16	2	7	1
Goals		1	2		2	2	19	5	17	14	17		1		1			2		8			

F.A. CUP

Round	Date	Opposition	Res.	Att.	Goalscorers	Quairney J.	Selkirk J.	Johnson P.	Marshall F.	Noble N.	Williams D.	Grainger J.	Henderson J.	Burke R.	Guest G.	Silman R.	Churms D.
3R	8 Jan	LEICESTER CITY	1-0	20428	Pell	1	2	3	4	5	6	7	8	9	10		11
4R	29	LUTON TOWN	1-5	21200	Guest	1	2	3	4	5	6	7	8	9	10	11	

Final League Table

		Pl.	Home W	D	L	F	A	Away W	D	L	F	A	F.	A.	Pts
1	Birmingham City	42	14	4	3	56	22	8	6	7	36	25	92	47	54
2	Luton Town	42	18	2	1	55	18	5	6	10	33	35	88	53	54
3	Rotherham United	42	17	1	3	59	22	8	3	10	35	42	94	64	54
4	Leeds United	42	14	4	3	43	19	9	3	9	27	34	70	53	53
5	Stoke City	42	12	5	4	38	17	9	5	7	31	29	69	46	52
6	Blackburn Rovers	42	14	4	3	73	31	8	2	11	41	48	114	79	50
7	Notts County	42	14	3	4	46	27	7	3	11	28	44	74	71	48
8	West Ham United	42	12	4	5	46	28	6	6	9	28	42	74	70	46
9	Bristol Rovers	42	15	4	2	52	23	4	3	14	23	47	75	70	45
10	Swansea Town	42	15	3	3	58	28	2	6	13	28	55	86	83	43
11	Liverpool	42	11	7	3	55	37	5	3	13	37	59	92	96	42
12	Middlesbrough	42	13	1	7	48	31	5	5	11	25	51	73	82	42
13	Bury	42	10	5	6	44	35	5	6	10	33	37	77	72	41
14	Fulham	42	10	5	6	46	29	4	6	11	30	50	76	79	39
15	Nottingham Forest	42	8	4	9	29	29	8	3	10	29	33	58	62	39
16	Lincoln City	42	8	6	7	39	35	5	4	12	29	44	68	79	36
17	Port Vale	42	10	6	5	31	21	2	5	14	17	50	48	71	35
18	Doncaster Rovers	42	10	5	6	35	34	4	2	15	23	61	58	95	35
19	Hull City	42	7	5	9	30	35	5	5	11	14	34	44	69	34
20	Plymouth Argyle	42	10	4	7	29	26	2	3	16	28	56	57	82	31
21	Ipswich Town	42	10	3	8	37	28	1	3	17	20	64	57	92	28
22	Derby County	42	6	6	9	39	34	1	3	17	14	48	53	82	23

SEASON 1955/56
DIVISION TWO

No.	Date	Opposition	Res.	Att.	Goalscorers	Quairney J.	Selkirk J.	Warner D.	Marshall F.	Noble N.	Williams D.	Grainger J.	Pell D.	Farmer T.	Guest G.	Wilson I.	Morgan L.	Moore R.	Keyworth K.	Johnson P.	Meadows F.	Dixon R.	Bambridge K.	Jordan B.	Simpson K.	Chums D.	Weakley B.	Jackson B.	Hussey M.	Kettleborough K.	Silman R.	Madden P.	Haynes E.
1	20 Aug	West Ham United	1-1	18952	O.G.	1	2	3	4	5	6	7	8	9	10	11																	
2	22	BRISTOL CITY	1-3	15409	Farmer	1	2	3	4	5		7		9	10	11	6	8															
3	27	PORT VALE	1-0	11944	Guest	1	2	3	4	5		7		9	10	11		8	6														
4	30	Bristol City	2-5	27142	Farmer, Grainger	1	2	3	4	5		7		9	10	11		8	6	3													
5	3 Sep	Doncaster Rovers	1-1	15284	Wilson	1	2	3	8	5		7		9	10	11			6	4													
6	5	BARNSLEY	0-0	18847		1	2	3		5		7		9	10	11		8	6	4													
7	10	Swansea Town	1-4	19957	Guest	1	2	3		5		7			10	11			6	4	8	9											
8	14	Barnsley	2-3	19446	Farmer, Marshall	1	2	3	8	5		7		9					6	4			11										
9	17	NOTTS COUNTY	1-1	10479	Selkirk	1	2	3				7		10	9	8			6	4			11	5									
10	24	Leeds United	1-4	23763	Moore	1	2	3			6	7		9	10			8	4				11	5									
11	1 Oct	FULHAM	2-3	12879	Grainger, Moore	1	2	3	4			7		9				8	6				11	5			10						
12	8	BRISTOL ROVERS	1-0	12399	Farmer	1	2		4	5		7		9	10			8	6	3			11										
13	15	Stoke City	0-1	17421		1	2		4	5		7		9	10			8	6	3			11										
14	22	NOTTINGHAM FOREST	2-1	11578	Bambridge, Farmer	1	2		4	5				9	8	10			6	3			11	7									
15	29	Liverpool	0-2	31810		1	2		4	5	6		8	9		10				3			11	7									
16	5 Nov	LEICESTER CITY	3-1	12030	Farmer, Keyworth, Wilson	1	2		4	5	6	7		9		10			8	3			11										
17	12	Lincoln City	1-1	12160	Weakley	1	2		4	5	6	9				10			8	3			11				7						
18	19	BLACKBURN ROVERS	3-2	12802	Grainger(2), Wilson	1	2		4	5	6	7				10			8	3		9	11										
19	26	Hull City	3-0	22830	Bambridge, Dixon, Wilson	1	2		4	5	6	7				10			8	3		9	11										
20	3 Dec	PLYMOUTH ARGYLE	0-0	11615		1	2		4	5	6	7				10			8	3		9	11										
21	10	Sheffield Wednesday	2-0	22530	Bambridge, Wilson	1	2		4	5	6	7		9		10			8	3			11										
22	17	WEST HAM UNITED	3-2	10293	Bambridge, Dixon, O.G.	1	2		4	5	6	7				10				3		9	11						8				
23	24	Port Vale	1-4	13023	Grainger	1	2		4	5	6	7				10				3		9	11						8				
24	26	BURY	1-3	11907	Wilson	1	2		4	5	6	7				10			8	3		9	11										
25	27	Bury	1-2	9529	Grainger	1	2			5	6	7		9						3			11						8	4			
26	31	DONCASTER ROVERS	3-3	15427	Wilson(2), Bambridge	1	2		4	5	6	7		9		10				3			11		8								
27	21 Jan	Notts County	2-1	12616	Bambridge, Grainger	1	2		8			7				10			6	9			11	5				4			3		
28	11 Feb	Fulham	1-1	9165	Grainger	1	2		8			7				10			6	9			11	5				4			3		
29	3 Mar	Nottingham Forest	0-1	14817		1	2					7		8		10			6	9			11	5				4			3		
30	10	SHEFFIELD WEDNESDAY	2-3	19865	Grainger, Wilson	1	2	8	3		6	7				10				9			11	5				4					
31	17	Leicester City	1-3	29029	Johnson	1	2		4	3	6	7				10				9			11	5				8					
32	24	LINCOLN CITY	2-2	9681	Johnson, Marshall	1	2		10	3	6	8								9			11	5			7	4					
33	31	Bristol Rovers	4-1	23301	Wilson(3), Grainger	1	2			5	6	7		8		10				9			11	3				4					
34	2 Apr	Middlesbrough	1-0	20803	Johnson	1	2			5	6	7		8		10				9			11	3				4					
35	3	MIDDLESBROUGH	2-1	13032	Wilson(2)	1	2			5	6	7		8		10				9			11	3				4					
36	7	HULL CITY	0-2	9619		1	2			5	6	7		8		10				9			11	3				4					
37	14	Plymouth Argyle	1-3	7856	Johnson	1	2			5	6	7				10				9			11					4		8		3	
38	21	LIVERPOOL	0-1	9225		1	2	3		5	6	7				10			4	9			11							8			
39	23	LEEDS UNITED	0-2	20013		1	2	3		5	6	7				10			4	9			11							8			
40	28	STOKE CITY	0-1	7383		1	2	3		5	6	7		9		10			4				11							8			
41	30	Blackburn Rovers	1-3	12635	Farmer	1	2			5	6	7		9		11		10	4				3							8			
42	3 May	SWANSEA TOWN	2-3	5415	Kettleborough, O.G.	1	2	3			6	7		9					4				11	5						8			10
		Apps.				42	42	14	26	36	25	41	2	21	20	32	1	16	22	34	1	7	33	15	3	2	2	10	5	5	3	1	1
		Goals					1		2			10		7	2	14		2	1	4		2	6										

F.A. CUP

No.	Date	Opposition	Res.	Att.	Goalscorers	Quairney J.	Selkirk J.	Warner D.	Marshall F.	Noble N.	Williams D.	Grainger J.	Pell D.	Farmer T.	Guest G.	Wilson I.	Morgan L.	Moore R.	Keyworth K.	Johnson P.	Meadows F.	Dixon R.	Bambridge K.	Jordan B.	Simpson K.	Chums D.	Weakley B.	Jackson B.	Hussey M.	Kettleborough K.	Silman R.	Madden P.	Haynes E.
3R	7 Jan	SCUNTHORPE	1-1	16144	Grainger	1	2	3	4	5	6	7				10				9			11					8					
3Rr	12	Scunthorpe	2-4	13222	Grainger, Marshall	1	2		10	5	6	7		8					3	9			11					4					

JACK GRAINGER

DANNY WILLIAMS

Still regular first-teamers during the 1955-56 season,
but now nearing the end of their football careers with United

Final League Table

	Pl.	Home W	D	L	F	A	Away W	D	L	F	A	F.	A.	Pts
1 Sheffield Wed.	42	13	5	3	60	28	8	5	41	34	101		62	55
2 Leeds United	42	17	3	1	51	18	6	3	12	29	42	80	60	52
3 Liverpool	42	13	4	3	52	25	7	3	11	33	38	85	63	48
4 Blackburn Rovers	42	13	4	4	55	29	8	2	11	29	36	84	65	48
5 Leicester City	42	15	3	3	63	23	6	3	12	31	55	94	78	48
6 Bristol Rovers	42	13	5	3	53	33	8	3	10	31	37	84	70	48
7 Nottingham Forest	42	9	5	7	30	26	10	4	7	38	37	68	63	47
8 Lincoln City	42	14	5	2	49	17	4	5	12	30	48	79	65	46
9 Fulham	42	15	2	4	59	27	5	4	12	30	52	89	79	46
10 Swansea Town	42	14	4	3	49	23	6	2	13	34	58	83	81	46
11 Bristol City	42	14	4	3	49	20	5	3	13	31	44	80	64	45
12 Port Vale	42	12	4	5	38	21	4	9	8	22	37	60	58	45
13 Stoke City	42	13	2	6	47	27	7	2	12	24	35	71	62	44
14 Middlesbrough	42	11	4	6	46	31	5	4	12	30	47	76	78	40
15 Bury	42	9	5	7	44	39	7	3	11	42	51	86	90	40
16 West Ham United	42	14	4	5	52	27	2	7	12	22	42	74	69	39
17 Doncaster Rovers	42	11	5	5	45	30	1	6	14	24	66	69	96	35
18 Barnsley	42	10	5	6	33	35	1	7	13	14	49	47	84	34
19 Rotherham United	42	7	5	9	29	34	5	4	12	27	41	56	75	33
20 Notts County	42	8	5	8	39	37	3	4	14	16	45	55	82	31
21 Plymouth Argyle	42	7	6	8	33	25	3	2	16	21	62	54	87	28
22 Hull City	42	6	4	11	32	45	4	2	15	21	52	53	97	26

SEASON 1956/57
DIVISION TWO

No.	Date	Opposition	Res.	Att.	Goalscorers	Quairney J.	Selkirk J.	Morgan L.	Neilson S.	Noble N.	Williams D.	Grainger J.	Kettleborough K.	Johnson P.	Slater B.	Hunter J.	Moore M.	Farmer T.	Scrivens W.	Marshall F.	Webster B.	Jordan B.	Jackson B.	Bambridge K.	Madden P.	Stephenson R.	Brown R.	Warner D.	Keyworth K.	Silman R.	Dixon R.	Ironside R.	Jackson R.	Lambert R.
1	18 Aug	SHEFFIELD UNITED	0-4	11865		1	2	3	4	5	6	7	8	9	10	11																		
2	22	Doncaster Rovers	1-1	14720	Farmer	1	2	3	4	5	6	7			10	11	8	9																
3	25	Bristol City	1-2	21241	Hunter		2	3	4	5	6	7			10	11	8	9	1															
4	27	DONCASTER ROVERS	0-1	8816		1	2	3		5	6	7			10	11	8	9		4														
5	1 Sep	BLACKBURN ROVERS	0-2	9789			2	3		5	6	9		8	10	11				1	4	7													
6	8	West Ham United	1-1	19448	Jackson	1	2	3	4	5	10	7		9									6	8	11									
7	15	NOTTINGHAM FOREST	3-2	12512	Grainger, Johnson, Williams	1	2	3	4		10	7		9									6	8	11									
8	22	Fulham	1-3	31104	Williams	1	2	3	4		10	7		9								8	6		11	5								
9	29	SWANSEA TOWN	6-1	13777	Brown(2), Grainger(2), Johnson(2)	1	2	3	4	5	6	7		9											11		8	10						
10	6 Oct	Stoke City	0-6	21590		1	2	3	4	5	6	7		9											11		8	10						
11	13	MIDDLESBROUGH	2-3	13644	Selkirk, Stephenson	1	2	3	4	5	6	7		9	11												8	10						
12	20	Bury	4-1	8933	Stephenson(2), Bambridge, Farmer	1	2	3		5	6	7			10			9		4					11		8								
13	27	BRISTOL ROVERS	0-0	11983		1	2	3		5	6	7		9	10									4	11		8								
14	3 Nov	Notts County	5-1	12870	Johnson(3), Stephenson(2)	1		3		5	6	7		9									10		11		8								
15	10	LIVERPOOL	2-2	11668	Grainger, Stephenson	1		3		5	6	7		9	10										11		8		2	4					
16	17	Leyton Orient	1-2	17859	Stephenson	1		3		5	6	7		9											11		8		2	4					
17	24	HUDDERSFIELD TOWN	3-3	12977	Johnson(2), Noble	1	2	3		5	6	7		9	8										11		8	10	2	4					
18	1 Dec	Leicester City	2-5	27914	Jackson, Grainger	1	2	3		5	6	7		9											11			10		4					
19	8	GRIMSBY TOWN	2-1	10800	Grainger, Stephenson	1	2	3		5	6	7		9									8		11			10		4					
20	15	Sheffield United	7-2	21609	Bmbrdge(2),Slatr(2),Graingr(2),Silmn	1		3		5	6	7		9	10								10		11		8			4					
21	22	BRISTOL CITY	6-1	4669	Grainger(2), Johnson(2), Slater(2)	1	2	3		5	6	7		9	10										11		8			4	2				
22	25	BARNSLEY	0-0	14332		1	2	3		5	6	7		9	10										11		8			4					
23	26	Barnsley	1-1	11031	Grainger	1	2	3		5	6	7		9											11		8			4					
24	29	Blackburn Rovers	2-3	24442	Johnson(2)	1	2			5	6	7		9	10										11		8	10		4					
25	1 Jan	PORT VALE	1-0	8120	Slater	1	2	3		5	6	7		9	10										11		8	11		4	3				
26	12	WEST HAM UNITED	0-1	11090		1	2	3		5	6	7		9	10										11		8			4					
27	19	Nottingham Forest	1-3	18580	Johnson	1	2	3		5	6	7		9						4				11		8								
28	2 Feb	FULHAM	4-3	10554	Bambridge(2), Dixon, Grainger	1		5			6	7												11		8	10						4		
29	9	Swansea Town	0-1	15611		1		5			6	7												11		8	10	2		3	9		4		
30	16	STOKE CITY	1-0	11675	Stephenson		2	5			6	7		10										11		8				3	9	1	4		
31	23	Middlesbrough	1-0	14829	Stephenson		2	5			6	7		10										11		8				3	9	1	4		
32	2 Mar	BURY	1-1	11101	Dixon		2	5			6	7		10										11		8				3	9	1	4		
33	9	Bristol Rovers	2-4	14954	Grainger, Keyworth			5			6	7		2										11		8				3	9	1			10
34	16	NOTTS COUNTY	0-0	9482				5			6	7		2										11		8			4	3	9	1			10
35	23	Liverpool	1-4	33307	Stephenson			5			6	7		2										11		8			4	3					10
36	30	LEYTON ORIENT	2-0	8198	Brown(2)		2	5			6	7												11		8	9		4	3					10
37	6 Apr	Huddersfield Town	0-1	13008							6	7		2	10									11		8	9		4	3			1		10
38	13	LEICESTER CITY	1-1	10927	Brown						6	7		2										11	5		9		4	3			1		8
39	19	Lincoln City	3-3	11150	Brown, Grainger, Lambert						6	7		2										11	5	10	9		4	3			1		8
40	20	Grimsby Town	2-3	13695	Farmer, O.G.						6	7		2					8					11	5	10	9		4	3			1		8
41	22	LINCOLN CITY	3-0	7646	Johnson, Stephenson, Williams			5			6			2					8				7	11		10	9		4	3			1		
42	27	Port Vale	1-2	7038	Farmer			5			6			2					8				7	11		10	9		4	3			1		
					Apps.	27	27	26	9	37	42	40	1	35	17	5	3	7	2	4	4	3	6	35	5	31	19	5	22	17	7	12	1	13
					Goals		1			1	3	14		14	5	1		4						2	5	12	6		1	1	2			1

F.A. CUP

	Date	Opposition	Res.	Att.	Goalscorers																													
3R	5 Jan	Bristol City	1-4	25045	Stephenson	1	2	3		5	6	7				10								11		8			4		9			

Final League Table

		Pl.	Home						Away						F.	A.	Pts
			W	D	L	F	A	W	D	L	F	A				
1	Leicester City	42	14	5	2	68	36	11	6	4	41	31	109	67	61
2	Nottingham Forest	42	13	4	4	50	29	9	6	6	44	26	94	55	54
3	Liverpool	42	16	1	4	53	26	5	10	6	29	28	82	54	53
4	Blackburn Rovers	42	12	6	3	49	32	9	4	8	34	43	83	75	52
5	Stoke City	42	16	2	3	64	18	4	6	11	19	40	83	58	48
6	Middlesbrough	42	12	5	4	51	29	7	5	9	33	31	84	60	48
7	Sheffield United	42	11	6	4	45	28	8	2	11	42	48	87	76	46
8	West Ham United	42	12	4	5	31	24	7	4	10	28	39	59	63	46
9	Bristol Rovers	42	12	5	4	47	19	6	4	11	34	48	81	67	45
10	Swansea Town	42	12	3	6	53	34	7	4	10	37	56	90	90	45
11	Fulham	42	13	1	7	53	32	6	3	12	31	44	84	76	42
12	Huddersfield Town	42	10	3	8	33	27	8	3	10	35	47	68	74	42
13	Bristol City	42	13	2	6	49	32	3	7	11	25	47	74	79	41
14	Doncaster Rovers	42	12	5	4	51	21	3	5	13	26	56	77	77	40
15	Leyton Orient	42	7	8	6	34	38	8	2	11	32	46	66	84	40
16	Grimsby Town	42	12	4	5	41	26	5	1	15	20	36	61	62	39
17	Rotherham United	42	9	7	5	37	26	4	4	13	37	49	74	75	37
18	Lincoln City	42	9	4	8	34	27	5	2	14	20	53	54	80	34
19	Barnsley	42	8	7	6	39	35	4	3	14	20	54	59	89	34
20	Notts County	42	7	6	8	34	32	2	6	13	24	54	58	86	30
21	Bury	42	5	3	13	37	47	3	6	12	23	49	60	96	25
22	Port Vale	42	7	4	10	31	42	1	2	18	26	59	57	101	22

SEASON 1957/58
DIVISION TWO

No.	Date	Opposition	Res	Att	Goalscorers	Quairney J.	Johnson P.	Silman R.	Lambert R.	Noble N.	Keyworth K.	Webster B.	Stephenson R.	Brown R.	Stephens M.	Bambridge K.	Partridge C.	Farmer T.	Jordan B.	Kettleborough K.	Morgan L.	Ironside R.	Madden P.	Burns B.	Williams D.	Simpson K.	Twidle K.	Broadbent A.	Jones G.	Sawyer B.	Jackson B.	Perry P.	Layne D.
1	24 Aug	DONCASTER ROVERS	2-1	12923	Keyworth, Stephenson	1	2	3	4	5	6	7	8	9	10	11																	
2	28	Middlesbrough	2-2	28696	Brown, Stephens	1	2	3	4	5	6	7	8	9	10	11																	
3	31	Ipswich Town	2-1	21436	Brown, Silman	1	2	3	4	5	6	7	8	9	10	11																	
4	5 Sep	MIDDLESBROUGH	1-4	13195	Webster	1	2	3	4	5	6	7	8	9	10	11																	
5	7	Huddersfield Town	3-1	20414	Stephens(2), Partridge	1	2	3	4	5	6		7	9	10		11		8														
6	18	LIVERPOOL	2-2	10443	Partridge, Webster	1	2	3	4	5	6	7	8		10		11		9														
7	21	Stoke City	1-4	20487	Layne	1	2	3	4			7	8				11		10			6											9
8	28	BRISTOL CITY	4-1	8850	Farmer(2), Stephenson, Webster	1	2	3	4	5	6	7	11				10	9															
9	5 Oct	Cardiff City	2-2	14390	Farmer, Webster	1	2		4	5	6	7	11				10	9		8	3												
10	12	BLACKBURN ROVERS	1-2	12599	Kettleborough	1	2		4	5	6	7	11				10	9		8	3												
11	19	Sheffield United	0-2	24936		1	2	3		5	6	7			10	11		9		8													
12	26	WEST HAM UNITED	1-2	8971	Johnson		2	3	4	5	6	7		9		11		10		8			1										
13	2 Nov	Barnsley	0-3	18943			2	3	4	5	6	7		9		11				8		10	1										
14	9	FULHAM	3-1	8785	Brown, Burns, Webster		2	3	4	5	6	7		9		11				8			1	10									
15	16	Swansea Town	3-1	12984	Burns, Keyworth, Webster		2	3		5	6	7		9		11				8			1	10	4								
16	23	DERBY COUNTY	0-2	12051		1	2	3		5	6	7		9		11		10		8				4									
17	27	Liverpool	0-2	37518		1	2			5	6	7		9						8	3			10	4			11					
18	30	Bristol Rovers	3-1	17624	Webster(2), Burns	1	2			5	6	7		9						8	3			10	4			11					
19	7 Dec	LINCOLN CITY	1-2	8393	Burns	1	2			5	6	7		9						8	3			10	4			11					
20	14	Notts County	0-1	10857		1	2			5	6	7		11	10					8	3				4	9							
21	21	Doncaster Rovers	2-3	10860	Brown, Keyworth	1	2			5	6	7		10		11			4	8	3								9				
22	25	Leyton Orient	2-6	13966	Brown, Twidle		2			5	6	7		10		11			4	8	3						9						
23	26	LEYTON ORIENT	2-2	11133	Brown, Kettleborough		2				6	7		10					4	8	3		1	5				11	9				
24	28	IPSWICH TOWN	1-4	11612	Kettleborough		2				6	7		9					4	8	3		1	5			11		10				
25	11 Jan	HUDDERSFIELD TOWN	1-1	8833	Broadbent	1	2			5	6	7		9					4	8	3						11		10				
26	18	Grimsby Town	1-3	12749	Broadbent	1	2			5	6	7		9					4	8	3						11		10				
27	1 Feb	STOKE CITY	0-2	8072		1	2	4			6	7		9						8	3				5			11	10			
28	8	Bristol City	1-0	25639	Broadbent	1	2	9			6	7								8	3				5			4	11	10		
29	15	GRIMSBY TOWN	2-0	9256	Jones, Kettleborough	1	2	9			6			7						8	3				5			4	11	10		
30	22	Derby County	4-3	17073	Webster(2), Kettleborough, Keywrth	1	2			5	6	7		9						8	3							4	11	10		
31	1 Mar	SHEFFIELD UNITED	1-6	17756	Broadbent	1	2			9	6	7								8	3				5			4	11	10		
32	8	West Ham United	0-8	25040		1	2			5	6	7								8	3							4	9	11	10		
33	15	BARNSLEY	4-1	11572	Broadbent(2), Kettleborough, Webstr		2			5	6	7								8	3	1						4	9	11	10		
34	29	SWANSEA TOWN	5-2	7064	Jones(2), Broadbent, Webstr, Twidle		2			5	6	7	8								3							4	9	11	10		
35	4 Apr	Charlton Athletic	0-4	19245		1	2			5	6	7	8								3							4	9	11	10		
36	5	Blackburn Rovers	0-5	22074				2			6	7									3	1		5				4	9	11	8		10
37	7	CHARLTON ATHLETIC	1-5	9758	Sawyer	1		2	5		6	7									3							4	9	10	8	11	
38	12	BRISTOL ROVERS	2-0	7131	Broadbent, Williams	1		2	6			7								5	3							4	9	10		11	
39	19	Lincoln City	0-2	9139		1		2	6			8								5	3				4	7	9		10		11	
40	21	CARDIFF CITY	3-1	8147	Jackson(2), Lambert	1		2	6				8	7							3				5			4	9	11			10
41	26	NOTTS COUNTY	1-3	7222	Broadbent	1		2	6				8	7							3				5			4	9	11			10
42	1 May	Fulham	1-3	7743	Layne				6		10	7					8		4		3				5			11				2	9
			Apps.			32	21	32	22	33	41	39	12	23	12	6	7	9	10	27	28	10	12	5	20	4	14	20	14	3	3	1	2
			Goals				1	1			4	12	2	6	3		2	3		6				4	1		2	9	3	1	2		2

F.A. CUP

Rd	Date	Opposition	Res	Att	Goalscorers	Quairney J.	Johnson P.	Silman R.	Lambert R.	Noble N.	Keyworth K.	Webster B.	Stephenson R.	Brown R.	Stephens M.	Bambridge K.	Partridge C.	Farmer T.	Jordan B.	Kettleborough K.	Morgan L.	Ironside R.	Madden P.	Burns B.	Williams D.	Simpson K.	Twidle K.	Broadbent A.	Jones G.	Sawyer B.	Jackson B.	Perry P.	Layne D.
3R	4 Jan	BLACKBURN ROVERS	1-4	11716	Stephens	1	2			5	6			9	10					8	3				4			11					

(Back):Lambert, Morgan, Kettleborough, Johnson, Quairney, Noble, Williams, Silman, Keyworth, Madden (Front): Webster, Stephenson, Brown, Farmer, Stephens.

Final League Table

		Pl	Home					Away					F.	A.	Pts
			W	D	L	F	A	W	D	L	F	A			
1	West Ham United	42	12	8	1	56	25	11	3	7	45	29	101	54	57
2	Blackburn Rovers	42	13	7	1	56	18	9	5	7	43	39	93	57	56
3	Charlton Athletic	42	15	3	3	65	33	9	4	8	42	36	107	69	55
4	Liverpool	42	17	3	1	50	13	5	7	9	29	41	79	54	54
5	Fulham	42	13	5	3	53	24	7	7	7	44	35	97	59	52
6	Sheffield United	42	12	5	4	50	16	7	5	7	37	28	75	50	52
7	Middlesbrough	42	13	3	5	52	29	6	4	11	31	45	83	74	45
8	Ipswich Town	42	13	4	4	45	29	3	8	10	23	40	68	69	44
9	Huddersfield Town	42	9	8	4	28	24	5	8	8	35	42	63	66	44
10	Bristol Rovers	42	12	5	4	52	31	5	3	13	33	49	85	80	42
11	Stoke City	42	9	4	8	49	36	9	2	10	26	37	75	73	42
12	Leyton Orient	42	14	2	5	53	27	4	3	14	24	52	77	79	41
13	Grimsby Town	42	13	4	4	54	30	4	2	15	32	53	86	83	40
14	Barnsley	42	10	6	5	40	25	4	6	11	30	49	70	74	40
15	Cardiff City	42	10	6	5	44	31	4	4	11	19	46	63	77	37
16	Derby County	42	11	3	7	37	36	3	5	13	23	45	60	81	36
17	Bristol City	42	11	4	6	37	29	2	4	13	28	57	63	88	35
18	Rotherham United	42	8	3	10	38	44	6	2	13	27	57	65	101	33
19	Swansea Town	42	8	3	10	48	45	3	6	12	24	54	72	99	31
20	Lincoln City	42	6	9	6	33	35	5	3	13	22	47	55	82	31
21	Notts County	42	9	3	9	24	31	3	3	15	20	49	44	80	30
22	Doncaster Rovers	42	7	5	9	34	40	1	6	14	22	48	56	88	27

SEASON 1958/59
DIVISION TWO

No.	Date	Opposition	Res.	Att.	Goalscorers	Ironside R.	Silman R.	Morgan L.	Lambert R.	Madden P.	Williams D.	Webster B.	Layne D.	Waterhouse K.	Jones G.	Broadbent A.	Perry P.	Kettleborough K.	Jordan B.	Foster B.	Quairney J.	Twidle K.	Sawyer B.	Bambridge K.	Seddon T.	Swann G.	Jackson B.	Gunthorpe K.	Robinson E.	Kirkman A.	Perry A.	Blakeman A.	Cooper D.
1	23	Bristol City	1-6	25253	Jones	1	2	3	4	5	6	7	8	9	10	11																	
2	28	CHARLTON ATHLETIC	4-3	11849	Webster(2), Broadbent, Jones	1		3	4	5	6	7		9	10	11	2	8															
3	30	CARDIFF CITY	1-0	11474	Webster	1			4	5	6	7		9	10	11	2	8															
4	4 Sep	Charlton Athletic	2-5	12062	Waterhouse(2)	1			4	5	6	7		9		11	2	8													3		
5	6	Huddersfield Town	0-3	14330		1	3		4		6	7		9	10	11	2	8	5												3		10
6	11	MIDDLESBROUGH	1-4	12089	Webster	1	3		4	5	6	7		9		11	2	10				8											
7	13	BARNSLEY	3-0	12747	Broadbent, Kettleborough, Webster		2	3	4	5		7	9	8		11		10	6	1													
8	17	Middlesbrough	2-1	34231	Broadbent, Twidle			3	4	5	2	7		8		11		10	6	1		9											
9	20	Scunthorpe United	0-2	13595				3	4	5	2	7	9	8		11		10	6	1		9											
10	27	Sheffield United	0-2	23339				3	4	5	2	7		8		11		10	6	1		9											
11	4 Oct	BRIGHTON & HOVE	0-1	7412				3	4	5	6	7		8	10	11	2			1		9											
12	11	LEYTON ORIENT	1-1	6890	Webster	3			4	5		7		9		10	2	8		1			11										
13	18	Derby County	1-1	16186	Layne			3	4	5	6	7	9			10	2	8		1			11								6		
14	25	BRISTOL ROVERS	3-3	8040	Broadbent, Layne, Webster				4	5	6	7	9			10	2	8		1			11										
15	1 Nov	Sheffield Wednesday	0-5	30468				3	4		6	7	9			10	2	8	5	1			11		3								
16	8	SWANSEA TOWN	3-3	7005	Broadbent, Jones, Webster			3	4	5	6	7	9		8	10	2			1			11										
17	15	Stoke City	0-3	15465				3	4	5	6	7			8	10	2			1			11										
18	22	SUNDERLAND	0-4	8801				3	5		6	7		10		2	8			1			9		11								
19	29	Lincoln City	0-1	7766				3	4	5	6	7				2	8			1			9		11	4							
20	6 Dec	FULHAM	4-0	7430	Twidle(2), Sawyer, Webster			3	4	5	6	8				11	2	10		1		9	7		11								
21	13	Ipswich Town	0-1	12126				3	4	5	6	8				11	2	10		1		9	7										
22	20	BRISTOL CITY	1-2	6653	Twidle			3	4	5	6	8				11	2	10		1		9	7										
23	26	LIVERPOOL	0-1	13092			2	3	4	5	6	7				10		8		1		9		11									
24	27	Liverpool	0-4	44729			2	3	4		6	7			8	10				1		9		11				5					
25	3 Jan	Cardiff City	0-1	17115			2	3	8	5	6	7		4		11		10		1		9											
26	31	Barnsley	1-1	13475	Cooper		2	3	4	5	6	7				11		8		1									10				9
27	7 Feb	SCUNTHORPE UNITED	1-1	9843	Cooper		2	3	4	5		6	7					8		1			11							10			9
28	21	Brighton & Hove Albion	0-3	18861			2	3	4		6	7						8		1			11							10			9
29	28	Swansea Town	0-3	11340			2	3	4	5	6	8			10					1		7	11				5			10			9
30	7 Mar	DERBY COUNTY	3-0	10061	Bambridge, Kettleborough, Webster		2	3		5	6	7	9	4		8		10		1			11										9
31	14	Bristol Rovers	1-4	10763	Kettleborough		2	3		5	6	7	9	4		8		10		1			11										9
32	21	SHEFFIELD WEDNESDAY	1-0	18221	Kirkman		2	3	4	5		7		6						1			11							10	8		9
33	27	Grimsby Town	1-1	15145	Kirkman		2	3	4	5		7		6				10		1			11							10	8		9
34	28	Leyton Orient	0-2	11883		1	2	3	4	5		7		6	11			10					11								8		9
35	30	GRIMSBY TOWN	2-1	8983	Cooper(2)	1	2	3	4	5		7		6				10						9							8		9
36	4 Apr	STOKE CITY	0-0	10294		1	2	3	4	5		7		6				10					11								8		9
37	11	Sunderland	1-1	19920	Kirkman	1	2	3	4	5		7		6									11								8		9
38	15	SHEFFIELD UNITED	2-2	13687	Cooper, Kirkman	1	2	3	4	5		7		6									11							10	8		9
39	18	LINCOLN CITY	1-0	11930	Webster	1	2	3	4	5		7		6									11							10	8		9
40	23	IPSWICH TOWN	1-2	13069	Webster	1	2	3	4	5		7		6									11							10	8		9
41	25	Fulham	0-4	17861		1	2	3	4	5		7		6			10						11								8		9
42	30	HUDDERSFIELD TOWN	0-1	10553		1		3	4	5		7		6			2	10					11								8		9
				Apps.		15	24	36	40	37	29	42	9	27	9	28	17	31	7	1	27	10	13	17	1	2	1	2	8	11	2	2	14
				Goals								12	2	2	3	5		3				4	1	1						4			5

F.A. CUP

	Date	Opposition	Res.	Att.	Goalscorers	Silman R.	Morgan L.	Lambert R.	Madden P.	Webster B.	Williams D.	Kettleborough K.	Foster B.	Twidle K.	Sawyer B.						
3R	10 Jan	Aston Villa	1-2	33357	Sawyer	2	3	4	5	8	7	6	10	1	9	11					

Final League Table

		Pl.	Home						Away						F.	A.	Pts
			W	D	L	F	A		W	D	L	F	A				
1	Sheffield Wed.	42	18	2	1	68	13		10	4	7	38	35		106	48	62
2	Fulham	42	18	1	2	65	26		9	5	7	31	35		96	61	60
3	Sheffield United	42	16	2	3	54	15		7	5	9	28	33		82	48	53
4	Liverpool	42	15	3	3	57	25		9	2	10	30	37		87	62	53
5	Stoke City	42	16	2	3	48	19		5	5	11	24	39		72	58	49
6	Bristol Rovers	42	13	5	3	46	23		5	7	9	34	41		80	64	48
7	Derby County	42	15	1	5	46	29		5	7	9	28	42		74	71	48
8	Charlton Athletic	42	13	3	5	53	33		4	12	5	39	57		92	90	43
9	Cardiff City	42	12	2	7	37	26		6	5	10	28	39		65	65	43
10	Bristol City	42	11	3	7	43	27		6	4	11	31	43		74	70	41
11	Swansea Town	42	12	5	4	52	30		4	4	13	27	51		79	81	41
12	Brighton & Hove A.	42	10	9	2	46	29		5	2	14	28	61		74	90	41
13	Middlesbrough	42	9	7	5	51	26		6	3	12	36	45		87	71	40
14	Huddersfield Town	42	12	3	6	39	20		4	5	12	23	35		62	55	40
15	Sunderland	42	13	4	4	42	23		3	4	14	22	52		64	75	40
16	Ipswich Town	42	12	4	5	37	27		5	2	14	25	50		62	77	40
17	Leyton Orient	42	9	4	8	43	30		5	4	12	28	48		71	78	36
18	Scunthorpe United	42	7	6	8	32	37		5	3	13	23	47		55	84	33
19	Lincoln City	42	10	5	6	45	37		1	2	18	18	56		63	93	29
20	Rotherham United	42	9	5	7	32	28		1	4	16	10	54		42	82	29
21	Grimsby Town	42	7	7	7	41	36		2	3	16	21	54		62	90	28
22	Barnsley	42	8	4	9	34	34		2	3	16	21	57		55	91	27

SEASON 1959/60

DIVISION TWO

No.	Date	Opposition	Res.	Att.	Goalscorers	Ironside R.	Silman R.	Morgan L.	Lambert R.	Madden P.	Waterhouse K.	Webster B.	Kirkman A.	Myerscough W.	Robinson E.	Bambridge K.	Sawyer B.	Kettleborough K.	Swann G.	Hughes H.	Williams D.	Perry P.	Quairney J.	O'Hara E.	Jackson B.
1	22 Aug	CHARLTON ATHLETIC	3-3	10257	Kirkman(2), Myerscough	1	2	3	4	5	6	7	8	9	10	11									
2	26	Derby County	1-1	20596	Kirkman	1	2	3	4	5	6	7	8	9	10	11									
3	29	Bristol City	3-2	20407	Kirkman(2), Robinson	1	2	3	4	5	6	7	8	9	10	11									
4	31	DERBY COUNTY	1-2	13787	Myerscough	1	2	3	4	5	6	7	8	9	10	11									
5	5 Sep	SCUNTHORPE UNITED	1-1	10764	Myerscough	1	2	3	4	5	6	7	8	9	10	11									
6	7	Plymouth Argyle	0-1	24745		1	2	3	4	5	6		8	9				7	10	11					
7	12	Leyton Orient	3-2	14044	Sawyer(2), Kirkman	1			4				8	9				7	10	11	3	6			
8	16	PLYMOUTH ARGYLE	1-1	9327	Sawyer	1	2	3	4	5			8	9				7	10	11		6			
9	19	Cardiff City	4-1	24392	Webster(2), Sawyer, O.G.	1	2	3	4	5		7			10	11	9	8				6			
10	26	HULL CITY	1-0	11646	Sawyer	1	2	3	4	5		7			10	11	9	8				6			
11	3 Oct	Sheffield United	3-2	26339	Bambridge, Myerscough, Sawyer	1	2	3	4	5		7			10	11	9	8				6			
12	10	HUDDERSFIELD TOWN	1-1	17179	Sawyer	1	2	3	4	5		7			10	11	9	8				6			
13	17	Ipswich Town	3-1	15783	Myerscough(2), Kettleborough	1	2	3	4	5		7			10	11	9	8				6			
14	24	BRISTOL ROVERS	3-0	10285	Sawyer(2), Kettleborough	1	2	3	4	5	6	7			10	11	9	8							
15	31	Swansea Town	2-2	15343	Kettleborough, Waterhouse	1	2	3	4	5	6	7			10	11	9	8							
16	7 Nov	BRIGHTON & HOVE ALB.	1-0	11660	Kettleborough	1	2	3	6	5		7			10	11	9	8			4				
17	14	Stoke City	3-2	10258	Myerscough(2), Webster	1	2	3	4	5		7	11	10			9	8				6			
18	21	PORTSMOUTH	2-1	15240	Kettleborough, Webster	1	3		4	5		7	11	10			9	8				6	2		
19	28	Sunderland	2-1	26909	Sawyer, Webster	1	3		4	5		7		10			9	8				6	2		
20	5 Dec	ASTON VILLA	2-1	20567	Myerscough, Sawyer	1	2	3	4	5		7		10			9	8				6			
21	12	Lincoln City	1-0	13950	Bambridge	1	2	3				7		10			9	8				6			5
22	19	Charlton Athletic	2-2	10192	Kettleborough, Sawyer	1	2	3	4	5		7		10			9	8				6			
23	26	MIDDLESBROUGH	0-2	19980		1	2	3	4	5		7		10			9	8				6			
24	28	Middlesbrough	0-3	36184		1	2	3	4	5		7	11	10			9	8				6			
25	2 Jan	BRISTOL CITY	3-1	13719	Kirkman, Webster, O.G.	1		3	4			7	11	10			9	8				6	2		
26	16	Scunthorpe United	1-2	12745	Kirkman		3	4	5	6		7	11	10			9	8					2	1	
27	23	LEYTON ORIENT	1-1	16246	Sawyer	1	2	3	4	5	8	7	11	10			9					6			
28	6 Feb	CARDIFF CITY	2-2	16525	Myerscough(2)	1		3	4	5	8	7	11	10			9						2		
29	13	Hull City	0-1	10171		1		3	4	5	6	7	11	10			9	8					2		
30	27	Huddersfield Town	1-1	19560	Sawyer	1		3	4	5	6	7		10			9	8					2	11	
31	2 Mar	SHEFFIELD UNITED	0-0	16920		1		3	4			7	8				9						2	11	5
32	5	IPSWICH TOWN	1-4	11454	Webster	1		3	4			7	8				9	10			6	2		11	5
33	12	Bristol Rovers	1-3	15142	Sawyer	1		3	8		6	7		10			9	4					2	11	5
34	19	SUNDERLAND	1-0	8867	Lambert	1		3	4	5	6	7					9				8			11	
35	26	Brighton & Hove Albion	0-0	13352		1		3	4	5		7	10	8			9	6					2	11	
36	2 Apr	STOKE CITY	3-0	8648	Kirkman, O'Hara, Sawyer	1		3	4	5		7	8			11	9	6					2	10	
37	9	Portsmouth	0-2	12981		1		3	4	5		7	8			11	9	6					2	10	
38	16	LINCOLN CITY	1-0	9887	O'Hara	1		3	4	5		7	8	9		11		6					2	10	
39	18	Liverpool	0-3	26776		1		3	4	5		7	8	9		11		6					2	10	
40	19	LIVERPOOL	2-2	10288	Kirkman, Waterhouse	1		3	4	5	6	7	8				9	10	11				2		
41	23	Aston Villa	0-3	32860		1		3	4		6	8	7				9	10	11				2		5
42	30	SWANSEA TOWN	1-1	7029	Sawyer	1		3	4			8	7				9	6	11				2	10	5
					Apps.	41	25	39	42	36	18	36	27	38	5	22	35	35	6	1	19	19	1	11	6
					Goals			1			2	6	10	11	1	2	18	6						2	

F.A. CUP

Round	Date	Opposition	Res.	Att.	Goalscorers	Ironside R.	Silman R.	Morgan L.	Lambert R.	Madden P.	Waterhouse K.	Webster B.	Kirkman A.	Myerscough W.	Robinson E.	Bambridge K.	Sawyer B.	Kettleborough K.	Swann G.	Hughes H.	Williams D.	Perry P.	Quairney J.	O'Hara E.	Jackson B.
3R	9 Jan	ARSENAL	2-2	24447	Myerscough, Sawyer	1		3	4	5		7	11	10			9	8				6	2		
3Rr	13	Arsenal	1-1	57598	Webster	1		3	4	5		7	11	10			9	8					2		
3R2r	18	ARSENAL*	2-0	56290	Kettleborough, Sawyer	1	2	3	4	5		7	11	10			9	8				6			
4R	30	BRIGHTON & HOVE ALB.	1-1	24750	Kirkman	1	2	3	4	5		7	11	10			9	8				6			
4Rr	3 Feb	Brighton & Hove Albion	1-1	23790	Sawyer	1		3	4	5		7	11	10			9	8				6	2		
4R2r	8	Brighton & Hove Albion**	0-6	32864		1		3	4	5		7	11	10			9	8				6	2		

* Played at Hillsborough
** Played at Highbury

Final League Table

		Pl.	Home W	D	L	F	A	Away W	D	L	F	A	F.	A.	Pts
1	Aston Villa	42	17	3	1	62	19	8	6	7	27	24	89	43	59
2	Cardiff City	42	15	2	4	55	36	8	10	3	35	26	90	62	58
3	Liverpool	42	15	3	3	59	28	5	7	9	31	38	90	66	50
4	Sheffield United	42	12	5	4	43	22	7	7	7	25	29	68	51	50
5	Middlesbrough	42	14	5	2	56	21	5	5	11	34	43	90	64	48
6	Huddersfield Town	42	13	3	5	44	20	6	6	9	29	32	73	52	47
7	Charlton Athletic	42	12	7	2	55	28	5	6	10	35	59	90	87	47
8	Rotherham United	42	9	9	3	31	23	8	4	9	30	37	61	60	47
9	Bristol Rovers	42	12	6	3	42	28	6	5	10	30	50	72	78	47
10	Leyton Orient	42	12	4	5	47	25	3	10	8	29	36	76	61	44
11	Ipswich Town	42	12	5	4	48	24	7	1	13	30	44	78	68	44
12	Swansea Town	42	12	6	3	54	32	3	4	14	28	52	82	84	40
13	Lincoln City	42	11	3	7	41	25	5	4	12	34	53	75	78	39
14	Brighton & Hove A.	42	7	8	6	35	32	6	4	11	32	44	67	76	38
15	Scunthorpe United	42	9	7	5	38	26	4	3	14	19	45	57	71	36
16	Sunderland	42	8	6	7	35	29	4	6	11	17	36	52	65	36
17	Stoke City	42	8	3	10	40	38	6	4	11	26	45	66	83	35
18	Derby County	42	9	4	8	31	28	5	3	13	30	49	61	77	35
19	Plymouth Argyle	42	10	6	5	42	36	3	3	15	19	53	61	89	35
20	Portsmouth	42	6	6	9	36	36	4	6	11	23	41	59	77	32
21	Hull City	42	7	6	8	27	30	3	4	14	21	46	48	76	32
22	Bristol City	42	8	3	10	27	31	3	2	16	33	66	60	97	27

1959-60 season

(Back): Steels, Hannah, Madden, Silman, Lancaster, D.Williams. (3rd row): Quairney, Waterhouse, Kirkman, Lambert, Morgan, Sawyer, B. Jackson, Ironside, Wilson (Trainer).
(2nd row):E. Jackson(Trainer), Hooper(Coach), Kettleborough, Hughes, Webster, Myerscough, Johnston(Man.)
(Front): Turner, Carver, Butler, Perry, Brown, Robinson, Hibbert.

1960-61 Season

(Back):Houghton, Smith, B.Jackson,Ironside, Wren, Valentine, Madden. (3rd row):E.Jackson(Trainer), Lambert, Waterhouse, Morgan, Poole, Coldwell, Kirkman, D.Williams, T.Johnston (Man.).
(2nd row):Wilson(Trainer), Sawyer, Lancaster, Robinson,Kettleborough, Perry,Webster, O'Hara, Holmes(Sec.).
(Front): Carver, Casper, Shevels, Butler.

SEASON 1960/61

DIVISION TWO

No.	Date	Opposition	Res.	Att.	Goalscorers	Ironside R.	Perry P.	Morgan L.	Lambert R.	Madden P.	Waterhouse K.	Webster B.	Kettleborough K.	Smith C.	Kirkman A.	Sawyer B.	Bambridge K.	Houghton K.	O'Hara E.	Jackson B.	Darwin G.	Weston D.	Wren J.	Swann G.	Lancaster R.	Caldwell D.	Butler I.
1	20 Aug	SOUTHAMPTON	1-0	10669	Kirkman	1	2	3	4	5	6	7	8	9	10	11											
2	24	Lincoln City	1-0	10859	Webster	1	2	3	4	5	6	7	8	9	10	11											
3	27	Leeds United	0-2	16480		1	2	3	4	5	6	7	8	9	10	11											
4	29	LINCOLN CITY	2-0	9606	Kirkman, Sawyer	1	2	3	4	5	6	7	8		10	9	11										
5	3 Sep	MIDDLESBROUGH	1-2	10568	Kettleborough	1	2	3	4	5	6		8		10	9	11	7									
6	7	BRISTOL ROVERS	4-0	8366	Kettleborough(2), Kirkman, Smith	1	2	3	4	5	6		8	9	10	7	11										
7	10	Brighton & Hove	0-1	14593		1	2	3	4	5	6	7	8		10	9	11										
8	12	Bristol Rovers	1-2	13071	Kirkman	1	2	3	4	5	6	7	8		10			9	11								
9	17	IPSWICH TOWN	1-1	8873	O'Hara	1	2	3	4	5	6		8		7	9	11		10								
10	24	Scunthorpe United	1-1	12724	Kettleborough	1	2	3	4		6	7	8		9			11	10	5							
11	1 Oct	LEYTON ORIENT	2-1	7453	Smith, Perry	1	2	3			7	6		9	8			11	10	5							
12	8	Portsmouth	2-2	7759	Kirkman, Smith	1	2	3			7	6		9	8			11	10	5							
13	15	HUDDERSFIELD TOWN	2-2	10961	Darwin, Webster	1	2	3	4			7	6	9				11	10	5	8						
14	22	Sunderland	1-1	19240	Darwin	1	2	3	4	5		7	6	9				11	10		8						
15	29	PLYMOUTH ARGYLE	0-0	8448		1	2	3	4	5			8	10	9			7	11		6						
16	5 Nov	Norwich City	1-3	22504	Sawyer	1	2	3	4	5			8	10				7	11	9	6						
17	12	CHARLTON ATHLETIC	2-3	7919	Houghton(2)	1	2	3	4	5			7	10				9	11	8	6						
18	19	Sheffield United	1-3	20462	Sawyer	1	2	3	4	5			7	10				9	8	11	6						
19	26	STOKE CITY	0-0	8450		1	2	3	4	5	6		10					7	9	11	8						
20	10 Dec	LUTON TOWN	5-2	6297	Houghton(2), Kirkman(2), Perry	1	2	3	4	5	6	7			8	9		11	10								
21	17	Southampton	2-3	13120	Sawyer, Webster	1	2	3	4	5	6				8	9		11	10								
22	26	Liverpool	1-2	39436	Kirkman	1	2	3	4	5	6	11			8	7					10	9					
23	27	LIVERPOOL	1-0	17915	Weston	1	2	3	4	5	6	11			8	7					10	9					
24	31	LEEDS UNITED	1-3	12557	Sawyer	1	2	3	4	5	6	11			8	7					10	9					
25	14 Jan	Middlesbrough	2-2	15638	Kirkman, Silman		2	3	4	5	6				8	7	11	10				9					
26	4 Feb	Ipswich Town	1-1	12225	Sawyer		2	3	4	5	6	7			8	9	11					10	1				
27	11	SCUNTHORPE UNITED	4-0	8225	Perry, Sawyer, Waterhouse, O.G.	1	2	3	4	5	6	7			9			11	10			8					
28	20	Leyton Orient	1-2	9613	Weston	1	2	3	4	5	6				8			11	10			9					
29	25	PORTSMOUTH	1-0	6284	Swann	1	2	3	4	5	6				8			11	10			9		7			
30	4 Mar	Huddersfield Town	1-0	15144	Houghton	1	2	3	4	5	6				7			9	11			10					
31	11	SUNDERLAND	0-0	10588		1	2	3	4	5	6				7			9	11	10		8					
32	14	Swansea Town	1-2	12594	Houghton	1	2	3	4	5	6				7			9	11	10		8					
33	18	Luton Town	1-2	10179	Kirkman	1	2	3	4	5	6				7			9	11	10		8					
34	25	NORWICH CITY	0-2	7352		1	2	3	4	5	6	7						9	11	10		8					
35	1 Apr	Stoke City	4-1	8244	Sawyer(2), Perry, Weston	1	2	3	4	5	6	7			10	9		11				8					
36	3	Derby County	0-3	12778		1	2	3	4	5	6	7			10	9		11				8					
37	4	DERBY COUNTY	1-1	6700	Lancaster	1	2	3		5	6				7	9		11	10			8			4		
38	8	SHEFFIELD UNITED	1-2	19549	Houghton	1	2	3		5	6				7	9		11	10			8			4		
39	15	Charlton Athletic	3-4	10351	Weston(2), Bambridge	1	2	3	4	5	6				10	7	11	9				8					
40	18	BRIGHTON & HOVE	5-2	7188	Weston(2), Houghton, Perry, Kirkman	1	2	3	4	5	6				10	7	11	9				8					
41	22	SWANSEA TOWN	3-3	6527	Houghton, Waterhouse, Weston	1		3	4	5	6				10	7	11	9				8				2	
42	29	Plymouth Argyle	3-3	11690	Houghton, Kirkman, Weston	1		3	4	5					10	7	11	9				8			6		11
					Apps.	41	41	42	40	38	33	25	19	9	35	34	31	23	9	11	2	21	1	2	3	1	1
					Goals		6				2	3	4	3	12	9	1	10	1		2	9		1	1		

F.A. CUP

Rnd	Date	Opposition	Res.	Att.	Goalscorers	Ironside R.	Perry P.	Morgan L.	Lambert R.	Madden P.	Waterhouse K.	Webster B.	Kettleborough K.	Smith C.	Kirkman A.	Sawyer B.	Bambridge K.	Houghton K.	O'Hara E.
3R	7 Jan	WATFORD	1-0	14854	Houghton	1	2	3	4	5	6				8	7	11	10	9
4R	28	Birmingham City	0-4	31932		1	2	3	4	5	6	7			8	9	11	10	

LEAGUE CUP

Rnd	Date	Opposition	Res.	Att.	Goalscorers	Ironside R.	Perry P.	Morgan L.	Lambert R.	Madden P.	Waterhouse K.	Webster B.	Kettleborough K.	Smith C.	Kirkman A.	Sawyer B.	Bambridge K.	Houghton K.	O'Hara E.	Jackson B.	Darwin G.	Weston D.
1R	26 Oct	Leicester City	2-1	6244	Darwin, Kettleborough	1	2	3	4	5		7	10			9	11			6	8	
2R	23 Nov	BRISTOL ROVERS	2-0	10912	Houghton, Kirkman	1	2	3	4	5	6		10		7	9		8	11			
3R	20 Dec	Bolton Wanderers	2-0	6594	Houghton, O.G.	1	2	3	4		6	7			8	9	11	10	5			
4R	13 Feb	PORTSMOUTH	3-0	11918	Weston(2), Houghton	1	2	3	4	5	6	7			8			11	10			9
SF1	21 Mar	SHREWSBURY TOWN	3-2	13397	Sawyer(2), Kirkman	1	2	3	4	5	6				7	9		11	10			8
SF2	29	Shrewsbury Town	1-1	16722	Weston	1	2	3	4	5	6	7			10	9	11					8

Final League Table

		Pl.	Home W	D	L	F	A	Away W	D	L	F	A	F.	A.	Pts
1	Ipswich Town	42	15	3	3	55	24	11	4	6	45	31	100	55	59
2	Sheffield United	42	16	2	3	49	22	10	4	7	32	29	81	51	58
3	Liverpool	42	14	5	2	49	21	7	5	9	38	37	87	58	52
4	Norwich City	42	15	3	3	46	20	5	6	10	24	33	70	53	49
5	Middlesbrough	42	13	6	2	44	20	5	6	10	39	54	83	74	48
6	Sunderland	42	12	5	4	47	24	5	8	8	28	36	75	60	47
7	Swansea Town	42	14	4	3	49	26	4	7	10	28	47	77	73	47
8	Southampton	42	12	4	5	57	35	6	4	11	27	46	84	81	44
9	Scunthorpe United	42	9	8	4	39	25	5	7	9	30	39	69	64	43
10	Charlton Athletic	42	12	3	6	60	42	4	8	9	37	49	97	91	43
11	Plymouth Argyle	42	13	4	4	52	32	4	4	13	29	50	81	82	42
12	Derby County	42	9	6	6	46	35	6	4	11	34	45	80	80	40
13	Luton Town	42	13	5	3	48	27	2	4	15	23	52	71	79	39
14	Leeds United	42	7	7	7	41	38	7	3	11	34	45	75	83	38
15	Rotherham United	42	9	7	5	37	24	3	6	12	28	40	65	64	37
16	Brighton & Hove A.	42	9	6	6	33	26	5	3	13	28	49	61	75	37
17	Bristol Rovers	42	13	4	4	52	35	2	3	16	21	57	73	92	37
18	Stoke City	42	9	6	6	39	26	3	6	12	12	33	51	59	36
19	Leyton Orient	42	10	5	6	31	29	4	3	14	24	49	55	78	36
20	Huddersfield Town	42	7	5	9	33	33	6	4	11	29	38	62	71	35
21	Portsmouth	42	10	6	5	38	27	1	5	15	26	64	64	91	33
22	Lincoln City	42	5	4	12	30	43	3	4	14	18	52	48	95	24

SEASON 1961/62
DIVISION TWO

No.	Date	Opposition	Res.	Att.	Goalscorers
1	19 Aug	Stoke City	2-1	11063	Kirkman(2)
2	26	BRISTOL ROVERS	4-0	8216	Kirkman(2), Houghton, Weston
3	30	Middlesbrough	1-5	11919	Waterhouse
4	2 Sep	Leeds United	3-1	12610	Kirkman(3)
5	9	NORWICH CITY	3-1	8622	Houghton, Perry, O.G.
6	15	Scunthorpe United	2-5	11953	Kirkman, O.G.
7	20	Charlton Athletic	2-0	9986	Kirkman, Weston
8	23	BRIGHTON & HOVE	2-1	8722	Perry, Weston
9	28	CHARLTON ATHLETIC	3-2	11316	Perry, Waterhouse, Weston
10	30	Bury	1-2	11038	Waterhouse
11	7 Oct	Walsall	0-5	12038	
12	14	DERBY COUNTY	2-2	12385	Houghton, Madden
13	21	Leyton Orient	1-1	10581	Perry
14	28	PRESTON NORTH END	2-2	10069	Houghton, Weston
15	4 Nov	Plymouth Argyle	5-2	10685	Kirkman(2), Perry, Taylor, Weston
16	11	NEWCASTLE UNITED	0-0	11552	
17	18	Swansea Town	2-2	11140	Houghton, Webster
18	25	SOUTHAMPTON	4-2	9607	Kirkman(2), Houghton, Webster
19	2 Dec	Luton Town	3-4	9886	Kirkman, Sawyer, Taylor
20	8	HUDDERSFIELD TOWN	3-3	10241	Taylor(2), Weston
21	16	STOKE CITY	1-2	15657	Perry
22	22	Bristol Rovers	2-4	8838	Kirkman, Sawyer
23	26	LIVERPOOL	1-0	13717	Weston
24	12 Jan	LEEDS UNITED	2-1	6207	Houghton, Kirkman
25	20	Norwich City	1-0	24269	Weston
26	2 Feb	SCUNTHORPE UNITED	0-1	12528	
27	10	Brighton & Hove	3-0	10369	Kirkman(2), Bennett
28	17	BURY	2-0	7432	Cassidy, Kirkman
29	24	WALSALL	2-2	7872	Butler, Kirkman
30	3 Mar	Derby County	1-1	12619	Weston
31	9	LEYTON ORIENT	2-1	10847	Houghton, Weston
32	17	Preston North End	0-2	12100	
33	24	PLYMOUTH ARGYLE	1-3	8547	Butler
34	28	Liverpool	1-4	32827	Weston
35	31	Newcastle United	0-1	21865	
36	3 Apr	MIDDLESBROUGH	0-1	6037	
37	7	SWANSEA TOWN	1-2	4120	Webster
38	14	Southampton	1-2	8107	Houghton
39	21	LUTON TOWN	1-1	3492	Kirkman
40	23	Sunderland	0-4	38903	
41	24	SUNDERLAND	0-3	8674	
42	28	Huddersfield Town	3-0	8679	Houghton, Kirkman, Webster

Appearance grid (shirt numbers worn)

No.	Ironside R.	Perry P.	Morgan L.	Lambert R.	Madden P.	Waterhouse K.	Webster B.	Weston D.	Houghton K.	Kirkman A.	Bambridge K.	Morritt G.	Sawyer B.	Butler I.	Lancaster R.	Wilson A.	Taylor B.	Cassidy W.	Jackson B.	Carver D.	Bennett A.	Haselden J.
1	1	2	3	4	5	6	7	8	9	10	11											
2	1	2	3	4	5	6	7	8	9	10	11											
3	1	2	3	4	5	6	7	8	9	10	11											
4	1	2	3	4	5	6	7	8	9	10	11											
5	1	2	3	4	5	6	7	8	9	10	11											
6	1	2	3	4	5	6	7	8	9	10	11											
7		2	3	4	5	9	7	8		10		1		11	6							
8		2	3	4	5	9	7	8		10		1		11	6							
9		2	3	4	5	10	7	9	8			1		11	6							
10		2	3	4	5	10	7	9	8			1		11	6							
11		2	3	4	5	6	7	8	9	10		1		11								
12		2	3	4	5			8	9	10		1		11	6		7					
13		2	3	4				8	9	10		1		11	6	5	7					
14		2	3	4		6		8	9	10		1		11	5	7						
15	1	2	3	4	5			10	8	9				11		6	7					
16	1	2	3	4	5			10	8	9				11		6	7					
17	1		3	4	5	6	7	8	9						10		11		2			
18	1		3	4	5		7	8	9						10	6	11		2			
19	1		3	4	5		7	10	8				9		6		11		2			
20	1	2	3	4	5		7	10	8	9					6		11					
21	1	2	3	4	5		7	10	8	9					6		11					
22			3	4	5		7	8		10		1	9		6		11		2			
23	1	2	3	4	5	6	7	8	10				9				11					
24	1	2			5	6	7	8	9	10					4		11		3			
25	1		3		5	6	7	8	10				9		4		11		2			
26	1		3		5	6	7	8	9	10					4		11		2			
27	1		3		5	6	7	8	10	11					4				2		9	
28	1		3		5	6	7	8		10							11	4	2		9	
29	1		3			6	7	8	9	10				11		5		4	2			
30	1		3		5	6	7	8	10	11			9					4	2			
31	1		3		5	6	7	8	9	11					10			4	2			
32	1		3		5	6	7	8	9	11					10			4	2			
33	1		3		5	6	7	8	9	11					10			4	2			
34	1		3		5	6	7	8	9	10							11	4	2			
35	1		3		5	6	7	8	9	10							11	4	2			
36	1		3		5	6	7	8		10	11							4	2	9		
37				4	5		7	8	6	10	11	1					3		2	9		
38			3	4	5		7	8				1			10	6	11		2	9		
39	1		3	4	5	6	7	8	9	10							11		2			
40	1		3	4	5	6	7	8	9	10							11		2			
41			3	4	5		7	9	8		11	1			10	6			2			
42			3	4		6	7	8	10		11	1							2		9	5
Apps.	28	21	39	29	38	32	33	34	30	39	14	14	5	14	18	5	25	17	18	2	6	1
Goals		6			1	3	4	12	10	22			2	2			4	1			1	

F.A. CUP

Rd	Date	Opposition	Res.	Att.	Goalscorers	Team (shirt numbers)
3R	9 Jan	Huddersfield Town	3-4	28071	Weston(2), Houghton	Perry 2, Morgan 3, Lambert 4, Madden 5, Waterhouse 6, Webster 7, Weston 9, Houghton 10, Kirkman 8, Morritt 1, Lancaster 11

LEAGUE CUP

Rd	Date	Opposition	Res.	Att.	Goalscorers	Team (shirt numbers)
1R	11 Sep	Darlington	1-0	8943	O.G.	Perry 2, Morgan 3, Lambert 4, Madden 5, Waterhouse 6, Weston 8, Houghton 9, Kirkman 10, Morritt 1, Butler 7, Lancaster 11
2R	4 Oct	Luton Town	0-0	6144		Perry 2, Morgan 3, Lambert 4, Madden 5, Waterhouse 6, Webster 7, Weston 8, Houghton 9, Kirkman 10, Bambridge 11, Morritt 1
2Rr	10 Oct	LUTON TOWN	2-0	5301	Houghton, O.G.	Perry 2, Morgan 3, Lambert 4, Madden 5, Waterhouse 6, Webster 7, Weston 8, Houghton 9, Kirkman 10, Bambridge 11, Morritt 1
3R	14 Nov	Preston North End	0-0	7870		Ironside 1, Perry 2, Morgan 3, Lambert 4, Madden 5, Webster 7, Lancaster 10, Wilson 11, Taylor 6
3Rr	28	PRESTON NORTH END	3-0	10078	Butler, Houghton, Webster	Ironside 1, Morgan 3, Lambert 4, Madden 5, Webster 7, Weston 8, Kirkman 10, Sawyer 9, Butler 11, Lancaster 6, Cassidy 2
4R	12 Dec	LEEDS UNITED	1-1	10899	Bambridge	Ironside 1, Perry 2, Morgan 3, Lambert 4, Madden 5, Webster 7, Weston 8, Houghton 9, Bambridge 11, Lancaster 10, Wilson 6
4Rr	15 Jan	Leeds United	2-1	6385	Webster, Weston	Ironside 1, Madden 5, Waterhouse 6, Webster 7, Weston 8, Kirkman 10, Bambridge 11, Wilson 9, Cassidy 4, Carver 3, Jackson 2
5R	6 Feb	BLACKBURN ROVERS	0-1	11065		Ironside 1, Madden 5, Waterhouse 6, Webster 7, Weston 8, Houghton 9, Kirkman 10, Bambridge 11, Cassidy 4, Carver 3, Jackson 2

LEAGUE CUP (from previous season)

Rd	Date	Opposition	Res.	Att.	Goalscorers	Team (shirt numbers)
F1	22 Aug	ASTON VILLA	2-0	12226	Kirkman, Webster	Ironside 1, Perry 2, Morgan 3, Lambert 4, Madden 5, Waterhouse 6, Webster 7, Weston 8, Houghton 9, Kirkman 10, Bambridge 11
F2	5 Sep	Aston Villa	0-3	31201		Ironside 1, Perry 2, Morgan 3, Lambert 4, Madden 5, Waterhouse 6, Webster 7, Weston 8, Houghton 9, Kirkman 10, Bambridge 11

Final League Table

		Pl.	Home W	D	L	F	A	Away W	D	L	F	A	F.	A.	Pts
1	Liverpool	42	18	3	0	68	19	9	5	7	31	24	99	43	62
2	Leyton Orient	42	11	5	5	34	17	11	5	5	35	23	69	40	54
3	Sunderland	42	17	3	1	60	16	5	6	10	25	34	85	50	53
4	Scunthorpe United	42	14	4	3	52	26	7	3	11	34	45	86	71	49
5	Plymouth Argyle	42	12	4	5	45	30	7	4	10	30	45	75	75	46
6	Southampton	42	13	3	5	53	28	5	6	10	24	34	77	62	45
7	Huddersfield Town	42	11	5	5	39	22	5	7	9	28	37	67	59	44
8	Stoke City	42	13	4	4	34	17	4	4	13	21	40	55	57	42
9	Rotherham United	42	9	6	6	36	30	7	3	11	31	46	70	76	42
10	Preston North End	42	11	4	6	34	23	4	6	11	21	34	55	57	40
11	Newcastle United	42	10	5	6	40	27	5	4	12	24	31	64	58	39
12	Middlesbrough	42	11	3	7	45	29	5	4	12	31	43	76	72	39
13	Luton Town	42	12	1	8	44	37	5	4	12	25	34	69	71	39
14	Walsall	42	11	7	3	42	23	3	4	14	28	52	70	75	39
15	Charlton Athletic	42	10	5	6	38	30	5	4	12	31	45	69	75	39
16	Derby County	42	10	7	4	42	27	4	4	13	26	48	68	75	39
17	Norwich City	42	10	6	5	36	28	4	5	12	25	42	61	70	39
18	Bury	42	9	4	8	32	36	8	1	12	20	40	52	76	39
19	Leeds United	42	9	6	6	24	19	3	6	12	26	42	50	61	36
20	Swansea Town	42	10	5	6	38	30	2	7	12	23	53	61	83	36
21	Bristol Rovers	42	11	3	7	36	31	2	4	15	17	50	53	81	33
22	Brighton & Hove A.	42	7	7	7	24	32	3	4	14	18	54	42	86	31

1961-62: (Back) Sawyer, Webster, Weston, Houghton, Kirkman, Bambridge.
(Back): Lambert, Waterhouse, Madden, Ironside, Morgan, Perry.

1962-63: (Back): Lambert, Jackson, Madden, Ironside, Lancaster, Morgan.
(Front): Weston, Kirkman, McIlmoyle, Houghton, Taylor.

SEASON 1962/63

DIVISION TWO

No.	Date	Opposition	Res.	Att.	Goalscorers
1	18 Aug	CHELSEA	0-1	11268	
2	22	Leeds United	4-3	14096	Kirkman(2), Weston(2)
3	25	Luton Town	3-2	8615	Kirkman(2), McIlmoyle
4	28	LEEDS UNITED	2-1	20013	Butler, Kirkman
5	1 Sep	SOUTHAMPTON	2-0	11289	Houghton, McIlmoyle
6	5	Sunderland	0-2	38172	
7	8	Scunthorpe United	0-1	13113	
8	11	SUNDERLAND	4-2	13064	Bennett(2), Houghton, Kirkman
9	15	BURY	1-5	11257	Kirkman
10	22	Walsall	0-1	10616	
11	29	Charlton Athletic	3-2	12744	Bennett, Houghton, Taylor
12	5 Oct	NORWICH CITY	0-3	12561	
13	13	Grimsby Town	2-1	10255	Bennett(2)
14	20	PLYMOUTH ARGYLE	3-2	9351	Houghton, Kirkman, Lambert
15	27	Preston North End	2-2	8863	Bennett, Lambert
16	3 Nov	PORTSMOUTH	0-0	9042	
17	10	Cardiff City	1-4	14199	Kirkman
18	17	HUDDERSFIELD TOWN	0-2	11589	
19	24	Middlesbrough	1-2	12478	Kirkman
20	30	DERBY COUNTY	2-2	9362	Casper, McIlmoyle
21	8 Dec	Newcastle United	1-4	21955	McIlmoyle
22	15	Chelsea	0-3	19735	
23	21	LUTON TOWN	2-1	8198	McCole(2)
24	26	STOKE CITY	1-2	11915	Waterhouse
25	23 Feb	Norwich City	2-4	15212	Bennett, Waterhouse
26	9 Mar	Plymouth Argyle	2-2	7455	Houghton, Waterhouse
27	16	PRESTON NORTH END	3-1	7270	Bennett(2), Butler
28	19	Bury	5-0	12000	Bennett(2), Houghton(2), McCole
29	23	Portsmouth	2-1	11493	Ashe, Bennett
30	29	CARDIFF CITY	2-1	9181	Bennett(2)
31	1 Apr	Stoke City	1-3	31289	Houghton
32	6	Huddersfield Town	0-1	14015	
33	13	MIDDLESBROUGH	4-1	8059	Bennett(2), Blain, Houghton
34	15	SWANSEA TOWN	2-1	8281	Bennett(2)
35	16	Swansea Town	2-2	10077	Bennett, McCole
36	20	Derby County	2-3	10017	McCole, Bennett
37	27	NEWCASTLE UNITED	3-1	9542	Butler, Houghton, O.G.
38	30	CHARLTON ATHLETIC	1-2	9773	Bennett
39	4 May	WALSALL	1-2	7899	Bennett
40	7	GRIMSBY TOWN	0-0	7765	
41	11	Southampton	0-1	10126	
42	17	SCUNTHORPE UNITED	1-0	7367	Bennett

Appearances (shirt numbers)

No.	Ironside R.	Jackson B.	Morgan L.	Lambert R.	Madden P.	Lancaster R.	Weston D.	Kirkman A.	McIlmoyle H.	Houghton K.	Taylor B.	Butler I.	Cassidy W.	Bennett A.	Bambridge K.	Casper F.	Waterhouse K.	Sawyer B.	Morritt G.	Haselden J.	McCole J.	Blain J.	Carver D.	Ashe N.	Tiler B.
1	1	2	3	4	5	6	7	8	9	10	11														
2	1	2	3	4	5	6	7	8	9	10		11													
3	1	2	3	4	5	6	7	8	9	10		11													
4	1	2	3	4	5	6	7	8	9	10		11													
5	1	2	3	4	5	6	7	8	9	10	11		2												
6	1		3	4	5	6	7	8	9	10	11		2												
7	1		3	4	5	6	7	8	9	10	11		2												
8	1		3	4	5	6	7	8		10			2	9	11										
9	1		3	4	5	6	7	8		10			2	9	11										
10	1		3	4	5	6	7	8		10	11		2	9											
11	1		3	4	5	6	10	7		8	11		2	9											
12	1		3	4	5	6	10	7		8	11		2	9											
13	1	2	3	4	5		10	7		8	11			9		6									
14	1	2	3	4	5		7	8		10	11			9		6									
15	1	2	3	4	5				9	10	11			8		6	7								
16	1	2	3	4	5		7	8		10				9	11	6									
17	1	2	3	4	5		7	8		10	11			9		6									
18	1	2	3	4	5		7	8		10	11			9		6									
19	1	2	3	4	5		9	7	8		11	10				6									
20		2	3	4			10	8	9		11					6		7	1	5					
21		2	3	4	5	6	10	8	9		11						7		1						
22		2	3	4	5	6	7	8			11								1		9	10			
23		2	3	4	5		7	8			11					6			1		9	10			
24		2	3	4	5			8			11					6	7		1		9	10			
25	1		3	4	5					10	11			8		6	7				9				
26	1		3	2	5	4				10	11			8		6	7				9				
27	1		3	2	5	4						11		8		6	7				9	10			
28	1		3	4	5	6				10	11			8							9	7	2		
29	1		3	4	5	6				10	11			8							9		2	7	
30	1		3	4	5	6				10				8							9		2	7	
31	1		3	4	5	6				10	11			8							9		2	7	
32	1		3	4	5	6				10	11			8							9		2	7	
33	1		3	4	5	6				10				8							9	7	2		
34	1		3	4		6				10	11			8						5	9	7	2		
35	1		3	4		6				10	11			8						5	9	7	2		
36	1		3	4		6				10	11			8							9	7	2		
37	1		3	4	5	6				10	11			9	8							7	2		
38	1		3	4	5	6				10	11			9	8							7	2		
39	1		3	4	5					10	11			9	8							7	2		6
40	1	6	3	4	5					10	11			9	8								2	7	
41	1	6	3	4	5					10				9	11	8							2	7	
42	1	6	3	4	5		9			10	11			8									7	2	
Apps.	37	20	42	42	39	28	19	26	12	37	17	23	8	29	4	8	13	1	5	3	14	13	15	6	1
Goals		2				2	10	4	10	1		3		23		1	3				5	1		1	

F.A. CUP

Round	Date	Opposition	Res.	Att.	Goalscorers
3R	20 Feb	Watford	0-2	5165	

Lineup: Ironside 1, Jackson 2, Morgan 3, Lambert 8, Madden 5, Lancaster 4, Weston 7, McIlmoyle 9, Houghton 10, Taylor 11, Casper 6

LEAGUE CUP

Round	Date	Opposition	Res.	Att.	Goalscorers
2R	25 Sep	Bristol City	2-1	7469	Taylor(2)
3R	16 Oct	WEST HAM UNITED	3-1	11581	Houghton, Kirkman, Weston
4R	14 Nov	Blackburn Rovers	1-4	7391	Waterhouse

2R lineup: Ironside 1, Morgan 3, Lambert 4, Madden 5, Lancaster 6, Weston 10, Kirkman 7, Taylor 11, Cassidy 2, Bennett 9, Casper 8
3R lineup: Ironside 1, Jackson 2, Morgan 3, Lambert 4, Madden 5, Weston 7, Kirkman 8, Houghton 10, Taylor 11, Bennett 9, Casper 6
4R lineup: Ironside 1, Jackson 2, Morgan 3, Lambert 4, Madden 5, Weston 7, Kirkman 8, Taylor 11, Butler 10, Bennett 9, Casper 6

Final League Table

		Pl.	Home					Away					F.	A.	Pts
			W	D	L	F	A	W	D	L	F	A			
1	Stoke City	42	15	3	3	49	20	5	10	6	24	30	73	50	53
2	Chelsea	42	15	3	3	54	16	9	1	11	27	26	81	42	52
3	Sunderland	42	14	5	2	46	13	6	7	8	38	42	84	55	52
4	Middlesbrough	42	12	4	5	48	35	8	5	8	38	50	86	85	49
5	Leeds United	42	15	2	4	55	19	4	8	9	24	34	79	53	48
6	Huddersfield Town	42	11	6	4	34	21	6	8	7	29	29	63	50	48
7	Newcastle United	42	11	8	2	48	23	7	3	11	31	36	79	59	47
8	Bury	42	11	6	4	28	20	7	5	9	23	27	51	47	47
9	Scunthorpe United	42	12	7	2	35	18	4	5	12	22	41	57	59	44
10	Cardiff City	42	12	5	4	50	29	6	2	13	33	44	83	73	43
11	Southampton	42	15	3	3	52	23	2	5	14	20	44	72	67	42
12	Plymouth Argyle	42	13	4	4	48	24	2	8	11	28	49	76	73	42
13	Norwich City	42	11	6	4	53	33	6	2	13	27	46	80	79	42
14	Rotherham United	42	11	3	7	34	30	6	3	12	33	44	67	74	40
15	Swansea Town	42	13	5	3	33	17	2	4	15	18	55	51	72	39
16	Portsmouth	42	9	5	7	33	27	4	6	11	30	52	63	79	37
17	Preston North End	42	11	6	4	43	30	2	5	14	16	44	59	74	37
18	Derby County	42	10	5	6	40	29	2	7	12	21	43	61	72	36
19	Grimsby Town	42	8	6	7	34	26	3	7	11	21	40	55	66	35
20	Charlton Athletic	42	8	4	9	33	38	5	1	15	29	56	62	94	31
21	Walsall	42	7	7	7	33	37	4	2	15	20	52	53	89	31
22	Luton Town	42	10	4	7	45	40	1	3	17	16	44	61	84	29

SEASON 1963/64

DIVISION TWO

No.	Date	Opposition	Res.	Att.	Goalscorers	Ironside R.	Jackson B.	Morgan L.	Lambert R.	Madden P.	Lancaster R.	Blain J.	Bennett A.	Kirkman A.	Houghton K.	Butler I.	Carver D.	Lyons B.	Tiler B.	Haselden J.	Casper F.	Clish C.	Morritt G.
1	24 Aug	Bury	2-4	8271	Bennett, Madden	1	2	3	4	5	6	7	8	9	10	11							
2	28	Leeds United	0-1	22517		1	2	3	4	5	6	7	8	9	10	11							
3	31	MANCHESTER CITY	1-2	11418	O.G.	1	2	3	4	5	6	7	8	9	10	11							
4	3 Sep	LEEDS UNITED	2-2	14381	Houghton(2)	1		3	4	5	6		8		10	11	2	7	9				
5	7	Swindon Town	1-3	19649	Bennett	1		3	4	5	6		8	9	10	11	2	7					
6	9	Middlesbrough	2-2	30013	Bennett, Jackson	1	6	3	4	5		7	8		10	11	2		9				
7	13	CARDIFF CITY	1-0	11568	Houghton	1	6	3	4			7	8		10	11	2		9	5			
8	17	MIDDLESBROUGH	2-1	12572	Butler, O.G.	1	6	3	4			7	8		10	11	2		9	5			
9	21	Norwich City	2-2	16465	Butler, Houghton	1	6	3	4	5		7	8		10	11	2		9				
10	28	SCUNTHORPE UNITED	2-1	8834	Butler, Tiler	1	6	3	4	5		7	8		10	11			9		2		
11	1 Oct	SOUTHAMPTON	2-3	10670	Madden, Tiler	1	6	3	4	5		7	8		10				9		2		
12	5	Portsmouth	1-2	11452	Tiler	1	6	3	4	5			8		10	11	2	7	9				
13	19	HUDDERSFIELD TOWN	3-1	8963	Bennett, Butler, Lancaster	1	6	3	2	5	4		8			11		7	9		10		
14	26	Swansea Town	2-4	9160	Butler, Houghton	1	6	3	2	5	4	7	8		10	11			9				
15	2 Nov	PLYMOUTH ARGYLE	3-1	7248	Bennett, Butler, Houghton	1	6	3	2	5	4		8		10	11		7	9				
16	9	Charlton Athletic	3-4	22759	Butler, Lancaster, Tiler	1	6	3	4	5			8		10	11	2	7	9				
17	16	GRIMSBY TOWN	1-0	7601	Bennett	1	6	3	4	5			8		10	11	2	7	9				
18	23	Preston North End	2-2	13883	Bennett, Madden	1	6	3	4	5			8		10	11	2	7	9				
19	30	LEYTON ORIENT	2-4	6526	Bennett(2)	1	6	3			5	4		9	10	11	2	7		8			
20	7 Dec	Derby County	4-1	10599	Houghton(2), Lyons(2)	1	6		4	5			8		10	11	2	7	9			3	
21	14	BURY	6-2	6769	Houghton(3), Bennett(2), O.G.	1	6		4	5			8		10	11	2	7	9			3	
22	21	Manchester City	1-6	11060	Lyons	1	6		4	5			8		10	11	2	7	9			3	
23	26	Northampton Town	3-1	15089	Bennett, Butler, Tiler	1	6		4	5			8		10	11	2	7	9			3	
24	28	NORTHAMPTON TOWN	1-0	10618	O.G.	1	6		4	5			8		10	11	2	7	9			3	
25	11 Jan	SWINDON TOWN	0-0	9369		1	6	3	4	5					10	11	2	7	9	8			
26	17	Cardiff City	1-2	8773	Houghton	1		3	4	5			8		10	11	2	7	6	9			
27	1 Feb	NORWICH CITY	4-0	7289	Bennett(2), Houghton, Lyons	1	6	3	2	5	4		8		10	11		7	9				
28	8	Scunthorpe United	3-4	7656	Butler, Lyons, Jackson	1	6	3	2	5	4		8		10	11		7	9				
29	15	PORTSMOUTH	4-2	6692	Butler(2), Houghton, Lyons		6	3	4	5					10	11	2	7	9		8		1
30	22	NEWCASTLE UNITED	2-3	8853	Tiler(2)		6	3	4	5					10	11	2	7	9		8		1
31	29	Grimsby Town	3-1	7623	Tiler(2), Lyons		6	3	4	5					10	11	2	7	9		8		1
32	7 Mar	SWANSEA TOWN	3-0	7574	Tiler(2), Lyons		6	3	4	5					10	11	2	7	9				1
33	20	CHARLTON ATHLETIC	5-0	8822	Tiler(2), Bennett, Butler, Houghton		6	3	4	5					10	11	2	7	9				1
34	27	Sunderland	0-2	56675			6	3	4	5					10	11	2	7	9				1
35	28	Huddersfield Town	3-0	10363	Tiler(2), Bennett		6	3	4	5						11	2	7	9		10		1
36	30	SUNDERLAND	2-2	21641	Casper, Lyons		6	3	4	5						11	2	7	9		10		1
37	4 Apr	PRESTON NORTH END	4-2	11803	Casper(2), Butler, Tiler		6	3	4	5					10	11	2	7	9		8		1
38	8	Newcastle United	2-5	18308	Butler, Houghton		6	3	4	5					10	11	2	7	9		8		1
39	11	Leyton Orient	2-0	7455	Butler, Houghton	1	6	3	4	5			8		10	11	2	7	9				
40	18	DERBY COUNTY	2-0	9936	Houghton, Tiler	1	6	3	4	5			8		10	11	2	7	9				
41	25	Plymouth Argyle	0-0	16716		1	6	3	4	5			8		10	11	2	7	9				
42	27	Southampton	1-6	12539	Tiler	1	6		3	5	4		8		10	11	2	7	9				
					Apps.	32	39	36	41	40	12	10	36	4	39	42	32	32	37	4	11	5	10
					Goals		2			3	2		16		18	15		9	18		3		

F.A. CUP

No.	Date	Opposition	Res.	Att.	Goalscorers	Ironside R.	Jackson B.	Morgan L.	Lambert R.	Madden P.	Lancaster R.	Blain J.	Bennett A.	Kirkman A.	Houghton K.	Butler I.	Carver D.	Lyons B.	Tiler B.	Haselden J.	Casper F.	Clish C.	Morritt G.
3R	4 Jan	Burnley	1-1	24948	Casper	1	6		4	5					10	11	2	7	9		10	3	
3Rr	7	BURNLEY	2-3	23813	Lyons(2)	1	6		4	5					10	11		7	9	2	10	3	

LEAGUE CUP

No.	Date	Opposition	Res.	Att.	Goalscorers	Ironside R.	Jackson B.	Morgan L.	Lambert R.	Madden P.	Lancaster R.	Blain J.	Bennett A.	Kirkman A.	Houghton K.	Butler I.	Carver D.	Lyons B.	Tiler B.	Haselden J.	Casper F.	Clish C.	Morritt G.
2R	25 Sep	Grimsby Town	3-1	6629	Blain, Butler, Tiler	1	6	3	4	5		7	8		10	11			9	2			
3R	4 Nov	COVENTRY CITY	4-2	7826	Houghton(2), Bennett(2)	1	6	3	4	5			8		10	11	2	7	9				
4R	27	MILLWALL	5-2	7195	Tiler(2), Bennett, Houghtn, Jackson	1	6	3	4	5			8		10	11	2	7	9				
5R	16 Dec	Stoke City	2-3	12988	Jackson, Tiler	1	6	3	4	5			8		10	11	2	7	9				

Final League Table

		Pl.	Home					Away					F.	A.	Pts
			W	D	L	F	A	W	D	L	F	A			
1	Leeds United	42	12	9	0	35	16	12	6	3	36	18	71	34	63
2	Sunderland	42	16	3	2	47	13	9	8	4	34	24	81	37	61
3	Preston North End	42	13	7	1	37	14	10	3	8	42	40	79	54	56
4	Charlton Athletic	42	11	4	6	44	30	8	6	7	32	40	76	70	48
5	Southampton	42	13	3	5	69	32	6	6	9	31	41	100	73	47
6	Manchester City	42	12	4	5	50	27	6	6	9	34	39	84	66	46
7	Rotherham United	42	14	3	4	52	26	5	4	12	38	52	90	78	45
8	Newcastle United	42	14	2	5	49	26	6	3	12	25	43	74	69	45
9	Portsmouth	42	9	7	5	46	34	7	4	10	33	36	79	70	43
10	Middlesbrough	42	14	4	3	47	16	1	7	13	20	36	67	52	41
11	Northampton Town	42	10	2	9	35	31	6	7	8	23	29	58	60	41
12	Huddersfield Town	42	11	4	6	31	25	4	6	11	26	39	57	64	40
13	Derby County	42	10	6	5	34	27	4	5	12	22	40	56	67	39
14	Swindon Town	42	11	5	5	39	24	3	5	13	18	45	57	69	38
15	Cardiff City	42	10	7	4	31	27	4	3	14	25	54	56	81	38
16	Leyton Orient	42	8	6	7	32	32	5	4	12	22	40	54	72	36
17	Norwich City	42	9	7	5	43	30	2	6	13	21	50	64	80	35
18	Bury	42	8	5	8	35	36	5	4	12	22	37	57	73	35
19	Swansea Town	42	11	6	4	44	26	1	5	15	19	48	63	74	33
20	Plymouth Argyle	42	6	8	7	26	32	2	8	11	19	35	45	67	32
21	Grimsby Town	42	6	7	8	28	34	3	7	11	19	41	47	75	32
22	Scunthorpe United	42	8	8	5	30	25	2	2	17	22	57	52	82	30

1963-64: (Back): Carver, Morritt, Ironside, Lambert, Jackson, Madden.
(Middle): Purshouse (Dir.), Wilcockson, Tiler, Haselden, Houghton, Lancaster, Williams (Man.)
(Front): Blain, Lyons, Ashe, McCole, Kirkamn, Casper.

1964-65: (Back): Carver, Lancaster, Ironside, Morritt, Bennett, Madden, Haselden.
(Middle): Houghton, Rabjohn, Wilcockson, Clish, Jackson, Butler, Casper, Lambert.
(Front): Tiler, Brandon, Chappell, Chambers, Roebuck, Lyons.

SEASON 1964/65

DIVISION TWO

Player columns (left to right): Ironside R., Carver D., Clish C., Lambert R., Madden P., Jackson B., Lyons B., Bennett A., Tiler B., Casper F., Butler I., Morritt G., Houghton K., Simpson O., Lancaster R., Haselden J., Pring K., Wilcockson H., Galley J., Hellawell J., Hardy R., Williams R., Chapman R., Massey R.

No.	Date	Opposition	Res.	Att.	Goalscorers
1	22 Aug	Preston North End	0-0	18038	
2	25	SWANSEA TOWN	4-2	11298	Bennett, Butler, Casper, O.G.
3	29	NORWICH CITY	4-0	9659	Bennett(2), Butler, O.G.
4	1 Sep	Swansea Town	3-0	11569	Bennett, Casper, Houghton
5	5	Crystal Palace	1-2	18200	Bennett
6	12	BURY	3-0	10510	Bennett, Houghton, Lyons
7	15	PORTSMOUTH	1-0	14755	Houghton
8	19	Leyton Orient	1-2	8888	Bennett
9	26	CHARLTON ATHLETIC	3-2	11808	Bennett(2), Madden
10	30	Portsmouth	0-2	11192	
11	3 Oct	Manchester City	1-2	15211	
12	6	CARDIFF CITY	3-1	12601	Houghton(3)
13	10	Ipswich Town	4-4	13756	Tiler(2), Bennett, Lyons
14	17	PLYMOUTH ARGYLE	4-2	11104	Bennett, Butler, Casper, Tiler
15	24	Bolton Wanderers	0-2	14173	
16	31	MIDDLESBROUGH	2-3	10552	Butler, Lyons
17	7 Nov	Newcastle United	1-3	32870	Butler
18	14	NORTHAMPTON TOWN	1-1	11273	Butler
19	21	Southampton	1-6	17035	Casper
20	28	HUDDERSFIELD TOWN	2-3	9116	Casper, Houghton
21	5 Dec	Coventry City	5-3	20058	Galley(3), Bennett, Butler
22	12	PRESTON NORTH END	2-2	9579	Galley, Houghton
23	19	Norwich City	0-3	14986	
24	28	DERBY COUNTY	1-1	8903	Galley
25	2 Jan	CRYSTAL PALACE	1-0	9657	Galley
26	6 Feb	Charlton Athletic	1-1	8447	Lyons
27	13	MANCHESTER CITY	0-0	10917	
28	20	IPSWICH TOWN	2-2	7333	Bennett(2)
29	27	Plymouth Argyle	1-1	12227	Bennett
30	6 Mar	COVENTRY CITY	0-2	8063	
31	13	Middlesbrough	5-3	10972	Bennett(3), Hardy, Tiler
32	20	NEWCASTLE UNITED	1-1	9992	Bennett
33	24	Derby County	2-2	11737	Bennett, Galley
34	27	Northampton Town	0-1	19488	
35	3 Apr	SOUTHAMPTON	1-3	7665	Bennett
36	6	LEYTON ORIENT	3-0	6795	Hellawell, Pring, Tiler
37	10	Huddersfield Town	0-1	12462	
38	16	Swindon Town	2-3	17480	Bennett(2)
39	17	BOLTON WANDERERS	0-0	7685	
40	19	SWINDON TOWN	1-0	5552	Casper
41	24	Cardiff City	2-3	9794	Massey(2)
42	27	Bury	1-0	4330	Hellawell

Apps.: Ironside 4, Carver 33, Clish 38, Lambert 38, Madden 38, Jackson 17, Lyons 36, Bennett 37, Tiler 30, Casper 32, Butler 22, Morritt 36, Houghton 20, Simpson 1, Lancaster 3, Haselden 4, Pring 14, Wilcockson 11, Galley 15, Hellawell 9, Hardy 17, Williams 3, Chapman 2, Massey 2

Goals: Lyons 1, Bennett 4, Tiler 24, Casper 5, Butler 6, Houghton 7, Galley 8, Pring 1, Hellawell 1, Hardy 7, Massey 2

F.A. CUP

Rd	Date	Opposition	Res.	Att.	Goalscorers
3R	9 Jan	LINCOLN CITY	5-1	12456	Bennett(2), Galley(2), Madden
4R	30	Wolverhampton Wanderers	2-2	29736	Bennett, Pring
4Rr	2 Feb	WOLVERHAMPTON WAND.	0-3	25104	

LEAGUE CUP

Rd	Date	Opposition	Res.	Att.	Goalscorers
2R	23 Sep	ROCHDALE	2-0	8834	Casper, Tiler
3R	14 Oct	SWANSEA TOWN	2-2	8993	Casper(2)
3Rr	28	Swansea Town	0-2	7566	

Final League Table

		Pl.	Home					Away					F.	A.	Pts
			W	D	L	F	A	W	D	L	F	A			
1	Newcastle United	42	16	4	1	50	16	8	5	8	31	29	81	45	57
2	Northampton Town	42	14	7	0	37	16	6	9	6	29	34	66	50	56
3	Bolton Wanderers	42	13	6	2	46	17	7	4	10	34	41	80	58	50
4	Southampton	42	12	6	3	49	25	5	8	8	34	38	83	63	48
5	Ipswich Town	42	11	7	3	48	30	4	10	7	26	37	74	67	47
6	Norwich City	42	15	4	2	47	21	5	3	13	14	36	61	57	47
7	Crystal Palace	42	11	6	4	37	24	5	7	9	18	27	55	51	45
8	Huddersfield Town	42	12	4	5	28	15	5	6	10	25	36	53	51	44
9	Derby County	42	11	5	5	48	35	5	6	10	36	44	84	79	43
10	Coventry City	42	10	5	6	41	29	7	4	10	31	41	72	70	43
11	Manchester City	42	12	3	6	40	24	4	6	11	23	38	63	62	41
12	Preston North End	42	11	8	2	46	29	3	5	13	30	52	76	81	41
13	Cardiff City	42	10	7	4	43	25	3	7	11	21	32	64	57	40
14	Rotherham United	42	10	7	4	39	25	4	5	12	31	44	70	69	40
15	Plymouth Argyle	42	10	7	4	36	28	6	1	14	27	51	63	79	40
16	Bury	42	9	4	8	36	30	5	6	10	24	36	60	66	38
17	Middlesbrough	42	8	5	8	40	31	5	4	12	30	45	70	76	35
18	Charlton Athletic	42	8	5	8	35	34	5	4	12	29	41	64	75	35
19	Leyton Orient	42	10	4	7	36	34	2	7	12	14	38	50	72	35
20	Portsmouth	42	11	4	6	36	22	1	6	14	20	55	56	77	34
21	Swindon Town	42	12	3	6	43	30	2	2	17	20	51	63	81	33
22	Swansea Town	42	9	7	5	40	29	2	3	16	22	55	62	84	32

SEASON 1965/66
DIVISION TWO

No.	Date	Opposition	Res.	Att.	Goalscorers	Morritt G.	Wilcockson H.	Clish C.	Hardy R.	Madden P.	Tiler B.	Lyons B.	Chappell L.	Galley J.	Williams R.	Pring K.	Jones R.	Haselden J.	Casper F.	Hellawell J.	Rabjohn C.	Massey R.	Simpson O.	Chambers D.	Allen D.	Harrity M.	Shepherd J.	Bennett J.
1	21 Aug	Bristol City	1-2	16801	Williams	1	2	3	4	5	6	7	8	9	10	11												
2	24	LEYTON ORIENT	2-1	7641	Chappell, Madden	1	2	3	4	5	6	7	8	9	10	11												
3	28	COVENTRY CITY	1-1	11134	Chappell	1	2	3	4	5	6	7	8	9	10	11												
4	30	Leyton Orient	4-1	7382	Galley(2), Chappell, Lyons	1	2	3	4	5	6	7	8	9	10	11												
5	3 Sep	Carlisle United	0-1	12551		1	2	3	4	5	6	7	8	9	10	11												
6	7	WOLVERHAMPTON WANDS.	4-3	11653	Williams(2), Lyons, Pring	1	2	3	4	5	6	7	8	9	10	11												
7	11	CARDIFF CITY	6-4	9211	Williams(2), Galley(2), Lyons	1	2	3	4	5	6	7	8	9	10	11												
8	13	Wolverhampton Wanderers	1-4	20012	Pring		2	3	4	5	6	7	8	9	10	11	1											
9	18	Derby County	3-1	11166	Galley(2), Williams	1	2	3	4		6	7	8	9	10	11		5										
10	25	SOUTHAMPTON	1-0	13159	Williams	1	2	3	4	5	6	7		9	10	11			8									
11	2 Oct	Bury	1-6	7015	Casper		2	3	4	5	6	7		9	10	11	1		8									
12	9	Middlesbrough	0-4	13152			2	3	4	5	6	7	12	9	10	11*	1		8									
13	16	HUDDERSFIELD TOWN	0-0	16939		1	2	3	4	5	6	7	11	9					8									
14	23	Crystal Palace	2-2	15833	Clish, Lyons	1	2	3	4	5	6	7	11	9					8									
15	30	PRESTON NORTH END	6-3	8634	Chappll(2), Glley(2), Csper, Wilcocksn	1	2	3	4	5	6	7	8	9	10				8									
16	6 Nov	Charlton Athletic	2-2	10098	Madden, Pring		2	3	4	5	6	7	8	9		11	1				10							
17	13	PLYMOUTH ARGYLE	2-0	9367	Chappell, Hellawell		2	3	4	5	6	7	8	9		11	1			12	10*							
18	20	Portsmouth	1-1	8657	Chappell		2	3	10	5	6	7	8	9		11	1				4							
19	27	BOLTON WANDERERS	2-1	9785	Galley(2)		2	3	4	5	6	7	8	9	10*	11	1				4							
20	4 Dec	Ipswich Town	0-0	10279			2	3	4	5	6	7	8	9	10*	11	1				12							
21	11	BIRMINGHAM CITY	3-4	10684	Chappell(2), Hardy		2	3	10*	5	6	7	8	9		11	1				4	12						
22	18	Huddersfield Town	0-4	17855			2*	3	10	5	6	7	8	9		11	1		12		4							
23	1 Jan	MIDDLESBROUGH	4-1	10922	Chappell(2), Rabjohn, O.G.		2	3	10	5	6	7	8	9		11	1				4							
24	8	Plymouth Argyle	2-5	12202	Chappell, Galley		2	3	10	5	6*	7	8	9		11	1		12		4							
25	12	Manchester City	1-3	25526	Galley		2	3	10	5		7	8	9		11	1				4							
26	15	CRYSTAL PALACE	3-0	8382	Chappell, Galley, O.G.		2	3		5	6	7	8	9		11	1		10		4							
27	29	BRISTOL CITY	1-2	10667	O.G.		2	3			6	7	8	9		11	1	5	10		4							
28	5 Feb	Coventry City	2-2	24932	Galley, Lyons		2	3			6	7	8	9		11	1	5	10		4							
29	26	Cardiff City	0-0	9184			2	3			6	7	8	9		11	1	5	10		4							
30	12 Mar	DERBY COUNTY	3-0	10856	Casper, Chappell, Galley		2	3			6	7	8	9		11*	1	5	10		4			12				
31	19	Southampton	1-1	15766	Casper		2	3			6	7	8	9			1	5	10		4			11				
32	25	BURY	2-1	11519	Clish, Lyons		2	3			6	7	8	9			1	5	10		4			11				
33	9 Apr	Preston North End	1-1	10733	Galley		2	3			6	7	8	9			1	5	10		4			11				
34	11	Norwich City	2-1	14707	Casper, Galley		2	3			6	7	8	9			1	5	10		4			11				
35	12	NORWICH CITY	2-1	11202	Casper(2)		2	3	12		6	7	8	9			1	5	10		4			11*				
36	16	PORTSMOUTH	3-3	8567	Chappell(2), Casper		2	3			6	7	8	9		11	1	5	10		4							
37	25	Bolton Wanderers	3-1	10622	Chambers, Lyons, Rabjohn		2	3	12		6	7	8			11*	1	5	10		4			9				
38	30	IPSWICH TOWN	0-0	9431			2	3			6	7	8			11	1	5	10					9				
39	4 May	MANCHESTER CITY	0-1	11685			2	3			6	7	8			11	1	5			4			10				
40	7	Birmingham City	0-3	11469			2				6	7	8	9			1	5	10					3	11	4*	12	
41	9	CHARLTON ATHLETIC	0-0	5585			2	3			6	7	8	9			1	5	10				4	11				
42	12	CARLISLE UNITED	3-3	4990	Casper, Galley, Wilcockson		2	3			6	7	8	9			1	5	10				4					11
					Apps.	12	42	41	25	25	41	42	39	40	16	31	30	18	25		20		2	9	1	1	1	1
					Subs.								2						1	1	1	1		1			1	
					Goals		2	2	1	2		7	16	18	8	3			9	1	2			1				

F.A. CUP

No.	Date	Opposition	Res.	Att.	Goalscorers	Morritt G.	Wilcockson H.	Clish C.	Hardy R.	Madden P.	Tiler B.	Lyons B.	Chappell L.	Galley J.	Williams R.	Pring K.	Jones R.	Haselden J.	Casper F.	Hellawell J.	Rabjohn C.
3R	22 Jan	SOUTHEND UNITED	3-2	10644	Rabjohn, Wilcockson, O.G.		2	3		5	6	7	8	9		11	1		10		4
4R	12 Feb	Manchester United	0-0	54263			2	3			6	7	8	9		11	1	5	10		4
4Rr	15	MANCHESTER UNITED	0-1				2	3			6	7	8	9		11	1	5	10		4

LEAGUE CUP

No.	Date	Opposition	Res.	Att.	Goalscorers	Morritt G.	Wilcockson H.	Clish C.	Hardy R.	Madden P.	Tiler B.	Lyons B.	Chappell L.	Galley J.	Williams R.	Pring K.	Jones R.	Haselden J.	Casper F.
2R	22 Sep	WATFORD	2-0	9051	Galley, Pring	1	2	3	4		6	7	8	9	10	11		5	
3R	13 Oct	Shrewsbury Town	5-2	8440	Galley(2), Casper, Chappell, Hardy		2	3	4	5	6	7	11	9	10		1		8
4R	3 Nov	WEST HAM UNITED	1-2	13902	Galley		2	3		5	6	7	8	9	10	11	1		4

Final League Table

		Pl.	Home					Away					F.	A.	Pts
			W	D	L	F	A	W	D	L	F	A			
1	Manchester City	42	14	7	0	40	14	8	8	5	36	30	76	44	59
2	Southampton	42	13	4	4	51	25	9	6	6	34	31	85	56	54
3	Coventry City	42	14	5	2	54	31	6	8	7	19	22	73	53	53
4	Huddersfield Town	42	12	7	2	35	12	7	6	8	27	24	62	36	51
5	Bristol City	42	9	10	2	27	15	8	7	6	36	33	63	48	51
6	Wolverhampton W.	42	15	4	2	52	18	5	6	10	35	43	87	61	50
7	Rotherham United	42	12	6	3	48	29	4	8	9	27	45	75	74	46
8	Derby County	42	13	2	6	48	31	3	9	9	23	37	71	68	43
9	Bolton Wanderers	42	12	2	7	43	25	4	7	10	19	34	62	59	41
10	Birmingham City	42	10	6	5	41	29	6	3	12	29	46	70	75	41
11	Crystal Palace	42	11	7	3	29	16	3	6	12	18	36	47	52	41
12	Portsmouth	42	13	4	4	47	26	3	4	14	27	52	74	78	40
13	Norwich City	42	8	7	6	33	24	4	8	9	19	25	52	52	39
14	Carlisle United	42	16	2	3	43	19	1	3	17	17	44	60	63	39
15	Ipswich Town	42	12	6	3	38	23	3	3	15	20	43	58	66	39
16	Charlton Athletic	42	10	6	5	39	29	2	8	11	22	41	61	70	38
17	Preston North End	42	7	10	4	37	23	4	5	12	25	47	62	70	37
18	Plymouth Argyle	42	7	8	6	37	26	5	5	11	17	37	54	63	37
19	Bury	42	12	5	4	45	25	2	2	17	17	51	62	76	35
20	Cardiff City	42	10	3	8	37	35	2	7	12	34	56	71	91	34
21	Middlesbrough	42	8	8	5	36	28	2	5	14	22	58	58	86	33
22	Leyton Orient	42	3	9	9	19	36	2	4	15	19	44	38	80	23

1965-66: (Back): Carver, Madden. Morritt, Clish. (Middle): Lambert, Casper, Galley, Tiler, Haselden, Wilcockson. (Front): Lyons, Hardy, Williams, Chappell, Pring.

1966-67: (Back): Hart, Bennett, Bradd, Harrity, Fallon, Shepherd, Hall.
(Centre): Clish, Allen, Swift, Hill, Jones, Surman, Simpson, Haselden, Hudson.
(Front): Chambers, Galley, Wilcockson, Lyons, Tiler, Chappell, Rabjohn, Casper, Pring.

SEASON 1966/67
DIVISION TWO

No.	Date	Opposition	Res.	Att.	Goalscorers	Jones R.	Wilcockson H.	Clish C.	Rabjohn C.	Haselden J.	Tiler B.	Lyons B.	Williams R.	Galley J.	Casper F.	Chappell L.	Hill A.	Simpson O.	Harrity M.	Pring K.	Chambers D.	Massey R.	Haddock A.	Shepherd J.	Surman L.	Bentley D.
1	20 Aug	MILLWALL	3-1	10031	Galley(2), Clish	1	2	3	4	5	6	7	8	9	10	11										
2	24	Bolton Wanderers	2-2	14214	Chappell, Galley	1	2	3	4	5	6	7	8	9	10	11										
3	27	Northampton Town	1-3	13954	Galley	1	2	3	4	5	6	7	8	9	10	11										
4	30	BOLTON WANDERERS	0-1	11567		1	2	3	4	5	6	7	8	9	10	11										
5	3 Sep	PLYMOUTH ARGYLE	4-2	9084	Lyons(2), Chappell, Galley		2	3	4	5	6	7	8	9	10	11	1									
6	6	Bury	2-5	5148	Chappell, Williams		2	3	4	5	6	7	8	9	10	11	1									
7	10	Hull City	0-1	25209			2	3	4	5	6	7	8	9	10	11	1									
8	17	PORTSMOUTH	0-1	9593			2	3	4	5	6	7	8	9	10	11	1									
9	24	Birmingham City	3-2	19515	Casper, Chappell, Lyons		2		4	5	6	7	8	9	10	11	1	3								
10	1 Oct	NORWICH CITY	2-1	9222	Casper(2)		2	3	4	5	6	7	8	9	10	11	1									
11	8	Charlton Athletic	0-2	11121			2	3	4	5	6	7	8	9	10	11	1									
12	15	DERBY COUNTY	0-0	10989			2	3	4	5	6	7	8	9	10*	11	1				12					
13	22	Crystal Palace	1-1	19486	Williams			3	4	5	6	7	8	9		10	1		2	11						
14	29	HUDDERSFIELD TOWN	4-2	13848	Chappell(2), Galley, Pring			3	4	5	6	7	8	9		10	1		2	11						
15	4 Nov	Cardiff City	0-0	6056				3	4	5	6	7	8	9		10	1		2	11						
16	12	WOLVERHAMPTON WANDS.	2-2	12373	Chappell, Galley			3	4	5	6		8	9		10	1		2	11						
17	19	Ipswich Town	2-3	12498	Chappell, O.G.			3	4	5			8	9		10	1		2	11	7					
18	26	BRISTOL CITY	3-3	8534	Chappell(2), O.G.		2	3	4	5			8	9	7	10	1			11	7					
19	3 Dec	Carlisle United	3-2	10766	Galley(3)		2	3		5	6		8	9	7	10	1		4	11						
20	10	BLACKBURN ROVERS	2-1	9343	Chappell, Williams		2	3	4	5*	6		8	9	7	10	1		12	11						
21	17	Millwall	0-2	11788			2	3	4	5	6		8	9	7	10	1			11						
22	26	Coventry City	2-4	31348	Massey, Williams		2	3	4	5	6		8	9		10	1		11			7				
23	27	COVENTRY CITY	1-1	13301	Massey	1	2	3	4	5	6		8	9		10			11			7				
24	31	NORTHAMPTON TOWN	1-2	9013	Chappell	1	2	3	4	5	6		8	9		10				11		7				
25	7 Jan	Plymouth Argyle	0-1	9981			2	3	4	5	6		8	9		10	1			11		7				
26	14	HULL CITY	1-1	17237	Galley		2	3	4	5	6			9	8	10	1			11		7				
27	21	Portsmouth	2-3	15253	Chappell, Galley		2	3	4	5	6			9	8	10	1			11		7				
28	4 Feb	BIRMINGHAM CITY	3-2	10440	Chambers(2), Williams		2	3	4	5	6*		8	9		10	1		12	11	7					
29	11	Norwich City	0-1	14167			2	3	7	5	6		8	9		10	1		4	11						
30	25	CHARLTON ATHLETIC	2-0	8078	Chappell, Pring		2	3	7	5	6			9		10	1		4	11	8					
31	4 Mar	Huddersfield Town	0-3	19859			2	3	8	5	6			9		10	1		4	11			7			
32	18	CRYSTAL PALACE	0-1	7916			2	3	8	5	6			9		10	1			11			7			
33	25	Derby County	0-2	14161			2	3	4	5	6			9	8	10	1			11			7			
34	27	PRESTON NORTH END	2-1	8243	Casper, Galley		2	3	4	5	6			9	8	10	1			11			7			
35	28	Preston North End	1-1	13797	Chappell		2	3	4	5	6			9	8	10	1			11			7			
36	1 Apr	CARDIFF CITY	4-1	8585	Casper, Clish, Massey, O.G.		2	3	4		6			9	8	10	1	11	5			7				
37	8	Wolverhampton Wanderers	0-2	32338			2	3	4					9	8	10	1	11	5		7					
38	15	IPSWICH TOWN	0-2	8477			2	3	4	5	6				8	10	1			7	11	9				
39	22	Bristol City	2-1	16888	Galley, Rabjohn		2	3	4	5	6			9		10	1			11		9		7		
40	29	CARLISLE UNITED	2-3	7641	Massey, Rabjohn		2	3	4	5	6				8	10				11		9		7		
41	6 May	Blackburn Rovers	1-1	8567	Chappell		2		4	5	6			9		10	1	3	11		8			7		
42	13	BURY	3-0	5362	Casper, Chappell, Galley		2		4	5	6			9	8	10	1	3	11*					7		12
			Apps.			6	37	39	41	40	42	15	28	40	25	41	35	3	17	24	7	13	4	4	1	
			Subs.															2			1						1
			Goals				1	3			3	5		15	6	17				2		4				

F.A. CUP

	Date	Opposition	Res.	Att.	Goalscorers	Wilcockson H.	Clish C.	Rabjohn C.	Haselden J.	Tiler B.	Williams R.	Galley J.	Chappell L.	Hill A.	Harrity M.	Pring K.	Chambers D.
3R	28 Jan	Nuneaton	1-1	17000	Chambers	2	3	4	5	6	8	9	10	1		11	7
3Rr	31	NUNEATON	1-0	22930	Wilcockson	2	3	4	5	6	8	9	10	1		11	7
4R	18 Feb	BIRMINGHAM CITY	0-0	15723		2	3	7	5	6	8	9	10	1	4	11	
4Rr	21	Birmingham City	1-2	35482	Galley	2	3	7	5	6		9	10	1	4	11	8

LEAGUE CUP

	Date	Opposition	Res.	Att.	Goalscorers	Wilcockson H.	Clish C.	Rabjohn C.	Haselden J.	Tiler B.	Lyons B.	Williams R.	Galley J.	Casper F.	Chappell L.	Hill A.	Chambers D.
2R	14 Sep	Sheffield Wednesday	1-0	20204	Casper	2	3	4	5	6	7	8	9	10	11	1	
3R	5 Oct	Northampton Town	1-2	5631	Lyons	2	3	4	5	6	7	8*	9	10	11	1	12

Final League Table

		Pl.	Home					Away					F.	A.	Pts
			W	D	L	F	A	W	D	L	F	A			
1	Coventry City	42	17	3	1	46	16	6	10	5	28	27	74	43	59
2	Wolverhampton W.	42	15	4	2	53	20	10	4	7	35	28	88	48	58
3	Carlisle United	42	15	3	3	42	16	8	3	10	29	38	71	54	52
4	Blackburn Rovers	42	13	6	2	33	11	6	7	8	23	35	56	46	51
5	Ipswich Town	42	11	8	2	45	25	6	8	7	25	29	70	54	50
6	Huddersfield Town	42	14	3	4	36	17	6	6	9	22	29	58	46	49
7	Crystal Palace	42	14	3	4	42	23	5	6	10	19	32	61	55	48
8	Millwall	42	14	5	2	33	17	4	4	13	16	41	49	58	45
9	Bolton Wanderers	42	10	7	4	36	19	4	7	10	28	39	64	58	42
10	Birmingham City	42	11	5	5	42	23	5	3	13	28	43	70	66	40
11	Norwich City	42	10	7	4	31	21	3	7	11	18	34	49	55	40
12	Hull City	42	11	5	5	46	25	5	2	14	31	47	77	72	39
13	Preston North End	42	14	3	4	44	23	2	4	15	21	44	65	67	39
14	Portsmouth	42	7	5	9	34	37	6	8	7	25	33	59	70	39
15	Bristol City	42	10	8	3	38	22	2	6	13	18	40	56	62	38
16	Plymouth Argyle	42	12	4	5	42	21	2	5	14	17	37	59	58	37
17	Derby County	42	8	6	7	40	32	4	6	11	28	40	68	72	36
18	Rotherham United	42	10	5	6	39	28	3	5	13	22	42	61	70	36
19	Charlton Athletic	42	11	4	6	34	16	2	5	14	15	37	49	53	35
20	Cardiff City	42	9	7	5	43	28	3	2	16	18	59	61	87	33
21	Northampton Town	42	8	6	7	28	33	4	0	17	19	51	47	84	30
22	Bury	42	9	3	9	31	30	2	3	16	18	53	49	83	28

SEASON 1967/68
DIVISION TWO

No.	Date	Opposition	Res.	Att.	Goalscorers	Hill A.	Wilcockson H.	Clish C.	Rabjohn C.	Thompson W.	Haselden J.	Chambers D.	Chappell L.	Tiler B.	Shepherd J.	Pring K.	Massey R.	Bradd L.	Sheffield L.	Harrity M.	Galley J.	Bentley D.	Surman L.	Swift T.	Hodgson W.	Burgin A.	Crickmore C.	Hague N.	Quinn J.	Wilson A.	Parker G.	Storrie J.	Watson D.	Watson G.	Leigh D.	Downes S.	Tunks R.
1	19 Aug	CRYSTAL PALACE	0-3	7661		1	2	3	4	5	6	7	8	9	10	11																					
2	26	Aston Villa	1-3	13663	Chappell	1	2	3	8	5	4		7	6		11			10	9																	
3	28	DERBY COUNTY	1-3	10775	Sheffield	1	2	3	8	5	4		7	6		11			10	9																	
4	2 Sep	QUEENS PARK RANGERS	1-3	7811	Tiler	1	2		7	5	4	12	8	6		11			10*	9	3																
5	5	Carlisle United	1-4	9496	Galley	1	2			5	4		10	6		7					9	3	8	11													
6	9	Plymouth Argyle	1-0	9323	Chambers	1	2			5	4	7	10	6							9	3	8	11													
7	16	CARDIFF CITY	3-2	5541	Chappell, Galley, Sheffield	1	2			5	4	7	10	6							9	3	8	11													
8	23	Portsmouth	1-1	19734	Sheffield	1	2			5	4	7	10	6							9	3	8														
9	26	Derby County	1-4	28251	Sheffield	1	2			5	4	7	10	6*		11					9	3	8														
10	30	NORWICH CITY	1-3	5987	Sheffield	1	2		8		4	7		6							9	3	10		5	11											
11	7 Oct	BLACKPOOL	1-2	6725	Galley	1	2		7	5		12	8	6						3*	10					11	4										
12	14	Huddersfield Town	0-2	11413		1	2		7	5			8	6						3	10					11	4										
13	21	BOLTON WANDERERS	2-2	6935	Galley(2)	1	2		4			5	8	6		7					9		10			11	3										
14	28	Birmingham City	1-4	21478	Galley	1	2		4			5	8	6		7					9		10			11	3										
15	4 Nov	BRISTOL CITY	1-0	5706	Chappell	1	2		4*			5							12	6		7	9			8				10	3	11					
16	11	Middlesbrough	1-1	16519	Sheffield	1	2		4			5							6			7	9			8				10	3	11					
17	18	IPSWICH TOWN	1-3	6068	Crickmore	1	2		4			5							6			7	9			8				10	3	11					
18	25	Millwall	0-0	13595		1	2		4			5	8	6							9								10	3	11	7					
19	2 Dec	HULL CITY	1-3	15258	Chappell	1	2		4			5	8	6							9							3	11	7	10						
20	9	Blackburn Rovers	1-3	10028	Bentley	1							8	6	10			9				2		11	5				3	4	7						
21	16	Crystal Palace	0-1	13541		1							8	6	9			2				11		5			12	3*	10	7	4						
22	23	ASTON VILLA	0-2	9946		1		12					8	3	9			2				10		5			11*		6	7	4						
23	26	Preston North End	2-2	17952	Shepherd, Wilson	1			4				8	3	9			2				10		5			11		6	7							
24	30	PRESTON NORTH END	1-0	12394	Clish	1		3					8	6	10			2				11		5				4	7	9							
25	6 Jan	Queens Park Rangers	0-6	16782		1		3					10	6	7			2				5					4	12	8*	9	11						
26	20	Cardiff City	2-2	8748	Bentley, Quinn	1							10	3	8			2				11		5				4	7		9	6					
27	3 Feb	PORTSMOUTH	1-1	11888	Storrie	1							8	6	10							11		2				3	4	7		9	5				
28	10	Norwich City	2-2	15258	Shepherd, Storrie	1							8	6	10							11		2				3	4	7		9	5				
29	24	Blackpool	1-1	13689	Tiler	1							6	10								11		2				3	4	7*		9	5	8	12		
30	2 Mar	HUDDERSFIELD TOWN	1-0	13672	Storrie	1							6									11		2				3	4			9	5	7	8	10	
31	16	Bolton Wanderers	2-0	8506	Dawnes, G.Watson	1						8	6									11		2				3	4			9	5	7*	12	10	
32	19	PLYMOUTH ARGYLE	1-0	16350	Tiler	1						8	6	7*								11		2				3	4			9	5	8	10		
33	23	BIRMINGHAM CITY	1-1	15711	Hague	1						6	8									11		2				3	4	12		9	5	7*	10	1	
34	29	Bristol City	1-0	19783	Downes	1						8	7	6								11		2				3	4			10	5		9		
35	6 Apr	MIDDLESBROUGH	0-1	15082		1						8	6				12					11		2				3	4			10	5	9*	7		
36	12	CHarlton Athletic	1-4	15082	Bentley	1						8	6									11		2				3	4			10	5	7	9		
37	13	Ipswich Town	0-2	22152		1						8	7	6			12					11		2*				3	4			10	5	9			
38	16	CHARLTON ATHLETIC	1-1	10684	Wilson	1								8					6*			11		2				3	4	7		10	5		12	9	
39	20	MILLWALL	2-0	12093	Downes, Wilson	1						6	8									11		2				3	4			10	5		9		
40	25	Hull City	1-2	20591	Downes	1							6*	8								11		2				3	4	7		10	5	7	12	9	
41	4 May	BLACKBURN ROVERS	1-0	8325	Bentley	1							6	8*								11		2				3	4	7		10	5		9		
42	11	CARLISLE UNITED	1-2	6646	Hague	1							6	9								11		2				3				8	5	10	4		
					Apps.	41	19	5	15	8	27	7	26	40	17	12		3	19	17	13	25		24	9	9	7	20	23	12	3	19	18	6	5	11	1
					Subs.			1				2	1								2						1	1		2				3		1		
					Goals						1	4	3	2					6			6	4					1	2	1	3		3		1		4	

F.A. CUP

No.	Date	Opposition	Res.	Att.	Goalscorers	Hill A.	Chappell L.	Tiler B.	Shepherd J.	Bentley D.	Swift T.	Hague N.	Quinn J.	Wilson A.	Storrie J.	Watson D.	Downes S.	Tunks R.
3R	27 Jan	WOLVERHAMPTON	1-0	14841	Storrie	1	8	6	10	11	5	3	4	7	9	2		
4R	17 Feb	Aston Villa	1-0	33481	Storrie	1	8*	6	10	11	2	3	4	7	9	5		12
5R	9 Mar	LEICESTER CITY	1-1	23500	Downes	1	6	8		11	2	3	4	7	9	5		10
5Rr	13	Leicester City	0-2	41856		1	6	8	7	11	2	3	4		9	5		10

LEAGUE CUP

No.	Date	Opposition	Res.	Att.	Goalscorers	Hill A.	Wilcockson H.	Clish C.	Rabjohn C.	Thompson W.	Haselden J.	Chambers D.	Chappell L.	Tiler B.	Shepherd J.	Pring K.	Massey R.	Sheffield L.	Harrity M.	Galley J.	Bentley D.	Surman L.	Swift T.	Tunks R.
1R	23 Aug	Notts County	1-0	4492	Bradd	1	2	3	8	5	4		10	6		11	7	9						
2R	13 Sep	Norwich City	1-1	12935	Galley	1	2			5	4	7	10	6				9	3	8	11			
2Rr	19	NORWICH CITY	0-2	7054			2			5	4	7	10	6			12	9	3	8	11*	1		

Final League Table

		Pl	Home					Away					F.	A.	Pts
			W	D	L	F	A	W	D	L	F	A			
1	Ipswich Town	42	12	7	2	45	20	10	8	3	34	24	79	44	59
2	Queen's Park Rgs.	42	18	2	1	45	9	7	6	8	22	27	67	36	58
3	Blackpool	42	12	6	3	33	16	12	4	5	38	27	71	43	58
4	Birmingham City	42	12	6	3	54	21	7	8	6	29	30	83	51	52
5	Portsmouth	42	13	6	2	43	18	5	7	9	25	37	68	55	49
6	Middlesbrough	42	10	7	4	39	19	7	5	9	21	35	60	54	46
7	Millwall	42	9	10	2	35	16	5	7	9	27	34	62	50	45
8	Blackburn Rovers	42	13	5	3	34	16	3	6	12	22	33	56	49	43
9	Norwich City	42	12	4	5	40	30	4	7	10	20	35	60	65	43
10	Carlisle United	42	9	9	3	38	22	5	4	12	20	30	58	52	41
11	Crystal Palace	42	11	4	6	34	19	3	7	11	22	37	56	56	39
12	Bolton Wanderers	42	8	6	7	37	28	5	7	9	23	35	60	63	39
13	Cardiff City	42	9	6	6	35	29	4	6	11	25	37	60	66	38
14	Huddersfield Town	42	10	6	5	29	23	3	6	12	17	38	46	61	38
15	Charlton Athletic	42	10	6	5	43	25	2	7	12	20	43	63	68	37
16	Aston Villa	42	10	3	8	35	30	5	4	12	19	34	54	64	37
17	Hull City	42	6	8	7	25	23	6	5	10	33	50	58	73	37
18	Derby County	42	8	5	8	40	35	5	5	11	31	43	71	78	36
19	Bristol City	42	7	7	7	26	25	6	3	12	22	37	48	62	36
20	Preston North End	42	8	7	6	29	24	4	4	13	14	41	43	65	35
21	Rotherham United	42	7	4	10	22	32	3	7	11	20	44	42	76	31
22	Plymouth Argyle	42	5	4	12	26	36	4	5	12	12	36	38	72	27

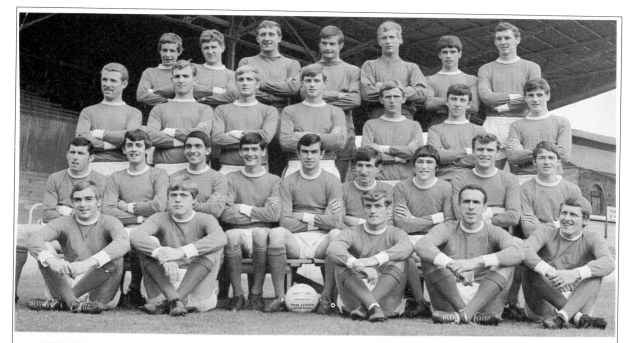

1967-68: (Back): Simms, White, Hill, Surman, Tunks, Rushby, Rabjohn. (2nd Row): Haselden, Wilcockson, Swift, Bradd, Wilson, McKernan, Hudson. (3rd row): Haddock, Shepherd, Chambers, Bentley, Tiler, Wilson, Lynn, Clish, Pring. (Front): Harrity, Hague, Chappell, Thompson, Simpson.

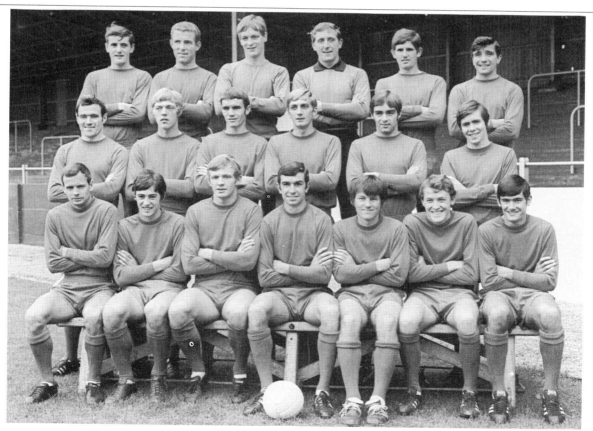

1968-69: (Back): Hudson, Haselden, Tunks, Hill, Leigh, Quinn. (Middle): Storrie, Hague, D.Watson, Swift, Harrity, Brogden. (Front): Leggatt, Downes, Gilliver, Tiler, Todd, G.Watson, Bentley.

SEASON 1968/69

DIVISION THREE

No.	Date	Opposition	Res.	Att.	Goalscorers	Hill A.	Swift T.	Harrity M.	Quinn J.	Watson D.	Tiler B.	Leggatt G.	Downes S.	Gilliver A.	Storrie J.	Bentley D.	Hague N.	Haselden J.	Leigh D.	Todd R.	Watson G.	Mealand B.	Furnell J.	Brogden L.	Marshall I.	Womble T.	Griffin W.	Mullen J.	Hudson C.
1	10 Aug	Leyton Orient	3-3	7979	Leggatt(2), Downes	1	2	3	4	5	6	7	8	9	10	11													
2	17	TRANMERE ROVERS	4-1	10285	Downes(2), Leggatt(2)	1	2		4	5	6	7	8	9*	10	11	3					12							
3	24	Luton Town	1-3	14163	Storrie	1	2		4	5	6		8		10		3				11								
4	27	GILLINGHAM	1-0	10478	Storrie	1	2		4		6	7	8	9		11	3	5			10								
5	31	BARNSLEY	0-0	14720		1	6		4	5	10	7	8*	12	9	11	3					2							
6	7 Sep	Brighton & Hove	2-2	10164	Bentley, Tiler		6		4	5	10	7	12	9	8*	11	3					2	1						
7	14	TORQUAY UNITED	1-0	9548	Leggatt		2		4	5	6	7	10*	9	8	11	3		12				1						
8	17	Oldham Athletic	0-0	4526			2		4	5	6	7	12	9	8	11*	3				10		1						
9	21	Mansfield Town	1-0	10033	Downes		2		4	5	6			9	8		3		10				1	7		11			
10	28	SOUTHPORT	3-1	10540	Hague, Quinn, Watson		6		4	5	10		8	9		11	3					2	1	7					
11	5 Oct	Northampton Town	0-1	8602			6		4	5	10			9	8		3		12			2	1	7	11*				
12	9	Gillingham	0-2	5525			6		4	5	10			9	8		3		12			2	1	7	11*				
13	12	BRISTOL ROVERS	3-2	9693	Brogden, Downes, Storrie		6		4	5	10			9	8		3		12			2	1	7	11*				
14	19	Shrewsbury Town	0-1	6636			6		4	5	10			9	8*	11	3					2	1	7			12		
15	26	BOURNEMOUTH	1-1	8639	Storrie		2*		4	5	6		11	9	8	10	3						1	7	12				
16	2 Nov	Walsall	0-0	4857			6		4	5	8	11		9	10		3					2	1	7					
17	4	Stockport County	1-3	6645	Brogden		2		4	5	6			9		11	3		10			2	1	7		8			
18	9	HARTLEPOOL	1-1	8657	Womble		2		4	5	6			9		11	3		10			2	1	7		8			
19	23	WATFORD	0-2	9013					4*	5	6	12		9		11	3		10			2	1	7		8			
20	30	Crewe Alexandra	0-1	4635						5	6			9	10	11	3		12	4		2	1	7*		8			
21	13 Dec	Bristol Rovers	1-1	5611	Brogden		6		4	5	10		8	9		11	3					2	1	7					
22	21	SHREWSBURY TOWN	1-0	6908	Swift		6		4	5	10*		8	9	12	11	3					2	1	7					
23	28	Bournemouth	0-1	8788			6			5			8	9		11	3			4		2	1	7					
24	11 Jan	WALSALL	0-1	7199			6		4	5				9	8*	11	12		3		10	2	1	7					
25	18	Hartlepool	3-0	3677	Brogden, Gilliver, Storrie		6		4	5				9	8	11			3			2	1	7				10	
26	21	NORTHAMPTON TOWN	0-1	8177			6		4	5				9	8	11			3			2	1	7				10	
27	25	STOCKPORT COUNTY	4-1	8571	D.Watson(2), Griffin, Storrie		6		4	5				9	8	11			3			2	1	7				10	
28	1 Feb	PLYMOUTH ARGYLE	0-1	9080			6		4	5		12		9	8	11*			3			2	1	7				10	
29	8	Watford	1-5	10678	Storrie		6		4	5				9	8	11			3			2	1	7				10	
30	22	Swindon Town	0-1	23500			6		4	5				9	8	12			3			2	1	7				10*	11
31	1 Mar	LEYTON ORIENT	3-1	6850	Mullen, Storrie, D.Watson		6		4	5				9	8	10			3			2	1	7					11
32	4	READING	4-1	7665	Leggatt(2), Mullen, D.Watson		6		4	5		7		9	8	10			3			2	1						11
33	7	Tranmere Rovers	0-0	4843			6		4	5				9	8	10			3			2	1	7					11
34	12	Plymouth Argyle	2-1	6605	Downes, Storrie		6		4	5				9	8	10			3			2	1	7					11
35	15	LUTON TOWN	2-2	9560	Quinn, Storrie		6		4	5				9	8	10			3			2	1	7					11
36	21	Barnsley	1-0	13260	Brogden		6		4	5				9	8	10			3			2	1	7					11
37	24	Reading	0-1	3316			6		4	5				9	8	10			3			2	1	7					11
38	29	BRIGHTON	1-1	7568	D.Watson		6		4	5				9	8	10			3			2*	1	7					11
39	4 Apr	Barrow	0-2	4892			6		4	5				9	8	10			3				1	7				11	2
40	5	Southport	0-0	4497			3			5			8	9	10		6		3				1	7			4	11	2
41	8	OLDHAM ATHLETIC	1-2	8705	Swift		6		2	5		12		9*	8	10			3				1	7			4	11	
42	12	MANSFIELD TOWN	3-0	6645	Brogden, Gilliver, D.Watson		6		4	5				9	8	10			3				1	7				11	2
43	15	BARROW	3-1	6867	Storrie(2), Quinn		6		4	5				9	8	10			3				1	7				11	2
44	19	Torquay United	0-1	6183			6		4	5		12		9	8	10			3			2	1	7*				11	
45	25	CREWE ALEXANDRA	3-0	6831	Brogden, Storrie, D.Watson		6		4	5		12			8	10			3			2	1	7*			9	11	
46	2 May	Swindon Town	1-1	9584	Storrie		6		4	5					8	10			3			2	1	7			9	11	
		Apps.				5	44	1	44	44	22	13	23	24	42	40	22	1	25	2	7	30	41	36	4	6	9	17	4
		Subs.										2	5	2	1		2		2	4					1				
		Goals					2		3	8	1	7	6	2	14	1	1							7			1	2	

F.A. CUP

No.	Date	Opposition	Res.	Att.	Goalscorers	Hill A.	Swift T.	Harrity M.	Quinn J.	Watson D.	Tiler B.	Leggatt G.	Downes S.	Gilliver A.	Storrie J.	Bentley D.	Hague N.	Haselden J.	Leigh D.	Todd R.	Watson G.	Mealand B.	Furnell J.	Brogden L.	Marshall I.	Womble T.	Griffin W.	Mullen J.	Hudson C.
1R	16 Nov	Hartlepool	1-1	6579	Womble		6		4	5	12			9		11*	3		10			2	1	7		8			
1Rr	19	HARTLEPOOL	3-0	11518	G.Watson(2), Storrie		2		4	5	6			9		11	3				10		1	7		8			
2R	7 Dec	MANSFIELD TOWN	2-2	10379	Gilliver(2)				4	5	6	8		12	9	11*	3		10			2	1	7					
2Rr	9	Mansfield Town	0-1	12876					4	5	6			8	9		10	11*			3	2	1	7			12		

LEAGUE CUP

No.	Date	Opposition	Res.	Att.	Goalscorers	Hill A.	Swift T.	Harrity M.	Quinn J.	Watson D.	Tiler B.	Leggatt G.	Downes S.	Gilliver A.	Storrie J.	Bentley D.	Hague N.	Haselden J.	Leigh D.	Todd R.	Watson G.	Mealand B.	Furnell J.	Brogden L.	Marshall I.	Womble T.	Griffin W.	Mullen J.	Hudson C.
1R	14 Aug	Scunthorpe United	1-2	4643	Quinn	1	2		4		6	7	8	9	10		3	5	11										

Final League Table

		Pl.	Home W	D	L	F	A	Away W	D	L	F	A	F.	A.	Pts
1	Watford	46	16	5	2	35	7	11	5	7	39	27	74	34	64
2	Swindon Town	46	18	4	1	38	7	9	6	8	33	28	71	35	64
3	Luton Town	46	20	3	0	57	14	5	8	10	17	24	74	38	61
4	Bournemouth	46	16	2	5	41	17	5	7	11	19	28	60	45	51
5	Plymouth Argyle	46	10	8	5	34	25	7	7	9	19	24	53	49	49
6	Torquay United	46	13	4	6	35	18	5	8	10	19	28	54	46	48
7	Tranmere Rovers	46	12	3	8	36	31	7	7	9	34	37	70	68	48
8	Southport	46	14	8	1	52	20	3	5	15	19	44	71	64	47
9	Stockport County	46	14	5	4	49	25	2	9	12	18	43	67	68	46
10	Barnsley	46	13	6	4	37	21	3	8	12	21	42	58	63	46
11	Rotherham United	46	12	6	5	40	21	4	7	12	16	29	56	50	45
12	Brighton & Hove A.	46	12	7	4	49	21	4	6	13	23	44	72	65	45
13	Walsall	46	10	9	4	34	18	4	7	12	16	31	50	49	44
14	Reading	46	13	3	7	41	25	2	10	11	26	41	67	66	43
15	Mansfield Town	46	14	5	4	37	18	2	6	15	21	44	58	62	43
16	Bristol Rovers	46	12	6	5	41	27	4	5	14	22	44	63	71	43
17	Shrewsbury Town	46	11	8	4	28	17	5	3	15	23	50	51	67	43
18	Orient	46	10	8	5	31	19	4	6	13	20	39	51	58	42
19	Barrow	46	11	6	6	30	23	6	2	15	26	52	56	75	42
20	Gillingham	46	10	10	3	35	20	3	5	15	19	43	54	63	41
21	Northampton Town	46	12	6	5	37	30	5	4	14	17	31	54	61	40
22	Hartlepool	46	12	6	5	25	29	4	7	12	15	41	40	70	39
23	Crewe Alexandra	46	11	4	8	40	31	2	5	16	12	45	52	76	35
24	Oldham Athletic	46	9	6	8	33	27	4	3	16	17	56	50	83	35

SEASON 1969/70
DIVISION THREE

No.	Date	Opposition	Res.	Att.	Goalscorers
1	9 Aug	BURY	4-3	7089	Bentley(2), Womble, O.G.
2	16	Shrewsbury Town	0-1	4627	
3	23	DONCASTER ROVERS	0-1	13801	
4	26	MANSFIELD TOWN	2-2	6266	Downes(2)
5	30	Bournemouth & BA	0-1	7293	
6	6 Sep	LEYTON ORIENT	0-0	6468	
7	13	Walsall	2-0	4826	Brogden, Mullen
8	15	Rochdale	2-4	6739	Storrie, Womble
9	20	GILLINGHAM	0-1	6318	
10	27	Barrow	2-1	3650	Leigh, Storrie
11	4 Oct	BRADFORD CITY	2-3	8595	Downes, Swift
12	7	SHREWSBURY TOWN	1-2	4981	Downes
13	11	Bristol Rovers	0-3	8807	
14	13	Stockport County	1-1	4009	Fantham
15	18	FULHAM	0-0	7699	
16	25	Reading	1-1	5617	
17	1 Nov	LUTON TOWN	1-1	8727	Leigh
18	8	Tranmere Rovers	2-2	3196	Leigh, Downes
19	22	Torquay United	0-0	5816	
20	25	BRIGHTON & H.A.	2-0	5984	Hague, Swift
21	2 Dec	BARNSLEY	2-0	12269	Downes, Swift
22	13	WALSALL	4-1	7703	Downes, Fantham, Hague, Leigh
23	20	Leyton Orient	1-1	4593	Downes
24	26	Doncaster Rovers	2-1	19742	Brogden, Lill
25	27	BOURNEMOUTH & BA	3-0	10663	Fantham(2), Womble
26	10 Jan	Gillingham	1-1	4794	Lill
27	13	STOCKPORT COUNTY	0-0	8161	
28	17	BARROW	5-0	8086	Womble(2), Hague, Lill, Mullen
29	24	Plymouth Argyle	3-0	8536	Hague(2), Lill
30	31	Bradford City	1-0	15880	Mullen
31	7 Feb	BRISTOL ROVERS	0-0	11668	
32	14	Bury	1-2	5026	Phillips
33	21	READING	1-1	12829	Hague
34	28	Fulham	2-3	8142	Brogden, Watson
35	3 Mar	Halifax Town	2-4	4429	Hague, Warnock
36	10	SOUTHPORT	2-0	6804	Phillips, Warnock
37	13	Barnsley	0-1	11327	
38	17	PLYMOUTH ARGYLE	1-0	6984	Lill
39	21	HALIFAX TOWN	1-1	7244	Phillips
40	23	TORQUAY UNITED	2-1	6774	Watson, O.G.
41	27	Luton Town	1-2	14315	Swift
42	28	Southport	1-2	3012	Swift
43	31	TRANMERE ROVERS	0-1	6312	
44	4 Apr	Mansfield Town	0-2	9166	
45	8	Brighton & H.A.	1-2	11297	Warnock
46	14	ROCHDALE	3-1	6020	Phillips(2), Leigh

Appearances (Apps / Subs / Goals):

Player	Apps	Subs	Goals
Furnell J.	35		
Mealand B.	14	1	
Leigh D.	44		5
Quinn J.	2		
Watson D.	41		2
Swift T.	37		5
Brogden L.	18		3
Womble T.	15	8	5
Downes S.	20	3	8
Bentley D.	42		2
Mullen C.	40	2	3
Hudson C.	23	3	
Griffin W.	5	1	
Storrie J.	9		2
Hague N.	41	5	8
Atkinson P.	3	2	
Warnock N.	33		3
Lill D.	25		5
Houghton W.	18		
Phillips T.	12		5
Tunks R.	11		
Fantham J.	18	2	4

F.A. CUP

No.	Date	Opposition	Res.	Att.	Goalscorers
1R	15 Nov	Notts County	3-0	8769	Downes(2), Hague
2R	6 Dec	WORKINGTON	3-0	8920	Downes, Fantham, Swift
3R	3 Jan	PETERBOROUGH	0-1	13146	

LEAGUE CUP

No.	Date	Opposition	Res.	Att.	Goalscorers
1R	12 Aug	Bradford PA	2-0	3980	Mullen, O.G.
2R	3 Sep	Bolton Wanderers	0-0	11043	
2Rr	9	BOLTON WANDERERS	3-3	7924	Brogden(2), Storrie
2R2r	11	BOLTON WANDERERS	1-0	9018	Womble
3R	24	BURNLEY	1-1	10069	Mullen
3Rr	30	Burnley	0-2	10319	

Final League Table

		Pl.	Home W	D	L	F	A	Away W	D	L	F	A	F.	A.	Pts
1	Orient	46	16	5	2	43	15	9	7	7	24	21	67	36	62
2	Luton Town	46	13	8	2	46	15	10	6	7	31	28	77	43	60
3	Bristol Rovers	46	15	5	3	51	26	5	11	7	29	33	80	59	56
4	Fulham	46	12	9	2	43	26	8	6	9	38	29	81	55	55
5	Brighton & Hove A.	46	16	4	3	37	16	7	5	11	20	27	57	43	55
6	Mansfield Town	46	14	4	5	46	22	7	9	24	27		70	49	53
7	Barnsley	46	14	6	3	43	24	5	9	9	25	35	68	59	53
8	Reading	46	16	3	4	52	29	5	8	10	35	48	87	77	53
9	Rochdale	46	11	6	6	39	24	7	4	12	30	36	69	60	46
10	Bradford City	46	11	6	6	37	22	6	6	11	20	28	57	50	46
11	Doncaster Rovers	46	13	4	6	31	19	4	8	11	21	35	52	54	46
12	Walsall	46	11	4	8	33	31	6	8	9	21	36	54	67	46
13	Torquay United	46	9	5	9	36	22	5	8	10	26	37	62	59	45
14	Rotherham United	46	10	8	5	36	19	5	6	12	26	35	62	54	44
15	Shrewsbury Town	46	10	12	1	35	17	3	6	14	27	46	62	63	44
16	Tranmere Rovers	46	10	8	5	38	29	4	8	11	18	43	56	72	44
17	Plymouth Argyle	46	10	7	6	32	23	6	4	13	24	41	56	64	43
18	Halifax Town	46	10	9	4	31	25	4	6	13	16	38	47	63	43
19	Bury	46	13	4	6	47	29	2	7	14	28	51	75	80	41
20	Gillingham	46	7	6	10	28	23	6	7	10	24	31	52	64	39
21	Bournemouth	46	8	9	6	28	27	4	6	13	20	44	48	71	39
22	Southport	46	11	5	7	31	22	3	5	15	17	44	48	66	38
23	Barrow	46	7	9	7	28	27	1	5	17	18	54	46	81	30
24	Stockport County	46	4	7	12	17	30	2	4	17	10	41	27	71	23

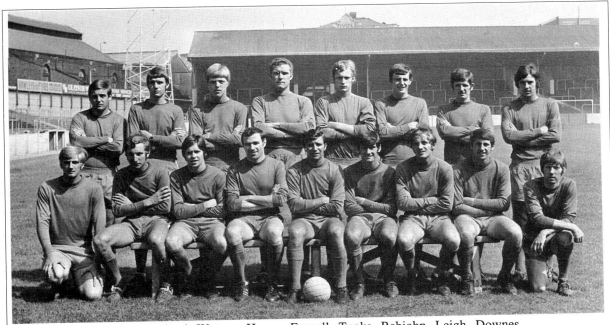

(Back): Mealand, Watson, Hague, Furnell, Tunks, Rabjohn, Leigh, Downes.
(Front): Swift, Warnock, Brogden, Storrie, Quinn, Bentley, Mullen, Womble, Griffin.

- 1969-70 -

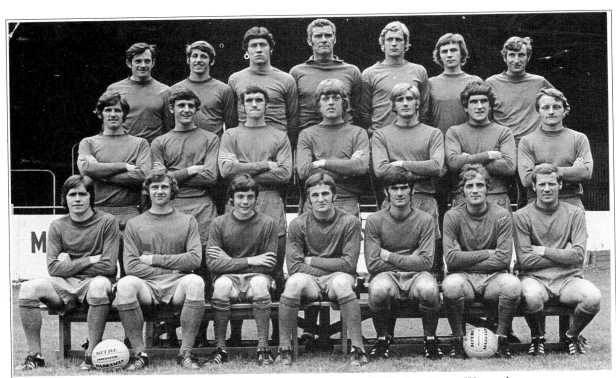

(Back): Fantham, Womble, McDonagh, Furnell, Tunks, Leng, Warnock.
(Middle): Leigh, Hudson, Watson, Hague, Swift, Lill, Houghton.
(Front): Brogden, Coop, Kulic, Phillips, Bentley, Mullen, Bettany.

- 1970-71 -

SEASON 1970/71
DIVISION THREE

Player columns (left→right): Tunks R., Houghton W., Leigh D., Bettany J., Watson D., Swift T., Brogden L., Hague N., Phillips T., Bentley D., Mullen J., Lill D., Fantham J., Womble T., Wright P., Warnock N., Johnson R., Hudson C., Mielczarek R., Quinn J., Gilbert C., McDonagh J., Ferguson E.

No.	Date	Opposition	Res.	Att.	Goalscorers	Tu	Ho	Le	Be	Wa	Sw	Br	Ha	Ph	Bn	Mu	Li	Fa	Wo	Wr	Wk	Jo	Hu	Mi	Qu	Gi	Mc	Fe
1	15 Aug	Shrewsbury Town	2-4	4656	Hague, O.G.	1	2	3	4	5	6	11	8	7	10		9*							12				
2	22	DONCASTER ROVERS	2-0	8285	Brodgen, Leigh	1	2	3	4*	5	6	7	8	9	10	11		12										
3	29	Brighton & H.A.	1-1	9849	Hague	1	2	3	4	5	6	7*	8	9	10	11	12											
4	1 Sep	BURY	3-2	6993	Bentley, Bettany, Watson	1	2	3	4*	5	6	7	8	9	10	11	12											
5	5	GILLINGHAM	0-0	7244		1	2	3	4	5	6	7	8	9	10	11												
6	12	Wrexham	1-1	8562	Brogden	1	2	3	4		5	7	6	9*	10	11						8		12				
7	19	ROCHDALE	5-1	6579	Watson(3), Brogden, Fantham	1	2	3	4	5	6	7	8		10*	11					9			12				
8	22	SWANSEA CITY	2-0	8068	Brogden, Watson	1	2	3	4	5	6	7*	8		10	11					9			12				
9	26	Plymouth Argyle	1-4	9081	Leigh	1	2	3	4	5	6	7	8		10	11*					9			12				
10	29	Halifax Town	3-1	5891	Brogden(2), Phillips	1	2	3	4*		5	7	6	9	10	11	8							12				
11	3 Oct	WALSALL	1-0	7337	Hague	1	2	3	4		5	7	6	9	10	11	8											
12	10	Burnley	1-2	14318	Warnock	1		3	4*	5	6	7	8	12	10					2	11			9				
13	17	SHREWSBURY TOWN	1-1	7103	Watson	1		3	4*	5	6	7	8	12	10					2	11			9				
14	20	TORQUAY UNITED	3-1	6039	Hague, Warnock, O.G.	1	2	3		5	6	7	4	9	10						11			8				
15	24	Port Vale	0-1	7215		1	2	3		5	6	7*	4	9	10						11		12	8				
16	31	BRISTOL ROVERS	1-1	7478	Hague	1	2	3		5	6	7	4	9	10			12			11*			8				
17	7 Nov	Bradford City	1-1	7445	Watson	1	2	3		5	6		4	7*	10	12	9				11			8				
18	9	Mansfield Town	1-1	7739	Watson	1	2	3		5	6		4	7	10		9				11			8				
19	14	FULHAM	1-1	9398	O.G.	1	2	3		5	6		4	9*		7	10	8			11		12					
20	28	READING	2-1	6940	Fantham, Watson	1	2	3	8	5	6		4			10	7	9			11							
21	4 Dec	Tranmere Rovers	0-5	2513		1	2	3	8*	5	6		4		10	12	7	9			11							
22	19	Doncaster Rovers	2-0	6471	Fantham, Leigh	1	2	3	4*		6		5		10	11	8	9			7			12				
23	26	CHESTERFIELD	1-2	14035	Swift	1	2	3			6		5		10	11	4	9			7	8						
24	9 Jan	HALIFAX TOWN	2-2	7446	Leigh, Johnson	1	2	3			6		5		10*	11		9	8		7	4	12					
25	15	Torquay United	1-3	5696	Phillips	1	2	3			6		5	11	10		12	9*	7			8	4					
26	23	ASTON VILLA	1-1	12648	Swift	1	2	3			6		5	12	10	11*		9	7			8	4					
27	30	Reading	2-4	4664	Mullen(2)	1	2	3			6		5		10	11		7				8	4	5				
28	6 Feb	TRANMERE ROVERS	2-0	6317	Hague, Mullen	1	2	3			6	7				11						10		5	4			
29	13	Aston Villa	0-1	27183		1	2	3			6	12	9			11		8*	7			10	5	4				
30	20	MANSFIELD TOWN	2-1	7361	Mullen, Womble	1	2	3			6	7	9			11			8*			10		5	4			12
31	27	Bristol Rovers	2-0	11092	Hague	1	2	3			6	7	9			11			8			10		5	4			
32	6 Mar	PORT VALE	2-1	6540	Womble, Mullen	1	2	3			6	7	9			11			8			10		5	4			
33	9	Swansea City	1-1	7262	Hague	1	2	3			6	7*	9		12	11			8			10		5	4			
34	13	Fulham	0-1	9627		1	2	3			6	7*	9			11			8			10		5	4			
35	16	PRESTON NORTH END	1-1	8291	Mullen	1	2	3			6	7*	9			11						10		5	4	12		
36	20	BRADFORD CITY	1-1	6581	Brogden	1	2	3			6	7	9			11		12				10		5	4	8		
37	27	Gillingham	1-2	2955	Mielczarek	1	2	3			6*		9			11		7				10		5	4	8		
38	3 Apr	BRIGHTON & H.A.	2-0	4374	Gilbert, Quinn	1	2	3			6		9			11		12	7*			10		5	4	8		
39	10	Chesterfield	1-1	10220	Quinn	1	2	3			6		9			11		12	7			10		5	4	8*		
40	12	WREXHAM	1-1	4888	Phillips		2	3				9*	12	8	11			7				10	6	5	4		1	
41	13	Walsall	1-0	4586	Mielczarek		2					9	8	6	11			7				10	3	5	4		1	
42	17	BARNSLEY	1-0	7328	Fantham		2					6	9*	8	11			7				10	3	5	4	12		
43	24	Rochdale	3-4	3526	Gilbert, Swift, O.G.		2				6		4	12	8	11*		7				10	3	5		9	1	
44	27	Bury	1-0	3708	Gilbert		2				6		4	11	8			7				10	3	5		9	1	
45	1 May	PLYMOUTH ARGYLE	1-1	4385	Gilbert	1	2				6		4	12	8			7				10	3	5		9*		11
46	4	Preston North End	0-3	28224		1	2				6		12		8	11*		7				10	3	5		9		4
				Apps		42	44	40	16	18	43	24	45	18	33	34	8	28	14	2	13	24	11	19	15	9	4	2
				Subs							1	1	6	1	2	4	3	2	3		7		2		1			
				Goals			4	1	9	3	7	9	3	1	6			4	2		2	1		2	2	4		

F.A. CUP

Rnd	Date	Opposition	Res.	Att.	Goalscorers	Tu	Ho	Le	Be	Wa	Sw	Br	Ha	Ph	Bn	Mu	Li	Fa	Wo	Wr	Wk	Jo	Hu	Mi
1R	23 Nov	Great Harwood	6-2	5138	Watson(2), Fantham, Bentley, Mullin	1	2	3	8*	5	6		4		10	7	12	9			11			
2R	12 Dec	Grantham	4-1	5560	Fantham, Hague, Watson	1	2	3	8*	5	6		4		10	7	12	9			11			
3R	11 Jan	LEEDS UNITED	0-0	24000		1	2	3			6		5	12	10*	11	8	9	7			4		
3Rr	18 Jan	Leeds United	2-3	36890	Bentley, Womble	1	2	3			6		5	12	10	11	8	9*	7			4		

LEAGUE CUP

Rnd	Date	Opposition	Res.	Att.	Goalscorers	Tu	Ho	Le	Be	Wa	Sw	Br	Ha	Ph	Bn	Mu	Li
1R	19 Aug	Barnsley	1-0	8260	Phillips	1	2	3	4	5	6*	7	8	9	10	11	12
2R	8 Sep	BRISTOL CITY	0-0	7384		1	2	3	4	5	6	7	8	9*	10	11	12
2Rr	15	Bristol City	0-4	9413		1	2	3	4		6	7		10	11*	8	9

Final League Table

		Pl	Home W	D	L	F	A	Away W	D	L	F	A	F.	A.	Pts
1	Preston North End	46	15	8	0	42	16	7	9	7	21	23	63	39	61
2	Fulham	46	15	6	2	39	12	9	6	8	29	29	68	41	60
3	Halifax Town	46	16	5	2	46	22	6	10	7	28	33	74	55	56
4	Aston Villa	46	13	7	3	27	13	6	8	9	27	33	54	46	53
5	Chesterfield	46	13	8	2	45	12	4	9	10	21	26	66	38	51
6	Bristol Rovers	46	11	5	7	38	24	8	8	7	31	26	69	50	51
7	Mansfield Town	46	13	7	3	44	28	5	8	10	20	34	64	62	51
8	Rotherham United	46	12	10	1	38	19	5	6	12	26	41	64	60	50
9	Wrexham	46	12	8	3	43	25	6	5	12	29	40	72	65	49
10	Torquay United	46	12	5	6	37	26	7	5	11	17	31	54	57	49
11	Swansea City	46	11	5	7	41	25	4	11	8	18	31	59	56	46
12	Barnsley	46	12	6	5	30	19	5	5	13	19	33	49	52	45
13	Shrewsbury Town	45	11	6	6	37	28	5	7	11	21	34	58	62	45
14	Brighton & Hove A.	46	8	10	5	28	20	6	6	11	22	27	50	47	44
15	Plymouth Argyle	46	6	12	5	39	33	6	7	10	24	30	63	63	43
16	Rochdale	46	8	8	7	29	26	6	7	10	32	42	61	68	43
17	Port Vale	46	11	6	6	29	18	4	6	13	23	41	52	59	42
18	Tranmere Rovers	46	8	11	4	27	18	2	11	10	18	37	45	55	42
19	Bradford City	46	7	6	10	23	25	6	8	9	26	37	49	62	40
20	Walsall	46	10	1	12	30	22	7	4	9	21	30	51	57	39
21	Reading	46	10	7	6	32	33	4	4	15	16	52	48	85	39
22	Bury	46	7	9	7	30	23	5	4	14	22	37	52	60	37
23	Doncaster Rovers	46	8	5	10	28	27	5	4	14	17	39	45	66	35
24	Gillingham	46	6	9	8	22	29	4	4	15	20	38	42	67	33

SEASON 1971/72

DIVISION THREE

No.	Date	Opposition	Res.	Att.	Goalscorers
1	14 Aug	Blackburn Rovers	1-2	7801	Phillips
2	21	BARNSLEY	3-0	6648	Hague(2), Phillips
3	28	Bournemouth	1-3	11876	Bentley
4	31	BRIGHTON	2-4	4782	Hudson, Johnson
5	4 Sep	TORQUAY UNITED	2-2	3956	Johnson, Quinn
6	10	Tranmere Rovers	0-0	2822	
7	18	BRADFORD CITY	2-0	4962	Gilbert, Mullen
8	25	Mansfield Town	1-0	4797	Johnson
9	28	SWANSEA CITY	4-0	5282	Gilbert(4)
10	2 Oct	YORK CITY	1-1	7024	Leigh
11	9	Aston Villa	2-1	30249	Gilbert, Phillips
12	16	BLACKBURN ROVERS	2-1	7256	Gilbert(2)
13	23	Shrewsbury Town	1-0	6295	Gilbert
14	30	WALSALL	1-1	7997	Ham
15	6 Nov	Halifax Town	1-1	5409	Ham
16	9	Bristol Rovers	2-1	13081	Ham, Mullen
17	13	PLYMOUTH ARGYLE	4-3	8443	Ham(2), Hague, Gilbert
18	27	WREXHAM	2-2	7548	Gilbert(2)
19	4 Dec	Rochdale	1-2	3384	Bentley
20	18	Torquay United	1-0	4620	Ham
21	27	OLDHAM ATHLETIC	3-1	9224	Gilbert(2), Ham
22	1 Jan	Bradford City	0-1	6862	
23	8	BOURNEMOUTH	0-0	9948	
24	22	Swansea City	2-0	8717	Ham, Mullen
25	29	BRISTOL ROVERS	0-0	7728	
26	12 Feb	SHREWSBURY TOWN	2-1	6045	Johnson, Swift
27	19	Walsall	0-0	4506	
28	26	HALIFAX TOWN	3-2	7595	Gilbert, Mielczarek, Phillips
29	4 Mar	Plymouth Argyle	1-2	8292	Swift
30	11	ASTON VILLA	0-2	16290	
31	14	NOTTS COUNTY	2-2	10146	Gilbert, Ham
32	18	Barnsley	1-1	7145	Eustace
33	22	Notts County	1-1	11522	Gilbert
34	26	TRANMERE ROVERS	0-0	5756	
35	31	York City	0-2	6117	
36	3 Apr	MANSFIELD TOWN	3-1	5518	Ham(2), Gilbert
37	8	CHESTERFIELD	0-1	5935	
38	12	Chesterfield	1-0	7140	Ham
39	15	Wrexham	0-0	4426	
40	18	PORT VALE	3-0	3764	Ham(2), Phillips
41	22	ROCHDALE	5-1	4182	Gilbert(2), Meilczarek, Swift, Ham
42	26	Brighton	1-2	27928	Ham
43	29	Bolton Wanderers	2-2	5345	Mullen, Swift
44	2 May	BOLTON WANDERERS	2-0	3945	Mullen, Womble
45	5	Oldham Athletic	1-5	4640	Swift
46	8	Port Vale	2-1	2743	Gilbert, Mullen

Appearance / Goals Summary

Players: Tunks R., Hudson C., Houghton W., Quinn J., Mielczarek R., Swift T., Phillips T., Johnson R., Gilbert C., Bentley D., Mullen J., Hague N., Leng M., Leigh D., Ham R., Womble T., Ferguson E., Breckin J., Brogden L., McDonagh J., Whitehead N., Eustace P., Henderson A.

	Tun	Hud	Hou	Qui	Mie	Swi	Phi	Joh	Gil	Ben	Mul	Hag	Len	Lei	Ham	Wom	Fer	Bre	Bro	McD	Whi	Eus	Hen
Apps.	37	15	2	30	39	41	26	41	36	37	37	6	11	34	34	8	20	7		9	11	6	
Subs.					1		8			2	1	1	6			4	2	1	1				1
Goals		1		1	2	5	5	4	21	2	6	3		1	16	1						1	

F.A. CUP

Round	Date	Opposition	Res.	Att.	Goalscorers
1R	20 Nov	Frickley Colliery	2-2	5824	Bentley, Mullen
1Rr	23	FRICKLEY COLLIERY	4-0	9793	Gilbert(3), Bentley
2R	11 Dec	YORK CITY	1-1	9212	Gilbert
2Rr	13	York City	3-2	10010	Ham(2), Womble
3R	15 Jan	Bury	1-1	9613	Gilbert
3Rr	24	BURY	2-1	14625	Gilbert, Swift
4R	5 Feb	Tottenham Hotspur	0-2	36903	

LEAGUE CUP

Round	Date	Opposition	Res.	Att.	Goalscorers
1R	17 Aug	SHEFFIELD WEDNESDAY	0-2	8983	

Final League Table

		Pl.	Home W	D	L	F	A	Away W	D	L	F	A	F.	A.	Pts
1	Aston Villa	46	20	1	2	45	10	12	5	6	40	22	85	32	70
2	Brighton & Hove A.	46	15	5	3	39	18	12	6	5	43	29	82	47	65
3	Bournemouth	46	16	6	1	43	13	7	10	6	30	24	73	37	62
4	Notts County	46	16	3	4	42	19	9	9	5	32	25	74	44	62
5	Rotherham United	46	12	8	3	46	25	8	7	8	23	27	69	52	55
6	Bristol Rovers	46	17	2	4	54	26	4	10	9	21	30	75	56	54
7	Bolton Wanderers	46	11	8	4	25	13	6	8	9	26	28	51	41	50
8	Plymouth Argyle	46	13	6	4	43	26	7	4	12	31	38	74	64	50
9	Walsall	46	12	8	3	38	16	3	10	10	24	41	62	57	48
10	Blackburn Rovers	46	14	4	5	39	22	5	5	13	15	35	54	57	47
11	Oldham Athletic	46	11	4	8	37	35	6	7	10	22	28	59	63	45
12	Shrewsbury Town	46	13	5	5	50	29	4	5	14	23	36	73	65	44
13	Chesterfield	46	10	5	8	25	23	8	3	12	32	34	57	57	44
14	Swansea City	46	10	6	7	27	21	7	4	12	19	38	46	59	44
15	Port Vale	46	10	10	3	27	21	3	5	15	16	38	43	59	41
16	Wrexham	46	10	5	8	33	26	6	3	14	26	37	59	63	40
17	Halifax Town	46	11	6	6	31	22	2	6	15	17	39	48	61	38
18	Rochdale	46	11	7	5	35	26	1	6	16	22	57	57	83	37
19	York City	46	8	8	7	32	22	4	4	15	25	44	57	66	36
20	Tranmere Rovers	46	9	7	7	34	30	1	9	13	16	41	50	71	36
21	Mansfield Town	46	5	12	6	19	26	3	8	12	22	37	41	63	36
22	Barnsley	46	6	10	7	23	30	3	8	12	9	34	32	64	36
23	Torquay United	46	8	6	9	31	31	2	6	15	10	38	41	69	32
24	Bradford City	46	6	8	9	27	32	5	2	16	18	45	45	77	32

(Back): Ferguson, Swift, Hudson, Tunks, McDonagh, Hague, Leigh, Houghton.
(Front): Womble, Bentley, Brogden, Quinn, Mullen, Johnson, Phillips.

-1971 -72 -

(Back): Baker(Coach), Swift, Mielczarek, Phillips, McDonagh,Tunks,Quinn,Leigh, Ferguson,Ham,Gilbert.
(Front): Mullen, Johnson, Leng, Whitehead, McAnearney (Manager),
Breckin, Bentley, Houghton, Womble, Falconer (Physio)

- 1972-73 -

SEASON 1972/73
DIVISION THREE

No.	Date	Opposition	Res.	Att.	Goalscorers
1	12 Aug	PLYMOUTH ARGYLE	1-0	5473	Ham
2	19	Grimsby Town	1-2	11727	Mullen
3	26	PORT VALE	7-0	4531	Gilbrt(3),Johnsn,Swft,Whtehead,Wmble
4	28	York City	1-0	4090	Mullen
5	2 Sep	Wrexham	0-1	5332	
6	9	CHARLTON ATHLETIC	2-1	4927	Houghton, Mullen
7	16	Swansea City	1-0	3645	Mielczarek
8	19	SHREWSBURY TOWN	2-0	5508	Ham(2)
9	23	HALIFAX TOWN	0-1	6568	
10	27	Watford	1-1	7769	Johnson
11	30	Oldham Athletic	0-1	6518	
12	7 Oct	Chesterfield	2-3	7632	Gilbert, Ham
13	10	BOURNEMOUTH	2-7	5110	Gilbert(2)
14	14	BRISTOL ROVERS	1-1	4463	Ham
15	21	Walsall	0-1	6136	
16	25	Notts County	0-2	6199	
17	28	SCUNTHORPE UNITED	2-1	4317	Ferguson, Womble
18	4 Nov	WATFORD	1-0	4055	Swift
19	11	Shrewsbury Town	1-1	2395	Womble
20	25	Bolton Wanderers	1-2	7980	Womble
21	2 Dec	ROCHDALE	0-0	4184	
22	15	Tranmere Rovers	0-2	3613	
23	23	BLACKBURN ROVERS	1-1	3231	Mielczarek
24	26	Halifax Town	1-0	3327	Ferguson
25	30	GRIMSBY TOWN	2-0	5691	Ferguson, Womble
26	13 Jan	Brentford	1-1	7440	Breckin
27	20	WREXHAM	1-1	2390	Mullen
28	27	Charlton Athletic	2-1	5877	Mullen(2)
29	30	NOTTS COUNTY	1-4	6201	Gilbert
30	3 Feb	Bournemouth	0-4	11216	
31	10	SWANSEA CITY	0-2	3042	
32	17	Plymouth Argyle	1-4	8454	Ham
33	24	TRANMERE ROVERS	1-2	2322	Ham
34	26	Port Vale	1-4	4433	Phillips
35	3 Mar	CHESTERFIELD	1-0	3749	Ferguson
36	6	BRENTFORD	2-1	2514	Ferguson, O.G.
37	10	Bristol Rovers	0-3	9469	
38	17	WALSALL	2-0	3204	Ham, Mielczarek
39	19	Southend United	0-1	6167	
40	25	Scunthorpe United	1-2	2199	Gilbert
41	31	BOLTON WANDERERS	1-0	6506	Wigg
42	7 Apr	Rochdale	1-0	1588	Mullen
43	14	SOUTHEND UNITED	1-0	3389	Bentley
44	20	Blackburn Rovers	1-2	15986	Gilbert
45	23	OLDHAM ATHLETIC	2-3	2951	O'Grady, Whitehead
46	28	YORK CITY	1-2	3936	Wigg

Player appearances (shirt number worn; * = substituted / substitute)

No.	Tunks R.	Houghton W.	Leng M.	Stowell B.	Mielczarek R.	Swift T.	Whitehead N.	Ham R.	Gilbert C.	Bentley D.	Mullen J.	Phillips T.	Johnson R.	Leigh D.	Ferguson E.	McDonagh J.	Wilkinson W.	O'Grady M.	Breckin J.	Buckley P.	Wigg R.	Womble T.
1	1	2	3	4	5	6	7	8	9	10*	11	12										
2	1	2			5	6	7	8	9		11	10	4	3								12
3	1	2			5	6*	7	8	9		11	10	4	3								
4	1	2		12	5	6	7	8	9		11	10*	4	3								
5	1	2		12	5		7	8	9*		11	10	4	3	6							
6	1	2		4	5		7	8	9		11		10	3	6							12
7	1	2		4	5	3*	7	8	9		11		10		6							12
8	1	2	3	4	5		7	8	9		11		10		6							12
9	1	2	3	4	5		7*	8	9		11		10		6							12
10	1	2	3	4	5			11	8	9			10		6							7
11	1	2	3	4	5	12	7*	8	9				10		6							11
12		2	12	4	5	6*	7	8	9			11		10		3	1					
13		2	3		5	6		8	9	4	11	7	10			1*					12	
14		2	3	4	5	6	7*	8	9		11		12	10		1						
15		2	3	4	5	6*		8	9		7	11	12	10		1						
16		2	3		5	6		8	9	10	11	7			4*	1						9
17		2	3		5	6		8	12	10	11*	7			4	1						9
18		2			5	6	7*	8	12	10		11			4	1		4	3			9
19		2		7	5	6		8		12	10	11*			4	1		4	3			9
20		2		7	5	6		8*		12	10	11			4	1		4	7	3	12	9
21		2			5	6			9		10	11*			4	1		4	7	3	11	8
22		2			10	5	6			9					4	1		4	7	3	11	8
23		2			5	6				10	11	8	7		4	1			3			9
24		2			5	6				10	11	8	7		4	1			3			9
25		2			5	6				10	11	8	7		4	1		5	3			9
26		2				6				10	11	8	7		4	1			3		12	9
27		2			5	6*				10	11	8	7		4	1		12	3			9*
28		2			5				12	10	11	8	7		4	1		6	3			9
29	2*				5					9	10	11	12	7	4	1		6	3			8
30		2			5					9	10	11	12	7*	4	1		6	3			8
31		2		10	5		7		12	9		11			4*	1		6				12
32		2			5					8	9	10	11			6	1	4*	7	3		
33		2	6		5			7	8	9*	10		12		4	1			11	3		
34		2	6		5			7	8		10		12	9*	4	1			11	3		
35	1	2			5				8	9*	10	11	12	6	4				7	3		
36	1	2			5				8	9	10	11			4				7	3		
37	1	2*			5				8	12	10	11			4				7	3		9
38	1				5	6*			8	12	10	11		4	2				7	3		9*
39	1				5	6			8	12	10	11*	7	4	2				7	3		8
40	1				5	6			8	9	11*	12	4		2				7	3		8
41	1	3			5	6			8		10	11		4	2			7				9
42	1	3			5	6			8		10	11		4*	2			7				9
43	1	3			5	6	12		8		10	11		4*	2			7				9
44	1	3*			5	6	12		8	9	10	11*		4	2			7	8			
45	1	3			5	6	12		8	9	10	11		4	2			11				9
46	1	3			5	6	7		8	9		10		4	2			11				9
Apps.	23	41	14	14	45	30	18	33	29	33	38	15	35	5	34	23	14	14	23	1	7	17
Subs.			1	2		1	3	1	8				9			1			1		2	5
Goals		1			3	2	2	8	9	1	7	1	2		5			1			2	5

F.A. CUP

Rd	Date	Opposition	Res.	Att.	Goalscorers
1R	18 Nov	SOUTH SHIELDS	4-0	4839	Swift(2), Mielczarek, Womble
2R	9 Dec	Stockport County	0-1	4539	

Rd	Houghton	Mielczarek	Swift	Whitehead	Ham	Mullen	Phillips	Ferguson	McDonagh	O'Grady	Breckin	Buckley	Womble
1R	2	4	5	6	8	10	11	7	1		3		9
2R	2		5	6	12	9	10		1	4	7*	3	11	8

LEAGUE CUP

Rd	Date	Opposition	Res.	Att.	Goalscorers
1R	16 Aug	Darlington	1-0	3180	Johnson
2R	6 Sep	BRENTFORD	2-0	4966	Ham(2)
3R	3 Oct	Arsenal	0-5	21241	

Rd	Tunks	Houghton	Leng	Stowell	Mielczarek	Swift	Whitehead	Ham	Gilbert	Mullen	Phillips	Johnson	Ferguson	Womble
1R	1	2	3*	4	5	6	7	8	9	11	12	10		
2R	1	2		4	5		7	8	9	11	10	3	6	12
3R	1	2	11	4	5	3	7	8	9*	10	6			12

Final League Table

		Pl.	Home W	D	L	F	A	Away W	D	L	F	A	F.	A.	Pts
1	Bolton Wanderers	46	18	4	1	44	9	7	7	9	29	30	73	39	61
2	Notts County	46	17	4	2	40	12	6	7	10	27	35	67	47	57
3	Blackburn Rovers	46	12	8	3	34	16	8	7	8	23	31	57	47	55
4	Oldham Athletic	46	12	7	4	40	18	7	9	7	32	36	72	54	54
5	Bristol Rovers	46	12	4	2	55	20	3	9	11	22	36	77	56	53
6	Port Vale	46	15	6	2	41	21	6	5	12	15	48	56	69	53
7	Bournemouth	46	14	6	3	44	16	3	10	10	22	28	66	44	50
8	Plymouth Argyle	46	14	3	6	43	26	6	7	10	31	40	74	66	50
9	Grimsby Town	46	16	2	5	45	18	4	6	13	22	43	67	61	48
10	Tranmere Rovers	46	12	8	3	38	17	3	8	12	18	35	56	52	46
11	Charlton Athletic	46	12	7	4	46	24	5	4	14	23	43	69	67	45
12	Wrexham	46	11	9	3	39	23	3	8	12	16	31	55	54	45
13	Rochdale	46	8	8	7	22	26	6	4	9	26	28	48	54	45
14	Southend United	46	13	6	4	40	14	4	4	15	21	40	61	54	44
15	Shrewsbury Town	46	10	10	3	31	21	5	4	14	15	33	46	54	44
16	Chesterfield	46	13	4	6	37	22	4	5	14	20	39	57	61	43
17	Walsall	46	14	3	6	37	26	4	4	15	19	40	56	66	43
18	York City	46	8	10	5	24	14	5	5	13	18	32	42	46	41
19	Watford	46	11	8	4	32	21	3	9	11	11	25	43	48	41
20	Halifax Town	46	9	8	6	29	23	4	7	12	14	30	43	53	41
21	Rotherham United	46	12	4	7	34	27	5	3	15	17	38	51	65	41
22	Brentford	46	12	5	6	33	18	3	2	18	18	51	51	69	37
23	Swansea City	46	11	5	7	39	29	3	4	16	14	44	51	73	37
24	Scunthorpe United	46	8	7	8	18	25	2	3	18	15	47	33	72	30

SEASON 1973/74
DIVISION FOUR

No.	Date	Opposition	Res.	Att.	Goalscorers
1	25 Aug	Northampton Town	1-3	4098	Phillips
2	1 Sep	SWANSEA CITY	1-0	2993	Wigg
3	8	Crewe Alexandra	8-1	2116	Phillips(3), Bntley(2), Wmble(2), Wigg
4	12	Bradford City	1-2	3440	O'Grady
5	15	HARTLEPOOL	2-2	3679	O.G., Wigg
6	18	GILLINGHAM	1-1	3660	Wigg
7	22	Newport County	0-1	3138	
8	29	BURY	1-0	3713	Crawford
9	3 Oct	Gillingham	1-1	5330	Wigg
10	6	Darlington	1-1	2019	Wigg
11	13	EXETER CITY	4-0	2958	Phillips(2), Johnson, Wigg
12	20	Brentford	1-1	4420	Wigg
13	23	BRADFORD CITY	2-1	4200	Bentley, Phillips
14	27	COLCHESTER UNITED	0-0	4594	
15	3 Nov	Chester	0-1	2385	
16	10	STOCKPORT COUNTY	1-2	3600	Crawford
17	13	TORQUAY UNITED	1-0	2965	Phillips
18	17	Reading	0-1	5475	
19	1 Dec	Mansfield Town	0-3	2778	
20	8	WORKINGTON	1-1	2383	Gilbert
21	22	Bury	1-3	2878	Womble
22	26	BARNSLEY	2-1	6047	Delgado, Wigg
23	29	CREWE ALEXANDRA	1-1	3410	Wigg
24	1 Jan	Swansea City	2-4	4961	Crawford, Gilbert
25	12	Hartlepool	0-2	1982	
26	20	NORTHAMPTON TOWN	1-2	4355	Goodfellow
27	27	Lincoln City	1-2	6157	Wigg
28	3 Feb	DONCASTER ROVERS	2-1	5957	Swift, Wigg
29	10	NEWPORT COUNTY	1-1	2933	Womble
30	23	DARLINGTON	0-1	2331	
31	3 Mar	Barnsley	0-1	6273	
32	8	Colchester United	1-0	5180	Goodfellow
33	16	BRENTFORD	1-1	2259	Finney
34	19	DONCASTER ROVERS	1-2	2440	Delgado
35	23	Stockport County	1-0	1789	Derrett
36	25	Peterborough United	0-2	7583	
37	30	CHESTER	3-2	1945	Phillips(2), Woodall
38	2 Apr	LINCOLN CITY	2-0	2350	Wigg(2)
39	6	Torquay United	0-3	2022	
40	13	READING	1-1	2293	Delgado
41	15	SCUNTHORPE UNITED	1-1	2341	O.G.
42	16	Scunthorpe United	0-3	2107	
43	20	Workington	2-0	950	Phillips, Woodall
44	27	MANSFIELD UNITED	2-1	2329	Phillips, Woodall
45	30	Exeter City	0-0	2945	
46	11 May	PETERBOROUGH UNITED	3-1	3100	Goodfellow, Womble, Woodall

Player appearances (League)

No.	Turks R.	Houghton W.	Breckin J.	O'Grady M.	Sjoberg J.	Swift T.	Womble T.	Wigg R.	Phillips T.	Bentley D.	Mullen J.	Mielczarek R.	Crawford A.	Wilkinson W.	Leng M.	Henderson A.	Gilbert C.	Johnson R.	Robinson F.	McDonagh J.	Ferguson E.	Murphy P.	Delgado R.	Derrett S.	Goodfellow J.	Woodall J.	Finney R.
1	1	2	3	4	5	6	7	8	9	10	11																
2	1		3	4	5	6	7*	8	9	10			2	11				12									
3	1		3	4	5	6	7	8	9	10			2	11													
4	1		3	4	5	6	7	8	9	10			2	11													
5	1		3	4	5	6	7	8	9	10			2	11													
6	1		3	4	5	6	7	8	9	10			2*	11				12									
7	1		3			6	7	8	9	10			2	11	4*	5		12									
8	1	2	3			6	7	8	9	10				11	4	5											
9	1	2	3			6	7	8	9	10				11	4	5											
10	1	2	3			6	7	8	9	10				11	4	5											
11	1	2	3			6	7	8	9	10		5		11				4									
12	1	2	3			6	7	8	9	10		5		11				4									
13	1	2	3			6	7	8*	9	10		5	12	11				4									
14	1	2	3			6	7	8	9	10		5	7	11				4									
15	1	2				6		8	9	10		5*		11	3	12	4	7									
16		2				6	7	8	9	10				11	3	5	4			1							
17		2	11			5	7	8	9	10					3		4			1							
18		2	11			5	7	8	9						3		4			1			6				
19		2	12			5	7			10				11	4	3		9		1			6		8*		
20		2				5	7	8		10				11	4	3		9		1			6				
21			3	10		5	7	8	9	12	11			2						1			6*		4		
22			3	4*		5	7	8	9	10	11			2						1			6				
23			3			5	7*	8	9	10				11	2		12			1			6				
24						6	7	8		10				11	4	3		9		1			5	2			
25						6	12	8		10	7			11*		3		9		1			5	2			
26		2				6	4	8	9					11	7					1			5	3	10		
27						6	7	8	9	4				11	3					1			5	2	10		
28						6	7	8	9	4				11	3					1			5	2	10		
29						6	7	8	9*	4				11	3			12		1			5	2	10		
30			3			6	7	8	9*	4				11				12		1			5	2	10		
31			12			6	9	8	7	4	11			3*						1			5	2	10		
32			3			6	7	8		4	11			12						1			5	2	10*	9	
33			3			6	4			10	7			11						1			5	2	10	9	8
34			3			6	4			10	7			11						1			5	2	10	9	8
35			3			6	7	8	11						4					1			5	2	10	9	
36			3			6	7	8	11						4					1			5	2	10	9	
37	1		3			6	7	8	11						4								5	2	10	9	
38	1		3			6	7	8	11						4								5	2	10	9	
39	1		3			6	7	8	11*					12	4								5	2	10	9	
40	1		3			6	7	8	11						2				4				5		10	9	
41	1		3			6	11	8	12				5*		2				7				4		10	9	
42	1		3			6	7	8	11					12	2				4*				5		10	9	
43	1		3			6	4	8	7					11	2								5		10	9	
44	1		6			5	4	8	7					11	3								2		10	9	
45	1		6			5	4	8	7					11	3								2		10	9	
46			3			6	8		7					11	4				1				5	2	10	9	
Apps	24	15	33	10	6	46	45	40	38	32	8	11	28	11	29	5	4	8	4	22	7	1	24	19	19	15	2
Subs		2						1		1					1	4	2					1					
Goals			1	1		5	14	12	3	3			3				2	1					3	1	3	4	1

F.A. CUP

Rnd	Date	Opposition	Res.	Att.	Goalscorers
1R	24 Nov	SOUTHPORT	2-1	2935	Phillips, Wigg
2R	15 Dec	Wrexham	0-3	4114	

Rnd	Houghton W.	Breckin J.	Swift T.	Womble T.	Wigg R.	Phillips T.	Bentley D.	Mullen J.	Mielczarek R.	Crawford A.	Wilkinson W.	Leng M.	Henderson A.	Delgado R.	Derrett S.
1R	2	11	5	7	8*	9	10			4	3	12		1	6
2R	12	4	6	7	8		10	11		2*	3	5	9	1	

LEAGUE CUP

Rnd	Date	Opposition	Res.	Att.	Goalscorers
1R	28 Aug	LINCOLN CITY	2-1	3455	Phillips, Sjoberg
2R	10 Oct	EXETER CITY	1-4	2559	Gilbert

Rnd	Turks R.	Houghton W.	Breckin J.	O'Grady M.	Sjoberg J.	Swift T.	Womble T.	Wigg R.	Phillips T.	Bentley D.	Mullen J.	Mielczarek R.	Henderson A.	Gilbert C.
1R	1	2	3	4	5	6	7	8	9	10	11*	12		
2R	1	2	3			6	7	4	9	10		11	5	8

Final League Table

		Pl.	Home W	D	L	F	A	Away W	D	L	F	A	F.	A.	Pts
1	Peterborough Utd.	46	19	4	0	49	10	8	7	8	26	28	75	38	65
2	Gillingham	46	16	5	2	51	16	9	7	7	39	33	90	49	62
3	Colchester United	46	16	5	2	46	14	8	7	8	27	22	73	36	60
4	Bury	46	18	3	2	51	14	6	8	9	30	35	81	49	59
5	Northampton Town	46	14	7	2	39	14	6	6	11	24	34	63	48	53
6	Reading	46	11	9	3	37	13	5	10	8	21	24	58	37	51
7	Chester	46	13	6	4	31	19	4	9	10	23	36	54	55	49
8	Bradford City	46	14	7	2	45	20	3	7	13	13	32	58	52	48
9	Newport County	46	13	6	4	39	23	3	8	12	17	42	56	65	45
10	Exeter City	45	12	5	6	37	20	6	3	13	21	35	58	55	44
11	Hartlepool	46	11	4	8	29	16	5	8	10	19	31	48	47	44
12	Lincoln City	46	10	8	5	40	30	6	4	13	23	37	63	67	44
13	Barnsley	46	15	5	3	42	16	2	5	16	16	48	58	64	44
14	Swansea City	46	11	6	6	28	15	5	5	13	17	31	45	46	43
15	Rotherham United	46	10	9	4	33	22	5	4	14	23	36	56	58	43
16	Torquay United	46	11	7	5	37	23	2	10	11	15	34	52	57	43
17	Mansfield Town	46	13	8	2	47	24	0	9	14	15	45	62	69	43
18	Scunthorpe United	45	12	7	3	33	17	2	5	16	14	47	47	64	42
19	Brentford	46	9	7	7	31	20	3	9	11	17	30	48	50	40
20	Darlington	46	9	8	6	29	24	4	5	14	11	38	40	62	39
21	Crewe Alexandra	46	11	5	7	28	30	3	5	15	15	41	43	71	38
22	Doncaster Rovers	46	10	7	6	32	22	2	4	17	15	58	47	80	35
23	Workington	46	10	8	5	33	26	1	5	17	10	48	43	74	35
24	Stockport County	46	4	12	7	22	25	3	8	12	22	44	44	69	34

(Back): McDonagh, Breckin, Sjoberg, Henderson, Swift, Wigg, Tunks.
(Middle): Womble, Phillips, Bentley, Houghton, Mullen, Mielczarek, Hudson, Gilbert.
(Front): Robinson, Abrahams, Leng, Crawford, O'Grady, Ferguson, Wilkinson, Johnson, Whitehead.

- 1973-74 -

(Back): Bell (Coach), Swift, McDonagh, Henderson, Peck, Womble, Haslam, Claxton (Coach).
(Middle): McGuigan(Man.), Delgado, Syrat, Spencer, Leng, Crawford, Robinson, Goodfellow, Smith(Physio)
(Front): Phillips, Finney, Wigg, Breckin, Davey, Woodall, Derrett.

- 1974-75 -

SEASON 1974/75
DIVISION FOUR

No.	Date	Opposition	Res.	Att.	Goalscorers	McDonagh J.	Derrett S.	Breckin J.	Leng M.	Delgado R.	Spencer T.	Finney R.	Wigg R.	Phillips T.	Goodfellow J.	Crawford A.	Swift T.	Womble T.	Woodall J.	Habbin R.	Wagstaff B.
1	17 Aug	Torquay United	3-0	3850	Crawford, Finney, Phillips	1	2	3	4	5	6	7	8	9	10	11					
2	24	READING	2-1	2721	Finney, Phillips	1	2	3	4	5	6	7	8	9	10	11					
3	30	Workington	2-0	1456	Wigg, Womble	1	2	3	4*	5	6	7	8		10	11	12	9			
4	7 Sep	LINCOLN CITY	2-2	3608	Breckin, Woodall	1	2	3	4	5	6	7			10	11		9	8		
5	14	Hartlepool	2-3	2346	Finney, Swift	1	2	3		5	6	7			10	11	4	9	8		
6	16	Brentford	4-3	5980	Wigg(2), Swift, Woodall	1	2	3		5	6	7	9			11	4	10	8		
7	21	DARLINGTON	1-1	3743	Crawford	1	2	3		5	6	7	9			11	4	10	8		
8	24	BRADFORD CITY	4-0	4781	Finney(2), Delgado, Womble	1	2	3		5	6	7	9			11	4	10	8		
9	28	Doncaster Rovers	0-0	4710		1	2	3		5	6	7	9			11	4	10	8		
10	1 Oct	SHREWSBURY TOWN	0-0	6495		1	2	3		5	6	7	9*	12		11	4	10	8		
11	5	Northampton Town	1-3	4934	Womble	1	2	3		5	6	7*	9		10	11	12	4	8		
12	12	Rochdale	2-1	1684	Crawford, Womble	1	2	3		5	6	7	9		10	11	4	8			
13	19	SOUTHPORT	3-0	4102	Womble(2), Crawford	1	2	3		5	6	7	9		10	11	4	8			
14	21	Stockport County	0-1	2275		1	2	3		5	6	7	9		10	11	4	8			
15	26	Scunthorpe United	3-0	2838	Swift, Wigg, Womble	1	2	3		5	6	7	9		10	11	4	8			
16	2 Nov	NEWPORT COUNTY	1-1	4642	Phillips	1	2	3	12	5	6		9*	7	10	11	4	8			
17	5	STOCKPORT COUNTY	3-0	3490	Breckin, Crawford, Finney	1	2	3		5	6	7			10	11	4	8			
18	8	Swansea City	2-0	2414	Finney, Womble	1	2	3		5	6	7	9		10	11	4	8			
19	16	EXETER CITY	1-1	4623	Breckin	1	2	3	4	5	6	7	9		10	11		8			
20	30	Cambridge United	0-0	2881		1	2	3		5	6	7	9		10	11		8			
21	7 Dec	CHESTER	1-2	4412	Woodall	1	2	3		5	6	7	9		10*	11	4	8	12		
22	21	Mansfield Town	1-1	8559	Crawford	1	2	3		5	6		9		10	11	4	8		7	
23	26	HARTLEPOOL	1-2	5643	Wigg	1	2	3		5	6		9		10	11	4	8		7	
24	11 Jan	Chester	1-0	5832	Wigg	1	2	3		5	6	7	9	8	10	11		4			
25	18	CAMBRIDGE UNITED	0-0	3957		1	2	3		5	6	7	9	8	10	11		4			
26	1 Feb	SWANSEA CITY	1-0	4123	Delgado	1	2	3		5	6	7		8	10	11		4		9	
27	4	BRENTFORD	3-0	4410	Crawford, Finney, Phillips	1	2	3		5	6	7		8	10	11		4		9	
28	8	Newport County	1-1	4161	Habbin	1	2	3		5	6	7			10	11	4	8		9	
29	15	CREWE ALEXANDRA	1-1	4364	Finney	1	2	3		5	6	7		8	10	11		4		9	
30	22	Exeter City	4-0	3548	Finney, Goodfellow, Habbin, Phillips	1	2	3		5	6	7		8	10	11		4		9	
31	25	Barnsley	1-1	7635	Habbin	1	2	3		5	6	7		8	10	11		4		9	
32	1 Mar	WORKINGTON	1-0	5052	Habbin	1	2	3*	7	5	6			8	10	11	12	4		9	
33	5	Crewe Alexandra	0-1	2883		1	2	3	7	5	6			8	10	11		4		9	
34	15	DONCASTER ROVERS	1-0	8049	Womble	1	2	3		5	6			8	10	11		7		9	4
35	18	TORQUAY UNITED	3-1	5730	Derrett, Finney, Habbin	1	2	3		5	6	7		8	10	11				9	4
36	22	Lincoln City	0-2	8031		1	2	3		5	6	7		8*	10	11		4		9	12
37	29	MANSFIELD TOWN	2-1	11669	Habbin, Womble	1	2	3		5	6	7			10	11		8		9	4
38	31	BARNSLEY	2-0	9989	Finney, Womble	1	2	3		5	6	7	12		10	11		8		9	4*
39	1 Apr	Darlington	1-0	2504	Finney	1		3	2		6	7			10	11	5	8		9	4
40	5	SCUNTHORPE UNITED	3-2	6469	Habbin, Spencer, Womble	1		3	2	5	6				10	11		8		9	4
41	8	Shrewsbury Town	1-3	6538	Womble	1	2	3		5	6	7			10	11		8		9	4
42	12	Northampton Town	1-1	3714	Finney	1	2	3		5	6	7			10	11		8		9	4
43	16	Bradford Town	1-1	3278	Finney	1	2	3		5	6	7			10	11		8		9	4
44	19	ROCHDALE	3-1	7509	Habbin(2), Womble	1	2	3		5	6	7			10	11		8		9	4
45	23	Reading	1-1	4326	Habbin	1	2	3		5	6	7			10	11		8		9	4
46	26	Southport	0-2	2657		1	2	3		5	6	7			10	11		8		9	4
					Apps.	46	44	36	19	45	46	40	18	21	40	46	19	44	10	21	11
					Subs.				1					2			3		1		1
					Goals		1	3		2	1	15	6	5	1	7	3	14	3	10	

F.A. CUP

Round	Date	Opposition	Res.	Att.	Goalscorers	McDonagh J.	Derrett S.	Breckin J.	Leng M.	Delgado R.	Spencer T.	Finney R.	Wigg R.	Phillips T.	Goodfellow J.	Crawford A.	Swift T.	Womble T.	Woodall J.	Habbin R.	Wagstaff B.
1R	23 Nov	CHESTER	1-0	5358	Delgado	1	2	3		5	6	7		9	10	11	4	8			
2R	14 Dec	NORTHAMPTON TOWN	2-1	4741	Wigg(2)	1	2	3		5	6		9		10	11	4	8		7	
3R	4 Jan	Stafford Rangers	0-0	8532		1	2	3		5	6	7	9		10	11	4		8		
3Rr	7	STAFFORD RANGERS	0-2	11262		1	2		3	5	6	7	9		10	11	4	8			

LEAGUE CUP

Round	Date	Opposition	Res.	Att.	Goalscorers	McDonagh J.	Derrett S.	Breckin J.	Leng M.	Delgado R.	Spencer T.	Finney R.	Wigg R.	Phillips T.	Goodfellow J.	Crawford A.	Swift T.	Womble T.	Woodall J.	Habbin R.	Wagstaff B.
1R	20 Aug	LINCOLN CITY	1-1	2725	Crawford	1	2	3	4		6	7	8	9	10	11	5				
1Rr	28	Lincoln City	1-1	3254	Swift	1	2	3	4	5	6	7	8	9*	10	11	12				
1R2r	3 Sep	LINCOLN CITY	2-1	3577	Finney, Womble	1	2	3	4	5		7			10	11	6	9			
2R	11	Reading	2-4	8971	Crawford, Finney	1	2	3	4	5	6	7			10	11		9	8		

Final League Table

		Pl.	Home					Away					F.	A.	Pts
			W	D	L	F	A	W	D	L	F	A			
1	Mansfield Town	46	17	6	0	55	15	11	6	6	35	25	90	40	68
2	Shrewsbury Town	46	16	3	4	46	18	10	7	6	34	25	80	43	62
3	Rotherham United	46	13	7	3	40	19	9	8	6	31	22	71	41	59
4	Chester	46	17	5	1	48	9	6	6	11	16	29	64	38	57
5	Lincoln City	46	14	8	1	47	14	7	7	9	32	34	79	48	57
6	Cambridge United	46	15	5	3	43	16	5	9	9	19	28	62	44	54
7	Reading	46	13	6	4	38	20	8	4	11	25	27	63	47	52
8	Brentford	46	15	6	2	38	14	3	7	13	15	31	53	45	49
9	Exeter City	46	14	3	6	33	24	5	8	10	27	39	60	63	49
10	Bradford City	46	10	5	8	32	21	7	8	8	24	30	56	51	47
11	Southport	46	13	7	3	36	19	2	10	11	20	37	56	56	47
12	Newport County	46	13	5	5	43	30	6	4	13	25	45	68	75	47
13	Hartlepool	46	13	6	4	40	24	3	5	15	12	38	52	62	43
14	Torquay United	46	10	7	6	30	25	4	7	12	16	36	46	61	42
15	Barnsley	46	10	7	6	34	24	5	4	14	28	41	62	65	41
16	Northampton Town	46	12	6	5	43	22	3	5	15	24	51	67	73	41
17	Doncaster Rovers	46	10	9	4	41	29	4	3	16	24	50	65	79	40
18	Crewe Alexandra	46	9	5	9	22	16	2	9	12	12	31	34	47	40
19	Rochdale	46	9	9	5	35	22	4	4	15	24	53	59	75	39
20	Stockport County	46	10	8	5	35	26	2	6	15	17	43	43	70	38
21	Darlington	46	11	4	8	38	27	2	6	15	16	40	54	67	36
22	Swansea City	46	9	4	10	25	31	6	2	15	21	42	46	73	36
23	Workington	46	7	5	11	23	29	3	6	14	13	37	36	66	31
24	Scunthorpe United	46	7	8	8	27	29	0	7	16	14	49	41	78	29

SEASON 1975/76
DIVISION THREE

No.	Date	Opposition	Res.	Att.	Goalscorers	McDonagh J.	Leng M.	Breckin J.	Wagstaff B.	Stancliffe P.	Spencer T.	Finney R.	Phillips T.	Habbin R.	Goodfellow J.	Crawford A.	Haslam G.	Derrett S.	Green J.	Eades K.	Rhodes M.	Watling B.	Womble T.	McAllister	Gwyther D.	Delgado R.
1	16 Aug	Brighton & H.A.	0-3	10138		1	2	3	4	5	6	7	8	9	10	11										
2	23	HEREFORD UNITED	1-1	3825	Breckin		2	3	4	5		7	8*	9	10	11	1	6								12
3	30	Southend United	2-1	4219	Finney, Leng		7	3	4	5		8		9	10	11	1	6	2							
4	6 Sep	BURY	3-3	4070	Finney(2), Habbin	1	7	3	4	5		8		9	10	11		6	2							
5	13	Crystal Palace	0-2	16431		1	7	3	4	5		8		9	10	11		6	2							
6	20	WREXHAM	2-1	3776	Spencer, Wagstaff	1	7	3	4	5	6	8		9	10	11			2							
7	23	Gillingham	0-0	5498		1	7	3	4*	5	6	8	12	9	10	11			2							
8	27	Peterborough United	3-1	6543	Habbin(2), Phillips	1	7	3		5	6	8	4	9	10	11			2							
9	4 Oct	SWINDON TOWN	0-2	4731		1	7	3		5	6		4	9	10	11		12	2	8*						
10	11	CARDIFF CITY	1-0	4272	O.G.	1	7	3		5	6	8	4	9	10	11			2							
11	18	Millwall	1-3	6327	Habbin	1	7	3		5	6	8	4	9	10	11			2							
12	21	Colchester United	0-0	3468		1	7	3		5	6	8	4	9	10	11		2								
13	25	ALDERSHOT	2-2	4428	Crawford, Stancliffe	1	7	3		5	6	8	4	9	10	11		2								
14	1 Nov	Port Vale	0-1	3921		1	7	3		5	6	8	4	9	10	11			2							
15	4	CHESTER	0-1	4282		1	7	3		5	6	8	4	9	10	11			2							
16	8	WALSALL	3-1	4454	Phillips(2), Finney	1		3		5	6	7	8	9	10	11			2		4					
17	15	Shrewsbury Town	2-0	3775	Phillips(2)	1		3		5	6	7	8	9	10	11			2		4					
18	29	Sheffield Wednesday	0-0	18961		1		3		5	6	7	8	9	10	11			2		4					
19	6 Dec	CHESTERFIELD	2-0	6474	Goodfellow, Rhodes	1*		3		5	6	7	8	9	10	11			2		4		12			
20	20	MANSFIELD TOWN	2-1	6067	Phillips, Spencer			3		5	6	7	8	9	10	11			2		4	1				
21	26	Grimsby Town	1-4	6919	Finney			3		5	6	7	8	9	10	11			2		4	1				
22	27	HALIFAX TOWN	0-1	7614			7	3		5	6	9	8		10	11			2		4	1				
23	10 Jan	SOUTHEND UNITED	2-0	4390	Finney, Womble			3		5	6	7	8		10	11			2		4	1	9			
24	13	Preston N.E.	2-3	6289	Finney, Womble		12	3		5	6	7	8*		10	11			2		4	1	9			
25	17	Wrexham	0-3	2897				3		5	6	7		8	10	11			2		4		9	1		
26	31	COLCHESTER UNITED	2-0	3943	Leng, Spencer		7	3		5	6	8		9	10	11			2		4			1		
27	3 Feb	CRYSTAL PALACE	4-1	7633	Finney(2), Rhodes, Spencer		7	3		5	6	8		9	10	11			2		4			1		
28	7	Chester	1-3	4573	Stancliffe		7	3		5	6	8	12	9*	10	11			2		4			1		
29	13	Walsall	1-5	4989	Habbin		12	3		5	6	7	8	9	10	11			2*		4			1		
30	21	SHREWSBURY TOWN	0-1	4947				3	4	5		7		8	10	11		6	2					1	9	
31	24	GILLINGHAM	2-0	4404	Gwyther, Habbin			3		5	6*	7		8	10	11		12	2		4			1	9	
32	28	Aldershot	0-3	3538				3		5		7		8	10	11			2		4			1	9	
33	6 Mar	PORT VALE	1-2	4280	Rhodes		12	3		5*		7		8	10	11		6	2		4			1	9	
34	9	Swindon Town	1-1	9866	Goodfellow			3	5				7		10	11		6	2		4		8	1	9	
35	13	Cardiff City	1-1	11072	Gwyther			3	5				7		10	11		6	2		4		8	1	9	
36	16	MILLWALL	1-1	4556	Womble		12	3	5				7		10	11		6	2		4		8*	1	9	
37	20	SHEFFIELD WEDNESDAY	1-0	13567	Habbin			3	6	5			8	7	10	11			2		4			1	9	
38	27	Chesterfield	0-1	5995				3	6	5	12		8*	7	10	11			2		4			1	9	
39	29	Mansfield Town	1-1	9098	Crawford			3	4	5	6			8	10	11			2		7			1	9	
40	3 Apr	BRIGHTON	1-1	4309	Spencer			3	4	5	6			8	10	11			2		7			1	9	
41	6	PETERBOROUGH UNITED	1-1	3872	Crawford			3	4	5	6	7*	12	8	10	11			2					1	9	
42	10	Bury	0-4	5141				3	4	5	6		7	8	10	11			2					1	9	
43	17	GRIMSBY TOWN	3-0	4414	Crawford(2), Finney			3	5		6	7		8	10	11		2			4			1	9	
44	19	Halifax Town	1-0	2614	Gwyther		12	3		5	6	7*	8		10	11			2		4			1	9	
45	20	PRESTON N.E.	1-1	4874	Crawford		7	3		5	6	9	8		10	11			2		4			1	9	
46	24	Hereford United	2-3	8950	Crawford, Finney		7	3		5	6	9	8		10	11			2		4			1	9	
		Apps.				17	21	46	18	42	34	37	26	40	46	46	2	16	38	1	28	5	6	22	15	
		Subs.				5					1		3					2						1		1	
		Goals				2	1	1	2	5	11	6	7	2	7						3		3		3	

F.A. CUP

	Date	Opposition	Res.	Att.	Goalscorers	McDonagh J.	Leng M.	Breckin J.	Wagstaff B.	Stancliffe P.	Spencer T.	Finney R.	Phillips T.	Habbin R.	Goodfellow J.	Crawford A.	Haslam G.	Derrett S.	Green J.	Eades K.	Rhodes M.	Watling B.	Womble T.
1R	22 Nov	CREWE ALEXANDRA	2-1	5080	Crawford, Stancliffe	1		3		5	6	7	8	9*	10	11			2		4		12
2R	13 Dec	BRADFORD CITY	0-3	7006		1		3		5	6	7	8	9	10	11	1		2		4		

LEAGUE CUP

	Date	Opposition	Res.	Att.	Goalscorers	McDonagh J.	Leng M.	Breckin J.	Wagstaff B.	Stancliffe P.	Spencer T.	Finney R.	Phillips T.	Habbin R.	Goodfellow J.	Crawford A.	Haslam G.	Derrett S.	Green J.
1R1L	19 Aug	NOTTINGHAM FOREST	1-2	4912	Crawford	1	2	3	4	5	6*	7	8	9	10	11		12	
1R2L	27	Nottingham Forest	1-5	7977	Goodfellow		7	3	4	5		8		9	10	11	1	6	2

Final League Table

		Pl.	Home				Away				F.	A.	Pts
			W	D	L	F A	W	D	L	F A			
1	Hereford United	46	14	6	3	45 24	12	5	6	41 31	86	55	63
2	Cardiff City	46	14	7	2	38 13	8	6	9	31 35	69	48	57
3	Millwall	46	16	6	1	35 14	4	10	9	19 29	54	43	56
4	Brighton & Hove A.	46	18	3	2	58 15	4	6	13	20 38	78	53	53
5	Crystal Palace	46	7	12	4	30 20	11	5	7	31 26	61	46	53
6	Wrexham	46	13	6	4	38 21	7	6	10	28 34	66	55	52
7	Walsall	46	11	8	4	43 22	7	6	10	31 39	74	61	50
8	Preston North End	46	15	4	4	45 23	4	6	13	17 34	62	57	48
9	Shrewsbury Town	46	14	2	7	36 25	5	8	10	25 34	61	59	48
10	Peterborough Utd.	46	12	7	4	37 23	3	11	9	26 40	63	63	48
11	Mansfield Town	46	8	11	4	31 22	8	4	11	27 30	58	52	47
12	Port Vale	46	10	10	3	33 21	5	6	12	22 33	55	54	46
13	Bury	46	11	7	5	33 16	3	9	11	18 30	51	46	44
14	Chesterfield	46	11	5	7	45 30	6	4	13	24 39	69	69	43
15	Gillingham	46	10	8	5	38 27	2	11	10	20 41	58	68	43
16	Rotherham United	46	11	6	6	35 22	4	6	13	19 43	54	65	42
17	Chester	46	13	7	3	34 19	2	5	16	9 43	43	62	42
18	Grimsby Town	46	13	7	3	39 21	2	3	18	23 53	62	74	40
19	Swindon Town	46	11	4	8	42 31	5	4	14	20 44	62	75	40
20	Sheffield Wed.	46	12	6	5	34 25	0	10	13	14 34	48	59	40
21	Aldershot	46	10	8	5	34 26	3	5	15	25 49	59	75	39
22	Colchester United	46	9	6	8	25 27	3	8	12	16 38	41	65	38
23	Southend United	46	9	7	7	40 31	3	6	14	25 44	65	75	37
24	Halifax Town	46	6	5	12	22 32	5	8	10	19 29	41	61	35

(Back): Swift, Stancliffe, Delgado, McDonagh, Wagstaff, Breckin, Spencer, Derrett.
(Front): Leng, Crawford, Phillips, Goodfellow, Finney, Habbin.

- 1975-76 -

(Back): Haslam, Habbin, Spencer, McDonagh, Green, McAlister, Stancliffe, Gwyther, Wagstaff, Breckin, Rhodes, Smith.
(Front): Bell (Coach), Goodfellow, Finney, Pugh, Womble, Phillips, Crawford, Nix, McGuigan (Man.)

- 1976-77 -

SEASON 1976/77

DIVISION THREE

No.	Date	Opposition	Res.	Att.	Goalscorers	McAlister T.	Stancliffe P.	Breckin J.	Pugh D.	Spencer T.	Wagstaff B.	Finney R.	Phillips T.	Habbin R.	Rhodes M.	Crawford A.	Smith I.	Goodfellow J.	Gwyther D.	Womble T.	Green J.
1	21 Aug	Peterborough United	2-0	6247	Phillips, Finney	1	2		3	5	6	7	8	4		11		10	9		
2	24	BURY	3-0	4707	Phillips(2), Gwyther	1	2*	12	3	5	6	7	8	4		11		10	9		
3	28	MANSFIELD TOWN	3-0	5358	Crawford, Finney, Gwyther	1	2		3	5	6	7	8	4		11		10	9		
4	4 Sep	Brighton & H.A.	1-3	16059	Crawford	1	2	3		5	6	7	8	4*	12	11		10	9		
5	11	OXFORD UNITED	1-1	4420	Phillips	1	2	3		5	6	7	8	4		11		10	9		
6	18	Preston N.E.	0-0	7899		1	2	3	4	5	6	7	8			11		10	9		
7	25	CHESTER	1-1	3913	Gwyther	1	2	3	4	5	6	7	8	12		11		10*	9		
8	2 Oct	GRIMSBY TOWN	3-2	3925	Crawford, Gwyther, Phillips	1	2	3	4	5	6	7	8			11		10	9		
9	9	York City	1-1	3811	Crawford	1	2	3	4	5	6		8			11		10	9	7	
10	16	TRANMERE ROVERS	1-2	4365	Crawford	1	2	3	4*	5	6		8	12		11		10	9	7	
11	23	Crystal Palace	1-2	13819	Gwyther	1	5	3	4	6	10		8			11			9	7	2
12	26	PORTSMOUTH	2-2	4428	Spencer(2)	1	5	3	4	6	10		8	12	4	11			9	7*	
13	29	Lincoln City	2-2	9318	Gwyther, Phillips	1	5	3	2	6		7	8		4	11		10	9		
14	2 Nov	Sheffield Wednesday	3-1	18204	Gwyther, Phillips, Spencer	1	5	3	2	6		7	8		4	11		10	9		
15	6	SHREWSBURY TOWN	1-0	4761	Crawford	1	5	3	2	6		7	8		4	11		10	9		
16	13	Swindon Town	4-2	7604	Crawford(2), Phillips(2)	1	5	3	2	6		7	8		4	11		10	9		
17	27	WALSALL	1-0	6180	Finney	1	5	3	2	6		7	8		4	11		10	9		
18	4 Dec	Gillingham	2-1	4715	Crawford, Phillips	1	5	3	2	6		7	8		4	11		10	9		
19	18	PORT VALE	1-1	4812	O.G.	1	5	3	2	6		7	8		4	11		10	9		
20	27	Northampton Town	4-1	6963	Crawford(2), Finney, Phillips	1	5	3	2	6		7	8		4	11		10	9		
21	28	CHESTERFIELD	1-0	9880	Crawford	1	5	3	2	6		7	8		4	11		10	9		
22	15 Jan	Bury	1-1	6575	O.G.	1	5	3	2	6		7	8		4	11		10	9		
23	22	PETERBOROUGH UNITED	0-0	6889		1	5	3	2	6		7	8		4	11		10	9		
24	1 Feb	Shrewsbury Town	0-0	5509		1	5	3	2	6		7	8		4	11		10	9		
25	5	Mansfield Town	1-3	11527	Crawford	1	5	3	2	6		7	8		4	11		10	9		
26	12	BRIGHTON & H.A.	0-0	9303		1	5	3	2	6		7	8			11		10	9	4	
27	15	WREXHAM	2-0	8375	Crawford, Phillips	1	5	3	2	6		7	8			11		10	9	4	
28	19	Oxford United	2-1	4956	Crawford, Womble	1	5	3	2	6		7	8			11		10	9	4	
29	26	PRESTON N.E.	2-0	8860	Crawford, Habbin	1	5	3	2	6			8	7		11		10	9	4	
30	5 Mar	Chester	3-1	6150	Crawford, Gwyther, Phillips	1	5	3	2	6			8	7		11		10	9	4	
31	8	LINCOLN CITY	1-0	10045	Crawford	1	5	3	2	6			8	7		11		10	9	4	
32	12	Grimsby Town	1-1	5792	Finney	1	5	3	2	6		7	8			11		10	9	4	
33	19	YORK CITY	1-1	7409	Crawford	1	5	3	2	6			8	7		11		10	9	4	
34	25	Tranmere Rovers	1-0	3738	Crawford	1	5	3	2	6			8	7		11		10	9	4	
35	2 Apr	CRYSTAL PALACE	1-1	8353	Gwyther	1	5	3	2	6			8	7		11		10	9	4	
36	9	Chesterfield	0-1	9088		1	5	3	2	6	12		8	7		11		10	9	4*	
37	11	NORTHAMPTON TOWN	2-0	7286	Crawford, Gwyther	1	5	3	2	6			8	7	4	11		10	9		
38	12	SHEFFIELD WEDNESDAY	0-1	17356		1	5	3	2	6	12	7	8		4	11		10*	9		
39	16	Portsmouth	1-5	10588	Phillips	1	5	3	2	6	10	7	8		4	11			9		
40	18	Wrexham	1-2	14622	Phillips	1	5	3	2	6		7	8			11			9	10	
41	23	SWINDON TOWN	1-1	5631	Phillips	1	5	3	2	6		7	8			11		10	4	9	
42	30	Walsall	1-0	5399	Finney	1	5	3	2	6		7	8	12		11		10	4	9*	
43	3 May	READING	1-2	4200	Gwyther	1	5	3	2	6		7	8	9*		11		10	4	12	
44	7	GILLINGHAM	1-0	3004	Phillips	1	5	3	2	6		7	8	9		11		10	4		
45	11	Reading	3-0	5680	Phillips(3)	1	5	3	2	6		7	8	9		11		10	4		
46	14	Port Vale	4-1	4271	Crawford(2), Habbin, Phillips	1	5	3	2	6		7	8	9		11		10	4		
		Apps.				46	46	43	44	46	13	34	46	17	18	46		42	46	18	1
		Subs.						1			2			4	1					1	
		Goals								3		6	21	2		23			11	1	

F.A. CUP

	Date	Opposition	Res.	Att.	Goalscorers	McAlister T.	Stancliffe P.	Breckin J.	Pugh D.	Spencer T.	Wagstaff B.	Finney R.	Phillips T.	Habbin R.	Rhodes M.	Crawford A.	Smith I.	Goodfellow J.	Gwyther D.	Womble T.	Green J.
1R	20 Nov	ALTRINCHAM	5-0	5969	Finney(2), Breckin, Crawfrd, Gwytr	1	5	3	2	6		7	8		4	11		10	9		
2R	11 Dec	YORK CITY	0-0	7076		1	5	3	2	6		7	8		4	11		10	9		
2Rr	14	York City	1-1	3996	Crawford	1	5	3	2	6		7	8		4	11		10	9		
2R2r	21	York City	2-1	6714	Crawford(2)	1	5	3	2	6		7	8		4	11		10	9		
3R	8 Jan	Wolverhampton Wands.	2-3	23605	Crawford(2)	1	5	3	2	6		7	8		4	11		10	9		

LEAGUE CUP

	Date	Opposition	Res.	Att.	Goalscorers	McAlister T.	Stancliffe P.	Breckin J.	Pugh D.	Spencer T.	Wagstaff B.	Finney R.	Phillips T.	Habbin R.	Rhodes M.	Crawford A.	Smith I.	Goodfellow J.	Gwyther D.	Womble T.	Green J.
1R1L	14 Aug	Chesterfield	1-3	4427	Phillips	1	2	3	4	5	6	7	8	9	10	11					
1R2L	17	CHESTERFIELD	3-0	3735	Crawford(2), Phillips	1	2		4	5	6	7	8	9	12	11	3*	10			
2R	1 Sep	MILLWALL	1-2	5005	O.G.	1	2	3		5	6	7	8	4		11		10	9		

Final League Table

		Pl.	Home					Away					F.	A.	Pts
			W	D	L	F	A	W	D	L	F	A			
1	Mansfield Town	46	17	6	0	52	13	11	2	10	26	29	78	42	64
2	Brighton & Hove A.	46	19	3	1	63	14	6	8	9	20	26	83	40	61
3	Crystal Palace	46	17	5	1	46	15	6	8	9	22	25	68	40	59
4	Rotherham United	46	11	9	3	30	15	11	6	6	39	29	69	44	59
5	Wrexham	46	15	6	2	47	22	9	4	10	33	32	80	54	58
6	Preston North End	46	15	4	4	48	21	6	8	9	16	22	64	43	54
7	Bury	46	15	2	6	41	21	8	6	9	23	38	64	59	54
8	Sheffield Wed.	46	15	4	4	39	18	7	5	11	26	37	65	55	53
9	Lincoln City	46	12	9	2	50	30	7	5	11	27	40	77	70	52
10	Shrewsbury Town	46	13	7	3	40	21	5	4	14	25	38	65	59	47
11	Swindon Town	46	12	6	5	48	33	3	9	11	20	42	68	75	45
12	Gillingham	46	11	8	4	31	21	5	4	14	24	43	55	64	44
13	Chester	46	14	3	6	28	20	4	5	14	20	38	48	58	44
14	Tranmere Rovers	46	10	7	6	31	23	3	10	10	20	30	51	53	43
15	Walsall	46	7	8	8	39	32	5	8	10	18	33	57	65	41
16	Peterborough Utd.	46	11	4	8	33	28	2	11	10	22	37	55	65	41
17	Oxford United	46	9	8	6	34	29	3	7	13	21	36	55	65	39
18	Chesterfield	46	10	6	7	30	20	4	4	15	26	44	56	64	38
19	Port Vale	46	9	7	7	29	28	2	9	12	18	43	47	71	38
20	Portsmouth	46	8	9	6	28	26	3	5	15	25	44	53	70	36
21	Reading	46	10	5	8	29	24	3	4	16	20	49	49	73	35
22	Northampton Town	46	9	4	10	33	29	4	4	15	27	46	60	75	34
23	Grimsby Town	46	10	6	7	29	22	2	3	18	16	47	45	69	33
24	York City	46	7	8	8	25	34	3	4	16	25	55	50	89	32

SEASON 1977/78

DIVISION THREE

No.	Date	Opposition	Res.	Att.	Goalscorers	McAlister T.	Forrest G.	Breckin J.	Gwyther D.	Green J.	Spencer T.	Finney R.	Phillips T.	Young T.	Goodfellow J.	Crawford A.	Rhodes M.	Stancliffe P.	Habbin R.	Womble T.	Matthews P.	Smith I.	Dawson R.	Nix P.	Pugh D.
1	20 Aug	Oxford United	3-2	4614	Goodfellow, Phillips, Spencer	1	2	3		5	6	7	8	9*	10	11	4		12						
2	27	Preston N.E.	2-3	5964	Finney(2)	1	2	3	.		6	7	8		10	11	4	5	9*	12					
3	3 Sep	CARLISLE UNITED	0-0	4052		1	2	11	9	3	6	7		8*	10		4	5		12					
4	10	Hereford United	3-2	4393	Crawford, Rhodes, Womble	1	2	3	9		6	7			10	11	4	5		8					
5	13	EXETER CITY	1-0	4889	Finney	1	2	3	9		6	7			10	11	4	5		8					
6	17	COLCHESTER UNITED	1-0	4906	Womble	1	2	3	9		6	7			10	11	4	5		8					
7	24	Cambridge United	1-1	4381	Phillips	1	2	3	9	12	6*	7	8		10	11	4	5							
8	27	Shrewsbury Town	1-4	4191	Finney	1	2	3	9	6		7	8		10	11	4	5							
9	1 Oct	BRADFORD CITY	2-1	5878	Breckin, Rhodes	1	2	3	9	6		7	8		10	11	4	5							
10	4	WALSALL	3-0	4848	Crawford(2), Stancliffe	1	2	3	9	6		7	8		10*	11	4	5		12					
11	8	Gillingham	1-2	7584	Phillips	1	2	3	10	6		7	8			11	4	5		9					
12	11	PLYMOUTH ARGYLE	1-2	6286	Phillips	1	2	3	9	6		7	8		10	11	4*	5		12					
13	15	CHESTER	1-1	4825	Crawford	1		3	9	6		7	8		10	11		5		2	4				
14	21	Tranmere Rovers	2-2	6215	Crawford, Finney	1	2	3	9	6		7	8		10	11		5			4				
15	29	LINCOLN CITY	0-0	5058		1	2	3	9	6		7	8		10	11		5			4				
16	5 Nov	Bury	1-1	5198	Phillips	1	2	3	9	6		7	8		10	11		5			4				
17	12	PETERBOROUGH UNITED	0-1	4200		1	2	3	9	6		7*	8		10	11		5		12	4				
18	19	Swindon Town	0-2	6024		1	2	3	9	6		7	8		10	11		5			4				
19	3 Dec	WREXHAM	2-2	5105	Crawford, Stancliffe	1	2	3*		6		7	8	9		11		5		4		12			
20	10	Portsmouth	3-3	9466	Gwyther(2), Finney	1	2	3	9	6		7	8		10	11		5		4					
21	26	CHESTERFIELD	1-2	6599	Phillips	1	2	3	9	6		7	8		10	11*		5		12	4				
22	27	Sheffield Wednesday	0-1	18973		1	2	3				7	8			11			4	6	5	9			
23	31	Port Vale	0-3	3861		1	2	3				7	8		10			11	4	9	5				
24	2 Jan	BURY	0-3	4609		1	5	3			6	7	8		10			4		9		2	11		
25	14	OXFORD UNITED	2-0	3542	Crawford, Dawson	1	5	3			6	7			10	8	4			2			9	11	
26	7 Feb	Carlisle United	1-2	5359	Gwyther	1	2	3	4	5	6	7	8		10								9	11	
27	25	Bradford City	0-3	6357		1	2		4	3	6	7	8		10	11	12	5*					9		
28	4 Mar	GILLINGHAM	2-0	3731	Finney, Nix	1	2	3	9	5	6	7	8		10			4						11	
29	8	Exeter City	0-1	4106		1	5	3	9	6		7	8		10		4							11	2
30	11	Chester	1-2	3741	Finney	1	5	3	9	6		7	8		10		4							11	2
31	14	CAMBRIDGE UNITED	1-0	3746	Finney	1	5	3	9	6		7	8		10		4							11	2
32	18	TRANMERE ROVERS	2-0	3655	Green, Rhodes	1	5	3	9	6		7	8		10		4							11	2
33	24	Lincoln City	3-3	5795	Gwyther(2), Finney	1	5	3	9	6		7	8		10		4							11	2
34	25	SHEFFIELD WEDNESDAY	1-2	12630	Finney	1	5	3	9	6		7	8	12	10		4							11*	2
35	27	Chesterfield	0-0	6960		1	2	3	9	6		7	8		10		4	5						11	
36	1 Apr	PORT VALE	2-0	3707	Finney, Goodfellow	1	2	3	9	6		7	8		10		4	5						11	
37	4	SHREWSBURY TOWN	0-0	4262		1	2	3	9	6		7	8		10		4	5						11	
38	8	Peterborough United	0-1	7098		1	2	3	9	6		7	8		10		4	5						11	
39	11	Plymouth Argyle	1-1	5018	Gwyther	1	2	3	9	6		7	8		10		4	5						11	
40	15	SWINDON TOWN	1-3	3824	Gwyther	1	2	3	9	6		7	8		10		4	5						11	
41	18	HEREFORD UNITED	1-0	3244	Finney	1	2	3	9	6		7	8		10	11	4	5*							12
42	22	Wrexham	1-7	16535	Phillips	1	2	3	9	6	5	7	8		10	11	4								
43	25	PRESTON N.E.	2-1	5646	Phillips, Stancliffe	1	4	3	9	6			8	12	10	11		5			7*			2	
44	29	PORTSMOUTH	0-1	3718		1	4	3	9	6			8	12	10	11		5			7*			2	
45	1 May	Walsall	1-3	4364	Gwyther	1		3	9	6		7	8		10	11	4	5						2	
46	3	Colchester United	0-0	2554		1	4	3	9	6		7	8	12	10	11		5*						2	
		Apps.				46	44	45	39	40	11	44	41	3	45	28	32	32	1	12	8	3	7	15	10
		Subs.								1									4		1	6	1			1
		Goals					1		8	1	1	13	8		2	7	3	3		2			1	1	

F.A. CUP

No.	Date	Opposition	Res.	Att.	Goalscorers	McAlister T.	Forrest G.	Breckin J.	Gwyther D.	Green J.	Spencer T.	Finney R.	Phillips T.	Young T.	Goodfellow J.	Crawford A.	Rhodes M.	Stancliffe P.	Habbin R.	Womble T.	Matthews P.	Smith I.	Dawson R.	Nix P.	Pugh D.
1R	26 Nov	MOSSLEY	3-0	4453	Finney, Gwyther, Phillips	1	2	3	9	6		7	8		10	11		5		12	4*				
2R	17 Dec	SPENNYMOOR	6-0	4788	Phillips(3), Crawford(2), Gwyther	1	2	3	9	6		7	8		10	11		5		4					
3R	7 Jan	MILLWALL	1-1	5337	Finney	1	2	3		6		7	8		10			5		4			9	11	
3Rr	10	Millwall	0-2	8051		1	5	3		6			8		10			7		2	4		9	11	

LEAGUE CUP

No.	Date	Opposition	Res.	Att.	Goalscorers	McAlister T.	Forrest G.	Breckin J.	Gwyther D.	Green J.	Spencer T.	Finney R.	Phillips T.	Young T.	Goodfellow J.	Crawford A.	Rhodes M.	Stancliffe P.	Habbin R.	Womble T.	Matthews P.	Smith I.	Dawson R.	Nix P.	Pugh D.
1R1L	13 Aug	YORK CITY	3-0	2462	Gwyther(2), Finney	1	2	3	4	5	6	7	8	9	10	11									
1R2L	16	York City	0-3	1671		1	2	3	4	5	6	7	8	9	10	11									
1Rr	23	York City*	6-5	2569	Crawford	1	2	3			6	7			10	11	4	5				8	9		
2R	31	West Bromwich Albion	0-4	15009		1	2	3	9		6	7	8		10	11	4	5							

* Full time 1-1, 6-5 after penalties -
scorers: Crawford, Finney, Habbin, Goodfellow, Forrest, Rhodes

Final League Table

		Pl	Home					Away					F.	A.	Pts
			W	D	L	F	A	W	D	L	F	A			
1	Wrexham	46	14	8	1	48	19	9	7	7	30	26	78	45	61
2	Cambridge United	46	19	3	1	49	11	4	9	10	23	40	72	51	58
3	Preston North End	46	16	5	2	48	19	4	11	8	15	19	63	38	56
4	Peterborough Utd.	46	15	7	1	32	11	5	9	9	15	22	47	33	56
5	Chester	46	14	8	1	41	24	2	14	7	18	32	59	56	54
6	Walsall	46	14	8	1	35	17	6	9	8	26	33	61	50	53
7	Gillingham	46	11	10	2	36	21	4	10	9	31	39	67	60	50
8	Colchester United	46	10	11	2	36	16	5	7	11	19	28	55	44	48
9	Chesterfield	46	14	6	3	40	16	3	8	12	18	33	58	49	48
10	Swindon Town	46	12	7	4	40	22	4	9	10	27	38	67	60	48
11	Shrewsbury Town	46	11	7	5	42	23	5	8	10	21	34	63	57	47
12	Tranmere Rovers	46	13	7	3	39	19	3	8	12	18	33	57	52	47
13	Carlisle United	46	13	7	3	32	26	4	10	9	27	33	59	59	47
14	Sheffield Wed.	46	13	7	3	28	14	2	9	12	22	38	50	52	46
15	Bury	46	7	13	3	34	22	6	6	11	28	34	62	56	45
16	Lincoln City	46	10	8	5	35	26	5	7	11	18	35	53	61	45
17	Exeter City	46	11	8	4	30	18	4	6	13	19	41	49	59	44
18	Oxford United	46	11	10	2	38	21	2	4	17	26	46	64	67	40
19	Plymouth Argyle	46	7	8	8	33	28	4	9	10	28	40	61	68	39
20	Rotherham United	46	7	9	7	26	19	2	8	13	25	49	51	68	39
21	Port Vale	46	7	11	5	28	23	1	9	13	18	44	46	67	36
22	Bradford City	46	11	6	6	40	29	1	4	18	16	57	56	86	34
23	Hereford United	46	9	9	5	28	22	0	5	18	6	38	34	60	32
24	Portsmouth	46	4	11	8	31	38	3	6	14	10	37	41	75	31

SEASON 1978/79

DIVISION THREE

No.	Date	Opposition	Res.	Att.	Goalscorers	McAlister T.	Forrest G.	Breckin J.	Rhodes M.	Green J.	Flynn J.	Finney R.	Phillips T.	Gwyther D.	Crawford A.	Smith D.	Vaughan I.	Dawson R.	Pugh D.	Stancliffe P.	Winn S.	Carr P.	Young T.	Mountford R.
1	19 Aug	Gillingham	0-0	4157		1	2	3	4	5	6	7	8	9	10	11								
2	26	BLACKPOOL	2-1	4572	Breckin, Finney	1	2	3	4	5	6	7	8	9	10	11								
3	2 Sep	Colchester United	0-0	2448		1	2	3	4	5	6	7	8	9	10	11								
4	5	HULL CITY	0-2	6389		1	2	3	4	5	6	7	8	9	10	11								
5	9	LINCOLN CITY	2-0	4427	Finney, Smith	1	2	3	4	5	6	7	8	9	10	11								
6	12	Swansea City	4-4	17065	Gwyther(3), Phillips	1	2	3	4	5	6	7	8	9	10	11								
7	15	Southend United	1-2	6527	Gwyther	1	2	3	4	5	6	7	8	9	10	11								
8	23	MANSFIELD TOWN	2-0	5350	Dawson, Finney	1	2	3		5			8	9	10	11	6*	7			12			
9	26	WATFORD	2-1	6442	Crawford, Gwyther	1	6	3		5		4	8	9*	10	11		7	2		12			
10	30	Plymouth Argyle	0-2	6705		1	6	3		5		4	8	9	10	11		7	2					
11	7 Oct	SHEFFIELD WEDNESDAY	0-1	13746		1	6	3		5		4	8	9	10	11		7	2					
12	14	Swindon Town	0-1	4476		1	2	3*		5	6	10	8	9	11	12		7		4				
13	17	BRENTFORD	1-0	3881	Flynn	1	2			6	3	10	8	4	11			7		5	9			
14	21	Carlisle United	1-1	5085	Phillips	1	2	3		6	10	7	8	4	11					5	9			
15	28	SHREWSBURY TOWN	1-2	4470	Phillips	1	2	3		6	10	7	8	4	11				12	5*	9			
16	4 Nov	Walsall	1-0	5456	Green	1	2	3		5	6	7	8	4	11	10					9			
17	11	COLCHESTER UNITED	1-0	3777	Finney	1	2	3		5	6	7	8	4	11	10			12		9*			
18	18	Blackpool	2-1	6085	Finney, Phillips	1	2	3		5	6	7	8	9	11	10				4				
19	2 Dec	Oxford United	0-1	3311		1	2	3		5	6	7	8	9	11	10				4				
20	9	CHESTERFIELD	1-0	4956	Gwyther	1	2	3		5	6	7	8	9	11	10				4				
21	23	TRANMERE ROVERS	3-2	3829	Phillips(2), Crawford	1	2	3		5	6	7	8	9	11	10				4				
22	26	Bury	2-3	5852	Phillips(2)	1	2	3		5	6	7	8	9	11	10				4				
23	3 Feb	Watford	2-2	12857	Gwyther, Phillips	1	2	3		5	6	7	8	9	11	10				4				
24	6	SOUTHEND UNITED	2-1	4478	Finney, Phillips	1	2	3		5	6	7	8	9	11	10				4				
25	10	PLYMOUTH ARGYLE	1-0	5237	Gwyther	1	2	3		5			8	9	11	10		7		4				
26	24	SWINDON TOWN	1-3	5128	Phillips	1	2	3		5	6	7*	8	9	11	10			12	4				
27	3 Mar	CARLISLE UNITED	1-3	3908	Finney	1	2	3		5	6	7	8	9	11	10				4				
28	6	SWANSEA CITY	0-1	3864		1	2	3		5	6	7	8	9	11	10				4				
29	14	Chester	1-0	2636	Gwyther	1	2	3		5	6	7	8	9	11					4		10		
30	24	Hull City	0-1	4717		1	2	3		5	6	7	8	9	11					4		10		
31	27	GILLINGHAM	1-1	3239	Phillips	1	2	3		5	6	7	8	9	11					4		10		
32	31	Exeter City	0-2	3349		1	2	3		5	6	7	8	9	11					4		10		
33	4 Apr	Lincoln City	0-3	3347		1	2	3		5	6	7	8	9	11					4		10		
34	7	OXFORD UNITED	0-0	2734		1	2	3	4	6		7	8		11					5	9	10		
35	14	BURY	2-1	3026	Gwyther, Rhodes	1	2	3	4	6		7	8	9	11					5		10		
36	16	Peterborough United	1-1	3807	Gwyther	1	2	3	4	6		7	8	9	11					5		10		
37	18	Tranmere Rovers	1-1	1254	Phillips	1	2	3	4	6		7	8	9	11					5		10		
38	21	CHESTER	0-1	2893		1	2	3	4	6		7	8	9	11					5		10		
39	23	Brentford	0-1	6710		1	2	3	4	6			8	9	11					5		10	7	
40	28	Chesterfield	0-1	4160		1	2	3	4	6		7		9	11					5		10	8	
41	1 May	PETERBOROUGH UNITED	1-1	2162	Finney	1	2	3	4	6		7	8		11					5		10	9	
42	5	EXETER CITY	2-1	2217	Gwyther, Young	1	2	3	4	6	12	7		9*	11					5		10	8	
43	7	Sheffield Wednesday	1-2	12094	Carr	1	2	3	4	6		7	8		11					5		10	9	
44	10	Shrewsbury Town	1-3	8450	Gwyther	1	2	3	4	6		7		9	11					5		10	8	
45	14	WALSALL	4-1	1996	Finney, Phillips, Smith, O.G.	1	2	3	4	6		7	8		11					5		10	9	
46	19	Mansfield Town	1-0	3913	Smith		2	3	4	6		7	8		11					5		10	9	1
		Apps.				45	46	45	20	46	29	41	46	41	39	31	1	7	3	33	6	18	8	1
		Subs.									1								3		2			
		Goals						1	1	1	1	9	14	13	2	3				1		1	1	

F.A. CUP

No.	Date	Opposition	Res.	Att.	Goalscorers	McAlister T.	Forrest G.	Breckin J.	Rhodes M.	Green J.	Flynn J.	Finney R.	Phillips T.	Gwyther D.	Crawford A.	Smith D.	Vaughan I.	Dawson R.	Pugh D.	Stancliffe P.
1R	25 Nov	WORKINGTON	3-0	3927	Gwyther(2), Breckin	1		3		5	6	7	8	9	11	10	2	12		4
2R	16 Dec	Barnsley	1-1	15491	Crawford	1	2	3		5	6	7	8	9	11	10				4
2Rr	9 Jan	BARNSLEY	2-1	15506	Gwyther, Phillips	1	2	3		5	6	7	8	9	11	10				4
3R	15	Manchester City	0-0	26209		1	2	3		5	6	7	8	9	11	10				4
3Rr	17	MANCHESTER CITY	2-4	13748	Breckin, Green	1	2	3		5	6	7	8	9	11	10				4

LEAGUE CUP

No.	Date	Opposition	Res.	Att.	Goalscorers	McAlister T.	Forrest G.	Breckin J.	Rhodes M.	Green J.	Flynn J.	Finney R.	Phillips T.	Gwyther D.	Crawford A.	Smith D.	Vaughan I.	Dawson R.	Pugh D.
1R1L	12 Aug	HARTLEPOOL	5-0	2341	Finney(3), Gwyther, Phillips	1	2	3	4	5	6	7	8	9	10	11			
1R2L	15	Hartlepool	1-1	1746	Crawford	1	2	3	4	5	6	7	8	9	10	11			
2R	30	ARSENAL	3-1	10481	Finney, Gwyther, Green	1	2	3	4	5	6	7	8	9	10	11			
3R	3 Oct	READING	2-2	6847	Crawford, Finney	1	2	3		5	6	4	8	9	10	11		7	
3Rr	11	Reading	0-1	12221		1	6	3		5		4	8	9	10	11		7	2

Final League Table

		Pl.	Home					Away					F.	A.	Pts
			W	D	L	F	A	W	D	L	F	A			
1	Shrewsbury Town	46	14	9	0	36	11	7	10	6	25	30	61	41	61
2	Watford	46	15	5	3	47	22	9	7	7	36	30	83	52	60
3	Swansea City	46	16	6	1	57	32	8	6	9	26	29	83	61	60
4	Gillingham	46	15	7	1	39	15	6	10	7	26	27	65	42	59
5	Swindon Town	46	17	2	4	44	14	8	5	10	30	38	74	52	57
6	Carlisle United	46	11	10	2	31	13	4	12	7	22	29	53	42	52
7	Colchester United	46	13	9	1	35	19	4	8	11	25	36	60	55	51
8	Hull City	46	13	9	2	36	14	7	2	14	30	47	66	61	49
9	Exeter City	46	14	6	3	38	18	3	9	11	23	38	61	56	49
10	Brentford	46	14	4	5	35	19	5	5	13	18	30	53	49	47
11	Oxford United	46	10	8	5	27	20	4	10	9	17	30	44	50	46
12	Blackpool	46	12	5	6	38	19	6	4	13	23	40	61	59	45
13	Southend United	46	11	6	6	30	17	4	9	10	21	32	51	49	45
14	Sheffield Wed.	46	9	8	6	30	22	4	11	8	23	31	53	53	45
15	Plymouth Argyle	46	11	9	3	40	27	4	5	14	27	41	67	68	44
16	Chester	46	11	9	3	42	21	3	7	13	15	40	57	61	44
17	Rotherham United	46	13	3	7	30	24	3	7	12	19	32	49	55	44
18	Mansfield Town	46	7	11	5	30	24	5	8	10	21	38	59	65	42
19	Bury	46	6	11	6	35	32	5	9	9	24	33	59	65	40
20	Chesterfield	46	10	5	8	35	34	3	9	11	16	31	51	65	40
21	Peterborough Utd.	46	8	7	8	26	24	3	7	13	18	39	44	63	36
22	Walsall	46	7	6	10	34	32	3	6	14	22	39	56	71	32
23	Tranmere Rovers	46	4	12	7	26	31	2	4	17	19	47	45	78	28
24	Lincoln City	46	5	7	11	26	38	2	4	17	15	50	41	88	25

(Back): Habbin, Pugh, Breckin, Smith, Forrest, Rhodes.
(Middle): McGuigan (Manager), Young, Gwyther, Stancliffe, McAlister, Green, Spencer, Bell (Coach).
(Front): Finney, Crawford, Phillips, Goodfellow, Womble, Eades, Nix.

- 1977-78 -

(Back): Tiler, McEwan, Gwyther, Mountford, Stancliffe, Winn, Flynn,
(Front): Breckin, Fern, Finney, Carr, Green, Gooding, Forrest, Smith, Rhodes.

- 1979-80 -

SEASON 1979/80

DIVISION THREE

No.	Date	Opposition	Res.	Att.	Goalscorers	Mountford R.	Forrest G.	Tiler K.	Rhodes M.	Green J.	Breckin J.	Gooding M.	McEwan W.	Gwyther D.	Fern R.	Finney R.	Flynn J.	Carr P.	Smith D.	Stancliffe P.	Nix P.	Dawson R.	Ogden C.	Henson P.	Brown G.	Halom V.	Owen G.	Taylor A.	Winn S.
1	18 Aug	Oxford United	1-5	3181	Rhodes	1	2	3	4			6	7	8	9	10	11	5											
2	21	MANSFIELD TOWN	2-1	4490	Fern, Finney	1	2	3	4	5	6	7	8	9	10	11													
3	25	COLCHESTER UNITED	3-0	3728	Fern, Finney, Gwyther	1	2	3	4	5	6	7	8	9	10	11													
4	1 Sep	Southend United	2-0	4765	Gwyther(2)	1	2	3	4	5	6	7	8	9	10	11													
5	8	SWINDON TOWN	3-0	4672	Gwyther(2), Tiler	1	2	3	4	5	6	7	8	9	10	11													
6	15	Blackpool	2-3	7807	Gwyther, Rhodes	1	2	3	4	5	6	7	8	9	10	11													
7	18	Carlisle United	1-3	3916	McEwan	1	2	3	4	5	6	7	8	9	10	11													
8	22	CHESTERFIELD	2-0	6174	McEwan(2)	1	2	3	4	5	6	7	8	9	10	11													
9	29	Blackburn Rovers	3-0	7435	Gwyther(2), Finney	1	2	3	4	5	6	7	8	9	10	11													
10	2 Oct	CARLISLE UNITED	4-1	6024	Fern(2), Finney, Gwyther	1	2	3	4	5	6	7	8	9	10	11													
11	6	SHEFFIELD UNITED	1-2	20355	Finney	1	2	3		5	6	7	8	9	10	11			4										
12	8	Mansfield Town	1-5	6308	Finney	1	2	3		5	6	7	8	9	10	11			4										
13	13	SHEFFIELD WEDNESDAY	1-2	18500	Finney	1	2	3	4	5	6		8	9	10	7					11								
14	20	Plymouth Argyle	0-1	4850		1	2	3	4		6	7	8	9	10	11				5									
15	23	HULL CITY	2-1	5917	Finney, Gwyther	1	2		4	6	3	7	8	9	10	11				5									
16	27	Grimsby Town	0-2	7702		1	2		4	6	3	7	8	9	10	11				5									
17	3 Nov	OXFORD UNITED	0-2	4365		1	2		4	6	3	7	8	9	10	11				5									
18	6	Hull City	1-1	5899	Nix	1	2		4	6	3		8	9	10	7				5	11								
19	10	Wimbledon	1-0	2798	Fern	1	2		4	6	3		8	9	10	7				5	11								
20	17	BRENTFORD	4-2	4709	McEwan(2), Finney, Green	1	2		4	6	3		8	9	10	7				5	11								
21	1 Dec	Exeter City	1-1	3354	O.G.	1	2		4	6	3		8	9	10	7				5	11								
22	8	GILLINGHAM	2-1	4648	Dawson, Stancliffe	1	2		4	6	3		8		10	7				5	11	9							
23	21	Chester	1-3	2727	Finney	1	2	3	4	6			8		10	7				5	11	9							
24	26	BURY	0-2	4892		1	2	12	4	6		3	7*	8	10	9				5	11								
25	29	Colchester United	1-1	3375	Gooding	1	2	4	8	6		3	7		10	11				5			9						
26	12 Jan	SOUTHEND UNITED	2-1	4092	Forrest(2)	1	2	4	8	6		3	7		10	11				5			9						
27	5 Feb	BLACKBURN ROVERS	1-3	4663	Finney	1	2	4	8	6		3	7*	12	10	11				5			9						
28	9	Chesterfield	0-3	9073			2	4	8	6		3	7	12	10	11*				5			9		1				
29	20	Reading	1-1	5208	Rhodes		2	4	10	6		3	7	8		11				5			9		1				
30	23	Sheffield Wednesday	0-5	20557			2	4	10	6		3	7	8	9					5					1	11			
31	1 Mar	PLYMOUTH ARGYLE	3-1	3840	Henson(2), Gooding		2	4	8	6		3	7		10					5				11	1	9			
32	4	Barnsley	0-0	13180			2	4	8	6		3	7		10					5				11	1	9			
33	8	GRIMSBY TOWN	0-0	9032			2	4	8	6		3	7		10					5				11	1	9			
34	15	Sheffield United	0-1	16646			2	4	8	6		3			10					5				11	1	9	7		
35	22	WIMBLEDON	0-0	3810			2	4	8	6					10*		12			5				11	1	9	7	3	
36	25	MILLWALL	2-1	3417	Carr(2)		2	4		6								10		5				11	1	9	7	3	8
37	29	Brentford	1-0	4990	Winn		2	4		6								10		5				11	1	9	7	3	8
38	1 Apr	CHESTER	2-0	4631	Forrest, Winn		2	4		6								10		5				11	1	9	7	3	8
39	5	Bury	0-1	3301			2	4		6			12					10		5				11*	1	9	7	3	8
40	7	BARNSLEY	1-1	9376	Henson		2	4		6			12					10		5				11	1	9	7*	3	8
41	12	Millwall	0-0	3996			2		4	6								10		5				11	1	9	7	3	8
42	15	Swindon Town	2-6	7439	Forrest, Halon		2		4	6								10		5				11	1	9	7	3	8
43	19	EXETER CITY	2-0	3241	Green, McEwan		2		4	6		7	8							5				11	1			3	9
44	26	Gillingham	1-0	3479	McEwan		2		4	6		7	8					10		5				11	1			3	9
45	3 May	READING	1-1	3061	Gooding		2		4	6		7	8					10*		5				11	1		12	3	9
46	6	Blackpool	0-2	4497			2		12	6		7	8						4*	5				11	1	9		3	10
		Apps.				27	43	34	38	44	33	32	30	21	37	28	1	8	1	33	7	3	17	16	14	9	12		11
		Subs.						1	1				2	2													1		
		Goals					4	1	3	2		3	7	10	5	11		2		1	1	1		3		1			2

F.A. CUP

No.	Date	Opposition	Res.	Att.	Goalscorers	Mountford R.	Forrest G.	Tiler K.	Rhodes M.	Green J.	Breckin J.	Gooding M.	McEwan W.	Gwyther D.	Fern R.	Finney R.	Flynn J.	Carr P.	Smith D.	Stancliffe P.	Nix P.	Dawson R.	Ogden C.
1R	24 Nov	Morecambe	1-1	4100	Finney	1	2		4	6	3		8	9	10	7				5	11		
1Rr	27	MORECAMBE	2-0	5671	Green, Stancliffe	1	2		4	6	3		8	9	10	7				5	11		
2R	15 Dec	ALTRINCHAM	0-2	6083		1	2		4	6	3		8		10	7				5	11	9	

LEAGUE CUP

No.	Date	Opposition	Res.	Att.	Goalscorers	Mountford R.	Forrest G.	Tiler K.	Rhodes M.	Green J.	Breckin J.	Gooding M.	McEwan W.	Gwyther D.	Fern R.	Finney R.
1R1L	11 Aug	Leicester City	2-1	11646	Finney, Gooding	1	2	3	4	5	6	7	8	9	10	11
1R2L	14	LEICESTER CITY	3-0	5179	Fern(2), Gooding	1	2	3	4	5	6	7	8	9	10	11
2R1L	28	Bristol City	0-1	6981		1	2	3	4	5	6	7	8	9	10	11
2R2L	4 Sep	BRISTOL CITY	1-1	7327	Fern	1	2	3	4	5	6	7	8	9	10	11

Final League Table

		Pl.	Home W	D	L	F	A	Away W	D	L	F	A	F.	A.	Pts
1	Grimsby Town	46	18	2	3	46	16	8	8	7	27	26	73	42	62
2	Blackburn Rovers	46	13	5	5	34	17	12	4	7	24	19	58	36	59
3	Sheffield Wed.	46	12	6	5	44	20	9	10	4	37	27	81	47	58
4	Chesterfield	46	16	5	2	46	16	7	6	10	25	30	71	46	57
5	Colchester United	46	10	10	3	39	20	10	2	11	25	36	64	56	52
6	Carlisle United	46	13	6	4	45	26	5	6	12	21	30	66	56	48
7	Reading	46	14	6	3	43	19	2	10	11	23	46	66	65	48
8	Exeter City	46	14	5	4	38	22	5	5	13	22	46	60	68	48
9	Chester	46	14	6	3	29	18	3	7	13	20	39	49	57	47
10	Swindon Town	46	15	4	4	50	20	4	4	15	21	43	71	63	46
11	Barnsley	46	10	7	6	29	20	6	7	10	24	36	53	56	46
12	Sheffield United	46	13	5	5	35	21	5	5	13	25	45	60	66	46
13	Rotherham United	46	13	4	6	38	24	5	6	12	20	42	58	66	46
14	Millwall	46	14	6	3	49	23	2	7	14	16	36	65	59	45
15	Plymouth Argyle	46	13	7	3	39	17	3	5	15	20	38	59	55	44
16	Gillingham	46	8	9	6	26	18	6	5	12	23	33	49	51	42
17	Oxford United	46	10	4	9	34	24	4	9	10	23	38	57	62	41
18	Blackpool	46	10	7	6	39	34	5	4	14	23	40	62	74	41
19	Brentford	46	10	6	7	33	26	5	5	13	26	47	59	73	41
20	Hull City	46	11	7	5	29	21	1	9	13	22	48	51	69	40
21	Bury	46	10	4	9	30	23	6	3	14	15	36	45	59	39
22	Southend United	46	9	8	6	33	23	3	4	16	14	35	47	58	38
23	Mansfield Town	46	10	7	6	31	24	1	7	15	16	34	47	58	36
24	Wimbledon	46	6	8	9	34	38	4	6	13	18	43	52	81	34

SEASON 1980/81
DIVISION THREE

No.	Date	Opposition	Res.	Att.	Goalscorers	Brown G.	Forrest G.	Breckin J.	Henson P.	Stancliffe P.	Vaughan I.	Gooding M.	Fern R.	Halom V.	Carr P.	Finney R.	Towner A.	Moore R.	Seasman J.	Mullen J.	Tiler K.	Rhodes M.	Mountford R.	Taylor A.	Winn S.
1	16 Aug	FULHAM	2-2	4436	Forrest, Moore	1	2	3		5	6	8		4		11	7	9	10						
2	20	Blackpool	0-0	10427		1	2	3		5		8		4	12	11*	7	9	10	6					
3	23	Portsmouth	1-3	14767	Gooding	1	2	3		5		8		4	11		7	9	10	6					
4	30	HUDDERSFIELD TOWN	0-0	6961		1	2	3		5		8		4		11	7	9	10	6					
5	6 Sep	BARNSLEY	2-0	10766	Finney, Moore	1	2	3		5		8				11	7	9	10	6	4				
6	13	Swindon Town	1-2	5498	Towner	1	2	3	12	5		8				11	7	9*	10	6	4				
7	16	Walsall	2-0	4500	Halom, Towner	1	2	3		5		8		9		11	7		10	6	4				
8	20	READING	2-0	4461	Moore(2)	1	2	3		5		8				11	7	9	10	6	4				
9	27	Sheffield United	2-1	17995	Finney, Rhodes	1	2	3		5		8				11	7	9	10	6		4			
10	30	WALSALL	2-1	6842	Moore, Seasman	1	2	3		5		8				11	7	9	10	6		4			
11	4 Oct	EXETER CITY	3-1	6889	Henson, Moore, Seasman	1	2	3	12	5		8				11*	7	9	10	6		4			
12	7	Chesterfield	0-2	10638		1	2	3	11	5		8					7	9	10	6		4			
13	11	Burnley	1-1	9691	Towner	1	2	3	11	5		8					7	9	10	6		4			
14	18	GILLINGHAM	2-0	5903	Forrest, Winn	1	2	3	11	5		8					7*	9	10	6		4			12
15	21	CHESTER	0-0	6635		1	2	3	11	5		8						9	10	6	7	4			
16	25	Colchester United	0-0	2623			2	3	11	5		8						9	10	6	7	4	1		
17	29	Oxford United	1-1	3064	Moore		2*	3	11	5		8						9	10	6	7	4	1		12
18	1 Nov	MILLWALL	3-0	5742	Moore(2), Henson			3	11	5		8*	7					9	10	6	2	4	1		12
19	4	CHESTERFIELD	0-0	11093				3	11	5		8	7					9	10	6	2	4	1		
20	8	Charlton Athletic	0-2	7338			2	3	11	5		8	7					9		6	10	4	1		
21	11	BLACKPOOL	4-0	6367	Moore(3), Gooding		2	3	11	5		8	7		10			9		6		4	1		
22	15	Fulham	1-1	4011	Fern		2	3	11	5		8*	7		10			9		6		4	1		12
23	29	NEWPORT COUNTY	1-0	5512	Moore		2	3	11	5		8	7*		10			9		6		4	1	12	
24	6 Dec	Plymouth Argyle	1-3	6155	Fern		2	3	11	5		8	7		10			9*		6		4	1		12
25	20	BRENTFORD	4-1	5913	Towner(2), Fern, Moore		2	3	11	5		8	10				7	9		6		4	1		
26	26	Hull City	2-1	8618	Gooding, Henson		2	3	11	5		8	10				7	9		6		4	1		
27	27	CARLISLE UNITED	3-0	8458	Moore(2), Fern		2	3	11	5		8*	10		12		7	9		6		4	1		
28	3 Jan	Gillingham	0-0	3748			2	3	11	5		8	10				7	9		6		4	1		
29	10	OXFORD UNITED	0-0	6705			2	3	11	5		8	10				7	9		6		4	1		
30	16	Newport County	1-0	4738	Fern		2	3	11	5		8	10				7	9		6		4	1		
31	24	Huddersfield Town	0-1	16687			2	3	11	5		8	10				7	9		6		4	1		
32	30	PORTSMOUTH	3-0	7588	Seasman(2), Towner		2	3	11	5			10				7	9	8	6		4	1		
33	7 Feb	SWINDON TOWN	1-0	7162	Gooding		2	3	11		5	10					7	9	8	6		4	1		
34	21	SHEFFIELD UNITED	2-1	11905	Moore, Towner		2	3	11		5	10					7	9	8	6		4	1		
35	28	Reading	1-1	5360	Fern		2	3	11	5	6		10				7	9	8			4	1		
36	18 Mar	Exeter City	1-2	4464	Moore		2	3	11	5			10				7	9	8	6		4	1		
37	21	Chester	1-0	3945	Fern		2	3	11	5			10				7	9	8	6		4	1		
38	28	COLCHESTER UNITED	2-0	7956	Moore(2)		2	3	11	5			10				7	9	8	6		4	1		
39	31	BURNLEY	1-0	9762	Moore		2	3	11	5			10				7	9	8	6		4	1		
40	4 Apr	Millwall	1-0	5041	Fern		2	3	11	5			10				7	9	8	6		4	1		
41	11	CHARLTON ATHLETIC	3-0	13515	Fern, Mullen, Seasman		2	3	11*	5		12	10				7	9	8	6		4	1		
42	18	Carlisle United	1-0	6788	Fern		2	3		5		11	10				7	9	8	6		4	1		
43	20	HULL CITY	1-1	11602	Seasman		2	3		5		11	10				7	9	8	6		4	1		
44	25	Brentford	1-2	6910	Moore		2	3		5		11	10				7	9	8	6		4	1		
45	28	Barnsley	0-1	25945			2	3	11	5			10				7	9	8	6		4	1		
46	2 May	PLYMOUTH ARGYLE	2-1	11497	Fern, Moore		2	3	11	5	4		10				7	9	8	6			1		
					Apps.	15	44	46	32	44	3	36	28	5	5	10	36	45	34	43	11	38	31		
					Subs.				2			1			2									1	5
					Goals		2	3				4	11	1		2	7	23	6			1		1	1

F.A. CUP

	Date	Opposition	Res.	Att.	Goalscorers	Brown G.	Forrest G.	Breckin J.	Henson P.	Stancliffe P.	Vaughan I.	Gooding M.	Fern R.	Halom V.	Carr P.	Finney R.	Towner A.	Moore R.	Seasman J.	Mullen J.	Tiler K.	Rhodes M.	Mountford R.	Taylor A.	Winn S.
1R	4 Nov	Boston United	4-0	6004	Moore(2), Carr, Taylor		2	3	11	5			7		10			9		6		4	1	8	
2R	13 Dec	BARNSLEY	0-1	15426			2	3	11	5		8	7					9	10	6		4	1		

LEAGUE CUP

	Date	Opposition	Res.	Att.	Goalscorers	Brown G.	Forrest G.	Breckin J.	Henson P.	Stancliffe P.	Vaughan I.	Gooding M.	Fern R.	Halom V.	Carr P.	Finney R.	Towner A.	Moore R.	Seasman J.	Mullen J.	Tiler K.	Rhodes M.	Mountford R.	Taylor A.	Winn S.
1R1L	9 Aug	BRADFORD CITY	1-3	3881	Forrest	1	2	3	4	5	6	7	8	9	10	11									
1R2L	13	Bradford City	0-0	4431		1	2	3		5	6	8		4	12	11	7	9	10*						

Final League Table

		Pl.	Home				Away					F.	A.	Pts
			W	D	L	F	A	W	D	L	F	A			
1	Rotherham United	46	17	6	0	43	8	7	7	9	19	24	62	32	61
2	Barnsley	46	15	5	3	46	19	6	12	5	26	26	72	45	59
3	Charlton Athletic	46	14	6	3	36	17	11	3	9	27	27	63	44	59
4	Huddersfield Town	46	14	6	3	40	11	7	8	8	31	29	71	40	56
5	Chesterfield	46	17	4	2	42	16	6	6	11	30	32	72	48	56
6	Portsmouth	46	14	5	4	35	19	8	4	11	20	28	55	47	53
7	Plymouth Argyle	46	14	5	4	35	18	5	9	9	21	26	56	44	52
8	Burnley	46	13	5	5	37	21	5	9	9	23	27	60	48	50
9	Brentford	46	7	9	7	30	25	7	10	6	22	24	52	49	47
10	Reading	46	13	5	5	39	22	5	5	13	23	40	62	62	46
11	Exeter City	46	9	9	5	36	30	7	4	12	26	36	62	66	45
12	Newport County	46	11	6	6	38	22	4	7	12	26	39	64	61	43
13	Fulham	46	8	7	8	28	29	7	6	10	29	35	57	64	43
14	Oxford United	46	7	8	8	20	24	6	9	8	19	23	39	47	43
15	Gillingham	46	9	8	6	23	19	3	10	10	25	39	48	58	42
16	Millwall	46	10	9	4	30	21	4	5	14	13	39	43	60	42
17	Swindon Town	46	10	6	7	35	27	3	9	11	16	29	51	56	41
18	Chester	46	11	5	7	25	17	4	6	13	13	31	38	48	41
19	Carlisle United	46	8	9	6	32	29	6	4	13	24	41	56	70	41
20	Walsall	46	8	9	6	43	43	5	6	12	16	31	59	74	41
21	Sheffield United	46	12	6	5	38	20	2	6	15	27	43	65	63	40
22	Colchester United	46	12	7	4	35	22	2	4	17	10	43	45	65	39
23	Blackpool	46	5	9	9	19	28	4	5	14	26	47	45	75	32
24	Hull City	46	7	8	8	23	23	1	8	14	17	49	40	71	32

(Back): Vaughan, Tiler, Mountford, Brown, McEwan, Stancliffe,
(Middle): Claxton (Coach), Fern, Breckin, Gooding, Green, Forrest, Rhodes, Halom (Coach).
(Front): Dawson, Winn, Henson, Porterfield, (Manager), Finney, Carr, Taylor.

- 1980-81 -

(Back): Hughes (Man.), Rhodes, Fern, Henson, Stancliffe, Mountford, Brown, Green, Moore,
Fleetwood, Taylor. (Middle): Winn, Vaughan, Forrest, Gooding, Breckin, Mullen, Towner,
Finney, Carr, Seasman, McEwan, Claxton (Coach). (Front): ? , ? , ? , Johnson, ? , ? .

- 1981-82 -

SEASON 1981/82
DIVISION TWO

No.	Date	Opposition	Res.	Att.	Goalscorers	Mountford R.	Forrest G.	Taylor A.	Green J.	Stancliffe P.	Mullen J.	Towner T.	Seasman J.	Moore R.	Fern R.	Henson P.	Breckin J.	Rhodes M.	Hughes E.	Gooding M.	Alexander I.	McEwan W.	Gow G.	Mimms R.	Carr P.
1	29 Aug	NORWICH CITY	4-1	8919	Fern(2), Moore, Seasman	1	2	3	4	5	6	7	8	9*	10	11				12					
2	5 Sep	Cambridge United	0-3	4385		1	2	3	4*	5	6	7	8	9	10	11				12					
3	8	Sheffield Wednesday	0-2	26826		1	2	3	4	5	6	7	8	9	10	11*				12					
4	12	CARDIFF CITY	1-0	7197	Moore	1	2	3	4	5	6	7	8	9	10	11*				12					
5	19	Watford	0-1	10644		1	2		4	5	6	7		9	10*	11	3			8					
6	22	LEICESTER CITY	1-1	7781	Moore	1	2		4	5	6	7		9	10	11	3			8					
7	26	BOLTON WANDERERS	2-0	6998	Green, Henson	1	2		4	5		7		9	10*	11	3			8	6	12			
8	3 Oct	Shrewsbury Town	1-2	4646	Forrest	1	2		6	5		7		9	10*	11	3	4							12
9	10	Crystal Palace	1-3	8021	O.G.	1	2		6	5		7	12	9		11	3	4		8*	10				
10	17	OLDHAM ATHLETIC	1-2	8034	Moore	1	2			5		7		9		11*	3	4		6	8	10			12
11	24	Newcastle United	1-1	19039	Gooding	1	2		6	5		7		9	10	11	3	4		8					
12	31	CHELSEA	6-0	10145	Fern(3), Moore(2), Breckin	1	2		6	5		7		9	10	11	3	4		8					
13	7 Nov	Queens Park Rangers	1-1	10949	O.G.	1	2		6	5		7		9		11	3	4		8					
14	14	BARNSLEY	2-4	18324	Moore(2)	1	2		6	5		7		9	10*	11	3	4		8		12			
15	21	CHARLTON ATHLETIC	2-1	7177	Fern, Moore	1	2	3	6	5		7		9	10	11		4		8					
16	28	Luton Town	1-3	11061	Fern	1	2	3	6	5		7	12*	9	10	11		4		8					
17	5 Dec	ORIENT	1-0	6346	Towner	1	2	3	6	5		7		9	10	11		4		8					
18	16 Jan	Norwich City	0-2	12750		1	2	3	6	5		7		9	10*	11		4		8		12			
19	23	Blackburn Rovers	0-2	7706		1		3	6	5		7	12	9				4		8*	2	10	11		
20	30	WATFORD	1-2	8189	Fern	1			6	5		7		9	10		3	4			2	11	8		
21	2 Feb	DERBY COUNTY	2-1	7487	Moore, O.G.	1			6	5		7		9	10		3	4			2	11	8		
22	6	Cardiff City	2-1	3823	Fern, Gow	1			6	5		7		9	10		3	4			2*	11	8		
23	9	Grimsby Town	2-1	8629	McEwan, Moore	1			6	5		7	10	9			3	4				11	8		
24	13	CAMBRIDGE UNITED	1-0	7312	O.G.	1	2		6	5		7		9	10		3	4				11	8		
25	16	SHREWSBURY TOWN	3-0	7497	Fern(2), Hughes	1	2		6	5		7		9	10		3	4	8			11			
26	20	Bolton Wanderers	1-0	9466	Seasman	1	2		6	5		7	10	9			3	4	8			11			
27	23	WREXHAM	2-0	9158	Fern, Moore	1	2		6	5		7		9	10		3	4				11	8		
28	27	CRYSTAL PALACE	2-0	10007	Moore, Towner	1	2		6	5		7		9	10		3	4				11	8		
29	6 Mar	Oldham Athletic	3-0	8640	Seasman(2), Moore	1	2		6	5		7	10	9			3	4				11	8		
30	13	NEWCASTLE UNITED	0-0	16905		1	2		6	5		7	10	9			3	4				11	8		
31	17	Leicester City	0-1	21123		1	2		6	5		7	10	9*		12	3	4				11	8		
32	20	Chelsea	4-1	11900	Moore(2), McEwan, Towner	1	2		6	5		7	10	9			3	4				11	8		
33	27	QUEENS PARK RANGERS	1-0	10472	Seasman	1	2		6	5		7	10	9			3	4				11	8		
34	2 Apr	Barnsley	0-3	23059		1	2		6	5		7	10	9			3	4				11	8		
35	10	GRIMSBY TOWN	2-2	10011	Fern, Seasman	1	2		6	5		7	10		9		3			12		11*	4	8		
36	12	Derby County	1-3	14080	Seasman	1	2		6	5		7	10	9*			3					11	12	8		
37	17	Charlton Athletic	2-1	5011	Moore, Seasman	1			6	5		7	10	9			3	4*	2	12		11	8		
38	24	LUTON TOWN	2-2	11290	Moore, Seasman	1			6	5		7	10	9			3	4*	2	12		11	8		
39	1 May	Orient	2-0	3009	Moore, Seasman	1			6	5		7	10	9			3	4	2			11	8		
40	4	SHEFFIELD WEDNESDAY	2-2	20513	Hughes, Moore	1	2		6	5		7	10	9			3	4				11	8		
41	8	BLACKBURN ROVERS	4-1	8333	Green(2), McEwan, Moore		2		6	5		7	10	9			12	3			4*	11	8	1	
42	15	Wrexham	2-3	3350	Moore, Stancliffe		2		6	5		7	10	9			3			4		11	8	1	
					Apps.	40	35	9	41	42	6	42	21	40	26	16	33	25	23	16	3	21	21	2	
					Subs.								4				2			1		6	5		2
					Goals				2	1		3	10	22	13	1	1		1	1		3	1		

F.A. CUP

No.	Date	Opposition	Res.	Att.	Goalscorers	Mountford R.	Forrest G.	Taylor A.	Green J.	Stancliffe P.	Mullen J.	Towner T.	Seasman J.	Moore R.	Fern R.	Henson P.	Breckin J.	Rhodes M.	Hughes E.	Gooding M.	Alexander I.	McEwan W.	Gow G.
3R	2 Jan	SUNDERLAND	1-1	11649	Towner	1	2	3	6	5		7		9	10	11		4		8			
3Rr	18	Sunderland	0-1	14865		1		3	6	5		7		9		11*		4	2	8		10	12

LEAGUE CUP

No.	Date	Opposition	Res.	Att.	Goalscorers	Mountford R.	Forrest G.	Taylor A.	Green J.	Stancliffe P.	Mullen J.	Towner T.	Seasman J.	Moore R.	Fern R.	Henson P.	Breckin J.	Rhodes M.	Hughes E.	Gooding M.	Alexander I.	McEwan W.	Gow G.
1R1L	1 Sep	Darlington	3-1	3042	Fern, Henson, O.G.	1	2	3	4	5	6	7	8	9	10	11							
1R2L	15	DARLINGTON	2-1	3894	Moore(2)	1	2		4	5	6	7		9	10	11	3			8			
2R1L	7 Oct	Sunderland	0-2	10450		1	2		4	5	6	7		9		11	3			8			
2R2L	27	SUNDERLAND	3-3	8179	Breckin, Fern, Gooding	1	2		6	5		7		9	10	11*	3	4		8	12		

Final League Table

		Pl.	Home					Away					F.	A.	Pts
			W	D	L	F	A	W	D	L	F	A			
1	Luton Town	42	16	3	2	48	19	9	10	2	38	27	86	46	88
2	Watford	42	13	6	2	46	16	10	5	6	30	26	76	42	80
3	Norwich City	42	14	3	4	41	19	8	2	11	23	31	64	50	71
4	Sheffield Wed.	42	10	8	3	31	23	10	2	9	24	28	55	51	70
5	Queen's Park Rgs.	42	15	4	2	40	9	6	2	13	25	34	65	43	69
6	Barnsley	42	13	4	4	33	14	6	6	9	26	27	59	41	67
7	Rotherham United	42	13	5	3	42	19	7	2	12	24	35	66	54	67
8	Leicester City	42	12	5	4	31	19	6	7	8	25	29	56	48	66
9	Newcastle United	42	14	4	3	30	14	4	4	13	22	36	52	50	62
10	Blackburn Rovers	42	11	4	6	26	15	5	7	9	21	28	47	43	59
11	Oldham Athletic	42	9	9	3	28	23	6	5	10	22	28	50	51	59
12	Chelsea	42	10	5	6	37	30	5	7	9	23	30	60	60	57
13	Charlton Athletic	42	11	5	5	33	22	2	7	12	17	43	50	65	51
14	Cambridge United	42	11	4	6	31	19	2	5	14	17	34	48	53	48
15	Crystal Palace	42	9	2	10	25	26	4	7	10	19	19	34	45	48
16	Derby County	42	9	8	4	32	23	3	4	14	21	45	53	68	48
17	Grimsby Town	42	5	8	8	29	30	6	5	10	24	35	53	65	46
18	Shrewsbury Town	42	10	6	5	26	19	1	7	13	11	38	37	57	46
19	Bolton Wanderers	42	10	4	7	28	24	3	3	15	11	37	39	61	46
20	Cardiff City	42	9	2	10	28	32	3	6	12	17	29	45	61	44
21	Wrexham	42	9	4	8	22	22	2	7	12	18	34	40	56	44
22	Orient	42	6	8	7	23	24	4	1	16	13	37	36	61	39

SEASON 1982/83
DIVISION TWO

Player columns (left to right): Mimms R. | Forrest G. | Breckin J. | Hughes E. | Stancliffe P. | Green J. | Towner A. | Gow G. | Fern R. | Seasman J. | McBride J. | Moore R. | Mountford R. | McEwan W. | Gooding M. | Henson P. | Walker P. | Lodge P. | Friar P. | Johnson N. | Arnott K. | Mitchell R. | Alexander I. | Conroy S.

No.	Date	Opposition	Res.	Att.	Goalscorers	Mim	For	Bre	Hug	Sta	Gre	Tow	Gow	Fer	Sea	McB	Moo	Mou	McE	Goo	Hen	Wal	Lod	Fri	Joh	Arn	Mit	Ale	Con
1	28 Aug	Fulham	1-1	7021	McBride	1	2	3	4	5	6	7	8	9	10	11													
2	31	LEICESTER CITY	1-3	9254	Gow	1	2	3	4	5	6	7	8		10	11	9												
3	4 Sep	CRYSTAL PALACE	2-2	6989	Hughes, Seasman	1	2	3	4	5	6	7	8		10	11	9												
4	7	Oldham Athletic	1-1	4261	Hughes		2	3	4	5*	6	7	8		10	11	9		1	12									
5	11	Burnley	2-1	9099	Fern(2)		2	3	4	5	6	7	8	9	10	11			1										
6	18	CAMBRIDGE UNITED	2-0	6654	Fern(2)		2	3	4	5	6	7*	8	9	10	11			1		12								
7	25	Wolverhampton Wanderers	0-2	16377			2	3	4	5	6		8	9	10*	11			1		7	12							
8	2 Oct	NEWCASTLE UNITED	1-5	12436	McBride		2	3	4	5	6		8	9	10	11			1		7								
9	9	Bolton Wanderers	2-2	6577	Gow, Seasman		2	3	4	5	6	7	8		10	11	9		1										
10	16	BARNSLEY	1-0	13791	Seasman		2	3	4	5	6	7	8		10	11	9		1										
11	23	Shrewsbury Town	0-2	3926			2	3	4	5	6	7	8	12	10*	11	9		1										
12	30	MIDDLESBROUGH	1-1	8135	Moore		2	3	4	5	6	7	8		10*	11	9		1		12								
13	6 Nov	QUEENS PARK RANGERS	0-0	7402			2	3	4	5	6	7	8		10	11	9		1										
14	13	Carlisle United	2-2	5294	Gooding, Green		2	3		5	6	7			10	11	9		1	8	4								
15	20	Charlton Athletic	5-1	6761	Moore(3), McBride, Towner		2			5	6	7	8		10	11	9		1	4		3							
16	27	CHELSEA	1-0	8793	Seasman		2			5	6	7	8		10	11	9		1	4		3							
17	4 Dec	Derby County	0-3	13149			2			5	6	7	8		10	11	9		1	12	4*	3							
18	11	LEEDS UNITED	0-1	13034			2			5	6	7	8		10	11	9		1	4		3							
19	18	Blackburn Rovers	0-3	6333			2	3		5	6	7	8	12	10	11	9*			4									
20	27	GRIMSBY TOWN	3-0	9231	Walker(2), O.G.		2			5	6	7	8		10	11	9		1	4		3	10						
21	28	Sheffield Wednesday	1-0	25024	McBride		2			5	6	7	8			11	9		1	4		3	10						
22	1 Jan	CHARLTON ATHLETIC	1-0	8798	Fern		2			5	6	7	8	10	12	11	9	1		4*		3							
23	3	Crystal Palace	1-1	7704	Gow		2			5	6	7	8	12	4	11	9*		1			3	10						
24	15	FULHAM	0-1	7667			2			5	6	7*		12	4	11	9	1				3	10	8					
25	22	Cambridge United	0-2	3090			2			5	6	7		9	4	11						3	10	8					
26	29	OLDHAM ATHLETIC	1-3	6392	Hughes		2			5	6	7	8	12	9	11			1			3	10	4*					
27	5 Feb	BURNLEY	1-1	6079	McBride		2			5	6	7	8			11	9		1			3	10	4					
28	19	BOLTON WANDERERS	1-1	5646	McBride	1	2			5	6	7	8			11	9			4			10	3					
29	26	Barnsley	1-2	13941	Moore	1	2			5	6	7	8			11	9			4			10	3					
30	5 Mar	SHREWSBURY TOWN	0-3	4810		1	2			5	6	7	8		12	11	9			4			10*	3					
31	12	Middlesbrough	1-1	8875	Hughes	1	2			5	6	7	8			11	9						10	3	4				
32	19	Queens Park Rangers	0-4	9541		1	2			5	6	7	8		9	11							10	3	4				
33	26	CARLISLE UNITED	1-2	5486	McBride	1	2			5		6		4		8	11	9						3	5	7	10		
34	2 Apr	SHEFFIELD WEDNESDAY	0-3	11250		1	2*			5				4		8	11	9		12				3	6	7	10		
35	4	Grimsby Town	2-1	7117	Arnott, McBride	1				5				4		8	11	9*		2				3	6	7	10	12	
36	9	WOLVERHAMPTON WANDS.	1-1	7286	Seasman	1				5		4				9	11	12		2				3	6	7	10	8*	
37	16	Leicester City	1-3	12978	McBride	1				5		4				9	11			2	12			3	6	7*	10	8	
38	20	Newcastle United	0-4	18447			2			5	6		4			8	11	9		12				3		7*	10		1
39	23	DERBY COUNTY	1-1	9646	Seasman		2			5			4			8	11	9		7				3	6		10		1
40	30	Chelsea	1-1	8674	Arnott		2			5			4			8*	11	9		12				3	6	7	10		1
41	7 May	BLACKBURN ROVERS	3-1	5871	Seasman(3)		2			5			4			8	11	9						3	6	7	10		1
42	14	Leeds United	2-2	14985	McBride		2			5			4			8	11	9*		12				3	6	7	10		1
		Apps.				13	39	15	32	13	36	30	37	7	31	42	35	24	18	6	18	10	4	15	11	9	10	2	5
		Subs.												5						5	3	2		2				1	
		Goals							4	1	1	3	5	9	11	5			1		2				2			

F.A. CUP

Rnd	Date	Opposition	Res.	Att.	Goalscorers	For	Sta	Gre	Tow	Gow	Sea	McB	Moo	McE	Hen	Wal
3R	8 Jan	Shrewsbury Town	1-2	6027	Seasman	2	5	6	7	8	10	4	11	9	1	3

MILK CUP

Rnd	Date	Opposition	Res.	Att.	Goalscorers	For	Bre	Sta	Gre	Tow	Gow	Sea	McB	Moo	McE	Goo	Mit	Ale
2R1L	5 Oct	QUEENS PARK RANGERS	2-1	5603	Green, Seasman	2	3	5	6	7	8	10	11	9	1	4		
2R2L	26	Queens Park Rangers	0-0	9653		2	3	5	6		8	10	11		1	4	9	7
3R	10 Nov	Liverpool	0-1	20412		2	3	5	6	7		10	11	9	1		8	4

Final League Table

		Pl	Home W	D	L	F	A	Away W	D	L	F	A	F.	A.	Pts
1	Queen's Park Rgs.	42	16	3	2	51	16	10	4	7	26	20	77	36	85
2	Wolverhampton W.	42	14	5	2	42	16	6	10	5	26	28	68	44	75
3	Leicester City	42	11	4	6	36	15	9	6	6	36	29	72	44	70
4	Fulham	42	13	5	3	36	20	7	4	10	28	27	64	47	69
5	Newcastle United	42	13	6	2	43	21	5	7	9	32	32	75	53	67
6	Sheffield Wed.	42	9	8	4	33	23	7	7	7	27	24	60	47	63
7	Oldham Athletic	42	8	10	3	38	24	6	9	6	26	23	64	47	61
8	Leeds United	42	7	11	3	28	22	6	10	5	23	24	51	46	60
9	Shrewsbury Town	42	8	9	4	20	15	7	5	9	28	33	48	48	59
10	Barnsley	42	9	8	4	37	28	5	7	9	20	27	57	55	57
11	Blackburn Rovers	42	11	7	3	38	21	4	5	12	20	37	58	58	57
12	Cambridge United	42	11	7	3	26	17	2	5	14	16	43	42	60	51
13	Derby County	42	7	10	4	27	24	3	9	9	22	34	49	58	49
14	Carlisle United	42	10	6	5	44	28	2	6	13	24	42	68	70	48
15	Crystal Palace	42	11	7	3	31	17	1	5	15	12	35	43	52	48
16	Middlesbrough	42	8	7	6	27	29	3	8	10	19	38	46	67	48
17	Charlton Athletic	42	11	3	7	40	31	2	6	13	23	55	63	86	48
18	Chelsea	42	8	8	5	31	22	3	6	12	20	39	51	61	47
19	Grimsby Town	42	9	7	5	32	26	3	4	14	13	44	45	70	47
20	Rotherham United	42	6	7	8	22	29	4	8	9	23	39	45	68	45
21	Burnley	42	10	4	7	38	24	2	4	15	18	42	56	66	44
22	Bolton Wanderers	42	10	2	9	30	26	1	9	11	12	35	42	61	44

(Back): Alexander, Vaughan, Fern, Moore, Mimms, Mountford, Stancliffe, Johnson, Forrest, Taylor.
(Middle): Morton (Youth Coach), Rhodes, McBride, Gow, Breckin, Green, Seasman, Towner, Gooding, Carr.
(Front): Cronly, Benton, Ingham, Durham, Brown, Fadzean.

- 1982-83 -

(Back): Walker, Crosby, Stevenson, Mountford, Mimms, Johnson, Green.
(Middle): Henson(Coach), McEwan(Coach), O'Dell, Mitchell, McBride, Forrest, Seasman, Rhodes, Kerr(Man.), Claxton(Asst.Man.), Campion(Sponsor). (Front):Friar, Alexander, Durham,Kilmore, McInnes.

- 1983-84 -

SEASON 1983/84

DIVISION THREE

No.	Date	Opposition	Res.	Att.	Goalscorers	Stevenson A.	Forrest G.	Crosby P.	O'Dell A.	Johnson N.	Green J.	McInnes I.	Kilmore K.	Moore R.	Mitchell R.	McBride J.	McEwan W.	Rhodes M.	Gooding M.	Donovan T.	Seasman J.	Friar P.	Raynes W.	Stone J.	Walker P.	Durham J.	Brown G.	Henson P.	Mimms R.	Trusson M.	Pickering M.	Dungworth J.	Simmons A.	Birch A.	McFadzean J.	Eley K.
1	27 Aug	Southend United	2-2	3114	Kilmore, Moore	1	2	3	4	5	6	7*	8	9	10	11		12																		
2	3 Sep	PORT VALE	2-1	4847	Kilmore, Moore	1	2	3	4	5			8	9	10	11*	6	7							12											
3	6	PLYMOUTH ARGYLE	2-0	4488	Kilmore, McBride	1	2	3	4*	5			8	9	10	11	6	7							12											
4	10	Exeter City	1-0	3193	Rhodes	1	2	3	4	5			8*	9	10		6	7	11						12											
5	17	LEYTON ORIENT	0-1	5518		1	2	3	4	5			8		10		6	7*	11	9					12											
6	24	Bolton Wanderers	0-2	5592		1	2	3	4*	5			8		10		6	7	11	9	12															
7	1 Oct	NEWPORT COUNTY	0-1	4099		1	2	3	12	5			8*		10		6	4	7	9	11															
8	8	WALSALL	0-1	3540		1	2	6	4	5			8		10*				7	12	9	3	11													
9	15	Scunthorpe United	2-1	3139	Gooding(2)	1	2			5			8		10		4		7	9	11	3		6												
10	18	MILLWALL	1-0	3461	Stone	1	2	3		5			8		10		4	12	7	9*	11			6												
11	22	Wimbledon	1-3	2579	Kilmore	1	2	3		5			8		10		4	11*	7					6	9	12										
12	29	BRADFORD CITY	1-0	4506	Durham	1	2	3		5			8		10		4	12	7				11*	6		9										
13	1 Nov	Bournemouth	2-4	3495	Gooding, Walker	1	2	3		5			8		10		4	12	7				11*	6	9											
14	5	BRISTOL ROVERS	2-2	3957	Gooding(2)	1	2	3	4	5			8*		10		6		7				11		9	12										
15	12	Preston North End	0-1	3916		1	2	3	7	5					10			4	8				11*		9		6								12	
16	26	Gillingham	2-4	4052	Raynes, O.G.	1	6	3	7	5			8		10			2	4		11		12		9											
17	3 Dec	BURNLEY	1-1	5544	Kilmore	1	2		7	5			8		3			4	10				11	6	9											
18	17	OXFORD UNITED	1-2	4000	Mitchell	1	2		7				8		3			4	10				11*	6	9	12		5								
19	26	Sheffield United	0-3	22756		1	2*	5	7				8		3			4	10		9		12	6				11								
20	27	HULL CITY	0-1	6298			2	3	7	5			8		3				7		9			6				11	1							
21	31	Wigan Athletic	1-2	3526	Johnson		2	3		5			8		10				7				11	6	9			4	1							
22	2 Jan	LINCOLN CITY	1-1	4595	Kilmore		2	6		5			8		10				7			3	11			9			1	4						
23	22	Leyton Orient	1-2	2204	Kilmore					5			8		3			10	7			2	11		12	9*			1	4	6					
24	4 Feb	Newport County	4-1	2391	Gooding(2), Kilmore, Rhodes	1	2			5			8		10		7	12	11			3			9					4*	6					
25	11	BOLTON WANDERERS	1-1	5043	Trusson	1	2	3		5			8*		10		7	12	11											4	6	9				
26	18	Bradford City	0-1	5020		1	2	3		5			8		10		7*	12	11											4	6	9				
27	25	WIMBLEDON	1-2	3141	Dungworth	1	2	3	12	5			8		10		7						11*							4	6	9				
28	3 Mar	Millwall	0-2	2985		1	2	3	11*	5			8		10		7						12							4	6	9				
29	6	Bristol Rovers	0-2	5264			2	3		5*		12	11		10			7											1	4	6	9	8			
30	10	PRESTON NORTH END	0-1	3256			2	3					11		10		12	4							8*				1	5	6	9	7			
31	17	Walsall	2-2	4915	Dungworth, Simmons		2	3		5			11		10			7											1	4	6	9	8			
32	20	Brentford	1-2	3391	Kilmore		2	3		5			11		10			7											1	4	6	9	8			
33	30	Plymouth Argyle	1-1	4736	Simmons		2	3		5			11		10														1	4	6	9	8	7		
34	2 Apr	Port Vale	3-2	3705	Birch(3)		2	3		5			11		10*			12											1	4	6	9	8	7		
35	7	BRENTFORD	4-0	3635	Birch, Mitchell, Simmons, Trusson		2	3		5			11		12			10											1	4	6*	9	8	7		
36	10	SOUTHEND UNITED	0-0	3722			2	3		5			11					10								9			1	4	6		8	7		
37	14	Burnley	2-2	4591	Birch, Kilmore		2	3		5			11		12			10											1	4	6	9*	8	7		
38	17	BOURNEMOUTH	1-0	3937	Simmons		2	3		5			11*		12			10											1	4	6	9	8	7		
39	21	SHEFFIELD UNITED	0-1	14177			2	3		5			11		12			10											1	4	6	9*	8	7		
40	23	Hull City	0-5	9799			2	3		5			11		12			10*											1	4	6	9	8	7		
41	28	GILLINGHAM	3-0	3198	Birch(2), Simmons		2	3		5			11		12			10											1	4*	6	9	8	7		
42	1 May	EXETER CITY	1-0	3636	Birch		2	3		5			11					10											1	4	6	9	8	7		
43	5	Lincoln City	1-0	2140	Kilmore		2	3		5			11*		12			10											1	4	6	9	8	7		
44	7	WIGAN ATHLETIC	4-1	3863	Simmons(2), Birch, Dungworth		2			5			11		3			10	12										1	4	6	9	8	7*		
45	12	Oxford United	2-3	9852	Kilmore(2)		2			5			11		3			10	12										1	4	6	9*	8	7		
46	15	SCUNTHORPE UNITED	3-0	4298	Birch, Simmons, O.G.		2	3		5			11						10										1	4*	6	9	8	7		12
					Apps.	24	45	39	15	43	1	1	45	4	36	3	17	28	24	5	7	5	11	10	10	4	1	4	22	25	24	21	18	14		
					Subs.				2						7		1	8	2	1	1		3		5	3									1	1
					Goals					1			13	2	2	1		2	7				1	1	1	1				2		3	8	10		

F.A. CUP

Rd.	Date	Opposition	Res.	Att.	Goalscorers	Stevenson A.	Forrest G.	Crosby P.	O'Dell A.	Johnson N.	Green J.	McInnes I.	Kilmore K.	Moore R.	Mitchell R.	McBride J.	McEwan W.	Rhodes M.	Gooding M.	Donovan T.	Seasman J.	Friar P.	Raynes W.	Stone J.	Walker P.	Durham J.	Brown G.	Henson P.	Mimms R.	Trusson M.	Pickering M.	Dungworth J.	Simmons A.	Birch A.	McFadzean J.	Eley K.
1R	19 Nov	HARTLEPOOL	0-0	3325		1	2	3	7	5			8*		10			12	4		11			6	9											
1Rr	23	Hartlepool	1-0	2635	Kilmore	1	2	3	7	5			8		10				4		11			6	9											
2R	10 Dec	HULL CITY	2-1	6885	Kilmore(2)	1	2		7				8		3			4	10				11*	6	9	12		5								
3R	7 Jan	WEST BROMWICH ALBION	0-0	8142			2	6		5			8		10				7			3	11*			9		12	1	4						
3Rr	11	West Bromwich Albion	0-3	12107			2	6		5			8		10				7			3	11			9*		12	1	4						

MILK CUP

Rd.	Date	Opposition	Res.	Att.	Goalscorers	Stevenson A.	Forrest G.	Crosby P.	O'Dell A.	Johnson N.	Green J.	McInnes I.	Kilmore K.	Moore R.	Mitchell R.	McBride J.	McEwan W.	Rhodes M.	Gooding M.	Donovan T.	Seasman J.	Friar P.	Raynes W.	Stone J.	Walker P.	Durham J.	Brown G.	Henson P.	Mimms R.	Trusson M.	Pickering M.	Dungworth J.	Simmons A.	Birch A.	McFadzean J.	Eley K.
1R1L	30 Aug	HARTLEPOOL	0-0	4384		1	2	3	4	5	6	7*	8	9	10	11		12																		
1R2L	14 Sep	Hartlepool	1-0	2321	Gooding	1	2	3	4*	5			8	9	10		6	7	11						12											
2R1L	4 Oct	LUTON TOWN	2-3	4035	Kilmore, Gooding	1	2	6	4	5			8		10				7		9	3	11													
2R2L	25	Luton Town	2-0	6755	Kilmore, Walker	1	2	3		5			8		10		4	12	7				11	6	9											
3R	8 Nov	SOUTHAMPTON	2-1	8821	Mitchell, Rhodes	1	2	6	7	5					10			4	8			3	11*		9										12	
4R	29	WIMBLEDON	1-0	6946	Kilmore	1	2		12	5			8		3			4	10		7*		11	6	9											
5R	18 Jan	WALSALL	2-4	14487	Kilmore(2)			6*	12	5			8		10			4	7			3	11		9	12			1							

ASSOCIATE MEMBERS CUP

Rd.	Date	Opposition	Res.	Att.	Goalscorers	Stevenson A.	Forrest G.	Crosby P.	O'Dell A.	Johnson N.	Green J.	McInnes I.	Kilmore K.	Moore R.	Mitchell R.	McBride J.	McEwan W.	Rhodes M.	Gooding M.	Donovan T.	Seasman J.	Friar P.	Raynes W.	Stone J.	Walker P.	Durham J.	Brown G.	Henson P.	Mimms R.	Trusson M.	Pickering M.	Dungworth J.	Simmons A.	Birch A.	McFadzean J.	Eley K.
1R	21 Feb	SHEFFIELD UNITED	0-1	3396		1	2	3	12	5		7	8						10*				11							4	6	9				

Final League Table

		Pl.	Home W	D	L	F	A	Away W	D	L	F	A	F.	A.	Pts
1	Oxford United	46	17	5	1	58	22	11	6	6	33	28	91	50	95
2	Wimbledon	46	15	5	3	58	35	11	4	8	39	41	97	76	87
3	Sheffield United	46	14	7	2	56	18	10	4	9	30	35	86	53	83
4	Hull City	46	16	5	2	42	11	7	9	7	29	27	71	38	83
5	Bristol Rovers	46	16	5	2	47	21	6	8	9	21	33	68	54	79
6	Walsall	46	14	4	5	44	22	8	5	10	24	39	68	61	75
7	Bradford City	46	11	9	3	46	30	9	2	12	27	35	73	65	71
8	Gillingham	46	13	4	6	50	29	7	6	10	24	40	74	69	70
9	Millwall	46	16	4	3	42	18	2	9	12	29	47	71	65	67
10	Bolton Wanderers	46	13	4	6	36	17	5	6	12	20	43	56	60	64
11	Orient	46	13	5	5	40	27	5	4	14	31	54	71	81	63
12	Burnley	46	12	5	6	52	25	4	9	10	24	36	76	61	62
13	Newport County	46	11	9	3	35	27	5	5	13	23	48	58	75	62
14	Lincoln City	46	11	4	8	42	29	6	6	11	17	33	59	62	61
15	Wigan Athletic	46	11	5	7	26	18	5	8	10	20	38	46	56	61
16	Preston North End	46	12	5	6	42	27	3	6	14	24	39	66	66	56
17	Bournemouth	46	11	5	7	38	27	5	2	16	25	46	63	73	55
18	Rotherham United	46	10	5	8	29	17	5	4	14	28	47	57	64	54
19	Plymouth Argyle	46	11	8	4	38	17	2	4	17	18	45	56	62	51
20	Brentford	46	8	9	6	41	30	3	7	13	28	49	69	79	49
21	Scunthorpe United	46	9	9	5	40	31	0	10	13	14	42	54	73	46
22	Southend United	46	8	9	6	34	24	2	5	16	21	52	55	76	44
23	Port Vale	46	10	4	9	33	29	1	6	16	18	54	51	83	43
24	Exeter City	46	4	8	11	27	39	2	7	14	23	45	50	84	33

SEASON 1984/85

DIVISION THREE

No.	Date	Opposition	Res.	Att.	Goalscorers	Mimms R.	Forrest G.	Crosby P.	Trusson M.	Johnson N.	Pickering M.	Birch A.	Simmons A.	Dungworth J.	Rhodes M.	Gooding M.	O'Dell A.	Raynes W.	Kilmore K.	Mitchell R.	Eley K.	McInnes I.	Donovan T.	Conroy S.	Richardson I.	Morris A.	Scott M.	Warburton R.
1	25 Aug	Reading	0-1	3733		1	2	3	4	5	6	7	8	9	10	11												
2	1 Sep	LINCOLN CITY	0-0	4161		1	2	3	4	5	6	7	8	9	10*	11			12									
3	8	Bournemouth	0-3	3106		1	2	3	4	5	6	7*	8	9	10	11			12									
4	15	BOLTON WANDERERS	3-1	3926	Dungworth(2), Gooding	1	2	3	4*	5	6	7		9	10	8			11	12								
5	18	BRENTFORD	1-1	3644	Birch	1	2	3	4	5	6	7		9	10	8			11*	12								
6	22	Preston North End	3-0	5063	Dungworth, Simmons, Trusson	1	2		4	5	6	7	10	9	12	8			11*	3								
7	29	BURNLEY	3-2	4646	Birch, Pickering, Trusson	1	2		4	5	6	7	10	9	12	8			11*	3								
8	2 Oct	Bristol City	1-0	6586	Birch	1	2		4	5	6	7	10	9		8			11	3								
9	7	Doncaster Rovers	1-0	10839	Simmons	1	2		4	5	6	7		9		8			11	3								
10	13	BRISTOL ROVERS	3-3	5177	Dungworth, Gooding, Simmons	1	2	5	4		6	7	10	9	12	8			11	3								
11	20	Plymouth Argyle	0-1	4067		1	2	5	4		6	7	10	9*	12	8			11	3								
12	23	NEWPORT COUNTY	1-0	4297	Kilmore	1	2	5	4		6	7	10	9	12	8			11*	3								
13	27	DERBY COUNTY	2-0	8508	Dungworth, Trusson	1	2	5	4		6	7	10	9		8			11	3								
14	3 Nov	Hull City	0-0	6837		1	2	5	4			7	10	9		8	6		11*	3	12							
15	10	Gillingham	1-2	3568	Dungworth	1	2	6	4	5		7	10*	9	12	8			11	3								
16	24	ORIENT	2-1	3932	Birch, Gooding	1	2	3	4	5	6	11		9		8			10	3								
17	1 Dec	Walsall	2-0	4538	Kilmore, Simmons	1	2	6	4		6	7	11	9	12	10			8*	3								
18	8	Newport County	2-0	2012	Kilmore(2)	1	2		4	5		7	11	9	12	10			8	3		6*						
19	15	YORK CITY	4-1	4716	Simmons(2), Birch, Gooding	1	2		4*	5	6	7	11	9	12	8			10	3								
20	22	WIGAN ATHLETIC	3-3	4462	Dungworth, Simmons, Trusson	1	2		4	5		7	11	9	6	8			10*	3			12					
21	26	Swansea City	0-1	3814		1	2	6	4	5		7	11	9	10	8*				3			12					
22	29	Cambridge United	2-0	2615	Gooding, Simmons	1	2	6	4	5		7	10	9		8				3			11					
23	1 Jan	BRADFORD CITY	1-2	9122	Dungworth	1	2	6	4	5		7	10*	9	12	8				3			11					
24	19	BOURNEMOUTH	1-0	4468	Simmons	1	2	6	4	5		7	10	9		8				3			11*					
25	26	Bolton Wanderers	0-2	5059		1	2		4			7	10	9		8				3		11*	12					
26	2 Feb	Burnley	0-7	3856		1	2	6	4			7	10	9	12	8*				3	5	11						
27	9	PRESTON NORTH END	3-0	3645	Simmons(2), Richardson	1	2	6	4	5		7*	10		12	8			11	3					9			
28	16	BRISTOL CITY	2-1	4901	Richardson, Simmons	1	2	6	4	5		7	10		12	8			11*	3					9			
29	23	HULL CITY	1-1	7068	Richardson	1	2	6	4			7	10		12	8			11*	3					9			
30	2 Mar	Derby County	1-1	10259	Gooding	1	2	6	4	5		7	10*		12	8			11	3					9			
31	9	PLYMOUTH ARGYLE	0-2	4111		1	2	6	4	5		7	10		12	8			11*	3					9			
32	13	Lincoln City	3-3	2157	Gooding(2), Kilmore	1	2	10	4	5	6	7	9*	12		8			11	3								
33	16	Bristol Rovers	0-1	4083		1	2	10	4	5	6		12	9		8			11	3		7*						
34	19	MILLWALL	0-0	3728		1	2	3	4		6	7	9	5		8			11	10								
35	23	DONCASTER ROVERS	2-3	5090	Gooding(2)	1	2	3	4	5	6	7	9	12		8			11	10*								
36	26	READING	3-0	2581	Birch, Raynes, Trusson	1	2		4	5		7*	12	9		8		11	10	3								
37	29	Millwall	0-0	7044		1	2	7	4	5	6		12	9		8		11*	10	3								
38	6 Apr	SWANSEA CITY	0-1	3145		1	2	4		5	6	7	9*			8		11	10	3			12					
39	8	Bradford City	1-1	8967	Kilmore	1	2	11	4	5*	6	7		9		8			10	3			12					
40	13	GILLINGHAM	1-0	3022	Trusson	1			4	5	6	7	2			8		11	10	3			9					
41	20	Orient	1-0	2087	Kilmore	1			4	5	6	7	2			8		11	10	3		9*				12		
42	23	Brentford	0-3	3019		1	2	11	4	5	6	7		9*		8			10	3			12					
43	27	WALSALL	0-1	2293		1	2	3	4	5	6	7				8			11*	10			12					
44	3 May	York City	0-3	3551		1	2		4	5	6	7	8	9					11	3					9		10*	12
45	6	CAMBRIDGE UNITED	0-1	1515		1	2		4	5	6	7	8	9					11	3							10	
46	11	Wigan Athletic	1-2	3012	Trusson	1	2		4	5	6		10	9		8			7	3	12						11*	
		Apps.				46	44	33	45	35	32	42	35	39	8	44	1	6	37	40	2	5	4		5		3	
		Subs.											3	7	12				2	2	4	2	3		1	1		
		Goals							7		1	6	12	8		10		1	7						3			

F.A. CUP

	Date	Opposition	Res.	Att.	Goalscorers	Mimms R.	Forrest G.	Crosby P.	Trusson M.	Johnson N.	Pickering M.	Birch A.	Simmons A.	Dungworth J.	Rhodes M.	Gooding M.	O'Dell A.	Raynes W.	Kilmore K.	Mitchell R.	Eley K.	McInnes I.	Donovan T.	Conroy S.	Richardson I.	Morris A.	Scott M.	Warburton R.
1R	17 Nov	Mansfield Town	1-2	4161	Gooding	1	2	3	4	5	6	7		9		8			10	11								

MILK CUP

	Date	Opposition	Res.	Att.	Goalscorers	Mimms R.	Forrest G.	Crosby P.	Trusson M.	Johnson N.	Pickering M.	Birch A.	Simmons A.	Dungworth J.	Rhodes M.	Gooding M.	O'Dell A.	Raynes W.	Kilmore K.	Mitchell R.	Eley K.	McInnes I.	Donovan T.	Conroy S.	Richardson I.	Morris A.	Scott M.	Warburton R.
1R1L	28 Aug	Darlington	2-1	1622	Simmons, Gooding	1	2	3	4	5	6	7	8	9	10	11			12									
1R2L	4 Sep	DARLINGTON	4-0	1861	Trusson(2), Birch, Forrest	1	2	3	4	5	6	7	8*	9	10	11												
2R1L	26	Stoke City	2-1	8221	Birch, Simmons	1	2		4	5	6	7	10	9		8			11	3								
2R2L	9 Oct	STOKE CITY	1-1	6898	O.G.	1	2		4	5*	6	7	10	9	12	8			11	3								
3R	30	GRIMSBY TOWN	0-0	8413		1	2	5	4		6*	7	10	9	12	8			11	3								
3Rr	6 Nov	Grimsby Town	1-6	7649	Birch	1	2	5	4			7	10*	9		8	6		11	3	12							

FREIGHT ROVER TROPHY

	Date	Opposition	Res.	Att.	Goalscorers	Mimms R.	Forrest G.	Crosby P.	Trusson M.	Johnson N.	Pickering M.	Birch A.	Simmons A.	Dungworth J.	Rhodes M.	Gooding M.	O'Dell A.	Raynes W.	Kilmore K.	Mitchell R.	Eley K.	McInnes I.	Donovan T.	Conroy S.	Richardson I.	Morris A.	Scott M.	Warburton R.
1R	22 Jan	CHESTERFIELD	1-1	2027	Trusson	1	2	6	4	5		7	10	14		8				3		11	9					
1Rr	5 Feb	Chesterfield	0-1	2809			2	6	4	5		7	10	12		8				3		11	9*					1

Final League Table

		Pl.	Home					Away					F.	A.	Pts
			W	D	L	F	A	W	D	L	F	A			
1	Bradford City	46	15	6	2	44	23	13	4	6	33	22	77	45	94
2	Millwall	46	18	5	0	44	12	8	7	8	29	30	73	42	90
3	Hull City	46	16	4	3	46	20	9	8	6	32	29	78	49	87
4	Gillingham	46	15	5	3	54	29	10	3	10	26	33	80	62	83
5	Bristol City	46	17	2	4	46	19	7	7	9	28	28	74	47	81
6	Bristol Rovers	46	15	6	2	37	13	6	6	11	29	35	66	48	75
7	Derby County	46	14	7	2	40	20	5	6	12	25	34	65	54	70
8	York City	46	13	5	5	42	22	7	4	12	28	35	70	57	69
9	Reading	46	8	7	8	31	29	11	5	7	37	33	68	62	69
10	Bournemouth	46	16	3	4	42	16	3	8	12	15	30	57	46	68
11	Walsall	46	9	7	7	33	22	9	6	8	22	33	55	55	67
12	Rotherham United	46	11	6	6	36	24	7	5	11	19	31	55	55	65
13	Brentford	46	13	5	5	42	27	3	9	11	20	37	62	64	62
14	Doncaster Rovers	46	11	5	7	42	33	6	3	14	30	41	72	74	59
15	Plymouth Argyle	46	11	7	5	33	23	4	7	12	29	42	62	65	59
16	Wigan Athletic	46	12	6	5	36	22	3	8	12	24	42	60	64	59
17	Bolton Wanderers	46	12	5	6	38	22	4	1	18	31	53	69	75	54
18	Newport County	46	9	6	8	30	30	4	7	12	25	37	55	67	52
19	Lincoln City	46	8	11	4	32	20	3	7	13	18	31	50	51	51
20	Swansea City	46	7	5	11	31	39	5	6	12	22	41	53	80	47
21	Burnley	46	6	11	6	30	24	5	5	13	30	49	60	73	46
22	Orient	46	7	7	9	30	36	4	6	13	21	40	51	76	46
23	Preston North End	46	9	5	9	33	41	4	2	17	18	59	51	100	46
24	Cambridge United	46	2	3	18	17	48	2	6	15	20	47	37	95	21

1984-85: (Back): Forrest, Dungworth, Trusson, Mimms, Johnson, Pickering, Crosby.
(Middle): Claxton (Asst.Man.), Kilmore, Simmons, Mitchell, Donovan, Walker, O'Dell, Henson (Coach).
(Front): Birch, Rhodes, McInnes, Kerr (Manager), Raynes, Durham, Gooding.

1985-86: (Back): Henson (Youth Man.), Barnsley, Smith, Conroy, O'Hanlon, Trusson,
Pickering, Claxton (Asst.Man.). (Middle): Forrest, Donovan, Simmons, Hunter (Man.), Tynan, Martin,
Crosby. (Front): Dungworth, Raynes, Enerson, Birch, Pugh, McInnes, Gooding.

SEASON 1985/86

DIVISION THREE

No.	Date	Opposition	Res.	Att.	Goalscorers	O'Hanlon K.	Barnsley A.	Crosby P.	Trusson M.	Smith K.	Pickering M.	Birch A.	Gooding M.	Tynan T.	Dungworth J.	Emerson D.	Forrest G.	Simmons A.	Pugh D.	Martin M.	Cowdrill B.	Eley K.	Pepper N.	Horner P.
1	17 Aug	Bolton Wanderers	1-1	5129	Trusson	1	2	3*	4	5	6	7	8	9	10	11		12						
2	24	LINCOLN CITY	1-0	3356	Smith	1			4	5	6	12	8*	9	3	11	2	10	7					
3	27	Chesterfield	0-2	5434		1			4	5	6	12		9	3	11	2	10		7*	8			
4	31	BRISTOL CITY	2-0	3134	Forrest, Tynan	1			4*	5	6	7	12	9	3	11	2	10			8			
5	7 Sep	Swansea City	0-1	3687		1			4	5	6	7	12	9	3	11	2	10*			8			
6	14	READING	1-2	3076	Simmons	1			4	5	6	7	12	9	3	11	2	10			8*			
7	17	Walsall	1-3	4681	Emerson	1			4	5	6	7	8	9	3	11	2	10						
8	21	DONCASTER ROVERS	2-1	5189	Birch, Simmons	1			4	5	6	7	8	9	3	11		10		2				
9	28	Brentford	1-1	3257	Gooding	1			4	5	6	7*	8	9	3	11	2	10	12					
10	1 Oct	CARDIFF CITY	3-0	2906	Gooding(2), Simmons	1			4	5	6	7	8	9	3	11	2	10						
11	5	WOLVERHAMPTON WANDS.	1-2	4015	Tynan	1			4	5	6	7	8*	9	3	11	2	10	12					
12	12	Bristol Rovers	2-5	3499	Birch, Tynan	1			4	5*	6	7	8	9	3	11	2	10	12					
13	19	PLYMOUTH ARGYLE	1-1	2942	Tynan	1			4	5	6	7	8*	9	3	11	2	10	12					
14	22	Newport County	0-0	1817		1			4	5	6	7		9	3	11	2	10	8					
15	26	York City	1-2	4444	Pugh	1			4	5	6	7		9*	3	11	2	10	8			12		
16	2 Nov	DERBY COUNTY	1-1	6030	Trusson	1			4	5	6	7	12	9		11*	2	10	8		3			
17	6	GILLINGHAM	1-1	2361	Birch	1			4	5	6	7		9	3	11	2	10	8					
18	13	Wigan Athletic	0-2	3084		1			4	5	6		8	9*	10	11	2	12	7		3			
19	23	BURY	2-0	3335	Birch, Tynan	1				5	6	7	4	9	3	8	2	10	11					
20	14 Dec	NOTTS COUNTY	1-0	3820	Birch	1	2		10	5	6	7	4	9	3	8			11					
21	17	Bournemouth	2-1	2489	Trusson, Tynan	1	2		10	5	6	7	4	9	3	8			11					
22	22	Lincoln City	0-0	3007		1	2		10	5	6	7	4	9	3	8			11					
23	26	Darlington	2-2	3725	Gooding, Pugh	1	2		10*	5	6	7	4	9	3	8		12	11					
24	28	CHESTERFIELD	1-2	4816	Birch	1	2		10	5	6	7	4*	9	3	8		12	11					
25	1 Jan	BLACKPOOL	4-1	4200	Dungwrth, Emersn, Gooding, Simmns	1	2			5	6	7	4	9	3	8		10	11*			12		
26	11	Bristol City	1-3	6672	Tynan	1	2			5*	6	7	4	9	3	8		10	11			12		
27	18	BOLTON WANDERERS	4-0	3821	Tynan(2), Emerson, Trusson	1	2	3	10		6	7*	4	9		8			11			12		
28	1 Feb	SWANSEA CITY	4-1	2932	Tynan(3), Gooding	1	2		10	5	6	7	4	9	3	8			11					
29	4	NEWPORT COUNTY	0-0	2975		1	2		10	5	6	7	4	9	3	8			11					
30	15	WALSALL	3-0	3516	Birch, Smith, Tynan	1	2		10	5	6	7	4	9	3	8			11					
31	1 Mar	BRENTFORD	1-2	3268	Gooding	1	2		10	5	6	7*	4	9	3	8		12	11					
32	8	Wolverhampton Wanderers	0-0	2898		1	2	3	10		6	7				5	8	9		11			4	
33	15	BRISTOL ROVERS	2-0	2734	Birch, Emerson	1	2	3		5	6	7		9*		8		10	11			12	4	
34	19	Reading	1-2	4970	Birch	1	2	3		5	6	7	12	9*		8		10	11				4*	
35	22	YORK CITY	4-1	3240	Birch(2), Emerson, Smith	1	2	3		5	6	7	4	9		8		10	11					
36	25	Cardiff City	3-2	1863	Simmons(2), Birch	1	2	3		5	6	7	4	9		8		10	11					
37	29	Blackpool	1-2	4007	Dungworth	1	2	3		5	6	7	4	9		8		10*	11					12
38	31	DARLINGTON	1-2	3041	Emerson	1	2	3		5	6	7	4	9		8		12	11					10*
39	4 Apr	Gillingham	0-3	4525		1	2	3	9	5*	6	7	4			11	8	12						10
40	8	Plymouth Argyle	0-4	13034		1	2	3	9		6	7	4			5		11					4	10
41	12	WIGAN ATHLETIC	0-0	3004		1	2		9	5	6	7	4		3	8		10	11					
42	15	Doncaster Rovers	0-0	3159		1	2		9	5	6	7	4		3	8		10	11					
43	19	Bury	0-2	2166		1	2		9	5	6	7	4		3	8		10*	11			12		
44	26	BOURNEMOUTH	4-0	2101	Emerson, Gooding, Simmons, Trusson	1	2		9*	5	6	7	4		3	8		10	11			12		
45	3 May	Notts County	0-1	3213		1	2	3	9	5	6	7*	4			10	8		11			12		
46	9	Derby County	1-2	21036	Trusson	1	2		9	5	6	7	4		3	8		10	11					
					Apps.	46	28	12	37	43	46	43	35	30	46	45	17	31	33	5	2		4	3
					Subs.								2	5					7	4		5	3	1
					Goals				6	3		12	8	13	2	7	1	7	2					

F.A. CUP

	Date		Res.	Att.	Goalscorers	O'Hanlon K.	Barnsley A.	Crosby P.	Trusson M.	Smith K.	Pickering M.	Birch A.	Gooding M.	Tynan T.	Dungworth J.	Emerson D.	Forrest G.	Simmons A.	Pugh D.	Martin M.	Cowdrill B.	Eley K.	Pepper N.	Horner P.
1R	16 Nov	WOLVERHAMPTON	6-0	3507	Brch(2), Goodng, Simmns, Smth, Tynan	1				5	6	7	4	9	3	8	2	10	11					
2R	7 Dec	BURNLEY	4-1	4264	Trusson(2), Birch, Tynan	1	2		10	5	6	7	4	9	3	8			11					
3R	4 Jan	Frickley Athletic	3-1	5923	Pugh, Gooding, Tynan	1	2			5	6	7	4	9	3	8		10	11					
4R	25	Arsenal	1-5	28490	Tynan	1	2		10	5	6	7	4	9	3	8			11					

MILK CUP

	Date		Res.	Att.	Goalscorers	O'Hanlon K.	Barnsley A.	Crosby P.	Trusson M.	Smith K.	Pickering M.	Birch A.	Gooding M.	Tynan T.	Dungworth J.	Emerson D.	Forrest G.	Simmons A.	Pugh D.	Martin M.	Cowdrill B.	Eley K.	Pepper N.	Horner P.
1R1L	20 Aug	SHEFFIELD UNITED	1-3	9087	Emerson	1			4	5	6	7*	8	9	3	11	2	10	12					
1R2L	3 Sep	Sheffield United	1-5	7486	Birch	1				5	6	7	4	9	3	11	2	10						

FREIGHT ROVER TROPHY

	Date		Res.	Att.	Goalscorers	O'Hanlon K.	Barnsley A.	Crosby P.	Trusson M.	Smith K.	Pickering M.	Birch A.	Gooding M.	Tynan T.	Dungworth J.	Emerson D.	Forrest G.	Simmons A.	Pugh D.	Martin M.	Cowdrill B.	Eley K.	Pepper N.	Horner P.
1R	14 Jan	York City	0-0	2122		1	2	3			6	7	4	9		5	8			11		10		
1R	21	HARTLEPOOL UNITED	3-0	1309	Emerson, Pugh, Trusson	1	2		4*	5	6		4	9	3	8			14	11		7		
2R	18 Feb	Wigan Athletic	0-3	2597		1	2			5	6	7	4	9	3	8			11					

Final League Table

		Pl.	Home					Away					F.	A.	Pts
			W	D	L	F	A	W	D	L	F	A			
1	Reading	46	16	3	4	39	22	13	4	6	28	29	67	51	94
2	Plymouth Argyle	46	17	3	3	56	20	9	6	8	32	33	88	53	87
3	Derby County	46	13	7	3	45	20	10	8	5	35	21	80	41	84
4	Wigan Athletic	46	17	4	2	54	17	6	10	7	28	31	82	48	83
5	Gillingham	46	14	5	4	48	17	8	8	7	33	37	81	54	79
6	Walsall	46	15	7	1	59	23	7	2	14	31	41	90	64	75
7	York City	46	16	4	3	49	17	4	7	12	28	41	77	58	71
8	Notts County	46	12	6	5	42	26	7	8	8	29	34	71	60	71
9	Bristol City	46	14	5	4	43	19	4	9	10	26	41	69	60	68
10	Brentford	46	8	8	7	29	29	10	4	9	29	32	58	61	66
11	Doncaster Rovers	46	7	10	6	20	21	9	6	8	25	31	45	52	64
12	Blackpool	46	11	6	6	38	19	6	6	11	28	36	66	55	63
13	Darlington	46	10	7	6	39	33	5	6	12	22	45	61	78	58
14	Rotherham United	46	13	5	5	44	18	2	7	14	17	41	61	59	57
15	Bournemouth	46	9	8	6	41	31	6	3	14	24	41	65	72	54
16	Bristol Rovers	46	9	6	8	27	21	5	4	14	24	54	51	75	54
17	Chesterfield	46	10	6	7	41	30	3	8	12	20	34	61	64	53
18	Bolton Wanderers	46	10	4	9	35	30	5	4	14	19	38	54	68	53
19	Newport County	46	7	8	8	35	33	4	10	9	17	32	52	65	51
20	Bury	46	11	7	5	46	26	1	6	16	17	41	63	67	49
21	Lincoln City	46	7	9	7	33	34	3	7	13	22	43	55	77	46
22	Cardiff City	46	7	5	11	22	29	5	4	14	31	54	53	83	45
23	Wolverhampton W.	46	6	6	11	29	47	5	4	14	28	51	57	98	43
24	Swansea City	46	9	6	8	27	27	2	4	17	16	60	43	87	43

SEASON 1986/87
DIVISION THREE

Players (columns, left to right): O'Hanlon K., Ash M., Crosby P., Gooding M., Smith K., Slack T., Trusson M., Emerson D., Tynan T., Douglas C., Pugh D., Dungworth J., Simmons A., Campbell W., McGinley J., Williams A., Philliskirk A., Evans G., Haycock P., Warburton R., Felgate D., Newcombe G., Green J., Scott M., Pepper N., Eley K., Morris A., Fleetwood S.

No.	Date	Opposition	Res.	Att.	Goalscorers
1	23 Aug	FULHAM	0-0	3329	
2	30	Port Vale	1-1	3684	Slack
3	6 Sep	GILLINGHAM	0-1	3243	
4	13	Bury	2-0	2394	Douglas, Emerson
5	16	Chesterfield	1-2	2850	Dungworth
6	20	BRISTOL ROVERS	0-1	2702	
7	27	Swindon Town	0-2	4055	
8	30	WIGAN ATHLETIC	0-2	2417	
9	4 Oct	MIDDLESBROUGH	1-4	4421	Douglas
10	11	Notts County	0-5	4132	
11	18	BOLTON WANDERERS	1-0	3430	Williams
12	21	Walsall	1-4	3663	Evans
13	25	York City	1-2	3216	Haycock
14	1 Nov	MANSFIELD TOWN	2-2	3385	Dungworth, Smith
15	4	CHESTER CITY	3-0	2439	Gooding, Haycock, Philliskirk
16	8	Blackpool	0-1	3578	
17	22	Bristol City	1-0	6750	Dungworth
18	30	BRENTFORD	2-3	3148	Douglas, Haycock
19	13 Dec	BOURNEMOUTH	4-2	2092	Campbell, Evans, Gooding, Trusson
20	20	Newport County	2-1	1760	Pugh, Trusson
21	26	DARLINGTON	0-0	3272	
22	27	Carlisle United	5-3	2381	Gooding(3), Campbell, Trusson
23	1 Jan	Doncaster Rovers	0-3	4652	
24	3	BRISTOL CITY	2-0	3270	Campbell, Evans
25	27	PORT VALE	1-1	2397	Trusson
26	31	BURY	2-1	2814	Evans(2)
27	3 Feb	Gillingham	0-1	3862	
28	7	CHESTERFIELD	0-1	3462	
29	14	Bristol Rovers	2-0	2467	Evans, Pugh
30	17	Fulham	1-1	2352	Campbell
31	21	SWINDON TOWN	1-2	3004	Dungworth
32	28	Wigan Athletic	1-2	3917	Dungworth
33	3 Mar	Mansfield Town	0-0	2455	
34	7	YORK CITY	0-0	2465	
35	14	Bolton Wanderers	0-0	3748	
36	17	WALSALL	1-0	2148	Haycock
37	21	NOTTS COUNTY	1-1	3787	Gooding
38	28	Middlesbrough	0-0	9569	
39	4 Apr	BLACKPOOL	1-0	2653	Haycock
40	11	Chester City	0-1	2174	
41	18	DONCASTER ROVERS	2-0	3687	Haycock, Williams
42	20	Darlington	1-1	1576	Gooding
43	25	NEWPORT COUNTY	3-1	2555	Evans(2), Williams
44	2 May	Brentford	0-2	3425	
45	4	CARLISLE UNITED	2-1	2598	Evans, Williams
46	9	Bournemouth	0-2	11310	

Apps. 40, 13, 34, 46, 16, 14, 17, 10, 2, 42, 46, 41, 1, 36, 1, 36, 6, 34, 21, 3, 6, 27, 12, 1, 1
Subs. 3, 1, 1, 3, 5, 1, 5, 1
Goals 8, 1, 1, 4, 1, 3, 2, 4, 4, 4, 1, 9, 6

F.A. CUP

1R	15 Nov	Chester City	1-1	2749	Gooding
1Rr	18	CHESTER CITY	1-1	2692	Evans
1R2r	24	Chester City	0-1	3203	

LITTLEWOODS CUP

1R1L	26 Aug	Doncaster Rovers	1-1	1434	Tynan
1R2L	2 Sep	DONCASTER ROVERS	4-1	2958	Douglas, Pugh, Simmons, Tynan
2R1L	23	Coventry City	2-3	6663	Douglas, Dungworth
2R2L	7 Oct	COVENTRY CITY	0-1	4694	

FREIGHT ROVER TROPHY

| GRP | 5 Dec | Halifax Town | 0-0 | 1150 | |
| GRP | 9 | MANSFIELD TOWN | 1-1 | 1317 | Evans |

Final League Table

		Pl.	Home W	D	L	F	A	Away W	D	L	F	A	F.	A.	Pts
1	Bournemouth	46	19	3	1	44	10	7	6	32	26	76	40	97
2	Middlesbrough	46	16	5	2	38	11	12	5	6	29	19	67	30	94
3	Swindon Town	46	14	5	4	37	19	11	7	5	40	28	77	47	87
4	Wigan Athletic	46	15	5	3	47	26	10	5	8	36	34	83	60	85
5	Gillingham	46	16	5	2	42	14	7	4	12	23	34	65	48	78
6	Bristol City	46	14	6	3	42	15	7	8	8	21	21	63	36	77
7	Notts County	46	14	6	3	52	24	7	7	9	25	32	77	56	76
8	Walsall	46	16	4	3	50	27	6	5	12	30	40	80	67	75
9	Blackpool	46	11	7	5	35	20	5	9	9	39	39	74	59	64
10	Mansfield Town	46	9	5	9	30	23	6	7	10	22	32	52	55	61
11	Brentford	46	9	7	7	39	32	6	8	9	25	34	64	66	60
12	Port Vale	46	8	6	9	43	36	7	6	10	33	34	76	70	57
13	Doncaster Rovers	46	11	8	4	32	19	3	7	13	24	43	56	62	57
14	Rotherham United	46	10	6	7	29	23	5	6	12	19	34	48	57	57
15	Chester City	46	7	9	7	32	28	6	8	9	29	31	61	59	56
16	Bury	46	9	7	7	30	26	5	6	12	24	34	54	60	55
17	Chesterfield	46	11	5	7	36	33	2	10	11	20	36	56	69	54
18	Fulham	46	8	7	5	35	41	4	9	10	24	36	59	77	53
19	Bristol Rovers	46	8	8	7	26	29	6	4	13	23	46	49	75	51
20	York City	46	11	8	4	34	29	1	5	17	21	50	55	79	49
21	Bolton Wanderers	46	8	5	10	29	26	2	10	11	17	32	46	58	45
22	Carlisle United	46	7	5	11	26	35	3	7	13	13	43	39	78	38
23	Darlington	46	6	10	7	25	28	1	6	16	20	49	45	77	37
24	Newport County	46	4	9	10	26	34	4	4	15	23	52	49	86	37

1986-87: (Back): Chambers (Youth Coach), Ash, Dungworth, Smith, O'Hanlon, Slack, McGinley, Crosby, Claxton (Asst.Man.). (Middle): Pugh, Williams, Douglas, Hunter (Man.), Evans, Campbell, Gooding. (Front): Eley, Scott, Haycock, Morris, Warburton, Pepper.

1987-88: (Back): Chambers (Youth Man.), Hunter (Manager), Douglas, Slack, Dungworth, O'Hanlon, Newcombe, Johnson, Green, Williams, Claxton (Asst.Man.), Breckin (Scout). (Middle): Scott, Campbell, Evans, Airey, Haycock, Pugh, Gooding, Crosby. (Front): Goodwin, Pepper, Morris, Warburton, Ash, Dennis, Burrows.

SEASON 1987/88

DIVISION THREE

No.	Date	Opposition	Res.	Att.	Goalscorers	O'Hanlon K.	Douglas C.	Scott M.	Campbell W.	Dungworth J.	Green J.	Tomlinson D.	Williams A.	Evans G.	Airey C.	Pugh D.	Johnson N.	Grealish A.	Pepper N.	Haycock P.	Crosby P.	Buckley J.	Cusack D.	Crichton P.	Wylde R.	Mendonca C.	Goodwin S.	Ash M.
1	15 Aug	Bristol Rovers	1-3	3399	Campbell	1	2	3	4	5	6	7	8	9#	10	11				14								
2	22	BURY	0-1	3017		1	2	3		5	6	7	8	9	10	11		4										
3	29	Port Vale	0-0	2895		1	2	3	11	5	6		8	9	10	7		4										
4	31	CHESTER CITY	5-2	2551	Airey(4), Campbell	1	2	3	11	5	6		8	9	10	7*		4		12								
5	5 Sep	Brentford	1-1	3604	Airey	1	2	3	11	5	6		8	9	10	7		4										
6	12	WALSALL	0-1	3325		1	2	3	11	5	6		8	9	10	7*		4		12								
7	16	Brighton	1-1	6945	Campbell	1	2	3	11*	5	6		8	9	10			4	7	12								
8	19	Preston N.E.	0-0	5124		1	2	3			6		8	9	10		5	4	7	11								
9	26	MANSFIELD TOWN	2-1	3829	Grealish, Williams	1	2	3	14		6		8	9	10	7	5	4	11#									
10	29	GRIMSBY TOWN	0-0	3375		1	2	3	4		6	7	8	9	10	11	5											
11	3 Oct	Chesterfield	2-3	2993	Evans, Grealish	1	2*	3	11	12	6		8	9	10	7	5	4										
12	11	NORTHAMPTON TOWN	2-2	5244	Airey, Grealish	1		3	11	2	6	14	8	9	10	7#	5	4										
13	16	Southend United	1-1	2217	Campbell	1		3	11	2	6	7	8	12	10	14	5#	4		9*								
14	20	York City	2-1	1932	Evans, Williams	1	2	3	11	5	6		8	9	10	7		4										
15	24	BRISTOL CITY	4-1	3397	Airey(2), Evans, O.G.	1	2	3	11	5	6		8	9	10	7		4*		12								
16	31	Wigan Athletic	0-3	3004		1	2	3	11	5	6		8	9	10	7		4										
17	3 Nov	NOTTS COUNTY	1-1	4157	Green	1	2	3	11	5	6		8	9	10	7*		4#		12	14							
18	7	Blackpool	0-3	3447		1	2	3	11	4	6		8	9		7	5			10								
19	21	FULHAM	0-2	3427		1	2			5	6		8	9	10	11*			4	12	3	7						
20	28	Aldershot	3-1	2549	Airey, Campbell, Williams	1	2		11		6		8	9	10		5	4			3	7						
21	12 Dec	GILLINGHAM	1-2	2557	Green	1	2		11	5	6	14	8	9*	10			4		12	3	7#						
22	20	Sunderland	0-3	20168		1	2		11	5	6	14	8	9	10			4	3#			7						
23	26	Mansfield Town	1-0	4763	Williams	1	2		11		5		8	9				4		10	3	7	6					
24	28	DONCASTER ROVERS	1-0	5840	Haycock	1	2		11		5		8	9				4		10	3	7	6					
25	1 Jan	PORT VALE	1-0	3913	Haycock	1	2#		11	14	5		8	9*	12			4		10	3	7	6					
26	2	Walsall	2-5	5051	Airey, Haycock	1			11	2	5		8	9	12			4		10*	3	7	6#					14
27	9	Bury	2-2	2230	Evans, Haycock	1			11	2	5		8	9				4		10	3	7	6					
28	16	PRESTON N.E.	2-2	4011	Haycock, Williams	1			11	2	5		8	9				4		10	3	7	6					
29	30	Chester City	0-1	2059		1			11	2	5		8	9*	12			4		10	3	7	6					
30	13 Feb	Doncaster Rovers	2-2	2769	Haycock(2)	1	2						8		9	11	5		4	10	3	7	6					
31	17	BRENTFORD	2-0	2572	Haycock, Pugh	1	2						8		9	11	5		4	10	3	7	6					
32	20	BRISTOL ROVERS	1-1	2966	Haycock	1	2		14	9			8			11#	5	4		10	3	7	6					
33	27	CHESTERFIELD	1-1	3440	Williams	1	2		11	9			8			7	5	4		10	3		6					
34	5 Mar	SOUTHEND UNITED	1-1	2531	Airey	1	2			9*			8		12	11	5	4		10	3	7	6					
35	8	Grimsby Town	1-2	3423	Haycock	1	2			9			8			11#	5	4	14	10	3	7	6					
36	11	Northampton Town	0-0	5432			2			12	14		8				5	4	11	10*	3	7#	6	1	9			
37	16	BRIGHTON	1-0	2562	Haycock		2					11				14	5	4	8	10	3	7#	6	1	9			
38	19	WIGAN ATHLETIC	1-1	3288	Wylde		2					11					5	4	8	10	3	7	6	1	9			
39	26	Bristol City	0-2	7517			2			11#	6				14		5	4	8	10	3	7		1	9*	12		
40	2 Apr	BLACKPOOL	0-1	3001			2				6				14	11	5	4	8	10*	3	7		1	9#	12		
41	4	Fulham	1-3	4402	Mendonca		2				6					11	5	4	8	10	3	7		1	9#	14		
42	8	YORK CITY	0-1	2942		1	2		11						9		5	4	8	10	3	7*	6			12		
43	23	Notts County	0-4	7021		1	2		11	8*	5				14			4		10	3	7	6			9		
44	30	ALDERSHOT	1-0	2818	Douglas	1	2	11#	8	6	5					7				10*	3	12				9	4	14
45	2 May	Gillingham	2-0	3015	Haycock, Mendonca	1	2		11	8	6					7	5			10	3					9	4	
46	7	SUNDERLAND	1-4	9374	O.G.	1	2		11#	8	6					7	5	4*		9	3	14				10	12	
					Apps.	40	40	19	31	29	36	6	36	28	25	27	23	38	14	27	27	24	18	6	6	4	2	
					Subs.				2	3	1	3		1	7	2			1	8	1	2				4	1	2
					Goals		1		5		2		6	4	11	1		3		12					1	2		

F.A. CUP

Round	Date	Opposition	Res.	Att.	Goalscorers	O'Hanlon K.	Douglas C.	Scott M.	Campbell W.	Dungworth J.	Green J.	Tomlinson D.	Williams A.	Evans G.	Airey C.	Pugh D.	Johnson N.	Grealish A.	Pepper N.	Haycock P.	Crosby P.	Buckley J.	Cusack D.	Crichton P.	Wylde R.	Mendonca C.	Goodwin S.	Ash M.
1R	14 Nov	Doncaster Rovers	1-1	3319	Dungworth	1	2	3	11	4	6		8	9		11	5			10								
1Rr	17	DONCASTER ROVERS	2-0	4530	Haycock(2)	1	2	3	11	12	6*		8	9		11	5	4		10								
2R	6 Dec	Macclesfield	0-4	4000		1	2		11	12	6		8	9#	10		5*	4		14	3	7						

LITTLEWOODS CUP

Round	Date	Opposition	Res.	Att.	Goalscorers	O'Hanlon K.	Douglas C.	Scott M.	Campbell W.	Dungworth J.	Green J.	Tomlinson D.	Williams A.	Evans G.	Airey C.	Pugh D.	Johnson N.	Grealish A.	Pepper N.	Haycock P.	Crosby P.	Buckley J.	Cusack D.	Crichton P.	Wylde R.	Mendonca C.	Goodwin S.	Ash M.
1R1L	18 Aug	HUDDERSFIELD TOWN	4-4	3353	Evans(2), Airey, Scott	1	2	3	4	12	6	7	8	9	10#	11	5*			14								
1R2L	25	Huddersfield Town	3-1	4528	Airey, Douglas, Evans	1	2	3	11	5	6		8	9	10	7		4										
2R1L	22 Sep	Everton	2-3	15369	Pepper, Scott	1	2	3		12	6		8	9	10	14	5	4*	7	11#								
2R2L	6 Oct	EVERTON	0-0	12955		1		3	11	2	6	14	8	9*	10	7#	5	4		12								

FREIGHT ROVER TROPHY

Round	Date	Opposition	Res.	Att.	Goalscorers	O'Hanlon K.	Douglas C.	Scott M.	Campbell W.	Dungworth J.	Green J.	Tomlinson D.	Williams A.	Evans G.	Airey C.	Pugh D.	Johnson N.	Grealish A.	Pepper N.	Haycock P.	Crosby P.	Buckley J.	Cusack D.	Crichton P.	Wylde R.	Mendonca C.	Goodwin S.	Ash M.
PR	13 Oct	SCARBOROUGH	1-0	2161	Green	1		3	4	2	6	7	8		10		5	4		9								
PR	24 Nov	Sunderland	1-7	6750	Dungworth	1	2		4	5	6*	7	8	9	10	11			14		3							
R1	25 Jan	Darlington	2-3	1354	Williams(2)	1	14		11	2*	5		8	9		12	6	4		10	3	7#						

RELEGATION PLAY OFF

Round	Date	Opposition	Res.	Att.	Goalscorers	O'Hanlon K.	Douglas C.	Scott M.	Campbell W.	Dungworth J.	Green J.	Tomlinson D.	Williams A.	Evans G.	Airey C.	Pugh D.	Johnson N.	Grealish A.	Pepper N.	Haycock P.	Crosby P.	Buckley J.	Cusack D.	Crichton P.	Wylde R.	Mendonca C.	Goodwin S.	Ash M.
1L	15 May	Swansea City	0-1	9148		1	2			8	6					11	5			9	3	7				10	4	
2L	18	SWANSEA CITY	1-1	5568	Johnson	1	2		7	8	6				10#		5	12		9*	3	11				14	4	

Final League Table

		Pl.	Home W	Home D	Home L	Home F	Home A	Away W	Away D	Away L	Away F	Away A	F.	A.	Pts
1	Sunderland	46	14	7	2	51	22	13	5	5	41	26	92	48	93
2	Brighton & Hove A.	46	15	7	1	37	16	8	8	7	32	31	69	47	84
3	Walsall	46	15	6	2	39	22	8	7	8	29	28	68	50	82
4	Notts County	46	14	4	5	53	24	9	8	6	29	25	82	49	81
5	Bristol City	46	14	6	3	51	30	7	6	10	26	32	77	62	75
6	Northampton Town	46	12	8	3	36	18	6	11	6	34	33	70	51	73
7	Wigan Athletic	46	11	8	4	36	23	9	4	10	34	38	70	61	72
8	Bristol Rovers	46	14	5	4	43	19	4	7	12	25	37	68	56	66
9	Fulham	46	10	5	8	36	24	9	4	10	33	36	69	60	66
10	Blackpool	46	13	4	6	45	27	4	10	9	26	35	71	62	65
11	Port Vale	46	12	8	3	36	19	6	3	14	22	37	58	56	65
12	Brentford	46	9	8	6	27	23	7	6	10	26	36	53	59	62
13	Gillingham	46	8	9	6	45	21	6	8	9	32	40	77	61	59
14	Bury	46	9	7	7	33	26	6	7	10	25	31	58	57	59
15	Chester City	46	9	8	6	29	30	5	8	10	22	32	51	62	58
16	Preston North End	46	10	6	7	30	23	5	7	11	18	36	48	59	58
17	Southend United	46	10	6	7	42	33	4	7	12	23	50	65	83	55
18	Chesterfield	46	10	5	8	25	28	5	5	13	16	42	41	70	55
19	Mansfield Town	46	10	6	7	25	21	4	6	13	23	38	48	59	54
20	Aldershot	46	12	3	8	45	32	3	5	15	19	42	64	74	53
21	Rotherham United	46	8	8	7	28	25	4	8	11	22	41	50	66	52
22	Grimsby Town	46	6	7	10	25	29	6	7	10	23	29	48	58	50
23	York City	46	4	7	12	27	45	4	2	17	21	46	48	91	33
24	Doncaster Rovers	46	6	5	12	25	36	2	4	17	15	48	40	84	33

SEASON 1988/89
DIVISION FOUR

No.	Date	Opposition	Res.	Att.	Goalscorers	O'Hanlon K.	Russell W.	Crosby P.	Grealish A.	Johnson N.	Green J.	Hazel D.	Williams A.	Williamson R.	Haycock P.	Heard P.	Buckley J.	Goodwin S.	Mendonca C.	Dempsey M.	Evans S.	Scott M.	Pepper N.	Barnsley A.	Ash M.	Thompson S.
1	27 Aug	DONCASTER ROVERS	3-0	4497	Heard, Russell, Williamson	1	2	3	4*	5	6	7	8	9	10#	11		14	12							
2	3 Sep	Rochdale	2-0	2071	Johnson, Williamson	1	2	3	4	5	6	7#	8	9	10	11			14							
3	10	WREXHAM	2-2	4498	Williamson(2)	1	2	3	4	5	6		8	9	10	11	7									
4	17	Grimsby Town	4-0	3467	Williamson(2), Heard, Williams	1	2	3*	4	5	6		8	9	10*	11	7	14	12							
5	20	LEYTON ORIENT	4-1	4289	Buckley, Grealish, Heard, Williams	1	2	3	4*	5	6		8	9	10	11	7		12							
6	24	Carlisle United	2-0	2862	Haycock, Williamson	1	2	3	4*	5	6		8	9	10	11	7									
7	1 Oct	EXETER CITY	0-1	4075		1	2	3		5	6	14	8	9	10*	11	7#	4	12							
8	4	Burnley	0-1	9283		1	2	3	4	5	6	7*	8	9	10	11				14						
9	8	Darlington	1-1	1746	Grealish	1	2	3*	8	5	6	10	4				7	14	12	11#						
10	15	TRANMERE ROVERS	0-0	4133		1	2	5			6	10	8	9	10		3	7		4						
11	22	Torquay United	2-1	2228	Goodwin, Crosby	1	2	6		5		11	8	9	10		3	7		4						
12	25	COLCHESTER UNITED	2-0	4066	Green, Williamson	1	2	6	12	5		11*	8	9	10		3	7		4						
13	29	Scarborough	0-1	4106		1	2	14		5	6	11	8	9	10#		3	7		4						
14	5 Nov	LINCOLN CITY	2-0	4506	Mendonca, Williams	1	2		4	5	6	11*	8	9			3	7	10	12						
15	8	SCUNTHORPE UNITED	3-3	5923	Goodwin, Hazel, O.G.	1	2		4*	5	6	11	8	9			3	7	10	12						
16	12	Cambridge United	1-1	2882	Dempsey	1	2	6	4			5	11	9			3	7#		8	10		14			
17	26	Hereford United	1-1	2058	Grealish	1	2	6	4		5	7		9			3			9*	8	10	11			12
18	3 Dec	STOCKPORT COUNTY	2-1	4105	Haycock, Hazel	1	2	6	4		5	7		9			3	12	11	8*	10					
19	16	York City	1-1	2656	Buckley	1	2	6*	4		5	7		9			3	12		8	10			11		
20	26	CREWE ALEXANDRA	1-2	7165	Williamson	1	2		4	5#	7			12	9*	6	14	3		8	10			11		
21	31	Halifax Town	2-0	5258	Buckley, Russell	1	2	6	4			12		9			3	7	11	14	8*	10#		5		
22	2 Jan	Hartlepool United	1-1	3370	Williamson	1	2	6	4			7		9			3	11	8	10				5		
23	7	Peterborough United	3-0	3368	Evans(2), Williamson	1	2	6	4			11		9#			3	7*	12	14	8	10		5		
24	14	ROCHDALE	3-1	4541	Williamson(2), Crosby	1	2	6	4			11		9			3	7#		14	8	10		5		
25	21	Doncaster Rovers	0-1	4432		1	2	6	4			11		9		12	3	7		14	8#	10*		5		
26	4 Feb	Leyton Orient	1-3	3290	Williamson	1		6	4		2	14		9		12	7#	11		8	10*	3		5		
27	11	CARLISLE UNITED	2-1	4111	Heard, Haycock	1		6	4			7				9	11*	12	8		10	3		5	2	
28	18	DARLINGTON	1-2	4228	Williamson	1	2	6	4#			7		9		12	14	7	8		10*	3		5		
29	25	Tranmere Rovers	0-0	6509		1	2	6	4			11		9		10			7			3		5		
30	28	Colchester United	1-1	3671	Grealish	1	2	6	4			11		9		10		12	8*	7			3	5		
31	4 Mar	TORQUAY UNITED	1-0	3791	Williamson	1	2	6	4			11		9		10		12	8*	7			3	5		
32	7	GRIMSBY TOWN	1-0	4888	Johnson	1	2	6	4	5		11		9#		14	12	8*		7	10			3		
33	11	Lincoln City	1-0	5186	O.G.	1	2	6	4	5		11		9				8		7	10			3		
34	14	SCARBOROUGH	1-1	6010	Hazel	1	2	6		5		11		9		4*	12	8		7	10	14		3#		
35	18	Wrexham	4-1	2929	Evans(2), Williamson(2)	1	2	3	4	5		11*		9		10#	12	8		7	14	6				
36	25	HARTLEPOOL UNITED	4-0	4915	Evans(2), Williamson, O.G.	1	2	3		5		11#		9		14	12	8		7	10	6				
37	27	Crewe Alexandra	3-1	5994	Williamson(3)	1	2	3		5		11		9				8		7	10	6		4		
38	1 Apr	YORK CITY	0-1	5926		1	2	3		5		11		9#		14	12	8		7*	10	6		4		
39	4	PETERBROUGH UNITED	1-1	4762	Williamson	1	2	3	7*	5		11		9		14	12	8			10#	6		4		
40	7	Halifax Town	1-1	2974	Williamson	1	2	6	4			11		9		10	14	8		7#				3	5	
41	15	Exeter City	0-0	2594		1	2		4	5		11		9		10	12	8		7*				3	6	
42	22	BURNLEY	3-1	5726	Williamson(2), Scott	1	2	12	4	5		11		9		10#		7			8	14		3	6*	
43	29	HEREFORD UNITED	6-0	5334	Bckley(2),Goodwn,Hycock,Hzel,Wlliamsn	1	2		4*	5		11#		9		10*		7			12	14		3	6	
44	1 May	Scunthorpe United	0-0	8775		1	2		4	5		11		9		10*		7			8	7		14	3	6
45	6	Stockport County	3-1	4313	Hazel(2), Goodwin	1	2		4*	5		11		9		10#		12			8	7		14	3	6
46	13	CAMBRIDGE UNITED	0-0	9567		1	2		12	5		11		9		10#		4			8*	7		14	3	6
					Apps.	46	44	36	36	26	21	39	15	41	27	28	19	33	5	24	19	18	1	27	1	1
					Subs.			1	3						3		1	6	2	17	8	5	3	6	1	1
					Goals		2	2	4	2	1	6	3	27	4	5	4	1	1		6	1				

F.A. CUP

Rd	Date	Opposition	Res.	Att.	Goalscorers	O'Hanlon K.	Russell W.	Crosby P.	Grealish A.	Johnson N.	Green J.	Hazel D.	Williams A.	Williamson R.	Haycock P.	Heard P.	Buckley J.	Goodwin S.	Mendonca C.	Dempsey M.	Evans S.	Scott M.	Pepper N.	Barnsley A.	Ash M.	Thompson S.
1R	19 Nov	BARROW	3-1	5495	Green, Williamson, O.G.	1	2	6	4		5	11		9*			3			12	8	10	11#	14		
2R	10 Dec	Grimsby Town	2-3	5676	Dempsey, Grealish	1	2	6	4		5	11				9	3	11		8	10					

LITTLEWOODS CUP

Rd	Date	Opposition	Res.	Att.	Goalscorers	O'Hanlon K.	Russell W.	Crosby P.	Grealish A.	Johnson N.	Green J.	Hazel D.	Williams A.	Williamson R.	Haycock P.	Heard P.	Buckley J.	Goodwin S.	Mendonca C.	Dempsey M.	Evans S.	Scott M.	Pepper N.	Barnsley A.	Ash M.	Thompson S.
1R1L	30 Aug	Grimsby Town	1-0	2517	O.G.	1	2	3	4	5	6	7	8	9	10*	11		12								
1R2L	6 Sep	GRIMSBY TOWN	1-0	3381	Grealish	1	2	3	4	5	6		8	9	10#	11*	7	12	14							
2R1L	27	MANCHESTER UNITED	0-1	13110		1	2	3	4#	5	6		8	9	10	11	7	14								
2R2L	12 Oct	Manchester United	0-5	20597		1	2	3		5		7	8	9	14	11	6	4	10#							

SHERPA VAN TROPHY

Rd	Date	Opposition	Res.	Att.	Goalscorers	O'Hanlon K.	Russell W.	Crosby P.	Grealish A.	Johnson N.	Green J.	Hazel D.	Williams A.	Williamson R.	Haycock P.	Heard P.	Buckley J.	Goodwin S.	Mendonca C.	Dempsey M.	Evans S.	Scott M.	Pepper N.	Barnsley A.	Ash M.	Thompson S.
PR	29 Nov	Grimsby Town	0-1	1194		1	2	6			5	7		9			3			4	8	10		11*		12
PR	13 Dec	DONCASTER ROVERS	2-1	1790	Haycock, Hazel	1	2	6	4		5	7		9			3	11	12		8	10*				
1R	17 Jan	Blackpool	3-4	1620	Buckley, Grealish, Hazel	1	2	6	4		5	11		9			3	7	12		8*	10				

Final League Table

		Pl.	Home					Away					F.	A.	Pts
			W	D	L	F	A	W	D	L	F	A			
1	Rotherham United	46	13	6	4	44	18	9	10	4	32	17	76	35	82
2	Tranmere Rovers	46	15	6	2	34	13	6	11	6	28	30	62	43	80
3	Crewe Alexandra	46	13	7	3	42	24	8	8	7	25	24	67	48	78
4	Scunthorpe United	46	11	9	3	40	22	10	5	8	37	35	77	57	77
5	Scarborough	46	12	7	4	33	23	9	7	7	34	34	67	57	77
6	Leyton Orient	46	16	2	5	61	19	5	10	8	25	31	86	50	75
7	Wrexham	46	12	7	4	44	28	7	7	9	33	35	77	63	71
8	Cambridge United	46	13	7	3	45	25	5	7	11	26	37	71	62	68
9	Grimsby Town	46	11	9	3	33	18	6	6	11	32	41	65	59	66
10	Lincoln City	46	12	6	5	39	26	6	4	13	25	34	64	60	64
11	York City	46	10	8	5	43	27	7	5	11	19	36	62	63	64
12	Carlisle United	46	9	6	8	26	25	6	9	8	27	27	53	52	60
13	Exeter City	46	11	4	5	46	23	4	2	17	19	45	65	68	60
14	Torquay United	46	15	2	6	32	23	2	6	15	13	37	45	60	59
15	Hereford United	46	11	8	4	40	27	3	8	12	26	45	66	72	58
16	Burnley	46	12	6	5	35	20	2	7	14	17	41	52	61	55
17	Peterborough Utd.	46	10	3	10	29	32	4	9	10	23	42	52	74	54
18	Rochdale	46	10	10	3	32	26	3	4	16	24	56	56	82	53
19	Hartlepool United	46	10	8	5	37	33	4	4	15	17	45	50	78	53
20	Stockport County	46	10	6	7	33	24	2	11	10	23	32	54	52	51
21	Halifax Town	46	10	7	6	42	27	3	4	16	27	48	69	75	50
22	Colchester United	46	8	7	8	35	30	4	7	12	25	48	60	78	50
23	Doncaster Rovers	46	6	9	8	32	32	4	4	15	17	46	49	78	49
24	Darlington	46	3	12	8	28	38	5	6	12	25	38	53	76	42

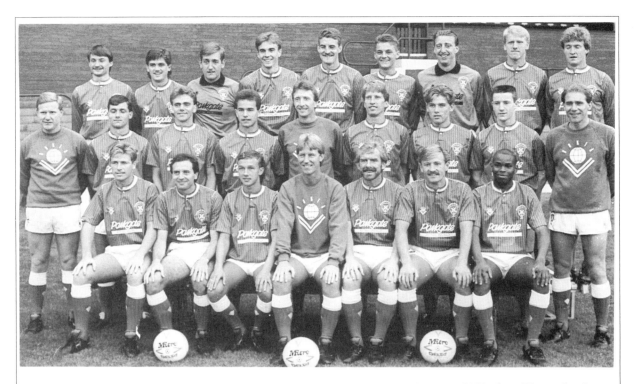

1988-89: (Back): Clarke, Pepper, Newcombe, Williams, Johnson, Warburton, O'Hanlon, Haycock, Green. (Middle): Breckin (Youth Coach), Ash, Buckley, Tomlinson, Henson (Asst.Man.), Russell, Thompson, Scott, Bailey (Physio). (Front): Heard, Williamson, Goodwin, McEwan (Man.), Grealish, Crosby, Hazel.

1989-90: (Back): Robinson, Johnson, Mercer, Evans, O'Hanlon, Haycock, Barnsley. (Middle): Bailey (Physio), Russell, Heard, Buckley, Thompson, Henson (Asst.Man.), Dempsey, Pepper, Richardson, Ainscow, Breckin (Youth Man.). (Front): Goodwin, Scott, Grealish, McEwan (Man.), Williamson, Mendonca, Hazel.

SEASON 1989/90
DIVISION THREE

No.	Date	Opposition	Res.	Att.	Goalscorers	O'Hanlon K.	Russell W.	Robinson R.	Grealish A.	Barnsley A.	Scott M.	Buckley J.	Dempsey M.	Williamson R.	Haycock P.	Hazel D.	Johnson N.	Mendonca C.	Pepper N.	Goodwin S.	Heard P.	Thompson S.	Ainscow A.	Evans S.	Goater S.	Mercer W.	Pickering A.	Cash S.	Ford S.	Richardson N.
1	19 Aug	PRESTON NORTH END	3-1	5951	Dempsey, Mendonca, Williamson	1	2	3	4	5	6	7	8	9	10#	11		14												
2	26	Wigan Athletic	3-0	2659	Buckley, Mendonca, Williamson	1	2	3	4#	5	6*	7	8	9		11	12	10		14										
3	2 Sep	WALSALL	2-2	5926	Buckley, Williamson	1	2	3	4#	5	6*	7*	8	9		11	12	10		14										
4	9	Tranmere Rovers	1-2	4912	Barnsley	1	2	6				7	8	9	12	11	10*		4											
5	16	BOLTON WANDERERS	1-0	6846	Heard	1	2		12	6		7*	8	9	10#	11	5			4	3	14								
6	23	Notts County	0-2	5891		1	2	3	4*	6	10	7#	8	9			5			12			11	14						
7	26	Bury	1-1	3276	Williamson	1	2	3	4	6	11	7	8	9		12	5	10*												
8	30	CARDIFF	4-0	4998	Williamson(3), Mendonca	1	2	3	4*	6	8	7		9		11#	5	10		12		14								
9	7 Oct	BIRMINGHAM CITY	5-1	4450	Williamson(3), Buckley, Scott	1	2	3	4	6	11	7		9			5	10		8										
10	14	Fulham	1-1	4375	Barnsley	1	2	3	4	6	11			9			5			8		10	7							
11	17	LEYTON ORIENT	5-2	5728	Mndonca(2),Bckley,Robinsn,Wlliamsn	1	2	3	4	6	11	7*		9			5	10		8			12							
12	21	Crewe Alexandra	0-0	3647		1	2	3	4	6	11	7		9			5	10*		8			12							
13	28	BLACKPOOL	1-1	5570	Johnson	1	2	3	4*	6	11	7		9		14	5	10#		8			12							
14	31	Swansea City	0-1	4077		1	2	3*	4	6	11			9		12	5	10#		8		7		14						
15	4 Nov	Northampton Town	2-1	3598	Buckley, Goodwin	1		4		2	3	7		9		11	5	10*		8	6			12						
16	11	CHESTER CITY	5-0	5216	Williamson(2),Buckley,Goodwin,Hazel	1		4		2	3	7		9		11	5			8	6			10*	12					
17	25	SHREWSBURY TOWN	4-2	5694	Evans, Johnson, Pepper, Williamson	1		3		2	6	7	4*	9		11	5		12	8				10#	14					
18	2 Dec	Bristol City	0-0	9509		1		3	4	2	6	7		9		11	5		8					10						
19	16	HUDDERSFIELD TOWN	0-0	6673		1		3	4	2*	6	7		9		11#	5	10		8	14			12						
20	26	Mansfield Town	1-3	6384	Goodwin	1	2	3	4#	14	6	7		9			5	10*		8	11			12						
21	30	Reading	2-3	3924	Barnsley, Williamson	1		3	4#	2	6	7		9		11	5	10	14	8										
22	1 Jan	BRISTOL ROVERS	3-2	7750	Evans, Hazel, Williamson		5	3	4	2	6	7*		9		11		5		12	8			10		1				
23	6	Brentford	2-4	5624	Goater, O.G.		5	3	4	2	6*			9		11	12			7#	8			10	14	1				
24	13	WIGAN ATHLETIC	1-2	6055	Goodwin	1		3	12	2	6			9		11	5	14	4	8	7*			10#						
25	20	Preston North End	1-0	6088	Evans	1	2	3	4	14	6	7	11#	9*		12	5			8				10						
26	27	TRANMERE ROVERS	0-0	6386		1	2	3			6	7	11*	9		12	5		4	8				10						
27	3 Feb	NOTTS COUNTY	1-2	7251	O.G.	1	2	3	4#	14	6	7		9		11	5			8				10*	12					
28	10	Bolton Wanderers	2-0	7728	Mendonca(2)	1	2	3	4		6	7*		9		12	5	10	11	8										
29	17	SWANSEA CITY	3-2	5062	Heard, Mendonca, Williamson	1	2	3	4*			7		9		12	5	10	11	8	6									
30	24	Shrewsbury Town	1-1	3282	Goodwin	1	2	3	4		6	7		9			5	10*	11	8				12						
31	3 Mar	BRENTFORD	2-1	5640	Goater, Williamson	1	2	3	4	14	6#	7		9		11	5			8				10						
32	10	Cardiff City	0-2	2888		1	2	3	4	6				9		11*	5			8		12		10		2				
33	10	BURY	1-3	5425	Goodwin	1	12	3	4	6				9			5		11*	8			14	10#		2				
34	17	Birmingham City	1-4	6985	Mendonca	1	2	3		5		7#	8	9		11*		10	4		6				12		14			
35	20	FULHAM	2-1	4511	Mendonca(2)	1	2	3				7	8	9			5	10	4	11	6									
36	24	Leyton Orient	1-1	3359	Heard	1	2	3				7	8	9		5		10	4		6						11			
37	31	CREWE ALEXANDRA	1-3	5613	Williamson	1	2	3				7	8	9		14	5	10#	4	6				12			11*			
38	3 Apr	BRISTOL CITY	1-2	5274	Buckley	1		3		2		7	8	9		14	5	10*	4	6#				12			11			
39	7	Blackpool	2-1	3505	Cash, Mendonca	1		6				7	8			5	10	11	4					12	9	2	3			
40	14	Bristol Rovers	0-2	6794				3		6		8*				5	10	11	4					12	9	2	3	1		
41	16	MANSFIELD TOWN	0-0	5096		1		6	8			7			12	11	5	9*	4					10		2	3			
42	21	Huddersfield Town	1-2	4963	Dempsey	1		6	4	14		11	8			5	10		7#							2	3			
43	24	READING	1-1	3719	Mendonca	1		6	4#		2	11	8*		12	5	10		7							2	3			
44	28	Chester City	0-2	3827		1		6		2		11	8	9#		12	5	10	7*	4				14			3			
45	1 May	Walsall	1-1	5697	Dempsey	1		6		2			8			11	5	10		4		14		9			7#			3
46	5	NORTHAMPTON TOWN	2-0	3420	Evans, Mendonca	1		6		2			8			11	5	10		4	12			9			7*			3

					Apps.	43	28	43	31	31	28	40	22	41	2	22	40	30	15	35	13	3		12	5	2	9	8	1	2
					Subs.		1			6				1				3	2	4	1	3		8	8		7	1		
					Goals			1		3	1	7	3	19		2	2	14	1	6	3			4	2		1			

F.A. CUP

Round	Date	Opposition	Res.	Att.	Goalscorers	O'Hanlon K.	Russell W.	Robinson R.	Grealish A.	Barnsley A.	Scott M.	Buckley J.	Dempsey M.	Williamson R.	Haycock P.	Hazel D.	Johnson N.	Mendonca C.	Pepper N.	Goodwin S.	Heard P.	Thompson S.	Ainscow A.	Evans S.	Goater S.
1R	18 Nov	BURY	0-0	6305		1		3	4	2	6	7		9		11	5			8				10	
1Rr	21	Bury	2-1	5009	Evans, Hazel	1	12	3	4	2	6	7		9		11	5			8*				10	
2R	9 Dec	Walsall	0-1	4240		1		3	4#	2	6	7		9		11	5		8	14				10*	12

LITTLEWOODS CUP

Round	Date	Opposition	Res.	Att.	Goalscorers	O'Hanlon K.	Russell W.	Robinson R.	Grealish A.	Barnsley A.	Scott M.	Buckley J.	Dempsey M.	Williamson R.	Haycock P.	Hazel D.	Johnson N.	Mendonca C.	Pepper N.	Goodwin S.	Heard P.	Thompson S.
1R1L	22 Aug	Sheffield United	1-1	11136	Mendonca	1	2	3	4	5	6	7	8	9		11		10				
1R2L	29	SHEFFIELD UNITED	1-0	11833	Williamson	1	2	3	4#	5	6	7	8	9		11		10		14		
2R1L	20 Sep	Norwich City	1-1	9531	Williamson	1	2	3	4	6		7	8	9	10		5				11	
2R2L	3 Oct	NORWICH CITY	0-2	9064		1	2	3	4	6	8*	11		9		7	5	10#		12	14	

LEYLAND DAF TROPHY

Round	Date	Opposition	Res.	Att.	Goalscorers	O'Hanlon K.	Russell W.	Robinson R.	Grealish A.	Barnsley A.	Scott M.	Buckley J.	Dempsey M.	Williamson R.	Haycock P.	Hazel D.	Johnson N.	Mendonca C.	Pepper N.	Goodwin S.	Heard P.	Evans S.	Goater S.
PR	28 Nov	Hartlepool United	4-1	818	Buckley, Grealish, Robinson, O.G.	1		3	4	2	6*	7		9		11#	5		12	8		10	14
PR	12 Dec	YORK CITY	3-1	1996	Barnsley, Grealish, Williamson	1		3	4	2	6	7#		9		11	5	12	14	8		10*	
1R	9 Jan	HUDDERSFIELD TOWN	3-0	3519	Hazel, Mendonca, Scott	1		3		2	6					11	5	10#	4	8	7	9	14
2R	31	Bolton Wanderers	0-1	6838		1	2#	3		14	6	7		9		11	5		4	8		10*	12

Final League Table

		Pl	Home					Away					F.	A.	Pts
			W	D	L	F	A	W	D	L	F	A			
1	Bristol Rovers	46	15	8	0	43	14	11	7	5	28	21	71	35	93
2	Bristol City	46	15	5	3	40	16	12	5	6	36	24	76	40	91
3	Notts County	46	17	4	2	40	18	8	8	7	33	35	73	53	87
4	Tranmere Rovers	46	15	5	3	54	22	8	6	9	32	27	86	49	80
5	Bury	46	11	7	5	35	19	10	4	9	35	30	70	49	74
6	Bolton Wanderers	46	12	7	4	32	19	6	9	8	27	29	59	48	69
7	Birmingham City	46	10	7	6	33	19	8	5	10	27	40	60	59	66
8	Huddersfield Town	46	11	5	7	30	23	6	9	8	31	39	61	62	65
9	Rotherham United	46	12	6	5	48	28	5	7	11	23	34	71	62	64
10	Reading	46	10	9	4	33	21	5	10	8	24	32	57	53	64
11	Shrewsbury Town	46	10	9	4	38	24	6	6	11	21	30	59	54	63
12	Crewe Alexandra	46	10	8	5	32	24	5	9	9	24	29	56	53	62
13	Brentford	46	11	4	8	41	31	7	3	13	25	35	66	66	61
14	Leyton Orient	46	9	6	8	28	24	7	4	12	24	32	52	56	58
15	Mansfield Town	46	13	2	8	34	25	3	5	15	16	40	50	65	55
16	Chester City	46	11	7	5	30	23	2	8	13	13	32	43	55	54
17	Swansea City	46	10	6	7	25	27	4	6	13	20	36	45	63	54
18	Wigan Athletic	46	10	6	7	22	22	3	8	12	19	42	48	64	53
19	Preston North End	46	10	7	6	42	30	4	3	16	23	49	65	79	52
20	Fulham	46	8	8	7	33	27	4	7	12	22	39	55	66	51
21	Cardiff City	46	8	9	6	30	35	5	5	12	21	35	51	70	50
22	Northampton Town	46	7	9	7	27	31	4	7	12	24	37	51	68	47
23	Blackpool	46	6	8	9	29	27	3	2	10	11	20	40	49	46
24	Walsall	46	6	8	9	23	30	3	6	14	17	42	40	72	41

SEASON 1990/91

DIVISION THREE

No.	Date	Opposition	Res.	Att.	Goalscorers	O'Hanlon K.	Forrest G.	Scott M.	Goodwin S.	Law N.	Robinson R.	Buckley J.	Spooner S.	Williamson R.	Mendonca C.	Hazel D.	Dempsey M.	Barnsley A.	Goater S.	Richardson N.	Thompson S.	Russell W.	Stancliffe P.	Jenkinson L.	Evans S.	Watts J.	Pickering A.	Mercer W.	Howard J.	Johnson N.	Taylor A.	Cullen A.	Duffield P.	Hodges M.	Pearson J.	
1	25 Aug	Stoke City	1-3	13048	Williamson	1	2	3	4	5	6	7*	8	9	10	11	12																			
2	1 Sep	SHREWSBURY TOWN	2-2	4817	Hazel, Law	1	2	3	4*	5		12	8	9	10#	11	7	6	14																	
3	8	Bury	1-3	2998	Mendonca	1	2	3		5#	10			9	8	11	7	4	14	6																
4	15	WIGAN ATHLETIC	5-1	4100	Evans(2), Hazel, Mendonca, O.G.	1		3			6		4	9*	12	7	8	2					5	11	10											
5	18	BRENTFORD	2-2	4298	Dempsey, Mendonca	1	2	3			6		4		9	7	8						5	11	10											
6	22	Leyton Orient	0-3	3496		1	2	3			6		4	9		7	8						5	11	10											
7	29	READING	0-2	4058		1	2		12	14	6		4*			7	8	3	9				5#	11	10											
8	2 Oct	Grimsby Town	1-2	6923	Dempsey	1	2		7	5	3		4		9#	12	8	6	14					11*	10											
9	6	Fulham	0-2	3428		1	2		7	5#	3		4		9*	11	8	6	12					14	10											
10	13	HUDDERSFIELD TOWN	1-3	6120	Buckley	1	2#		8		3	7	10			11*			9				5	12	14	4	6									
11	20	PRESTON NORTH END	1-0	4599	Mendonca		2	3	7		6			9	10	11*	8		14		12	4#				5		1								
12	23	Bolton Wanderers	0-0	4692			2	3	7		6			9	10*	11	8				12	4				5		1								
13	27	Cambridge United	1-4	4142	Williamson		2	3	7		6			9	10	11	8				12	4*				5		1								
14	3 Nov	BRADFORD CITY	0-2	6057			2	3	7		6			9	10#	11	8				12	4*			14	5		1								
15	10	Bournemouth	2-4	5442	Goater, Scott		2	3	7		6		12			14	8*		10		11	4			9#	5		1								
16	24	MANSFIELD TOWN	1-1	3729	Evans		2	3	7	5					10*	11	8				12	4			9	6		1								
17	1 Dec	SOUTHEND UNITED	0-1	3465			2	7	8	5	3		14			11			10*			4#			9	6		1	12							
18	15	Birmingham City	1-2	4735	Law		2		7	3			8		9	11		6#	10		14	4						1		5						
19	22	Exeter City	0-2	3752			6		7	3			4		9	11#		2	14		8	12			10			1*		5						
20	26	CHESTER CITY	2-1	3547	Evans, Spooner	1	2		7	6	3		4		9	11					8				10					5						
21	29	TRANMERE ROVERS	1-1	4316	Mendonca	1			7	6			4		9	11		2			8	3			10					5						
22	1 Jan	Swansea City	0-5	5938		1	14		7	6			4		9	12	11	2#			8	3			10*					5						
23	12	Shrewsbury Town	0-0	2800		1	2		7	6					9	11	8			4	10	3								5						
24	19	STOKE CITY	0-0	6236		1	2		7#	5	6		14		10	11	8		9		4	3														
25	2 Feb	Brentford	2-1	5540	Cullen, Dempsey	1	2		7	12	6					11	8#	3	9	4					14					5*		10				
26	5	LEYTON ORIENT	0-0	4056		1	2			5	6					11	8	3	9	4	7*				12							10				
27	23	BOURNEMOUTH	1-1	4107	Johnson	1	2				6				10	11	4		9*			3			12					5		7				8
28	1 Mar	Southend United	1-2	5622	Hazel	1	2				6				10	11	7		9*	4		3			12					5						8
29	5	BURY	0-3	3658		1					6				10	11	7		14	4#		3			9					5				2		8
30	9	BIRMINGHAM CITY	1-1	5015	Mendonca	1	2				6				9	11	7			4		3								5			10			8
31	12	GRIMSBY TOWN	1-4	5542	Mendonca	1	2#				6				9	11	7			4		3								5			10	14		8
32	16	Reading	0-2	3250		1			7	6	3		14		9	11			12	4		2								5			10*			8
33	19	Huddersfield Town	0-4	4578		1			7	6	3		4		9			2	11											5			10			8
34	23	FULHAM	3-1	3180	Duffield, Goater, Goodwin				4	6	3					7		2	9		14							1		5			10			8
35	26	Wigan Athletic	0-2	1929			14		4	6	3							2	9		7#							1		5			10			8
36	30	Chester City	2-1	1079	Duffield, Pearson		7		4	6	3					11		2										1		5			10		9	8
37	1 Apr	EXETER CITY	2-4	3701	Hathaway, Pearson		3		4	6	5					11		2	14									1					10		9	8
38	5	Tranmere Rovers	2-1	7398	Pearson(2)	1	7		4	6	3					11		2															10	5	9	8
39	9	CREWE ALEXANDRA	1-1	4141	Duffield	1	7		4	6	3				14	11#		2*															10	5	9	8
40	13	SWANSEA CITY	2-3	3510	Duffield, Richardson	1	3		7	5	6				10		8			4		2											11		9	
41	20	Preston North End	2-1	4069	Goodwin, Mendonca	1			7	5	6				10					4		2									3		11		9	[illegible]
42	23	Mansfield Town	2-1	4041	Pearson, Mendonca	1			7	5	6				10					4		2									3		11		9	8
43	27	BOLTON WANDERERS	2-2	8045	Duffield, Goodwin	1			7	5	6				10					4		2									3		11		9	[illegible]
44	30	Crewe Alexandra	1-3	4086	Barrick	1			7*	5	6				10					4		2									3		11		9	[illegible]
45	4 May	CAMBRIDGE UNITED	3-2	5402	Hazel, Mendonca, Richardson	1				5	3				10	7				4		2				6							11		9	[illegible]
46	11	Bradford City	0-1	6354		1				5	3				10	7				4		2				6							11		9	[illegible]
					Apps.	33	32	13	33	30	39	2	15	9	32	36	25	19	13	16	9	25	5	5	14	10	1	13		17	4	3	17	3	11	
					Subs.		2		1	2		1	4		2	3	1		9		7	1		2	6				1					1		
					Goals			1	3	2	1	1		3	10	3	3		2	2					4					1		1	5		5	

F.A. CUP

1R	17 Nov	STOCKPORT COUNTY	1-0	4501	Dempsey		2	3	7	5						11	8		10*		12	4			9	6		1							
2R	11 Dec	HALIFAX TOWN	1-1	2906	Goater		2		7	5	3		10*			11	8		9		14				12	6	4#	1							
2Rr	17	Halifax Town	2-1	2132	Evans, Johnson		6		7	3			4		9	11	12	2			8*				10			1		5					
3R	5 Jan	Swansea City	0-0	6478		1	2		7	6					9	11	8			4	10	3								5					
3Rr	21	SWANSEA CITY	4-0	4233	Mendonca(2), Demspey, Goater	1	2				6		7		10	11	8		9#		4	3			14					5					
4R	26	Crewe Alexandra	0-1	6057		1	2		7		6				10	11	8	3	9*		4				12					5					

RUMBELOW'S CUP

1R1L	28 Aug	Doncaster Rovers	6-2	3665	Williamson(3), Hazel(2), Goodwin	1	2	3	4	5	6	12	8	9	10*	11	7																		
1R2L	4 Sep	DONCASTER ROVERS	2-1	3448	Dempsey, O.G.	1	2	3	14	5			8#	9		11*	7	4	10	6	12														
2R1L	25	BLACKBURN ROVERS	1-1	4213	O.G.	1	2#	3	12		6		4	9*		7	8	14			11		5		10										
2R2L	9 Oct	Blackburn Rovers	0-1	4664		1	2	6	8		3	7	10			11			14						9#	4	5								

LEYLAND DAF TROPHY

PR	5 Nov	Halifax Town	1-1	956	Thompson		2	3	7		6		10	9*		11	8				12					5	4	1							
PR	27	SCARBOROUGH	1-1	1182	Scott		2	11	8	5	3				10	7						4			9	6		1							
1R	15 Jan	Tranmere Rovers	0-3	2997		1	2			6	5		7		9	11	8			4*	10	3			12										

Final League Table

		Pl.	Home W	D	L	F	A	Away W	D	L	F	A	F.	A.	Pts
1	Cambridge United	46	14	5	4	42	22	11	6	6	33	23	75	45	86
2	Southend United	46	13	6	4	34	23	13	1	9	33	28	67	51	85
3	Grimsby Town	46	16	3	4	42	13	8	8	7	24	21	66	34	83
4	Bolton Wanderers	46	14	5	4	33	18	10	6	7	31	32	64	50	83
5	Tranmere Rovers	46	13	5	5	38	21	10	4	9	26	25	64	46	78
6	Brentford	46	12	4	7	30	22	9	9	5	29	25	59	47	76
7	Bury	46	13	6	4	39	26	7	7	9	28	30	67	56	73
8	Bradford City	46	13	3	7	36	22	7	7	9	26	32	62	54	70
9	Bournemouth	46	14	6	3	37	20	5	7	11	21	38	58	58	70
10	Wigan Athletic	46	14	3	6	40	20	6	6	11	31	34	71	54	69
11	Huddersfield Town	46	13	3	7	37	23	5	10	8	20	28	57	51	67
12	Birmingham City	46	8	9	6	21	21	8	8	7	24	28	45	49	65
13	Leyton Orient	46	15	2	6	35	19	3	8	12	20	39	55	58	64
14	Stoke City	46	9	7	7	36	29	7	5	11	19	30	55	59	60
15	Reading	46	11	5	7	34	28	6	3	14	19	38	53	66	59
16	Exeter City	46	12	6	5	35	16	4	3	16	23	36	58	52	57
17	Preston North End	46	11	5	7	33	29	4	6	13	21	38	54	67	56
18	Shrewsbury Town	46	8	7	8	29	22	6	3	14	32	46	61	68	52
19	Chester City	46	10	3	10	27	27	4	6	13	19	31	46	58	51
20	Swansea City	46	8	6	9	31	33	5	3	15	18	39	49	72	48
21	Fulham	46	8	8	7	27	22	2	8	13	14	34	41	56	46
22	Crewe Alexandra	46	6	9	8	35	35	5	2	16	27	45	62	80	44
23	Rotherham United	46	5	10	8	31	38	5	2	16	19	49	50	87	42
24	Mansfield Town	46	5	8	10	23	27	3	6	14	19	36	42	63	38

1990-91: (Back): Robinson, Barnsley, Haycock, Johnson, O'Hanlon, Ford, Mercer, Evans, Law, Watts, Richardson. (Middle): Russell, Williamson, Dempsey, Buckley, Henson (Asst.Man.), Howard, Pickering, Mendonca, Spooner, Hodges. (Front): Breckin (Youth Man.), Thompson, Goater, Forrest, McEwan (Manager), Scott, Hazel, Goodwin, Bailey (Physio).

1991-92: (Back): Watts, Johnson, Ford, Evans, Mercer, Law, Goater.
(Middle): Russell(Youth Coach),Hazel,Robinson, Breckin(Asst.Man.), Richardson,Pickering, Bailey(Physio)
(Front): Hathaway, Thompson, Hutchings, Henson (Manager), Goodwin, Barrick, Taylor.

SEASON 1991/92
DIVISION FOUR

No.	Date	Opposition	Res.	Att.	Goalscorers	MerW	HutC	RobR	RicN	JohN	LawN	GooS	BarD	CunA	PagD	HazD	GoaS	WatJ	HatI	ForS	TayA	TodM	WilR	PicA	RusW	McKA	BarS	SnoG	HowJ
1	17 Aug	BURNLEY	2-1	6042	Cunningham, Johnson	1	2	3	4	5	6	7		8	9	10	11												
2	24	Lincoln City	2-0	4134	Cunningham, Robinson	1	2	3	4	5	6	7		8	9	10	11												
3	31	CREWE ALEXANDRA	1-2	4362	Johnson	1	2	3	4	5	6	7		8	9	10	11												
4	3 Sep	Carlisle United	3-1	2346	Goodwin, Page, Richardson	1	2	3	4	5	6	7#		8	9	10	11*	12	14										
5	7	HEREFORD UNITED	0-0	3778		1	2	3	4#	5				8	9	10	11		14	7									
6	13	Halifax Town	4-0	2613	Cunninghm, Goater, Hutchings, Wilsn		2			5	6			8	9	10	11*		14		1	3	4	7					
7	17	Rochdale	1-1	4033	Hutchings		2				6			8	9	10	11	5			1	3		7	4				
8	21	MAIDSTONE UNITED	3-3	3870	Page(2), Hazel		2				6	7*		8	9	10	11	12	5		1	3			4				
9	28	Blackpool	0-3	5356			2				6	7		8	9	10	11	12	5		1	3	4						
10	12 Oct	Chesterfield	1-1	6137	Cunningham	1*	3				6	7			9	10	11	12	5			4	8	2					
11	25	YORK CITY	4-0	4677	Cunningham(2), Hutchings, Page		3			5	6	7#		14	9	10	11					4	8	2		1			
12	2 Nov	NORTHAMPTON TOWN	1-0	3146	Cunningham		3			5	6	7			9	10	11					4	8	2		1			
13	6	Doncaster Rovers	1-1	3507	Wilson		3				6	7	12		10		11	9	5			4*	8	2		1			
14	9	Scunthorpe United	0-1	4175		1	3				6	7	8	9	10	11	4	5						2					
15	22	WALSALL	2-1	4192	Cunningham, Watts	1	3				6	7	8	9	10	11		5						2					
16	30	Cardiff City	0-1	3551		1	3			5	6	7		10*	11	12						4		2					
17	14 Dec	GILLINGHAM	1-1	3137	Cunningham	1	3			5	6	7		8#	9	10*	12	11		14		4		2					
18	21	LINCOLN CITY	1-1	3293	Cunningham	1	3			5	6	7			9	10	11	8				4		2					
19	26	Burnley	2-1	13812	Cunningham, Page	1	3			5	6	7		8	9	10	11					4		2					
20	28	Crewe Alexandra	1-0	4490	Hazel	1	3			5	6	7		8	9	10	11					4		2					
21	1 Jan	CARLISLE UNITED	1-0	4850	Page	1	3			5	6	7		8	9	10	11					4		2					
22	4	SCARBOROUGH	0-2	4497		1	3			5	6	7		8	9	10	11					4		2					
23	11	Barnet	5-2	3552	Page(3), Goodwin, Todd	1	3			5	6	7		8	9	10	11					4		2					
24	18	MANSFIELD TOWN	1-1	6454	Hazel	1	3			5	6	7		8	9	10	11					4		2					
25	8 Feb	York City	1-1	3526	Todd	1	3			5	6	7		8	9	10	11					4*	12	2					
26	11	CARDIFF CITY	1-2	3827	Hazel	1	3			5	6	7		8#	9	10	11		14			4		2					
27	15	Gillingham	1-5	2486	Goater	1	3			5	6	7#		8	9		11	10	14			4		2					
28	22	BARNET	3-0	3841	Cunningham, Hutchings, Page	1	3		8	5	6	7		9	10	11						4		2					
29	29	Scarborough	3-0	2604	Hazel, Page, Richardson	1	3		8	5	6	7		9	10	11						4		2					
30	3 Mar	Mansfield Town	0-1	5713		1			8	5	6	7		9	10	11						4		2			3		
31	7	WREXHAM	3-0	3562	Cunningham(2), Howard	1	3			5	6	7		9	10#	11											8		14
32	10	DONCASTER ROVERS	3-1	4883	Cunningham(2), Howard	1	3			5	6	7		9		11											8		10
33	14	Northampton Town	2-1	2561	Barrick, Goodwin	1	3		4	5	6	7	8	9#		11		14*					12	2					10
34	21	SCUNTHORPE UNITED	5-0	4528	Goater(3), Goodwin, Howard	1	3		8	5	6	7	11			9		14				4*	12	2#					10
35	28	Walsall	2-0	3524	Goater, Hazel	1	3		8*	5	6	7	11			12	9					4		2					10
36	31	HALIFAX TOWN	1-0	4517	Wilson	1	3#		8*	5	6	7	11			12	9		14			4		2					10
37	4 Apr	Hereford United	0-1	1868		1	3		8*	5	6	7	11			12	9					4		2					10
38	11	ROCHDALE	2-0	5086	Goater, Goodwin	1	3		4	5	6	7	8			11	9							2					10
39	18	Maidstone United	0-0	1744		1	3		4	5	6	7	8		12	11	9*							2					10
40	20	BLACKPOOL	2-0	8992	Cunningham, Hazel	1	3		4	5	6	7	8		12	14	11	9						2*					10#
41	28	Wrexham	3-0	3477	Goater(2), Hazel	1	3		4	5	6	7	8		9	11	10				2								
42	2 May	CHESTERFIELD	1-1	8193	Cunningham	1	3		4	5	6	7	8	9	12	11	10*				2								
					Apps.	35	41	5	18	35	42	39	32	34	29	34	17	7	2	4	6	23	11	27	6	3		3	9
					Subs.								2	2	2	4	5	2	6					3					1
					Goals		4	1	2	2		5	1	18	11	8	9	1				2	3						3

F.A. CUP

Rd	Date	Opposition	Res.	Att.	Goalscorers	MerW	HutC	RobR	RicN	JohN	LawN	GooS	BarD	CunA	PagD	HazD	GoaS	WatJ	HatI	ForS	TayA	TodM	WilR	PicA
1R	16 Nov	Scunthorpe United	1-1	4511	Cunningham	1	3				6	7		8	9	10	11	4	5					2
1Rr	26	SCUNTHORPE UNITED	7-6*	4892	Page(2), Goodwin	1	3				6	7		8	9	10	11*	12	5			4		2
2R	7 Dec	Burnley	0-2	9775		1	3			5	6	7		8*	9	10	11	12				4		2

* Score after penalties, 3-3 after extra time. Scorers: Todd, Goodwin, Cunningham, Barrick, Hutchings, Goater, Pickering

RUMBELOWS CUP

Rd	Date	Opposition	Res.	Att.	Goalscorers	MerW	HutC	RobR	RicN	JohN	LawN	GooS	BarD	CunA	PagD	HazD	GoaS
1R1L	20 Aug	GRIMSBY TOWN	1-3	3839	Robinson	1	2	3	4	5	6	7	8*	9	10	11	12
1R2L	27	Grimsby Town	0-1	3637		1	2	3	4	5	6	7	8	9	10*	11	12

AUTOGLASS TROPHY

Rd	Date	Opposition	Res.	Att.	Goalscorers	MerW	HutC	JohN	LawN	CunA	PagD	HazD	GoaS	WatJ	HatI	TayA	TodM	WilR	PicA	SnoG
1R	21 Jan	CHESTER CITY	3-0	2543	Page, Goater, Wilson	1	3	5	6	8	9*	10#	11	12		4	7	2		14
2R	18 Feb	BURNLEY	2-4*	2578	Hazel	1	3	5	6	8	9	12	11	10*	14		4#	2		

* Score after penalties, 1-1 after extra time. Scorers: Cunningham, Law.

Final League Table

		Pl.	Home					Away					F.	A.	Pts
			W	D	L	F	A	W	D	L	F	A			
1	Burnley	42	14	4	3	42	16	11	4	6	37	27	79	43	83
2	Rotherham United	42	12	6	3	38	16	10	5	6	32	21	70	37	77
3	Mansfield Town	42	13	4	4	43	26	10	4	7	32	27	75	53	77
4	Blackpool	42	17	3	1	48	13	5	7	9	23	32	71	45	76
5	Scunthorpe United	42	14	5	2	39	18	7	4	10	25	41	64	59	72
6	Crewe Alexandra	42	12	6	3	33	20	8	4	9	33	31	66	51	70
7	Barnet	42	16	1	4	48	23	5	5	11	33	38	81	61	69
8	Rochdale	42	12	6	3	34	22	6	7	8	23	31	57	53	67
9	Cardiff City	42	13	5	3	42	26	4	12	5	24	27	66	53	66
10	Lincoln City	42	9	5	7	21	24	8	6	7	29	20	50	44	62
11	Gillingham	42	12	5	4	41	19	3	7	11	22	34	63	53	57
12	Scarborough	42	12	5	4	39	28	3	7	11	25	40	64	68	57
13	Chesterfield	42	6	7	8	26	28	8	4	9	23	33	49	61	53
14	Wrexham	42	11	4	6	31	26	3	5	13	21	47	52	73	51
15	Walsall	42	5	10	6	28	26	7	3	11	20	32	48	58	49
16	Northampton Town	42	5	9	7	25	23	6	4	11	21	34	46	57	46
17	Hereford United	42	9	4	8	31	24	3	4	14	13	33	44	57	44
18	Maidstone United	42	6	9	6	24	22	2	9	10	21	34	45	56	42
19	York City	42	6	9	6	26	23	2	7	12	16	35	42	58	40
20	Halifax Town	42	7	5	9	23	35	3	3	15	11	40	34	75	38
21	Doncaster Rovers	42	6	2	13	21	35	3	6	12	19	30	40	65	35
22	Carlisle United	42	5	9	7	24	27	2	4	15	17	40	41	67	34

SEASON 1992/93

DIVISION TWO (Formerly Division Three)

No.	Date	Opposition	Res.	Att.	Goalscorers	Mercer W.	Wilder C.	Hutchings C.	Banks I.	Johnson N.	Law N.	Taylor A.	Goodwin S.	Todd M.	Cunningham A.	Goater S.	Barrick D.	Hazel D.	Page D.	Clarke M.	Richardson N.	Pickering A.	Currie D.	Kite P.	Howard J.	Campbell D.	Flounders A.	Buckley J.	Gridelet P.	Varadi I.	Marginson K.
1	15 Aug	Exeter City	2-0	3362	Cunningham, Goater	1	2	3	4	5	6		7	8	9	10#	11		14												
2	22	HARTLEPOOL UNITED	0-0	4355		1	2	3*	4	5	6		7	8	9	10#	11	12	14												
3	29	Burnley	1-1	9684	Cunningham	1	2		4	5	6	3	7	8	9		10	11													
4	1 Sep	Port Vale	2-4	5370	Goodwin, Todd	1	2		4	5	6	3	7	8	9*	10	11	12													
5	5	WIGAN ATHLETIC	2-3	3806	Goater, Todd	1	2	3	4	5	6		7#	8	9	10	11		14												
6	12	BOLTON WANDERERS	2-1	5227	Goater(2)	1	2	3	4	5	6			8	9	10	11	7													
7	16	Reading	1-3	2481	Goater	1	2	3	4	5	6			8	9	10	11	7													
8	19	Hull City	1-0	4780	Barrick	1	2#	3	4	5	6			8	9	10	11	7	14												
9	26	BLACKPOOL	3-2	4408	Banks, Cunningham, Hazel	1*		3	4	5#	6			8	9	10	11	7	14		12	2									
10	3 Oct	HUDDERSFIELD TOWN	1-0	5459	Goater	1		3	4	5	6			8	9#	10	11	7	14			2									
11	10	Bournemouth	0-0	4761		1		3	4	5	6			8	9	10	11#	7	14			2									
12	17	BRIGHTON	1-0	4404	Cunningham	1		3*	4	5	6			8	9		11	7	12			2	10								
13	24	West Bromwich Albion	2-2	13170	Todd(2)			3	4#	5	6		14	8	9		11	7				2	10	1							
14	31	MANSFIELD TOWN	2-0	5030	Banks, Currie	1		3	4	5	6			8	9		11	7				2	10								
15	3 Nov	CHESTER CITY	3-3	4188	Barrick(2), Hazel	1		3	4	5	6		14	8#	9*		11	7				2	10			12					
16	7	Plymouth Argyle	1-2	6519	Currie	1		3	4	5	6			8#	9		11	7			14	2	10								
17	21	PRESTON NORTH END	1-0	4246	Pickering	1		3	4	5	6		8		9		11	7				2			10						
18	28	Bradford City	3-0	9004	Barrick, Cunningham, Hazel	1		3	4	5	6			8	9		11	7				2			10*	12					
19	12 Dec	Fulham	1-0	3629	Johnson	1		3	4	5	6			8	9		11#	7	12		14	2			10*						
20	18	SWANSEA CITY	0-0	4600		1		3	4	5	6			8	9	14	11	7				2			10#						
21	28	Stoke City	0-2	21714		1		3	4	5	6			8	9	14	11#	7				2			10						
22	9 Jan	READING	3-2	4492	Cunningham(2), Howard	1		3	4	5	6			8	9	7	11					2			10						
23	16	Blackpool	0-2	6144		1	12	3	4	5	6			8	9	7	11					2			10*						
24	26	BURNLEY	0-1	4989		1	7	3	4	5	6			8	9	10#	11		14			2									
25	30	Hartlepool United	2-0	3992	Johnson, Wilder	1	7	3	4	5	6			8		10	11					2			9						
26	6 Feb	EXETER CITY	1-1	4210	Goater		7	3	4	5	6			8		14	10	11		1		2			9#						
27	9	HULL CITY	0-1	3660			7	3	4*	5				8			10	11	12	14	1	6	2		9#						
28	13	Wigan Athletic	1-1	1902	Page		7	3	4	5	6	12	8			10	11*		9	1		2									
29	20	PORT VALE	4-1	5545	Flounders(2), Howard, Wilder	1	7	3	4	5	6		8			10*	11					2					12	9				
30	26	BOURNEMOUTH	1-2	4401	Wilder	1	7	3	4	5	6			8			11	12				2#					10*	9	14		
31	2 Mar	STOCKPORT COUNTY	0-2	4280		1	7		4#	5*		3	8				11	12			6	2			10		9	14			
32	6	Huddersfield Town	1-1	5235	Varadi		3		4		5						14	7		1		2					9	11#	6	10	
33	9	Leyton Orient	1-1	4401	Hazel		3		4		5						11	7		1		2					9		6*	10	
34	13	PLYMOUTH ARGYLE	2-2	4276	Wilder, O.G.		3		4#		5						11	7		1	12	2			14		9	8*	6	10	
35	19	Chester City	2-1	2265	Varadi, Wilder		3	8	4		5						11	7	9	1		2							6	10	
36	23	BRADFORD CITY	2-0	4447	Varadi(2)		8	3	4		5						11	7	9	1		2							6	10	
37	27	Preston North End	2-5	4859	Banks, Wilder		8		4		5	3				9	11#	7	10	1		2			14				6		
38	30	Bolton Wanderers	0-2	7985		1	3		4*		5				8	9#		11	10		12	2			14				6		
39	3 Apr	LEYTON ORIENT	1-1	3083	Hazel	1	3		4		5				8	14	11	7	9#			2							6	10	
40	6	FULHAM	1-1	3065	Page	1	3		4		5				8		11	7	9			2							6	10	
41	9	Stockport County	2-2	5440	Banks, Law	1	3		4		5				9		11	7	12		6	2								10*	
42	12	STOKE CITY	0-2	9021		1	4			5	3				9		11	7	12		6	2								10*	
43	17	Swansea City	0-2	4658		1	8		4		5				9*		11	7	10		6	2									12
44	24	Brighton	2-1	7841	Hazel, Wilder	1	3		4		5				8		11	7	10		6	2									
45	1 May	WEST BROMWICH ALBION	0-2	8059		1	3		4		5				9#	14	11	7	8		6	2								10	
46	8	Mansfield Town	3-1	3833	Hazel, Law, Wilder	1	3		4		5				9		11	7	8		6	2								10	
		Apps.				36	31	30	45	31	44	6	28	16	31	20	45	31	11	9	8	38	5	1	12		6	2	9	11	
		Subs.				1						1	2		2	3	1	5	13		5			5	1		2				1
		Goals				8	4		2	2	1		4	7	7	4	7	4	2			1	2		2		2			4	

F.A. CUP

1R	14 Nov	WALSALL	4-0	4201	Goodwin(2), Cunningham,	1		3	4	5	6		8		9		11	7				2			10						
2R	5 Dec	HULL CITY	1-0	6118	Cunningham	1		3	4	5	6		8		9		11	7				2			10						
3R	12 Jan	Northampton Town	1-0	7256	Howard	1	12	3	4	5	6		8		9*	7	11					2			10						
4R	23	NEWCASTLE UNITED	1-1	13405	Johnson	1	12	3	4	5	6		8		9	10	11	7*				2									
4Rr	3 Feb	Newcastle United	0-2	29005		1	7	3	4	5#	6			8			10	11				14	2		9						

COCA COLA CUP

1R1L	18 Aug	Hull City	2-2	3226	Banks, Todd	1	2	3	4	5	6		7	8	9	10	11														
1R2L	25	HULL CITY	1-0	3565	Todd	1	2		4*	5	6	3	7	8	9	10	11	12													
2R1L	23 Sep	EVERTON	1-0	7736	Goater	1			4*	5	6		12	8	9#	7	11		14			2									
2R2L	7 Oct	Everton	0-3	10302		1		3	4	5	6			8	9	10#	11	7	14			2									

AUTOGLASS TROPHY

GR	1 Dec	Lincoln City	1-0	1066	Cunningham	1		3	4	5	6			8	9		11	7				2			10						
GR	8	SCUNTHORPE UNITED	3-1	1634	Barrick, Cunningham, Hazel	1		3	4	5	6			9			11	7	12		14	2			10*	8#					
2R	19 Jan	WIGAN ATHLETIC	4-5*	1704	Cunningham, Goodwin, Hazel	1	12	3	4*	5	6			9	10	11	7#					14									

* Score after penalties, 3-3 after extra time.

Scorers: Goater, Cunningham, Law, Barrick

Final League Table

		Pl.	Home					Away					F.	A.	Pts
			W	D	L	F	A	W	D	L	F	A			
1	Stoke City	46	17	4	2	41	13	10	8	5	32	21	73	34	93
2	Bolton Wanderers	46	18	2	3	48	14	9	7	7	32	27	80	41	90
3	Port Vale	46	14	7	2	44	17	12	4	7	35	27	79	44	89
4	West Bromwich Alb.	46	17	3	3	56	22	8	7	8	32	32	88	54	85
5	Swansea City	46	12	7	4	38	17	8	6	9	27	30	65	47	73
6	Stockport County	46	11	11	1	47	18	8	4	11	34	39	81	57	72
7	Leyton Orient	46	16	4	3	49	20	5	5	13	20	33	69	53	72
8	Reading	46	14	4	5	44	20	4	11	8	22	31	66	51	69
9	Brighton & Hove A.	46	14	4	5	36	24	7	5	11	27	35	63	59	69
10	Bradford City	46	12	5	6	36	24	6	9	8	33	43	69	67	68
11	Rotherham United	46	12	8	3	37	30	7	8	8	30	33	60	60	65
12	Fulham	46	9	5	9	28	22	7	8	8	29	33	57	55	65
13	Burnley	46	11	8	4	38	21	4	8	11	19	38	57	59	61
14	Plymouth Argyle	46	11	6	6	38	28	5	6	12	21	36	59	64	60
15	Huddersfield Town	46	10	6	7	30	22	7	3	13	24	39	54	61	60
16	Hartlepool United	46	8	6	9	19	23	6	9	8	23	37	42	60	54
17	Bournemouth	46	7	10	6	28	24	5	7	11	17	28	45	52	53
18	Blackpool	46	9	5	9	40	30	3	6	14	23	45	63	75	51
19	Exeter City	46	5	8	10	26	30	6	9	8	28	39	54	69	50
20	Hull City	46	9	5	9	28	28	4	6	13	18	43	46	69	50
21	Preston North End	46	8	4	11	41	47	5	3	15	24	47	65	94	47
22	Mansfield Town	46	7	8	8	34	34	4	3	16	18	46	52	80	44
23	Wigan Athletic	46	8	8	7	25	22	2	5	16	18	50	43	72	41
24	Chester City	46	6	2	15	30	47	2	3	18	19	55	49	102	29

(Back): Ridenton, Cunningham, Richardson, Law, Mercer, Clarke, Johnson, Rockett, Goater, Curtis.
(Centre): Russell (Youth Coach), Hazel, Howard, Banks, Breckin (Asst.Man.), Pickering, Gleeson, Page, Bailey (Physio). (Front): Taylor, Todd, Hutchings, Henson (Manager), Goodwin, Barrick, Hathaway.

- 1992-93 -

(Back): Howard, Banks, Richardson, Law, Mercer, Johnson, I.Breckin, Goater, Curtis, Roberts.
(Middle): Hutchings (Coach), Russell (Youth Coach), Jacobs, Marginson, Wilder, Pickering, Hazel, Smith, J.Breckin (Asst.Man.), Bailey (Physio).
(Front): Page, Todd, Varadi, Henson (Manager), Dolby, Goodwin, Hurst.

- 1993-94 -

SEASON 1993/94

DIVISION TWO

No.	Date	Opposition	Res.	Att.	Goalscorers	Mercer W.	Pickering A.	Jacobs W.	Banks I.	Richardson N.	Law N.	Hazel D.	Goodwin S.	Helliwell I.	Goater S.	Wilder C.	Page D.	Marginson K.	Clarke M.	Varadi I.	Hutchings C.	Williams A.	Howard J.	Kiwomya A.	Whitworth N.	Dolby C.	Brien A.	Todd M.	Hurst P.	Marshall S.	Roberts G.	Barras A.	Smith S.	Breckin I.
1	14 Aug	Wrexham	3-3	5570	Banks, Goater, Goodwin	1	2	3	4	5	6	7	8	9		10	11																	
2	21	HUDDERSFIELD TOWN	2-3	5540	Varadi, Wilder	1	2	3	4	5	6	7	8	9			11			11														
3	28	York City	0-0	4674		1	2	3	4*	5	6	7	8	9	12	11					10													
4	31	BURNLEY	3-2	5533	Varadi(2), Helliwell	1	2	3	4	5	6	7	8*	9	12	11					10													
5	4 Sep	BRENTFORD	2-0	4333	Hazel(2)	1	2	3	4	5	6	7	8	9		11					10													
6	11	Cambridge United	1-0	3804	Varadi	1	2	3	4	5	6	7	8	9		11					10													
7	14	Plymouth Argyle	2-4	6293	Varadi(2)	1	2	3	4	5	6	7	8	9		11					10													
8	18	BRISTOL ROVERS	1-1	4000	Varadi	1	2	3	4	5	6	7*	8	9	12	11#					10	14												
9	25	Stockport County	0-2	4903			2*		4	5	6		8	9	7			11	1	10	12													
10	2 Oct	BLACKPOOL	0-2	3770		1		3	4	5	6		8	9	12	2				10	7		11											
11	9	Leyton Orient	1-1	3304	Varadi	1	2	3	4	5			8	9		11		7		10				6										
12	16	SWANSEA CITY	1-1	3178	Goodwin	1	2	3		6			8	9*	12	11		7#		10			5	14	4									
13	23	Brighton	2-0	5104	Goodwin, Pickering		2	3		5			8	9		11		1		10	7		6		4									
14	30	PORT VALE	0-2	4786		1		3		5#		2	8	9	12			11*		10	7		6		4	14								
15	2 Nov	READING	2-2	3171	Hazel, Whitworth	1		3				7	8	9	12			11*		10	2		6		5	4								
16	6	Hull City	1-4	4860		1		3				11	8	9#	14	2				10	7		6		5	4								
17	20	FULHAM	1-2	2667	Todd	1		3					8		9	2					7	10	11	6	5	4								
18	27	Barnet	1-2	1938	Goodwin	1			4				14	8	12	9		2				3	7	10#	11*	6								
19	11 Dec	Huddersfield Town	1-2	4994	Varadi	1*							7	8	9			2	GK	10	3	4			5			11	6					
20	17	WREXHAM	2-1	2664	Brien, Marshall		14					7*	8		9#	2			1	10	3	4		12		5	11		6					
21	27	Bradford City	1-2	7765	Goodwin		14					7	8		9*	2			1	10	3#	4		12		5	11		6					
22	1 Jan	Hartlepool United	0-2	2101				3				7	8			12	2		1	10	4		9		5	11*		6						
23	3	CARDIFF CITY	5-2	3395	Varadi(3), Goater, Goodwin			3	7				8		9*	2			1	10	4		12		5			6	11					
24	14	Swansea City	0-0	3271				3	7				8	12	9*	2			1	10	4				5			6	11					
25	22	LEYTON ORIENT	2-1	3392	Goater, Wilder			3					8		9	2			1	10	4				5	7		6	11					
26	5 Feb	BRIGHTON	0-1	3773				3					8	14	9	2			1	10	4				5	7#		6	11					
27	12	Exeter City	1-1	3113	Helliwell			3	7				8	9*	12	2			1	10	4				5			6	11					
28	19	YORK CITY	2-1	3816	Goodwin, Jacobs			3	7				8	9*	12	2			1	10	4				5	14		6#	11					
29	26	Brentford	2-2	4980	Jacobs, Varadi			3	7				8	9	12	2			1	10	4				5					11*	6			
30	5 Mar	CAMBRIDGE UNITED	3-0	3266	Banks, Brien, Goater			3	7				8	9*	10	2			1		4	12			5					11	6			
31	8	BOURNEMOUTH	1-2	2884	Helliwell			3	7				8	9	10	2			1		4	12			5	11*					6			
32	12	Bristol Rovers	2-0	4224	Barras, Roberts			3	7				8	9	10	2			1		4				5					11	6			
33	15	PLYMOUTH ARGYLE	0-3	2982				3	7				8	9	10	2			1		4				5					11	6			
34	19	STOCKPORT COUNTY	1-2	3755	Goater			3	7	6			8	9	12	2			1	10	4				5					11*				
35	26	Blackpool	2-1	3588	Goater(2)			3	7*	6		14	8#	9	11	2			1	10	4				5					12				
36	29	Cardiff City	0-1	3583				3	7	6			8	9		2			1	10	4	11*			5			12					
37	2 Apr	BRADFORD CITY	2-1	4604	Goater, Williams			3		6			7	8	9	11	2		1	10*	4	12			5								5	
38	5	Bournemouth	0-0	3097				3		6			7	8	9	11	2		1	10#	4									14			5	
39	9	HARTLEPOOL UNITED	7-0	2792	Goater(4), Varadi(2), Goodwin			3		6			7	8#	9*	11	2		1	10	4	12			14								5	
40	12	Port Vale	1-2	6804	Banks				8	6			7		9	11			1	10	4	10#						3		14		2	5	
41	16	Reading	0-0	6295					8	6			7		9	11			1	10	4						3				2	5	
42	19	EXETER CITY	3-0	2804	Goater, Varadi, Williams			3	8	6			7		9	11			1	10	4											2	5	
43	23	HULL CITY	1-0	4944	Varadi			3	8	6			7		9	11			1	10	4											2	5	
44	26	Burnley	0-0	10806				3	8	6			7		9	11			1	10	4											2	5	
45	30	Fulham	0-1	5217				3	8	6			7		9#	11	14		1	10	4											2	5	
46	7 May	BARNET	1-1	3674	Varadi			3	8	6			7		9	11#	14		1	10	4											2	5	
					Apps.	17	12	40	31	27	10	26	38	37	25	35	6	29	38	5	34	4	4	8	25	9	3	10	11	5	7	10		
					Subs.		2					4		3	10	2			1	1		2				3		1	1	2	1	2		
					Goals		1	2	3			3	8	3	13	2				19		2			2	1			2	1	1	1		

F.A. CUP

No.	Date	Opposition	Res.	Att.	Goalscorers	Mercer	Pickering	Jacobs	Banks	Richardson	Law	Hazel	Goodwin	Helliwell	Goater	Wilder	Page	Marginson	Clarke	Varadi	Hutchings	Williams	Howard	Kiwomya	Whitworth	Dolby	Brien	Todd
1R	13 Nov	STOCKPORT COUNTY	1-2	4836	Wilder	1		3	11	5			8	9			2			10	7				6	4		

COCA COLA CUP

No.	Date	Opposition	Res.	Att.	Goalscorers	Mercer	Pickering	Jacobs	Banks	Richardson	Law	Hazel	Goodwin	Helliwell	Goater	Wilder	Page	Marginson	Clarke	Varadi	Hutchings	Williams	Howard	Kiwomya
1R1L	17 Aug	Wigan Athletic	1-0	1531	Hazel	1	2	3	4	5	6	7	8	9		10	11							
1R2L	24	WIGAN ATHLETIC	4-2	2009	Banks, Law, Varadi, O.G.	1	2	3	4	5	6	7*	8	9	12	11					10			
2R1L	21 Sep	PORTSMOUTH	0-0	3866		1	2	3	4	5	6		8	9	7*			11		10			12	
2R2L	5 Oct	Portsmouth	0-5	4589		1		3	4#	5	6		8	12	9*	11	7			10	2			14

AUTOGLASS TROPHY

No.	Date	Opposition	Res.	Att.	Goalscorers	Mercer	Pickering	Jacobs	Banks	Richardson	Law	Hazel	Goodwin	Helliwell	Goater	Wilder	Page	Marginson	Clarke	Varadi	Hutchings	Williams	Howard	Kiwomya	Whitworth	Dolby	Brien	Todd	Hurst
1R	18 Oct	Doncaster Rovers	2-1	1626	Marginson, O.G.	1	2	3	5				8	9	10			7							14	6	11#		
1R	9 Nov	HUDDERSFIELD TOWN	1-1	1598	Varadi	1		3					11#	8			2			10	7	9	14	6		5		4	
2R	7 Dec	Chester City	0-1	1500		1						7	8	12	9*					10	3	4			5		11	6	

Final League Table

		Pl.	Home					Away					F.	A.	Pts
			W	D	L	F	A	W	D	L	F	A			
1	Reading	46	15	6	2	40	16	11	5	7	41	28	81	44	89
2	Port Vale	46	16	6	1	46	18	10	4	9	33	28	79	46	88
3	Plymouth Argyle	46	16	4	3	46	26	9	6	8	42	30	88	56	85
4	Stockport County	46	15	3	5	50	22	9	10	4	24	22	74	44	85
5	York City	46	12	7	4	33	13	9	5	9	31	27	64	40	75
6	Burnley	46	17	4	2	55	18	4	6	13	24	40	79	58	73
7	Bradford City	46	13	5	5	34	20	6	8	9	27	33	61	53	70
8	Bristol Rovers	46	10	8	5	33	26	10	2	11	27	33	60	59	70
9	Hull City	46	9	9	5	33	20	9	5	9	29	34	62	54	68
10	Cambridge United	46	11	5	7	38	29	8	4	11	41	44	79	73	66
11	Huddersfield Town	46	9	8	6	27	26	8	6	9	31	35	58	61	65
12	Wrexham	46	13	4	6	45	33	4	7	12	21	44	66	77	62
13	Swansea City	46	12	7	4	37	20	4	5	14	19	38	56	58	60
14	Brighton & Hove A.	46	10	7	6	38	29	5	7	11	22	38	60	67	59
15	Rotherham United	46	11	4	8	42	30	4	9	10	21	30	63	60	58
16	Brentford	46	7	10	6	30	28	6	9	8	27	27	57	55	58
17	Bournemouth	46	8	7	8	26	27	6	8	9	25	32	51	59	57
18	Leyton Orient	46	11	9	3	38	26	3	5	15	19	45	57	71	56
19	Cardiff City	46	10	7	6	39	33	3	8	12	27	46	66	79	54
20	Blackpool	46	12	9	2	41	37	4	3	16	22	38	63	75	53
21	Fulham	46	7	6	10	20	23	7	4	12	30	40	50	63	52
22	Exeter City	46	8	7	8	38	37	3	5	15	14	46	52	83	45
23	Hartlepool United	46	8	3	12	28	40	1	6	16	13	47	41	87	36
24	Barnet	46	4	6	13	22	32	1	7	15	19	54	41	86	28

SEASON 1994/95

DIVISION TWO

No.	Date	Opposition	Res.	Att.	Goalscorers	Clarke M.	Smith S.	Hurst P.	Wilder C.	Breckin I.	Richardson N.	Hazel D.	Goodwin S.	Goater S.	Varadi I.	James M.	Brien A.	Helliwell I.	Mercer W.	Williams A.	Hayward A.	Williams C.	Todd M.	Pike M.	Foran M.	Monington M.	Dolby C.	Roberts G.	Marginson K.	Davison R.	Roscoe A.	Ayrton M.	McGlashan J.	Peel N.	Farrelly G.
1	13 Aug	SHREWSBURY TOWN	0-4	3762		1	2*	3	4	5	6	7	8	9	10	11	12																		
2	20	Crewe Alexandra	1-3	3505	Varadi		2					6	7	8	11#	10	3	5	1	4	9*	12	14												
3	26	BOURNEMOUTH	4-0	2306	Goater(2), Hayward, O.G.	1	2				7#		8		11					10	4	9	6	3	5				14						
4	30	Brentford	0-2	4031		1	2				7		8		11					10	4	9	6	3*	5				12						
5	3 Sep	Cambridge United	1-2	2885	Goater	1	2				7		8	14	11#					10	4	9*	6	3	5				12						
6	10	BRISTOL ROVERS	0-3	2596		1	2	5			7			8	10	11				10	4	9	6	3											
7	13	BIRMINGHAM CITY	1-1	3799	O.G.	1	2	5			7*	8	10				6	9		4	11	3							12						
8	17	Hull City	2-0	4431	Goater, Goodwin	1	2	5			7	8	10			3	6	9		4	11														
9	24	Peterborough United	2-2	4894	Goater, Goodwin	1	2	5			7	8	10			3	6	9		4	11														
10	1 Oct	BLACKPOOL	0-2	3517		1	2	5			7	8	10	12	3		6	9*		4	11														
11	8	Stockport County	0-1	4991		1	2	5				8	10			7	6			4	14	11#3					9								
12	15	YORK CITY	2-1	3380	Goater, Goodwin	1	2	5			7#	8	10			11	6			4	14	3					9								
13	22	LEYTON ORIENT	2-0	2700	Goater, Marginson	1	2	5				8	10	12	3		6			4	7							11	9*						
14	29	Brighton	1-1	6734	Davison	1	2	5			8#		10	12	3		6			4	7							14	9*	11					
15	1 Nov	Swansea City	0-1	2511		1	2	5					10	9	3		6			4	7							8		11					
16	5	PLYMOUTH ARGYLE	3-1	2848	Goater(2), Varadi	1		14	2	5			10	9	3		6			4	7							8#		11					
17	19	Oxford United	1-2	5801	Helliwell	1	7		2	5	12		10	9*	3		6	8#		4	14									11					
18	26	CHESTER CITY	2-0	2949	Goater(2)	1		14	2	5	8		10*	12	3		6		4#									9	11						
19	10 Dec	CREWE ALEXANDRA	2-2	2907	Hayward, McGlashan	1		11	2		4		10		3	6					7				5				9			8			
20	16	Shrewsbury Town	0-1	3243		1		11	2	4			10		3						7				5				9			8			
21	26	BRADFORD CITY	3-1	5400	Davison, Goater, Roscoe	1		14	2	6	4		10		3		12				7#				5				9'#	11		8			
22	27	Huddersfield Town	0-1	15557		1			2	6	4	12	10		3						7				5				9	11*		8			
23	31	CARDIFF CITY	2-0	3064	Breckin, Monington	1		14	2	6	4	12	10		3						7				5				9*	11#		8			
24	7 Jan	Leyton Orient	0-0	2796		1			2	6	4#	10			3		12				7				5				14	9*	11	8			
25	14	WYCOMBE WANDERERS	2-0	3537	Hayward, O.G.	1			2	6	4		10*		3						7				5				9	11		8			
26	21	Plymouth Argyle	0-0	5484		1			2	6	4		10	14	3						7				5				9#	11		8			
27	4 Feb	Chester City	4-4	1794	McGlashan(2), Monington, Wilder	1			2	6	4	12	10		3						7*				5				9	11		8			
28	11	SWANSEA CITY	3-3	2858	Davison, Hayward, Roscoe	1			2	6	4*	12	10		3						7				5				9	11		8			
29	18	Wycombe Wanderers	0-2	5153		1			2	6			10	14	3						7				5				12	9#	11	8*			
30	21	OXFORD UNITED	1-1	2833	Goater	1			2	6	4	7	10		3						5				5				9	11					
31	25	Blackpool	2-2	5043	Davison, Goater	1			2	6	4	7	10		3						5				5				9	11					
32	4 Mar	PETERBOROUGH UNITED	0-0	3123		1			2	6	4		10#	14	3*						5				5				9	11					
33	7	CAMBRIDGE UNITED	1-0	2208	Goater	1		3		2	6	4	10	14							7				5				9#	11					
34	11	Bournemouth	1-1	5666	Goater	1		3		2	6	4	10								7		9		5					11					
35	14	Wrexham	1-3	1823	Goater	1		3		2	6	4	10								7#		9		5		8			11					
36	18	BRENTFORD	0-2	2974		1	2	3			6	4#	7	10	9*						12		14							11			8		
37	22	Bristol Rovers	0-2	4420		1		3		2	6	4*	10	14							7#		9							11			8		12
38	25	HULL CITY	2-0	3692	Peel, Roscoe	1			2	6			10			3					7				5					11			8	9	4
39	28	BRIGHTON	4-3	2316	Breckin, Goater, Peel, Roscoe	1			2	6			10			3	5				7				5					11			8	9	4
40	1 Apr	Birmingham City	1-2	16077	Goater	1			2	6			10			3					7	14								11			8	9#	4
41	8	Cardiff City	1-1	6412	Peel	1			2	6			10			3	5				7									11			8	9	4
42	15	HUDDERSFIELD TOWN	1-1	6687	Hayward	1			2	6			10			3					7				5					11			8	9	4
43	17	Bradford City	3-0	3535	Farrelly, Hayward, Peel	1			2	6*	12		10#			3					7				5				14	11			8	9	4
44	22	WREXHAM	0-1	2628		1			2	6			10			3					7				5				14	11			8	9#	4
45	29	York City	0-2	3183		1	14		2	6	5		10			3					7#									11			8	9	4
46	6 May	STOCKPORT COUNTY	1-0	3469	Farrelly	1			2	6			10			3					7									11			8	9	4
					Apps.	45	3	8	45	41	23	16	10	45	6	40	16	10	1	17	33	12	7	3	25	5	19	31	27	9		19	31	27	9
					Subs.		1	5			2	5		11			1	2		4	2	2			2	2	3	2						1	
					Goals			1	2			3	19	2		1		6			2				1	4	4				3	4	2		

F.A. CUP

						Clarke M.	Smith S.	Hurst P.	Wilder C.	Breckin I.	Richardson N.	Hazel D.	Goodwin S.	Goater S.	Varadi I.	James M.	Brien A.	Helliwell I.	Mercer W.	Williams A.	Hayward A.	Williams C.	Todd M.	Pike M.	Foran M.	Monington M.	Dolby C.	Roberts G.	Marginson K.	Davison R.
1R	12 Nov	York City	3-3	4020	Goater(2), Helliwell	1	8		2	5			10	9	3*	6	12	4						7		11				
1Rr	22	YORK CITY	3-0	4391	Davison(2), Goater	1		11	2	5	8		10	12	3	6		4	7									9*		
2R	3 Dec	Wrexham	2-5	4521	Davison, Hurst	1	4	11	2	5	8		10		3	6	14		7#									9		

COCA COLA CUP

						Smith S.	Hazel D.	Goodwin S.	Goater S.	Varadi I.	James M.	Brien A.	Helliwell I.	Mercer W.	Williams A.	Hayward A.	Williams C.
1R1L	16 Aug	CARLISLE UNITED	1-0	2055	Varadi	2	6	7	8	11*	10	3	5#	9	1	4	12 14
1R2L	23	Carlisle United	1-3	5004	Hayward	2	6		7	8	10*	3	5		1	4	9 12 11

AUTO WINDSCREENS SHIELD

						Clarke M.	Hazel D.	Goodwin S.	Goater S.	Varadi I.	James M.	Brien A.	Helliwell I.	Williams A.	Hayward A.	Roberts G.	Marginson K.	Davison R.	McGlashan J.
1R	27 Sep	Scunthorpe United	3-1	1404	Goater, Helliwell, Todd	1		2	5		7	8	10#9	3	6	9	4	11	
1R	18 Oct	CHESTERFIELD	1-1	1585	Goater	1		2	5			10		3	6	4	7	11	8 9
2R	30 Nov	WIGAN ATHLETIC	1-3	1587	Goater	1	14	11*	2	5	8		10	12	3	6	7	9	4#

Final League Table

		Pl.	Home W	D	L	F	A	Away W	D	L	F	A	F.	A.	Pts
1	Birmingham City	46	15	6	2	53	18	10	8	5	31	19	84	37	89
2	Brentford	46	14	4	5	44	15	11	6	6	37	24	81	39	85
3	Crewe Alexandra	46	14	3	6	46	33	11	5	7	34	35	80	68	83
4	Bristol Rovers	46	15	7	1	48	20	7	9	7	22	20	70	40	82
5	Huddersfield Town	46	14	5	4	45	21	8	10	5	34	28	79	49	81
6	Wycombe Wanderers	46	13	7	3	36	19	8	8	7	24	27	60	46	78
7	Oxford United	46	13	6	4	30	18	8	6	9	36	34	66	52	75
8	Hull City	46	13	6	4	40	18	8	5	10	30	39	70	57	74
9	York City	46	13	4	6	37	21	8	5	10	30	30	67	51	72
10	Swansea City	46	10	8	5	23	13	9	6	8	34	32	57	45	71
11	Stockport County	46	12	3	8	40	29	7	5	11	23	31	63	60	65
12	Blackpool	46	11	4	8	40	36	7	6	10	24	34	64	70	64
13	Wrexham	46	10	7	6	38	27	6	8	9	27	37	65	64	63
14	Bradford City	46	8	6	9	29	32	8	6	9	28	32	57	64	60
15	Peterborough Utd.	46	7	11	5	26	29	7	7	9	28	40	54	69	60
16	Brighton & Hove A.	46	9	10	4	25	15	5	7	11	29	38	54	53	59
17	Rotherham United	46	12	6	5	36	26	2	8	13	21	35	57	61	56
18	Shrewsbury Town	46	9	5	9	34	27	4	5	14	20	35	54	62	53
19	Bournemouth	46	9	4	10	30	34	4	7	12	19	35	49	69	50
20	Cambridge United	46	8	9	6	33	28	3	6	14	19	41	52	69	48
21	Plymouth Argyle	46	7	6	10	22	36	5	4	14	23	47	45	83	46
22	Cardiff City	46	5	6	12	25	31	4	5	14	21	43	46	74	38
23	Chester City	46	5	6	12	23	42	1	5	17	14	42	37	84	29
24	Leyton Orient	46	6	6	11	21	29	0	2	21	9	46	30	75	26

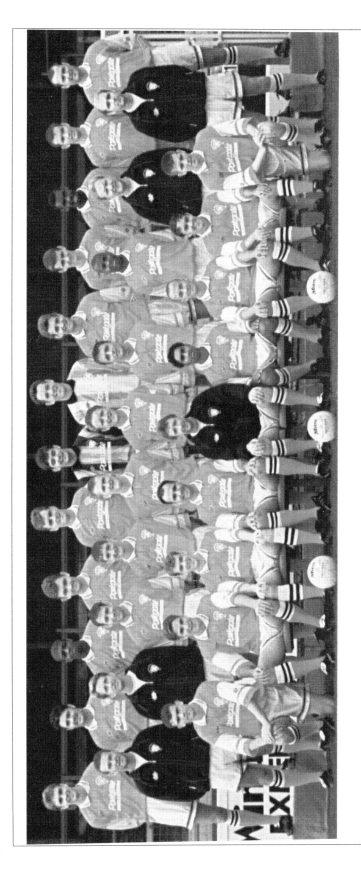

(Back): A.Williams, Brien, C.Williams, Richardson, Helliwell, Mercer, Clarke, Johnson, I.Breckin, Goater, Barnard, Pike. (Middle): Hutchings(Coach), Russell(Youth Coach), Howard, Green, Marginson, Wilder, James, Hazel, J.Brackin(Asst.Man.) Bailey(Physio). (Front):Smith, Roberts, Todd, Varadi, Henson(Man.), Dolby, Goodwin, Hurst, Hilton.

- 1994-1995 -

ADVANCED SUBSCRIBERS

Rotherham United F.C. (Presentation copy)

Willy Østby - Norway
Chris, Sheila, Mary Hooker
Jonny Stokkeland Kvinesdal - Norway
Christer Svensson
David Ernshaw
Richard Wells
Gordon Macey
Alan Davies
G. Painter, Castle Cary
Graham Spackman
Mark Tyler, Rayleigh, Essex
J. Ringrose
Dave Windross
Moira & Frederick Furness
Michael John Griffin
Dave McPherson, Colchester
L.A. Zammit
W.D. Phillips
David Keats, Thornton Heath
Philip H. Whitehead
M.J. Cripps
David Richard Downs
A.N. Other
Steve Emms
Robert M. Smith
Fred Lee, Plymouth Argyle
John Motson
Donald Noble, Dunkeld, Perthshire
Duncan Watt
Peter Cogle, Aberdeen
Raymond Shaw
G.T. Allman
David Jowett
Harry Kay, Bingley, Yorkshire
P.J. Newport
Svein Borge Pettersen (Sandefjord)
A.H. Atkins, Canada
Doug Lamming
Colin Cameron
Stephen Kieran Byrne
Andrew Anderson
Dave Smith
Bob Lilliman
Dave Parine
Gordon Small
B.H. Standish
Jack Retter
Michael Campbell
Geoffrey Wright
Martin Simons, Belgium
Phil Hollow
Ray Bickel
Derek Hyde
Brian Tabner
Örjan Hansson
Peter Baxter - Reading

To Mark, Merry Christmas
Peter Pickup, Pudsey, Yorkshire
Reg White
Reiner Sawitzki - Germany
Bill Blackburn, Claremont Television
Brian Chapple, Ehled Geordie
E. Beeley, Rotherham
Walter Pratt, Mintoe Man
Patricia Hope, Tickhill
Les Payne, Travelling colleague
Yasmin Elaine Brookes, Rotherham
R. Nettleton, Rotherham
Mike Todd, London Millers
Chris Taylor, Swinton
Richard Rylett, Kimberworth, Rotherham
Mr. Ben Bennett
Des Pejko, Rotherham/Tickhill
Andrew Westgarth, Wath, Rotherham
Matt Norcliffe, Moulin Rouge
Claire Westgarth, Wath, Rotherham
David O. Dutton, Ickwell, Beds.
Phil Tooley, Chesterfield
John Wallbank, Edenthorpe, Doncaster
Mark. L. Simmons, Hull
Richard Wareham, Streatham, London
Malcolm Neale, Morden, Surrey
Jeffrey G. Spencer
Guy Holroyd, New York
Stephen Eyre
Richard Eyre
David Eyre
Garry Mark Bray
Calum Jordan Bray
Mike Jolly, Sheffield S11
Joan Davies, Sheffield
Gareth Davis, Rawmarsh
Hugh Vaughan, Moulin Rouge
Terry Kelly, Munsboro
Lee Rowbotham, Kimberworth, Rotherham
Kevin Hood, Sunnyside, Rotherham
David Brett Clark, Swinton
Rachel Clyna Barnes
Tom, Joe, Jack Barnes
Matthew Twigg, Kimberworth, Rotherham
Eric Twigg, Moorgate, Rotherham
Dave Woods, A Bristol Babe
Richard W. Lane, Newark
Christopher John Burrows, Newark
Jim Poucher, Malta
Harold Mosby, Broom, Rotherham
Eleanor & Roselyn Peers, Rotherham
Roger Mortimer, Rawmarsh
Mick Lister, Rotherham
David Haywood, Rotherham Harriers
Darren Peers, Rotherham
Mark Thomas, Maltby, Liverpool

Antony Greenwood, The Perishers
Allan Beighton, Bramley, Rotherham
P.D. Appleby, Rotherham
Chas. B. Robinson, Wentworth
Tom Sharp, Kimberworth, Rotherham
Tony Jones, Kimberworth, Rotherham
Neil Liversidge, Bolton-on-Dearne
Glynn and Michael Coates
David John Roden, Rotherham
Joanne Bott
Neil Sharman, Kimberworth, Rotherham
Steve, Chapeltown
Deborah Stanton, Clifton, Rotherham
Christopher Hoyland, Bahrain
Michael & Tessa Longden, Rotherham
Roy Jennison, Saxilby
Wayne Houghton, Rotherham
D. Hough, Rotherham
Neil McLean, Clifton, Rotherham
E.J. Davis
Greg Artell, Kimberworth, Rotherham
Steve Exley, Derby
Mike Oldham, Sandal, Wakefield
Laurence Bradley, Maltby
Bernard Davies, Rockingham, Rotherham
Craig Asbridge, Kimberworth, Rotherham
Jennifer Ansley, Munsbrough, Rotherham
Tony Ainscough, Brinsworth, Rotherham
Stephen Willey, Balby, Doncaster
Dave Taylor, Swinton
Aland & Daniel Ramsden, Greasbrough
Graham and James Symonds
Graham & Phil Kyte, Royston
John Harrison, Carlton-in-Lindrick
Brian Exley, Worksop
Peter John Exley, Worksop
Martin Simmons, Belton
Mick Seddons, Rotherham
Joanne No. 1 Fan
Adam Geofrey Tyler, Greasbro
Barrie Dalby, Conisbrough
Trevor Wootton, Broom, Rotherham
Robert Lee Walkington, Kimberworth
Mark Foster, Aston
Charles H. Brett, Rawmarsh
Nigel Pease, Swinton, Mexborough
George Hutchinson, Rawmarsh, Rotherham
Mr. W. Grier
Peter Kirby, Maidstone
Andrew Marshall, Brislington, Bristol
John Rawnsley
Keith Coburn
Roger Wash
David Lumb
Trond Isaksen, Norway
Arran and Nicholas Matthews